sustainable residential interiors

SECOND EDITION

Annette K. Stelmack

Associates III:
Kari Foster *and*
Debbie Hindman

WILEY

Dedicated to my 'Grosseltern' (grandparents).
—Annette K. Stelmack

Cover Images: (Top row, left) Private residence, San Francisco, California: Interior designer, Joshua Mogal, eco + historical, inc.; Architect, Jonathan Feldman, Bridgett Shank, Feldman Architecture; Photographer, Paul Dyer Photo. (Top row, right) Wellness Loft, Delos' pilot project, Manhattan, New York: Developer, Delos' WELL Building Standard. (Bottom row, left) Private residence, Lake Creek, Colorado: Interior designer, Annette Stelmack, Kari Foster, Associates III; Photographer, David O. Marlow. (Bottom row, right) Private residence, Aspen, Colorado: Interior designer, Wendy Silverman; Architect, Sarah Broughton, Rowland + Broughton Architecture and Urban Design; Brent Moss Photography.
Cover design: Wiley

For general information about our other products and services, please contact our Customer Care Department within the United States at (800) 762-2974, outside the United States at (317) 572-3993 or fax (317) 572-4002.

Wiley publishes in a variety of print and electronic formats and by print-on-demand. Some material included with standard print versions of this book may not be included in e-books or in print-on-demand. If this book refers to media such as a CD or DVD that is not included in the version you purchased, you may download this material at http://booksupport.wiley.com. For more information about Wiley products, visit www.wiley.com.

Library of Congress Cataloging-in-Publication Data:

Foster, Kari.
    Sustainable residential interiors / Kari Foster, Annette Stelmack, ASID, Debbie Hindman, Associates III.—
Second edition.
        pages cm
        Includes index.
        ISBN 978-1-118-60368-0 (hardback) — ISBN 978-1-118-88974-9 (epdf) — ISBN 978-1-118-89693-8 (epub)
        1. Sustainable design—United States.   2. Ecological houses—Design and construction.   3. Sustainable engineering—United States.   4. Interior architecture—United States.   I. Stelmack, Annette.   II. Hindman, Debbie.   III. Title.
    TH4860.F67 2014
    729.028'6—dc23
                                                                                2013047828

Printed in the United States of America
10 9 8 7 6 5 4 3 2 1

CONTENTS

PREFACE

When we heal the earth, we heal ourselves.
—DAVID ORR

As residential interior designers, we create "home" for our clients. Our responsibility is to serve them in one of the most personal and profound expressions of their world—where they live. We are privileged to engage with them on an intimate level, listening to their needs and dreams for "home," where they welcome us into their living rooms, dining rooms, kitchens, bedrooms, bathrooms, home offices, and closets.

Since the first edition of this book, residential interior designers have developed a greater consciousness and appreciation for green and healthy design issues. In fact, the market transformation has seen an explosion of sustainable ideas, principles, and practices, including eco-friendly and healthier products. Green building rating systems are being adopted nationwide, and product certifications are standard practice for many manufacturers, who are following the leaders in the commercial sector of the industry.

This new edition provides comprehensive and reliable information on how to apply sustainable design principles and practices on projects. We celebrate your interest in integrating environmentally responsible design into your practice, and it is an honor to offer this book to the design community.

Our intention in *Sustainable Residential Interiors* is to support you as you question the status quo, to ignite your spirit as a catalyst for change, to present you with information and processes, and to encourage you to ask well-informed questions as you start down the path to creating healthy, high-performing, eco-friendly, meaningful, nurturing residences that positively impact our clients and the world we live in. Designers around the world are integrating sustainable, healthy, and high-performing strategies into their daily practice; it is no longer an added value, it is inherent to their work. In fact, we implore you to act now, and live differently, for if we don't, who will?

Consumers, too, are more aware of the environmental issues affecting their homes and lifestyles, and they increasingly ask designers, architects, and builders to incorporate healthy indoor air quality and sustainability into their projects. To help meet this increased demand, this book provides design professionals with a comprehensive, easy-to-understand sustainable resource guide. It will:

- Answer why we must become catalysts for change.
- Share inspiring stories about today's environmental champions.

- Give visual examples of sustainable projects and applications.
- Examine why the health, safety, and welfare of our clients matter.
- Address the most hazardous chemicals that are consistently in our lives.
- Explore the health impacts of traditional building.
- Encourage critical thinking about environmental issues within homes.
- Present strategies for incorporating sustainable design into work and projects.
- Provide a practical, hands-on approach to sustainable design.
- Offer guidelines for clients and project teams.
- Provide helpful checklists for greening projects and specifications.
- Give in-depth information to promote understanding and assist in specifying interior finishes and furnishings.
- Raise questions for manufacturers and vendors.
- Share effective methods of marketing sustainable design services.
- Discuss what's next with industry leaders.

Years ago, our eyes, minds, and hearts were opened to the inspirational world of sustainable design. Since then, we have been on a quest, searching for ways to exemplify integrity in our work, as articulated through the details of a project—asking how long finishes will last and which adhesives to specify, addressing indoor air quality, ensuring that woods are from certified sources, finding low-impact materials, conserving energy and water, supporting construction teams in reducing waste, providing information regarding healthy cleaning methods, assisting clients with multiple chemical sensitivities to create a healthy interior—all while exceeding the client's expectations.

We know that healthy, eco-friendly design might not always be what our clients want initially, but we believe they will come to value and appreciate it in the long run. And it is for the future that we do this, for the future health of the Earth and its inhabitants, for future generations, indeed, for the future of humanity and our planet. We, the authors, have found that when something is right, there is always consensus, and we have agreed that this is the right way to practice the business of interior design.

Our goal for *Sustainable Residential Interiors* is to create a reference tool for interior designers who are beginning to embrace green design strategies. What is a healthy, green building? Simply, sustainable building takes steps to create homes that are socially and environmentally responsible while supporting the health and prosperity of families, communities, and the environment. Whether renovating an existing residence or designing a new home for your clients, keep in mind these three fundamental goals:

- Be mindful about using limited resources, such as wood and water, to limit waste, pollution, and environmental damage.

- Build and remodel with energy efficiency in mind to save money, create a more responsible home, and reduce air pollution and global warming.
- Choose healthy materials and construction methods to prevent indoor air pollution from formaldehyde, mold, toxins, and other contaminants.

The residential design industry is moving briskly in the direction of sustainable building for many vital reasons, among them:

- *Higher quality.* Most green building products and materials are now developed to perform better than their conventional counterparts.
- *Greater durability and less maintenance.* Green building encourages the use of longer-lasting products that don't require an inordinate amount of time or the use of harsh chemicals to maintain. Less frequent replacement puts less of a burden on natural resources and landfills.
- *Greater comfort and lower utility bills.* Energy-efficient upgrades can reduce the rate of energy consumption, lowering energy bills while providing a comfortable living space.
- *Healthier products and practices.* Green building promotes the use of products and construction practices that avoid introducing harmful chemicals and other pollutants into the home.
- *Natural resource conservation.* Protecting the environment is yet another compelling reason for committing to build green.

This book is a continuation of a journey that started so many years ago. It presents a logical and sequential process for creating healthy, sustainable residential interiors that meet the goals of the homeowner as well as the goals of green design. Step by step, it will take you through an integrated design process, exemplifying how sustainable principles, strategies, and practices can be applied at each level of interior design. These principles and practices can be utilized in any residential project to create a home that is healthy, functional, comfortable, sustainable, and beautiful.

Imagine if:

- We learned how to be eco-friendly from our parents and grandparents, our grade schools, middle schools, high schools, and colleges.
- Clients came to us asking for homes and products that were Earth- and family-friendly.
- We, as residential interior designers, ascribed to the medical profession's charge, "First, do no harm," and recommended and specified only Earth-friendly and healthy materials and products.
- We were able to provide net-zero-energy homes that were truly restorative for our clients and for the planet.
- Residential contractors and architects seamlessly and routinely integrated green principles and strategies into their everyday best practices.

- Government mandated environmentally sustainable construction for residences.
- The core principle of all manufacturers of residential products included healthy ingredients as well as environmental and social responsibility.
- All materials were safe and their contents healthy.
- There was a practical, positive book to assist residential interior designers in converting their practice into one that is socially and environmentally responsible.

Well, here it is!

Our challenge, and opportunity, is to learn how we can leave a lighter footprint on the planet—or better yet, no footprint at all—and have a positive impact on our clients in order to create a thriving future for generations to come. As interior designers, we must actively promote change, transparency, and progress in the building industry—change that will support our clients' vision and respect the environment, fully integrating environmentally responsible design. On each project we are motivated to create designs that are appropriate to the client and that meet traditional goals—the homeowner's needs, budget, schedule, and aesthetics—as well as to give back more than we take from the surrounding environment.

Thank you for taking time to read this book. Whether you are taking your first steps toward adopting sustainability or are well along on your journey, we hope that you will find it informative and helpful and that it will inspire you to act now. We are truly honored to share with you how much our design and building profession is transforming and moving in a better direction. We look forward to engaging in conversations with you about healthy, intelligent, high-performing design, and with that in mind we welcome your feedback, your insights, and your questions. Hope to hear from you soon!

ACKNOWLEDGEMENTS

I am sincerely thankful to everyone who contributed their time, dedication, expertise and knowledge to make this book possible.

To Tom Stelmack, I am endlessly grateful for your never-ending love as my remarkable life partner of more than thirty-five years: You are *my* home. In particular, thank you for believing in me, always, and for encouraging me while we endured a tumultuous year of family illnesses, epic flooding, and the passing of dear loved ones. Your feedback and gracious support helped me through the challenges, the long days and evenings, and the countless weekends of hard work. Thanks for holding down the home front, babe.

My love always to my family, especially my son, daughter-in-law, and grandson, who cheered me on and gifted me with special family time to relax, laugh, love, and celebrate the next generation. Also to my parents and grandparents, for instilling values I deeply cherish, especially your profound love and joy for family, your exquisite caring for nature and her bounty, and your risk-taking spirit that embraces everything the universe offers and proves that life is indeed magnificent.

Thank you to my clients, who continually open their hearts and minds to allow me to help them create healthy, nurturing, high-performing, and vitalizing interiors that reflect their essence and support their health, safety, and well-being.

I want to acknowledge my U.S. Green Building Council family, both near and far: Thank you for teaching and inspiring me. What an amazing professional arena in which to connect, collaborate, inspire, advocate, and educate. To my fellow LEED faculty members: Thank you for sharing your passion, commitment, and expertise. A special shout out to Holley Henderson, who in my moments of weakness took time to brainstorm and clarify the direction of the new chapters; thank you, my Yoda sister.

A huge thanks to the early adopters and pioneers that I've stalked for more than fifteen years. I've had the immense good fortune to connect and work with you and deeply appreciate the motivation, guidance, passion, and knowledge you've graciously shared with me: Bill Reed, Ann Edminster, Ed Mazria, Kristen Richie, William McDonough, Dr. Marilyn Black, Peter Yost, Linda Sorrento, Alex Wilson, Paula Baker-Laporte, Bill Browning, Mary Cordaro, David Bergman, Rachel Gutter, Tom Lent, Penny Bonda, Nadav Malin, Nancy Clanton, Lance Hosey, Leigh Anne Van Dusen, Jay Hall, Jill Salisbury, Michael Lehman, and Susan Szenasy, and, in loving memory, Greg Franta, Ray Anderson and Malcolm Lewis. My heart and mind are overflowing thanks to each and every one of you, and so many more, who have respectfully challenged me and provided opportunities for tremendous personal and professional growth. You are thought-leaders on the cutting edge of the industry, truly being the difference!

Initially, our passion as environmental stewards was nurtured by trailblazers from all walks of life; Buckminster Fuller, Daniel Quinn, David Suzuki, Julia Butterfly Hill, Judith Helfand, Michael Braungart, Paul Hawken, Sarah Susanka, and Sym Van der Ryn are among them. We are thrilled that many have contributed to our book: Bert Gregory, Hunter Lovins, Janine Benyus, Paula Baker-Laporte, Steve Badanes, Trudy Dujardin, and William McDonough. Thank you for your unwavering commitment to creating a better world. You inspire us daily to do our part in creating healthy and nurturing environments.

A special note of gratitude to my exceptional reviewers. To Teen Rollins, who jumped in head first to provide guidance, clarity, and organization for the new chapters. Thank you for reining me in as the material was growing exponentially and for reviewing existing information for necessary updates. To Kari Foster, Debbie Hindman, and Amy DePierre at Associates III: thank you for your valuable review and editing of the draft manuscript and for your feedback, comments, and patience, and particularly for encouraging me to fly solo on this second edition. Namaste dear friends, I treasure our long-standing and enduring friendships.

My phenomenal research team—Rena Goodwin, Jessica Levy, Teen Rollins, Sheena Roddy, Briar Sawkins, Erica Smith, Bethany Strothman, Lisa Taylor, and Lori Tugman—provided in-depth examination and confirmed updates–tracking down all the material I needed to create the new chapters and advance the existing ones, and securing images and permissions. Your dedication, staying power, commitment, thoroughness, and patience were outstanding. I loved working with all of you and appreciate you immensely.

To the interior designers, architects, and project teams who submitted their cutting-edge, healthy, and high-performing residential projects: Thank you for your enthusiasm and the wealth of expertise and creativity you share through your work, which illustrates that sustainable, healthy principles and practices are beautiful, culturally rich, and ecologically sound.

My editor, Lauren Poplawski, has been understanding and patient this year, especially when my personal life got in the way of writing. Thank you for your compassion and for being there when I needed your guidance and expertise.

Finally, I want to thank you, our readers, for expanding your commitment to healthy, sustainable interior design. Knowledge empowers change; I am honored to be part of your process. I hope to hear from you as you transform your approach, communication, and design process in your projects.

—ANNETTE K. STELMACK, INSPIRIT-LLC

We are eternally grateful to Annette Stelmack for her incredible hard work in spearheading the research, writing, and rewriting of this second edition of *Sustainable Residential Interiors* and in updating it with the many changes that have occurred in the few short years since we collaborated together on the first edition. It's gratifying to see the new wealth of information available to us all in creating healthy, responsible, beautiful, and life-enhancing interior spaces. A special mention and thank you to Amy DePierre, an integral part of the Associates III team, for her supreme effort and diligence in the review of the content and written word.

—KARI FOSTER AND DEBBIE HINDMAN, ASSOCIATES III, INC.

CHAPTER 1

why be sustainable?

There is no greater potential for personal expression than building one's own shelter. For this reason alone, home construction should be sustainable for generations to come. And to be truly sustainable, it is not enough to minimize damage to the environment; the construction must have a net positive impact on it.

—DENNIS WEDLICK, AIA

The answer to the question why, as residential designers, our work should be sustainable is simple: There is only one planet Earth, and if we destroy its ability to sustain life, our planet will become uninhabitable. Numerous speeches have been made and publications written by credible sources who, over the past decades, have been leading the market transformation in the building industry. This book will share knowledge and provide motivation from another perspective—that of the residential interior design community.

Through our experiences and the information that we have gathered and organized, we will demonstrate to residential design professionals that it is possible to build a home that is beautiful, pleasing, functional, healthy, safe, affordable, and life-sustaining. The time is now to 'BE' the catalyst for change within the residential design community and to integrate sustainable residential design into our work.

Interior designers are resourceful beings; they are information-gathering, solution-seeking, innovative creatures, and these are ideal characteristics for promoting healthy, high-performing, sustainable design. Our profession is a natural for revolutionizing the industry by transforming environments. It is, after all, what we do. By focusing our creative energy and implementing sustainable design, we become instruments of beneficial change. If we are resolute in our belief that each positive action makes a difference, our contribution to a healthy planet is guaranteed.

Before us lies a remarkable opportunity to connect where we are with where we have been to inform where we need to be going. Creating healthy, life-enhancing design is an invigorating prospect. Is it challenging? Absolutely! It's challenging, doable, exciting—and, of course, the right thing to do.

Let's begin by asking why everything considered good for us is termed "alternative"—alternative health care, alternative medicine, alternative food. Indeed, sustainable design should no longer be considered an alternative; it is, simply, the responsible way to conduct good business. In fact, states and municipalities have passed legislation mandating high-performing and healthy building standards. It benefits us all to work together toward better solutions that "respect all of the children of all of the species, for all times," to quote renowned architect William McDonough, principal and founder of William McDonough + Partners and MBDC.

Sustainability is transforming the building industry, and expertise in sustainable design is now highly regarded and regularly sought after. Clients, architects, and contractors value the knowledge and skills that we bring to the table as part of the professional services team; as designers, we can offer numerous possibilities for creating eco-friendly homes. The finishes in a home can exemplify environmental responsibility, support our clients' health, and be beautiful as well. By combining materials in a unique and environmentally responsible way, we have a rich opportunity to make a difference.

As interior designers and architects, we have the power—and the responsibility—to create environments that sustain life on the planet. The methods that we employ, often beyond the realm of other professions, compel us to practice sustainable design. By doing so, we are, as defined nearly three decades ago by the Brundtland Commission in 1987, "meeting the needs of the present without compromising the ability of future generations to meet their own needs."

Designers have much to teach the world. Of all people, we understand that there is never only one right way to design anything. Searching for new solutions, creatively adapting what we know to what we need, and solving problems is what designers do. Perhaps, then, we as designers need to expand our vision to include sustainability and start showing ordinary people how to look at the world from a green design point of view.

—FROM DANIEL QUINN, ISHMAEL: AN ADVENTURE OF THE MIND AND SPIRIT (BANTAM, 1995)

There are countless opportunities for design professionals and those we work with to make a significant difference. Green building practices and strategies, coupled with constantly emerging technologies, are transforming our industry and, subsequently, the buildings that we live and work in. By applying principles, strategies, and practices that sustain our natural resources, we can ensure a healthier life on our planet for future generations.

As we all were taught, for every action there is an equal reaction; similarly, for every choice we make there is a consequence. By practicing sustainable design, we catalyze change in our industry by gathering information, learning new strategies, attending conferences, questioning the status quo, sharing information, and aligning with like-minded individuals, project teams, and clients.

Market transformation begins with individuals who integrate sustainability into the core of their interior design process—one step at a time, one material at a time, one project at a time, and one question at a time. We can and do make a difference. (See the sidebar on Ray Anderson, page 50.)

What Are Green Buildings?

The U.S. Environmental Protection Agency (EPA) describes green building as the practice of creating structures and using processes that are environmentally responsible and resource-efficient throughout a building's life cycle, from siting to design, construction, operation, maintenance, renovation, and deconstruction.[1] Green buildings, including residences, exhibit a high level of environmental, economic, and engineering performance, including:

- Energy efficiency and conservation
- Indoor environmental quality
- Resource and materials efficiency
- Occupant health, safety, welfare, and productivity
- Transportation efficiency
- Improved environmental quality including air, water, land, limited resources, and ecosystems

The U.S. Green Building Council (USGBC) states that the built environment is expected to double by 2050. Buildings have a major impact on the environment as a whole in that they account for:

- 39 percent of total energy use and percent of electricity consumption
- 30 percent of greenhouse gas emissions
- 30 percent of raw materials use

---

[1] www.epa.gov/greenbuilding/pubs/about.html

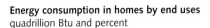

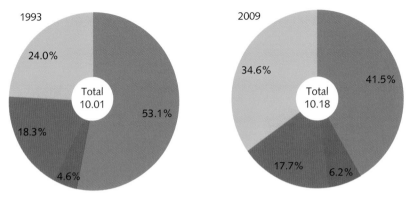

Figure 1.2   ■ space heating   ■ air conditioning   ■ water heating   ▨ appliances, electronics, and lighting

- 30 percent of waste output (136 million tons annually)
- 12 percent of potable water consumption

Various other resources note that:

- Nearly 40 percent of total U.S. energy consumption in 2012 was consumed in residential and commercial buildings, or about 40 quadrillion British thermal units (Btus).
- 50 percent of all global energy is used to cool, light, and ventilate buildings.
- More than 50 percent of all resources are used in construction.

The EPA notes that if every American home replaced their five most frequently used light fixtures or the bulbs in them with Energy Star–qualified lighting, we would save close to $8 billion each year in energy costs, and together we'd prevent the greenhouse gases equivalent to the emissions from nearly ten million cars.

In addition, statistics show that the United States, though it comprises less than 5 percent of the world's population, consumes nearly 20 percent of the world's energy—and as of 2012 generates 16 percent of the world's global emissions. Our ecological footprint is enormous compared with that of other countries. If everyone in the world enjoyed the American standard of living, we would need four to five Earths to sustain us.

Buildings account for around half of the global output of the greenhouse gas carbon dioxide as well as half of the output of sulfur dioxide and nitrogen oxide, both components of acid rain. The building industry therefore shares responsibility for environmental disasters related to energy production: oil spills, nuclear waste, the destruction of rivers by hydroelectric dams, the runoff from coal mining, the mercury emissions from burning coal—the list goes on and on.

This is motivation enough to rethink the way that we practice design. By designing and adapting the places where we live in an ecologically responsive style, we can contribute to the well-being of our clients as well as our planet and its limited natural resources. To encourage, inform, and assist you in navigating all this, we have assembled some of the most compelling reasons for sustainable design in the key areas where residential interior designers can actively improve the current state of the industry and the planet—before it is too late and the damage to the planet and its ecosystems become irremediable. They include:

- Environmental stewardship and the improved environmental quality of the planet, including air, water, and land, and protecting limited resources and ecosystems
- Good design supported by the Council for Interior Design Accreditation (CIDA) and the American Institute of Architects (AIA)
- Natural resource and materials conservation that minimizes the use of nonrenewable natural resources, and building with low-impact materials
- Improved indoor air and environmental quality
- Energy efficiency, lower energy consumption, and the promotion of renewable energy sources
- Water efficiency and conservation
- Waste reduction and management
- Optimized operational and maintenance practices
- A healthy planet for future generations

ENVIRONMENTAL STEWARDSHIP

For the children and the flowers are my sisters and my brothers, come and stand beside me, we can find a better way.

—JOHN DENVER, COFOUNDER, WINDSTAR

Nature is the precious source of life. As such, living in and engaging with nature should be treated as a privilege. All Earth's citizens must develop a broader perspective and become stewards of our planet. If we do not, the results promise to be disastrous. There is long-established evidence, for example, that we are headed for the dire consequences of global climate change. We would be foolish to wait for a calamity such as a dramatic rise in sea levels—predicted to be nearly five feet within a few generations—before we take action.

How Did the Ecology Movement Begin?

Over one hundred years ago, John Muir wrote to the editor of *Century* magazine, "Let us do something to make the mountains glad." Together, John Muir, Theodore Roosevelt, and David R. Bower founded the Sierra Club, the first major organization in the world dedicated to preserving nature, and the modern ecology movement was born.

Throughout his life, Muir was concerned with the protection of nature both for the spiritual advancement of humans and, as he said so often, for nature itself. These two concerns still inform the ecology movement and continue to inspire millions to think of themselves as a part of nature. Though the arguments in favor of ecological thinking are often couched in scientific terms, the basic impetus remains as Muir stated it: "When we try to pick out anything by itself, we find it hitched to everything in the universe."[2]

How Did the Environmental Movement Begin?

When, in 1962, Rachael Carson wrote the book *Silent Spring*, it made the public aware of nature's vulnerability to human intervention. In it, she made a radical proposal: that at times, technological progress is so fundamentally at odds with natural processes that it must be curtailed. Prior to the book's publication, there had never been broad public interest in conservation, for until then few people had worried about the disappearing wilderness. But the threats Carson outlined—the contamination of the food chain, cancer, genetic damage, the extinction of entire species—were too frightening to ignore. For the first time, the need to regulate industry in order to protect the environment became widely accepted, and environmentalism emerged.

Carson was well aware of the larger implications of her work. Appearing in a CBS documentary about *Silent Spring* shortly before her death from breast cancer in 1964, she remarked:

> Man's attitude toward nature is today critically important simply because we
> have now acquired a fateful power to alter and destroy nature. But man is
> a part of nature, and his war against nature is inevitably a war against him-
> self....[We are] challenged as mankind has never been challenged before to
> prove our maturity and our mastery, not of nature, but of ourselves.

The message of *Silent Spring*, one of the landmark books of the twentieth century, continues to resonate loudly more than four decades after its publication. Equally inspiring is the example of Rachel Carson herself. Against overwhelming difficulties and adversity, and motivated by her unabashed love of nature, she rose like a gladiator to its defense.

Environmental Stewardship

What is environmental stewardship, and how does it relate to sustainable design? Sustainability is a concept with definitions that vary across national borders and over time, but most agree that at its core is societal advancement balanced by the social, economic, and environmental needs of current and future generations. Here are two examples:

- The Environmental Protection Agency bases sustainability on a simple principle: Everything that we need for our survival and well-being depends, either

The more clearly we can focus our attention on the wonders and realities of the universe about us, the less taste we shall have for destruction.

—RACHEL CARSON, © 1954
REPRINTED WITH PERMISSION
FROM THE NATURAL RESOURCES
DEFENSE COUNCIL

---

[2] www.ecotopia.org/ecology-hall-of-fame/john-muir/biography/

directly or indirectly, on our natural environment. Sustainability creates and maintains the conditions under which humans and nature can exist in productive harmony and that permit fulfilling the social, economic and other requirements of present and future generations. Sustainability helps ensure that we have and will continue to have the water, materials, and resources to protect human health and our environment.[3]

- The Energy Alternative defines environmental stewardship as the "wisest use of both finite and reusable energy resources to produce the most work guided by a principle of causing the least known harm to the environment and driven by a desire to aid in the restoration of a healthier environment."[4]

PERSONAL RESPONSIBILITY

Never doubt that a small group of thoughtful, committed people can change the world; indeed, it's the only thing that ever has!

—Margaret Mead

As interior designers, we must make a commitment to become environmental champions; it is, after all, men and women who make things happen and get things done who will 'BE' the significant difference in the world.

Change occurs by the actions we take and the choices we make. We can be change agents who set an example by demonstrating environmental responsibility through our work and business practices. We, collectively, have the power to drive change within our industry. By specifying interior finishes that are timeless, healthy, and include recycled content; selecting woods that are responsibly harvested; and ensuring that the materials we specify do not contribute to outgassing and exacerbate human health problems, we can reshape our industry's traditions while we accelerate acceptance and implementation of environmental principles and practices. As environmental champions, we can welcome the challenge to be innovative risk-takers and push beyond the status quo. We may experience an occasional setback, but if we continue to challenge the industry we can help raise it to the next level of environmental performance.

By seeking reliable information and surrounding ourselves with like-minded people, we nurture our environmental aspirations. But first we need to recognize how directly our actions affect the environment, both positively and negatively. Then we must acquire the skills we need to further develop our personal commitment to improving the environment, safety, health, and well-being of our clients.

On a personal level, identify what inspires you to take on environmental issues and to make change happen. Then proactively, respectfully, enthusiastically, and tenaciously pursue your goal of sustaining the environment. Influence others through your involvement with professional organizations such as the American Society of

---

[3] www.epa.gov/sustainability/basicinfo.html
[4] www.theenergyalternative.com/glossary.html

Environmental Champion: Ray Anderson

Ray Anderson's personal commitment to the environment changed the floor-covering industry. In 1994, as CEO of Interface, the world's largest commercial floor-coverings producer, Anderson was invited to give the keynote address to Interface's newly formed environmental task force. He was reluctant to accept because his environmental vision ended with obeying the law. Then he received Paul Hawkens's *The Ecology of Commerce* (1994). Anderson recalled, "I read it, and it changed my life. It hit me right between the eyes. It was an epiphany. I wasn't halfway through it before I had the vision I was looking for. . .and a powerful sense of urgency to do something." After this chance introduction to environmental issues, Anderson embarked on a mission to make Interface a sustainable corporation by leading a worldwide war on waste and by pioneering the processes of sustainable development within his company and beyond.

Interior Designers (ASID), the International Interior Design Association (IIDA), the American Institute of Architects (AIA), the AIA Committee on the Environment (AIA COTE), Architects/Designers/Planners for Social Responsibility (ADPSR), and the U.S. Green Building Council (USGBC). As part of the larger movement, you can integrate environmental consciousness at all levels, both personally and professionally. Make the very personal decision to take moral responsibility for what you do as a designer of the built environment, and then put that commitment into action on all projects.

GOOD DESIGN

Good design and sustainable design are one and the same—synonymous with each other. Integrating sustainable design principles and practices is creative and rewarding and opens doors to vast possibilities for personal expression and personal growth for the designer, the client, and the project team.
  —ADAPTED FROM DENNIS WEDLICK, AIA, DENNIS WEDLICK ARCHITECT, LLC

Designers are trained to become habitually conscientious creatures, and we accept responsibility for creative design solutions for every interior. Our professional organizations provide codes of ethics that specify our responsibilities as designers regarding function, safety, codes, and aesthetics. We are required to find solutions to design questions and to prepare drawings and specifications that illustrate how we intend to implement these solutions. And the subject of sustainability is now being included in the education of interior designers.

On January 1, 2006, the board of directors for the Council for Interior Design Accreditation (CIDA, formerly the Foundation for Interior Design Educations Research, or FIDER) adopted revisions to its professional standards. This set in motion the addition of sustainability to the curricula for interior education programs and launched the sustainable initiative that all interior design programs must include to be accredited. (These standards were updated in 2011 and again in 2014.) CIDA's vision and leadership continue to have far-reaching effects for interior design education and professional practice.

These revisions strengthened the expectations for student learning in sustainability and communication. The new standards maintain that every student who graduates from a CIDA-accredited school must demonstrate his or her understanding of the concepts, principles, and theories of sustainability as they pertain to building methods, materials, systems, and occupants.

These standards are also supported by the AIA, whose board of directors also adopted position statements to promote sustainable design and resource conservation. In order to achieve a 70 percent reduction of the current consumption level of fossil fuels used to construct and operate buildings by 2015, and an 80 percent reduction by 2020, the AIA will collaborate with other national and international organizations as well as scientists and public health officials. As part of this initiative, the AIA will also develop and promote the integration of sustainability into the curricula for the education of architects and architecture students so this core principle becomes a guide for current and future architects.[5]

AIA Public Policy Position Statement

Architects are Environmentally Responsible

The creation and operation of the built environment requires an investment in the Earth's resources. Architects must be environmentally responsible and advocate for the sustainable use of those resources.

Supporting Position Statements

1. Energy and the Built Environment

    The AIA supports governmental policies, programs, and incentives to encourage energy conservation as it relates to the built environment as well as aggressive development and harvesting of energy from renewable sources. Architects are encouraged to promote energy efficiency and waste reduction in the built environment,

---

[5] www.aia.org

encourage energy-conscious design and technology, plus support a national program for more efficient use and recycling of nonrenewable resources and carbon-neutral design strategies.

2. Sustainable Built Environment

The AIA supports governmental and private-sector policy programs and incentives to encourage a built environment that embodies the advantages of sustainable architecture.

3. Sustainable Architectural Practice

The AIA recognizes a growing body of evidence that demonstrates current planning, design, construction, and real estate practices contribute to patterns of resource consumption that will inhibit the sustainable future of the Earth. Architects, as the leaders in design of the built environment, are responsible to act as stewards of the Earth. Consequently, we encourage communities to join with us to take the leadership to change the course of the planet's future and support legislative and regulatory strategies that implement sustainable design practices to advance the goal of achieving carbon-neutral buildings by the year 2030.

4. Sustainable Building Codes, Standards, and Rating Systems

The AIA supports the development, evaluation, and use of codes, standards and evidence-based rating systems that promote the design, preservation, and construction of sustainable communities and high-performance buildings

Source: American Institute of Architects

Additionally the AIA Committee on the Environment (COTE) works to advance, disseminate, and advocate—to the profession, the building industry, the academy, and the public—design practices that integrate built and natural systems and enhance both the design quality and environmental performance of the built environment. COTE is the voice of AIA architects regarding sustainable design, building science, and performance.

COTE reflects the profession's commitment to provide healthy and safe environments for people and is dedicated to preserving the Earth's capability of sustaining a shared high-quality of life. The committee's mission is to lead and coordinate the profession's involvement in environmental and energy-related issues and to promote the role of the architect as a leader in preserving and protecting the planet and its living systems.

What Is Next for Sustainable Design?

Authentic experiences are grounded in what is real, what is enduring, and what we can experience directly. As such, experiential design is less focused on buildings as objects and interior architecture as abstract composition, instead prioritizing direct, sensual experience and the narrative of place. In addition to engaging traditional sustainability measures such as energy efficiency, daylighting, and the use of healthy materials, the following are key to a holistic and experientially based sustainable design approach:

- *Focus on experiential qualities*. Experiential design is sensual, tactile, and revealed over time as spaces respond to the dynamics of the seasons and the time of day.
- *Connect with cultural history*. Design can keep stories about the past alive by preserving and/or reusing artifacts or by leaving traces of the past through the use of architectural palimpsests.
- *Engage the natural world*. In a natural setting, this may mean organizing space to capture views or finding opportunities to open up to the outdoors. In urban settings, this may mean creating a bit of nature indoors with living walls, roof terraces, and pocket parks.
- *Seek out diversity*. Rather than seeking beauty in uniformity and a tightly controlled palette, seek out materials, colors, and textures that create beauty through diversity.
- *Demonstrate interconnectedness*. Develop building systems that are multifunctional and interconnected, like systems in the natural world.
- *Cultivate resilience*. Be aware that efficiency has its limits, and the use of redundant systems can be beneficial in the long run to increase longevity.
- *Use local materials*. Explore the use of locally sourced natural materials, reused materials, and unique or artisanal materials that have meaning to building occupants.

Source: Sandy Mendler, AIA, in *Contract* magazine. http://www.contractdesign .com/contract/design/What-Is-Next-for-Sus-7749.shtml

COTE provides the AIA with knowledge about environmental issues and advises the Institute on environmental policy matters affecting the practice of architecture. The committee supports cooperation with educators and institutions of learning, manufacturers, government agencies, environmental organizations, and industry groups to advance environmentally sound design processes and standards as well as environmentally innovative materials and integrated systems.

All of this is great news for the entire built community. Through ingenuity, drive, and commitment, we can make sustainability and design ideal partners. Coupled with the support of the higher educational system, the accelerated implementation of a healthy, high-performing built environment and interior design is a certainty.

LOW-IMPACT BUILDING MATERIALS

Mountain men left no physical trace of their lives upon the Western land-scape—they moved so lightly upon the world that only the land and the river remain a witness to those shining times.

—1838 RENDEZVOUS ASSOCIATION

The AIA requires the reduced use of nonrenewable natural resources through the reuse of existing structures and materials, reductions in construction waste, promotion of recycled content materials, and use of materials independently certified as from sustainable sources. This strong stance will change how every building is created going forward and, because we work so closely with architects, it will likewise change our approach to projects.

Conventional building practices consume large quantities of wood, stone, metal, and other natural resources that lead unnecessarily to their depletion. Wood, for example, one of the most frequently used building materials, is often inefficiently utilized. Reports indicate that we have already harvested 95 percent of this nation's old-growth forests. Plainly, this practice cannot continue.

According to the Worldwatch Institute, the USGBC, and the United Nations Environment Programme, buildings have a significant measurable impact on the environment.

- Buildings use about 40 percent of global energy, 25 percent of global water, and 40 percent of global resources.
- The building sector is the largest contributor to global greenhouse gas emissions, emitting approximately one-third of all greenhouse gas emissions.
- As much as 10 percent of the global economy is dedicated to buildings: their construction, operation, and the equipping of these homes and offices.
- Buildings account for 40 percent of the materials entering the global economy each year. Three billion tons of raw materials are turned into foundations, walls, pipes, and building finishes.

- Buildings consume enormous resources: one-quarter of the world's wood harvest and two-fifths of the world's material and energy flows.

- Residential and commercial buildings consume approximately 60 percent of the world's electricity.

- Existing buildings represent significant energy-saving opportunities because their performance level is frequently far below current efficiency potentials.

- In developing countries, new green construction yields enormous opportunities. Population growth, prosperity, and increasing urbanization fuel building and construction activities, which represent up to 40 percent of GDP.

- In the United States, nearly 650,000 new housing units are built each year, approximately 80 percent of which are single-family homes.

- A typical 1,700-square-foot wood-frame home requires the equivalent of clear cutting one acre of forest in the United States.

Products specified for the design and construction of homes consume resources and energy and produce air and water pollution and solid waste during manufacturing. Finite raw materials such as granite and marble are in decline and, therefore, prices for such products are rising faster than inflation. Following installation, these products and materials also require maintenance and periodic replacement, and when the building is demolished they are usually disposed of in landfills.

Resource efficiency must therefore become common practice. Durable, reusable building materials that minimize the use of natural resources are key to sustainable building practices. Consider the following overarching criteria when researching, specifying, and selecting materials.

Sustainable Management Practices

Companies that adopt sustainable management practices are becoming easier to find; look to organizations that pursue certification programs and standards like the International Standards Organization's ISO 14000 category, which addresses a variety of environmental management characteristics. ISO 1400 provides practical tools for companies and organizations that want to control their environmental impact and constantly improve their environmental performance through life-cycle analysis, communication, and auditing.

Look for manufacturers whose policies responsibly address the triple bottom line: people, profit, and planet. Do they prominently display their sustainable practices in their website and literature? Qualify the strategies they employ, such as source, waste water and energy reduction, voluntary testing programs, improved corporate image, and waste management.

Resource Efficiency

A fundamental strategy for resource-efficient building is to build less square footage, use smaller quantities of materials, and design the smallest footprint possible while still meeting the customer's needs. The most cost-effective conservation strategy is to buy fewer products and to use those products more resourcefully.

Source Reduction

The EPA defines source reduction as the design, manufacture, purchase, or use of materials (such as products and packaging) that reduce the amount or toxicity of garbage generated. Source reduction reduces waste-disposal and handling charges because the costs of recycling, municipal composting, landfilling, and combustion are diminished. Source reduction conserves resources and reduces pollution.

Reused Materials

Reused material is an element, product, or material that has been reprocessed or repurposed from another location or for a different purpose. Many durable products such as doors, cabinets, and other easily removed millwork, as well as some architectural metals and glass, can be readily salvaged and reused. This practice has typically been limited to restoration work, but deconstruction for building and renovation projects is now common practice in many parts of the country. Salvaging requires a plan to cost-effectively reclaim quality materials such as old-growth hardwood flooring. Labor costs are often partially or even entirely offset by savings on new materials, transportation, and landfill tipping fees.

Recycled Content

The Leadership in Energy and Environmental Design (LEED) rating system categorizes recycled materials:

- *Postconsumer material* is the percentage of a product's material made from waste generated by end users (such as households or commercial, industrial, and institutional facilities) and can no longer be used for its originally intended purpose. It has been recycled into raw material for a new product.

- *Preconsumer/postindustrial content* is the percentage of a product's material that has been diverted from the waste stream during a manufacturing process. Excluded from this category are materials such as scrap that were generated during a certain process and can be reclaimed during that same process.

- *Internal manufacturing reclamation* refers to materials such as rework, regrind, or scrap that can be reused in the same process during which they were generated.

  Using products made with recycled content keeps materials out of the waste stream. There are many building products with a high percentage of recycled materials on the market.

Rapidly Renewable

Rapidly renewable materials must have a harvest cycle of ten years or less. Wood, plant fibers, wool, bamboo, agrifibers, cork, linoleum, soy, cotton, and corn-based products are examples of rapidly renewable materials. When these materials come from animals, like wool, they need to do no harm to the animal.

Climate-Specific

Certain types of construction and materials are more appropriate for certain climates. For example, utilizing thermal mass in building design has important energy and comfort benefits in the Southwest, where daily temperature swings can be extreme. In a hot, humid climate like that of the Southeast, lightweight construction and high ceilings may be more beneficial.

Regional Products

Specifying products made with local materials and labor can mean lower embodied energy consumption and reduce or even eliminate transportation costs. Regional products and materials should be extracted, harvested, and manufactured within a set distance of your project; LEED requires materials to come from within a 500-mile radius of the site.

Durable and Timeless

Good design and green design are synonymous and translate into a home that is the most durable and high-performing possible. The building envelope and assemblies, systems, interior finishes, and furnishings need to work together seamlessly to make a home healthy, efficient, safe, durable, and timeless. Durability is a strategy that should be adopted at the onset of the design, carried through material research and selection, and implemented throughout construction; it yields aesthetics and serviceability that lasts and adds to the value of the home. By integrating energy efficiency, indoor air quality, moisture management, and materials selection, the home will be inherently timeless and durable.

Multi-Attributes

Multi-attribute products carry numerous certifications that take into account a broad assessment of environmental, health, and even social measures. Some may include a full life-cycle evaluation. Others may simply use life-cycle philosophy to inform the priorities within a certification.

Manufacturer Transparency

Product transparency informs project teams about their products' health, environmental, and social impacts. Asking for a comprehensive report on a product's health effects, material sourcing, chemical makeup, sustainability, life cycle, and societal impact is a human right. This detailed level of transparency about a products ingredients will continue to move the industry in the right direction. Look for more on this subject in chapter 8, "Certifications and Standards."

Life-Cycle Cost

Over the useful life of a building, which can be one hundred years or more, most materials will require maintenance and be replaced more than once. When the costs over a building's entire life cycle are considered, a material's higher initial cost may be justified if the product compares favorably with others' durability.

Resource Recovery and Recycling

Beyond a material's initial use, it has the potential to be recovered, repurposed, and recycled:

- Metals are recyclable if they can be separated by type. Steel and aluminum building elements are easily recyclable. Approximately 50 to 70 percent of the pollution from and energy used in steel production can be eliminated through recycling; as much as 85 percent of the energy used in and pollution from aluminum manufacturing can be eliminated by re-melting it.

- Most plastics are technically recyclable, but the wide variety of plastics in use makes them difficult to separate; additives, coatings, and colorants impede recycling as well. Some plastics, such as pure polyvinyl chloride (PVC), would be recycled from buildings more often if they were designed for easy removal.

- Glass products are recyclable if separated and uncontaminated; however, few glass building products are currently recycled. Recycled glass products are made with consumer container glass salvaged from the waste stream. Although re-melting glass offers only marginal energy and pollution reduction, it reduces the use of virgin materials.

- Heavy timber is recyclable by salvaging and re-sawing it. Engineered structural wood products, wood panels, and millwork are candidates for salvage and reuse, particularly if they are fastened in such a way that they can be easily removed.

- Concrete, clay, ceramics, and other masonry products are difficult to salvage and reuse. They are sometimes recycled by crushing them for use as granular fill in road and sidewalk bases.

- Furniture, area rugs, and artwork can be recovered and repurposed. Most quality casework pieces, although they can be expensive, become future collectibles.

Ecologically minded design requires that we consider a product's environmental impact. By conserving natural resources, we will begin the rebuilding and restoration of our natural capital—the natural resources and ecological systems that provide vital life-support services to our planet.

INDOOR AIR QUALITY

A nation that destroys its soils destroys itself. Forests are the lungs of our land, purifying the air and giving fresh strength to our people.

—FRANKLIN ROOSEVELT

Healthy interiors are organic by nature. They feel good, live well, look great, and are sustaining for all. We are all part of the integrated system called nature, and more than any other species, what we do affects the health and longevity of life on the planet.

Why Does Indoor Air Quality Matter?

The air quality of our indoor environments affects our health and often contributes to structural degradation and building failures.

According to the American Lung Association of Minnesota, elements within our home and workplaces have been increasingly recognized as threats to our respiratory health. The most common pollutants are radon, combustion products, biologicals (molds, pet dander, pollen), volatile organic compounds (VOCs), lead dust, and asbestos.

The Environmental Protection Agency lists poor indoor air quality as the fourth-largest environmental threat to our country.

There are an estimated 40 million individuals in the United States affected by allergies, so knowing how to reduce a home's allergen levels is important. People who suffer from asthma or have other respiratory illness can be at a greater risk for health complications associated with poor air quality in their home.

The prevalence rate of pediatric asthma has increased from 40.1 to 69.1 percent—a 72.3 percent increase. Asthma is the sixth-ranking chronic condition in the United States and the leading serious chronic illness in children.

In the house itself, poor indoor air quality can result in structural rot from excess moisture within the walls and attic and around window framing. And common pollutants can enter our houses through air leaks in the structure. Typical problems or failures include musty odors and mold growth, window condensation, structural rot, peeling paint, back-drafting appliances, damp basements, ice dams and ice buildup on the edge of a roof, and high utility costs.

Source: American Lung Association, http://www.lung.org/associations/charters/mid-atlantic/air-quality/indoor-air-quality.html

In our efforts to build energy-efficient homes, we have inadvertently created indoor air problems due to poor ventilation and the use of toxic materials and finishes. Poor indoor air quality is caused by the off-gassing of chemicals found in many building materials as well as mold and mildew that build up in poorly designed and maintained heating and cooling systems. Statistics indicate that we spend 90 percent or more of our time indoors, further heightening the effects of indoor air quality (IAQ). The consequence of polluted indoor environments is an overall deterioration in health and well-being. The EPA reports that the air in new homes can be 2 to 5 times more polluted than outdoor air and occasionally 100 times worse than outdoor air. The World Health Organization (WHO) reports that as many as 30 percent of our buildings exhibit signs of what is referred to as sick building syndrome (SBS).

According to the *New England Journal of Medicine*, 40 percent of children will develop respiratory disease due in part to the chemicals in their homes. Children breathe more rapidly and inhale more air per breath than adults, and because they are more physically active than adults when outdoors, they are exposed to more outdoor air pollution. Because their breathing zone is lower than adults, they are more exposed to vehicle exhausts and heavier pollutants that concentrate at lower levels in the air. Children also spend up to 80 percent of their time indoors and are therefore also exposed to high amounts of indoor air contaminants.

The choices we make in designing homes and the materials we select have long-term consequences on the indoor environment. Interior designers can therefore contribute positively to creating a safer, healthier environment, and good indoor air quality must be an important consideration throughout the design process.

Fortunately, IAQ becomes a priority for clients once they understand that it is possible to build a home that provides a healthy environment for their family. Delivering an indoor environment that celebrates health, productivity, and happiness; aims to not cause headaches, watery eyes, or raspy throats; and ensures that children with allergies and asthma can breathe more easily is paramount to good design. By choosing wisely the strategies, systems, and products that we specify, we can produce a healthy environment that supports healthier air quality.

INDOOR ENVIRONMENTAL QUALITY

We must also consider indoor environmental quality (IEQ), which has a significant impact on the health, comfort, and productivity of a home's inhabitants as well. A sustainable building should therefore maximize daylighting and a connection to nature, provide appropriate ventilation and moisture control to minimize the opportunity for microbial growth, utilize the least toxic and lowest emitting materials, provide an adequate fresh air supply, and utilize ergonomic tactics.

Common Factors That Affect IAQ

- People (exhalation, body odors, diseases)
- Human activities that use cleaning products, correction fluids, carbonless paper, pest control products,
- Personal activities such as wearing fragrances and smoking
- Technology (photocopiers and laser printers)
- Furnishings (furniture, draperies, floor coverings)
- Finishes (paint, varnish, vinyl wall coverings)
- Building materials (caulking compounds, adhesives, wood laminates)
- Outdoor air quality
- Inadequate or contaminated air-handling units
- Inadequate cleaning practices

Source: Carpet & Rug Institute, www.carpet-rug.org

One of the most common indoor pollutants is formaldehyde, a volatile organic compound (VOC) and a known human carcinogen. When combined with urea, an organic compound, it can emit toxic VOCs at room temperature. Common culprits include kitchen cabinets, countertops, shelving, and furniture, all typically constructed from particleboard held together by formaldehyde-based adhesives. The formaldehyde continues to be released into the home for years after these products have been installed, and its emissions have an adverse effect on human health. These emissions are also easily absorbed by soft materials, including carpets and fabrics, that reemit VOCs at a later time, thereby prolonging residents' exposure.

Paints, finishes, solvents, and adhesives also contain unhealthy VOCs. What is commonly called a "new house smell" is caused by the off-gassing of these compounds and is a good indication that harmful chemicals are present. Children are at a greater risk than adults, as their bodies and brains are still developing, hence more susceptible to damage from these chemicals.

Potentially harmful substances come from every room in the home. Indoor air quality is affected by:

- The building assembly
- Interior finishes and furnishings
- Volatile organic compounds

- Existing hazards such as lead, mold, and asbestos
- Cooking and cooking appliances
- People and occupant behavior
- Pets
- Toiletries
- Cleaning supplies
- Environmental tobacco smoke
- Pollen and dust
- Back drafts
- Moisture and mold
- VOCs from paints and finishes
- Formaldehyde emissions from cabinets
- HVAC and filtration systems
- Petroleum and pesticides tracked in from outside
- IAQ of adjacent rooms like a garage or shed

Thanks in large part to green building rating systems, the building products industry has risen to the challenge of improving indoor air pollution by developing adhesives, paints, and finishes with lower levels of VOCs and emissions. The next step is to eliminate toxic content and harmful chemicals.

We designers must practice the precautionary principle when specifying interior finishes and furnishings. The Science and Environmental Health Network best defines the precautionary principle: "When an activity raises threats of harm to the environment or human health, precautionary measures should be taken even if some cause and effect relationships are not fully established scientifically."[6] Ultimately, if the effects of a product, strategy, practice, or process are disputed or unknown, it should be avoided.

Many finishes and furnishings contain potentially hazardous chemicals that range from somewhat to extremely unhealthy, and when combined they can create a veritable chemical soup. It is far easier—and less costly—to prevent indoor contamination from the outset. This means including strategies for good IAQ within the design and construction process. This will reduce the need for mitigation cleanup and lower the risk of potential liability issues. (See "Understanding IAQ," page 21.)

By designing responsibly—following a set of guidelines for good indoor air quality and using low-emission materials and pollutant source control—we can deliver healthy, clean, nontoxic homes.

---

[6]www.sehn.org/Volume_3–1.html

CONSERVATION OF ENERGY AND WATER

Energy

I believe that the average guy in the street will give up a great deal if he really understands the cost of not giving it up. In fact, we may find that while we're drastically cutting our energy consumption, we're actually raising our standard of living.

—David R. Brower

Understanding IAQ

Indoor Air Quality Sources
The quality of indoor air depends on the interaction and impact of many complex factors. With potentially hundreds of different contaminants present in indoor air, identifying indoor air quality problems and developing solutions is difficult. The ways in which these factors contribute to IAQ are summarized below.
Construction Materials, Furnishings, and Equipment
These items may emit odors, particles, toxic content, and total volatile organic compounds (TVOCs), absorbing and releasing VOCs known as semi-VOCs (suspended particles that are airborne). Individual VOCs from a specific material may combine with VOCs from other materials to form new chemicals. VOCs and particulates can cause health problems for occupants that are exposed to them. In the presence of adequate heat and moisture, some materials produce nutrients that support the growth of molds and bacteria, which produce microbial volatile organic compounds (MVOCs).   These organisms can affect occupants adversely if fungal spores containing mycotoxins and allergens or the MVOCs themselves are inhaled. Much research remains to be done to identify individual metabolic gases, their odors, the microbes that produce them, and the human response to molds and fungi.
Building Envelope
The envelope makes up the outer shell of the building and provides protection from the exterior elements. The design of building components that separate conditioned living areas from unconditioned spaces must consider climate, ventilation, and energy consumption. Through the design and specification of HVAC systems, doors, windows, and insulation, the envelope provides thermal comfort by regulating temperature, air speed, and humidity; controls the infiltration of outside air, moisture control, and humidity levels; and regulates air pressure changes.
Ventilation Systems
Filtration and acoustical materials in HVAC systems may contribute to indoor air pollution in the same way as construction materials. Ventilation systems also control the distribution, quantity, temperature, and humidity of air.

(Continued)

Understanding IAQ (*Continued*)

Maintenance
Lack of maintenance allows dirt, dust, mold, odors, and particles to accumulate. The use of high-VOC cleaning agents pollutes the air.
Occupants
The number of occupants and the amount of equipment contribute to indoor air pollution. People and pets are major sources of microorganisms and airborne allergens in indoor environments. Occupant activities also can pollute the air.
Electric and Magnetic Fields
Electric and magnetic fields (EMFs) are invisible areas of energy, often referred to as radiation, associated with the use of electrical power and various forms of natural and man-made equipment as well as lighting. Electromagnetic hypersensitivity (ES) is a physiological disorder caused by exposure to electromagnetic fields, also known as electro-pollution. It produces neurological and allergic-type symptoms. Symptoms may include headache, eye irritation, dizziness, nausea, skin rash, facial swelling, weakness, fatigue, joint and muscle pain, tinnitus, numbness, abdominal pressure and pain, difficulty breathing, and irregular heartbeat. Exposure to electronics, fluorescent lights, dimmers, or a new home or work environment can elicit symptoms.
Health and Indoor Air Quality Issues
Poor indoor air quality can cause short- and long-term illness; symptoms range from minor irritations to life-threatening diseases. They are classified as follows:
Sick Building Syndrome
Sick building syndrome is a collection of usually short-term symptoms experienced by occupants that may disappear after they leave the building. The most common symptoms are sore throat, fatigue, lethargy, dizziness, difficulty concentrating, respiratory irritation, headaches, eye irritation, sinus congestion, dryness of the skin, and other cold-, influenza-, and allergy-type symptoms.
Building-Related Illnesses
Building-related illnesses are clinically verifiable diseases attributable to a specific source or pollutant within a building. Examples include cancer and Legionnaires' disease.
Multiple Chemical Sensitivities
Multiple chemical sensitivity (MCS) is a medical condition characterized by a heightened sensitivity to chemicals. People who have MCS become ill when exposed to a variety of chemical sources, many of which are commonly part of the environment. Some people have mild chemical sensitivities, while others have a more severe form of the illness. Substances that can cause symptoms include pesticides, fresh paint, new carpets, countless building materials, solvents, fresh ink, smoke, vehicle exhaust, industrial fumes, many cleaning products, and perfume, cologne, and other scented products such as air fresheners, fragrance-emitting devices, fabric softener, potpourri, incense, essential oils, and most soaps, shampoos, hair products, skin lotions, and laundry detergents.

Understanding IAQ

Symptoms can occur after inhaling, touching, or ingesting these substances. Reactions to scented products can occur even in people who cannot smell them. Because people with MCS react to chemicals at levels that do not ordinarily affect others, chemical sensitivity is similar to an allergy, but the symptoms and mechanism are not the same as those of traditional allergies to pollen, animals, and dust. Many of the above substances can make anyone sick at high concentrations, but chemically sensitive people can be harmed by exposure levels considered safe for the general population. Some of the symptoms reported by people with MCS are similar to known toxic reactions such as those listed on the manufacturer's material safety data sheets (MSDSs), but many chemically sensitive people experience symptoms different from typical toxic reactions. This individual variability and exquisite sensitivity can be so pronounced many scientists and doctors find it hard to accept as real.

Typical Indoor Air Pollutants

Poor indoor air quality is caused by outdoor and indoor sources of gaseous and particulate air pollutants that exceed the capacity of the building's ventilation and filtration equipment to remove or dilute to an acceptable level. Although many pollutants originate outdoors or from occupant activities, equipment, and processes, others are generated by materials.

Indoor air pollutants include:

- VOCs emitted by interior materials and their components
- VOCs emitted by cleaning and maintenance products periodically used with those materials
- Fiber shed from textiles, insulation, and panel products
- Soil, biological materials (e.g., fungi and bacteria), and gases released by biological activity
- Dust and other particulates from spraying, sanding, or finishing

These material-based pollutants may affect the health and productivity of building occupants, maintenance personnel, and construction tradespeople.

Emission Levels

Review emission levels from building products at the following stages of a project:

- *Installation*. To prevent emission exposure to tradespeople and building occupants during construction or renovation, information on potential hazards is documented in MSDSs, which are legally required for any material that may have health risks. However, these sheets typically do not disclose a full list of contents or proprietary blends. Additional information is available from the Occupational Safety and Health Administration (OSHA).
- *Building occupancy*. To prevent exposing building occupants to toxic emissions, gather the emissions data for materials during building use. Obtain product emissions data from manufacturers and coordinate with the mechanical engineer so that ventilation rates will protect building occupants while ensuring the design and performance are feasible.
- *Maintenance and removal*. Review emission levels to prevent exposure of building occupants and tradespeople during maintenance procedures, removal, or demolition. Maintenance and removal risks are reasonably well known for many conventional materials.

(Continued)

Understanding IAQ (*Continued*)

Consider these additional materials issues and effects:

■ *Sink effect*. Rough and porous materials may contain microscopic planes and cavities that can absorb airborne molecules. When these molecules, which may be pollutants, are released—or "desorbed"—from the material after several hours or days, it is known as the "sink effect." Hard, smooth, and nonporous surfaces typically have a low sink effect.

■ *Moisture and temperature*. Moisture and heat in materials increase their rate of deterioration and the emission of pollutants. Moisture also supports microbial growth.

■ *Soiling and cleaning*. Improper cleaning practices may disturb dirt and expose tradespeople to chemicals in cleaning products. Soft floor coverings such as carpeting are more susceptible to improper cleaning than nonporous flooring with minimal seams and low-maintenance coatings.

■ *Natural materials*. There is a common perception that natural materials are better for the environment and pose fewer health risks than man-made or synthetic materials, but this is not always the case. Toxicity and emissions testing will clarify which are, in fact, safer. However, predicting all potential health effects is not always possible.

Source: U.S. Environmental Protection Agency, www.epa.gov; Greenguard Certification from UL Environment, www.greenguard.org

Building Energy Consumption

Buildings consume more energy than any other sector. According to the U.S. Energy Information Administration (EIA), the building sector consumes nearly half (47.6 percent) of all energy produced in the United States. Nearly three-quarters (74.9 percent) of all the electricity produced in the United States is used just to operate buildings. Globally, these percentages are even greater.

Buildings are the largest contributor to climate change. Because so much blamed is heaped on transportation emissions, many people are surprised to learn that the building sector was responsible for nearly half (44.6 percent) of the United States' CO_2 emissions in 2010. By comparison, transportation accounted for 34.3 percent of CO_2 emissions and industry just 21.1 percent.

The health of the economy is tied to the building sector. The nation's economy hinges on a healthy building sector. The building sector touches nearly every industry (from steel, insulation, and

The United States, home to only about 4.5 percent of the world's population, consumes about 20 percent of the world's energy and generates 19 percent of global greenhouse gas pollution—six times that of automobiles in the United States. The United States is also the largest contributor to CO_2 emissions and, therefore, to climate change.

As members of the construction and design industry, residential interior designers have a responsibility to advocate for the highest efficiency appliances, lighting, and entertainment and office equipment.

Energy efficiency is one of the cornerstones of all high-performing building projects, and for residential designers, high-efficiency appliances, equipment, and lighting are a primary focus. The generation and use of energy are major contributors to air pollution and climate change. With the world's supply of fossil fuel dwindling, concerns for energy security increasing, and the global climatic impact of greenhouse gases growing, it is essential to find ways to reduce loads, increase efficiency, and utilize renewable energy.

We can begin by targeting energy savings when specifying appliances, entertainment and office equipment, ceiling fans, and light fixtures and light bulbs. Aided by the U.S. Department of Energy (DOE) minimum efficiency standards, the federal Energy Star program, and the efforts of the Consortium for Energy Efficiency (CEE), manufacturers have made tremendous strides in increasing the energy efficiency of their products. Energy-efficient choices can save families money on their energy bills while reducing greenhouse gas emissions.

caulking to mechanical and electrical equipment, glass, wood, metals, tile, fabrics, and paint) across all sectors of the economy, from architecture, planning, design, engineering, banking, and development to manufacturing, construction, wholesale, retail, and distribution.

The goal of reducing fossil fuel use by 50 percent was inspired, in part, by recent work by Santa Fe, New Mexico, architect Edward Mazria, AIA, who modified some standard assumptions made in analyzing U.S. energy use by economic sector. By including the energy embodied in building materials and some other adjustments, Mazria found that the share of energy use attributable to buildings grows dramatically, from 27 percent to nearly 50 percent. Mazria argues that to avoid a global catastrophe, global fossil fuel use must immediately be cut by 50 percent and emissions reduced even more than that by 2030. Other actions on the list include collaborating with organizations to integrate sustainability into architecture school curricula, documenting the contributions to humankind and the planet from sustainable design practices, and advocating globally for sustainable design. (See www.architecture2030.org for more information.)

Designers must always specify products that meet or exceed Energy Star requirements. Look for durable, easy-to-maintain products that conserve energy and water, are designed for disassembly, and come with long-term warranties.

One resource that identifies superefficient products is TopTen USA (www .toptenusa.org), which is a member of the TopTen International Group, a global alliance of TopTen organizations dedicated to product efficiency.

It's also important to discuss alternative energy sources with the client and project team. Consider wind, geothermal, and photovoltaic power with a goal of zero energy usage after ensuring that the home has a high-performing envelope.

There are different definitions of zero energy. Here is how the Net-Zero-Energy Home Coalition, a multi-stakeholder group in Canada comprised of corporations and nonprofit organizations, defines it:

> A net-zero-energy home at a minimum supplies to the grid an annual output of electricity that is equal to the amount of power purchased from the grid. In many cases the entire energy consumption (heating, cooling, and electrical) of a net-zero-energy home can be provided by renewable energy sources.

Water

For many of us, water simply flows from a faucet, and we think little about it beyond this point of contact. We have lost a sense of respect for the wild river, for the complex workings of a wetland, for the intricate web of life that water supports.

—SANDRA POSTEL, *LAST OASIS: FACING WATER SCARCITY* (2003)

We use purified drinking water to flush our toilets and water our lawns. That doesn't make any sense. In an era of scarcity, we won't need to limit whether we have water to boil pasta or take a bath. But we will think differently about a whole portfolio of water. There will be different kinds of waters for different uses. And water itself will get smart.

—CHARLES FISHMAN, THE BIG THIRST

How much water is used in a typical home?

- Approximately 400 billion gallons of water are used in the United States per day.

- Americans use about 100 gallons of water per day.

- Americans use more water each day by flushing the toilet than they do by showering or any other activity.

- Fifty to 75 percent of all residential water use occurs in the bathroom.

- Older toilets use between 3.5 and 7 gallons of water per flush. However, toilets with the EPA's "WaterSense" label require 75 to 80 percent less water.

- A leaky toilet can waste about 200 gallons of water every day.

- A bathroom faucet generally runs at 2 gallons of water per minute. By turning off the tap while brushing your teeth or

In many parts of this country and around the globe, freshwater has become a limited resource. Current studies indicate that the building industry consumes one-sixth of the world's freshwater supply, according to the USGBC and Worldwatch Institute. A sustainable building aims to reduce, control, or treat site runoff, use water efficiently, and reuse or recycle water for on-site use.

To protect and conserve water, designers can recommend the following:

- WaterSense flow and flush fixtures
- Low-flow faucets and showerheads
- Flow reducers on faucets and showerheads
- Ultra-low or dual-flush toilets
- Energy Star laundry appliances and dishwashers
- Chlorine filters on showerheads
- Water filtration units on faucets
- Hot water on-demand systems

The convenience of plumbing fixtures has made them the biggest water guzzlers in a typical family home. We must therefore specify water-conserving plumbing fixtures and fittings. In addition, retrofitting most devices in older buildings is cost-effective way to supports water efficiency by reducing water usage and

shaving, a person can save more than 200 gallons of water per month.

- High-efficiency washing machines can conserve large amounts of water. Traditional models use between 27 and 54 gallons of water per load, but new, energy- and water-conserving models (front-loading, top-loading, or those without agitators) use less than 27 gallons per load.
- Washing the dishes with an open tap can use up to 20 gallons of water, but filling the sink or a bowl and turning off the tap saves 10 of those gallons.
- Keeping a pitcher of water in the refrigerator instead of running the tap until it gets cold saves time and water.
- Not rinsing dishes prior to loading the dishwasher can save up to 10 gallons per load.

Source: U.S. Environmental Protection Agency and WaterSense

wastewater; such devices will pay for themselves within one to three years of installation.

In homes, bathrooms offer the greatest opportunity for saving water. Toilets use more water than any other household fixture. Nearly all flushed water in North America starts as clean, drinkable water.[7] The American Water Works Association Research Foundation examined water use in approximately 1,200 homes in 14 North American cities and found that an average household uses approximately 146,000 gallons of water annually, 42 percent indoors and 58 percent outdoors. In households where water-conserving plumbing fixtures have not been installed, toilets use an average of 20.1 gallons of water per day, or 26.7 percent of total indoor water use. In homes with water-conserving fixtures, toilets use an average of 9.6 gallons per day, or 19.3 percent of the total—though plumbing leaks account for another 10 to 14 percent of water use, and much of that is due to toilets.

Another water-saving device from the world of plumbing is the hot water on-demand system. Running cold water down the drain while waiting for hot water to reach the faucet wastes more than 10,000 gallons each year in an average American household. Hot water on-demand systems rapidly distribute hot water to the faucet while cold water is pumped back to the water heater. A pump attaches easily under the sink, and its heat sensor shuts off the unit after the water gets hot.

Preserving water is paramount, and new products on the market make it easier than ever to do. By reducing gallons per flush (GPF) and gallons per minute (GPM), we can achieve dramatic reductions in water use.

WASTE REDUCTION AND MANAGEMENT

The packaging for a microwavable dinner is programmed for a shelf life of maybe six months, a cook time of two minutes, and a landfill dead-time of centuries.

—DAVID WANN, *BUZZWORM*

> *Instead of defining success as getting the most materials, we need to move to a new standard: getting the most from them. Recycling 60 percent of U.S. solid waste would save the energy equivalent to 315 million barrels of oil each year.*
>
> —*WORLDWATCH INSTITUTE*

We live in a run away, throw away society that is leaving its mark on the Earth for future generations, who will have to clean up after their predecessors.

A green building includes waste reduction and management techniques from its inception to its completion. The best waste-reduction strategy embraces the three r's: reduce, reuse, and recycle, incorporating a comprehensive green building approach that includes resource conservation, material reuse, construction and demolition debris recovery and the use of recycled content materials. Such a strategy is vital to reducing pressure on landfills, saves money by reducing landfill tipping fees, provides raw materials for future building products, helps the environment, and enhances the bottom line.

---

[7] Per a report from *Environmental Building News* (EBN), January 2004.

Those in the building industry must be challenged to incorporate waste-reduction and recycling-specification language into their projects. Consider the following facts.

In 2011, Americans generated about 250 million tons of trash:

Paper and paperboard: 28 percent
Yard trimmings and food waste: 28 percent
Plastics: 13 percent
Metals: 9 percent
Rubber, leather, and textiles: 8 percent
Wood: 6 percent
Glass: 5 percent
Miscellaneous waste: 3 percent

Fortunately, times have changed. We recycled and composted almost 87 million tons of this material, equivalent to a 34.7 percent recycling rate. On average, we recycled and composted 1.53 pounds of our individual waste generation of 4.40 pounds per person per day. Recycling and composting prevented 86.9 million tons of material from being thrown away in 2011, up from 15 million tons in 1980.

At a minimum, these materials should be addressed by the project's waste management plan. Begin by estimating the types and quantities of the materials to be generated on-site. Target at least 50 percent of the construction and/or demolition debris for recycling. Then contact local haulers and recycling facilities for their terms and conditions.

Many cities have adopted regulations for construction waste management. For example, San Jose, California, requires contractors to recycle 75 percent of construction waste to receive a final certificate of occupancy, thereby reducing the amount of construction and demolition (C&D) waste sent to landfills. Look into your projects' local ordinances to learn what is available and/or required for construction and waste demolition.

Unused materials from the job site can also be donated. Salvaged materials, such as leftover wood, windows, doors, and other uninstalled items, can be donated to organizations such as Habitat for Humanity, local programs like ReSource (www.resourceyard.org), regional art programs, and design or architecture schools.

C&D debris occupies a large percentage of space in our landfills, and the steady growth of building activities is a major reason why landfill volumes have been increasing, despite expanding recycling efforts. In Alameda County, California, for example, where citizens recycle a high percentage of their waste, more than 355,000 tons of construction and demolition materials are nonetheless disposed of in county landfills annually.

Check out the Recycling Certification Institute, which oversees the national certification program that ensures integrity, transparency, accuracy, and reliability in the recovery/recycling reports of participating C&D recycling facilities. It provides a list of certified facilities along with evaluation reports and evaluation statements available on their website. The evaluation reports detail the activities conducted in the evaluation of the certified C&D recycling facility and outline the findings of the evaluators (www.recyclingcertification.org).

Landfills are expensive to build, and no one wants to live near one. The more we reduce waste, the less need we have for building new landfills. Waste reduction on the job site saves money, and hiring source reduction and reuse and/or recycling contractors can reduce expenses. By working with the contractor to develop a waste management plan and developing resources to assist in the diversion of C&D materials, we support environmental stewardship.

OPERATION AND MAINTENANCE

The practice of sustainable design does not end when construction is complete. After the homeowner moves in, the home must operate as it was designed to. Prior planning, recommended cleaning products, and long-term system maintenance guidelines all determine how well a home will perform over its useful life. Incorporating operating and maintenance considerations into the design of a home greatly contributes to healthy and safe living environments, quality of life, and the reduced use of energy and other resources.

To that end, specify materials and systems that are cost-effective and require less water, energy, toxic chemicals, and cleaners to maintain. Providing guidelines that address all aspects of maintaining a home will help a well-designed building function as intended.

Environmental Performance Index Ranks the United States Thirty-third

The 2014 Environmental Performance Index is a joint project between the Yale Center for Environmental Law and Policy (YCELP) and the Center for International Earth Science Information Network (CIESIN) at Columbia University, in collaboration with the World Economic Forum and The Environmental Performance Index (EPI) is calculated from an aggregate of twenty indicators reflecting national-level environmental data. These indicators are combined into nine issue categories, each of which fit under one of two overarching objectives.

The 2014 EPI ranked countries based on nine issues and twenty indicators related to environmental health, air quality, water and sanitation, water resources, agriculture, forests, fisheries, biodiversity and habitat, and climate and energy. Switzerland scored first among all countries, earning 87.67 out of 100 possible points. The United States scored 67.52 points, coming in behind most of Western Europe, Canada, Singapore, United Arab Emirates, Japan, Australia, and New Zealand. (The full report is available online at http://epi.yale.edu/.)

FOR FUTURE GENERATIONS

We do not inherit the Earth from our ancestors; we borrow it from our children.

—NAVAJO PROVERB

I do not believe that the process of human life on this globe has degenerated to a point of no return. I do believe, however, that we are fast approaching that point and we must redirect and correct our course in life to ensure health and a good life for the seventh generation coming. This legacy is passed down not to ensure the present, but to guarantee the future. Thinking of future generations is an enormous responsibility that requires vision.

—CHIEF OREN LYONS, AUGUST 1997

Protecting the environment and preserving the planet for future generations is without doubt one of the primary benefits of sustainable design. There are many definitions of sustainability:

- The ability to provide for the needs of the world's current population without damaging the ability of future generations to provide for themselves. When a process is sustainable, it can be carried out over and over without negative environmental effects or impossibly high costs to anyone involved (www .sustainabletable.org).
- To keep in existence, maintain; meeting the needs of future generations…. The ability to provide a healthy, satisfying, and just life for all people on Earth, now and for generations to come, while enhancing the health of ecosystems and the ability of other species to survive in their natural environments (www .earthethics.us).
- The Seventh Generation Principle states that we should make decisions about how we live today based on how our decisions will impact the next seven generations. We must be good caretakers of the Earth, not simply for ourselves, but for those who will inherit the Earth and the results of our decisions. This value is found in the Iroquois Great Law of Peace (Haudenosaunee Gayanashagowa) and is common among a number of indigenous peoples in the Americas. It is a sound principle should guides our policies and practices (www.woodbinecenter.org/node/27).

There are common threads to these definitions. Sustainability requires meeting environmental, economic, and community needs simultaneously. All three are essential to ensuring that quality of life continues for living systems and future generations.

What if residential interior designers embraced the message from Catherine Ryan Hyde in her 1999 novel *Pay It Forward*? The book advocates continually passing on good deeds. But does this have to be fiction?

In the book, Reuben St. Clair, the teacher-protagonist, starts a movement with this voluntary, extra-credit assignment: Think of an idea for world change, and put it into action.

Trevor, the twelve-year-old hero, thinks of quite an idea. He describes it to his mother and teacher this way:

> "You see, I do something real good for three people. And then when they ask how they can pay it back, I say they have to pay it forward. To three more people. Each. So nine people get helped. Then those people have to do twenty-seven." He turned on the calculator, punched in a few numbers. "Then it sort of spreads out, see. To 81. Then 243. Then 729. Then 2,187. See how big it gets?"

This concept could become a successful catalyst for healing the planet and creating a change in the marketplace. What if each of us, in our role as designers, implemented three great things for the environment on each of our projects and then asked project team members to "pay it forward"? The positive effects on the environment would grow exponentially....

Conclusion

William McDonough's sustainability design challenge is inspiring:

> We need a new design assignment and we need a new design. In order to do this we need to ask new questions. "How do we love all the children, of all species, for all time?" Please notice that I am not just saying *our* children; I am saying *all* of the children. And notice I am not just saying *our* species, I am saying *all* species. And notice I am not just saying *now*, I am saying *for all time*. When we integrate this question into our designs, wonderful and beautiful things begin to happen.

RESOURCES

"It's the Architecture, Stupid!" Edward Mazria, AIA. www.architecture2030.org.

"Shades of Green." Anita Baltimore, FASID. *Interiors & Sources*, April 2005.

"What Makes a Product Green." The GreenSpec Team. *Environmental Building News*, February 2012

"Why Green Design Matters." Penny Bonda, ASID. *Icon*, May 2003.

inspiring stories

Inspiration comes through experiences that touch our hearts and open our minds to new ways of thinking and new ways of doing. In acknowledgment of the power of such experiences in our own lives, we invited some of our mentors and associates to share their personal stories of inspiration.

William McDonough: Designing the Future

William McDonough is a world-renowned architect and designer and winner of three prestigious national awards: the Presidential Award for Sustainable Development (1996), the Presidential Green Chemistry Challenge Award (2003), and the National Design Award (2004). Time *magazine dubbed him a "hero for the planet" in 1999.*

Photo courtesy of William McDonough.

Founding principal of William McDonough + Partners Architecture and Community Design, a design firm practicing ecologically, socially, and economically intelligent architecture and planning in the United States and abroad, William is also the cofounder and principal, with German chemist Michael Braungart, of McDonough Braungart Design Chemistry (MBDC), which employs a comprehensive cradle-to-cradle design protocol to chemical benchmarking, supply-chain integration, energy and materials assessment, clean-production qualification, and sustainability issue management and optimization.

MY LIFE IN DESIGN HAS BEEN INFLUENCED STRONGLY BY EXPERIENCES I HAD ABROAD, beginning in Japan, where I spent my early childhood. Although land and resources were scarce there, I mainly recall the beauty of traditional Japanese homes, with their paper walls and dripping gardens, their warm futons and steaming baths. I also remember quilted winter garments and farmhouses with thick walls of clay and straw that kept the interior warm in winter and cool in summer.

Later, in college, I accompanied a professor of urban design to Jordan to develop housing for the Bedouin who were settling in the Jordan River Valley. There, I was struck again by how simple and elegant good design can be, especially when it is suited to the locale. The tents of woven goat hair the Bedouin had used when nomads drew hot air up and out, creating not only shade but a refreshing interior breeze. When it rained, the fiber swelled and the structure became tight as a drum. This ingenious design, locally relevant and culturally rich, contrasted sharply with modern home design, which applied universal solutions to local circumstances and sharply separated indoors and out. The Bedouin tent, on the other hand, was in constant, intelligent dialog with place; only a permeable membrane separated the landscape from the interior. Imagine if American homes and interiors were designed to make equally good use of the particular gifts of particular locales—the varieties of sunlight, wind, terrain, and vegetation that show what works in each place and make shelter a living, breathing presence in the landscape.

After graduate school, I apprenticed with a New York firm esteemed for its socially responsible urban housing, and then founded my own architectural firm in 1981. Three years later we were commissioned to design the offices of the Environmental Defense Fund, which became the first green office in New York. I worked on indoor air quality, a subject almost no one had studied in depth. Of particular concern to us were volatile organic compounds, carcinogenic materials, and anything else in paints, wall coverings, carpeting, flooring, and fixtures that might cause indoor air problems or multiple chemical sensitivity.

With little or no research available, we turned to manufacturers, who often told us the information was proprietary and gave us nothing beyond vague safeguards in the material data safety sheets mandated by law. We did the best we could at the time. We used water-based paints. We tacked down carpet instead of gluing it. We provided 30 cubic feet per minute of fresh air per person instead of the standard 5. We had granite checked for radon. We used wood that was sustainably harvested. We did our best, but I hoped for more. I wanted to design buildings and materials that were completely beneficial for people and nature. I wanted to make things that celebrated human creativity and the abundance of the natural world.

A meeting with Michael Braungart, the world-renowned German chemist, launched the design protocol that made this possible. Both Michael and I wanted to challenge the entrenched idea that industry and commerce inevitably damage the natural world. We saw pollution, toxicity, and waste as signals of design failure that could be positively addressed by design. Michael was highly skilled at analyzing the chemistry of materials and identifying the human and ecological health effects of plasticizers, polyvinyl chloride, heavy metals, and many other harmful substances. My practice and my design sensibility complemented Michael's scientific knowledge, and we were soon helping some of the world's most successful companies make products that were both environmentally safe and highly profitable. Moreover, those products were conceived so that, after their useful lives, they provided nourishment for something else, becoming either biological nutrients for the soil or technical nutrients for industry.

We called our approach "cradle-to-cradle design." One of the companies I designed products with was DesignTex, which worked with the Rohner textile mill in Germany to make Climatex Lifecycle, an upholstery fabric that blends wool free of pesticide residue and organically grown ramie dyed and processed entirely with nontoxic chemicals. The fabric is so safe that the trimmings from the mill become mulch for local gardens, returning the material's biological nutrients to the soil. And instead of producing dangerous effluents, the fabric solved the mill's hazardous waste problem: When the mill made Climatex Lifecycle, the processing water flowing out of the mill was as clean as the water flowing in. Meanwhile, companies taking up cradle-to-cradle design began to make technical nutrients for interiors: perpetually recyclable synthetic fabrics, carpet yarns, carpet tiles, and other household materials that can be recovered and used in generation after generation of high-quality products—not simply used in a product of lesser value, as in conventional recycling.

The things I make, and the way we make things, are a part of my story because they are the product of my influences and my hope for the future. They are part of this particular story because good design is transforming the materials we use in our homes. Interior designers still have to work hard to find materials that will be safe and beneficial for their clients, but thankfully, they are easier to find today than they were when I designed the Environmental Defense Fund's offices more than twenty years ago. Since then, our collective knowledge has grown, numerous high-quality, environmentally safe products have entered the marketplace, and the demand for them has expanded immensely. As young designers well schooled in the principles of ecological design enter the profession, demand and expertise will continue to grow. The future looks bright indeed—but only if we create the future with intention.

We can all be innovators and market catalysts today. We can imagine what a world of prosperity and health will look like and begin designing it right now. We can make things and places so intelligent and safe they leave an ecological footprint to delight in rather than lament. This will not be easy, of course. Creating a sustaining world is going to take us all, and it's going to take forever. But then, that's the point.

Used with permission and adapted especially for this book from *Cradle to Cradle: Remaking the Way We Make Things* (New York: North Point Press, 2002).

Hunter Lovins: Thinker of Sustainability

President of Natural Capitalism Solutions in Longmont, Colorado, Hunter Lovins is a professor of business and sustainability at the Bainbridge Graduate Institute and Bard College. Hunter has helped create a variety of for-profit and nonprofit companies, including Tree People in California, and the Rocky Mountain Institute (RMI) and E Source, both in Colorado. Through "natural capitalism," Hunter and her team implement the ideas of greater sustainability for companies and governments around the world and build the new intellectual capital we need to advance these ideas. She is also working with edu-cational institutions in the United States and abroad to inject the ideas of sustainability into all of the disciplines.

Photo courtesy of Hunter Lovins.

IN SOME WAYS, I AM NOT SURE THAT I HAD MUCH CHOICE OF A CAREER. My parents were both activists. My mother organized in the coalfields of West Virginia with John L. Lewis. My father helped to mentor Martin Luther King, Jr., and Cesar Chavez. I was carried as a baby to my first demonstration, in support of the Quakers who were sailing the boat *The Golden Rule* into the South Pacific to try to stop the atmospheric testing of nuclear bombs. My mom and dad taught me to leave the world a better place than I found it, to believe that not only *could* I make a difference but that I had a responsibility to do so.

Growing up on a small farm gave me a connection with natural and growing things, and I am still most comfortable outdoors. My parents gave me the blessing of knowing that there were things worth protecting. They never put limits on me and gave me the sense that anything was attainable if I wanted it badly enough. This made me a bit rebellious against the stupider parts of "the system" at an early age but also developed the recognition that I was devoting my life to causes that were larger than my passing desires.

My own activism started in about 1963, working in such movements as fair housing and civil rights, then moved into organizing anti-Vietnam War protests, human rights work, and environmental protection. I resigned from the Sierra Club in protest at the first firing of Dave Brower and went with him to Friends of the Earth. In 1970, I planted a tree on the first Earth Day.

Lots of things inspire me. It's been an enormous honor to be able to travel to many beautiful places, from my own beloved Colorado mountains to the Hindu Kush in Afghanistan, from the jungles of Jamaica to the veldt of Africa. Many people inspire me, from my friends and mentors Dave Brower and Dana Meadows, the two greatest environmental luminaries of our age, to such current colleagues as Lester Brown, Gwen Hallsmith, Paul Hawken, Denis Hayes, and Janine Benyus.

Rather than spend all my time with like-minded people, I find it is good to be exposed to different kinds of thinking. People tend to think in ways that are comfortable, and so we get into ruts. I try to spend as much time as I can with young people who don't know what is impossible, who have not had limits set on their ability to be creative and freethinking. Alan Savory, founder of Holistic Management, advises us to assume we are wrong and to always question our assumptions. The great activist Saul Alinsky, and Andy Lipkis, founder of Tree People, both taught me to engage in conversations with people from their perspective, not from my own. So I have a history of working with people from varying backgrounds, from the military and corporations to community activists, academicians, and politicians. Each brings a perspective that we need if we are to craft solutions that can tackle the sorts of challenges now facing us.

This is especially important when seeking to convey the idea that green design can work. Understanding what it is that people care about, and speaking to that, can enable advocates to show people how green design can enhance their quality of life. Visuals are also very important and communicate these ideas in a compelling way. My presentations use lots of pictures and relatively few words. In the design and environmental field we tend to focus more on the precise technical information, but this is much harder to learn from. We took great care when building RMI to create a structure that was beautiful and comfortable—as well as efficient. It was a technically fascinating house, the first to integrate passive solar and superefficient construction. But what sold the concept was that people could walk in from a snowstorm in February and see luscious tomatoes being grown. They could come in out of the dry Colorado clime and feel the humidity. The beauty of hand-painted Mexican tile and rubbed oak did a better job than we did of selling efficient passive and active solar architecture within a superinsulated environment.

It is important to get the numbers right, but it is equally important to demonstrate a higher quality of life. A sustainable future can solve such challenges as climate change, but people are more likely to embrace sustainability if they realize that our unsustainable society of material wealth has brought with it an inner poverty that no amount of Wal-Marts selling cheaper products can fill. This was brought home to me during my work in Afghanistan, where despite crushing poverty, the people have a closeness in their families and friendships, an oral tradition that values conversation and listening that our commercial media cannot match, and a dignity and happiness that does not derive from how much stuff they possess. Simple things—they love to fly kites—bring great enjoyment. When was the last time that you flew a kite with the entire neighborhood? There is much that we can do to use sustainable means to meet basic human needs for energy, water, housing, sanitation, and so on. But the Afghans have given me far more, in lessons in how to be truly happy.

My friend folksinger Kate Wolf said, "Find what you really care about and live a life that shows it." It is a great honor to have been given the opportunity to do this. Will you join me?

Paula Baker-Laporte: Designer of EcoNests

Hailed by Natural Home *magazine in 2005 as one of the top ten green architects in the United States, Paula leads the EcoNest design team in Ashland, Oregon. She is the primary author of* Prescriptions for a Healthy House: A Practical Guide for Architects, Builders, and Homeowners *(New Society Publishers, Gabriola Island, BC, 2008), is coauthor, with Robert Laporte of* EcoNests: Creating Sustainable Sanctuaries of Clay, Straw, and Timber *(Gibbs Smith, Layton, UT, 2005), and is a contributing author to several other books. Paula graduated from the University*

Photo courtesy of Paula Baker-Laporte.

of Toronto School of Architecture in 1978 and moved to Santa Fe in 1981 and to Ashland in 2011, where she currently lives with her husband, Robert Laporte. Paula has been designing fine custom homes since 1986, and her design and consulting work has taken her all over North America. She is an instructor for the International Institute for Building Biology and Ecology, where she has introduced courses on Natural Healthy Building. In 2007, she became a Fellow of the American Institute of Architects in recognition of her significant contribution to the profession.

I AM A RESIDENTIAL ARCHITECT WHO HAS ALWAYS CARED DEEPLY ABOUT THE NEEDS OF MY CLIENTS. However, I never understood how much I could influence their health and well-being until I realized that my own inexplicable chronic illness was caused by a home I had once lived in. I had multiple chemical sensitivities, or environmental illness. That was twenty-one years ago. Until that time, designing with health and environmental considerations in mind had been of only peripheral concern to me. I, like many architects, considered myself an artist, not a technician. Facing the daunting task of creating a chemical-free sanctuary in which I could regain my own health came with much soul-searching. I began to realize that the standard building practices on which I had built my career were often destructive, not only to the health of the occupants but to the environment as well. Together with my physician, Dr. Erica Elliott, and John Banta, a dedicated building scientist, I wrote my first book, *Prescriptions for a Healthy House*, in the hopes of influencing other architects, builders, and homeowners to build healthier homes. I wanted to make the process accessible and easier than it had been for me.

It was during the time of my recovery that I became a student of Bau-biologie, the philosophy of building for human and planetary health that originated in Germany and is practiced throughout Northern Europe but is, as yet, little known in the United States. I was discouraged by the lack of opportunities for actually designing in this way in this country. Then one day I read about the work of natural homebuilder Robert Laporte. He had developed a building system that embodied the concepts of Bau-biologie. His buildings were made of natural unprocessed materials—breathable, low in embodied energy, energy-efficient, and free of toxins and harmful waste products. The clay/straw timber-frame wall systems that he had perfected were not only ecological, they were finely crafted. I found the timber frame to be a powerful and challenging design element.

I attended one of his hands-on workshops in 1992 and came away with the distinct feeling that our futures would be intertwined. I felt a calling to work with him, although I must admit he was, at first, pretty oblivious to this possibility (*men!*). Before any real clients materialized, we collaborated on a series of conceptual plans, and one home at a time our collaboration began to bear fruit. Our work evolved into a body of homes that we dubbed "EcoNests."

In March 1999, Robert and I were married in our own newly completed "nest." Previously, my knowledge about the benefits of a natural home had been intellectual. From that day on it became visceral as well. Just as motherhood has made me a better person, with its lessons in patience, nurturing, compassion, and deep love, living in a natural and healthy home has embraced me and sheltered me so profoundly that I have become a more avid environmentalist, crusader, lecturer, hostess, tour guide, writer, and teacher in an effort to share this deeply satisfying experience with as many people as I can reach.

Together, Robert and I work to create humble dwellings that are designed for human health and comfort, energy efficiency, and to sustain the environment and its natural resources.

In September 2005, we had the great privilege of publishing the fruits of our collaboration to date in a book called *EcoNests: Creating Sustainable Sanctuaries of Clay, Straw, and Timber*. At the time of this writing we have just resettled in our newly built nest in Ashland and are collaborating on our second EcoNest book.

Janine Benyus: Biologist at the Design Table

Janine Benyus is the author of several remarkable books, including Biomimicry: Innovation Inspired by *Nature (New York: Harper Perennial, 2002) and is cofounder of Biomimicry 3.8, a hybrid social enterprise comprised of a for-profit B corporation and a 501(c)(3) not-for-profit corporation under a single brand and integrated management strategy. The company's mission is to train, equip, and connect engineers, educators, architects, designers, business leaders, and other innovators to sustainably emulate nature's 3.8 billion years of brilliant designs and strategies. These "biologists at the design table" offer innovation consulting, professional training, and educational program and curriculum development.*

Photo courtesy of Janine Benyus.

WHEN I WAS NINE OR TEN, I HAD AN EARLY EXPERIENCE WITH GRIEF THAT SHAPED THE REST OF MY LIFE. As development and building expanded in New Jersey, where we lived, my parents would move us farther and farther beyond the edge of the suburbs so we could be surrounded by nature. Each time we moved, my dad would need to commute farther to work, but it was important to him that my sister and I have a forest in which to wander.

In the mixed hardwood forest behind our home, in a ravine too steep to build on, I discovered a secret, miraculous world of vines and nests and box turtles. There I read books, pored over field guides, pressed plants, and tried to learn the names of all the critters in my world. I observed animals through all of the seasons over several years. I got to know when nestlings would hatch and where bats would roost. Magnifying glass in one hand, test tubes in the other, I was (as the desk sign—a gift from my dad—read), "Janine Benyus, Microscopist"—the naturalist sleuth! I brought home owl pellets and pond water and insect wings to share with my equally curious and indulgent parents.

It was my *Watership Down, Wind in the Willows* experience if ever there was one. My most magical experiences took place outdoors, and they were my initial inspiration to do what I have been doing all my life.

One day, while picking wild strawberries in the open meadow next to my ravine, I came across some orange flags on wooden stakes. Following their trail led me to a summer of watching bulldozers roll up the sod, scrape the land bare, and replace the thrumming meadow with a housing subdivision. I watched day by day and slowly, the grief from what was happening settled in my cells. I was convinced that the casual destruction was simply caused by a lack of understanding. If these men on the machinery only knew what I knew about this meadow, I thought, if only I could have shown them the wonders of this place, they would have turned off the bulldozers.

I knew that my affection for the natural world—the breath-held-in-wonder feeling when I walked outside—was something I wanted to share with others. By doing so, I thought I could engender a wider appreciation for nature—and that indeed became my raison d'être. I love to write; I've written six books to date and am already planning a new one. The story I try to tell is about the wonders of the natural world and how we can learn so much from it. I feel as though I'm holding something precious in my hand, like a robin's egg, and uncurling my fingers to share it with others.

I had no design knowledge before writing *Biomimicry*. I realized that in my books I had been asking questions about the adaptive genius in the natural world for years, commenting that maybe doctors could use a certain strategy, or architects could learn from a certain design. I wrote a lot about the elegant functionality in nature. As I learned more about our materials science, energy systems, medicine, business, and sustainable agriculture,

I began to see how nature's designs could inform our own. Biomimicry—the idea of going to nature for advice—is an attractive idea, and like any successful meme, it's been spreading rapidly. That's because looking to nature is a powerful method of innovation. Life has been adapting to the Earth for 3.8 billion years. By adopting nature's design principles—by asking, how would nature do it?—we find not only solutions that work but also problems worth solving, problems that are important to the survival of all life.

Jane Jacobs is an essayist whose writing I'd admired for years. In 1997, she recognized that biomimicry was relevant to urban design. She, among others, helped me recognize that it is an idea whose time has come. I had an opportunity, and when she asked, What do you want to do with your moment? I decided that biomimicry was what I needed to do, what was important to me.

Then Paul Hawken began touting my book at conferences, telling others that *Biomimicry* talks about ideas that matter. My life began to change. I hadn't been prepared for the changes that writing the book would bring to my world. I was comfortable as I was, content to work hard and write books in my secluded home in Montana. But I began to see the value of speaking and brainstorming in person with designers, engineers, and architects. When businesses ask Biomimicry Guild biologists to come to the design table, something new happens. We're exploring what's possible for us as a species by looking at what other species have already learned.

Designers are some of my favorite people, and I love good design. I couldn't always define it, but I knew I loved things that work well. I always have. And that's what I look for in the natural world—things that work well over the long haul, for both the organism and the ecosystem. This new career, called "biologist at the design table," gives biologists a chance to share their best practices with designers. Every week more people are calling, asking if they can get involved in bioinspired design. I tell them, This is not mine; it is ours. Collaboration is key.

So we're doing a lot of teaching these days. Dayna Baumeister, my partner in the Biomimicry Guild, conducts workshops where innovators get to practice bioinspired design in places like Costa Rica and Montana—so many great ideas just outside my door! The people who come to these workshops in turn inspire me.

Writing *Biomimicry* changed the path of my life, a path that is still unfolding, just as the story of our species is. If we see nature as a teacher, a wise mentor, it will change our relationship with the natural world. As apprentices, we'll come to admire and respect the organisms that teach us. I truly believe the words of Bab Dioum, a Senegalese conservationist: "In the end, we will conserve only what we love. We will love only what we understand. We will understand only what we are taught."

Trudy Dujardin: Harmony in Myself and with the Environment

Trudy Dujardin, ASID, is the president of Dujardin Design Associates of Greenwich, Connecticut, and Nantucket, Massachusetts. She is an award-winning designer and national expert on nontoxic building materials and sustainable design.

Photo courtesy of Trudy Dujardin.

ONE OF THE PRINCIPLES I LIVE BY IS THAT THERE IS NO WELL-BEING IN BODY AND MIND IF THE HEALTH OF OUR HOMES, PROPERTY, AND PLANET EARTH IS NEGLECTED. We are all as fragile as the Earth itself, and to maintain the beauty of our land and our lives we must work to sustain a clean, toxin-free environment. As an interior designer, that has always meant beginning with the homes I design.

My personal story and my own quest for health have always been intertwined with my search for meaning and the inner peace that comes from doing the right thing. Although I became even more passionate about sustainable design after my struggle with multiple chemical sensitivity, my commitment to living gently on the Earth began long before my diagnosis, when I wanted more than anything to protect the beauty of the island of Nantucket, Massachusetts, and the harbor I could see from my home.

As a child, I lived on a farm in South Carolina and was continually exposed to pesticides and crop dusting. I was the first and long-awaited grandchild and treasured by my grandparents, who would give me the best place to sleep, on a cot by a bank of windows, to catch the cool evening breeze. To protect me from mosquitoes, they would spray the window screens with a Flit gun filled with a DDT-based solution. Even as a child, I knew something was terribly wrong with this. Since I could barely stand the smell, I would try to hold my breath and keep my hands over my nose and mouth all night. And so, unknowingly, my quest for a healthy environment began.

As an adult, I spent many years on construction sites where little or no attention was paid to the toxicity of the materials being used or the health of the tradesmen. In 1987, I purchased land on the harbor of Nantucket Island overlooking the town, a delicate site within a very fragile ecosystem. And I vowed to build my home mindful of the environment, using only nontoxic materials. I was determined not to add to the pollution with construction runoff.

Nantucket Island is a world unto itself. My passion for green design derived from a desire to live in harmony with my environment. That meant having as little impact on that environment as possible—and ensuring the construction work would be promote the health of the construction workers, too.

I began to plan my dream house. My first mentor was Paul Bierman-Lytle. He led me toward less toxic building materials. It was the beginning of a five-year research project that would ensure a healthy new home.

At the same time, I began developing a condition known as multiple chemical sensitivity, or environmental illness. I was diagnosed in the mid-1990s. Together with Dr. Phillip J. Cohen and Dr. Adrienne Buffaloe Sprouse of the American Academy of Environmental Medicine in Prairie Village, Kansas, we uncovered potential causes. The pesticide exposures in my child-hood, my studio classes in art school, when I worked with oil-based products, and the toxic products on many construction sites where I had worked were all suspect.

Many days it was difficult for me to work, to concentrate, to go to the office, even to get out of bed. I could no longer go to construction sites or be around clients who were wearing perfume or whose clothes smelled like tobacco. I was having allergic reactions to many, many things, and my world shrank more and more each day.

This story has a happy ending. After almost two years of living in my healthy house full-time, I got better. I'm active again and free to move about in the world. My firm is thriving. I'm on several boards. I've become a Leadership in Energy and Environmental Design accredited professional in interior design and construction (LEED AP ID+C) and a passionate educator on environmental issues; I'm an adjunct professor at Fairfield University in Connecticut and teach sustainable design online at Keane University in New Jersey. I use my blog (www.holistichouse.com) to promote beautiful design and holistic living. My healing process was an educational journey, one I now feel lucky to be able to share with others.

Since then, I have lovingly renovated two more of my own homes, which are both completely green. Built with sustainable materials and painted, finished, and furnished with nontoxic products, they are as pure and health-giving as I could make them. The land they rest on is not sprayed or coated with poisons—neither insecticides, fungicides, nor fertilizers—which bestows the small creatures who visit my garden and lawn the same right to health as I claim for myself. I am proud to have completed homes in many shades of green for my clients as well.

This is an ongoing journey. Saving the planet, protecting the health of every person and all Earth's beautiful creatures, requires constant vigilance and much effort. We must continue to question the role of coal-burning factories and mercury toxicity; our dependence on fossil fuels; the conse-quences of air pollution, acid rain, climate change, food laden with chemicals and pesticide residue, and product manufacturing techniques harmful to the workers who make those products.

The overwhelming forces of climate change and global warming continue to impel the work of top environmental scientists worldwide. I am committed, today more than ever, to educate my clients and the public about ways to live in harmony with the Earth, to create sustainable homes that support health and well-being, and to make a difference while I can."

Bert Gregory: Greening Architectural Interiors

As Chairman and CEO of Mithun, Bert Gregory has led the two-hundred-person firm to national recognition for concept-based, environmentally intelligent design. He is renowned as an expert in the development of resource-efficient structures and communities and advocates for sustainable building and urbanism across the country. His interdisciplinary approach merges architecture, science, and design in order to create lasting urban places for the future. Bert currently serves on the board of directors of Forterra, which creates prosperous, vibrant communities and conserves natural and working landscapes in Washington's central Cascades and Olympic regions, and the Urban Land Institute Transit-Oriented Development Council, is part of the Technical Resource Group of the Clinton Climate Initiative's Climate-Positive Development Program, and is on the faculty of the Portland Institute of Sustainability's EcoDistrict Institute.

Photo courtesy of Bert Gregory.

GROWING UP IN A RAILROAD FAMILY IN DENVER, COLORADO, I GOT TO SEE MUCH OF THE UNITED STATES AS A YOUNGSTER. Trains took me to exciting cities where I saw large, astonishing buildings. I have vivid memories of elegant, beautiful, dramatically huge spaces. I'd go on a trip seeing my hometown through a certain lens and it would look completely different when I returned.

All that influenced my interest in the physical built world. My dad and I put together miniature train sets, and I would build the toy buildings. When I was in seventh grade, two architects moved onto our street, and their presence was an awakening for me. I realized that grownups actually did the kind of things I was interested in.

The wilderness of Colorado, Utah, and Wyoming was just as much a part of my world. My family spent lots of time skiing and backpacking in the mountains. Throughout high school and college, I continued to explore outdoors. My fascination with buildings and cities as well as nature drew me to green architecture.

My studies began at the University of Colorado in the late 1960s and early 1970s, when a new awareness of the importance of the natural world started seeping in the popular consciousness. My professors included Richard Whittaker, who was part of the team that designed Sea Ranch, a milestone project for harmonizing architecture with the environment. Core curricula included the study of the works of Ian McHarg, who wrote the seminal book *Design with Nature* (New York: John Wiley & Sons, 1995), which discussed how to situate buildings in the natural landscape. And I spent a semester studying Buckminster Fuller, who came to Colorado for a few days and shared lots of creative ideas about "Spaceship Earth," his metaphor for our planet, where we must work together as a crew, he said, if we were to survive. I was further influenced by another professor who had worked with Louis Kahn; he shared his thoughts on the integration of design with nature, the meaning of buildings, and terms such as *silence* and *light*.

After three years of college, I became a ski bum for five years and worked in a ski shop, completely immersing myself in the mountains until my need to be creative drew me to Montana State University to complete my degree. Bozeman merged the best of both worlds: rigorous design in a beautiful place. It was there that I won a competition for sustainable design sponsored by Reynolds Aluminum. Applying careful analysis to an available resource, I designed a solar energy collector out of beer cans that gathered heat during the day and released it at night, using paraffin as a phase-change medium for energy storage. The concept is inexpensive and works in many different climates.

Seattle was my next destination: I liked the idea of living where you could power a boat with wind instead of an engine. In 1985, I joined Mithun, which already had a reputation for innovative technology, respect for the land, and the design of buildings that made occupants feel as though they were outdoors. Mithun has since pioneered the design of outdoor learning centers for children such as IslandWood and Zoomazium in Seattle.

Environmental stewardship is increasingly important as the changes occurring on our planet become better understood. Scientific research has revealed that our world is a global, interconnected system, and this has driven me to find new ways to merge science and design. Design provides the intuitive aspect of what makes great buildings while science reveals the cause-and-effect relationship of our actions and gives us better options for making intelligent choices. For example, architects, civil engineers, biologists, and landscape designers must work together not only to create but also to restore habitats. I have an eleven-year-old daughter. By the time she approaches my age, the world's population will be 50 percent larger. We are at a turning point. It is especially important that we do everything we can to deliver a healthy environment for future generations, and we must make sure our kids become environmental stewards themselves.

Curitiba, Brazil, is an example of a major city that is incorporating innovative sustainable principles into its daily routines by developing incentives for community cooperation that match the needs and culture of its citizens. Jaime Lerner, Curitiba's former mayor and chief architect of the city's master plan, says, "You teach the parents by teaching the children."

As designers, the lines we draw, the materials we specify, the types of energy or light bulbs we recommend all influence the future of the planet. Each one of us has the responsibility and the power to create positive change. On a personal level, we should start by calculating our individual carbon footprints and find strategies to offset and then reduce them.[1]

At times I feel tremendously optimistic, and at others overwhelmed by the magnitude of the challenges we're confronting. Buckminster Fuller trusted in the ingenuity of humankind to ensure a positive future. But the future is approaching rapidly. We design professionals must all contribute to powering that change so that it happens fast enough.

Steve Badanes: Jersey Devil

Steve Badanes's commissions have included private homes, artist's studios, and the winning entry, "The Fremont Troll," in the Hall of Giants 1990 Competition in Seattle, Washington.

"Jersey Devil" is the name bestowed on the work of Badanes, John Ringel, and Jim Adamson, as well as others who have contributed to their diverse projects. This loose-knit group of designer-builders has eschewed convention both in the process of making architecture and in the accepted definitions of architecture itself. Jersey Devil's architecture

Photo courtesy of Steve Badanes.

---

[1] See www.climatetrust.org

*shows a concern for craft and detail, an attention to the expression of the
construction materials, and a strong environmental consciousness. For over
twenty-five years, the members of Jersey Devil have been constructing their
own designs while living on-site, in tents or Airstream trailers, and making
adjustments to their structures in response to problems encountered during
the building process.*

I'VE BEEN INSPIRED BY A LOT OF PEOPLE I'VE MET, ESPECIALLY TWO ELDERS OUTSIDE OF THE
ARCHITECTURAL COMMUNITY. The first is Toshiko Takaezu, a ceramic artist in New
Jersey. She makes world-class art and cooks delicious food and grows amaz-
ing flowers—a combination of talents that I love and admire.

The other is Meng Huang—an artist from China who worked in Hong
Kong illegally building movie sets. On a trip back to China to see his
family, he was caught, his passport was seized, and he was nearly killed.
Subsequently, he spent twenty years in China, where artists were unable
to work freely. I met him in Seattle after one of his children had helped him
emigrate. He was seventy. He had filled his Section 8 apartment with incredible masks and creatures that he made out of castoffs and recycled garbage.
Meng traveled with us on Jersey Devil jobs—to Hawaii, California, Florida,
and Mexico, and did amazing work with construction scraps; he also taught
school kids to make recycled art. The life he had lived in China would have
destroyed many, but it made him stronger. He was always in a good mood
and had a great sense of humor. Meng passed away in 2011 at age eighty-
eight, but his legacy lives on.

People are at the heart of what we do—not the architecture. Most architects and designers typically work at the top of the food chain. We are given
a gift, but we usually squander that gift on the wealthiest 2 percent of the
population who can afford to hire us. But that gift comes with social, political, and environmental responsibilities. Architecture has the potential to make
all our lives better and should benefit everyone equally.

We're at a crisis point. Buildings are responsible for half of the greenhouse gases that cause global warming. In the next ten to fifteen years, cars
will become more efficient and we'll be manufacturing them in more productive ways. However, buildings last forty to fifty years, and we can't just
replace them with bigger, more inefficient versions. Production of oil and gas
has peaked, and the only energy source we have left is coal—and burning
coal accelerates global warming.

Architecture has the potential to harness environmental forces and give
them form and to provide solutions to social problems. We need to meet the
challenge and do it with sustainability and with social justice, to be the heroes
who provide hope rather than the villains who exacerbate the problem.

There are those who have pointed out the right path to take: Wendell Barry in Kentucky, Marjory Stoneman Douglas in the Florida Everglades, and Malcolm Wells, the father of underground buildings.

I was born in New York and grew up in New Jersey. My dad was a builder, which influenced me early on. I realized I was good at art and mathematics and drew well, and gravitated to the study of architecture, which ideally synthesizes art and building. And although computer-aided design (CAD) is a widely employed tool, it's an abstraction of hand drawing (itself an abstraction of a building) and has less character. Everyone's drawing looks the same after you press that print button. A hand-drawn sketch is unique and taps into our emotions: drawing connects the hand and the heart, and that bar of soap we push around often short circuts the connection.

I was in school in the late 1960s, when the ecology movement was taking shape. Three of us created Jersey Devil right after graduating from college. We had no money, so the university construction shop, which was a separate building on a remote part of campus, became our office. It was an intense time—the Bobby Kennedy and Martin Luther King Jr. assassinations, the Vietnam War, the civil rights movement, feminism, revolutionary music and lifestyles, the polarization of the old and the young. We tried to take the political energy of the 1960s—all our community-based design, environmental activism, and desire for social justice—and turn it into something useful for the environment.

I enjoy my work tremendously. Lecturing about it is an opportunity to positively influence a lot of people. I condense thirty years of work into an hour and a half and present my message of environmentalism with humor rather than taking a strident, gloom-and-doom approach.

I've found that engaging students in their design/build studios stimulates them at a deep level and can change the course of their careers. In the Neighborhood Design/Build Studio at the University of Washington, students plan community facilities for nonprofit groups in Seattle. We built a library for Laotian refugees who had escaped their villages, which had been burned and bombed after the Vietnam War, and immigrated to Seattle. We have also taken teams of students to work in impoverished communities in Mexico, Cuba, Ghana, and India. These projects create empathy and understanding for other cultures and give students hands-on skills and the ability to work as a team. But the skilled workers in these countries often earn only a few dollars a day. In the United States, where laborers can earn $25 an hour and skilled workers far more, student labor can make a huge difference on outreach projects without the embodied energy of shipping them half way around the world. The old saying "Think globally, act locally" is a meaningful guidepost.

There is a need to make people both laugh and think, for us to become heroes and provide hope. Do I feel that I inspire others? I've heard that I do. Former students tell me, "I just completed a great project; it was your class that gave me the courage to do something different." That, in turn, inspires me, keeps me going, makes me feel good when an awful lot of things seem to be going wrong.

I'd like to be remembered as someone who stuck to my guns and had fun doing it. It's gratifying to look back and know that, over twenty-five years later, we were on the right path. I'd tell you to have a positive attitude, have a sense of humor, and don't take yourself too seriously. Being involved in the design profession is a gift that comes with social and environmental obligations. Without art or nature, after all, there isn't much left.

Ray C. Anderson: Mid-Course Correction

Ray C. Anderson was the chairman and CEO of Atlanta-based Interface, Inc., one of the world's largest commercial interior furnishings companies, which he founded in 1973 after graduating from the Georgia Institute of Technology with a degree in industrial engineering. Ray and his company revolutionized the carpet and floor-covering industry. He ultimately embarked on a mission to make Interface a sustainable corporation by leading a worldwide war on waste and pioneering the processes of sustainable development. He is the author of Mid-Course Correction: Toward a Sustainable Enterprise—The Interface Model *(Atlanta: Peregrinzilla Press, 1999), and* Business Lessons from a Radical Industrialist *(New York: St. Martin's/Griffin, 2011).*

Photo courtesy of Ray C. Anderson.

Ray passed away in 2011. He will always be remembered as a pioneer in the industry. The following essay, which he wrote in 2006, tells the amazing story of his sustainability awakening.

WHEN I WAS SIXTY YEARS OLD AND MY COMPANY, INTERFACE, BASED IN ATLANTA, GEORGIA, WAS TWENTY-ONE YEARS OLD, we began hearing rumblings from our customers: "When it comes to the environment, Interface just doesn't get it." Looking back at how I responded, I'm amused that I asked, "Interface doesn't get what?"

In just ten years, and a sea of change later, this company, the world's largest manufacturer of commercial carpet and other interior finishes, has become a leader in industrial ecology: It is a company on a different course, developing new technologies and rethinking everything we do, from the way we source raw materials and manufacture our products to how we sample, transport, install, maintain and—importantly—reclaim them.

Back in 1994, I wasn't all that different from most industrialists. But reading Paul Hawken's *The Ecology of Commerce* (New York: Harper Collins, 1994) put me on a different path. Hawken's thesis, that the Earth and all natural systems are in decline and that business and industry are both the biggest culprits and the only forces pervasive and powerful enough to reverse the decline was at once crystal clear and completely compelling. It was like a spear in my chest—a painful, powerful awakening.

As I read Hawken's book, I was dumbfounded by how much I didn't know about the environment and the impacts of the industrial system on it—the industrial system of which my "successful" company and I were an integral part. A new definition of success crept into my consciousness, and a latent sense of legacy asserted itself. I got it. I was a plunderer of the Earth, and that is not the legacy I wanted to leave behind.

I remember clearly the visceral nature of my own awakening, and I have come to believe that the transformation of society into a sustainable society for the indefinite future depends completely and absolutely on a complete shift in attitude, a shift that will occur one person at a time, one organization at a time, one technology, one building, one company, one university cur- riculum, one community, one region, one industry at a time, until the entire system coexists in ethical balance with Earth's natural systems.

The fundamental realization behind this transformation is that industrialism—of which we are each a part—developed in a different world from the one we live in today: fewer people, more plentiful natural resources, simpler lifestyles. The resultant take/make/waste system, so common today, simply cannot go on and on and on in a finite world with an ever-increasing population and diminishing resources.

At Interface, our journey began when our customers asked us a question. Now I ask you: When will your journey begin?

inspiring projects

These inspiring homes, which all adhere to guidelines for healthy and sustainable design, demonstrate that eco-friendly designs can also be high-performing, cost-effective, functional, and beautiful. In the hands of creative designers, intelligent, Earth-friendly materials provide a rich experience that echoes the natural world. Enjoy.

Associates III, Denver, Colorado

Figure 3.1
Photos: David O. Marlow

53

HIGH IN THE ROCKY MOUNTAINS STANDS A HOME THAT TREADS LIGHTLY ON THE LAND, where guests experience the natural environment in a rare setting. The design takes its inspiration from a legend that gave the design team the ultimate stimulus to create a new "old" home.

The fable begins with a family settling in a high mountain meadow in the late 1800s. The first structure they build is a log cabin, in 1873. The following spring they erect a barn and begin farming the valley below. The family grows, so in 1892 they build a two-story farmhouse with a hearth kitchen, bedrooms, and bathrooms. The family prospers; in 1910 they travel to Europe, where they are inspired by the great halls. Upon their return, they create a grand lodge and join the original log cabin with the farmhouse. In 1921, the last addition connecting the barn to the main house is built.

The design team extensively researched these building types. They expressed the distinctiveness and authenticity of each building type through millwork, finishes, light fixtures, furnishings, artwork, and accessories and achieved their environmental goals by using reclaimed woods, antiques, adhesives low in volatile organic compounds (VOCs), water-based finishes, long-life interior materials, locally sourced materials, Energy Star appliances, and an energy-efficient envelope and systems.

▲ *Figure 3.2*

◀ *Figure 3.3*

The home realizes the owners' dream of bringing the legend to life for themselves and their guests, who are overcome by the beauty and spirit of the surroundings. Inspired by turn-of-the-century Western lodges such as the Old Faithful Inn in Yellowstone National Park and Awahnee in Yosemite, the home is in harmony with the grandeur of the natural mountain landscape.

Standing dead timbers form the log cabin, while reclaimed silver oak was used in the barn; the natural patina of the woods ground the interior spaces. The farmhouse's interior is brighter, with integral color plaster walls between wood timbers, pickled wood floors, an antique brick hearth, and reclaimed terra-cotta tile floors. Throughout, handcrafted reclaimed wood with varying finishes are used for floors, walls, ceilings, timbers, and cabinetry. The great hall was erected with massive hand-hewn timbers that support the high ceilings; they are complemented by a massive regional rock fireplace with seating alcove.

Figure 3.4

Figure 3.5

In the bathrooms, an antique clawfoot tub and porcelain vanity are the only remnants of the past. The bathrooms were upgraded using contemporary products by a fifth-generation family member now living on the property.

The case goods, rugs, lighting, and accent pieces are mostly antiques; reproductions are made from reclaimed woods. Custom soft goods use both antique and natural fabrics. The quilts, blankets, and rugs were all crafted locally.

Figure 3.6

Delos, New York, New York

IN JUNE 2011, DELOS, THE PIONEER OF WELLNESS REAL ESTATE AND FOUNDER OF THE WELL BUILDING STANDARD, UNVEILED THE WORLD'S FIRST-EVER WELLNESS LOFT, located in the heart of lower Manhattan's Meatpacking District. The loft—Delos's pilot project—was commissioned by the organization's founder, Paul Scialla; it was envisioned as a home that could both enhance the residents' lives and optimize their health. The elegantly decorated loft features ergonomic design, more than seventy-five wellness amenities, and twenty-three pathways to improved air, water, light, nutrition, and sleep. The home also addresses residents' cardiovascular and cognitive health. Many of these features, which are invisible to the naked eye, support a home that not only promotes healthy living but also features elegant decor and design. The Meatpacking Loft is the world's first wellness home and an iconic step forward for real estate and wellness living.

Delos has combined medical research with architectural and engineering expertise to develop a comprehensive template for better living; it supports inhabitants' health through toxin- and allergen-free building materials and improved indoor air quality, lighting quality, and water quality, as well as optimal thermal and acoustic comfort. The Delos home supports every major domain of health, including sleep, respiratory, cardiovascular and cognitive health. The residents of Delos homes benefit from exclusive wellness programs, provided in partnership with leaders in the medical community.

Figure 3.7
Photos: Delos

Figure 3.8

The loft is the result of six years of research by Columbia University doctors, scientists, architects, designers, and wellness thought leaders on developing integrated modalities that are protective and therapeutic for residents. Delos has reshaped how homes are built as the company places wellness at the center of all its design and construction decisions by incorporating dynamic and holistic solutions to many of today's health problems.

Since the completion and success of the this loft, Delos has grown tremendously. In September 2012, at the annual meeting of the Clinton Global Initiative, former president Bill Clinton introduced Delos's Well-Building Standard, the world's first building standard for enhancing people's health and well-being through evidence-based techniques. Shortly thereafter, the company expanded into the hospitality sector, designing forty-two hotel rooms at the MGM Grand Hotel and Casino in Las Vegas built to that standard; in fall 2013, Delos designed to those specifications the first office for CBRE (in Los Angeles) and restaurants for LYFE Kitchen Restaurants (in Tarzana, California, and Chicago).

Figure 3.9

Delos completed its flagship development in winter 2013: the first ever Well-Building Standard–certified residential community in New York City's Greenwich Village. The project incorporates over seventy-five wellness features into the architecture and design that aim to reduce stress, ensure restful sleep, increase energy and vitality, improve blood circulation and posture, optimize digestion, and enhance the immune system and respiratory health. Through an exclusive collaboration with the Cleveland Clinic, a nonprofit academic medical center, its residents will have access to web-based programs designed to help improve sleep and nutrition and reduce stress.

Figure 3.10

Currently, Delos is also working on a public housing project, an orphanage in Haiti, and the first Well-certified city block, among other projects.

Delos envisions a future in which the interaction between building and person provides unprecedented insight into and control of residents' well-being. A holistic and preventative approach to wellness requires the kind of individualized recommendations that are only possible through quantifiable data about our health status; algorithms will power intelligent monitoring systems and controls that dynamically manage our interior environment, including lighting, beds, HVAC systems, flooring, and furniture. All of these features will be integrated into an information-gathering and communications system that will connect health-care provision.

Figure 3.11

eco+historical and Feldman Architecture, San Francisco, California

Figure 3.12
Design: eco+historical,
inc. Architecture: Feldman
Architecture. Photos: Paul Dyer.

BUILT AS ONE OF THE FIRST WORKERS' COTTAGES IN HORNER'S ADDITION, A NEIGHBORHOOD OF SAN FRANCISCO now known as Noe Valley, this charming 1889 Stick Victorian cottage has survived earthquakes and fires largely intact; it's missing just a few interior walls and the original wood-burning fireplace, covered over during a the addition of a kitchen and bath in the 1950s. At roughly 1,000 sq ft, it wasn't large enough for a contemporary family, and with its brick foundation, lack of insulation, and old leaky windows, it was in need of serious renovation.

Unlike the grand homes of San Francisco's Pacific Heights and Nob Hill, the cottages of Noe Valley were small and featured little in the way of fine woodwork or other finishes. This home was no different, with common hardware and inexpensive finishes that had suffered years of paint layering (with lead-based paint, no doubt) and smokers.

Figure 3.13

From 2010 to 2012, eco+historical undertook a gut rehab and expansion of the home, retaining its original facade and much of its framing but turning it into a LEED Platinum contemporary family home with traditional detailing that didn't mimic its Victorian past but did honor it. eco+historical partnered with Feldman Architecture for the scoping and design of the revised plans to excavate the lower level and add a small third-story and a garage that took the building from a tiny two-bedroom, one-bathroom cottage to a more flexible five-bedroom, four-bathroom home. eco+historical handled the design of the interior and exterior finishes as well as the green specifications.

The project scope was driven by the needs of contemporary family life. Because many people entertain at home and have home offices, families need more space today than they did in the late nineteenth century.

While the size grew from 1,000 to 2,600 sq ft, save a color change from mauve to white, the home looked largely unchanged from the sidewalk out front; the new third story is just barely visible, even from across the street. Thus the neighborhood character remained intact, despite the home's state-of-the-art water delivery system, energy efficiency, and use of sustainable and nontoxic materials and finishes.

Figure 3.14

This home was the first in San Francisco to use Aquatherm Green Pipe in place of copper piping throughout. Made of polypropylene that doesn't leech, Green Pipe is nontoxic, recyclable, nonconductive, and insulating, and has just a fraction of the embedded energy of other piping systems. The home also uses a GE GeoSpring hot water heat pump that extracts heat from the surrounding air and puts it into the water, and EPA-approved WaterSense faucets and toilets, thereby reducing its water demands. And some of the water it does use is piped from the master bathroom through a gray-water system that reuses shower and tub wastewater to water rear-yard trees. The rest of the drought-tolerant garden is lined with dry-stack walls made up of broken-up concrete from the original patio, and the plants are fed via a multizone drip system moderated by a rain and solar radiation sensor.

Figure 3.15

Figure 3.16

To manage electrical loads economically, the lights in the house are all on motion-sensing vacancy dimmers that turn off automatically when the rooms are unoccupied. Dimmable LED lighting further reduces the electrical load and microinverter solar panels on the thermoplastic polyolefin (TPO) cool roof provide megawatts of power every month.

To further minimize waste materials, the original roof rafters were cut down and rebuilt into planters for the front roof deck garden, and the original brick chimney was reused to lay a warm patio outside the ground-floor garden bedroom. New materials were specified to be Forest Stewardship Council (FSC) certified where possible, and even the backsplash tile, Fireclay Tile's Debris Series, included over 60 percent recycled material and nontoxic glazes. A breakfast nook chandelier (found on Etsy.com) made from rescued silverware adds whimsy.

Figure 3.17

Completed in March of 2012, the house received its LEED Platinum certification eight months later.

Susan Fredman Design Group, Chicago, Illinois

WHEN HEALTHY HOME 2010 OPENED TO THE PUBLIC IN SEPTEMBER OF THAT YEAR IN SUBURBAN CHICAGO, IT SET A PRECEDENT FOR GREEN, HEALTHFUL LIVING and raised the bar for healthier indoor air. Healthy Home 2010 was created to be a designer showcase and tour as well as a cutting-edge initiative for sustainable design that focuses on healthier indoor environments. Healthy Home 2010 was the first designer show house in the nation to bridge the gap between traditional green building and healthy interiors by implementing a new interior

Figure 3.18
Photos: Susan Fredman
Design Group

design protocol developed by a distinguished advisory board consisting of industry leaders in sustainable design.

Healthy Home 2010 was also the first house in the United States to incorporate elements of the Greenguard Environmental Institute's first-ever indoor environmental quality (IEQ) management plan for residential construction, a system for designing, from the ground up, buildings that contribute to healthier indoor air. The plan is an innovative supplement to sustainable building programs like the U.S. Green Building Council's LEED rating system. Healthy Home 2010 featured dozens of Greenguard-certified low-emitting products and building materials, including paints, wallboard, flooring, countertops, tile, and furnishings. By meeting some of the world's most stringent indoor air quality standards, Greenguard-certified products help reduce the number of airborne volatile organic compounds (VOCs) in the home's interior, thereby creating healthier indoor air.

With the needs of a young family in mind, Healthy Home 2010 was situated in Palatine, a quaint subdivision much like many suburban communities throughout the United States. But Palatine's healthy living standards set it apart as a model for future construction and design standards. The home featured a wealth of sustainable design—from landscaping to building to healthful interiors. Each material and product was preapproved by Healthy Home 2010's Interiors Advisory Board (IAB).

Figure 3.19

A team of industry leaders established the vision of Healthy Home 2010. The project was spearheaded by Victoria Di Iorio, education outreach coordinator for Healthy Child Healthy World, and Jill Salisbury, principal and founder of el: Environmental Language. Di Iorio noted that in building this home, "We are going beyond the notion of what is sustainable to create a home that has human health at the heart of our objectives."

A board of product and design experts comprised the IAB; they were responsible for vetting all materials, furnishings, and products under consideration by the building and design team for inclusion in the home. Each material and product used was approved only after meeting a rigorous set of criteria that ensured sustainable, healthier standards. The IAB established healthy interiors guidelines that were used to direct the design process as well as a series of standards that promote nontoxic, healthier homes.

Figure 3.20

Members of the IAB included:

- Penny Bonda, FASID, LEED fellow, partner, Ecoimpact Consulting
- Annette K. Stelmack, USGBC LEED faculty, LEED AP BD+C, sustainable design consultant, educator, principal, Inspirit-llc
- Leslie Gage, LEED AP, formerly with the Greenguard Environmental Institute
- Leigh Anne Vandusen, owner, O Ecotextiles
- Jill Salisbury, principal and founder, el: Environmental Language
- Victoria Di Iorio, education outreach coordinator, Healthy Child Healthy World

"By embracing the healthy interiors guidelines, homeowners can foster well-being for their families, which will inherently benefit the environment as well," Jill Salisbury remarked in 2011 when the house first opened.

Healthy Home 2010 also sought to develop sustainable and healthful solutions via a collaborative build-and-design approach. Dior Builders and the Susan Fredman Design Group teamed up to bring together traditional green building with healthy, beautiful interiors. The Healthy Home featured energy-efficient products, innovative technologies, green building materials, and furniture and accessories in order to foster a healthful living environment and showcase some of the highest standards of environmental integrity.

Dior Builders oversaw the design and construction of Healthy Home 2010. Its open floor plan and exclusive use of low-emitting materials complemented the home's focus on sustainable family living. Artful windowscaping brought in plenty of natural light and allowed for picturesque vistas.

Figure 3.21

The interior design direction and the home's furnishings selections were made by the Susan Fredman Design Group. The aesthetic is grounded in nature and combines natural elements and unexpected details with a palette of earth tones. Sustainable, nontoxic materials and furnishings were also featured throughout the home.

Susan Fredman, founder and CEO of the Susan Fredman Design Group, was excited to be part of the project, saying, "Our design team is proud to be at the forefront of an emerging design movement that not only encompasses all the elements of green design but also shows consumers how they can create a healthy home from the inside out."

Figure 3.22

About Healthy Child Healthy World

Healthy Child Healthy World (http://www.healthychild.org) is the nation's preeminent nonprofit organization that advocates for and protects children's health by designing cleaner, healthier indoor environments for children and their families.

Heidi Mendoza, re.dzine, Denver, Colorado

FROM ITS FOUNDATION TO THE ROOF, THE GREEN CUBE WAS PLANNED AND BUILT WITH LEED PLATINUM CERTIFICATION IN MIND. Its unique location combines walkability and convenience for true green living; its solar array returns energy to the grid, and healthier materials, paints, finishes, and natural lighting round out one truly green cube.

Figure 3.23
Photos: Heidi Mendoza,
RE.DZINE

Figure 3.24

This single-family residence in the sought-after Highlands neighborhood is a contemporary, energy-efficient home. It is designed to make a positive, sustained impact on homeowners and the environment. This small site called for a compact square footprint that incorporates an attached garage. The main floor is open and provides views of the downtown skyline. The upper floor houses the sleeping area and home office and features a rooftop patio.

The project raised funds to support an annual scholarship for North High School students wishing to pursue a career in the green building industry and also to educate visitors about affordable, sustainable building through tours, open houses, seminars, and special events showcasing its green vendors.

This project was a collaboration of local talent with a passion for sustainable building.

When I saw the initial concept for the Green Cube project, I immediately knew I was going to be part of something amazing. My role was to work on the interiors alongside 2B Studios. I was responsible for choosing materials for the entire home, for the design of the second-floor master bedroom, and for the office and master bedroom layout and design. I was also in charge of contacting local artists and furniture makers about showcasing their work in Green Cube during an art event night and parade of homes. Local green businesses outfitted every aspect of the solar-powered home with environmentally friendly and sustainable products, from materials and finishes to a green wall that produces vegetables year-round and helps filter the house naturally, improving the air quality.

Green Cube also features granite countertops, radiated heat floors, and swamp coolers instead of an air-conditioning unit—all of which help improve the indoor air quality.

Figure 3.25

Figure 3.26

Rowland + Broughton, Aspen, Colorado

Figure 3.27
Photos: Brent Moss
Photography

Figure 3.28

THIS MODERN RANCH IS A RENOVATION OF A 1969 DUPLEX located on the Aspen municipal golf course. The lot is surrounded by mature trees and magnificent views of Independence Pass and Maroon Bells, two peaks in the nearby Elk Mountains. The existing house is a typical ranch with low, sloping roofs and exposed wood beams. The program for the renovation is a mountain vacation home for the extended family, which spans three generations. The floor plan was reworked to provide each family member with his or her own bedroom/bathroom suite. A loft addition was created specifically for the grandchildren as a hideaway to play, read, and sleep in. The addition was designed to work with both the neighboring duplex unit roof lines and the original roofs.

The exterior color palette consists of painted gray siding in alternating directions, dark gray windows, dark gray beams, and preweathered Galvalume roof and fascia. The chimney has been reoriented and covered in a warm, dark metal. The dark gray beams extend inside and contrast with the modern light interiors. The interior design is a combination of warm textures and natural materials. Special considerations were taken for all building materials to create a healthy home.

Figure 3.29

Figure 3.30

Sustainable components of this project include the following:

■ An existing property was remodeled and reused.

■ High-efficiency windows and wall assemblies create an efficient core and shell.

■ All rift-sawn white oak used for millwork, floors, and doors is FSC certified.

■ Paint contained no volatile organic compounds (VOCs).

■ Sixty percent of the original roof and walls were retained.

■ Mature trees on the lot were retained.

■ 400 sq ft solar panel array was installed.

■ Photovoltaic panels produce 4.2 kW of energy per hour.

■ Much of the construction debris, including cardboard, wood, metal scrap, was recycled.

■ Replaced all old windows and doors with new energy-efficient models.

■ Replaced old furnace with efficient boiler/radiant heat system.

■ Metal siding and roof are durable and low maintenance.

■ Roof color qualifies for Energy Star compliance for cool roofs and can save up to 40 percent in heating and cooling costs.

■ Roof is nonvented and superinsulated, with a very efficient insulating value of R56.

- Roof material is made with 30 percent recycled content
- Rough-in for radon mitigation system will improve indoor air quality should radon be detected.
- Clerestory windows, glass sliding doors, and skylights increase natural daylight, reducing dependency on artificial light.
- Flooring uses Lyptus wood, which is made from eucalyptus trees, a renewable resource that regrows quickly.
- Countertops are Caesarstone, which is made with crushed quartz, a by-product of the mining industry.
- Master bath contains local Colorado Yule marble.

Building materials list includes:

- Homasote blown-in insulation
- Concrete slab and foundation without chemical additives
- Redwood sill plates
- Pure silicone sealants
- Kiln-dried lumber
- Trex decking
- FSC-certified Lumber
- Cork flooring
- Formaldehyde-free cabinet and work substrate

Figure 3.31

Figure 3.32

Carolyn Tierney, ECOterior Solutions, Dutchess County, New York

A MODEST DUTCHESS COUNTY FARMHOUSE FOUND NEW LIFE WITH A YOUNG FAMILY. The design team resurrected the one-hundred-year-old farmhouse so that it would accommodate a growing family.

Over its lifetime, the small house had been subjected to awkward additions. The space had to be enlarged to accommodate contemporary desires such as a large open kitchen and dining room and a master suite. The clients and the design team wanted to keep the intention of the original house by restoring the beauty of the existing elements while expanding the house in a way that respected its heritage.

Figure 3.33
Photos: Carolyn Tierney,
ECOterior Solutions

Figure 3.34

The two entrances were restored to the previous beauty. The fireplace was refurbished and brought to life; the woodwork was cleaned, polished, and painted. Energy-efficient lighting was added behind beams to light what had been a dark space. We brought the spaces to life with antiques and new furniture, while the reuse and repurposing of antiques allowed us to complement the home's history. The sign that sits on the mantle came from the side of the barn. It displays the farm's original name; we could not resist using it as artwork.

The chestnut mantle required only a good scrubbing and a coat of wax to uncover its original luster. The room was then furnished with upholstery made at a local upholstery shop that follows sustainable manufacturing processes; a side table made of recycled wine staves; and antique accessories such as Dietz Lanterns manufactured in New York City at the turn of the century; and an antique area rug found in Lancaster, Pennsylvania. The study is in the older part of the home; we were able restore the existing windows' lovely hand-blown panes. To combat drafts, we added insulation linings to the drapery. While this was not the most efficient solution, it allowed us to retain something beautiful and old.

The addition to the home houses a new kitchen, dining room, and family room. The cabinetry and fireplace mantle were designed using reclaimed chestnut selected for its beauty and also to blend the new and old. The radiant floor is detailed with a pattern of stone and reclaimed chestnut. Radiant flooring was the optimal solution for heating the new large space efficiently. Energy-efficient windows assist with the heating and cooling of the space.

When selecting furniture throughout the home we carefully considered where it was made, where the materials were sourced, and its finish.

Figure 3.35

The barstools, for example, were fabricated in a small shop in Pennsylvania and finished in natural VOC-free milk paint.

Figure 3.36

Figure 3.37

The reclaimed wood floors pair nicely with the existing floors in the original part of the house. The stone for the fireplace was sourced from a local property to match the tones and colors and to blend with the landscape, which can be viewed from this room. Timbers from a barn on the property taken down during construction were used as decorative beams and for the large mantel—a wonderful reuse of a product that traveled only 100 yards.

The interior furnishings are also sustainable. The upholstery was made by a North Carolina company that uses FSC wood frames and is attentive to the off-gassing of elements used as fillers and adhesives during production. The antique rug found in Pennsylvania blends old and new to create a warm, inviting space. While the Adirondack barrel chair by the fireplace is new, it was made by Old Hickory, an American company founded in 1892 that continues to make furniture. The superb twig chandeliers are from artisan Deanna Wish and are made of locally sourced hickory branches and roots.

Figure 3.38

The covered porch, which also uses repurposed beams from the property, makes the home appear like it has always been a comfortable farmhouse. Local stone for the fireplace and flooring add to the house's warmth. A chandelier made of shed antlers and created by a small craftsman lends a romantic atmosphere to the room. The chairs and sofa are all made from recycled plastics and covered in outdoor Sunbrella fabric. An antique trunk functions as a coffee table, while an antique iron table base with a new top finds new life as the dining table. The artwork above the fireplace is a large shutter from an antique store in an adjoining county.

Dujardin Design, Long Island Sound, Connecticut

Figure 3.39
Photos: Dujardin
Design

ON A GENTLE RISE OVERLOOKING LONG ISLAND SOUND ON
CONNECTICUT'S COASTLINE stands Trudy Dujardin's lovingly renovated holistic house. A testament to her passion for green products, paints, finishes, and
energy conservation, its elegance and warmth reveal her painstaking attention
to sustainable building and design. Having fully recovered from the multiple
chemical sensitivity she once suffered from, she is passionate about eco-friendly
homes and educating others about a holistic lifestyle. The Connecticut chapter
of the American Society of Interior Designers (ASID) selected this home for an
award of excellence, choosing her work as the best example of green creativity,
ingenuity, and design.

The renovation began with raising the roofline and adding shed dormers
to enlarge what had been a second-floor attic. Throughout, she selected low-
toxicity building materials, including steel support beams (instead of glue-
laminated wooden beams) and exterior grade CDX plywood for the subfloor.
For insulation, she used a cotton batting treated with boric acid. The HVAC
system used both a HEPA filter to minimize mold, dander, and pollen, and a
carbon filtration unit to eliminate VOCs and other gases. Every twenty minutes,
an energy recovery ventilation system exchanges interior air with outside air

that is filtered and conditioned (either heated or cooled) before being returned into the living spaces, ensuring good indoor air quality.

Filled with seafaring art and artifacts, it feels like a summerhouse. Natural light is key to the ambiance: awash in sunlight, the house minimizes energy usage. Low-wattage fiber optics light the staircase and niches for displaying art; interior windows allow sunlight to stream from room to room.

The clean, classic design celebrates both the home's intrinsic beauty and its allergen-free interior. Green amenities include cabinetry made from solid wood (without either particleboard or pressboard, which contain formaldehyde) and walls covered with a water-based latex paint that contains no biocides, pesticides, or preservatives. The custom cabinetry is made of solid wood, and only water-based glues were used. Cabinets original to the house were stripped and repainted with no-VOC paints as were all the remaining surfaces.

Upholstered pieces were custom made of 100 percent natural materials and filled with organic cotton and wool. Dujardin selected rock maple, a terpene-free wood, for solid pieces such as the fireplace mantel and bedroom built-ins.

Floors are an important component of a home devoted to clean air. In the dining room, a hand-painted floor in a stunning harlequin pattern obviates the need for rugs that can host dust mites and toxic chemicals in finishes, dyes, and backings. Upstairs, the floor on the landing is made of glass tiles inset into the wood to mimic the color and textures of a carpet. Where rugs are used, they are made only from natural materials. In the library, Dujardin commissioned a faux finish that mimics grass cloth, as grass cloth is often made with pesticide-laden materials. Here, as in other rooms, she made generous use of antique furniture: Any off-gassing took place years ago.

Figure 3.40

Figure 3.41

Figure 3.42

Figure 3.43

In this house, the bedrooms are the cleanest spaces in the home. Dujardin's bed and bedding and the air in the bedroom are chemical- and dust-free, allowing the body to detox at night. The mattress is filled with organic wool and covered in organic cotton free from any chemical contamination, including fire retardants. The window treatments are wood shutters, finished in a water-based, no-VOC paint.

The house exterior has been carefully considered as well. Due to its proximity to Long Island Sound, there are three oil separators installed in the driveway, designed to prevent car oil from washing into stormwater runoff and snowmelt and contaminate nearby waterways.

Dujardin purchased this property due in part because the previous owner also had environmental sensitivity. The house and property had never been sprayed with pesticides. For the past decade, she has made her home and property a sanctuary for life: bees buzz through the flowers, trees are home to birds, and the lawn is safe for little paws.

CHAPTER 4

healthy interiors

Figure 4.1 A client with multiple chemical sensitivities resides in this healthy home. All exterior and interior assemblies, including building materials, finishes, and furnishings, were fully vetted to ensure a healthy indoor environment.

Photo courtesy of Rowland + Broughton. Designed by Rowland + Broughton and Wendy Silverman with product vetting by Annette Stelmack.

Can we agree that if toxic chemicals from a building material are showing up in babies, then that is not a green building material?
—BILL WALSH, HEALTHY BUILDING NETWORK

Our health is inextricably connected to the home environment we create; what we design, specify, and provide for our clients matters. Unfortunately, studies indicate that there has been a steady increase in respiratory conditions, from asthma to allergies to a variety of illnesses, that link health concerns directly to the indoor environmental quality of a home.

The interior finishes, furnishings, materials, and products used to build homes are polluting their indoor air. Global organizations recognize that human health is being compromised by the homes we build, and important bodies of research point to the negative health effects of exposure to indoor chemicals. According to the World Health Organization (WHO), "There are many potentially hazardous compounds released indoors due to combustion, emissions from building materials, household equipment, and consumer products."[1]

Sustainable, green materials and products are a step in the right direction, but we must also consider the potential health consequences of using these materials and products in the spaces where we live, work, and play. Focus on the indoor emissions: toxic off-gassing that is odorless and harmful to health, and toxic particulates that may be released into the indoor air we breathe. We should not assume a material or product represented or sold as healthy, eco-friendly, or green actually is unless it has been vetted through rigorous testing protocols: Most products that are used in a residential environment have *not* been tested and deemed safe. Making informed choices when researching and specifying materials, finishes, and products is essential to minimizing our clients' chemical exposure.

Green Building Framework

Over the past few decades, green building has been adopted by governments at the federal, state, and municipal levels as well as by developers as green building rating systems, product certifications, and standards have proliferated. Some practices, like working with local and renewable materials or passive solar design, date back centuries. The Mesa Verde cliff dwellings in southern Colorado are exquisite examples; they were built in the twelfth century by the Anasazi and remain standing beneath the overhanging cliffs. While some were one-room buildings, others had more than 150 rooms. Villages in the Southwest built by the Anasazi were designed to capture passive solar heat during the winter, which warmed the spaces.

Today's green building efforts were born of a desire for energy efficiency and eco-friendly building practices. In the 1970s, oil prices increased at alarming

---

[1] http://www.euro.who.int/__data/assets/pdf_file/0007/78613/AIQIAQ_mtgrep_Bonn_ Oct06.pdf

rates, prompting research on energy efficiency and the use of renewable energy. Experiments with green building techniques emerged from the environmental movement of the 1960s and 1970s. "Earthships" were some of the first radically sustainable buildings embodying sustainable design and construction strategies. Earthships aimed for balance among the different strategies for homebuilding—generating their own water and power, conserving and reusing water, using local, recycled materials and passive heating and cooling, and growing food on site. By the late 1990s, these design and construction methods were delivering a radically different home—built with recycled materials and providing shelter, utilities, and food—for much the same cost as a conventional home.

In the 1990s, the industry reached several significant milestones: the American Institute of Architects (AIA) formed the Committee on the Environment (1989); the U.S. Environmental Protection Agency (EPA) and the Department of Energy (DOE) launched the Energy Star program (1992); the city of Austin, Texas, introduced the country's first local green building program (1992); the U.S. Green Building Council (USGBC) was founded (1993); the Clinton Administration announced the "Greening of the White House" (1993); and the USGBC established its Leadership in Energy and Environmental Design (LEED) program (1998).

Congress and federal agencies also got into the act: The Energy Policy Act of 2005 included sustainable performance standards for all federal buildings, the Federal Green Construction Guide for Specifiers was made available in the Whole Building Design Guide (WBDG), and the Office of Management and Budget (OMB) unveiled an "environmental scorecard" for federal agencies focused on sustainable building (2006).

These programs, publications, and legislation led the building industry, especially the commercial sector of the building industry, to begin adopting and implementing green building practices. By 2013, LEED registered and certified projects numbered 44,000 in the United States alone and totaled nearly 52,500 globally. Sustainability is here to stay. It is considered best practice by many and has become the norm in numerous places.

While the adverse environmental impact of building decreased, buildings still account for a lot of the total resources use in the United States. According to the USGBC, building, operating, and maintaining buildings accounts for 73 percent of all electricity consumption and 41 percent of overall energy use; consumes 14 percent of all potable water—15 trillion gallons per year; is responsible for 38 percent of all CO_2 emissions; and use 40 percent of raw materials globally.

The energy crisis of the 1970s in part inspired the ingenuity and passion that moved green building from exploration and development to actuality; architects, designers, and builders had found a way to make a difference. The initial focus was decreasing our dependence on fossil fuels through high-performing buildings and the use of renewable energy, then embraced water efficiency, sustainable site strategies, resource effectiveness for materials specified, and the comfort and health of the indoor environment.

Green commercial buildings consume less energy when compared with their counterparts. LEED Gold buildings in the General Services Administration's portfolio generally consume 25 percent less energy and 11 percent less water, cost 19 percent less to maintain, score 27 percent higher in occupant satisfaction, and emit 34 percent less greenhouse gases.

The building industry has begun to ameliorate the negative environmental impacts and to address the health and comfort of occupants. What other steps can we take to design and build healthy, high-performing, and intelligent homes that support the health, safety, and well-being of our clients? Addressing the indoor environment as well is key, not just because people spend 85 to 90 percent of their time indoors but because it is the right thing to do.

Let's enumerate what actions will have a net-positive effect on the health of our clients and that of future generations and the planet. We need to demand products and materials that support and improve health. Why aren't we asking for zero-hazard materials instead of settling for products that merely contain *fewer* toxins and contaminants? Why do we continue to spec systems that reduce energy and water consumption by just a small percentage? Wouldn't we rather have more stringent industry standards?

In the last fifty years, over eighty thousand industrial chemicals have been registered in the United States, yet only one thousand have been tested to determine if they are carcinogenic. And only five types of chemicals have been banned by the EPA under the Toxic Substances Control Act (TSCA): polychlorinated biphenyls (PCB), fully halogenated chlorofluoroalkanes, dioxin, asbestos, and hexavalent chromium. The use of four new chemicals used in metalworking fluids has also been forbidden. Worse, when two new chemicals mix in the environment they can create a new, potentially toxic chemical and add to the already increased level of burden on our bodies.

Volatile organic compounds (VOCs) are cancer-causing agents that off-gas from finishes, furnishings, and building materials; they include arsenic in pressure-treated wood, asbestos in old insulation, formaldehyde in composite wood products, and benzene in cigarette smoke.

Reproductive and developmental toxins affect fertility and fetal development and can cause birth defects and health problems later in life. These toxins, also found in finishes, furnishings, and building materials include phthalates in vinyl sheet flooring, acrylamide in adhesives, 1- and 2- bromopropane in coatings, and ethylene glycol in cleaning products.

Endocrine disruptors mimic the body's hormonal system, and even at low levels of exposure can affect the body adversely. These toxins include phthalates in vinyl sheet flooring, bisphenol A (BPA) in epoxies, PCBs in caulk and old light fixtures, halogenated flame retardants in foam furniture and mattresses, and dioxins and various pesticides.

Carcinogenic and endocrine-disrupting pesticides have been detected in more than 50 percent of those tested; fire-retardant chemicals (polybrominated diphenyl ethers, or PBDEs) were found in nearly all everyone. BPA was found in 90 percent of urine samples; women had higher levels than men or children.

Greenguard, a third-party certifier of products relating to indoor air quality, sampled and tested more than twenty-five untinted paints over a two-week period using dynamic environmental testing chambers. The products' stated content of VOC levels ranged between 0 grams per liter (g/l) up to 150 g/l. They also found that seven of the samples off-gassed formaldehyde above California's limit on dry product emissions and that two samples contained ethylene glycol emissions 50 percent above that limit. (This sample testing demonstrates that VOC content cannot be correlated to VOC emissions; more on that later in this chapter.)

The American Society of Interior Designers' Position on Sustainable Design

The American Society of Interior Designers, or ASID, endorses the following principles of environmental stewardship:

Advocacy for safe products and services: Interior designers should advocate with their clients and employers the development of buildings, spaces, and products that are environmentally benign, produced in a socially just manner, and are safe for all living things.

Protection of the biosphere: Interior designers should eliminate the use of any product or process that is known to pollute air, water, or earth.

Sustainable use of natural resources: Interior designers should make use of renewable natural resources and protect vegetation, wildlife habitats, open spaces, and wilderness.

Waste reduction: Interior designers should minimize waste through the reduction, reuse, or recycling of products and encourage the development and use of reclaimed, salvaged, and recycled products.

Wise use of energy: Interior designers should reduce energy use, adopt energy-conserving strategies, and choose renewable energy sources.

Reduction of risk: Interior designers should eliminate the environmental risk to the health of the end users of their designs.

ASID believes that interior designers should endeavor to practice sustainable design whenever feasible. Interior designers should meet present-day needs without compromising the ability to meet the needs of future generations.

Source: American Society of Interior Designers, http://www.asid.org/content/asid-position-sustainable-design

The primary issues of health, safety, and welfare for our clients should be non-negotiable. William McDonough said it best: "Don't poison people; tell the truth and let them know. Don't tell me it's impossible to make a safe, healthy interior. Instead tell me you weren't able to do it because you aren't able to find materials and products to create a healthy space."

Our homes and the homes of our clients are sanctuaries, the places we go to regenerate and that shelter us from storms, literally and figuratively, providing a shield from adverse external conditions. Shouldn't they also support the health of the occupants and construction tradespeople?

Let's examine why health matters and look at the issues of indoor air quality (IAQ), safety, and well-being. Then we'll discuss mitigation strategies and recap the benefits of alternative principles and practices that will hopefully become industry standards.

Why Health Matters

Our clients' welfare is contingent on their physical, mental, and emotional well-being; the aesthetic qualities of the texture, colors, and patterns that surround them; as well as their access to daylight and views. How can professional interior designers create healthy interior environments? Healthy home objectives involve material science and composition, ergonomics, daylighting and artificial lighting, indoor environmental and air quality, and acoustics, and embrace a connection to nature. To ensure safety, we must consider function and layout as well as circulation and egress patterns; source control of chemicals and pollutants; and the products and building systems necessary to minimize physical risks and accidents.

We must therefore research interior finishes and furnishings and then specify healthy ones. This section examines the shortcomings of some chemicals whose use is widespread in the building industry and explores chemical sensitivities and the electro-pollution surrounding us.

We spend 85 to 90 percent of our time indoors, and the level of indoor air pollutants can be two to five times higher than pollutants measured outdoors, even outside large and industrial cities. Greenguard noted in their "Children's Health Statistics" report that we are exposed to the highest levels of VOCs at home. Indoor air pollution has been linked to cancer, respiratory and heart disease, and headaches, lethargy, and dizziness.[2]

But what causes indoor air pollution? Household cleaners, adhesives, carpets, paints, perfumes, air fresheners, synthetics, resins, ducts, formaldehyde, adhesives, heavy metals, upholstery, cabinetry, sealers, particulates, VOCs, substrates, candles, finishes, allergens, ventilation systems, equipment—the list goes on and on.

---

[2] http://www.greenguard.org/Libraries/GG_Documents/GG_1008_IS_16_Childrens HealthStats_SHORT_ONLINE.sflb.ashx

So, what can we do about it?

Many organizations are researching the answer. Renowned architecture firm Perkins+Will compiled a comprehensive study for the National Institutes of Health's Division of Environmental Protection as part of a larger effort to promote health in the built environment. The government, regulatory agencies, and academic sources have identified 374 substances linked to asthma; 75 of them are found in paints and adhesives which are used in nearly every home constructed. This data will allow us to minimize their use in building materials and furnishings.

The study from Perkins+Will also reports that 23 million Americans suffer from asthma, 7.1 million of whom are children, and the numbers are growing exponentially. And according to the Global Initiative for Asthma, more than 10 percent of the U.S. population have been diagnosed with asthma.[3] In fact, asthma is one

---

Each appears on at least six reference lists

(2-Aminoethyl) ethanolamine	Isophorone diisocyanate (IPDI)
1,1'-Methylenebis (4isocyanatobenzene) MDI	Latex
4-Methylmorpholine	Maleic anhydride
Azoicarbonamide (1-1' - Azobisformamide)	Methyl Methacrylate
Chloroamine T	Methyl tetrahydrophtalic anhydride
Chromium	Mites
Chromium Compounds	N,N-Dimethylethanolamine
Chromium, Hexavalent	Napthalene Diisocyanate
Cobalt	Nickel
Colophony (Rosin)	Papain
Crab	Penicillins (Ampicillin)
Diazonium salt	Piperazine dihydrochloride
Egg Protein	Polymethylene Polyphenyl isocyanate (PPI)
Ethanolamine (2-Aminoethanol)	Polyvinyl Chloride
Ethylenediamine (1,2-Diaminoethane)	Psyllium
Formaldehyde	Spiramycin
Gluaraldehyde (aka Cidex)	Styrene
Hard Metal	Toluene diisocyanate (TDI)
Hexamethylene diisocyanate (HDI)	Triethylene Tetramine
Hydralazine	Tungsten carbide
Isocyanates	Wood dust

Figure 4.2 This insert from the study prepared by Perkins+Will and the National Institutes of Health enumerates substances linked to asthma and the frequency with which they appear on research reference lists.

Source: Perkins+Will (http://transparency.perkinswill.com/Media); National Institutes of Health (http://www.nems.nih.gov/Sustainability/Documents/NIH%20Asthma%20Report.pdf)

---

[3] www.ginasthma.org/local/uploads/files/GINABurdenSummary.pdf.

of the most common chronic diseases worldwide, affecting an estimated 300 million people. And it doesn't stop there. The rate of asthma increases as developing countries westernize. By 2025, it is estimated that more than half of the world's population will live in urban areas, and there is therefore likely to be a marked increase in the number of asthmatics worldwide over the next two decades: an additional 100 million individuals. Already, the number of children under 17 affected by asthma has doubled in 20 years to nearly 10 percent as of 2011.[4]

The World Health Organization (WHO) has partnered with the United Nations Environment Programme (UNEP) to identify health issues related to building materials (see sidebar). Their in-depth study points to commonly specified building materials as major sources of endocrine-disrupting chemicals (EDCs). According to the report, "Over the past decade it has become clear that humans, in particular small children, are...exposed to EDCs via dust and particles in indoor environments like homes, schools, childcare centres, and offices."[5] The report also notes that a large number of chemicals are used as additives in indoor materials as well as other products found in our homes. These chemicals can leak into dust particulates or food. They have called for full disclosure of chemical contents in materials and products, pushing the industry toward transparency in ingredients. And the Healthy Building Network has reported that health issues impacted by EDCs are on the rise. The table below indicates the primary areas of concern:

Clearly, our indoor environments of the buildings where we live, work, learn, and play are adversely affecting our health and well-being; the rise of asthma,

Rising Incidences of Health Impacts Associated with Endocrine Disrupting Chemicals	
Autism	**1:110 in 2007** Increased from under 5:10,000 in 1970, globally
Childhood Asthma	**Doubled in 20 years, to 9.4% in 2010** U.S. children, 0-17 years of age
Testicular Cancer	Up to **400% rise** Since 1967 in Baltic countries
Preterm Births	**30% increase** Since 1981 in US, UK & Scandinavia
Low Birth Weight	**19% increase** From 1990 to 2010 in US
Pediatric Brain Cancer	**7% increase** From 1995 to 2007 in US

Healthy Building Network
Source: *State of the Science of Endocrine Disrupting Chemicals – 2012, WHO/UNEP, 2013*

Figure 4.3 This table from the Healthy Building Network shows the rising incidences of health issues impacted by endocrine-disrupting chemicals.

Source: Healthy Building News.

---

[4] www.childstats.gov/americaschildren/tables.asp.
[5] http://www.healthybuilding.net/news/130225-who-edcs.html

reproductive difficulties, respiratory diseases, developmental conditions, cancer, and chemical sensitivities are just a few examples of how. We can no longer question whether indoor environments affect our health.

Chemical Concerns

Our endocrine system regulates the release of certain hormones essential for metabolism, growth and development, sleep, and mood. Substances known as endocrine-disrupting chemicals, or EDCs, can alter the function(s) of this hormonal system, thus increasing the risk of adverse health effects. Some EDCs occur naturally, while synthetic varieties can be found in pesticides, electronics, personal care products, and cosmetics. They can also be found as additives or contaminants in food. These chemicals contribute to the development of nondescended testes in young males, breast cancer in women, prostate cancer in men, developmental effects on the nervous system in children, attention deficit hyperactivity disorder (ADHD) in children, and thyroid cancer.

EDCs can enter the environment through industrial and urban discharges, agricultural run-off, and the burning and release of waste. We can be exposed to them via food and water, inhaling gases and particles in the air, and skin contact.

In 2013, the World Health Organization and the United Nations Environment Programme released *The State of the Science of Endocrine Disrupting Chemicals* 2012, a joint report that found that many synthetic chemicals that have never been tested for their disruption of the hormone system might have significant health implications and presents the current scientific knowledge on exposure to and the effects of EDCs.

Dr. Maria Neira, WHO's director for public health and environment, says, "We urgently need more research to obtain a fuller picture of the health and environment impacts of endocrine disruptors."

The report calls for more research on the associations between EDCs and specific diseases and disorders, noting that more comprehensive assessments and better testing methods could reduce disease risks, saving both lives and money that would be spent on treatment.

Everywhere we go we are surrounded by chemically laden products. It's time that we demand transparency in product content.

Source: World Health Organization http://www.who.int/mediacentre/news/releases/2013/hormone_disrupting_20130219/en/

HEALTH AND INDOOR AIR QUALITY

Poor indoor air quality (IAQ) can cause headaches, fatigue, nausea, dizziness, productivity issues, difficulty concentrating, and irritation of the eyes, nose, throat, and lungs. Asthma has been linked to specific air contaminants and damp indoor environments. Long-term exposure to asbestos, formaldehyde, and radon can cause cancer. Reproductive and developmental issues have been linked to unhealthy indoor air complicated by poor ventilation issues.

IAQ is affected by the building and site interface, the home's mechanical and plumbing systems, the indoor space and materials, as well as lifestyle patterns and choices. While the EPA has established limits for outdoor pollutants, there are no regulations on indoor chemicals and irritants. Moisture in the buildings envelope and interiors also contribute to poor IAQ.

Designers have the opportunity create a healthy, happy home, but we can also unintentionally do the opposite. Our first motto should be to do no harm. Avoiding toxins and chemicals of concern is best practice and the starting point for evaluating products and materials. Always review available data on the emissions from volatile organic compounds (VOCs) semivolatile organic compounds (SVOCs), and the VOC content labeling for all interior finishes, furnishings, and building envelope components. And look for third-party certifications that address IAQ (see chapter 8, "Certifications and Standards").

IAQ certifications address health problems such as sick building syndrome, chemical sensitivity, and respiratory problems. Testing involves a series of sealed-chamber tests that determine the amount of compounds that the product releases into the air over a certain period of time. The preferred methodology is to test all primary compounds separately. By evaluating the toxicity of a product based on its ingredients and/or by measuring emissions, its affect on IAQ protocols can be verified.

Some VOCs, SVOCs, and nonvolatile compounds exempt from testing potentially affect health adversely, and few manufacturers evaluate SVOC levels, so we inquire about them proactively.

- *VOCs:* These are gases that enter the environment (indoor/outdoor) through building and household products, including paints and pesticides, copiers and printers, interior finishes and furnishings, arts and crafts supplies, and cleaning products. As these chemicals vary greatly, it's important to understand the potentially hazardous VOC content and emissions for each product specified, as some manufacturers may not be measuring their emissions. VOC levels are measured in grams per liter (g/L). Wet-applied products like paint, stains, and adhesives emit VOCs after they're applied and taper off within a few weeks. Flooring, carpet, furniture, cabinetry and other interior finish products release VOCs more slowly, over a longer, unknown period of time.
  - *Content labeling.* Required for wet-applied materials, but the labels do not indicate off-gassing levels, don't explain how the product interacts

with the substrate to which it's being applied, and do not address SVOCs.

- *Emissions testing and certifications.* A manufacturer may—or may not—choose to pursue testing through a third party of indoor off-gassing. Many such tests do not include SVOCs or provide information on how the product interacts with the substrate to which it's being applied, and they can miss some emissions.

- *SVOCs.* Carbon-based substance that release gases from various materials, including phthalates, glycol-based solvents, halogenated flame retardants, and plasticisers that turn into persistent bioaccumulative toxins, or PBTs. Used in cleaning products and coatings, they attach to dust particulates that are then absorbed or inhaled.

- *Exempt VOCs.* Unregulated compounds are not usually included in a product's VOC content labeling; that means even zero-VOC products may contain exempt VOCs hazardous to one's health. Review all the ingredients for interior finishes and furnishings, request and review all ingredients from the manufacturer to ensure they are free of hazardous chemicals like formaldehyde, styrene, benzene, toluene, and various forms of chloride.

Understanding VOC emissions and content, SVOCs, and exempt VOCs will help you avoid specifying toxic materials such as persistent organic pollutants (POPs), which are extremely hazardous to human health and the environment. The threat they pose is understood globally, and we must eliminate their production and use.

Dioxins (PVC-based products) and furans (unintended industrial by-products) are of the utmost concern. Their production and incineration, especially those containing chlorine, contributes to the formation of PBTs, which remain in the environment for a long time (persist) and concentrate in the humans and animals exposed to them (bioaccumulate). All of us have been exposed to them. Designers, project teams, and homeowners must all understand that PBTs, even at low levels, are a potential source of serious human health issues and are detrimental to the environmental as well.

In 2012, the EPA's Toxic Substances Control Act (TSCA) identified eighty-three chemicals for risk assessment, and in the following year began testing 23 most commonly used chemicals. A wide range of these chemicals of concern are acknowledged carcinogens, harmful to our respiratory systems, and can cause developmental, reproductive, and neurological effects. Flame retardants; heavy metals like lead, mercury, manganese, arsenic, and cadmium; organic solvents (methylene chloride, glycol ethers, trichloroethylene); pesticides (atrazine, chlorpyrifos, parathion, lindane, DDT); environmental tobacco smoke and nicotine; and polychlorinated biphenyls (PCBs) all fall into this category. Chemicals that release endocrine disruptors are especially problematic because they are reactive and toxic at very low levels. Unfortunately, typical regulatory standards do not set acceptable levels that are low enough.

We are exposed daily to vast amounts of chemicals from products off-gassing and leaching and then attaching themselves to dust particulates. This dust gets on our hands and food, which we then ingest. The most vulnerable are children, the elderly, and those with compromised immune systems. Infants' and toddlers' breathing zones are closer to the ground, where there is a heavier concentration of chemicals and dust. Because they often put their hands in their mouth and they breathe more rapidly, they inhale more air—and more particulates—and ingest more chemicals. Their organs are still developing, which significantly increases their level of exposure to toxins. Always identify substances that may adversely affect your client's health. When designing for a family with small children, paying close attention to toxic chemicals is paramount.

Chemicals of Concern can be difficult to prioritize but important to the health of manufacturers, trades and residents. The first step in the process is to identify substances that may be of concern or have a serious effect on your client's health. Do they have specific chemical sensitivities to address? Work first to replace known substances of concern by progressively finding alternatives with equal performance and durability. If asthma is a trigger, avoid known asthmagens. Avoid PBTs in your designs along with VOCs that cause cancer and filter for chemicals that negatively affect our nervous systems, reproduction and human development. Simply put, aim to avoid as many chemical hazards as possible, but don't drive yourself crazy in the process.

With ever-present exposure to hazardous chemicals, human health can be compromised and for some severely threatened. It's important to know that chemicals can cause cancer, asthma, allergens, and respiratory issues, and that they can act as reproductive and developmental toxicants, endocrine disruptors, mutagens, and neurotoxins, potentially throwing our systems out of balance. It's always best to be cautious and avoid the worst offenders.

COMMON CHEMICALS OF CONCERN TO AVOID

The list of chemicals of concern varies from country to country. In the United States there are between forty and fifty chemicals on the list. Greenguard generally tests around two hundred chemicals for their IAQ certification. Germany lists around eight hundred chemicals of concern. Gather information from a variety of resources; start by avoiding the following short list of common hazards and toxins.

- Antimicrobials: Synthetic, broad-spectrum chemicals used as a substance or mixture of substances to destroy or suppress the growth of harmful microorganisms, including bacteria, viruses, and fungi. Triclosan is a common antimicrobial. It is a biocide and used as an additive in paint, carpet, countertops, cutting boards, wall coverings, door hardware, textiles, mattresses, and personal items to inhibit the growth of mold.
  - Antimicrobials bioaccumulate in fatty tissues.
  - They are endocrine disruptors.

Red List

The Living Building Challenge envisions a future where all materials in the built environment are replenishable and have no negative impact on human and environmental health. The precautionary principle should guide all material choices. A project pursuing the Living Building Challenge cannot contain any of the following Red List materials or chemicals:

Asbestos

Cadmium

Chlorinated polyethylene or

Chlorosulfonated polyethylene*

Chlorofluorocarbons (CFCs)

Chloroprene (Neoprene)

Formaldehyde (added)

Halogenated flame retardants*

Hydrochlorofluorocarbons (HCFCs)

Lead (added)

Mercury

Petrochemical fertilizers and pesticides*

Phthalates

Polyvinyl chloride (PVC)

Wood treatments containing creosote, arsenic or pentachlorophenol

*There are temporary exceptions for these Red List items due to economic concerns related to those materials economy. Refer to the dialogue section within the Living Building Challenge platform for complete, up-to-date listings.

Source: www.living-future.org

- Bacteria can develop cross-resistance to them.
- There may be long-term effects for chemically sensitive clients.
- Biocides: These substances kill or control the growth of living organisms and include pesticides, herbicides, fungicides, and antibacterials. They are added to paints, drywall, textiles, and hardwood flooring as a preservative to inhibit

microorganisms or control pests. Biocides typically contain permethrin, a member of the pyrethroid class of pesticides that can cause long-term health problems.

- Permethrin is classified as a likely carcinogen and known to be an endocrine disruptor, neurotoxin, and developmental and reproductive toxin.
- Biocides are often not listed on a material safety data sheet (MSDS).

- Bisphenol-A (BPA): A toxic, industrial chemical found in plastic, polycarbonate plastic, the resinous lining of food cans, and resins in epoxy paint coatings, adhesives, and sealants.

- BPA migrates into food and can mimic estrogen, affecting reproduction.
- It is on the EPA's restricted list of chemicals of concern.
- It may lead to developmental problems in children as well as systemic toxicity.
- Canada was the first country to designate BPA as toxic and banned it in consumer products.

- Cadmium: A toxic heavy metal, found in ores and used in baking enamels, television phosphors, and pigmentations for textiles and wall coverings.

- Categorized as a PBT.
- The Occupational Health and Safety Administration (OSHA) has declared cadmium and its compounds as highly toxic. Exposure to this metal is known to cause cancer and targets the body's cardiovascular, renal, gastrointestinal, neurological, reproductive, and respiratory systems.

- Carbon black: An additive used as a UV light stabilizer and found in products containing polyethylene, polypropylene, polyurethane, styrene, and PVC.

- Classified as a carcinogen by the International Agency for Cancer Research (IARC) and the State of California.

- Diisocyanate: Both methylene diphenyl diisocyanate (MDI) and toluene Diisocyanate (TDI) are found in polyurethane foams and resins, spray foam insulation, coatings, sealants, and adhesives.

- A known asthmagen, they cause lung damage, skin irritation, harm to the immune system, and chemical sensitivities.

- Formaldehyde: A colorless, water-soluble, pungent gas created primarily by resins of urea-formaldehyde (UF), a VOC that freely off-gases, but also by phenol formaldehyde (PF). Both are used in foam insulations, binding adhesives in wood composites, furnishings, and textile treatments.

- Formaldehyde is classified as a human carcinogen by multiple agencies.
- Short-term exposure to formaldehyde can be fatal.

- Long-term exposure to low levels of formaldehyde may cause respiratory difficulty, mucous membrane irritation, eczema, and chemical sensitivity.
- The construction industry uses 70 percent of all formaldehyde-based products.

- Flame retardants (FRs): Brominated, chlorinated, or halogenated compounds are added to furniture foam, textiles, upholstery, insulation, and electronics to meet flammability requirements of California's Technical Bulletin 177. Polyethylene, polypropylene, polyurethane, and styrene are typically used in FRs. Ironically, during a fire, FRs increase the amount of carbon monoxide and release toxic gases and smoke known to be harmful and at times fatal to both occupants and firefighters.
  - FRs are released into the air, attaching themselves to particulates that are then inhaled or ingested.
  - They are categorized as PBTs and have been linked to cancer, reduced fertility, and thyroid disruption.
  - The European Union has already banned some halogenated flame retardants, but the United States lags behind.
  - California is considering altering its building codes so that it no longer has to be used in construction.

- Hexavalent chromium: A harmful environmental pollutant used primarily for leather tanning, pigments and dyes, chrome plating and as wood a preservative (see chapter 19, "Furnishings"), this toxic component is a by-product of steel production.
  - A carcinogen, and can damage the respiratory system if inhaled.

- Isocyanates: Chemicals used to make polyurethane foam, coatings and insulation, and engineered wood.
  - An occupational hazard leading to asthma and respiratory sensitizers.

- Lead: A toxic heavy metal; exposure even at low levels can be harmful. Be careful when specifying faucets, as you can still come across products containing lead. Avoid solder containing lead for use near potable water.
  - A PBT, lead harmful if breathed or swallowed and can cause cancer and developmental and reproductive toxicity.
  - Specify 100 percent lead-free solder.

- Mercury: A toxic heavy metal found in thermometers, fluorescent and high-intensity discharge light bulbs, and some electrical switches. If inhaled, consult a physician immediately.
  - Categorized as a PBT and neurotoxicant, it may also be a developmental toxicant.

- The EPA has published disposal protocols for broken compact fluorescent lamps (CFLs).

- Nanomaterials: Minuscule particles, they can be 100,000 times thinner than a strand of hair and measure 1 to 100 nanometers. They are used in paints, fabrics, cosmetics, treated wood, electronics, and sunscreen.

  - Avoid as a precaution, especially with clients with chemically sensitivities.

- Perfluorochemicals (PFCs): Extremely stable, persistent, toxic chemicals that accumulate in the atmosphere as greenhouse gas. They can be detected in nearly all of us. PFCs are used as water and grease lubricant surface treatments and stain repellent in cookware, plus coatings, some personal care products, and carpet and textile treatments. Many PFCs break down into perfluorooctanoic acid (PFOA) or sulfonates (PFOS) in the environment the human body. PFOS is a PBT; PFOA is very persistent, does not biodegrade, hydrolyze, or photolyze in typical environmental conditions.

  - Associated with testicular, breast, liver, and prostate cancer, reproductive and developmental defects; and immune system suppression.

  - Of every twenty children tested for PFOA, nineteen had blood contaminated with PFOA.[6]

- Phthalates: Common industrial chemical used in PVC plastics, solvents, nail polish, and synthetic fragrances, including air fresheners. Often referred to as plasticizers, they're added to vinyl or PVC-based products for flexibility and durability. Phthalates do not chemically bind to such products and are eventually released into the air as SVOCs on dust particulates.

  - Categorized as a reproductive hazard and endocrine disruptor. The chemical leaches from the plastic, after which it is ingested, inhaled, or absorbed through the skin from dust particulates. It has recently been linked to asthma and allergies.

  - On the EPA's restricted list as a chemical of concern.

  - Introduced in the 1930s, they are now ubiquitous. In 2000, the Centers for Disease Control (CDC) tested 289 people and found high levels of phthalates in all of the subjects' blood.

- Polyvinyl chloride (PVC): A notorious upstream toxin, it releases phthalates while in use and dioxin when burned. PVC is found in many types of plastic

---

[6]http://www.ewg.org/research/pfcs-global-contaminants/pfoa-pervasive-pollutant-human-blood-are-other-pfcs

and in numerous building products, including carpet backing, upholstery, vinyl flooring, window shades, sealants, adhesives, and coatings.

- Dioxin is one of the most toxic substances known to exist.
- PVC and PVC by-products contain known carcinogens and developmental and reproductive toxicants.
- Vinyl chloride, used in manufacturing, is an acknowledged asthmagen. It was the subject of *Blue Vinyl*, a documentary film about "Cancer Alley," the ominous nickname for that section of the banks of the Mississippi River with elevated rates of cancer.

Perkins+Will's Precautionary List; the Healthy Building Network's Pharos Lens; information from the Health Product Declaration Collaborative; the Living Building Challenge Red List; LEED v4; GreenScreen for Safer Chemicals; and the European Union's Registration, Evaluation, Authorization, and Restriction of Chemicals (REACH) are all tools that can inform and guide you when evaluating products and materials.

CHEMICAL SENSITIVITIES

We unfortunately carry a wide range of chemicals in our bodies. Multiple chemical sensitivities (MCS) is an adverse physical reaction to low levels of many common chemicals. People can become hypersensitive to a broad range of synthetic pollutants, such as exhaust gases, formaldehyde, artificial fragrances, solvents, VOCs, perfumes, gasoline, diesel fuel, plastic materials, paints, and adhesives. The condition can be aggravated by pollen, dust mites, or pet dander. Someone is not typically born with MCS; it usually develops after exposure to various pollutants—either a large amount of pollutants at one time, or after exposure to low levels over a long period.

Chemical sensitivity is a generally accepted phenomenon, but debate over whether MCS should be classified as an illness continues. There are a number of other names for MCS, including twentieth-century disease, environmental illness, total allergy syndrome, and chemical AIDS.

Theories about the cause of MCS include allergy, dysfunction of the immune system, neurobiological sensitization, and various psychological issues. That the incidence of MCS is on the rise supports the theory that it is linked to the frequent exposure or overexposure of our immune systems to toxic, synthetic chemicals that are nearly impossible to avoid today. For a healthy individual, exposure to a toxic chemical may not become a substantial health risk, but for the chemically sensitized person, that same exposure—even a brief or low-level exposure—can cause regular, multiple symptoms or reactions. (Exposure to inert materials like sand, silica, gold, titanium, and water, typically provoke no reaction.) The most sensitized individuals will show a pronounced reaction to formaldehyde, isocyanates, epoxy resins, ammonia, peanuts, shellfish, sulfur dioxide, and others. If a client is sensitized to a particular chemical compound, exposure of any kind can be very serious—even fatal.

Figure 4.4 Living room with safe and luxurious fabrics from O Ecotextiles.

Photo courtesy of O Ecotextiles.

Formaldehyde, in particular, is omnipresent in the built environment, home products, and even in our cars. It is readily available to manufacturers, inexpensive, and used in numerous everyday building products, including wall insulation, medium-density fiberboard (MDF), plywood, fabric and carpet treatments, body care products (shampoo, toothpaste, etc.), glues, paints, plastics, and electrical equipment. Becoming sensitized to a chemical like formaldehyde is very disabling because it shows up in so many places. Symptoms may include flushing, rashes, stinging eyes and throat, and respiratory difficulties like breathlessness.

For anyone with MCS, the best strategy is to avoid whatever chemicals trigger their symptoms. But pinning down exactly which materials are problematic can be difficult. It is therefore important for the MCS sufferer to avoid exposure to as many pollutants and chemical toxins as possible. But it's also challenging at best to completely eradicate pollutants from our indoor environments. By following the precautionary principle, we can positively impact our clients' lives by avoiding the use of trigger chemicals where they live, eat, sleep, play, and work.

Their home especially should be a sanctuary where they can retreat and heal; the bedrooms, living room, and kitchen are a priority, as that is where clients will spend most of their time. Giving them a clean space where they can restore and regenerate will benefit them physically and psychologically.

Many chemical- and/or allergen-sensitive individuals have been treated like enigmas. By listening with empathy to their needs and concerns, acknowledging their apprehensions, and addressing the design process accordingly, you will gain their trust and earn credibility. If you are working with a sensitive client, clarify the source of their sensitivity, as your strategies will differ with each influencing factor.

In addition to following the precautionary principle, allow the client to sample all materials and finishes being considered. It is ultimately the client's responsibility to ensure that all interior finishes and furnishings elicit no problematic reactions. To test wet finishes, apply them to a clean piece of glass to limit chemical interaction or ask the client to sample the end product at another site. In addition, you can consult the following IAQ testing standards and certifications. (There are more details about these in chapter 8, "Certifications and Standards.") Remember that some exempt toxicants may not be listed on the manufacturer's MSDS.

- California Department of Public Health (CDPH) Section 01350 is a standard that has been adopted by the following bodies of certification:
  - National Sanitation Foundation (NSF) 140 Carpet
  - NSF 332 Resilient Flooring
  - Underwriters Laboratory Environment (ULE) 100 Gypsum
  - ULE 102 Doors
  - ULE 105 Ceiling Tiles
  - ULE 115 Insulation
  - ULE 106 Luminaries
- Greenguard Gold under the ULE label:
  - Rigorous testing performed by Air Quality Sciences (ACS); emission thresholds for formaldehyde, TVOC, and other compounds
- CRI Green Label Plus:
  - Emission thresholds in formaldehyde, total volatile organic compounds (TVOC), some other compounds
- Global Organic Textile Standard:
  - The leading standard for the processing of textile goods using organic fibers, including environmental and social criteria, it is universally recognized by more than 2,750 certified textile processing, manufacturing, and trading operators in more than five countries

- Floor Score:
    - Certification programs developed by Scientific Certification Systems (SCS) based on California protocols
- SCS Indoor Advantage Gold (including residential):
    - Introduced by SCS; based on the more rigorous California protocols

Creating healthy, vital spaces is as important to the work that we do as interior designers as are the aesthetics, performance, beauty, and function of those spaces. Doing so is meaningful, value-driven work, and the service that you provide to your clients will provide satisfaction for you as well.

ELECTRO-POLLUTION

Electromagnetic sensitivity is a global problem that worsens as the number of electromagnetic fields (EMFs) and radio frequencies (RF) that surround us increases. Our digital culture demands we constantly use and be in close contact with electrically powered devices like cell phones, computers, and tablets.

Electrical currents move through a wire or conductor and generate a flow of energy that creates fields of humming vibrations all around us. These fields of electromagnetic energy are produced indoors by heavy equipment, lighting and switching systems, smart meters, small and large appliances, digital devices, and wiring; exterior sources include power lines and substations, and wireless and radio frequencies. Electro-pollution can seem mysterious because we can't touch, taste, smell, or see it, even though we are encircled by more electromagnetic radiation (EMR) today then ever before because of the technology on which we increasingly rely. EMFs are one to two hundred million times greater than they were a century ago, and they affect each one of us differently, sometimes even disrupting the balance in our body chemistry.

Our bodies are themselves powered by (much smaller) electrical charges, like those that keep the heart pumping blood through our circulatory system. External EMFs interact directly with our bodies, surrounding us with a potent magnetic field and influencing our well-being—and sometimes causing disease. Electro-pollution can unbalance our body's system and become a hormone disruptor and carcinogen; it can also lead to heart disease, brain dysfunction, fibromyalgia, and respiratory distress.

Electro-pollution is also an endocrine disruptor that creates an imbalance in our body's melatonin. In addition to regulating the body's sleep/wake cycle, melatonin is a natural antioxidant that seeks out free radicals, improves thyroid function, strengthens the immune system's cancer-fighting cells, balances our energy, and prevents allergic reactions.

As with MCS, there is an ongoing debate in the medical field about the impact of EMFs. Studies indicate that they can be harmful, even causing cancer, and that sensitive individuals display compromised immune systems. While EMFs continue to a be a controversial topic concerning occupant health, much of the evidence leads us to adopting the precautionary path of avoidance and minimize homeowners' and residents' exposure to them, especially in children's rooms, as some studies indicate an elevation in childhood leukemia and cancers from exposure to EMFs.

When a client has electromagnetic sensitivities, be sure to include an EMF specialist on the project team to meet the goals and consider implementing the following strategies to mitigate common sources of EMFs:

- Code compliant wiring of three-way switches to avoid creating an electrical current loop. Also check for wiring errors like crossing neutral wires with other neutral or ground wires during installation or remodeling. Use twisted electric cable or have the electrician twist the cables during installation.

- Locate current-dense service panels, the main electrical cable that runs from the electric meter to the power panel, and the wires that run from the power panel to electrical equipment (like the range, and water heaters, which emit high levels of EMFs) away from heavily used interior spaces, especially bedrooms, to minimize high-current wiring that runs along the most used areas of the home.

- Check for low-level magnetic fields from currents running on water pipes and gas lines due to currents on the electrical grounding system. Avoid accidental grounding of metal-sheathed electrical cable to grounded water pipes.

- When remodeling, replace old knob-and-tube wiring (which will also address other safety concerns).

- Keep electronic devices that generate significant magnetic fields away from headboards, including wired clocks, radios, electric blankets, hair dryers, and telephones.

- Locate beds as far as possible from wall outlets and wires inside the wall. Do not install wires behind headboards. Metal conducts electricity—the metal mattress springs in a mattress and upholstered seating, or metal countertop, will become an energy conductor.

- Design computer work areas with as much distance as possible between the user and the equipment, including transformers, printers, and power strips. Use extension power cable to plug-in the computer away from the user's space, and push the monitor to the back of the desk.

- Suggest your client use a separate keyboard for a laptop and not place it on his or her lap. Studies have shown that the EMFs may cause reproductive problems.

- Advise clients to consider nonchemical, radiation-free computers.

- Avoid microwaves and induction cooking appliances. Specify the lowest energy-use rating for all appliances. Increasing the distance between such appliances and seating will lower EMF risks.

- Avoid electric heating systems, including baseboard heaters and radiant floor or ceiling heaters.

- Light-emitting diodes (LEDs) generate the lowest levels of EMFs; compact fluorescent lamps (CFLs) emit slightly more.

- Avoid dimming and adjustable switching, as the electrical current continues to flow, either through the bulb or through the rheostat. This constant flow of current is where the the EMF is most potent. The distance between an individual and the EMF current is inches rather than feet.

- Provide an easily accessible connection to the outdoors where clients can go barefoot to reconnect with the earth.

- Reject smart meters, as the wireless emissions have been known to cause arrhythmias and sleeping problems.

- Install an all-off switch so that the wireless frequencies in the home can be turned off at night.

- Personal shielding and protection devices are available for computers, cell phones, entertainment equipment, and appliances.

- Specify products with the lowest energy use ratings.

- Use a gauss meter, or magnetometer, to measure the strength of magnetic fields in the home prior to insulation and drywall installation to ensure that any issues are corrected first. According to industry experts, a level below 1 to 3 milligauss (mG) is acceptable for long-term EMF exposure.

Wireless frequencies can disturb cellular communication, cause oxidative stress in the body, and even thicken the blood; research is needed to determine the people most at risk when exposed to EMF and RF fields. Additionally, the EPA warns "there is reason for concern" and advises "prudent avoidance." Even though there is uncertainty about health risks from EMFs, evidence suggests that thoughtful preventative strategies can minimize homeowner exposure to these fields. Until there is a precise scientific assessment, the precautionary principle is best practice to protect our clients.

Resources

"Exposure to Radio Frequency Electro-Magnetic Fields," www.epa.gov/EPA-IMPACT/2003/September/Day-08/i22624.html
"Electromagnetic Pollution," www.buildingbiology.net/elpo.html
The Collaborative on Health and the Environment, www.healthandenvironment.org
Electromagnetic Health, www.electromagnetichealth.org
American Academy of Environmental Medicine, Electromagnetic and Radiofrequency Exposure, September, 2012.

Safety and Well-Being

Homes built today are usually considered safe living environments that support health and well-being. Unfortunately, the potential for injuries, exposure to hazardous materials and poor indoor environmental quality, and/or ergonomics may not be addressed by the home's design, construction, operation, and maintenance of a home.

As professional interior designers, it is our responsibility to protect our clients' health, safety, and welfare (HSW) by creating comfortable spaces that nurture and heal all of the building's users. Projects that prioritize users' HSW commit to design choices that "first, do no harm." Every decision impacts not only the environment but also the individuals who use the interior space, from the interior finishes and furnishings that we specify, to the function and layout of the interiors, to the lighting, acoustics, and air quality, to the personalized ergonomic strategies.

Even though we are not the subject matter experts on all of the building and its systems, we must understand all overarching principles and ensure they are addressed in the design. To realize the physical and psychological benefits of healthy buildings, we need to design them with a proactive approach that anticipates and protects the construction team, building occupants, materials and resources, structure, and continuity of operations.

Defining Health, Safety, and Welfare

In a recent study published in *The Interior Design Profession's Body of Knowledge* health, safety, and welfare as it relates to the practice of interior design is defined as follows:

> *Health:* Interior designers create interior environments that support people's soundness of body and mind, protect their physical, mental, and social well-being, and prevent disease, injury, illness, or pain that could be caused by occupancy of interior environments.
>
> *Safety:* Interior designers create interior environments that protect people against actual or perceived danger, protect against risk from crime, accidents, or physical hazards, and prevent injury, loss, or death that could be caused by occupancy of interior environments.
>
> *Welfare:* Interior designers create interior environments that support people's physical, psychological, social, and spiritual well-being and assist with or contribute to their financial or economic management, success, and responsibility.

Source: Denise A. Guerin and Caren S. Martin, *The Interior Design Professions Body of Knowledge*, www.idbok.org.

An integrated design and development process should specifically address HSW as enumerated by the following checklist while supporting the client's goals:

- Create a home that is safe and secure by physically protecting the occupants and possessions from climate and natural hazards.

- Provide a healthy home environment with an efficient, state-of-the-art heating, ventilating, and air-conditioning (HVAC) system that exceeds ASHRAE standards and considers indoor relative humidity. Ensure that equipment requires little maintenance and is energy efficient.

- Locate all outside air intakes away from building exhaust fumes, septic tanks, ground maintenance, vehicle exhaust, and other sources of harmful particulates that could compromise IAQ.

- Plan for a high-performing envelope that balances moisture and avoids accumulation, delivers an airtight structure to reduce energy demand, and interacts with HVAC pressurization to control airflow as desired.

- Eliminate hazards to decrease potential accidents and injuries from slips, trips, and falls. Specify interior and exterior flooring that keeps occupants safe from falls.

- Deliver a superior indoor environmental quality (IEQ) that considers the impact of indoor air quality, daylighting and views, visual and thermal comfort, connection with nature, and potable water quality on human health and well-being.

- Support a relationship with nature by intentionally arranging interior spaces and functions to connect with the outdoors, and provide accessible openings for easy access between the interior and exterior spaces.

- Design for optimal indoor air quality by balancing superior ventilation and air exchange with nontoxic interior finishes and furnishings. Avoid heavy metals, formaldehyde, fire retardants, fiberglass, VOCs, and asbestos; thoroughly evaluate chemicals of concern; and mitigate the potential for radon and carbon monoxide.

- Control the tracking in of contaminants from outdoors with doormats and shoe storage at all of the home's major entry points. Prevent fumes from entering living spaces with the pressurized storage of chemicals, a detached or pressurized garage, and by banning smoking on the jobsite and in the home.

- Provide maximum access to natural daylight and views with appropriate controls for glare, light levels, and privacy. Daylight creates a visually stimulating and productive environment and reduces total building energy costs by nearly a third.

- Plan for optimal user comfort that allows for adjustments to thermal, lighting, acoustics, and furniture to meet individual needs. Balance thermal comfort, radiant and ambient temperature, humidity, and air speed. Provide multiple and adjustable lighting sources and nighttime pathway lighting to and from bathrooms. Control acoustics with finishes and fabrics to manage noise levels and reverberation.

- Design for highly functional spaces to meet present and future needs; optimize organization and accommodate storage; and support ergonomic design for musculoskeletal health by providing the ability to adjust occupants' space to meet their personal preferences in an aesthetically pleasing manner.

- Provide flexible access to current technologic and communication needs with built-in capacity as well as adaptability for potential future technologies.

- Accommodate known and unforeseen special needs by embracing accessibility and all levels of ability and mobility. The space should be adaptable to future needs, including aging-in-place strategies. Apply universal design principles so that every family member—regardless of age, size, ability, or health—can fully enjoy the home.

- Enhance the physical, psychological, and social experience by listening to clients' needs, confirming their requests, and then reaching beyond their words to respond to their physical and emotional needs.

- Fully comply with life safety and local building codes, including fire protection. Planning for fire protection involves a systemic analysis of all the building's systems and components as part of a total fire safety system package.

- Incorporate integrated pest management strategies that avoid the use of pesticides, including landscape and turf management.

- Track and provide a comprehensive owner's manual for the operation and maintenance of all systems and interior finishes and furnishings. Ensure that owners understand how to operate systems as they were designed to work.

- Implement resiliency measures to adapt to ever-changing climatic, ecological, and social conditions to maintain or regain livable conditions after a disturbance or interruption due to natural disasters, loss of power, or interruptions in other services.

- Use life cycle assessments when evaluating the environmental and health impacts of a material or building through its entire life cycle—from its initial production through to its eventual reuse, recycling, or disposal.

These tactics require a successful integrated design approach that involves multiple project team members, professional subject matter experts, and even community stakeholders, all of whom will impact the design and operational criteria. By mitigating risks to health, security, and injury, we can design a truly safe home for generations to come.

There are other strategies for designing a home that ensures its occupants' HSW. For example, textured fabric may be an aesthetic preference but is a trap for contaminants that can be released back into the air. Work closely with the mechanical engineer or HVAC contractor to ensure that the system is balanced to support healthy air quality. Specify interior finishes and furnishings that minimize the potential for injuries due to slippery floors or fires that result from faulty electrical systems. Vistas and endpoints establish spatial orientation and provide connection opportunities with each other and nature. A flexible space allows a family to meet its ever-changing needs. The layout, placement, and selection of furnishings should optimize balance and well-being. Appropriate heights for seating and working ensure an ergonomic experience. Appropriate surface materials and finishes take function into account. Views can be celebrated while managing glare and balancing light to avoid eye fatigue. Superior IAQ is managed with healthy materials and products balanced by appropriate ventilation.

Our education and experience allows us to enhance the function and quality of interior spaces for the purpose of improving quality of life, increasing productivity, and protecting the HSW of the occupants. Interior designers inherently understand the importance of HSW measures and work across disciplines to ensure the design and construction delivers a safe living environment.

Healthy, High-Performing Strategies

According to Architecture 2030, the building industry consumes more energy (49 percent) than the transportation industry (28 percent) or manufacturing industry (23 percent). Energy demands can be dramatically reduced with a high-performing envelope that also supports the occupants' HSW. Tight buildings increase levels of interior chemicals and particulates by leaving them nowhere to escape. To mitigate potential HSW issues, let's now look to the building science aspects of the design and construction process, then at recommendations for vetting materials and products.

UNDERSTANDING BUILDING SCIENCE

A well-built, durable building envelope should last hundreds of years. As the physical separation between the interior and exterior of the building, the envelope is durable, manages moisture; insulates, raises R-values at the walls, roof, and glazing; and addresses thermal comfort, indoor air quality, and indoor environmental quality. A superior building envelope deflects bulk water, drains off and out any water that hits the envelope, supports drying when the building envelope gets wet, and is built with the most durable materials permitted by the budget.

The building envelope, also known as the enclosure, must respond to the natural forces of rain, snow, wind, and sun and protect its occupants and their assets. Multiple components and materials create a barrier not only to the elements but also to insects, sound, and ultraviolet rays; control access and egress; insulate and supports interior and exterior finishes; controls moisture and humidity; regulates temperature and ventilation; controls air pressurization—and uses energy to do so.

You can address project pitfalls by addressing the following overarching principles and strategies with your project team.

Building Envelope. An envelope serves the home by keeping out and managing bulk water and dealing with moisture both inside and outside the home. It provides thermal comfort with a barrier of exterior rigid materials and cavity insulation. It manages air movement through interior material selection of sheet goods, caulks, sealants, tapes and foams; controls vapor movement, heat flow, and the sun's energy and radiation; and addresses vapor profiles. It also supports a healthy indoor environment with superior IAQ, invites in and manages natural daylight, and provides a connection to nature and daylighting while reducing energy needs.

Follow this sequence of steps:

1. Seal for air leaks first.

2. Manage heat and water flow.

3. Manage moisture (water) and energy with balanced and equal intensity with exterior flashing (weather-lapping) and shielding (overhangs, awnings).

4. Retard vapor, typically with a specific vapor barrier or retarder.

5. Address vapor profiles and perm ratings to ensure the structure to dry.

Moisture Management. To keep moisture out of the house and maintain a dry structure and interior, take the following steps:

1. Ensure window and door flashing is properly installed so that weather-lapping allows water to run off the home and away from the foundation; roof overhangs, awnings, and window caps provide shielding from moisture.

2. Seal all roof and wall penetrations, including chimneys and vent stacks. Sealing the air movement will prevent leakage, which encourages water to travel along with it (leakage) and brings potential air pollutants indoors.

3. Retard vapor with a house-wrap weather barrier.

4. Understand vapor profile and product perm ratings to ensure building enclosure and structural and interiors assemblies can dry out.

5. Vent all wall and roof assemblies to allow water to drain and air to circulate, encouraging drying.

6. Know and understand vapor profiles of the assemblies (see details below).

7. Integrate mechanical systems, envelopes, and assemblies to control humidity, a form of moisture. Include dehumidification systems if all else fails.

To ensure that the above steps are addressed and integrated on the project, the entire team must be involved in the design strategies, decisions, and management of these methods throughout design and construction if these strategies are to be deployed successfully.

Controlling potential moisture issues moderate the development of pollutants like mold and dust mites. Specify that the contractor protect sensitive products from potential moisture damage and exposure to dust and VOCs throughout the construction process. If a susceptible product like drywall gets wet, the contractor must promptly remove the damaged materials. Best practice is to sequence the construction so that absorptive materials do not arrive on site until the building is closed in; they should then be stored in a dry space and covered until needed.

Vapor profiles. As interior designers, it is vital that we know and understand vapor profiles are the most important aspect of the building's assembly. A vapor profile assesses the vapor permeability of each component in a building assembly—the wall, ceiling, and roof. This assessment determines the drying potential of the building assembly and its components and in which direction the components will dry. The vapor profile shows whether all layers of the building assembly will protect themselves from getting wet and then how they will dry after they do.

To understand vapor profiles, we first have to understand perm ratings. Vapor perm ratings assess a product's permeability—its ability to allow liquids or gases to pass through it:

- 0.1 or less is nonpermeable
- 0.5 to 5 is retarding
- 5 to 10 is semipermeable
- 10+ is permeable

Wall, roof, and ceiling assemblies need to dry out when they get wet. The team needs to know which way the assembly will dry—from the inside out, from the outside in, or in both directions simultaneously. A wall assembly must not trap moisture between the exterior finishes and the interior finishes: it will not dry and will invite rot, mold, and mildew.

EVALUATING THE VAPOR PROFILE OF NEW ASSEMBLIES

Typically the building industry focuses on the vapor permeability of just one component in building assemblies—that of the vapor retarder or vapor barrier. But all the components in an assembly determine how water vapor moves, or does not move, through an assembly. The team must compare the vapor permeability of all components in an assembly to ensure that drying can occur in at least one direction, whether to the interior, the exterior, or both.

Moisture performance, also called vapor profile, is an important aspect of the assembly, and how an assembly is designed to dry out is just as important as how it is designed to keep from getting wet. Vapor profiles are also important to consider when closed-cavity insulation fill is used for thermal performance of wall and roof assemblies.

This illustration demonstrates that the building assemblies can dry in both directions:

1. They can dry toward the inside because all the components are permeable with a rating of 10+.

2. Even though the oil, with a 0.6 perm rating makes it a vapor retarder, the assembly can dry to the outside because the wood siding is installed with airspace behind it, and the lapped installation provides gaps in which the air can circulate.

An interior designer should take the following four steps in order to assess a home's vapor profile:

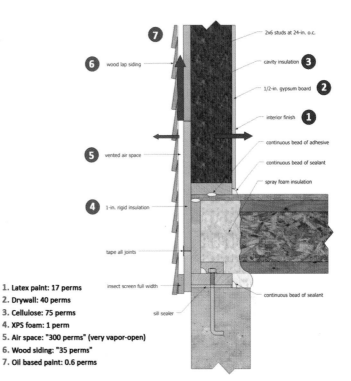

1. Latex paint: 17 perms
2. Drywall: 40 perms
3. Cellulose: 75 perms
4. XPS foam: 1 perm
5. Air space: "300 perms" (very vapor-open)
6. Wood siding: "35 perms"
7. Oil based paint: 0.6 perms

1. Determine the vapor permeability of each component. Manufacturers may provide you with this information for their products, but building product manufacturers are not necessarily consistent in the way they measure and report vapor permeability. And the vapor permeability of many building materials is not constant—it can change as the material's moisture content rises and falls. Make sure that you get numbers for every material or component in your assembly, and obtain the actual test used and units reported. A good start is the "Building Materials Property Table" available from the Building Science Corporation (www.buildingscience.com).

2. Identify the least vapor-permeable component(s)—those that most restrict the wetting and drying potential of the assembly. To understand the assembly's ability to withstand moisture accumulation, you must know how many low-perm materials there are and where they are located.

   The next two steps are not necessarily sequential. Consider them together with your contractor and team; they'll tell you how to keep things from getting wet and also about letting them dry.

3. Assess the extent and direction of vapor drive to determine if a vapor retarder is needed somewhere in the assembly to restrict the movement of vapor into the assembly. Consider the following:

   a. *Outdoor conditions*, including temperature, relative humidity, and how extreme and sustained the expected temperature differences will be with respect to the building interior. For more information, refer to the Climate Consultant Tool from UCLA, which connects weather data to home building design (http://www.energy-design-tools.aud .ucla.edu/).

b. *Indoor conditions*, including interior moisture loads, interior set points, and the type and extent of space conditioning (active heating, cooling, humidification and dehumidification, ventilation). Generally, in hot humid climates, the moisture is driven inside when the air conditioning is on as moisture moves toward the colder air. The opposite is true in cold climates: Colder outside air drives moisture from inside into the wall assembly (similar to how moisture condenses on windows in cold climates in the winter).

4. Assess the moisture storage capacity and drying potential of the assembly. Is there at least one way for vapor (moisture) to get out of the assembly? An assembly with two vapor retarders or barriers on opposite sides of the assembly means that there is little to no drying potential in either direction. That will become a serious problem unless you design and detail for extraordinary moisture management to keep this assembly from wetting.

Consider another example. What if you installed a mirror or nonpermeable wall covering on an exterior wall assembly like the one illustrated above? What will happen? The moisture performance will be compromised because both materials are nonpermeable and would seal moisture inside the wall cavity, potentiating mold growth because the assembly is unable to dry out.

Foundations. Typically the foundation's floors and walls, especially in basements, need to dry to the inside. To maintain a dry environment and avoid mold growth, foundations should be finished with a breathable interior material to allow drying to the inside. Ensure that all transition points between the concrete foundation and the framing materials for floors and walls are tightly sealed to prevent air leaks and manage moisture. If insulating foundation walls are on the interior, proper moisture control will be critical for the interior insulation of foundation walls. Ensure that the foundation dries to the inside and that wall finish assemblies breathe by examining the materials' vapor profiles.

Air leakage. Minimize air movement throughout the envelope of the house. Air infiltration carries and gathers pollutants, moving them into the home. Particulates from outside migrate in, carrying mold spores that deposit themselves inside the home. Common places for air leaks are between floor joists and in recessed lights, wiring and electrical holes, plumbing and appliance vents, HVAC and fireplace flues, basements, and attics. Pressurizing the home to balance ventilation, venting, and IAQ is standard practice.

Insulation. Use the healthiest alternatives available in the market place. As part of the wall and ceiling assemblies, insulation can directly contribute to the IAQ. Formaldehyde binders in foam insulation put construction workers at risk and may leach into the indoor environment. Insulation is one component in the wall assembly that can dramatically help to lower energy bills and mitigate cold and dampness. Balancing the thermal insulation properties with energy sources is vital to a healthy home environment.

Whole-house ventilation system. A whole house ventilation system, whether mechanical, natural, or combined, is critical to ensuring healthy interiors. A quality ventilation system provides adequate fresh air exchanges that help to lower airborne infectious diseases and decrease off-gassing, cooking odors, and indoor pollutants.

In homes, the air change rate is generally far lower and occupancy longer than in a commercial environment. This may lead to higher emissions of VOCs from materials unless a healthy air exchange rate is planned for the ventilation system.

Improve indoor air quality by installing ducts and equipment that minimize condensation problems. Whole-house and spot ventilation help dilute and exhaust indoor pollutants, and air filtration removes airborne particulates.

Indoor air quality. By definition, IAQ is the healthfulness of an interior environment. IAQ is affected by the building assembly, interior finishes and furnishings, existing hazards like lead, mold, and asbestos, cooking and cooking appliances, people, pets, toiletries, cleaning supplies, occupant behavior, environmental tobacco smoke (ETS), pollen and dust, back drafting, moisture and mold, emissions of VOCs and formaldehyde, HVAC equipment, ventilation and filtration, tracking in petroleum, pesticides and other contaminants from outside and adjacent rooms such as garages and storage sheds. And this just lists a few IAQ offenders!

Interior finishes can effect the performance of the building assembly and vapor profiles, IAQ, and occupant health. If a designer specifies an impermeable wall covering in a hot, humid climate, condensation on the back of the wall covering could result in mold growth on the paper facings of the gypsum board and even rot if the wall is a wood-frame assembly.

Work closely with the team to specify the filters that will be used on the project. Look for a minimum efficiency reporting value (MERV) rating on a scale of 1 to 20 and balance accordingly with the size of HVAC system and airflow capabilities. Filters with high resistance (higher numbers) let fewer particles through but also less air, so the system has to work harder to push air through. High efficiency particle arrestor (HEPA) filters capture at least 99 percent of airborne particles 0.3 microns or larger, but they require a lot of energy to push a lot of air through the tightly woven fiberglass filter. They are also noisy and need to be replaced regularly.

Always design with air quality in mind when specifying ventilation and filtration systems, materials selection, construction cleaning methods, and cooking appliances. Here are four building strategies:

1. Isolate attached garages; adjacent rooms have poor insulating and air sealing details. The air and thermal barriers must be complete and continuous between the two spaces, or the garage space must be depressurized with a high-efficiency exhaust fan, or both.

2. Store all toxic chemicals away from living spaces. Harmful chemicals can escape from lawn and garden products, gas cans, and used cans of paint. Hazardous materials should be stored in fire-safe, carefully sealed storage units located in well-ventilated garages or storage sheds. Encourage homeowners not to keep older chemicals in their homes or garages; such materials can often be disposed of during hazardous-waste collection days at municipal solid waste facilities.

3. Back drafting is an IAQ problem in which potentially dangerous combustion gases escape into the house instead of going up the chimney. To prevent back drafting of heating equipment, woodstoves, and fireplaces by maintaining heating equipment and inspecting annually. Avoid atmospherically vented appliances, including woodstoves and fireplaces, in new construction. Lastly, minimize depressurization by reducing exhaust fan sizes and balancing airflows in heating, cooling, and ventilation systems.

4. Protect residents from potential exposure to combustion gases by installing direct-vented or power-vented gas- and oil-fired equipment, properly vented fireplaces, and carbon monoxide alarms.

The air quality must be tested prior to move-in for clients with chemical sensitivities. Testing kits measure particulates (respirable suspended particulate matter), total VOCs (TVOCs), and SVOCs, and some include third-party testing for formaldehyde emissions.

Pest management. Provide a first-line defense against pest problems by fully sealing, caulking, or screening likely pest entry points. Pesticide use can be reduced if these physical barriers are combined with proper pest management techniques.

Radon mitigation. Test for radon to find out if mitigation will be needed. A colorless, odorless, radioactive gas, radon is the second leading cause of lung cancer in the United States. It comes from the natural decay of uranium found in nearly all soils. It typically moves up through the ground and into a home through cracks and holes in the foundation. Drafty homes, airtight homes, homes with or without a basement—any home can potentially have a radon problem.

Provide radon-resistant construction in areas with a high potential for radon. This includes gravel and plastic sheeting below slabs, fully sealed and caulked foundation penetrations, plastic vent pipe running from below slab through the roof, and an attic receptacle for easily adding an electric fan to the vent pipe if needed. Install a radon mitigation system with an exhaust fan that runs 24/7 to pull soil gases up and out of the conditioned space of the house.

Home commissioning/home-performance audit. Home commissioning is the process of testing a home after a construction project to ensure that all of the home's systems are operating correctly and at maximum efficiency. Similarly, a home performance audit assesses the building's envelope and mechanical systems. The building envelope components that manage water, air, and heat must be continuous and complete. A combination of visual inspections, a blower door test, infrared technology, and moisture meters can identify issues in the water, air, and thermal barrier systems. The assessment evaluates the air, water, and vapor permeability of individual components and the assembly as a whole.

Additionally, an energy audit can be combined with a home-performance audit to inspect, test, and assess moisture flow, combustion safety, thermal comfort, indoor air quality, and durability. Clients can dramatically improve the overall energy performance of the home with the following energy use assessment tools:

1. Energy bill analysis. Review all bills—electric, gas, fuel oil, cordwood, and so on—for at least one full year. It's actually best to analyze energy use over several years.

2. Install an energy feedback or logging device, such as the Energy Detective, to measure electricity usage and inform the homeowner about potential behavior modifications.

3. Do a performance audit.

Construction IAQ tool. A resourceful tool for the project team, and particularly for the contractor, is the I-BEAM tool developed by the EPA's Indoor Air Quality division. It can be used for both new construction and renovation to address IAQ during both the design and the construction phases. Additionally, products with the EPA's Indoor airPLUS label can be used in tandem with the Energy Star for Homes program. This program has thirty-plus design and construction strategies that improve indoor air quality for the home, including the following:

Proper installation sequence for materials
Respond to site context
Effective programmatic layout
Proper ventilation design and zoning
Low-emitting material specifications
Wet before dry: Beware of the sink effect!
Protect your ventilation
Temporary ventilation during construction
Employ a moisture and IEQ manager
Encourage good housekeeping for all on-site workers
Pre-occupancy indoor air quality test: flush out building or perform air testing
Green procurement guidelines
Establish a high-performance cleaning program
Educate staff on green housekeeping procedures
Establish regular HVAC and moisture management plans
Perform regular IAQ testing

Summing Up Building Science

For a healthy and high-performing home enclosure, work closely with the project team to ensure all these measures are addressed. Because it keeps the elements out and regulates the interior environment, consider a proactive, integrated approach to evaluating the building enclosure. A designer may not be the subject-matter expert in any of these areas, but we can initiate the conversation and advocate for the healthiest solutions possible for our clients.

VETTING MATERIALS AND PRODUCTS

We are witnessing dynamic changes in the manufacturing of products—certifications and standards, life cycle assessment, environmental product declarations, green chemistry, social equity, and health product declarations—all of which are contributing to a large-scale market transformation.

This chapter has discussed why health matters, what chemicals to avoid, and how to best design for HSW, and we've taken a high-level look at building science principles. Occupant health is nonnegotiable, and we must therefore eliminate the use of products that have negative health impacts on the homeowners and their family members, friends, and visitors. We now understand that health concerns are paramount, especially in the interior environments that we create.

As designers, we live in a world of products and materials. Understanding that a healthy, high-performing home is intentionally designed and not driven by a device or particular product is a vital first step. So where do we go from here?

To "first, do no harm" is to evaluate and make conscious, well-informed decisions that support the health of human and natural systems. Take the precautionary route when researching and specifying materials that do little or no harm to people, land, air, and water in the course of extraction, harvesting, processing, manufacturing, and transporting them.

Start by researching materials that adhere to the project's goals and objectives; this will narrow the vetting process. Present only nontoxic, low-emitting products and materials to your client during the design process, and ensure that they meet or exceed the most current emissions standards for IAQ (see chapter 8, "Certifications and Standards"). Next, avoid chemicals of concern by confirming what chemicals a material or product contains. Start with the MSDS information, but remember: There are many exempt chemicals that lead to toxic emissions. Eliminate the use of long-emitting chemicals like formaldehyde and PBTs. Ask manufacturers for full, transparent disclosure that can provide public reporting to back up their claims. Inquire about a manufacturer's social equity and whether they provide a healthy environment for manufacturing.

Material transparency. Ask for full disclosure of all product ingredients through either a manufacturer's declared disclosure or a third-party report. LEED v4 will be

targeting 20 percent or more products be used on projects based on the total value/costs of the interior materials. This will encourage the manufacturers to share their ingredients and also reward manufacturers who do provide intentional and significant chemical disclosure and do not manufacture their building products with toxic chemicals.

We are our clients' consumer informants. It is our responsibility to request transparency from manufacturers for building materials, interior finishes, and furnishings. Honest, open information sharing between manufacturers, designers, and trades begins a respectful dialogue that will lead to meeting the project's goals.

Manufacturers recognize the influence designers have with consumers. Through their engagement with the design/build community, they have begun to recognize the importance of health and environmental issues to the building industry and the consumer. They can now use relevant and cutting-edge transparency tools like the Health Product Declaration (HPD) and the Pharos Project (see chapter 8, "Certifications and Standards") to make full disclosure of their products' chemical makeup as well as specific health and environmental hazards. You will find that some building material manufacturers are reluctant to reveal information they consider proprietary. If so, share the project goals and objectives to win them over.

The way we ask matters. Learn about the company, welcome an open-ended information exchange without oppositional inquiries, and use familiar terms. By respectfully asking for product transparency, we can convince influential chemical companies to work with, rather than against, this crucial shift the industry is making. Check out the Healthy Building Network (www.healthybuilding.net), which is tracking the strategic initiatives of companies in the building materials market—those that avoid toxic chemicals, and those that do not.

Chemicals of concern. If it is made from hazardous components, do you really want your client to sleep and live with it? The time is now to challenge any attempt by manufacturers to cover up chemicals of concern in their products. The good news is that not all companies aim to screen proprietary, potentially hazardous materials. In fact, some leading manufacturers are working in tandem with consumers, embracing transparency and the opportunity to invest in long-term change.

Material and product manufacturers need to hear from their consumers about the value we place on supporting our clients' health. Think about how you can *be* the momentum behind product transparency. Manufacturers will eventually listen to you, their customer. Explain the importance of avoiding chemical hazards to your clients, trades in the field, and the environment. And specify manufacturers who meet the safe use of chemical requirements of the European REACH Chemical Safety Program.

Here are a few questions you can ask to begin a dialogue with manufacturer representatives. Remember, if we are all respectfully persistent and share our project goals and objectives, more and more manufacturers will address these critical issues sooner.

- Does your company provide reporting for the full disclosure of product material contents, including chemicals of concern?
- Does your company adopt the LEED v4 credit for toxic chemical disclosure and avoidance?
- Are your products evaluated by a third-party entity (like the Pharos Project or Cradle-2-Cradle regarding chemical ingredients?
- Does your company use the Health Product Declaration (see chapter 8)?

Vetting tools. The information available to project teams is imperfect, and researching product specific components can be time-consuming and frustrating. We can look to the following for a variety of information necessary for evaluating potential products:

- Material safety data sheets (see chapter 6, "Greening Specifications")
- VOC emissions testing and certifications
- VOC content labeling
- Third-party certifications
- Multiattribute certifications
- Environmental product declarations
- Health product declarations
- Pharos
- Declare
- GreenSpec

Making selections. Given the many tools and resources available for evaluating and identifying environmentally preferable materials, a preplanned process for product selection is essential. Search out accurate claims of sustainability, transparent material content, and full disclosure of any product toxicity.

Selecting healthy and environmentally preferable materials requires research, critical evaluation, and common sense. Issues such as aesthetics and availability must be balanced with warranties and the products' track record. Materials new to the market must be considered cautiously.

Take the following steps when determining if a material or product supports human health and is environmentally preferable:

- Utilize and request the tools outlined above.
- Check materials performance criteria and record of performance.
- Determine the expectations for the material or system.
- Request corporate environmental policy statements from the manufacturers under consideration.

Material Selection Rules

Tom Lent (Healthy Building Network) and Robin Guenther (Perkins+Will) came together to develop twelve rules for material selection. This straightforward advice for vetting building materials is also a call to action regarding toxicity. And it provides a basis for productive dialogue with manufacturers:

1. If it stinks, don't use it!
2. If they won't tell us what's in it, you probably don't want what's in it.
3. Just because almost anything can kill you doesn't mean building products should.
4. If it starts as hazardous waste, you probably don't want it in your building.
5. Avoid materials that are pretending to be something they are not.
6. Use carbohydrate-based materials when you can. (These embrace decay and transformation.)
7. Question materials that make healthy claims.
8. Pay more, use less.
9. If it is cheap, it probably has hidden (externalized) costs.
10. Regard "space-age" materials with skepticism.
11. Use materials made from substances you can imagine in their raw or natural state.
12. Question the generation of hazardous waste instead of where to use it in your building.

And here are a few to add to the list:

How about asking what products heal us?

What are we using today that we don't yet know is making us sick tomorrow?

How can we give back to Mother Nature what we take?

How about taxing pollutants instead of profits?

How about using only products that can be infinitely repaired rather than those whose obsolescence is preplanned?

Do you want your child growing up in Cancer Alley?

Isn't it time for us to just say no to toxic materials?

Source: ASID/HBN Webinar Series, 2013

- Be a respectful skeptic of environmental claims (both positive and negative) that have not been substantiated by independent sources.
- Look for materials that provide multiple benefits.

Through careful analysis, you can identify durable, timeless, and healthy products (like an earth-based plaster wall finish) or an organic and rapidly renewable material that biodegrades (like organic wool carpet with natural jute and rubber backing). This intelligent material selection process supports health, performance, and the environment.

Two terrific commercial projects have adopted health as their top priority in the design, construction, and operations of their buildings and are leading the way in the industry. Their vetting process is intense and purposeful and aims to deliver the project's goals and objectives. They are healthy, high-performing role models. We encourage you to study the VanDusen Botanical Gardens in Vancouver, British Columbia, and Google's corporate campus in Mountain View, California. Both took material transparency to heart and screened materials for hazardous ingredients. They avoid depleting natural resources and extend the life of the resources they do use through reuse and recycling. They used a detailed framework for product information and ingredients, including the inputs and outputs of resources and emissions through all stages of the product's life, using meticulous life cycle assessment analysis.

One final note on vetting products. The industry rarely studies the interaction of two or more chemicals in a laboratory testing environment; doing so is both complex and costly. We are exposed to multiple chemicals at low doses every day, yet we cannot be certain about their effects on our bodies. Taking the precautionary route is best practice where health is concerned. If you wish to explore toxicology further, check out *Toxicology for Non-Toxicologists* by Mark Stelljes (Lanham, MD: Government Institutes, 2007).

Team Integration

It takes an integrated project team to make intelligent decisions when designing a healthy, high-performing home. At the project's outset, organize the team, clarify the project mission and goals, and confirm the commitment of all project team members to align with and deliver those objectives. Rather than working in a traditional, siloed fashion, members of all disciplines on the project team should work collaboratively.

Preventing and solving air quality problems is an integrated task that involves designers, contractors and subcontractors, trades, and the homeowners themselves. Architectural and design decisions will set up the initial healthy conditions, and all other factors will tie directly into them, so the interior designer should be contracted and consulted at the project's onset. Unless mechanical and natural ventilation systems, moisture management, and green materials are building through the use of advanced building science, the home's indoor air quality is at risk.

If each member of the project team has an equal opportunity to contribute to the building as a whole, the team's collective wisdom will create a dynamic synergy contributing to the project's success. The team will need to be diligent during design, specifications development, and most importantly, during construction, when substitutions and other changes to the original plan may be necessary. An integrated approach allows health, safety, and welfare to become a goal of all phases of a home's life cycle, from planning, design, and construction to operations, maintenance, and renovation. For more on an integrated approach and for detailed strategies and scenarios, refer to chapter, "Greening Projects."

It is challenging at best to quantify a "healthy interior." Open and respectful communication among the key members of the team will help define challenges, expectations, and opportunities, clarify each team member's role, and ensure a successful project.

Benefits

The benefits of a healthy home are immeasurable. Who wouldn't want an environment that supports the health and well-being of family and friends? Now more than ever, healthy, high-performing interior design is an ethic that must be at the forefront of all projects. With human health supported by ethical interior at the core of a sustainable mission design, a home can even restore the health of a home's occupants.

Ethical interior design also supports economic and social growth while contributing to a cleaner environment. Our quality of life is rooted in nature's magnificence and complemented by the beauty that we create through our design solutions. And nature itself is a road map for our journey back to a balanced world that not only gives us back the natural cycles of a healthy life but even lowers costs for healthcare and insurance.

It is an honor and a profound responsibility to enhance the well-being and nurturing the lives of our clients—one that we must welcome and embrace as an opportunity to make a difference, both for the current generation and for many generations to come.

As our ethical design work benefits our clients, it ripples out to our project teams, the community—and boomerangs right back to us. We thereby ultimately regenerate our own spirits.

In 1992, William McDonough and Michael Braungart crafted the Hannover Principles in which they eloquently insist on "the rights of humanity and nature to co-exist." Those principles continue to resonate powerfully, calling on us to care for one another and the world at large and to embrace social equity, environmental stewardship, and balanced prosperity. They state that human health, our economy, and the well-being of our planet are undeniably, intrinsically linked.

The Hannover Principles

As an architect and designer, I spend time thinking about how we can ensure a future of abundance for our children. In 1991, at the suggestion of Dr. Michael Braungart, I was commissioned by the City of Hannover, Germany, to craft sustainable design principles for Expo 2000, the World's Fair. The result was the Hannover Principles: Design for Sustainability, which was officially presented by the City of Hannover as a gift to the 1992 Earth Summit's World Urban Forum in Rio de Janeiro, Brazil.

If design is the first signal of human intention, our intention today can be to love all ten billion people who will live on our planet by 2050. We can do this. If we imagine and embrace our cities as part of the same organism as the countryside, the rivers, and the oceans, then we can celebrate ourselves, all species, and the natural systems that we support and that support us. This is our design assignment. If we are principled and have positive goals, we can rise to this occasion. It will take us all; it will take forever—but that is the point.

1. Insist on the right of humanity and nature to coexist in a healthy, supportive, diverse, and sustainable condition.

2. Recognize interdependence. The elements of human design interact with and depend upon the natural world, with broad and diverse implications at every scale. Expand design considerations to recognize even distant effects.

3. Respect relationships between spirit and matter. Consider all aspects of human settlement—including community, dwelling, industry, and trade—in terms of existing and evolving connections between spiritual and material consciousness.

As the Hanover Principles eloquently state, our connection to nature is essential to our health and well-being. Biophilic design achieves a healthier, more natural architecture that reconnects the built environment with nature. By relying on biophilic design pillars, we can further improve the places we live, work, play, and heal. Our productivity increases and the number of sick days we take decline merely with the addition of natural daylight and fresh air.

Nature is celebrated using specific strategies within the built environment. Use plants and water, creating a visual connection with nature and welcoming daylight.

4. Accept responsibility for the consequences of design decisions upon human well-being, the viability of natural systems, and their right to co-exist.

5. Create safe objects of long-term value. Do not burden future generations with requirements for maintenance or vigilant administration of potential danger due to the careless creation of products, processes, or standards.

6. Eliminate the concept of waste. Evaluate and optimize the full life cycle of products and processes, to approach the state of natural systems, in which there is no waste.

7. Rely on natural energy flows. Human designs should, like the living world, derive their creative forces from perpetual solar income. Incorporate this energy efficiently and safely for responsible use.

8. Understand the limitations of design. No human creation lasts forever, and design does not solve all problems. Those who create and plan should practice humility in the face of nature. Treat nature as a model and mentor, not as an inconvenience to be evaded or controlled.

9. Seek constant improvement by the sharing of knowledge. Encourage direct and open communication between colleagues, patrons, manufacturers, and users to link long-term sustainable considerations with ethical responsibility and reestablish the integral relationship between natural processes and human activity.

The Hannover Principles should be seen as a living document committed to the transformation and growth in the understanding of our interdependence with nature so that they may adapt as our knowledge of the world evolves.

Source: William McDonough, see more in chapter 22, "What's Next?"

Evoke nature using natural and fractal patterns, materials, and objects. Vary spatial configurations to connect with aspects of nature through surprising vistas and safe havens, much like a walk through a forest.

Finally, employ a whole-systems design approach to achieve lasting, sophisticated, and economical solutions with multiple benefits. A holistic, integrated approach helps us rise above philosophical debates and align with the common goal of delivering a healthy home. When we step outside ourselves and look at the big picture, we can better understand how to serve the greater good.

Initially, this method may be more challenging. It takes patience to allow a respectful and engaging team process to unfold. By relying on creativity and intuition as well as teamwork, the appropriate solutions will surface to support intelligent, healthy, and high-performing design.

Next Steps

Our actions and choices have a dynamic impact on our clients, project teams, manufacturers, and the industry. Seeking out products, materials, and services that consider the combined impacts on human and environmental health will ultimately affect the products offered to us and to general consumers.

Ask the industry to step up. Our objectives—and the money we spend to reach them—ripples out to manufacturers, suppliers, and contractors, driving and modeling positive change, which will yield a greater choice of appropriate products and materials.

What will you do to make a difference?

- Ask manufacturers for transparent information about their products' ingredients.
- Let them know that we will not specify their products if they contain hazardous chemicals.
- Be a respectful skeptic but ask a lot of questions about a product's makeup.
- Don't accept the information provided to you at face value; double-check it using tools like HPDs and Pharos.
- Specify only healthy materials and systems.
- Adopt restorative and regenerative design practices and solutions for the health of the planet and, ultimately, for our own health.

These are the most important actions responsible designers can take. The good news is that manufacturers are proving to be up to the challenge and are researching and designing the kinds of materials and products we're asking for.

What an amazing impact we will make when we work together as a community, to *be* part of the change we want to see!

Don't you want a healthy home for your clients, for your family and friends?

RESOURCES

BuildingGreen Staff. *Avoiding Toxic Chemicals in Commercial Building Projects: A Handbook of Common Hazards and How to Keep Them Out.* Brattleboro, VT: BuildingGreen, Inc., 2012.
David Suzuki. http://davidsuzuki.org/issues/health/science/toxics/chemicals-in-your-cosmetics—-triclosan/.
Environmental Working Group. www.ewg.org.
European Chemicals Agency, REACH. http://echa.europa.eu/web/guest.
Greenguard. www.greenguard.org.

Green Science Policy. www.greensciencepolicy.org/consumers.

Healthy Building Network. www.healthybuilding.net.

International Living Future Institute. www.ilbi.org.

Perkins+Will Precautionary List. http://transparency.perkinswill.com.

Pharos Project, www.pharosproject.net.

Safer Chemicals, Healthy Families. http://www.saferchemicals.org/resources/EPA-and-SCHF-Chemicals-of-Concern.html.

U.S. National Library of Medicine, Toxicology Data Network. www.toxnet.nlm.nih.gov.

greening projects

Figure 5.1
Photo © Cesar Rubio Photography.
Architect: John Cary.

Earth provides enough to satisfy every man's need, but not every man's greed.

—Mohandas K. Gandhi, quoted in E. F. Schumacher,
Small Is Beautiful

Getting Started on a Green Project

The world of design is about making statements. What if designers regarded each project as a platform from which we could not only serve client needs, enhance design expertise, and deliver a project that incorporates health, safety, and welfare but that also achieves the advanced objective of contributing to saving the environment?

Within the interior design industry, the choices we make on each project have far-reaching consequences for the near and distant future. By making sustainable choices, we can without a doubt help ensure that we *have* a future. In this way, we can make our planet's continued existence the fundamental component in the design process, along with implementing principles, strategies, and practices in the built environment critical to sustaining our natural resources, air and water quality, energy sources, and humanity.

Therein lies the principle value to begin doing good: Sustainable design sustains life. Sustainable design strategies begin to reduce environmental and health impacts. What if a home could actually do more than that by first repairing environmental damage and then restoring the impacts? How amazing would it be to consider how we can restore surrounding ecosystems, increase biodiversity, and improve health?

If we look at sustaining life as the launching point, are designs that simply sustain us and life enough? Not in our book. Our designs must first sustain, then move to being restorative, and in the end create regenerative environments for both the residents and the planet. Regenerative design is an exciting principle and can be challenging in practice. What a great aspiration to work toward.

Regenerative interior design considers the relationships between the interior built environment and the surrounding community and natural systems. We already understand the we are placing increased demands for energy, water, and resources on a limited natural world. Let's take the next step and go beyond doing less harm, or being less bad to doing the best for our own health and well-being. Everything is connected, and ultimately, we depend on the health and well-being of natural systems to support us.

To regenerate means to create again. Systems that are regenerative make no waste and their output is equal to or greater than their input. Waste becomes input and, like a tree, the cycle is continuous. Regenerative design inherently plans for the future existence of itself, its surrounding community, and the constant evolution of all species, including humans. Designed with both people and the environment in mind, projects are now adopting zero-impact strategies that not only support but also celebrate health. Successful regenerative design models on commercial projects are forging the way in systems-based thinking to move projects from a resource-negative design where we use more resources than we return to the environment toward a resource-positive design. When we provide interiors that improve our clients' health while restoring ecosystems, we heal the planet and begin to regenerate natural and social capital.

Customary green building methods have focused on reductive principles by using less energy, water, resources, and materials and toward lowering emissions and greenhouse gases. Admittedly, that was where we needed to start. Today, cutting-edge thought leaders in the building industry are erasing the traditional equation to systemically change how we approach projects. For a glimpse into how this is occurring, here is a high-level overview of a regenerative design process. Starting with integrating a deep level of systems thinking where all stakeholders—owner, design team, engineers, contractor, trades, users, facility managers, community, lender—work together meticulously as an integrated team. The project objectives start with, but are not limited to, the following:

- Decrease the amount of resources (energy, water, and materials) needed for the building with judicious conservation measures. For example, by applying passive design strategies and designing an extremely high-performing envelope, less energy is needed from the onset. For materials, look to regional sources and select dimensional sizes that work with the size of the application for no waste.

- Purposefully and methodically reclaim and repurpose any output resources coming from the building. For example, capture heat from the air and use it to heat domestic hot water.

- Pinpoint and tap into the buildings' combined effects, or synergies. Take building outputs and use them for building inputs. For example, collect gray water and use it to flush plumbing fixtures, thereby reusing water.

- Identify and evaluate renewable sources to supply the remaining input demand. For example, use passive solar design with materials that retain the heat and radiate the warmth back into the home after the sun sets.

More and more evidence demonstrates the benefits of designing and building using sustainable, restorative, and regenerative principles and practices:

- Healthy indoor environment
- Repairing environmental damage
- Net-positive impact
- Zero to low dependency on energy sources
- Highest performing systems, materials, and products
- Buildings that breathe
- Higher-quality, longer-life materials
- Healthy, nontoxic indoor air quality
- Effective operations and maintenance in buildings

- Prevention of pollution and waste generation
- Improved recycling and repurposing of building materials
- Restoring ecosystems
- No impact and multiattribute materials
- Responsible sourcing of raw materials
- Diverting landfill disposal, waste incineration, and associated pollution
- Net-positive, net-zero, and optimized energy performance
- Resource positive design beyond simply conservation and management
- Conservation and reuse of precious water
- Effective and efficient lighting quality
- Celebrate and enhance biodiversity
- No waste output
- Trained building constructors, managers, and users
- Lower operating costs
- Higher comfort levels
- Healing individuals and the environment
- Reduced life-cycle costs
- Zero-emitting materials
- Commissioning of buildings and systems
- Stewardship for future generations
- Increased property value

Now it is viable and even easy for designers to make a personal and professional commitment to embrace sustainable design principles. There is no better time than now to join your peers by adopting healthy, high-performing design into your practice. Once you make that decision, start with education to deepen your knowledge.

EDUCATING YOURSELF

Educating yourself, gaining the knowledge available in the field of green, sustainable, and regenerative design, is crucial to moving forward. Education can take many forms. Invite environmental consultants into your office or workspace for brown-bag lunches, attend conferences, research products, surf the Internet, become REGREEN trained, align with like-minded individuals, read books and publications with a focus on sustainable strategies, become a LEED Accredited Professional, and investigate local groups offering programs on green, sustainable, and regenerative design.

Once you have a firm grasp on the underlying principles, take the next step and begin to integrate them so they become an intuitive part of the process. Consider, as starting points, doing the following during the overall design of your projects:

- Minimize the size of a residence.
- Integrate design aspects for diverse function, adaptive reuse, and/or disassembly.
- Design for climate and region.
- Design for durability and longevity.
- Specify low-impact materials and use resources most efficiently.
- Use local and regional resources.
- Use products with recycled or salvaged content.
- Specify the least toxic materials and manufacturing processes available.
- Integrate energy conservation and direct solar energy collection or passive solar, such as daylighting.
- Consider alternative energy sources such as wind power.
- Specify alternative, environmentally friendly materials made from renewable content.
- Design for optimal indoor air quality and human health.
- Specify woods from sustainable, certified forestry.
- Research and specify products that are recyclable.
- Adopt the seven *R*'s: reduce, reuse, recycle, recover, repair, repurpose, and respect.
- Integrate stringent water conservation strategies.

Next, begin to research all the attributes of the products you are considering for inclusion in your specifications. To that end, seek out products that emit low or no volatile organic compounds (VOCs), contain no chemicals of concern, and support health. Information is readily available through manufacturers; continue to push the envelope of transparency by asking tough questions. As a starting point, learn to interpret the material safety data sheet (MSDS) for each product and to understand its components. (Chapter 6, "Greening Specifications," has more information about MSDS.)

With a greater awareness and comprehension of these products, you will reach a heightened comfort level in specifying and working with them. Step by step, your experience will transform into knowledge. The voice—your voice—of healthy, sustainable design will emerge.

When a new project is pending, get involved as early as possible; introduce the subject of health, performance, and sustainability at the outset—ideally, during the schematic design phase of the architectural planning. Address sustainability with the entire team—client, architect, and contractor—to encourage the early adoption of an environmental focus on the project. From that point on, you can proceed as an integrated team to establish the mission, vision, and goals for the project.

ESTABLISHING THE PROJECT MISSION, VISION, AND GOALS

A successful team generates synergy through collective wisdom, respect for subject matter experts, and recognition that the whole is greater than the sum of its parts. Set the tone and gain commitment from all members of the project team by holding a kick-off meeting at which the team develops the project mission, vision, and goals *together*.

The mission, reflecting foresight and vision, provides the overarching incentive that motivates the design and construction team to move forward. To establish the mission, the team should brainstorm and agree upon the organizing principles of the project, as these will ultimately lead to the creation of goals.

Goals establishment, the next stage in the process, will help to determine the project parameters, including aspects of health, performance, net-positive environmental impacts, and restorative and life-giving design. Stated clearly, it will ensure that everyone rallies to support and achieve them. To that end, when planning the project goals, combine the client's programming and functional requirements and design vernacular with an emphasis on the environmental and health impacts on the family, community, and ecological systems. Initiate brainstorming sessions to determine how you plan to develop the green principles outlined previously and how to effectively incorporate these strategies into the project. Examples of straightforward goal statements are:

- Establish budget parameters.
- Adopt an integrated design approach.
- Assign an environmental champion.
- Quantify measurements of net-positive success.
- Design for resourceful energy and water performance.
- Integrate renewable resources.
- Plan for construction waste management.
- Design for a healthy, happy home.

Interior designers can make a significant impact on a project by stepping forward to be the champion guiding the goals and objectives on a project with focused efforts around the healthy, high-performing, resourceful objectives. By taking on this role, we are charged to inspire and question how we, as a team, are practicing social equity, environmental stewardship, and meeting the human right of a non-toxic built environment throughout the project. Doing so steps up the implementation of these principles and practices and is an effective way to move beyond the status quo by raising the bar of environmental and healthy interior performance.

Integrated Design Approach and Criteria

Integrated design is an interconnected approach that centers on how to engage all disciplines to work as a committed, coordinated, and collaborative team. The American Institute of Architects (AIA) says it best:

> Integrated Project Delivery (IPD) leverages early contributions of knowledge and expertise through the utilization of new technologies, allowing all team members to better realize their highest potentials while expanding the value they provide throughout the project life cycle.

AIA's IPD guide outlines principles and techniques and explains how to apply IPD practices in design and construction. At its best, the approach integrates people, systems, and practices into a collaborative process harnessing the collective wisdom and participant talents to optimize results, increase value to the owner, reduce waste, minimize natural resources, and maximize efficiency through all phases of design, fabrication, and construction (www.aia.org).

To successfully create a high-performance residence, a cooperative approach to the design process is essential. The central philosophy behind integrated design is to involve all individuals responsible for the design, implementation, construction, and operations of the home to interact closely with each other throughout the process, from the launch of the design process, during construction, and into occupancy. This differs from a traditional approach where the client, architects, engineers, designers, contractors, and consultants talk to each other periodically, within a linear or solo process during which they occasionally attend the same meetings. In an integrated approach, each individual involved spends time with each other to ensure that everyone fully comprehends the issues and concerns of all other parties and is part of problem solving and finding solutions.

Integrated design demands a "whole-systems thinking" approach to create a platform for taking a holistic approach to the design of a project. According to Merriam-Webster's dictionary, "holistic" relates to or is concerned with wholes or with complete systems rather than with the analysis of, treatment of, or dissection into parts. For example, holistic medicine attempts to treat the mind as well as the body, and holistic ecology views humans and the environment as a single system. The Rocky Mountain Institute states that "whole-systems design typically reveals lasting, elegantly frugal solutions with multiple benefits, which enable us to transcend ideological battles and unite all parties around shared goals." Systems thinking opens us to new potential solutions in the problem-solving process while shedding light on linkages among problems. This helps us to build on one solution to generate even more.

A holistic design approach ensures that everyone involved in a project understands that all building systems are interdependent. By interconnecting the materials, the systems and products of a building overlap; the result is a successful whole-building design whose result is greater than the sum of its parts.

A whole-systems design approach asks all members of the team to look at the materials, systems, and assemblies from different perspectives to optimize the entire system. At first this may be difficult, as we evaluate all levels, including, but not limited to, quality of life and health, future flexibility, efficiencies, costs, environmental impacts, creativity, and indoor air quality, possibly taking us beyond our comfort zone. It takes commitment, creativity, insight, and teamwork. Every system, material, and product must be considered simultaneously to expose useful interfaces. A review of interdependencies in this way produces a more effective, healthier, and more cost-efficient house. For example, the mechanical system might impact the indoor air quality, the ease of maintenance, global climate change, operating costs, whether the windows are operable and, in turn, what type of window coverings to use. Similarly, the size of the mechanical system would take into account how the space should be organized, the type of lighting system to use, the availability of natural daylight, the finishes and materials to specify, and the local climate.

THE CHARRETTE

Invite everyone who is significant to the success of the project to the first all-inclusive design meeting, or *charrette*. At a minimum, the client, architect, mechanical engineer, interior designer, lighting consultant, and contractor should be part of this first meeting and, ideally, as many subsequent meetings as possible.

Typically, a charrette is a collaborative and interactive brainstorming session that establishes an open forum for exchanging ideas and information, thereby allowing integrated solutions to be considered and to take shape. Each team member is given the floor, in turn, for the purpose of exchanging ideas and discussing problems within and beyond his or her field of expertise. This interactive approach establishes a team culture early on and engenders respect for all participants. An effective charrette process is based on action defining the problem(s), discovering and creating many possibilities, refining selected directions, and problem-solving avenues toward executing the winning solutions that serve the project's original objective. This process may be repeated as often as needed throughout the design and construction of the project.

Ideally, several charrettes will be held throughout the key phases of the design process to ensure that the group efforts are on track and meeting or exceeding goals. As part of the process, participants have the opportunity to become further educated about the issues to better enable them to serve the project mission, goals, and objectives. The collective wisdom of the team informs and expedites the design, usually identifying issues more quickly and solving problems proactively.

Another benefit of the charrette process is that all attendees connect with one another as well as with the project mission; they begin to inspire each other to meet the agreed-upon goals and objectives: to integrate sustainable, healthy, and restorative designs into the work and collaborate with the entire team. This leads to two other projectwide benefits: lower costs and, most importantly, high-performance, healthy buildings. Ultimately, this enables professionals, working together, to transform the industry one building at a time through harmonious, holistic designs.

Compare these outcomes to those that result from thinking and working on an insular level, which isolates professionals from each other and the bigger picture. When we aim to create integrated, holistic designs that take into account all players and disciplines on a project, the process becomes thoughtful and filled with intention, with all project goals in mind at all times. This is a worthy journey, and one that leads to success.

CHALLENGES OF INTEGRATION

Working on a project where the team collaborates as described above is a rewarding experience. There may also be challenges that arise, and these, too, must be recognized from the outset so that they do not delay or derail the project.

Occasionally, individual team members will resist deviation from the traditional approach. When this happens, first remind the team of the project's mission and goals. Solicit the help of the environmental champion, or call upon a team member who has had experience in the area of contention to share how he or she has previously addressed the issue. For example, perhaps a contractor or subcontractor is hesitant to use a specified nontoxic finish. Here are some recommended approaches:

- Provide the contractor/subcontractor with a quart of the alternative material to test (and abuse) in the field prior to applying it to the entire project.

- Ask a supplier to substantiate or stand behind the product to ease concerns about the product's performance.

- Bring in an expert to work with the contractor/subcontractor, to demonstrate how new methods can be used successfully in lieu of traditional and often unhealthy ways.

- If there is a language barrier, provide specifications and instructions in the contractor's/subcontractor's native language. This is not only respectful but will also facilitate an open exchange of ideas and solutions.

- Explain the personal health benefits of using the product in question. Note that specifying products that are nontoxic and healthier to live with also respects the health of the workers in the field who are applying and installing these products.

Interior Designer's Role

Conviction, passion, and creativity are integral to the character of interior designers who are committed to healthy, high-performing, sustainable design, enabling them to craft environments and products that look good, last long, function well, enrich lives, and support client needs. Traditional practice, which thoughtlessly takes from the Earth to make products and buildings for a single purpose, produces an inordinate amount of waste and creates manufacturing and user toxins. A sustainable, renewing design shifts the perspective to one that respects and works in tandem with nature, supports abundance and health, and is economically viable. This groundbreaking vision, which represents a transformative business model of human and environmental effectiveness, has been eloquently described by William McDonough and Michael Braungart from McDonough Braungart Design Chemistry (MBDC) as "cradle to cradle." They guide us by first taking into account the outcome from the Industrial Revolution:

> Consider looking at the Industrial Revolution of the nineteenth century and its aftermath as a kind of retroactive design assignment, focusing on some of its unintended, questionable effects. The assignment might sound like this.
>
> Design a system of production that:
>
> - Puts billions of pounds of toxic material into the air, water, and soil every year.
> - Produces some materials so dangerous they will require constant vigilance by future generations.
> - Results in gigantic amounts of waste.
> - Puts valuable materials in holes all over the planet, where they can never be retrieved.
> - Requires thousands of complex regulations to keep people and natural systems from being poisoned too quickly.
> - Measures productivity by how few people are working.
> - Creates prosperity by digging up or cutting down natural resources and then burying or burning them.
> - Erodes the diversity of species and cultural practices.
>
> Does this seem like a good design assignment?
>
> Even though none of these things happened intentionally, we find this "design assignment" to be a limited and depressing one for industries to perpetuate—and it is obviously resulting in a much less enjoyable world.
>
> We are proposing a new design assignment where people and industries set out to create the following:
>
> - Buildings that, like trees, are net energy exporters, produce more energy than they consume, accrue and store solar energy, and purify their own waste water and release slowly in a purer form.
> - Factory-effluent water that is cleaner than the influent.

- Products that, when their useful life is over, do not become useless waste, but can be tossed onto the ground to decompose and become food for plants and animals, rebuilding soil; or, alternately, return to industrial cycles to supply high-quality raw materials for new products.

- Billions, even trillions, of dollars worth of materials accrued for human and natural purposes each year.

- A world of abundance, not one of limits, pollution, and waste.

Welcome to the next industrial revolution.

McDonough and Braungart's words are still inspiring today. Where do you begin? One place might be to look at what you are already doing that makes an environmental difference and reach first for the low-hanging fruit. This translates to taking the simple, easier steps until your comfort level begins to rise. Then, on your next project, perhaps research and specify zero-VOC, no-impact paints, and natural carpet that can biodegrade at the end of its life. As you become more confident, continue to build on your experiences and successes. Consider specifying nontoxic adhesives and water-based finishes that do no harm. Next jump into the world of multiattribute materials with zero or no impact to the environment and home-owner and explore the numerous options that can be offered to the client. Use your designer's creativity to continue to push the envelope.

On project teams, embody the role of collaborator and environmental champion with the client, consultants, contractor, architect, and manufacturer. Become the health advocate and ecological cheerleader, rallying the team as they gain knowledge and experience. Learn together; invite experts in the field to coach all the players through process stages where knowledge or experience is lacking or where adversity, in the form of the aforementioned challenges, presents itself.

Examine the goals and objectives monthly to ensure that the project is on track and progressing as envisioned. As you become well informed about and comfortable with the principles and practices of healthy, green design, educating clients and collaborators will further increase your abilities and establish you as a credible resource within the industry.

The quality of life for future generations lies in the palms of our hands. Contributing to the well-being of all contributes to our own. On a daily basis we can support the continuation and improve the quality of life on this planet. And while on this course of action, we will become more fulfilled as human beings. We invite you to "BE" the difference through your work in interior design.

Job Site Measures

A resource-effective project must include a waste management plan, one that is outlined from the inception of the project design through its completion. A comprehensive approach addresses more than construction and demolition debris management—that is, recycling and repurposing on the project site. It challenges us to look at conserving resources *during* design, making use of recycled content and repurposed products and salvaging valuable materials removed during construction and demolition.

An environmental consultant can be brought to the project before the construction begins to provide guidance, options, and training that support conservation measures in the field. By inviting them to the jobsite throughout the process, the carpenters and other tradespeople can learn new, improved, and healthier techniques and applications. Schedule brown-bag lunches with the construction team to share ideas, and never stop asking whether there are better, more sustaining, or healthier ways to fabricate residences. By first identifying opportunities to prevent the generation of waste on construction sites, you will actually generate less waste, which means that there will be less to recycle or reuse.

Next, focus on diverting jobsite waste from landfills by finding various alternatives for end uses of the waste. Develop a construction and demolition (C&D) diversion plan that includes a high targeted percentage of diverting waste. Include recycling, reuse, and repurpose on site, donation for reuse on another site, or resale as starting strategies. These diversion methods for C&D materials reduces the environmental impact of producing new materials, avoids sending them to landfills and the associated impacts, creates job opportunities, and may reduce overall project expenses as typical disposal costs and landfill tipping fees are higher than recycling, perhaps resulting in a net gain.

Implementing a construction waste management (CWM) plan will depend greatly on your contractor's experience and commitment plus project-specific conditions that are conducive to a CWM plan and regional services to support the plan. If there is local infrastructure to support the process, it will be straightforward, as a CWM will more than likely be standard best practice. If local services are available, aim for a high diversion rate of 75 percent or more. In fact, we know contractors who divert 99 percent of their C&D material and don't allow dumpsters on their jobsites!

In rural or remote areas, it may be challenging to find recyclers, salvage yards, or haulers. The flip side is that this creates an opportunity for local businesses to consider this and support C&D diversion, requesting that services be brought into their area.

If your contractor routinely manages their C&D debris responsibly, their experience and commitment will provide for easy implementation. On the other hand, if they are new to a CWM plan ensure that education is provided to the contractors and subcontractors. Work with the contractor to identify C&D materials that can be utilized as commodities in new building projects. Typical C&D debris generated during new construction, renovation, and demolition of buildings includes concrete, wood, asphalt shingles, gypsum from drywall, metal, brick, glass, and plastics, most of which can now be recycled. Salvaged building components, such as doors, windows, cabinets, hardware, and light fixtures, can be reused on other projects or donated.

It is also important to work with the contractor to develop waste management strategies and resources to assist in the diversion of C&D materials from landfills.

Compile a list of materials for which recycling programs are relatively easy to find, such as cardboard, clean dimensional wood, beverage containers, land-clearing debris, concrete, bricks, concrete masonry units (CMUs), asphalt, and metals from various sources.

From the outset of the major phases of construction, brainstorm with the construction team to decide on strategies and agree on solutions. Request signage designating jobsite policies; make sure these are translated into all languages used on the jobsite. Set up discussions to solicit best practices, and encourage tradespeople to talk to their counterparts who have had success with new products and better installation methods.

Incorporate the storage and collection of recyclables, not only on the job site but also in the completed home. Setting up a recycling center can be as simple as designating collection bins for commonly recycled materials such as paper, glass,

Construction Waste Management Strategies

- Ensure that the infrastructure for recycling of C&D materials is in place and operating from the outset of the project; identify in advance where different materials should be taken for recycling.

- Establish a CWM plan that sets goals to divert, recycle, or salvage a minimum of 50 percent (by weight or volume) of construction, demolition, and land-clearing waste. Then aim for 75 to 90 percent on your next project.

- Set up an on-site system to collect and sort waste for recycling or reuse, and monitor the system throughout all phases of construction.

- Consistently track the amount of waste production during construction, and measure it against preexisting goals and guidelines.

- Mark bins clearly for various types of usable wood scraps like kindling, sawdust for compost, and materials for art projects.

- Purchase materials in the sizes needed rather than cutting them to size.

- Minimize packaging waste; ask suppliers to avoid excessive packaging, or leave packaging at the point of purchase.

- Centralize cutting operations to reduce waste and simplify sorting.

- Educate the work crew regarding recycling procedures; emphasize that this is an environmentally friendly effort.

- Donate salvaged materials to charity and cultural groups such as low-income housing projects and Habitat for Humanity.

plastic, metals, and corrugated cardboard. Making it convenient and educating the site team about its use will yield positive results.

If demolition is part of the project, it is usually relatively easy to responsibly deconstruct the building's components so that they can be donated, repurposed, reused, or recycled. Remember that reuse of an existing home saves resources and cuts down on waste outputs.

For more specific information check with your state agencies for requirements and programs for C&D debris management.

Client's Role and Responsibilities

The major ingredient in any successful green project is the role of the client. If a client is motivated as an environmental steward from the outset, team integration of environmental priorities will fall naturally into place in support of the client's vision. Put another way, the client's position sets the tone for the project and creates energy leading to the successful integration of healthy, eco-friendly,

---

Helpful Home Maintenance Measures for Clients

- Develop a plan for regular maintenance of vents, filters, plumbing, and combustion equipment (gas heater, stove, dryer).

- Institute a no-smoking policy for the home, especially during construction. Cigarette smoke is a major indoor air pollutant, containing formaldehyde, carbon monoxide, and other carcinogens. Once introduced, cigarette odors are difficult to remove.

- Recommend the use of low-toxic or citrus-based cleaning products and the elimination of all solvent-based products. Ideally, choose products that are biodegradable and ammonia- and chlorine-free. For light cleaning, use vinegar, baking soda, or borax. The best options are products labeled nontoxic, nonpetroleum-based, water-based, free of ammonia, phosphates, dye, or perfume and that are readily biodegradable and using recyclable containers. Avoid products with the words: "warning," "caution," "danger," "flammable," "poison," or "reactive" unless there are compelling reasons for their use.

- Use pump sprays rather than aerosol cans, which contain chemical propellants.

high-performing design. In this ideal project scenario the entire team works effectively together to serve the client's programming requests.

If you encounter a client who is resistant to healthy and sustainable strategies, the best approach is to first ask qualifying questions in order to better align with their goals, values, desires, and expectations. This allows the design team and homeowners to align through an important value-bonding process:

- What are their expectations to meet their lifestyle?
- Would they like a healthy home for their family?
- How long are they planning to live in the house?
- Do they want a high-performing home to save energy, water, and resources?
- Are there family health issues to take into account?
- Would they like their energy bills to be less?
- Do they have chemical sensitivities?
- What quality of finishes and furnishings are they looking for?
- Would they like a connection with nature and access to natural light?

- Use high-efficiency particulate arrestance (HEPA)–filtered vacuum cleaners. Eliminate excessively wet carpet cleaning to help reduce particulate and mold buildup.
- Purchase products with less packaging by ordering supplies in bulk or in concentrated form.
- Utilize a properly vented separate storage area for cleaning supplies, paints, and other toxic materials. Locate storage areas away from air intakes and windows and thoroughly seal and isolate them from living spaces. Follow safe handling, disposal, and storage practices.
- Eliminate pesticide and herbicide use on and around the home, as they can be harmful to plants, animals, and local waterways.
- Create a well-designed in-house recycling center, or recycle items that can be diverted from landfills.
- Compost fruit, yard, and vegetable clippings. This produces excellent yard mulch and reduces material sent down the drain or to the landfill.
- Encourage clients to check their electricity, natural gas, water, and waste billing records to determine operating efficiency.
- Encourage clients to discuss and evaluate their energy use, water consumption, and waste generation with their family members.

- What thermostat setting do they use in the summer? In the winter?
- How involved are they in the operations, maintenance, and cleaning of their home?

Every step taken in the direction of "greening" a project is important. The first step is to consider how the home will ultimately be utilized and cared for once the client moves in. With this heightened level of consciousness through-out the progression of design and construction, think about the operation and maintenance methods that can be implemented to support the health of the occupants and the environmental priorities. Through prior planning, green designs will markedly improve the living environment and quality of life for the client, supporting health, safety, and welfare and reducing energy, water, and resource costs. Specify materials and systems that simplify and lower mainte-nance requirements. Designs and techniques that conserve water and energy, that use nontoxic chemicals and cleaners to maintain, and that are cost-effective reduce costs over the lifetime of the home.

Prior to occupancy, assist the client in establishing care and maintenance pro-cedures to ensure that the home performs optimally. Take into account cleaning products and techniques, long-term system maintenance, and owner awareness to determine how well the home will perform in accordance with design intent throughout the life of the home. Provide them with a homeowner's manual docu-menting the final systems, interior finishes, and furnishings, including how to oper-ate and maintain the property.

Green Builder Programs

We've said it before, but it bears repeating: Buildings consume vast amounts of our resources and threaten the ecological systems that support life as we know it, from dissipating the ozone layer to depleting the world's forests. Shifting and changing building practices is essential, and renewed commitment to using resources wisely is paramount to our future.

In recognition of that fact, municipalities throughout the country are rapidly adopting green building programs, codes, and regulations. From Alameda County, California, to Boulder, Colorado, and New York City, there are guidelines and regu-lations advising, and even requiring, the practice of green design.

Many of the programs take into consideration national and regional issues such as weather and precipitation zones; recycling infrastructure; energy and water conservation options; renewable, biodegradable, and locally produced mate-rials; and waste and pollution prevention methods. The intent of these programs is toward market transformation within the building and manufacturing industries—to lower our impact toward the net-positive and to continue raising the bar on an ongoing basis.

The mission of many of these programs is to increase the effectiveness of the local building industry, to share knowledge, and provide information to the building trades in order to preserve our natural resources. Most programs allow for flexibility in design criteria to accommodate a wide range of alternatives for creating better buildings. Generally, they promote the reduction of construction waste, the use of renewable resources, energy optimization, improved and healthier indoor air quality, use of renewable energy, water conservation, and more efficient building techniques. As the cost of using our natural resources continues to increase, resource efficiency will become more cost-effective. This fact alone drives our industry toward more rapid market transformation.

Most environmental or efficient building programs are point-based, and the number of points required to achieve a green building rating relates to the size and type of the project. Points are awarded for incorporating efficient use of materials, water, and energy; climate-appropriate landscaping and siting; and other issues relative to producing a high-performance building. Typically, green building source books or resource guides are made available for use in conjunction with these programs. These publications provide information relevant to the targeted metrics.

Some programs are voluntary, offering savings to homeowners when applying for permits; others are mandatory, meaning penalties are imposed if they are not followed. The environmental initiatives offered by these programs help to shift thinking and, thus, encourage the building industry to develop better, healthier, more economical options for the homeowner, thereby accelerating market transformation.

For more detailed information, check out chapter 7, "Green Building Rating Systems."

Green Building Cost Considerations

The initial reaction to green building strategies is that they are good in theory but cost more in practice. It is true that costs may be slightly higher for energy-efficient HVAC and appliances, energy- and water-conserving construction, and nontoxic and environmentally friendly building materials. These up-front costs typically balance out over the lifetime of the residence, often saving costs in the long run.

The U.S. Green Building Council prepared a study to better understand the costs and financial impacts of green buildings: *Cost of Green Revisited: Reexamining the Feasibility and Cost Impact of Sustainable Design in the Light of Increased Market Adoption*. This 2006 study shows there is no significant difference in average costs for green buildings as compared to traditional buildings.

Revisiting the question of the cost of incorporating sustainable design features into projects, this paper builds on the work undertaken in the earlier paper "Costing Green: A Comprehensive Cost Database and Budget Methodology," released in

Table 5.1. Costs and Financial Benefits of Green Buildings

Financial Benefits of Green Buildings, Summary of Findings	
Category	20-Year-Net Present Value ($ /sq. ft.)
Energy savings	5.80
Emissions savings	1.20
Water savings	0.50
Operations and maintenance	8.50
Productivity and health benefits	36.90–55.30
Subtotal	52.90–71.30
Average extra cost of green building	<−3.00– −5.00>
Total 20-year net benefit	50.00–65.00

Source: U.S. Green Building Council, 2006. The entire study can be found at http://www.usgbc.org/resources/cost-green-revisited.

2004, and looks at the developments that have occurred over the past three years, as sustainable design has become more widely accepted and used.

In another study of 40 green buildings selected because of the solid cost data that was available, the results clearly showed that despite an average $4 per square foot green cost premium, the total financial benefit was more than 10 times the average initial investment. Tracking sustainable attributes and strategies on projects provides vital feedback the industry can utilize to effectively sell and promote green designs to clients.

From California to New York, more states are offering significant tax rebates, incentives, and credits for "going green." These incentives encourage development and construction of smarter, more sustainable homes and communities, help conserve undeveloped land, reduce air and water pollution, improve public health, reduce traffic congestion, ensure more efficient water usage, and reduce energy bills and transportation costs. Green building and environmental benefits add value to the client's home in the form of energy efficiency, improved indoor air quality, a healthier home for the family, and durability. In short, green design does not need to cost more than conventional methods. So when it comes to addressing cost issues, rather than focusing on the up-front costs (materials and installation) involved in incorporating green features into a home, focus on the benefits and the return on investment. Rather than questioning how much more a green building will cost, ask what is most important to the client and the project: quality of life, sustaining the environment, a healthy home, flourishing ecosystems, enhanced biodiversity, saving the Earth?

The aim of designing green buildings is to achieve a higher level of performance and quality. This is based on the choices we make in the design process, how we use materials, and the construction process we follow. Coupled with the creativity and knowledge of the entire team, including the owner, determine the quality standards for the home, striving for something different, better, healthier, and greener. High-performing, healthy building improves overall performance of the home, creating a long-life building and increased owner satisfaction. These are all quantifiable attributes that typically save money, time, and environmental resources through reduced maintenance, replacement, and energy costs. We have the opportunity to do something truly meaningful—create residences that we can leave to our children without trepidation, without a toxic environment, and without guilt. Let's make it happen. "BE" the difference!

RESOURCES

Green by Design: Creating a Home for Sustainable Living. Angela M. Dean, AIA, LEED AP. Salt Lake City, UT: Gibbs Smith, 2003.

"Turning Green through LEED." Penny Bonda. *Interior Design*, May 2005.

"The Whole Building Design Approach." Don Prowler, FAIA. *Whole Building Design Guide*, April 2006.

Rocky Mountain Institute. www.rmi.org.

U.S. Green Building Council. www.usgbc.org.

greening specifications

Figure 6.1
Photo courtesy of BDAL. Architect: BDAL.

To waste, to destroy our natural resources, to skin and exhaust the land instead of using it so as to increase its usefulness, will result in undermining in the days of our children the very prosperity which we ought by right to hand down to them amplified and developed.
—THEODORE ROOSEVELT, FROM SEVENTH ANNUAL MESSAGE
TO CONGRESS, DECEMBER 3, 1907

In addition to meeting the client's needs, budget, schedule, and design vision, ecologically intelligent and healthy design requires that we carefully consider the environmental and health implications of the products and materials that we specify. This chapter will dive into the nitty-gritty of how to approach a healthy, high-performing home interior by highlighting the vetting benchmarks.

We know materials and products have a tremendous impact on the environment throughout their entire life cycle. From manufacturing, to transportation, to installation, to use and after their useful life, they negatively impact the environment by polluting communities and using natural resources and, in due course, affect humans, too, by causing ailments and chemical sensitivities. The industry is working toward reporting more detailed product information (see chapter 8, "Certifications and Standards") but until then, it is challenging to measure the toxicity of a building's interiors and its environmental impacts.

Beauty company Aveda, mission-driven to care for the world, once used the following criteria to decide whether to design, specify, buy, or use a product:

1. Do we need it? Can we do without it?

2. Can we borrow, rent, or get it gently used?

3. Is the project designed to minimize waste? Can it be smaller, lighter, or made from fewer materials?

4. Is it designed to be durable or multifunctional?

5. Is it available in a less toxic form? Can it be made with nontoxic materials, no VOCs, or certified organic?

6. Does it use renewable resources?

7. Is reuse practical and encouraged?

8. Is the product and/or packaging refillable, recyclable, or repairable?

9. Is it made with postconsumer recycled or reclaimed materials? How much?

10. Is it available from a socially and environmentally responsible company?

11. Is it made locally?

12. Again, do we need it? Can we live without it?

Consider first that we need to do no harm. The health, safety, and welfare of our clients is nonnegotiable. The materials and products we specify need to be nontoxic, support human and planetary health, provide ingredient transparency, disclose impacts, and be socially just, supporting equal opportunity and fair-trade policies.

Best practice is to use the precautionary principle (see sidebar) to guide your product and material research and decisions. Use the following set of criteria to monitor your research, selection, and specification process—whether specifying fixed interior finishes, designing furniture, or selecting fabrics—applicable to all:

- Sustainability reporting
- Product declarations (environmental and health)
- Product transparency
- Certifications
- No chemicals of concern
- Zero- or low-emitting materials
- Zero- or low-impact materials
- Indoor air quality performance
- Effective water use
- Optimal energy performance
- Reduced material content
- Recycled/repurposed material content
- Renewable material content
- Regional material content
- Ergonomic design
- Durability and long-lived
- Adaptable and reusable
- Biodegradable
- Product take back/recycling
- Reduced packaging
- Shipping and handling

Product Criteria

Locating and identifying products and materials can be challenging. Becoming familiar with the language, definitions, and consequences of using materials and products may seem daunting at first, but after applying the preceding principles a few times, it becomes second nature. Rather than replacing or providing an alternative structure to your design process, this health and environmental overlay enhances your creative and problem-solving capabilities, and human- and earth-friendly design becomes a natural, logical extension of your work. Soon you won't remember how to design in any other manner, and you'll take the responsibility to heart.

This section outlines, in turn, each of the key overarching principles listed above in qualifying products. Meeting the criteria for a product is not a black-and-white process; it is more like balancing a scale, evaluating the pros and cons and selecting the appropriate solution to meet the project's mission, vision, and objectives. An understanding of these principles is the first step on the path to fully incorporating them into your project specifications.

SUSTAINABILITY REPORTING

To meet this criterion requires searching for manufacturers and companies committed to the triple bottom line of people, profit, and planet, plus process and products. Many large-scale manufacturers have corporate sustainability reporting (CSR) programs in place. Sustainability reporting helps measure, understand, and communicate not only a company's economic, environmental, and social impact but also its governance performance, which includes assessment of positive or negative impacts, raw material extraction, and source acquisition, to name a few.

The Global Reporting Initiative (GRI) provides a framework and guidelines for corporations and manufacturers to report their level of sustainable stewardship and has become a standard worldwide.[1] The process acknowledges that it is a journey, beginning with the initial setting of goals, then measuring performance, and followed by implementing sustainable principles and strategies.

The first step is to understand and reduce a company's impact on the natural environment. Policies and programs will vary from company to company. Support suppliers that have adopting sustainability as a corporate priority, who "walk their talk" by embracing the use of environmentally friendly, nonhazardous, clean materials and practices within their business, from the front door to the back door. Start by asking these opening questions:

- Do they incorporate waste diversion and reduction, energy optimization, renewable energy, recyclable packaging, and other environmental initiatives into their plan?
- How do they evaluate their products, and at what stage of design do they begin the evaluation?
- What is the material chemistry, or are there any chemicals of concern in their products?
- What about the ease of disassembly and recyclability of their products?

---

[1] www.globalreporting.org

A good indicator of a manufacturer's commitment is its employee bathrooms. They provide insight into the company's culture—specifically, how they value the safety, health, and quality of life of their team members and visitors. Do you find eco-friendly supplies and benign cleaning products under the sink?

Similarly, the design of the building may directly reflect a company's commitment to environmental values. Is the building LEED-certified? What approach do they take to the working relationships with their customers, vendors, and peers? In all areas, does the company seek to raise the health and environmental consciousness and standards of the industry?

Seek out vendors that push the envelope with their operations and policies, manufacturing products without reducing the capacity of the environment to provide for future generations and delivering products that support health. If a company actively tracks and publishes its improving results, it is most likely on an intelligent and responsible path.

PRODUCT DECLARATIONS

Evolution is the name of the game when it comes to product declarations. Currently there are two types: environmental product declaration (EPD) and health product declaration (HPD).

Manufacturers have the opportunity to be proactive about sharing product information by providing a summary of the environmental and/or health characteristics of a product. The goal is to standardize reporting so that it is easy to understand, provides consistency across the industry, and allows us to compare products. Both EPDs and HPDs work with product category rulings (PCR), which define environmental performance with specific rules for different product types or groups.

EPDs are essential based on a life-cycle assessment (LCA) that aims to measure the product's impacts from extraction of raw materials through the end of its life. For the most part, EPDs do not yet address human health or social impacts, nor do they provide much information on environmental impacts, either.

HPDs are based on the transparency of product ingredients for a fair and comparable evaluation. Some require open disclosure of ingredients from the manufacturer, including any hazardous content, for 100 percent of its ingredients. More and more designers need comprehensive, truthful information for reporting details to a third-party building rating system or for a client who has chemical sensitivities, in order to honor our commitment to deliver safe, healthy, and high-performing interiors.

"I often compare it to food," says Anthony Ravitz, Google's Green Team leader for real estate and workplace services. "At the supermarket, you can read a nutrition label and learn how a product might impact you. We lack the power as individuals to make those decisions about building materials."[2]

---

[2] Jennifer Atlee and Paula Melton, "The Product Transparency Movement: Peeking Behind the Corporate Veil," *Environmental Building News*, January 2012.

It's now imperative that we know what is in a product—its ingredients, the health and environmental impacts, full disclosure—before we specify it. Product declarations are a step in the right direction and, optimistically, will in time lead to a form of consistent product labeling. For more specific details on product declarations refer to chapter 8, "Certifications and Standards."

CERTIFICATION

For a product to achieve any sort of certification, there must first be a standard that provides the specific criteria for evaluating the product. Certification is a proclamation that the product meets certain outlined metrics and criteria and helps in the vetting process. There are various types of certification:

- *Multiattribute certifications* distinguish products that meet a stringent set of comprehensive criteria through a sequence of metrics regarding environmental and health impacts. Most use a life-cycle philosophy to identify primary goals that the certification implements while others adopt a full life-cycle assessment methodology. Multiattribute certifications help to identify products that excel in key areas like material composition, manufacturing impacts, emissions, and energy use.

- *Single-attribute certifications* describe the majority of green building product certifications. They focus on one area of performance, like water efficiency, forestry stewardship, or product emissions.

- *Third-party certification* is a comprehensive process by which a product, process, or service is reviewed by a reputable, independent, and unbiased third party and meets an established set of criteria, claims, and standards. It is the most rigorous of the certification tiers. The independent third party leads the product testing and awards the certification. An ANSI-approved certifier offers an additional layer of quality control and objectivity. ANSI is the American National Standards Institute, a private, nonprofit organization that oversees the development of voluntary consensus standards for products, services, processes, and systems in the United States.

- *Second-party certification* is the next tier down from third-party certification. The level of standards for a certain group of manufacturers or suppliers (e.g., Good Weave certifies area rugs and carpets) is set by an industry trade association. In this process, manufacturers regularly supply documentation and evidence that certain levels are adhered to and maintained, although there is no guarantee against potential conflicts of interest.

- *First-party declaration* is a manufacturer's marketing claim for its own products or operations as set forth in product brochures, specifications, and material safety data sheets (MSDS). None of this information is confirmed, validated, or independently tested by others.

Precautionary Principle

"When an activity raises threats of harm to the environment or human health, precautionary measures should be taken, even if some cause-and-effect relationships are not fully established scientifically."

This is the root of the Precautionary Principle, which directly relates to human and environmental health. Our moral responsibility is to protect, preserve, and restore the global ecosystems which all life, including ours, needs to survive.

Numerous organizations are working to advocate and implement the precautionary principal globally. The Science and Environmental Health Network is implementing it thorough environmental and public health policies.

> When an activity raises threats of harm to human health or the environment, precautionary measures should be taken even if some cause-and-effect relationships are not fully established scientifically. In this context, the proponent of an activity, rather than the public, should bear the burden of proof. The process of applying the precautionary principle must be open, informed, and democratic and must include potentially affected parties. It must also involve an examination of the full range of alternatives, including no action.*

Clean Production Action (www.cleanproduction.org) has a unique role in industry to design and deliver strategic solutions for green chemicals, sustainable materials, and environmentally preferable products. They translate a systems-based vision of clean production into the tools and strategies that nongovernmental organizations (NGOs), governments, and businesses need to advance green chemicals, sustainable materials, and environmentally preferable products. They also promote the precautionary principle as a paradigm of decision making based on taking precautionary action before scientific certainty of cause and effect is established; setting goals; seeking out and evaluating alternatives; shifting burdens of proof; and developing more democratic and thorough decision-making criteria and methods.

> In order to protect the environment, the precautionary approach shall be widely applied by States according to their capabilities. Where there are threats of serious or irreversible

damage, lack of full scientific certainty shall not be used as a reason for postponing cost-effective measures to prevent environmental degradation.[†]

The Center for Health, Environment, and Justice has launched the Environmental Health Alliance campaign to implement the precautionary principle in order to protect our health, environment, and economy for ourselves and future generations. The campaign promotes a platform based on four principles:

1. Heed early warning signs.
2. Put safety first.
3. Exercise democracy.
4. Choose the safest solutions.[**]

Thought-leading design firm Perkins+Will launched their transparency website, which is full of groundbreaking insights into environmental materials manufactured in accordance with the precautionary principle. It is the first free database that pushes the industry toward greater transparency around building materials containing substances that are known or suspected to be associated with an adverse finding in relation to human and environmental health. Perkins+Will has spent years reviewing government scientific papers that identify substances known or suspected to cause harm to humans and the environment. The list is an impressive tool for practitioners because it also drives the building products industry toward transparency from extraction to end of life, including manufacturers and deconstructors. Perkins+Will has classified substances through multiple regulatory entities as being detrimental to the health of humans and the environment and provides updates as new relevant data emerges.[‡]

These resources offer insight that can further empower us to make informed decisions about specifying, maintaining, and disposing of building products while protecting human and environmental health.

[*] Wingspread Statement on the Precautionary Principle, January 1998. http://www.sehn.org/precaution.html
[†] Rio Declaration 1992, United Nations Conference on Environment and Development
[**] Clean Production/Green http://cleanproduction.org/Steps.Precautionary.php
[‡] For more on the Perkins+Will transparency site, see www.transparency.perkinswill.com.

Multiattribute and third-party certifications, along with consensus standardization, help eliminate the need for government to create bureaucratic laws and regulations that may restrict market access and delay the introduction of new technologies. Third-party certifications have been successfully used for decades and, more recently, multiattribute certifications now focus multiple lenses on a single product. Light fixtures, stovetops, and safety equipment listed by Underwriters Laboratory (UL) are examples of products that are third-party certified. Other third-party certification organizations include the Forest Stewardship Council (FSC), Green Seal, Greenguard, Energy Star, and Cradle to Cradle.

Some of the certification bodies offer comprehensive product databases, such as Greenguard and the Green Product Guide from SCS Global, which has also been certifying products to its original multiattribute Environmentally Preferable Products (EPP) certification. For more information, see chapter 8, "Certifications and Standards."

AVOID CHEMICALS OF CONCERN

The objective of this criterion is to drive serious market transformation by asking for and specifying products that contain no toxic chemicals. There are over 85,000 chemicals in use in the United States alone—approximately 1,100 of which are manufactured in quantities of more than 1,000 pounds annually—that lack adequate toxicology studies that evaluate their health effects on humans and wildlife. In the United States, an additional 2,000 new chemicals introduced into the market yearly—seven new chemicals every day.

By encouraging the development and use of healthy building materials and products, we promote responsible design on countless levels. Do we really want products on the market that are harmful to humans, animals, and the environment? Of course not. It is our responsibility to provide interiors that promote the health, safety, and welfare of a building's occupants. Mindful of the precautionary principle, we need to inform our clients of potential risks and provide them with alternatives so they can make knowledgeable decisions. Due to the enduring impact materials and products can have on the occupants and the environment, designers must thoroughly vet the materials and products they specify by providing alternatives to clients whenever possible.

Scientists and toxicologists are identifying more and more "emerging chemicals of concern" (ECCs). There are limitations on ECCs in chemicals regulatory systems at the state, national, and international level. These emerging chemicals are toxic in some way, are building up in the environment, or are detected in humans or other living organisms and may cause adverse effects on public health or the environment.

Some examples of ECCs include bisphenol-A, phthalates, arsenic, perchlorate, nonylphenols, synthetic musks and other personal care product ingredients, nitrosodimethylamine, brominated flame retardants, nanoparticles, pharmaceutical wastes, and industrial chemical additives, stabilizers, and adjuvants.[3]

California adopted new Safer Consumer Product Regulations in October 2013. They call for product manufacturers utilizing one or more chemicals that are considered hazardous by the California Department of Toxic Substances Control (DTSC) to eliminate that chemical or analyze the feasibility of substituting a safer alternative. As consumers from California represent one-eighth of the American market, this state mandate will affect the ingredients of products and materials in the global supply chain.

GreenScreen is a valuable tool for assessing whether materials and product design and development meet regulatory and non-regulatory requirements. It includes standards, scorecards, and eco-labels. The GreenScreen for Safer Chemicals is a comparative process that uses chemical hazard assessment (CHA) to identify chemicals of particular concern and safer alternatives. Industry, government, and NGOs

Figure 6.2
Source: Clean Product Action,
http://cleanproduction.org/
StepsChart.html.

---

[3] http://www.dtsc.ca.gov/assessingrisk/emergingcontaminants.cfm

use the platform to support healthy, responsible product design and development; define materials procurement meeting client demand to eliminate chemicals of concern; and find safer alternative chemicals for product formulations.[4]

ZERO- OR LOW-EMITTING MATERIALS

When it comes to environmental product statements, there's a big difference between marketing claims and meeting standards. And we must, for example, dive deep into the information provided by manufacturers to ensure that everything inside the waterproofing assembly of a home—interior finishes, furnishings, insulation, drywall and substrates—have been evaluated to deliver the highest quality interior environment.

Smog-causing pollutants and particulate matter have serious health and environmental implications. The amended Clean Air Act of 1990 established standards issued by the Environmental Protection Agency (EPA) to control emissions and toxic pollutants. These standards strive to reduce the emissions of more than 100 airborne toxins. When fully implemented, these standards reduce toxic emissions by about 1.5 million tons per year—almost 15 times the reductions achieved prior to 1990.

Some air toxins are also smog-causing VOCs (e.g., toluene) or particulate matter (e.g., chromium), and these air toxin regulations have the added benefit of reducing ground-level ozone (urban smog) and particulate matter. In addition, various technologies and practices designed to control air toxins also reduce VOCs or types of particulate matter that are not among the 188 air toxins listed.

Look to manufacturers that comply with standards and testing by reporting their VOC emissions levels and test for total VOC (TVOC) emissions. For clients with chemical sensitivities, ask for information on suspended VOCs (SVOCs), carbon-based substances that become gaseous under certain conditions and are released through particulates in the air. SVOCs can include glycol-based solvents, nonylphenol surfactants, phthalates, and some flame retardants. For wet-applied products, look for reporting that includes both VOC content and emissions testing.

Refer to product standards compliant with the California Department of Public Health Standard Method v1.1 (specification 01350), and the California Air Resource Board ultra-low emitting formaldehyde (ULEF). For details refer to chapter 8, "Certifications and Standards."

LOW-IMPACT MATERIALS

Low-impact materials or products are often derived from natural sources such as wood, agricultural or nonagricultural plant products, and mineral products such as natural stone and slate shingles. They are subject to minimal processing, and often selected because they are low-emitting, strong, and beautiful. It typically requires

---

[4]http://www.cleanproduction.org/Greenscreen.php

less energy to make a usable product from them, and they are also less likely to off-gas chemicals or VOCs during manufacture or when disposed of.

INDOOR AIR QUALITY PERFORMANCE

People are sometimes surprised to learn that indoor air can be a greater health hazard than the air outdoors; this is of particular concern because we spend an average of 90 percent of our time indoors.

The IAQ of any building is measured against government guidelines that establish baseline efficiency for air purification and filtration systems. IAQ assessment covers microbial contaminants (mold, bacteria), chemicals (carbon monoxide, radon), allergens, fibers (asbestos), and any mass or energy stressor that can affect the heath of people or animals.

Techniques for analyzing IAQ include collecting air samples and samples from building surfaces and computer modeling the airflow inside buildings. This analysis can lead to an understanding of the sources of the contaminants and, ultimately, to strategies for removing the unwanted elements from the air.

Utilize tools like the EPA's Indoor Air Quality Building Education and Assessment Model (I-BEAM), which can be employed for the design and construction phase of both new construction and renovations. Balance ventilation and filtration with a high exchange of fresh air in the home, ensure that vapor profiles support drying of building assemblies, and install radon mitigation equipment. Then search out products with no toxic chemicals of concern and zero- to low-emitting products. (See chapter 8, "Certifications and Standards," for further information.)

EFFECTIVE WATER USE

Use WaterSense to find products that meet or exceed water-efficiency and performance requirements. Depending on the local code and jurisdictions of your project, advocate for graywater use and recovery systems and rainwater collection to reduce the need for and conserve potable water. Whenever possible, think water-smart by using the right type of water for the right application—graywater rather than drinking water to flush your fixtures, for example. (For more information, refer to chapter 8, "Certifications and Standards" and to chapter 17, "Mechanical: Plumbing.")

OPTIMIZE ENERGY PERFORMANCE

Work closely with the project team to optimize energy use and ensure that energy consumption is the lowest it can be while still meeting the client's needs. Best practice is to begin with a computer-generated energy model to determine how various design elements will affect the project's energy efficiency. From this starting point, design a high-performing building envelope—windows, doors, walls, insulation, and roof assemblies—followed by the efficient energy-consuming systems, appliances, and equipment. Look to Energy Star for a threshold to qualify appliances and equipment, then aim to exceed those performance standards to conserve even more. Balance the high-performing envelope with renewable on-site energy like solar or wind power, working toward net-zero energy whenever possible.

REDUCED MATERIAL CONTENT

The goal for this criterion is to encourage specification of finishes and furniture that are made simply, processed minimally, and inherently part of the construction. Most furniture and case pieces are assembled with screws, nuts, bolts, or other fasteners that loosen with age. A sustainable alternative is to utilize the inherent strength of wood with a system of self-locking joinery to hold furniture together. With dove-tailed connection, components slide and lock into one another, allowing for the seasonal movement of wood with minimal warping or loosening of the structure. Using simple methods of construction and minimal processing also allows for ease of maintenance and repair.

Choosing a stronger material for one component may result in a reduced need for materials for the assembly as a whole. An engineered assembly presents a stronger and less material-intensive option than using individual components for a particular application. Utilize the attributes of a material for more than one purpose, thereby resulting in a reduced use of materials. Concrete, for example, can be used as both the structure and finish of flooring.

RECYCLED/REPURPOSED MATERIAL CONTENT

Recycling and/or repurposing is the process of collecting, processing, marketing, and ultimately reusing materials that have traditionally been discarded. Antiques and collectible furniture exemplify the beauty of repurposing and refurbishing.

Products made with recycled and/or repurposed materials offer countless benefits, among them:

- Increase innovation to create processes for reuse
- Reduce the volume of waste sent to landfills and incinerators
- Decrease the demand for virgin or raw materials thereby lessening the environmental impacts associated with the extraction and harvesting of materials
- Result in business expansion and additional jobs as new product technologies emerge

Benefits associated with recycling cannot be realized, however, unless a market exists for recycled content products. Specify products with recycled material content to ensure that the recycling movement continues. Creating a demand for recycled content can and will shift entire manufacturing markets.

Begin by looking for products that contain postconsumer material. Preconsumer/postindustrial material is the next best, followed by closed-loop recycling, and lastly, down-cycling. (Refer to the glossary for definitions.) All have positives and negatives, depending on the project goals. The more often a material can be reutilized without losing integrity, the better. The longer a material can be recycled and kept out of the landfill, the better.

RENEWABLE MATERIAL CONTENT

Renewable materials have relatively short harvest rotations—typically less than ten years—and are therefore able to replenish themselves quickly. Bamboo is an example of a material that is self-sustaining; it can be harvested every five to ten years. Other examples include wheat board, wool, cotton, coir and jute fabrics, linoleum, and cork.

A building's environmental impact can be reduced through the use of renewable materials. These are often agriculturally based materials, which consume less energy in their preparation and are less problematic to dispose of at the end of their useful life. Look for products that are grown without pesticides, require minimal machinery to harvest, are indigenous (or, at the very least, not invasive) to the growing area, do not deplete topsoil or contaminate waterways, are biodegradable, and have lower VOC emissions.

When it comes to deciding whether to use a renewable material, first ask how quickly the resource is renewed. Then confirm that the material lasts longer in application than it takes to replace the amount used. And research the environmental impacts associated with the cultivation, collection, and harvest of the renewable material.

REGIONAL MATERIALS

Specifying and purchasing regional products reduces the significant environmental impacts of the energy needed to transport materials long distances. This practice also encourages a building style vernacular that supports the local economy and is climate appropriate. When a product's entire life cycle occurs within the same regions it connects users directly with the impact of their choices.

ERGONOMIC/UNIVERSAL DESIGN

Ergonomic design ensures that an environment works comfortably and healthily for its occupants. Intelligent, healthy, and high-performing designs are by nature human-centric and usable. Ergonomic and universal design addresses the limitations and capabilities of occupants, meets and supports their needs by aligning finishes, furnishings, equipment and tasks accordingly. Think of creating multigenerational spaces with easy-to-grip handles and switches, accessible door widths, smooth flooring transitions for walkers or wheelchairs, and motion detector lighting.

DURABLE AND LONG-LASTING

Durable, low-maintenance products are environmentally friendly because they need to be cared for and replaced less frequently. These qualities vary, however, depending on the standard and quality of the product and its application. Tile, stone, and concrete are examples of products that, once manufactured and installed, will last indefinitely.

Specifying durable, high-quality goods translates into a longer product life outside of the landfill. Durable goods may cost a little more up front, but they will typically save money in the long run. Note that because a product is durable doesn't mean that it is green or a better environmental choice.

ADAPTABLE AND REUSABLE

Designing for future reuse and adaptability is a creative and an interesting challenge from an interior designer's perspective. To that end:

■ Reconfigure planned or existing space to more deeply meet the clients' needs without adding square footage or resources.

■ Consider designing a piece of furniture that can be adapted for multiple uses—for example, a coffee table that also serves as an ottoman and/or storage.

■ Choose materials and components for products that can be reused or recycled after their useful life.

■ Think about repairing, selling, or donating items to reduce waste.

Furniture and area rugs are examples of products that have a long life and can be reused over and over again.

BIODEGRADABLE

Merriam-Webster's dictionary defines "biodegradable" as being capable of decomposing by biological agents or capable of being broken down, especially into harmless products, by the action of living things, such as microorganisms. Something that decomposes without leaching toxins or polluting the area is biodegradable.

Carpet mills are producing wall-to-wall carpeting and area rugs from 100 percent biodegradable, all-natural materials, including wool, hemp, jute, and natural rubber. The carpeting is typically nonwoven and uses a 100 percent biodegradable adhesive to bond the wool to a hemp-cotton primary backing and then to a secondary backing of jute fibers. No chemical treatments are used, and color variation is achieved through the selection of naturally pigmented wool.

PRODUCT TAKE-BACK

A number of manufacturers have take-back programs so a product and/or packaging can be physically returned at the end of its useful life. A comprehensive and successful program requires diligent design and planning, incremental implementation, can be disassembled, refurbished, reused, or recycled, and incentivizes its return.

Most take-back programs in the United States are voluntary. Legislation in many European countries requires manufacturers to take back their products, and even pay for their return.

REDUCED PACKAGING

In most regions of the developed world, packaging waste represents as much as one-third of the nonindustrial solid waste stream. As living standards are raised, countries in the developing world are seeing significant growth in their packaging waste. At least twenty-eight countries worldwide have laws designed to encourage the reduced use of packaging and greater recycling of packaging discards. Many of these countries require manufacturers to take back packaging discards or to pay for their recycling.

By using products and materials with reduced packaging and encouraging manufacturers to reuse or recycle their original packaging materials, materials are diverted from disposal at the landfill, and the use of raw materials is reduced. The associated reduction in waste and disposal cost translates into cost savings for the contractor and owner.

There are no U.S. federal mandates requiring manufacturers to take back their packaging discards or to pay for their recycling. New types of containers further complicate recycling efforts, and there is growing concern at the state and local levels regarding packaging waste. More recently, government reductions in recycling subsidies and a growing demand for materials from abroad have increased pressure on domestic recyclers, especially plastics recyclers, who are competing fiercely for limited materials. New methods of increasing the recovery of materials from the landfill, including packaging and plastics in particular, are needed.

Packaging can be made more sustainable by applying the principles of product stewardship, including eliminating toxic components, using less material, making packaging more reusable, including more recycled content, and making packaging more easily recyclable.

Responsible design practice requires asking manufacturers to package their products in an environmentally accountable fashion. Specifically request:

- Minimal packaging
- Use of only recycled-content materials
- Biodegradable peanuts and bubble wrap made from 100 percent recycled plastic that is in turn 100 percent recyclable
- Packing and boxing materials that are 90 percent postconsumer waste material and are themselves 100 percent recyclable
- Packaging materials that can be returned for their reuse

Blue Angel Mark

The Blue Angel Mark is an environmental label system promoted by the German government for numerous products, including furniture and finishes. This mark is attached to an item to let consumers know that it meets certain standards.

Economical use of raw materials, production, usage, service life, and disposal—all these factors are considered. Products that meet these specifications bear the logo of the Blue Angel directly on the product, and service companies include it on sales materials advertising their services.

It is the manufacturer who is responsible for the entire life cycle of the product—forever. The manufacturer maintains a program for recycling the product in concert with the guiding principles of the Blue Angel program (www.blauer-engel.de).

SHIPPING AND HANDLING

According to the EPA, the transportation sector is the second largest producer of carbon dioxide emissions, accounting for 33 percent of total greenhouse gas production. Heavy-duty freight trucks, which account for only 1 percent of the vehicles on the road, create 20 percent of the total greenhouse gasses.

The EPA's Smartway Transport Partnership (www.EPA.gov/smartway) challenges freight companies to improve their environmental performance. Since 2004, SmartWay partners have saved 65 million barrels of oil. This is equivalent to taking over 5 million cars off the road for an entire year.

The ability to move air product by ground and ground product by rail produces significant reductions in energy use, fuel consumption, and emissions. Environmentally efficient modes of transport will eventually lessen the impact on climate change.

Utilize shipping companies committed to reducing greenhouse gas emissions and improving the fuel efficiency of ground freight transportation. Companies that strive for the highest operational efficiencies, thus minimizing the impact on the environment, lead the way. Responsibility for the environment ranges from the construction, maintenance, and operation of facilities to the maintenance and operation of vehicles and aircraft to the conservation of resources. Request corporate sustainability reports to confirm the company works toward balancing economic, social, and environmental objectives.

Samples

From fabrics to finishes, the world of design creates a surplus of samples. It takes approximately 1 quart of oil and 2 gallons of water to produce the nylon fiber necessary to make a typical carpet sample. After the short-term use of these resources, most end up in the landfill.

Throughout the design process, consider how to be resource-efficient within the sampling process to reduce waste and inefficiency. Here's how:

- Encourage manufacturers to sample initially via Internet or email distribution during the schematic design process.
- Insist that showrooms take back all samples and catalogs for reuse.
- Donate excess samples to design and architectural schools.

Vetting Products

Designers delight in researching the latest and greatest sources and products available in our field; we thrive when seeking innovative solutions. Our creative juices flow as we begin to develop cutting-edge original designs. Our newly acquired knowledge of healthy, high-performing and environmentally sound solutions and green product criteria and design concepts gives us a fresh and exciting arena in which to explore the many possibilities in creating environmentally conscientious designs.

As we set out on this exciting venture, William McDonough and Michael Braungart of MBDC challenge us to ask two very basic questions about any product:

- Where does it come from?
- Where does it go?

Beginning our research with these two straightforward questions takes our thinking to the next level of inquiry. Consider the following general issues as you move into researching products and alternative design solutions:

- Will this product make the home more energy-efficient and/or comfortable?
- Will this product save water?
- Does this product contain toxic compounds or off-gas harmful chemicals?
- Is this product safe for the client and his or her family during and after installation?

- Is this product durable, so that it won't need to be frequently repaired or replaced?

- Is this product made from recycled materials?

- Is this product manufactured in an environmentally friendly way?

- Is this product made locally?

- What is *not* sustainable about this product?

- Is the design timeless or trendy?

Understanding the properties of materials—their sources and composition, whether dangerous or toxic—informs the search for better materials and products, thus benefiting quality of life.

Materials Safety Data Sheets

A materials safety data sheet (MSDS) is an informational document developed by the product manufacturer to provide safety information; it is primarily intended for its installers and contains instructions for the safe handling, storage, and disposal of the products. It also includes important information about the characteristics and actual or potential hazards of a substance.

The Occupational Health and Safety Administration (OSHA) requires an MDSD for all hazardous materials. Each MSDS contains the general composition of the product, as well as the known health effects, proper handling, recommended storage of the material, and methods to achieve uniform product performance. Most, but not all, manufacturers are required to provide an MSDS outlining the product's chemicals, chemical compounds, and chemical mixtures and list potentially hazardous ingredients, but the reporting requirements themselves are minimal.

As best practice, interior designers must search for or request the MSDS for all products used in the residential design process. Manufacturers and distributors can provide MSDS documents for nearly every product they sell that may contain hazardous materials. Almost all are available online on the manufacturers' websites. Make a digital or physical file containing the MSDSs for all products used on the project accessible so everyone on site is informed about proper storage, handling, and safety precautions.

The MSDS assists designers and clients in making product choices based on their safety or potential for ecological and human harm. They may be technical and sometimes difficult to decipher: There are many thousands of chemicals in existence, and no one can know about all of them. The MSDS can be used as a compass to point toward relative safety or danger. A product with an MSDS devoid of listed hazards and known negative health effects is likely to be much safer, for example, than one that requires a respirator for application and contains cancer-causing agents.

Top Twenty Hazardous Substances List

Section 104 (i) of the Comprehensive Environmental Response, Compensation, and Liability Act (CERCLA), as amended by the Superfund Amendments and Reauthorization Act (SARA), requires the Agency for Toxic Substances and Disease Registry (ATSDR) and the EPA to prepare a list, in order of priority, of substances commonly found at facilities on the National Priorities List (as determined by the above agencies) that pose the most significant potential threats to human health due to their known or suspected toxicity and potential for human exposure at these NPL sites. This list represents the top twenty substances from a total of 275. For the most current list, refer to the source link below. (Note: This is not a list of "most toxic" substances but rather a prioritization of substances based on a combination of their frequency, toxicity, and potential for human exposure at NPL sites.)

Substance	Examples of some common products
1. Arsenic	Wood preservatives
2. Lead	Batteries, metal products
3. Mercury	Light bulbs
4. Vinyl chloride (PVC)	PVC piping, PVC siding, packaging
5. Polychlorinated biphenyls (PCB)	Coolants, insulation for electrical equipment

That said, it is inadvisable to make decisions based solely upon the MSDS. Manufacturers provide us with the bare minimum to meet regulatory standards, and therein lies the problem. Because manufacturers' reporting requirements are minimal, disclosure levels are inconsistent at best. GreenSpec products editor Brent Ehrlich said, "I was curious about [name withheld]'s claims, so I decided to check out the MSDS. It's a beautiful piece of non-information. Poetic in its near complete absence of substance."[5]

Proprietary information is usually excluded from the MSDS, thereby leaving out important information about ingredients considered trade secrets. Inert components, which often comprise the bulk of the product, are also exempt from inclusion—but that they are inert does not mean they are safe for humans or the environment. The safe levels of exposure to chemicals, as listed on the MSDS, are determined through

---

[5]Jennifer Atlee, "A Tale of Two Material Safety Data Sheets," *BuildingGreen*, February 29, 2012.

Substance	Examples of some common products
6. Benzene	Dyes, rubber, detergents
7. Cadmium	Batteries, pigments, plastics, metal coatings
8. Benzo(a)pyrene	Incomplete combustion from coal, oil, and wood-burning
9. Polycyclic aromatic hydrocarbons (PAH)	Dyes, plastics, roofing tar
10. Benzo(b)fluoranthene	Stoves and furnaces
11. Chloroform	Swimming pools, plant growth chemicals
12. Aroclor 1260	PCB waste materials and products in landfills
13. DDT, p,p'-	Pesticides
14. Aroclor 1254	Rubber and synthetic resin plasticizers, adhesives, sealants, caulks
15. Dibenzo(a,h)anthracene (DbahA)	Product of incomplete combustion
16. Trichloroethylene (TCE)	Adhesives, paints, paint removers
17. Chromium, hexavalent	Leather tanning, wood preserving, dyes, pigment
18. Dieldrin	Insecticide
19. Phosphorus, white	Pesticides, fireworks
20. Hexachlorobutadiene	By-product of chlorinated hydrocarbon synthesis disposed of through incineration

Source: Agency for Toxic Substances and Disease Registry (ATSDR) http://www.atsdr.cdc.gov/spl/

limited testing on one substance at a time, but this is not the scenario in the real world. The MSDS is primarily intended to educate workers about the risks while the product is being used or applied; it does not adequately address the long-term risks that might occur after the curing, drying, or deterioration of the product.

Use the MSDS as a guideline for specifications or purchases, not as a mandate. Steer toward products with the least amount of risk and highest amount of product transparency, and away from those with serious safety, human health, or environmental limitations.

Even though the content of an MSDS is dictated by OSHA, the format can vary. However, the MSDS will contain pertinent information about the following, whatever the format, when required by OSHA:

- Product name(s), manufacturer contact info, emergency phone number.
- Hazardous ingredients that make up more than one percent of the substance, including all known carcinogens. In general, the smaller the amount

of recommended exposure, the more dangerous the chemical; anything expressed in parts per million (ppm) should be highly suspect. The hazards may be expressed in several different ways, including but not limited to the following:

- Formally regulated OSHA permissible exposure limit, or PEL

- Recommended limits, from the National Institute for Occupational Safety and Health (NIOSH), recommended exposure limit (REL), or the American Conference of Governmental Industrial Hygienists (ACGIH) threshold limit value (TLV)

- Parts per million (ppm) of dust or vapor per cubic meter of air (mg/m^3)

- Time-weighted average (TWA), a concentration averaged over an eight-hour day

- Short-term exposure limit (STEL), a 15-minute TWA that should not be exceeded

- Ceiling limit (c), which should not be exceeded at any time.

- Physical characteristics of the material, such as whether it can vaporize (vapor pressure), what it might smell or look like, its boiling or melting point, flammability, and off-gassing potential (expressed as "volatile organic content").

- Health hazards through normal exposure or overexposure. Most health risks are determined through testing on animals, which is a cruel and unnecessary practice. "Acute" exposure is short-term, while "chronic" is long-term or sustained.

- Emergency and first-aid measures for eye contact, skin contact, inhalation, ingestion, and so on.

- Recommendations for safe handling, storage, accidental release (leaks or spills), and fires.

- Exposure controls and personal protection such as recommendations to wear gloves, a respirator, dust mask, or other protective item.

- Chemical and physical properties as well as stability and reactivity to help determine which chemicals should not be used together or in close proximity.

- Toxicological information and ecological information about the substance's potential for harming humans, plants, animals, and the environment.

- Disposal considerations to help determine appropriate or allowable disposal methods.

- Transport information and regulatory information, both detailing additional regulations.

While technical, the content of an MSDS is an essential starting place; the format and information will become easier to understand after you work with a few products. MSDSs will help you specify safer and healthier materials, especially if used in tandem with the above criteria.

More importantly, circle back to the project goals and objectives to determine the chemical screen issues specific to the project. Utilize the resource platform outlined in chapter 8, "Certifications and Standards," to dig deeper into a product's chemical makeup. The Pharos Chemical and Material Library, a members-only website, is a user-friendly platform that helps designers evaluate the chemicals listed in an MSDS. Through this library, you can learn about known hazards lurking in a given chemical based on its CAS number on the MSDS. The CAS Registry Number is assigned to a material by the Chemical Abstracts Service (CAS) of the American Chemical Society (ACS). This can provide a bit more information until manufacturers agree to100 percent product transparency.

An MSDS is a next step toward ascertaining what is in a product, unless it contains proprietary ingredients. You may come across a "New Jersey Trade Secret" (NJTS number): ingredients exempt from disclosure because they trade secrets. When working with chemically sensitive clients, you can call the manufacturer's research and design department to ask whether a product includes specific ingredients that cause your client's symptoms.

The time has passed for our industry to require transparent information from the manufacturers that we work with. We must continue to demand detailed, transparent product ingredients, a comprehensive health product declaration, and a list of the chemicals of concern being used until the manufacturing industry accedes to those demands.

Questions for Manufacturers and Suppliers

Over the years, we have developed numerous questionnaires in order to determine if a product meets health, environmental, and social strategies. But manufacturers' and suppliers' answers to the simplified lists of questions below may get you the information you need more quickly. The questionnaires are organized, as are the subsequent chapters of this book, using the Construction Specifications Institute (CSI) MasterFormat, the most widely used standard for organizing specifications and other written information for commercial and institutional building projects in the United States and Canada. Use this format in preparing specifications in order to best serve the architectural and construction teams and the clients with whom you are working.

The CSI MasterFormat provides a master list of divisions with section numbers and titles within each division to organize information and specifications regarding a building's construction requirements and associated activities.

Standardizing the presentation of project specifications in this same manner improves communication among everyone involved in residential construction projects. This approach also assists the project team in delivering a consistent, organized structure to owners tailored to meet their requirements, timelines, and budgets.

Because so many participants interact on a building project, its details must be carefully documented and communicated. The process begins with identifying the owner's needs, to which the architect and design team give shape. In turn, the design team takes an integrated approach to engage the engineers, contractors, specifiers and other consultants to develop the project's particulars.

Specifications are the detailed written data about a structure's materials, products, and systems, ranging from a description of the HVAC system to the kind of window glass to the type of doorknobs. A building's specifications are contained in its project manual, developed by architects, interior designers, specifiers, and engineers. The construction team uses the project manual to bid on the project, and the winning bidder uses the manual to construct the building.

This format enhances communications among everyone involved in delivering construction projects.

Table 6.1 offers a glimpse at the CSI divisions that are relevant to the practice of residential interior design. It is accompanied by key questions for manufacturers and suppliers. Use these lists as a starting point and guide, then build on them. They will assist you in finding answers to the key questions regarding a product: "Where does it come from?" and "Where does it go?"

FIXED RESIDENTIAL INTERIOR FINISHES

Interior finishes, reflected in the CSI outline, are the finishes applied in the field to the floors, walls, and ceilings of the home. They are the most prominent aspects of a residential project where we, as interior designers, are able to offer sustainable solutions as we interface with the other design disciplines: zero- to low-emitting stains and finishes on FSC millwork and cabinetry, long-lasting and colorful 100 percent recycled glass tiles in baths and kitchens, and natural earthen-based plasters on walls throughout the home. This is also the place where designers can encourage the team to create a healthy, eco-friendly home. Here we have the opportunity to model and share important information with project team members—architects, engineers, contractors, and subcontractors—regarding high-performing, healthy, and sustaining practices and materials. This information demonstrates the added value that we bring to the project.

We can combine design details and a unique use of sustainable materials in unique and creative applications. By being conscientious specifiers, we become change agents in our industry.

Table 6.1. Questions for Manufacturers

CSI Division 3: CONCRETE
✓ Where is it fabricated?
✓ Is fly ash used, and if so, what percentage is used?
✓ How is it colored, stained, or sealed?
✓ Can you recommend or use adhesives, grout, mortar, or sealants without solvents, additives, or formaldehyde?
✓ How does the manufacturing process use water and energy efficiently?
✓ Where does the waste go?
✓ How is the waste disposed of safely or reused?
✓ Does the product or its waste emit toxins into the land at disposal?
✓ What recycling programs are in place to assist in the recycling of this product?

CSI Division 4: MASONRY

Stone

✓ Where is it quarried?
✓ How rare is it?
✓ What is the process used for quarrying?
✓ What percent of it, if any, is reclaimed?
✓ How does the quarry give back to the land, town, community?
✓ Where is it fabricated and finished?
✓ How is it packaged and transported?
✓ Can it be dry-stacked?
✓ Can you recommend or use adhesives, grout, mortar, or sealants without solvents, additives, or formaldehyde?
✓ How does the manufacturing process use water and energy efficiently?
✓ What sustainable manufacturing processes do you use?
✓ How is it packaged and shipped?
✓ How can packaging be returned for reuse?
✓ Where does the waste go?
✓ How is the waste safely disposed of or reused?
✓ What programs are in place that assist in the reuse of this product?

Brick

✓ What are the materials used?
✓ Where is it fabricated?
✓ What portion of it, if any, is reclaimed?
✓ Do you have salvaged brick?
✓ Can it be dry-stacked?
✓ Can you recommend or use adhesives, grout, mortar, or sealants without solvents, additives, or formaldehyde?

(Continued)

Table 6.1. Questions for Manufacturers (*Continued*)

✓ How does the manufacturing process use water and energy efficiently?

✓ What sustainable manufacturing processes do you use?

✓ How is it packaged and shipped?

✓ Can packaging be returned for reuse?

✓ Where does the waste go?

✓ How is the waste safely disposed of or reused?

✓ Are there programs in place that assist in the reuse of this product?

CSI Division 5: METALS

✓ Where does the metal originate?

✓ What percentage of this product is from recycled content?

✓ How is waste handled?

✓ How is it finished and sealed?

✓ How does the manufacturing process use water and energy efficiently?

✓ What sustainable manufacturing processes do you use?

✓ How is it packaged and shipped?

✓ Can packaging be returned for reuse?

✓ Where does the waste go?

✓ How is the waste safely disposed of or reused?

✓ Does the product or its waste emit toxins into the land at disposal?

✓ Are there recycling programs in place that assist in the recycling of this product?

CSI Division 6: WOOD AND COMPOSITES

Wood

✓ Where does the wood come from?

✓ If a hardwood, is the wood third-party-certified?

✓ If not, how is it farmed/logged?

✓ If you use medium-density fiberboard or particleboard, is it formaldehyde-free?

✓ Is it treated with chemicals (e.g., chromated copper arsenate)?

✓ Does the company participate in reforestation?

✓ If reclaimed, where is it from? Barn? Railroad? Other?

   ■ Is it free of lead, nails, tar, creosote, and so on?

✓ How does the manufacturing process use water and energy efficiently?

✓ What sustainable manufacturing processes do you use?

✓ Does the product off-gas or emit toxins to installers or end users?

✓ How is it packaged and shipped?

✓ Can packaging be returned for reuse?

✓ Where does the waste go?

✓ How is the waste safely disposed of or reused?

✓ Are there recycling programs in place that assist in the recycling of this product?

Table 6.1. Questions for Manufacturers (*Continued*)

Composites
✓ Where do the components of the material or product come from? What are they?
✓ Where does the product itself come from?
✓ Does it include any binders or adhesives? What are they made from?
✓ Is it formaldehyde-free?
✓ Is it treated with chemicals or preservatives?
✓ Where is it fabricated?
✓ How does the manufacturing process use water and energy efficiently?
✓ Does the product off-gas or emit toxins to installers or end users?
✓ Is it, or would you consider getting it, Greenguard-certified?
✓ What sustainable manufacturing processes do you use?
✓ How is it packaged and shipped?
✓ Can packaging be returned for reuse?
✓ Where does the waste go?
✓ How is the waste safely disposed of or reused?
✓ Does the product or its waste emit toxins into the land at disposal?
✓ Are there recycling programs in place that assist in the recycling of this product?

CSI DIVISION 8: OPENINGS (Doors and Windows)
✓ If new wood, is it third-party-certified?
■ Is it formaldehyde-free?
■ Is solid or engineered wood used?
✓ If reclaimed wood, where is it from? Barn? Railroad? Other?
■ Is it free of lead, nails, tar, creosote, and so on?
✓ What are the components in composite-made frames?
■ Are they formaldehyde free?
✓ What are the glues, dyes, glazes, paints, or other ingredients used?
■ Are they water-based or low-VOC?
✓ What is the R-value of the door or window?
✓ What is the R-value of the glazing?
■ Is the window or door rated by National Fenestration Rating Council (NFRC)?
■ Is it Energy Star–rated?
✓ Do you take back old frames for reuse or remanufacture?
✓ How does the manufacturing process use water and energy efficiently?
✓ Does the product off-gas or emit toxins to installers or end users?
✓ What sustainable manufacturing processes do you use?
✓ How is it packaged and shipped?
✓ Can packaging be returned for reuse?
✓ Where does the waste go?
✓ How is the waste safely disposed of or reused?
✓ Does the product or its waste emit toxins into the land at disposal?
✓ Are there recycling programs in place that assist in the recycling of this product?

(*Continued*)

Table 6.1. Questions for Manufacturers (*Continued*)

CSI Division 9: FINISHES

Plaster and Gypsum Board

✓ Where is it made?

✓ What are the material(s) contents?

✓ What happens to any by-products of manufacturing?

✓ How does the manufacturing process use water and energy efficiently?

✓ Does the product off-gas or emit toxins to installers or end users?

✓ What sustainable manufacturing processes do you use?

✓ How is it packaged and shipped?

✓ Can packaging be returned for reuse?

✓ Where does the waste go?

✓ How is the waste safely disposed of or reused?

✓ Does the product or its waste emit toxins into the land at disposal?

✓ Are there recycling programs in place that assist in the recycling of this product?

Tile

✓ Where is it made?

✓ What are the material(s) contents?

✓ What happens to any by-products of manufacturing?

✓ What dyes or paints are used?

✓ Is there recycled content?

✓ Can the tile be recycled?

✓ How does the manufacturing process use water and energy efficiently?

✓ Does the product off-gas or emit toxins to installers or end users?

✓ What sustainable manufacturing processes do you use?

✓ How is it packaged and shipped?

✓ Can packaging be returned for reuse?

✓ Where does the waste go?

✓ How is the waste safely disposed of or reused?

✓ Does the product or its waste emit toxins into the land at disposal?

✓ Are there recycling programs in place that assist in the recycling of this product?

Flooring

Stone Tile or Flooring

✓ Where is it quarried?

✓ How rare is it?

✓ What is the process used for quarrying?

✓ What percent of it, if any, is reclaimed?

✓ How does the quarry give back to the land, town, community?

✓ Where is it fabricated and finished?

✓ Can you recommend or use adhesives, grout, mortar, or sealants without solvents, additives, or formaldehyde?

Table 6.1. Questions for Manufacturers (*Continued*)

✓ How does the manufacturing process use water and energy efficiently?

✓ Does the product off-gas or emit toxins to installers or end users?

✓ What sustainable manufacturing processes do you use?

✓ How is it packaged and shipped?

✓ Can packaging be returned for reuse?

✓ Where does the waste go?

✓ How is the waste safely disposed of or reused?

✓ Does the product or its waste emit toxins into the land at disposal?

✓ Are there recycling programs in place that assist in the recycling of this product?

Terrazzo

✓ Where does the material or product come from?

✓ Does it include any binders or adhesives? If so, what are they made from?

✓ Is it formaldehyde-free?

✓ Is it treated with chemicals or preservatives?

✓ How does the manufacturing process use water and energy efficiently?

✓ Does the product off-gas or emit toxins to installers or end users?

✓ What sustainable manufacturing processes do you use?

✓ How is it packaged and shipped?

✓ Can packaging be returned for reuse?

✓ Where does the waste go?

✓ How is the waste safely disposed of or reused?

✓ Does the product or its waste emit toxins into the land at disposal?

✓ Are there recycling programs in place that assist in the recycling of this product?

Bamboo

✓ Where does the bamboo come from?

✓ Is it made using sustainable manufacturing practices?

✓ What other components or materials are added to the product?

✓ Does this product impact indoor air quality?

✓ What finishes and/or dyes are used?

✓ Can you recommend or use adhesives or sealants without solvents, additives, formaldehyde?

✓ How does the manufacturing process use water and energy efficiently?

✓ Does the product off-gas or emit toxins to installers or end users?

✓ Is it, or would you consider getting it, Greenguard-certified?

✓ What sustainable manufacturing processes do you use?

✓ How is it packaged and shipped?

✓ Can packaging be returned for reuse?

✓ Where does the waste go?

✓ How is the waste safely disposed of or reused?

✓ Does the product or its waste emit toxins into the land at disposal?

✓ Are there recycling programs in place that assist in the recycling of this product?

(Continued)

Table 6.1. Questions for Manufacturers (*Continued*)

Leather

✓ Where do the hides for your leather products come from?

✓ Do these hides come from humanely and organically raised animals?

✓ What sustainable manufacturing processes do you use?

✓ How is your leather tanned? Do you use chromium in your tanning process? Do you use vegetable-based tanning agents?

✓ What types of dyes do you use on your leathers? Do your dyes contain any toxic substances? Do you use any natural vegetable and mineral dyes?

✓ Are your leathers treated with any surface treatments (stain repellents, etc.)?

✓ How does the manufacturing process use water and energy efficiently?

✓ Does the product off-gas or emit toxins to installers or end users?

✓ How is it packaged and shipped?

✓ Can packaging be returned for reuse?

✓ Where does the waste go?

  ■ How do you handle the chemical and protein-based waste products that result from the manufacturing of your leather?

  ■ How is the waste safely disposed of or reused?

✓ Does the product or its waste emit toxins into the land at disposal?

✓ Are there recycling programs in place that assist in the recycling of this product?

Cork

✓ Where does this product come from?

✓ How is this product harvested?

✓ What sustainable harvesting practices are used in acquiring the cork?

✓ How is the cork cleaned and processed once it has been harvested?

  ■ Are any toxic substances used to clean or process the cork?

✓ Is a binder added to the cork? If so, what is the binder made of?

✓ Is a backing used on the cork? If so, what is the backing made of?

✓ Is the surface of the cork product finished or unfinished?

  ■ If it has been finished, what kind of finish has been used?

✓ How does the manufacturing process use water and energy efficiently?

✓ Does the product off-gas or emit toxins to installers or end users?

✓ Is it, or would you consider getting it, Greenguard-certified?

✓ What sustainable manufacturing processes do you use?

✓ How is it packaged and shipped?

✓ Can packaging be returned for reuse?

✓ Where does the waste go?

✓ How is the waste safely disposed of or reused?

✓ Does the product or its waste emit toxins into the land at disposal?

✓ Are there recycling programs in place that assist in the recycling of this product?

Table 6.1. Questions for Manufacturers (*Continued*)

Wood

✓ Where does the wood come from?

✓ If a hardwood, is the wood third-party-certified?

✓ If not, how is it farmed/logged?

✓ If you use MDF or particleboard, is it formaldehyde-free?

✓ Is it treated with chemicals (e.g., chromated copper arsenate)?

✓ Does the company participate in reforestation?

✓ If reclaimed, where is it from? Barn? Railroad? Other?

   ■ Is it free of lead, nails, tar, creosote, and so on?

✓ How does the manufacturing process use water and energy efficiently?

✓ What sustainable manufacturing processes do you use?

✓ Does the product off-gas or emit toxins to installers or end users?

✓ How is it packaged and shipped?

✓ Can packaging be returned for reuse?

✓ Where does the waste go?

✓ How is the waste safely disposed of or reused?

✓ Are there recycling programs in place that assist in the recycling of this product?

Linoleum

✓ Where does this product come from?

✓ What is this product made of? Does this product contain PVC-vinyl?

✓ Has a surface finish been applied to this product? If so, what kind?

✓ How is this product maintained?

✓ How does the manufacturing process use water and energy efficiently?

✓ Does the product off-gas or emit toxins to installers or end users?

✓ What sustainable manufacturing processes do you use?

✓ How is it packaged and shipped?

✓ Can packaging be returned for reuse?

✓ Where does the waste go?

✓ How is the waste safely disposed of or reused?

✓ Does the product or its waste emit toxins into the land at disposal?

✓ Are there recycling programs in place that assist in the recycling of this product?

Carpet

✓ Does the product meet or exceed the Carpet and Rug Institute Green Label Plus standards?

✓ Where is this product manufactured?

✓ What is the backing made from?

✓ What are the adhesives used?

✓ Does this product have a high recycled-material content?

(*Continued*)

Table 6.1. Questions for Manufacturers (*Continued*)

✓ Does this product have low or zero VOC content?

✓ What is this product's total life-cycle cost, including durability and embodied energy?

✓ Does this product have a high cleanability rating?

✓ Does this product have a high durability rating?

✓ How does the manufacturing process use water and energy efficiently?

✓ Does the product off-gas or emit toxins to installers or end users?

✓ Is it, or would you consider getting it, Greenguard-certified?

✓ What sustainable manufacturing processes do you use?

✓ How is it packaged and shipped?

✓ Can packaging be returned for reuse?

✓ Where does the waste go?

✓ How is the waste safely disposed of or reused?

✓ Does the product or its waste emit toxins into the land at disposal?

✓ Are there recycling programs in place that assist in the recycling of this product?

Wall Coverings

✓ Where is this product manufactured?

✓ What is it made of (vinyl, paper, etc.)?

✓ Does it contain recycled material content?

✓ Does it contain renewable material content (e.g., wood pulp from managed forests)?

✓ Is this product compostable or biodegradable?

✓ What types of dyes are used in the making of this product?

✓ Are any toxins emitted in the manufacturing of this product?

✓ Can you recommend or use adhesives without solvents, additives, or formaldehyde?

✓ How is this product maintained—that is, what type of cleansing agents must be used?

✓ How durable is this product?

✓ How does the manufacturing process use water and energy efficiently?

✓ Does the product off-gas or emit toxins to installers or end users?

✓ Is it, or would you consider getting it, Greenguard-certified?

✓ What sustainable manufacturing processes do you use?

✓ How is it packaged and shipped?

✓ Can packaging be returned for reuse?

✓ Where does the waste go?

✓ How is the waste safely disposed of or reused?

✓ Does the product or its waste emit toxins into the land at disposal?

✓ Are there recycling programs in place that assist in the recycling of this product?

Table 6.1. Questions for Manufacturers (*Continued*)

Paints, Finishes, Coatings, and Adhesives
✓ Does this product exceed EPA standards?
✓ Is this product water-based or biodegradable?
✓ Is it silicone-based?
✓ Is it considered low- or no-VOC?
✓ How does the manufacturing process use water and energy efficiently?
✓ Does the product off-gas or emit toxins to installers or end users?
✓ What sustainable manufacturing processes do you use?
✓ How is it packaged and shipped?
✓ Can packaging be returned for reuse?
✓ Where does the waste go?
✓ How is the waste safely disposed of or reused?
✓ Does the product or its waste emit toxins into the land at disposal?
✓ Are there recycling programs in place that assist in the recycling of this product?
CSI DIVISION 10: SPECIALTIES
Fireplaces
✓ Where is this product manufactured?
✓ What are the primary materials used in the manufacturing of this product?
✓ Does this product contain any recycled materials (steel, for example)?
✓ What type of fuel is used in this product?
✓ Does this product rely on a secondary energy source to ignite?
✓ How energy-efficient is this product?
✓ If a masonry stove:
■ Does this product come equipped with a catalytic converter?
■ What is the hourly smoke emission rate?
✓ How does the manufacturing process use water and energy efficiently?
✓ Does the product off-gas or emit toxins to installers or end users?
✓ What sustainable manufacturing processes do you use?
✓ How is it packaged and shipped?
✓ Can packaging be returned for reuse?
✓ Where does the waste go?
✓ How is the waste safely disposed of or reused?
✓ Does the product or its waste emit toxins into the land at disposal?
✓ Are there recycling programs in place that assist in the recycling of this product?

(*Continued*)

Table 6.1. Questions for Manufacturers (*Continued*)

CSI DIVISION 11: EQUIPMENT (Appliances and Equipment)

✓ Where is the appliance manufactured?

✓ What are the main components of the appliance made of?

✓ Are any toxins emitted in the manufacturing or end-use of this product?

✓ Is the appliance Energy Star–rated? How much energy is used?

✓ If the appliance uses water:

  ■ Is it a water-conserving appliance?

  ■ How much water is used?

✓ How durable is this appliance? What is its average life span?

✓ How much of the appliance can be disassembled and recycled?

✓ What type of materials or products are used or needed in the maintenance of this appliance?

✓ How does the manufacturing process use water and energy efficiently?

✓ Is it, or would you consider getting it, Greenguard-certified?

✓ What sustainable manufacturing processes do you use?

✓ How is it packaged and shipped?

✓ Can packaging be returned for reuse?

✓ Where does the waste go?

✓ How is the waste safely disposed of or reused?

✓ Does the product or its waste emit toxins into the land at disposal?

✓ Are there recycling programs in place that assist in the recycling of this product?

CSI DIVISION 12: FURNISHINGS

Cabinetry

✓ If a hardwood, is the wood third-party-certified? If not, how is it farmed/logged?

✓ If you use medium-density fiberboard or particleboard, is it formaldehyde-free?

✓ Where does the wood come from?

✓ Is it treated with chemicals (e.g., chromated copper arsenate)?

✓ Does the company participate in reforestation?

✓ If reclaimed, where is it from? Barn? Railroad? Other?

  ■ Is it free of lead, nails, tar, creosote, and so on?

✓ What are the elements (drawer fronts, box, etc.) made from?

✓ Are the adhesives or finishes toxic?

✓ How does the manufacturing process use water and energy efficiently?

✓ Does the product off-gas or emit toxins to installers or end users?

✓ Is it, or would you consider getting it, Greenguard-certified?

✓ What sustainable manufacturing processes do you use?

✓ How is it packaged and shipped?

✓ Can packaging be returned for reuse?

✓ Where does the waste go?

Table 6.1. Questions for Manufacturers (*Continued*)

✓ How is the waste safely disposed of or reused?

✓ Does the product or its waste emit toxins into the land at disposal?

✓ Are there recycling programs in place that assist in the recycling of this product?

Textiles/Fabrics

✓ What is the fabric made of? Where does it come from?

✓ Where is the fabric manufactured?

✓ If it is a natural fabric or fiber:

  ■ Were any chemicals used in the growing process of this fiber?

  ■ How was the natural fiber cleaned and processed?

✓ If it is a synthetic fabric:

  ■ Is it made from recycled content?

  ■ Is it recyclable?

  ■ Is it made from renewable content—that is, bio-based fibers?

  ■ Is it biodegradable/compostable in any way?

✓ What types of dyes were used in the fabric?

✓ Do you use flame retardants or other chemical finishes on the fabrics?

✓ How is the fabric maintained or laundered?

✓ How durable is the fabric?

✓ How does the manufacturing process use water and energy efficiently?

✓ Does the product off-gas or emit toxins to installers or end users?

✓ What sustainable manufacturing processes do you use?

✓ How is it packaged and shipped?

✓ Can packaging be returned for reuse?

✓ Where does the waste go?

✓ How is the waste safely disposed of or reused?

✓ Does the product or its waste emit toxins into the land at disposal?

✓ Are there recycling programs in place that assist in the recycling of this product?

Leather

✓ Where do the hides for your leather products come from?

✓ Do these hides come from humanely and organically raised animals?

✓ What sustainable manufacturing processes do you use?

✓ Are your leathers treated with any surface treatments (stain repellants, etc.)?

✓ How is your leather tanned? Do you use chromium in your tanning process? Do you use vegetable-based tanning agents?

✓ What types of dyes do you use on your leathers? Do your dyes contain any toxic substances? Do you use any natural vegetable and mineral dyes?

✓ How does the manufacturing process use water and energy efficiently?

✓ Does the product off-gas or emit toxins to installers or end users?

✓ How is it packaged and shipped?

(*Continued*)

Table 6.1. Questions for Manufacturers (*Continued*)

✓ Can packaging be returned for reuse?

✓ Where does the waste go?

■ How do you handle the chemical and protein-based waste products that result from the manufacturing of your leather?

■ How is the waste safely disposed of or reused?

✓ Does the product or its waste emit toxins into the land at disposal?

✓ Are there recycling programs in place that assist in the recycling of this product?

Case Pieces

✓ If a hardwood, is the wood FSC- or third-party-certified? If not, how is it farmed/logged?

✓ If you use medium-density fiberboard or particleboard, is it formaldehyde-free?

✓ Where does it come from?

✓ What are the glues, paints, or finishes used?

■ Are they water-based or low-VOC?

✓ Are any recycled or reclaimed materials used?

✓ What happens to by-products of manufacturing?

✓ How does the manufacturing process use water and energy efficiently?

✓ Does the product off-gas or emit toxins to installers or end users?

✓ Is it, or would you consider getting it, Greenguard-certified?

✓ What sustainable manufacturing processes do you use?

✓ How is it packaged and shipped?

✓ Can packaging be returned for reuse?

✓ Where does the waste go?

✓ How is the waste safely disposed of or reused?

✓ Does the product or its waste emit toxins into the land at disposal?

✓ Are there recycling programs in place that assist in the recycling of this product?

Upholstery

✓ Are woods used for the frames FSC- or third-party-certified?

✓ What are the main components and what are they made of?

✓ Are components formaldehyde-free?

✓ What are the glues, paints, or finishes?

■ Are they water-based or low-VOC?

✓ How does the manufacturing process use water and energy efficiently?

✓ Does the product off-gas or emit toxins to installers or end users?

✓ Is it, or would you consider getting it, Greenguard-certified?

✓ What sustainable manufacturing processes do you use?

✓ How is it packaged and shipped?

✓ Can packaging be returned for reuse?

✓ Where does the waste go?

Table 6.1. Questions for Manufacturers (*Continued*)

✓ How is the waste safely disposed of or reused?

✓ Does the product or its waste emit toxins into the land at disposal?

✓ Are there recycling programs in place that assist in the recycling of this product?

Bath/Bedroom Linens

✓ What is the fabric made of? Where does it come from?

✓ Where is the fabric manufactured?

✓ If it is a natural fabric or fiber:

- Were any chemicals used in the growing process of this fiber?
- How was the natural fiber cleaned and processed?

✓ If it is a synthetic fabric:

- Is it made from recycled content?
- Is it recyclable?
- Is it made from renewable content (i.e., bio-based fibers)?
- Is it biodegradable/compostable in any way?

✓ What types of dyes were used?

✓ Do you use flame retardants or other chemical finishes?

✓ How is the fabric maintained or laundered?

✓ How durable is it?

✓ How does the manufacturing process use water and energy efficiently?

✓ Does the product off-gas or emit toxins to installers or end users?

✓ What sustainable manufacturing processes do you use?

✓ How is it packaged and shipped?

✓ Can packaging be returned for reuse?

✓ Where does the waste go?

✓ How is the waste safely disposed of or reused?

✓ Does the product or its waste emit toxins into the land at disposal?

✓ Are there recycling programs in place that assist in the recycling of this product?

Area Rugs

✓ Is the product Rugmark-certified?

✓ Where is the rug made or manufactured?

✓ If the rug is made of a natural fiber:

- Were any chemicals used in the growing process of this fiber?
- How was the natural fiber cleaned and processed?
- What types of fabric treatments/or enhancements has the fabric been treated with?

✓ If the rug is made of synthetic fibers:

- Are they made from recycled content?
- Are they recyclable?
- Are they made from renewable content (i.e., bio-based fibers)?
- Are they biodegradable or compostable in any way?

(*Continued*)

Table 6.1. Questions for Manufacturers (*Continued*)

✓ What types of dyes were used?

✓ What is the backing made of?

✓ What, if any, adhesives are used?

✓ How is the rug maintained or cleaned?

✓ How does the manufacturing process use water and energy efficiently?

✓ Does the product off-gas or emit toxins to installers or end users?

✓ Is it, or would you consider getting it, Greenguard-certified?

✓ What sustainable manufacturing processes do you use?

✓ How is it packaged and shipped?

✓ Can packaging be returned for reuse?

✓ Where does the waste go?

✓ How is the waste safely disposed of or reused?

✓ Does the product or its waste emit toxins into the land at disposal?

✓ Are there recycling programs in place that assist in the recycling of this product?

Window Treatments

✓ Where is the product made?

✓ Is it made from a natural or renewable source?

✓ What is the process used in manufacturing it?

✓ Does the product contain low- or no-VOC contents?

✓ Does the product contain formaldehyde?

✓ What are the energy savings to be gained by using this product, or its R-value?

✓ How is the material maintained or laundered?

✓ How does the manufacturing process use water and energy efficiently?

✓ Does the product off-gas or emit toxins to installers or end users?

✓ Is it, or would you consider getting it, Greenguard-certified?

✓ What sustainable manufacturing processes do you use?

✓ How is it packaged and shipped?

✓ Can packaging be returned for reuse?

✓ Where does the waste go?

✓ How is the waste safely disposed of or reused?

✓ Does the product or its waste emit toxins into the land at disposal?

✓ Are there recycling programs in place that assist in the recycling of this product?

Art and Framing

✓ Are woods used FSC-certified, third-party-certified and/or formaldehyde-free?

✓ What are the components in composite-made frames?

✓ What are the glues, dyes, glazes, paints, or other ingredients used?

　■ Are they water-based or low-VOC?

✓ Do you take back old frames for reuse or remanufacture?

Table 6.1. Questions for Manufacturers (*Continued*)

✓ How does the manufacturing process use water and energy efficiently?
✓ Does the product off-gas or emit toxins to installers or end users?
✓ What sustainable manufacturing processes do you use?
✓ How is it packaged and shipped?
✓ Can packaging be returned for reuse?
✓ Where does the waste go?
✓ How is the waste safely disposed of or reused?
✓ Does the product or its waste emit toxins into the land at disposal?
✓ Are there recycling programs in place that assist in the recycling of this product (frames)?

Accessories

✓ Where is the product manufactured?
✓ What is the product made of? (Depending on the materials used—wood, glass, metal, fabric, etc.—see other manufacturer questions.)
✓ Is any part of this product made from recycled content?
✓ Is any part of this product made from renewable content?
✓ Is this product biodegradable?
✓ Is this product recyclable?
✓ Can this product be disassembled and reused in any other way after the end of its useful life?
✓ Does this product contain any toxic materials?
✓ How does the manufacturing process use water and energy efficiently?
✓ Does the product off-gas or emit toxins to installers or end users?
✓ What sustainable manufacturing processes do you use?
✓ How is it packaged and shipped?
✓ Can packaging be returned for reuse?
✓ Where does the waste go?
✓ How is the waste safely disposed of or reused?
✓ Does the product or its waste emit toxins into the land at disposal?
✓ Are there recycling programs in place that assist in the recycling of this product?

CSI DIVISION 22: MECHANICAL (Plumbing)

✓ Where is the product made?
✓ What happens to any by-products or waste from manufacturing?
✓ How is the waste safely disposed of or reused?
✓ Are any of the ingredients toxic?
✓ How is the product finished and sealed?
✓ Is there recycled content in the fixture?
✓ Can the fixture be recycled?

(Continued)

Table 6.1. Questions for Manufacturers (*Continued*)

✓ How does the manufacturing process use water and energy efficiently?

✓ Does the product off-gas or emit toxins to installers or end users?

✓ What sustainable manufacturing processes do you use?

✓ How is it packaged and shipped?

✓ Can packaging be returned for reuse?

✓ Does the product or its waste emit toxins into the land at disposal?

✓ Are there recycling programs in place that assist in the recycling of this product?

CSI DIVISION 26: ELECTRICAL (Lighting/Light Fixtures)

✓ Where is the product made?

✓ What happens to any by-products of manufacturing?

✓ Are the dyes, glazes, paints, and ingredients toxic?

✓ If wood:

- If a hardwood, is the wood FSC- or third-party-certified?

- If not, how is it farmed/logged?

- If you use MDF or particleboard, is it formaldehyde-free?

✓ If metal:

- Is any recycled content used?

- How do you handle waste?

- How is it finished and sealed?

✓ Is there recycled content in the fixture?

✓ Does it have an Energy Star rating?

✓ What kinds of lamps (bulbs) are recommended?

- Are they energy-efficient, or can the fixture be retrofitted to use energy-efficient lamps?

✓ How does the manufacturing process use water and energy efficiently?

✓ Does the product off-gas or emit toxins to installers or end users?

✓ Is it, or would you consider getting it, Greenguard-certified?

✓ Is it UL-listed?

✓ What sustainable manufacturing processes do you use?

✓ How is it packaged and shipped?

✓ Can packaging be returned for reuse?

✓ Where does the waste go?

✓ How is the waste safely disposed of or reused?

✓ Does the product or its waste emit toxins into the land at disposal?

✓ Are there recycling programs in place that assist in the recycling of this product?

FIXED INTERIOR SPECIFICATIONS GUIDELINES

As the schematic design and research phases begin, continue to explore product options that meet the mission, goals, and project objectives. Utilizing the preceding questions for manufacturers and suppliers, refer to the recommendations and guidelines for the types of products to specify, or not specify, in the following chapters.

Armed with knowledge about the certifications and standards for product compliance (chapter 8) and followed by the various finishes and fixed components (see chapters 14 and 15) begin questioning your suppliers about their products (see table 6.1). Recommendations, derived from lessons learned in practice, are provided to assist with vetting products; they are not intended to be comprehensive or the most critical factors—that will depend on the focused initiatives for the project you are working on. Add to these checklists and questionnaires and then share with others—and with us—what you learn through your own practice.

Employ a cohesive and comprehensive format when writing specifications for finishes. Highlight healthy, sustainable metrics as needed to ensure thorough communication to the design and construction team. Work directly with your suppliers and installers to create respectful, close working relationships, which will benefit all of your projects.

FURNITURE SPECIFICATIONS GUIDELINES

When it comes to furniture and fabrics, push the envelope by continually asking for products with healthy, sustainable attributes. Increased market demand continues to result in a steady growth in available options. If you also practice commercial design, you know that available options have grown exponentially; the U.S. Green Building Council's LEED rating systems are a part of the market transformation.

The information here can be applied to furnishings just as easily as it can be applied to fixed interior finishes. By following the same guidelines, create specifications for fabrics and furnishings that incorporate healthy, eco-friendly strategies. Begin by asking questions of the manufacturers or suppliers long before you begin writing the specification or purchase order. Question their methodology as well as the ingredients in their products. The more you know, the easier it will be to suggest alternatives for manufacturers to consider in making their pieces more environmentally friendly and healthy. You may have better luck, at the outset, with smaller custom manufacturers who are traditional builders and already have some of these practices in place.

As with fixed interior finishes, focus on long-life, durable, adaptable, timeless, and healthy furnishings that meet your project's goals and objectives. Whether you are considering repurposed antiques and collectibles, eliminating a manufacturing process, or working with regionally produced furniture that requires less energy and resources to transport to the project site, the strategies that you adopt will guide and inform you throughout the project.

In Summary

The assessment process can feel like comparing cantaloupe to kiwis. You may find yourself comparing the resource-extraction impacts of one product, for example, with the manufacturing impacts of another and the indoor-air-quality impacts of a third. All have varying degrees of environmental impact and there are no black and white answers. But the effort you make to meet the challenge inherent in qualifying and evaluating products is well worth it and will result in intelligent, responsible project specifications.

Designing a healthy, eco-friendly, high-performing home is a balancing act. Even in the greenest project, it is likely that you will have to use products that are not themselves green. They may, however, be used in a manner that helps reduce the overall environmental impacts of the building as a whole. A well thought out design that substitutes intelligent, eco-friendly, benign products for conventional ones can make the difference between a good building and a great one.

Seeking out training on sustainable, high performing strategies, and learning about the options available to you will boost your confidence and your credibility. The payoffs are infinite.

Penny Bonda, in *Green Design Matters* (2005), written for the American Society of Interior Designers, said it well:

> As interior designers you know, instinctively, how influential you are in the marketplace.
>
> Now you must accept responsibility for that influence and use your colossal purchasing power to create safer, better furnishing materials. It's time for each designer to think about himself or herself as an active participant in reshaping the old industrial marketplace into a cleaner postindustrial system. Here's how you do that, each one of you, separately, and collectively as a group:
>
> Remember that big order for ergonomic chairs you signed recently? Did you ask your supplier if the chairs were designed for disassembly, if they had recycled content, if the factories that made the parts were known for polluting the water and air, if the parts were made by semi-slave labor, if the chairs were shipped long distances and used up a great deal of energy to reach their destination? These are questions that consumers— especially large-volume consumers like interior designers—are beginning to ask today. Your questions will be welcomed by many manufacturers who are looking to please you, their valued clients. And you will understand how powerful you can be as an agent of change in a marketplace looking to fit into the twenty-first century.

If interior designers insist on making environmentally informed material choices, the profession will have a crucial role in society. To achieve this noble goal, you need to become true collaborators with manufacturers—many of whom still think of you as part of their sales teams—and use your understanding of people to create better, more relevant products. You also need to see yourselves as experts trained to safeguard the health and welfare of people in the kind of life-supporting environments you so ably plan and design. This way of thinking is the way of leaders. You are poised to take on the mantle of that important design leadership. But if you ignore the deep and wide social need for safer materials, among other people-oriented issues, your profession will surely go the way of kings and queens.

Resources

"Avoiding Toxic Chemicals in Commercial Building Projects." *Building Green*, 2012.

"Chemistry for Designers: Understanding Hazards in Building Products." Jennifer Atlee. *Environmental Building News* 19, no. 3 (March 2010).

"Evaluating Green." Mark Ryan. *ED+C*, January 2004.

"Finding Products for LEED v4: A Guide." *Environmental Building News* 22, no. 9 (September 2013).

"Navigating the Maze of Environmentally Preferable Products." *Environmental Building News* 12, no. 11 (November 2003).

"A Simple Formula for Change." Michael Washburn and Christina Koch. *Eco-Structure*, September/October 2004.

CHAPTER 7

green building rating systems

A green building rating system sets ecological, occupant health, ergonomic, and aesthetic conditions and parameters for the design and construction of a structure, then measures the completed project against them. There are green building rating systems for renovation and new construction of both residential and commercial projects. The majority of rating systems or green building programs set benchmarks for designated attributes, and award points according to a level of achievement that then corresponds to a certification level. The most common assessment categories are energy efficiency, indoor air quality, materials, water conservation, and site management.

Similar to product eco-labels, green building rating systems can be first-, second-, or third-party certified. This designation defines the level of separation between the verification process and building. First-party certification is self-declaration and includes self-reported information that is not verified by an outside party (e.g., homeowner survey). With second-party certification, an entity participates in the verification process (e.g., authenticating performance results) or collects revenue such as a membership fee. Third-party certification indicates that all aspects of the verification and certification process are conducted by an independent, unbiased body that only receives a fee for assessment services. Third-party certification is therefore the most rigorous and credible endorsement.

The first-ever rating system, Building Research Establishment Environmental Assessment Methodology (BREEAM), was launched in 1990, but new programs continue to emerge. While carbon footprint and CO_2 emissions are important elements for a sustainable building, some of the newer programs embrace a more holistic approach by also taking into account beauty, physical fitness, and social equity, an exciting evolution.

There are a variety of reasons why designers, builders, and homeowners pursue green building certifications. The first and perhaps the most compelling is that they are committed to the preservation of the environment and natural resources. Some individuals were already building, designing, and living sustainably well before the launch of BREEAM or Leadership in Energy and Environmental Design (LEED). Green building rating systems validate that life choice.

Occupant health is a strong motivator for pursuing third-party certification. Research has linked the rise of asthma to volatile organic compounds (VOCs) and formaldehyde, which have been ubiquitous in our home furnishings and cabinetry. Today's design students are taught the importance of sourcing nontoxic building materials and furniture, fixtures, and equipment (FF&E), and that designing interiors that support human health is fundamental. Building rating systems include criteria that support and contribute to healthy indoor air quality, thus making certification a logical means to that end.

Select government entities require green certification for new construction and legally obligate builders in those jurisdictions to build to a higher standard. For example, the federal government requires that, at a minimum, new construction and substantial renovation of federally owned facilities be LEED Gold–certified. While municipalities laud the environmental benefits of these programs, many are hesitant to require certification because of the extra time and expense of the certification process. Certain government officials also feel that their authority to approve building permits and occupancy certificates would be usurped by an outside organization. A number of cities have opted instead to adopt more stringent building codes or expedite certified projects.

Designers, architects, and builders who are energized by a challenge see third-party certification simply as a different way to do business. Changing the paradigm brings a new set of ideas to the table and offers a fresh perspective. Some professionals master one rating system, then tackle a different, more rigorous, program. The specialized knowledge gained from working with a variety of rating systems can help advance one's professional career. Serving as lead on certified projects differentiates you in project interviews and bolsters your credibility if you decide to strike out on your own.

When homeowners choose to certify their project it takes "keeping up with the Joneses" to a whole new level. Homeowners can demonstrate that their house is more energy-efficient than their neighbors' by displaying a plaque and publishing their accomplishment as a case study. In addition to bragging rights, homeowners reap financial benefits from lower operating costs and realizing a higher resale value. A 2011 Earth Advantage study found that certified new homes sold for 8 percent more on average than noncertified green homes and resales of green homes sold for an average of 30 percent more than conventional homes.[1]

---

[1] Earth Advantage Institute, "Certified Homes Outperform Non-Certified Homes for Fourth Year," June 8, 2011. http://www.earthadvantage.org/resources/library/research/certified-homes

As with any emerging technology, folks will undoubtedly devise a way to game the system. One such trend is to build to a rating system's standards without going through the certification process and then refer to the home as "LEED certifiable." This assertion should be viewed cautiously. Without independent verification, this claim has no credibility and is essentially a form of "greenwashing." This practice can, however, have a positive result. Homeowners who tackle renovations themselves can utilize green building standards as a guide to reduce their home's environmental impact. They can use the benchmarks within a rating system to start a dialogue with their contractor in order to generate solutions and align the project team with their sustainability goals. Building to the standards of a green building rating system without committing to full certification is controversial but may ultimately lead to market transformation.

National and International Programs

The abundance of building rating systems demonstrates that green building is not merely an industry fad but that it is here to stay. On the following pages, you will find information on the top programs being used around the country plus a few that reach international communities.

The 2030 Challenge

Organization: Architecture 2030

Website: http://www.architecture2030.org/ 2030_challenge/the_2030_challenge

Buildings are the major source of global demand for energy and materials that produce by-product greenhouse gases (GHG). Slowing the growth rate of GHG emissions and then reversing it is the key to addressing climate change and keeping global average temperature below 2°C above preindustrial levels. To accomplish this, Architecture 2030 issued the 2030 Challenge, asking the global architecture and building community to adopt fossil fuel reduction targets. Architecture 2030.org

Challenge details: All new buildings, developments, and major renovations shall be designed to meet a fossil fuel, GHG-emitting, energy consumption performance standard of 60 percent below the regional (or country) average/median for that building type.

Fossil Fuel Reduction

70 percent in 2015

80 percent in 2020

90 percent in 2025

Carbon-neutral in 2030

How to Participate in the 2030 Challenge

- Adopt the challenge. The challenge has been adopted by individuals, firms and organizations, local governments, state governments, and sectors of the federal government.

- Meet the challenge targets on building projects through sustainable design strategies, on-site renewable power, and/or purchasing up to 20 percent renewable energy.

- Use the Environment Project Agency (EPA) Target Finder Calculator to determine if your project is meeting the targets of the 2030 challenge.

FAQs

http://architecture2030.org/about/design_faq

Resources

Architecture 2030 publications: http://architecture2030.org/multimedia/publications

EPA Target Finder Calculator: http://www.energystar.gov/buildings/service-providers/design/step-step-process/evaluate-target/epa%E2%80%99s-target-finder-calculator

2030 Challenge for products: http://architecture2030.org/2030_challenge/products

Case Studies

2030 Case Studies http://architecture2030.org/index.php

2030 Challenge Design Award

http://blog.betterbricks.com/design/2011/11/riddle-me-this-the-2030-challenge-design-awards/

2030 Palette (beta release)

http://www.2030palette.org/

This is an online tool developed by Architecture 2030 to help designers, architects, and industry professionals implement the 2030 challenge.

BREEAM

Organization: Building Research
Establishment, Ltd. (BRE)

BREEAM®

Website: http://www.breeam.org

Number of certified projects: 250,000

Launched in 1990, BREEAM is the world's first sustainability rating system
for the built environment. It is based in the United Kingdom and used in
more than fifty countries, making it the most widely used green building standard in the world. While BREEAM's environmental assessment
methods encompass all stages of a building's lifecycle, its complementary
categories extend to the building quality, performance, and value. BRE has
adapted its archetypical rating system to other countries' climate, construction practices, and codes, establishing culture-specific schemes across
the globe.

Certification Programs	Certification Levels	Assessment Areas
BREEAM New Construction UK BREEAM Refurbishment UK	Outstanding Excellent Very good Good Pass	Energy and CO_2 Emissions Water Materials Surface water run-off* Waste Health and well-being Pollution Management Ecology*

*New construction only

Process and Details

BREEAM originally addressed only the commercial sector but broadened
its scope to include the residential market in 2000 with the creation of the
EcoHomes rating system. EcoHomes was used to certify both new homes and
renovation projects. In 2007, the Code for Sustainable Homes (CSH) replaced
EcoHomes as the assessment standard for new construction in England,
Wales, and Northern Ireland. BREEAM Domestic Refurbishment (BDR) was
launched in 2012 to certify projects in existing homes, replacing EcoHomes,
which officially expired on July 1, 2014.

The CSH has nine sustainable design assessment areas, with mandatory performance requirements from the first six categories. Performance requirements for pollution, management, and ecology are flexible. Energy efficiency and conservation are heavily weighted because the UK is committed to reducing CO_2 emissions by 80 percent by 2050.

BDR was developed to provide standards for more cost-effective renovations that improve the sustainability and environmental performance of existing homes. The refurbishment program uses seven assessment categories and allows innovation credits for exemplary performance in a specific area. BDR requires a minimum level of performance in the areas of energy efficiency, water, flooding, ventilation, and legal sourcing of timber.

The two-part BREEAM certification process uses independent, licensed assessors. An initial assessment at the design stage is based on detailed documentary evidence and commitments which result in an interim certificate of compliance. Final assessment and certification at the postconstruction stage includes confirmation of interim compliance, review of site records, and visual inspection.

Case Studies

http://www.breeam.org/case-studies.jsp

http://www.breeam.org/podpage.jsp?id=393

Developments

BRE Global updated BREEAM UK New Construction in 2014.

Earth Advantage

Organization: Earth Advantage

Website: http://www.earthadvantage.org/
residential/

Based in Portland, Oregon, Earth Advantage created the Northwest's first green residential building rating system in 2000. The initial program, which is a second-party certification, covered new construction only but has been expanded to include renovations; net-zero, multifamily units; and small commercial buildings. Earth Advantage (EA) also specializes in technical training and professional development for architects, designers, contractors, remodelers, developers, real estate agents and brokers, appraisers, lenders, auditors, and home inspectors.

Certification Programs	Certification Levels	Assessment Categories
Certified Home	Platinum	Energy
Remodel	Gold	Health
Net-Zero	Silver	Land
Net-Zero Ready		Materials
Multifamily		Water

The Earth Advantage Certified Home program for new construction includes prerequisites and minimums for each category. A project can attain a higher certification level (silver, gold, platinum) for achieving more points than the minimum score of 60 required for simple certification. Initial evaluation by an EA Green Building Consultant (GBC) and verification by an EA field technician are required.

Earth Advantage Certified Homes are also Energy Star–certified because they are rated to Northwest Energy Star program energy-efficiency standards. Energy Star homes save at least 15 percent more energy when compared with a home built to code. Typical best practices include effective insulation systems, high-performance windows, sealed ducts, efficient heating and cooling equipment, and Energy Star–qualified lighting and appliances.

Earth Advantage Net Zero homes generate as much energy on site as they use and must first meet Earth Advantage Platinum certification requirements. The program assumes normal homeowner behavior and occupancy and uses REM/Rate energy modeling to determine net-zero threshold. The threshold for Net Zero will be determined using REM/Rate, which is an energy model that includes annual total energy consumption figures and assumes normal homeowner behavior and occupancy. EA Net Zero Ready certification must meet the same specifications as EA Net Zero, including proper roof orientation/pitch/area and EPA solar-ready compliance, but does not require installation of the actual renewable energy systems.

Earth Advantage Remodel includes the flexibility of allowing a home or project to be certified in one assessment area or all five and uses the CakeSystems software to calculate energy-modeling points. A home can be certified to one or more pillars at a time or receive full certification in all five pillars. It requires an initial evaluation by an accredited EA remodeler who determines the pathway to certification. The program also requires that the renovation be carried out by an EA remodeler. Homeowners have the choice of becoming an accredited EA remodeler by going through EA's half-day Remodel Certification Program or by selecting an accredited EA remodeler from a list on their website (http://www.earthadvantage.org/certification/

earth-advantage-remodel). After work is completed, a third-party inspection by an EA rater is required to verify and certify the project.

Resources

Energy Trust of Oregon: http://www.earthadvantage.org/assets/documents/Trade_Ally_Application.pdf

Northwest Energy Star: http://www.northwestenergystar.com/partners/join-the-program/builder-enrollment

Articles and Case Studies

Cannon Beach Residence: http://www.buildinggreen.com/hpb/overview.cfm?projectid=428

Ducts Inside Case Studies: http://www.ductsinside.org/

Energy Star

Organization: U.S. Environmental Protection Agency and U.S. Department of Energy

Website: http://www.energystar.gov/

Number of projects: 1,510,998 certified homes built (as of summer 2013).

Established in 1992, Energy Star is a joint program of the U.S. Environmental Protection Agency (EPA) and U.S. Department of Energy (DOE). The building rating system for new and existing single-family homes as well as low-rise multifamily homes, can verify that a home is 15 to 30 percent more energy-efficient. The government label also rates commercial buildings with of the online, interactive benchmarking tool called "Portfolio Manager," which tracks energy and water consumption. Many Americans identify Energy Star as the eco-label for energy-efficient appliances.

Assessment Categories

Energy Efficiency

Thermal Enclosure

HVAC System Quality Installation

Water Management System

Energy Star is a binary label, third-party certification: There are no levels of certification for homes, and certification performance is verified through independent home energy raters. Energy Star certification does not expire.

According to the program website, Energy Star–certified homes built in the United States in 2012 are the equivalent of:

- Eliminating emissions from 45,453 vehicles

- Saving 187,972,166 lbs of coal

- Planting and growing 5,555,330 coniferous trees for 10 years

- Saving the environment 481,394,596 pounds of CO_2

These data are based on national averages: http://www.energystar.gov/index.cfm?fuseaction=new_homes_partners.locator.

Energy Star sets rigorous requirements for home certification. These requirements include core efficiency requirements plus the following system inspection checklists, which cover critical efficiency and comfort details:

- Thermal enclosure system checklist (for home energy rater)

- HVAC system quality installation checklist (for rater)

- HVAC system quality installation checklist (for contractor)

- Water management system checklist (for builder)

Energy Star partners may use the logos in promotional materials and on certified homes. Partners are listed online and are eligible for various recognition awards from Energy Star. Partnership is free and completed online (www.energystar.gov/homes). To participate, builders, raters, and HVAC contractors must meet certain training requirements. Certification typically takes two to three days. The cost of third-party verification varies by geographic region, rater availability, and availability of applicable incentives. For more information on certification see: http://www.energystar.gov/index.cfm?c=new_homes.nh_verification_process.

Resources

Energy Star Products: http://www.energystar.gov/index.cfm?c=products.pr_find_es_products&s=mega

Energy Star Home Performance: http://www.energystar.gov/index.cfm?fuseaction=hpwes_profiles.showSplash&s=mega

Case Studies

Energy Star twenty-year milestone report: http://www.energystar.gov/index.cfm?c=about.20_years

Energy Star Blue Hills case study: http://www.energystar.gov/ia/partners/bldrs_lenders_raters/downloads/case_study_blue_hills.pdf

Green Globes

Organization: Green Building Initiative

Website: http://www.thegbi.org

Process and Details

The Green Globes system originated in Canada and has been adapted for the United States through a consensus-based process approved by the American National Standards Institute (ANSI). The Green Building Initiative received ANSI accreditation as a standards developer in 2005 and has begun the process to establish Green Globes as an official ANSI standard. Currently, the rating system can be used to assess multifamily residential buildings but not single-family dwellings.

Certification Programs	Certification Levels (% of total points)	Assessment Areas
New construction (NC) Continuing improvement of existing buildings (CIEB)	1 globe = 35–54 2 globes = 55–69 3 globes = 70–84 4 globes = 85–100	Project management (NC only) Site (NC only) Energy Water Materials and resources Emissions Indoor environment Environmental management (CIEB only)

Green Globes assesses a building's environmental impact with weighted criteria on a 1,000-point scale. NC evaluates across seven categories; CIEB has six categories (see sidebar). The energy category can account for up to 39 percent of the maximum total points and offers four paths for evaluating energy performance, including Energy Star and the advanced life-cycle-based assessment of ASHRAE Building Energy Quotient (bEQ).

The unique features of Green Globes include no prerequisites, allowance for nonapplicable criteria such as regional variations and conflicts with state or local jurisdictions, and partial credit deemed appropriate by the third-party assessor. The certification process usually takes about four months. Buildings certified under CIEB must be recertified every three years, while NC certification is good during the life of the program.

Case Studies: http://www.greenglobes.com/casestudies.asp

LEED for Homes

Organization: U.S. Green Building Council

Website: http://www.usgbc.org/leed/
rating-systems/homes

Leadership in Energy and Environmental Design
(LEED) is a voluntary, consensus-based program that
has transformed the building market in the United
States. Launched in 2000, it was the first and is the
most prevalent green building rating system in North
America. The LEED for Homes program, piloted in 2005 and chartered
in 2008, primarily addresses new residential construction, but can also
be applied to whole-house renovations. A LEED-certified home is 20 to
60 percent more energy-efficient than a home built to code.

Certification Levels	Credit Categories
Platinum	Location and linkages
Gold	Sustainable sites
Silver	Water efficiency
Certified	Energy and atmosphere
	Materials and resources
	Indoor environmental quality
	Awareness and education
	Innovation
	Regional priority

The U.S. Green Building Council, which developed LEED, has evolved
into a membership organization focused on green education and advocacy. It has a network of seventy-seven chapters across the United States.
Independent, third-party certification for LEED rating systems and credentials
is conducted by the Green Building Certification Institute. LEED also offers
third-party certification for commercial buildings and entire neighborhoods as
well as individual accreditation (LEED AP and Green Associate).

To earn certification, homes must satisfy all LEED prerequisites and earn
a minimum of 45 points on a 136-point LEED rating system scale. LEED for
Homes differs from other LEED rating systems because it does not utilize
the LEED Online software for certification. Instead, a LEED verification team
consisting of a LEED for Homes Provider and Green Rater work together to
provide the required onsite verification and oversee the certification process.

Historically, LEED certification has been heavily weighted toward energy efficiency. However, LEED v4 increases the importance of materials, resources, and indoor air quality. Significantly, these are the categories in which interior designers are involved on a LEED project.

How to certify: http://www.usgbc.org/leed/certification/homes

Resources

LEED case studies: http://www.usgbc.org/projects/homes

LEED project directory: http://www.usgbc.org/resources/leed-homes-certified-projects

Case Studies

AIA top ten: OS House: http://www2.aiatopten.org/hpb/overview.cfm?ProjectID=1935

Special No. 9 House: http://www.buildinggreen.com/hpb/overview.cfm?projectid=1736

Upcoming LEED v4: http://www.usgbc.org/v4

LEED version 4 (v4) was finalized and approved in 2013 and, for the first time, included updates to the LEED for Homes rating system. USGBC will be transitioning its certification, training, and testing programs throughout 2014. During the transition period, projects will be able to certify under LEED for Homes 2008 or v4 before USGBC completely converts to v4. Improvements under LEED for Homes v4 include more stringent metrics for water efficiency, material-efficient framing, indoor environmental quality, and environmentally preferable products.

Living Building Challenge

Organization: International Living Future Institute (ILFI)

Website: http://living-future.org/lbc

Number of certified projects: 9 (as of February 2014)

The Living Building Challenge (LBC) is currently the most rigorous performance standard for the built environment. The program establishes nature as the inspiration to certify building projects that arebenign, healthy, beautiful, and efficient and strives to diminish the gap between current limits and ideal solutions.

Process and Details

The Living Building Challenge third-party rating system can be applied to the renovation or new construction of residential and commercial buildings, infrastructure (nonconditioned development), landscaping, or neighborhood. Projects must meet ambitious performance requirements, including net-zero energy, waste, and water. LBC is the only rating system that requires a minimum of twelve months of occupancy before certification to demonstrate operational achievement under inhabited conditions. Certification fees are based on project type and size and must be paid prior to audit.

Certification Programs	Performance Areas	
Living status	Site	Water
Petal recognition	Energy	Health
Net-zero energy building	Materials	Equity
	Beauty	

Living Building Challenge version 2.1 includes seven performance areas called "petals" that are subdivided into twenty "imperatives" that focus on a specific sphere of influence. For example, the materials petal is subdivided into five imperatives:

- **Red list:** Prohibits the use of specific toxic materials and chemicals such as halogenated flame retardants, PVCs, or added formaldehyde.

- **Embodied carbon footprint:** Accounts for total carbon footprint from construction to project boundary.

- **Responsible industry:** Uses third-party certified products and fair labor practices.

- **Appropriate sourcing:** Source labor and materials close to project.

- **Conservation and reuse:** Reduces or eliminates waste and conserves natural resources.

Full certification requires all twenty imperatives to be met and therefore has no prerequisites. Petal recognition requires three petals and certain imperatives. Net-zero energy building certification requires five specific imperatives, including net-zero energy. Projects can elect a two-part certification process through which imperatives unrelated to performance can be audited prior to the twelve-month operational phase.

Projects that achieve living status or petal recognition receive a physical award that functions as a door handle, allowing individuals entering the certified building to experience the award physically. Certified projects also earn a case study on the International Living Future Institute website as well as promotion at workshops, lectures, and conferences. The LBC certification does not expire.

Case Studies

http://living-future.org/living-building-challenge/case-studies/certified-projects

Future Developments

While the Living Building Challenge fosters a holistic regenerative approach for buildings, ILFI is also helping transform the market for products and companies through transparency. The Declare program, launched in 2012, is a "nutrition label" for building materials and interiors products. Declare lists a product's ingredients, location of final assembly (city, state, country), life expectancy, end-of-life options, and LBC criteria such as LBC red list–free. A database of Declare products is available at http://www.declareproducts.com/. Announced at Living Future 2013 was a social equity disclosure program (see chapter 21, "What's Next?"). The label rates companies on gender and ethnic diversity, wage equity, workplace safety, employee benefits, community involvement, and stewardship (http://living-future.org/just). Both of these transparency programs will tie into LBC version 3.0, which is expected to launch in 2014.

NGBS Green

Organization: Home Innovation Research Labs

Website: http://www.homeinnovation.com/green

Number of Certified Projects: 30,639

NGBS Green is the only ANSI-approved green building rating system developed specifically for residential buildings. Certification is based on compliance with the ICC 700 National Green Building Standard (NGBS) versions 2008 and 2012. The standard provides best practices for the design, construction, and certification of new single-family and multifamily homes, as well as renovations. It is also used to preapprove products used in conjunction with the certification.

NGBS Certification Programs	Certification Levels	Assessment Areas
Multifamily	Emerald	Site design
Single-family	Gold	Resource efficiency
Remodeling	Silver	Energy efficiency
	Bronze	Water efficiency
		Indoor environmental quality
		Building operation and maintenance

Process and Details

Home Innovation Research Labs is an independent subsidiary of the National Association of Home Builders (NAHB). Originally founded in 1964 as the NAHB Research Center, Home Innovation changed its name in early 2013 to better reflect the full-service market research, consulting, product testing, and accredited third-party certification firm it has become.

The NGBS Green certification requires buildings to meet minimum point thresholds for each of the six assessment areas. To earn higher certification, a project must meet higher point minimums in every category, not simply excel in one. This requirement is designed to ensure that projects attaining higher certification levels are designed and perform at more rigorous thresholds in every aspect of green building.

In 2012, NGBS there were 700 green practices and 1,300 attainable points for the four certification levels. The 2012 standard introduced certification for a single-room project such as a bathroom or kitchen remodel. (There are no separate certification levels for small remodeling projects.)

Each certification program requires registration and two inspections by an independent third party. A list of accredited NGBS verifiers is located on the Home Innovation Research Labs website. New construction projects must be scored using the NGBS scoring tool and inspected prior to drywall installation; a second inspection follows the completion of construction. Renovation certifications require an energy and water use audit by a building professional before and after construction in addition to the two inspections and verifications by an accredited verifier.

Certification fees are based on building type and NAHB membership. Verification fees are set by the third-party verifier and vary by market. Certification does not expire, but date of certification is listed on the certificate. Recognition includes online listing, use of certification mark, and Home Innovation marketing materials.

Case Studies

http://www.homeinnovation.com/services/certification/green_homes/green_home_gallery

PHIUS+

Organization: Passive House Institute U.S. (PHIUS)

Website: www.passivehouse.us

Number of Certified Projects: 82 (as of September 2013)

Passive House Institute US

A Passive House exploits solar energy through passive architectural design to heat and cool its interior and power appliances and fixtures. PHIUS+ certification is available for both new construction and retrofits of residential and commercial buildings. Hallmark features of a passive building include superinsulation, airtight construction, optimum placement and sizing of triple-glazed windows, balanced energy recovery ventilation, and limited thermal bridging.

Certification Programs	Performance Areas
PHIUS+ Certified	Energy model
	Moisture control
	On-site verification

Process and Details

A Passive House is designed to remain comfortable with minimal active heating or cooling during extreme climate conditions. PHIUS+ certification is performance-based rather than prescriptive and is one of the most rigorous energy standards developed in the United States. When properly implemented, the principles and standards for a Passive House decrease energy consumption as much as 90 percent.

The PHIUS+ certification program combines a thorough passive house design verification protocol with a stringent quality assurance and quality control (QA/QC) program. Certification requirements include a complete energy model known as Wärme- und Feuchtetransport instationär (WUFI; "transient heat and moisture transport"); Passive or Passive House planning package; comprehensive construction drawings; specifications for all windows, doors, insulation, appliances, HVAC and DHW systems; blower door test, ventilation commissioning report; contractor declaration; and PHIUS+ on-site checklist. In 2013, DOE Challenge Home and Energy Star for Homes became prerequisites for PHIUS+ certified residential projects.

Verification is performed by a qualified third-party PHIUS+ rater—a Residential Energy Services Network (RESNET) rater who has successfully completed PHIUS passive house rater training. Most PHIUS+ projects receive a RESNET Home Energy Rating (HERS) Index score, the leading industry standard by which a home's energy efficiency is measured. Many local, state, and federal financial incentive programs require a HERS Index score to demonstrate compliance.

Precertification, a consulting process with revision cycles during the design phase, can take anywhere from one to twelve months. Final certification is determined by the project schedule and awarded upon completion of the built project and a review of on-site documentation. Fee structure is based on project size. Discounted fees are available for Certified Passive House Consultants (CPHCs) and Passive House Alliance United States (PHAUS) members.

PHIUS+ certification never expires. Recognition for certification includes a certificate, plaque, and online listing in the PHIUS+ Certified Projects Database. Because PHIUS works in conjunction with the DOE and EPA, PHIUS+ certified projects also receive recognition from these and other organizations.

Case Studies

http://www.passivehouse.us/projects.php

Future Developments

The PHIUS+ standard will soon be adjusted to climate-specific criteria rather than maintaining one set of standards for all of North America.

WELL Building Standard

Organization: Delos Living, LLC

Website: www.delosliving.com

Number of certified projects: 4

The WELL Building Standard is an emerging performance-based interiors guideline for protecting human health. The comprehensive program not only takes an aggressive approach to limiting pollutants, toxins, and environmental conditions that pose immediate and long-term threats to health, but also factors nutrition, stress, ergonomics, and fitness into the equation. WELL is rooted in medical research from Columbia University and is designed to work in conjunction with other sustainable building programs such as LEED and Living Building Challenge.

WELL Programs	Assessment Areas
Delos Wellness Home	Air
Stay Well Hotel Room	Water
Delos Wellness Office	Light
	Nourishment
	Fitness
	Comfort
	Mind

Process and Details

One of the challenges of a green building program is that it must balance its priority, environmental protection, with human health. While the preponderance of current programs focus on the reduction of energy consumption and greenhouse gas emissions, this nascent program is singularly concentrated on "built environments that are holistically good for people, nurturing their emotional and physical needs simultaneously," as noted by Jason F. McLennan the founder of the Living Building Challenge.

The WELL program takes evidence-based design to the next level by developing an implementation standard grounded in research. Its foundational framework stems from medical literature relating health to indoor environmental quality, architecture, behavioral psychology, and building technologies. Delos organized over a thousand peer-reviewed studies in a database that correlates WELL's seven assessment areas to specific environmental conditions that link to twelve categories of human health: cardiovascular, cosmetic, respiratory, emotional, metabolic, gastrointestinal, health literacy, longevity and aging, immune, sleep, musculoskeletal, and cognitive. Strategies such as water filtration, air purification, electromagnetic field protection, and full-spectrum light therapy address evidence-based health and wellness elements.

WELL is currently being piloted and its implementation guidelines are only available to Delos partners; it remains to be seen whether it will become a third-party certification. It is encouraging, that industry is looking to fill this important niche in green building.

Case Studies: http://delosliving.com/projects/residential/

Future Developments:

Delos will continually expand and refine its database as new research and technology emerges.

Regional Programs

Throughout the country, numerous regional programs have received recognition for their leadership and efforts to standardize green building within their communities. Check for your local programs—and ensure that they adopt high standards similar to the national programs outlined above. A few such programs are described below.

Program Name	Categories/Areas of Focus
Austin Energy Green Building Rates the sustainability of new and remodeled buildings for three markets: single family, multifamily and commercial. www.my.austinenergy.com	Planning process, site, design, material efficiency, construction waste management, thermal envelope, moisture, pest control, plumbing, mechanical, electrical, indoor environmental quality, outdoor living and landscaping, and innovations.
California: Build It Green The GreenPoint Rated label is the mark of quality for green home construction. It is a recognizable, independent seal of approval that verifies a home has been built or remodeled according to proven green standards. www.builditgreen.org/greenpoint-rated/	Energy efficiency, resource conservation, indoor air quality, water conservation, and community.
Atlanta Earth Craft House In 1999, the Greater Atlanta Home Builders Association and Southface launched EarthCraft House, a residential green building program that addresses the climate in the Southeast. Since 1978, Southface has worked with the construction and development industry, government agencies and communities to promote sustainable homes, workplaces and communities. A blueprint for creating and maintaining energy- and resource-efficient living environments, the EarthCraft House program is intended for single-family detached homes, townhomes, and duplexes. www.earthcraft.org	Site planning, construction waste management, resource efficiency, durability and moisture management, indoor air quality, high-performance building envelope, energy-efficient systems, water efficiency, education and operations, and innovation.
Florida Green Building Coalition (FGBC) Green Home Standard The FGBC is a nonprofit Florida corporation dedicated to improving the built environment. The FGBC Green Home Standard sets forth the criteria that a new or existing home must meet to be designated green. Certifying agents can guide designers, builders, and homebuyers through the process of qualifying and documenting green homes. www.floridagreenbuilding.org/homes	Energy, water, lot choice, site, health, materials, disaster mitigation, and general.

(Continued)

(Continued)

Program Name	Categories/Areas of Focus
Wisconsin Environmental Initiative Green Building Home "Green-Built Home" certifies new home and remodeling projects that meet sustainable building and energy standards. By promoting building practices and products that reduce the ecological footprint of new home construction, WEI hopes to encourage sustainable community development. Support for Green Built Home comes from organizations that promote green building and energy efficiency in Wisconsin. www.greenbuilthome.org	Siting and land use, landscape conservation and stormwater management, energy efficiency, materials selection, indoor air quality, plumbing and water conservation, waste reduction, recycling, disposal, building operations, and efficient use of space.

Frameworks and Guidelines

There are also several green building frameworks and guidelines developed by various organizations that don't fit into other categories:

GSA Report A report by the General Services Administration's Office of Federal High-Performance Green Buildings comparing three major building rating systems. www.gsa.gov/portal/category/103391	Overview comparing Green Globes, LEED, and Living Building Challenge.
Living Environments in Natural, Social, & Economic Systems (LENSES) Framework The Institute for the Built Environment has brought together a network of scientists, economists, built-environment professionals, and community members to develop the LENSES Framework, which is designed to shift mind-sets toward regenerative thinking and action; it is a tool that guides and develops capacity within teams and encourages dialogue and action toward regenerative practices. LENSES provides a visual model that helps people to see interconnections and envision beneficial, regenerative ideas and potential solutions. www.ibe.colostate.edu/lenses.aspx	The Foundation Lens represents the overarching philosophy and guiding principles of sustainability, including respecting limits, interdependence, living economy, social justice, intergenerational views, nature as model, health, spirit, and stewardship. Built Environment Lens addresses the social, environmental, and economic aspects layered over the Foundation Lens, including land use, transportation, energy use, water use, materials use, health and comfort, operations and maintenance, community, education, beauty, and financing. Flows Lens shows the resources that flow into and out of a built environment, including water, air, heat, light, people, ideas, money, food, materials, transport, services, waste, and energy.

(Continued)

REGREEN Residential Remodeling Program The REGREEN program was created through a partnership between the ASID Foundation and the USGBC. It is a set of best practice guidelines and resources for designers, contractors, and homeowners, but it is not a rating system. www.regreenprogram.org	With nearly two hundred strategies, the program is based on project types like basement, bathroom, bedroom, kitchen, and live/work plus deep energy retrofits, gut rehabs, and home performance. Each project type can be sorted by the design or construction phase of the project. Strategy topics are covered by the following overarching categories: innovative design process, site of the home; water efficiency, energy and atmosphere, material and resources, and indoor environmental quality.

Holistic Communities

There are several prominent programs that address sustainable communities:

- **The Natural Step:** The Natural Step Network serves U.S.-based business, governmental, and educational organizations interested in using the Framework for Strategic Sustainable Development, a planning framework that provides a comprehensive, shared mental model of sustainability by helping people across organizations, disciplines, and cultures to communicate effectively, build consensus, and ultimately move toward their vision. It is openly published and free for all to use and has helped hundreds of different organizations around the world integrate sustainable development into their strategic planning and create long lasting transformative change. The systems approach to problem solving helps their partners understand and coordinate how daily decisions can support the larger system in which we all live. www.thenaturalstep.org/en/usa

- **The Noisette Foundation:** Partnering with the City of North Charleston, South Carolina, the Noisette Community Master Plan set forth a vision for "a vibrant, healthy city embracing its heritage and celebrating its role in the community, ecosystem and marketplace." The plan is a blueprint for building healthy communities. http://noisettefoundation.org/vision/

- **Whole Measures:** Whole Measures is a framework developed by the Center for Whole Communities that offers a flexible approach to planning, implementing, and measuring the change they seek to create in their communities and organizations. The Whole Measures framework helps participants understand how to plan and evaluate their work in a holistic way. When applied to a social or environmental change initiative, Whole Measures can serve as guide to a highly integrated, whole systems approach that embraces a wide variety of values. www.wholecommunities.org/whole_measures/

Tools and Resources

The building industry has raised the bar for healthy, sustainable, high-performing design through the use of green building rating systems. There are also tools and resources to aid the research, design, and construction process that can streamline our professional lives. Here are a few:

- **ATHENA Impact Estimator:** This whole-building, life-cycle assessment tool is used by design teams to explore the environmental footprint of different material choices and core-and-shell system options. www.athenasmi.org/our-software-data/impact-estimator/

- **Building for Environmental and Economic Sustainability (BEES):** BEES analyzes all stages in the life of a product: raw material acquisition, manufacture, transportation, installation, use, and recycling and waste management. The BEES software ads in the selection of cost-effective, environmentally sound building products. Developed by the National Institute of Standards and Technology Engineering Laboratory, the tool is based on consensus standards and designed to be practical, flexible, and transparent. BEES Online, aimed at designers, builders, and product manufacturers, includes actual environmental and economic performance data for 230 building products. www.nist.gov/el/economics/BEESSoftware.cfm

- **Practical Evaluation Tools for Urban Sustainability (PETUS):** This resource has been developed to help people who are involved with or affected by building and infrastructure consider impacts on the environment, society, and the economy. This website includes information that can be used to analyze and improve the sustainability of urban infrastructure, whatever the size or type. Categories focus on energy, waste, water and sewage, transportation, green blue (landscape), and buildings and land use. www.petus.eu.com

- **Whole Building Design Guide (WBDG):** The goal of whole building design is to create a successful high-performance building by applying an integrated design and team approach to the project during the planning and programming phases. Categories include integrated design approach, design objectives of whole building, accessible, aesthetics, cost-effective, functional/operational, historic preservation, productive, secure/safe, and sustainable. www.wbdg.org

RESOURCE

Earth Advantage Institute. "Certified Homes Outperform Non-Certified Homes for Fourth Year." June 8, 2011. www.earthadvantage.org/resources/library/research/certified-homes-outperform-non-certified-homes-for-fourth-year.

CHAPTER 8

certifications and standards

How times have changed! Every building industry magazine now features green products, all the major product directories include green selections, and suppliers try to position almost every product as green. This proliferation of green claims makes validation and certification essential.

—NADAV MALIN, PRESIDENT, BUILDING GREEN, INC., 2011

With the number and variety of green and/or healthy products growing every day, standards and certifications are essential to ensure that the quality, value, and safety of these products are upheld and verified. Additionally, these certifications help to streamline decision making by revealing which products come from a viable source.

What Are Green Certifications and Standards and Why Are They Important?

Green claims make validations and certifications vital to the product selection process. Reputable standards and certifications scrutinize the environmental and health claims of a product based on their impacts to humankind, the planet, and society, building on the foundation of significant and relevant claims that are crucial to our design decisions.

Standards are essential to any industry because they create a benchmark for expectations. A standard is a guideline or set of criteria for judging and determining the quality, safety, value, and health of a product or service. A green certification confirms and validates that certain green product standards and claims have been met and have been documented.

Two of the primary authorities on standards are the International Standards Organization (ISO) and the American National Standards Institute (ANSI). Many of the standards produced by these organizations become law or provide the foundation for industry norms.

There are many green standards and certifications that relate to the built environment and the home. Some of the certifications cover a broad spectrum of products and evaluate a variety of health and life-cycle concerns. Other certifications are specific to only one sector of the building industry and may only focus on one standard or one health concern.

New certifications enter the marketplace annually, continually raising the bar for designers, manufacturers, and project teams. What follows are suggestions for evaluating green certifications—a useful roadmap for navigating the ever-growing world of green products and manufacturers.

GREENWASHING

As sustainable design has become more widely embraced, the green design industry has grown. As with any industry, growth and recognition yield both positive and negative results.

Unfortunately, with the popularity of going green has come the potential for being misled by companies and clever marketing campaigns that want you to believe a product is more green than it really is. This is called "greenwashing," and it's something that all designers and consumers need to be aware of. TerraChoice, part of the Underwriters Laboratory (UL), produced the 2010 "Sins of Greenwashing Report" in which they define greenwashing as "the act of misleading consumers regarding the environmental practices of a company or the environmental benefits of a product or service."

Types of Greenwashing[1]:

- **Vague or undefined.** A company may claim that its product is "100 percent natural" or "nontoxic"—broad, generic claims that mean nothing without further definition.

- **Lack of proof.** Any company can make environmental claims, but unless they are backed up with evidence or valid second- or third-party verification, these claims hold no real value.

- **Association.** An organization may imply that its products are green through association or through iconic imagery by using a remote, nature-filled setting in advertising or nature-related imagery on the packaging, leading consumers to infer that the product is green or healthy.

---

[1] TerraChoice, "The Seven Sins of Green Washing." http://sinsofgreenwashing.org/index .html

- **Hidden tradeoffs.** A company advertises that its product's packaging is 100 percent recycled. What it doesn't tell you is that the actual material itself has very high volatile organic compound (VOC) emissions and contributes to poor indoor air quality. A product may have one green attribute, but it must be considered as whole.

- **Disconnection between a claim and the conclusion.** A company may have a valid, proven environmental claim about one of their products, but then they may imply or conclude that this valid claim is a basis for another, unproven claim. For example, a claim of mold resistance does not necessarily support a claim of better indoor air quality.

- **Green by comparison.** A product is not green simply because it is not as bad as similar product.

- **Lies.** It's more likely manufacturers will resort to manipulation and obfuscation, but some tell outright lies. Some products are advertised as having earned a certification or rating it does not have; others are packaged with deceptive labels that look similar to the logo of a valid certification.

FIRST-, SECOND-, OR THIRD-PARTY?

Part of what validates a green standard or certification is the level of separation between the manufacturer and the certifier. There are three levels of certification:

- **First-party or self-certification.** Offered by manufacturers for their own products or services, this information has not been confirmed or validated by an independent source.

- **Second-party certification:** An industry trade association or an outside consulting firm sets a level of standards for a certain group of manufacturers or suppliers. Manufacturers supply documentation and evidence that they are adhering to those standards.

- **Third-party certification:** A more comprehensive process wherein a product, process, or service is reviewed by a reputable, independent, and unbiased third-party. According to the *ISO Guide 65: General Requirements for Bodies Operating Product Certification Systems*, a third-party certification must not have any conflict of interest with or provide any advice or consultation to the company being reviewed; conduct an impartial and transparent review process; document the review method; give equal treatment to each product reviewed; and provide certification based on data.

Certifying organizations can become ANSI-accredited to demonstrate that they meet these requirements. However, there are some trusted and successful proprietary industry standards associated with groups and organizations that have verified environmental credentials.

The ISO also has a labeling system:

- Type I/ISO 14024 is a seal of approval that provides guidance on developing programs that verify the environmental attributes of a product. Evaluate and understand what type of requirements the manufacturer sets forth, and clarify if it addresses your specific issues.

- Type II/ISO 14021 is a demonstrated, single-attribute environmental claim. Confirm the standardized testing used for products emissions, recycled content, or energy consumption, plus the third-party certifying organization.

- Type III/ISO14025 is fundamentally an environmental product declaration (EPDs). EPDs typically provide all-inclusive, thorough product information; they are most often found and adopted in Europe.

In the United States, most ISO labels are Type I and Type II unless the product is made by an international manufacturer based here.

Certification Resources

Navigating the growing world of green products and certifications can be complicated and overwhelming. Fortunately, green product searches and eco-claim validation services can streamline your research.

GREEN PRODUCT SEARCHES

Declare http://www.declareproducts.com/product-database
    At its core, Declare is an ingredients label for building products. There is a growing database of products compliant with the Living Building Challenge (LBC) rating system. Subject-matter experts vet manufacturers and pronounce them compliant with avoiding chemicals on the "red-list." This is a key resource for project teams pursuing the LBC, providing them with a materials guide for product specification.

Green Spec http://greenspec.buildinggreen.com
    Developed by Building Green, this product guide lists over 2,200 environmentally preferable products. Building Green has been the industry leader in vetting products since 1997, consistently delivering the highest quality reports on products. They scrutinize manufacturers' claims, feature only products that meet its high standards, and make the standards and certifications those products meet accessible.
    In 2011, they published the comprehensive *Green Building Product Certifications: Getting What You Need*. The report, available for a nominal fee, identifies and details the key green certifications spanning multiple

building product sectors and product groups, with a sector-by-sector look at certifications.

Green Building Advisor www.greenbuildingadvisor.com

This website provides great information about designing, building, and remodeling sustainable, energy-efficient homes. It utilizes the Green Spec product directory specific to residential design. The site also provides CAD drawings for green residential projects and case studies and in-depth blogs on building practices and strategies.

Green Seal http://www.greenseal.org/FindGreenSealProductsAndServices.aspx

Green Seal is a third-party certification and labeling program with an extensive product list that includes everything from household goods to personal products to building products. The database is searchable by Green Seal standard.

Green Building Pages http://www.greenbuildingpages.com

This useful tool provides green search criteria based on the following categories: production/manufacture, installation/maintenance, end of product life, company social profile, certifications, testing, and sustainable achievements.

GreenFormat http://www.csinet.org/Home-Page-Category/Formats/GF

The Construction Specification Institute (CSI) provides GreenFormat as a platform for comparing sustainability attributes for multiple building products. GreenFormat lays out a sustainability information structure that works with CSI MasterFormat. A voluntary program, it aims to communicate the sustainability features of building materials, products, systems, and technologies.

Green2Green www.green2green.org

Green2Green was started by GreenBlue, a nonprofit that provides resources for making projects more sustainable. Compare products side by side, get advice from green experts, and locate green products by source.

Green Wizard www.greenwizard.com

Green Wizard's WORKflow Pro software helps designers and contractors define green goals, create and document a LEED checklist, evaluate project energy use, and find products based on environmental product declarations, health product declarations, life-cycle analysis, and cradle to cradle.

ecoScorecard www.ecoscorecard.com

This website allows you to search products, evaluate products against rating systems, and look at detailed manufacturer product documentation. There are also ecoScorecard plug-ins for building information modeling (BIM) software, including Autodesk Revit and SketchUp, so that green decision making can be implemented during the design process.

Healthy House Institute www.healthyhouseinstitute.com

The Healthy House Institute is dedicated to helping consumers find information about green products and services for greening their home. It views the home as an ecosystem and considers indoor environmental quality as a whole. Search for building products and services based on category and locale.

Oikos Green Building www.oikos.com

This organization looks at a house as an ecosystem. It has a green library that focuses on energy efficiency, environmentally sound construction, airtight construction, ventilation, daylighting, and water conservation.

Pharos Project http://www.pharosproject.net

From the nonprofit Healthy Building Network, Pharos is a materials selection tool that relies on manufacturer participation and disclosure as well as the independent research of the Pharos team. Its goal is to make the building materials market more transparent. It scores products based on VOCs, toxic content, manufacturing toxics, renewable materials, renewable energy, and reflectance values. Evaluate and compare details on alternative products according to the project's needs or objectives and identify health hazards relating to material contents.

Rate It Green http://www.rateitgreen.com

This user-based, peer-reviewed resource has a growing database of green building products and feedback about them from consumers and manufacturers.

U.S. Green Building Council's Green Home Guide www.greenhomeguide.com

USGBC's Green Home Guide created this platform so those in the residential market can share information about certification programs, tips and advice for greening the home, and articles from subject matter experts about green products and green design techniques.

ECO-CLAIM VALIDATION AND STANDARDS FOR SUSTAINABLE ORGANIZATIONS

Green Seal Claim Verification Program www.greenseal.org

Use this optional program by Green Seal to further verify the environmental, health, and social impacts of products, services, or organizations using a third-party verification system.

National Sanitation Foundation www.nsf.org

The National Sanitation Foundation (NSF) is a nonprofit organization that acts as an independent, third-party verification and certification company based on single-attribute claims. It tracks information about the safety of food, water, and household products and also certifies green living and building products. NSF discloses the details of its verification process.

Underwriters Laboratories Environmental Claim Validation http://www
.ul.com/global/eng/pages/offerings/businesses/environment/services/
ecv/

Underwriters Laboratories (UL) provides claim validation and third-
party verification for the following green product categories: recycled content, regional materials, rapidly renewable content, recyclability, volatile
organic compounds, reclamation, mold resistance, landfill waste diversion,
and energy-saving power strips.

Ecologo and multi-attribute certifications covering the product's environmental performance throughout its lifecycle are available. These
certifications identify products that meet sustainability goals. These voluntary, multi-attribute, life-cycle-based environmental certifications indicate
that a product has undergone rigorous scientific testing and/or exhaustive
auditing to prove its compliance with stringent third-party environmental
performance standards.

Sustainable Organizations Standard (LEO-1000) http://www.leonardoaca
demy.org/services/standards.html

The Leonardo Academy is a nonprofit organization that develops sustainable standards and provides third-party verification. It specializes in sustainability
training, emissions, sustainable agriculture, and sustainable buildings. This new
pilot standard is designed to evaluate organizations in three areas: environmental stewardship, social equity, and economic prosperity.

Indoor Environmental Quality

Americans spend about 90 percent of their lives indoors, underscoring the
importance of the built environment to the health and well-being of the occupants. Indoor environmental quality (IEQ) refers to all the factors that contribute
to how we experience, interact with, and are affected by the built environment.
These factors include indoor air quality (IAQ), lighting and daylighting, connection to nature (biophilia), thermal comfort and control, and electromagnetic fields
(EMFs).

Indoor air quality deals with ventilation, chemicals and toxins, microbes, dust,
particulates, smoke, and VOCs. In an enclosed space, the combination of stale
air, chemicals, and mold or dust can create an unhealthy, even toxic environment
whose inhabitants can develop sick building syndrome or chemical sensitivities
(see chapter 4, "Healthy Interiors.")

Product standards and certifications number in the hundreds and address
diverse criteria, from recycled content to renewable resources to sustainable manufacturing processes. As health-focused designers, we seek out products that prioritize IAQ; products that don't off-gas toxins and create indoor health risks.

Precautionary Principle

When an activity raises threats of harm to the environment or human health, precautionary measures should be taken even if some cause-and-effect relationships are not fully established scientifically until the activity is proven safe.

To streamline the process of understanding and adopting certifications and standards, this section specifically refers to emissions that impact IAQ. To improve IAQ within a home, account for all the components from the envelope to the finishes, furnishings, and cleaning products. Look for and specify products with the lowest emissions of VOCs and that contain the least amount of hazardous chemicals while still performing durably. If you're working with a client with chemical sensitivities, look for certifications that take semivolatile organic compounds (SVOCs) into account in addition to the toxicity of the chemicals in the product. (See chapter 4, "Healthy Interiors.")

California Department of Public Health Special Environmental Requirements, Standard Method, Section 01350 http://www.calrecycle.ca.gov/green building/specs/section01350/

This government environmental standard pertains specifically to protecting human health through improving IAQ. The standard includes product guidelines, emissions testing, and VOC testing for building and interior finish products. California Section 01350 is integrated into the testing protocols of other certifications, addresses long-term exposure through its testing methods, and provides specification guidance.

The 01350 standard brings some of the best current research to bear on the impact of product emissions on chronic health problems. This testing protocol is required for the following: NSF 140 Carpet, NSF 332 Resilient Flooring, ULE 100 Gypsum, ULE 102 Doors, ULE 115 Insulation, and ULE 106 Luminaries.

Greenguard www.greenguard.org

The Greenguard Environmental Institute has created third-party certification programs geared toward reducing chemical emissions for new and recently installed products. The program assures designers and users that products for indoor spaces meet stringent chemical emissions limits, thereby making manufacturers' claims credible with specific scientific data from an unbiased, third-party organization.

Greenguard Gold is the more rigorous certification based on California Section 01350 and incorporates chronic reference exposure levels (CRELs).

for illustrative purposes only

The exposure levels for individual volatile organic compounds focuses on the most vulnerable individuals, including children and elderly. A product that achieves this level is fit for use in healthy interior environments like homes, schools, and health-care facilities.

Note that various building programs, standards, and specifications indicate that Greenguard certifications can contribute to the score of a building rating system (for more information, see chapter 7, "Green Building Rating Systems").

Eco-Certified Composite Sustainability Standard http://www.decorative surfaces.org/cpa-green/go-ecc-green.html

The Composite Panel Association (CPA) developed this standard for green composite wood panel products. The certification considers life cycle, including carbon footprint, recycled content, renewable resources, sustainably sourced wood, and low-emissions. Its Eco-Certified Composite (ECC) products must comply with the formaldehyde emissions regulation of the California Air Resources Board (CARB). Melamine resins that are urea-formaldehyde based must meet CARB ATCM 93120 requirements for ultra-low-emitting formaldehyde (ULEF) resins.

Carpet and Rug Institute (CRI) Green Label http://www.carpet-rug .org/commercial-customers/green-building-and-the-environment/ green-label-plus/

A second-party certification from the Carpet and Rug Institute. CRI Green Label is for carpet cushioning and CRI Green Label Plus is for carpet and adhesives with low-VOC emissions that comply with the California Section 01350 standard emissions criteria. Undergoing this third-party emissions testing lends credibility to CRI's programs even though it has not been independently certified by such a third-party organization.

Floorscore IAQ Certification www.rfci.com

A third-party certification addressing emissions for resilient and hard surface flooring and adhesives. The Resilient Floor Covering Institute (RFCI) and Scientific Certification Systems (SCS) created this flooring certification program specifically to address emissions, IAQ, and VOCs. The certified products meet California Section 01350 standard emissions criteria. These products are recognized by many green building rating systems, including LEED for Homes.

Scientific Certification Systems Indoor Advantage http://www.scsglobal services.com/certified-indoor-air-quality?scscertified=1

Scientific Certification Systems is a third-party sustainability certifier that offers Indoor Advantage and Indoor Advantage Gold certifications for office furniture, paints and coatings, adhesives, sealants, insulation, wall coverings, furnishings, and other interior products. The products that meet the Indoor Advantage Gold standard are also compliant with the California Section 01350 standard emissions criteria.

Master Painter's Institute Extreme Green http://www.paintinfo.com/MPInews/ExtremeGreen_Jan2010.shtml

A second-party standard for paint that requires durability, low-emissions, and VOC levels below 50 grams per liter. Look for products that meet the more rigorous X-Green standard, which uses third-party testing for VOC emissions and meets requirements for California Section 01350 standard emissions criteria.

OEKO-TEX Standard 100 https://www.oeko-tex.com

Tests and certifies manufactured, domestic, and household textiles to ensure they do not contain or off-gas harmful substances and chemicals. More stringent testing is employed for products that come in contact with children or human skin.

South Coast Air Quality Management District (SCAQMD) 1113 Standard www.aqmd.gov

This government standard from the South Coast Air Quality Management District from Orange County, California, deals with the smog VOC emissions of interior and exterior architectural coatings, including roof coatings, concrete sealers, and aerosol coatings. Confirm that the contents of these product types are healthy, too. Search out "supercompliant" paints, ideally with less than 10 grams per liter of VOCs. SCAQMD provides a listing on their website for compliant products.

Air Resources Board Airborne Toxic Control Measure http://www.arb.ca.gov/toxics/compwood/compwood.htm

California continues to lead the industry in market transformation. The California Air Resources Board (ARB) released this Airborne Toxic Control Measure (ATCM) to reduce formaldehyde emissions from composite wood products: hardwood, plywood, particleboard, and medium-density fiberboard, or MDF. The standard is also known as California 93120 compliant. ATCM's phase-two emissions limits have become the industry standard for composite woods. They cap formaldehyde emissions at .05 parts per million for plywood.

If a manufacturer of hardwood plywood, particleboard, and medium density fiberboard uses no-added-formaldehyde (NAF) based resins or ultra-low-emitting formaldehyde (ULEF) resins it is exempted from some of the testing requirements when regularly below applicable phase-two emissions standards.

Life-Cycle Assessment

In addition to prioritizing indoor air quality (IAQ), we need to be aware of the entire life cycle of a product or material. A product may be harvested sustainably but then during the manufacturing process, it may be treated with harmful chemicals.

For example, to ward off fungal staining, some unfinished wood floors are treated with preservatives containing biocides. These toxic chemicals, developed to attack living organisms, expose us to reproductive and developmental toxicants plus carcinogens, which are then released into the air, compromising its quality.

A life-cycle assessment (LCA) takes a quantitative and qualitative assessment of all phases of a product's life into consideration: raw material extraction/harvesting, material processing, environmental impacts, manufacturing/assembly, usage, and end of life. It is challenging to interpret and calculate the environmental and health impacts for every input and output of a product's life. But doing so will help manufacturers, project teams, and consumers make more fully informed decisions. Fortunately, LCA is gaining traction in industry sectors searching for a standard methodology to evaluate and disseminate the results of these quantitative and qualitative assessments.

Manufacturers must first assess a product's impacts and the components that are primary IAQ offenders. To understand the full, cradle-to-grave impacts of their products, companies must adopt LCA's holistic approach and share the results with the rest of the industry through transparent reporting. LCA models should always follow international ISO-14044 and ISO-14044 standards.

Pursuit of reliable, scientifically rigorous and analytical LCA results will empower designers, manufacturers, and consumers to make healthier decisions. A comprehensive LCA strives to evaluate an extensive list of impacts, including environmental toxins that compromise ecosystems, reduction of natural resources, freshwater stewardship, degradation of ecosystems and habitat destruction, social responsibility, and toxic chemicals affecting human health.

Companies must be clear about the goals of an LCA to successfully communicate the results relevant to their manufacturing processes. To be useful to consumers, LCAs must be standardized; ideally, the products being compared have been certified by the same third-party organization.

The best place to start is to "be" part of the change by asking manufacturers to provide transparent product information that accounts for their product's impact on people and the planet. The following certifications consider various LCA data in the development of their certification or standard.

Cradle to Cradle Certification http://www.c2ccertified.org

Developed by McDonough Braungart Design Chemistry (MBDC), Cradle to Cradle is a third-party certification that requires achievement across multiple attributes meeting government regulations: materials that are safe for human health and the environment through all use phases; product and system design for material reutilization; the use of renewable energy and carbon management; water stewardship, including efficient use of water and maximum water quality associated with production; and company strategies for social fairness. There are five levels of Cradle to Cradle certification: basic, bronze, silver, gold, and platinum. Textiles, flooring, furniture, building materials, household goods, and many other products can get certified.

Environmentally Preferred Product (EPP), SCS Certified http://www
.scsglobalservices.com/environmentally-preferable-product

EPP is a third-party certification for multi-attribute products based
on life-cycle assessments that have lower environmental impacts such as
resource depletion, land use ecology, greenhouse gas and black carbon
emissions, regional emissions, human health, and risks from untreated hazardous and radioactive wastes.

SCS Global Services is an internationally recognized third-party certifier
that employs a rigorous scientific review process. Their LCA standard is
currently undergoing a public, ANSI review.

Environmental Product Declaration (EPD) http://www.environdec.com/en/
What-is-an-EPD/#.Uc9X7L_7V0o

To meet the stringent requirements for an EPD, companies must first
fully reveal what is typically confidential information regarding how their
products are made. Next, they perform a comprehensive life-cycle assessment according to ISO 14040 and 14044 standards. The LCA information
is then used to develop an EPD based on ISO 14025 standards. Both the
EPD and the LCA then go through third-party verification to get certified
as quantified environmental data for a product with preset categories of
parameters. Communicating through an EPD ensures that the product's
impacts are relevant, verified, and provide comparable information within
product category rulings (PCRs). PCR categories identify the type of information released as well as the testing and calculation protocols for various
product sectors.

SMaRT Certified Products http://www.mts.sustainableproducts.com/
SMaRT_product_standard.html

A third-party certification and ANSI-accredited standard, this program
was developed by the Institute for Market Transformation to Sustainability
(MTX) for products with multiple attributes. The rating system has four
tiers and certifies a vast array of building products (claiming they apply to
80 percent of the world's products).

As a multi-attribute, third-party product certification, SMaRT includes
environmental, economic, and social criteria for building products, fabric,
textiles, and flooring. A SMaRT certification requires an ISO 14040 LCA
for all four tiers: sustainable, silver, gold, and platinum. The sustainable
and silver certifications are reviewed by a SMaRT consultant gold and platinum certification levels are audited by Ernst & Young Global Sustainability
Auditing Group.

SMaRT requires 28 points for the entry level of certification and 156
points, the maximum achievable, for platinum; 15 of those points come
from prerequisites. SMaRT covers all product stages, is ISO-compliant, and
incorporates over 40 single-attribute standards.

There are tools and calculators that enable you to perform a do-it-yourself assessment on products you're considering for a project. The following ones are free:

- The **Athena EcoCalculator** provides LCA results for hundreds of common building assemblies using a structured Excel spreadsheet workbook with worksheet tabs for various categories of structural assemblies (columns and beams, floors, etc.). http://www.athenasmi.org/our-software-data/ecocalculator/

- The Green Design Institute of Carnegie Mellon University created the **Economic Input-Output Life Cycle Assessment (EIO-LCA)**. This tool allows you to compare various environmental impacts, including greenhouse gases, toxicity, energy, and water use for a variety of products; the tool estimates the resources required and the environmental emissions. This website takes the EIO-LCA method and transforms it into a user-friendly online tool to quickly and easily evaluate a commodity or service as well as its supply chain. http://www.eiolca.net/

- openLCA is a professional Life Cycle Assessment (LCA) and Footprint software with a broad range of features and many available databases, created by GreenDelta. Their goal is to provide a well-designed, consistent, high-performance, modular framework for sustainability assessment and life-cycle modeling. http://www.openlca.org/

Carbon Footprint

In response to the uptick in dramatic weather events and changing climatic patterns, manufacturers have begun reexamining the greenhouse gas emissions their products generate, providing yet another lens through which we as designers should look at the products we consider specifying. Companies like Interface, the world's largest designer and maker of carpet tile, are striving for climate neutrality leading the marketplace with this third-party certification based on life-cycle assessment.

Climate Neutral Business Network (CNBN) http://www.climateneutral.com/index.html

CNBN offers a third-party certification toward measurable climate-neutral assessment that aims for net-zero greenhouse gas (GHG) emissions associated with a product's life cycle. Offsetting GHG emissions reduces a product's potential contribution to climate change. This model has been adopted by Interface.

CarbonFree http://www.carbonfund.org/

The National Sanitation Fund (NSF), driven by consumer demand for product information from environmentally minded companies, established its CarbonFree Product Certification to make available transparent, readily available reporting on the level of a product's carbon footprint. NSF's technical capabilities and third-party verification are a reliable source of this information and permit designers to choose products that help decrease carbon impacts, and offset lingering emissions.

Carbon Reduction Label http://carbonreductionlabel.com.au/

The UK Carbon Trust launched this program in 2007 to help companies reduce greenhouse gas emissions during the production of their products. Planet Ark partnered with the UK Carbon Trust to bring this label to Australia as well. There are many certified products, including food, household goods, appliances, and the Dyson Airblade hand dryer.

Compostable

For biodegradable products, look to a viable certification program that tests to ASTM standards D6400 for compostable plastics and D6868 for biodegradable plastics used as coatings on compostable substrates. Currently, available certifications and products are limited.

Biodegradable Products Institute (BPI) Certified Compostable Program http://www.bpiworld.org

BPI recognizes products that meet ASTM D6400 (for plastics) or ASTM D6868 (for fiber-based applications) and that will compost satisfactorily in commercial composting facilities. For a product to be certified, it must disintegrate quickly, with no residue; convert to carbon dioxide, water, and biomass; support plant growth; and not introduce high levels of metals into the soil. The products include food service items, packaging, and compostable resins.

Certifications and Standards by Category/Material Type

The following sustainable products have been organized into categories according to their CSI division to correspond with the other chapters in this book. Many of these certifications cover a wide span of products, so they have been listed under the categories that correspond most closely to their primary products or specializations.

GENERAL BUILDING AND HOUSEHOLD PRODUCTS

U.S. Department of Agriculture (USDA) BioPreferred Program http://www .biopreferred.gov/Labeling.aspx

A government labeling program created by the USDA promotes the purchase and use of bio-based products. Based on the BioPreferred program created by the 2002 U.S. Farm Bill, its aim is to increase the purchase and use of bio-based products in an effort to reduce petroleum consumption and carbon footprint and increase the use of renewable resources.

The Food Conservation and Energy Act of 2008 built upon the existing preferred purchasing program and resanctioned this voluntary labeling program for consumer bio-based products. The USDA's "bio-preferred" designation applies to diverse product categories, from multipurpose cleaners to fibers and fabrics to millwork and flooring.

Canadian Standard Association Group Sustainability Mark http://www.csagroup.org/us/en/about-csa-group/certification-marks-labels/sustainability-marks

The Canadian Standard Association, or CSA Group, is an international standards development and testing certification organization. Its sustainability mark designates that a product has been evaluated according to the following: presence of toxic materials, energy consumption, manufacturing processes, product performance, and end of life cycle. The testing applies to electrical and electronic products, gas-fired products, plumbing products, personal protective equipment, and a variety of other products.

Design for the Environment (DfE) Safer Product Labeling Program http://www.epa.gov/dfe/

The DfE advances the EPA's mission to protect human health and the environment. The program uses the EPA's resources and knowledge of chemicals to label products that are safer for people and the planet without any compromise in quality or performance. Design for the Environment labels a variety of chemical-based products, from all-purpose cleaners and laundry detergents to carpet and floor-care products.

EcoLogo http://www.ecologo.org/

The EcoLogo Program is a type 1 eco-label as defined by ISO 14024. Companies comply with specific criteria that compare products and services with others in the same category. The rigorous and scientifically relevant criteria address the entire product life cycle. EcoLogo is third-party certified by Underwriters Laboratory, for which an extensive variety of sustainable products meet stringent environmental standards.

European Union EcoLabel http://ec.europa.eu/environment/ecolabel/

This label, created by the European Union (EU), is administered by each member state who is required to designate a Competent Body to administer the type I certification. EU EcoLabel covers a wide range of products, including finishes, furnishings, household goods, and building materials.

Green Seal http://www.greenseal.org/

Green Seal is an independent, nonprofit that substantiates manufacturers' claims. Its certification covers multiple attributes and targets tangible reductions in the environmental footprint in compliance with ISO type 1 (14024). Its list of certified products ranges from household goods to food packaging to construction materials.

Greener Product Certification Seal www.greenerproduct.com/default.aspx

The Greener Product Certification Seal demonstrates that a product has been vetted and complies with LEED for Homes and National Association of Home Builders' (NAHB) green building standards. Building products are evaluated utilizing environmental qualifiers specific to energy conservation and renewables, regionally produced materials, air quality, certified wood, recycled content, and reused and renewable materials. Environmental claims are reviewed and verified through third-party certification and/or supporting documentation stating that products comply with LEED-H rating systems and NAHB building standards.

National Sanitation Foundation (NSF) International http://nsf.org/

Since 1944, the NSF has protected consumers through the certification of products and by writing standards for food, water, and consumer goods. It is an independent nonprofit organization committed to public health, safety, and welfare as well as the environment. It provides standards development, product certification, verification, education, and risk management. The products it certifies include food safety products, resilient flooring, carpet, wall coverings, home products, appliances, toiletries, and plumbing materials.

Underwriters Laboratory Environment http://www.ul.com/global/eng/pages/offerings/businesses/environment/index.jsp

UL Environment supports the growth and development of sustainable products, services, and organizations worldwide through standards development, educational services, and independent third-party assessment and certification. It provides specific environmental services, including environmental claims validation, sustainable products certification, energy-efficiency certification, environmental product declarations, and advisory services. It also hosts a database available for researching sustainable products and verifying UL Environment certification claims.

It also verifies compliance of environmental product declarations with ISO 14024 and aggregate life cycle assessment data into a comprehensive package. As a program operator, UL Environment also helps develop product category rules (PCRs).

It is a third-party certifier for a variety of green product certifications; two of its most recognized programs include EcoLogo and Greenguard.

CONCRETE, MASONRY, AND METALS

Other than multi-attribute criteria, there are no applicable environmental, social, or health standards or certifications specific to concrete, masonry, and metals.

WOOD AND COMPOSITES

There are a variety of wood programs in place to guide your research and selection process of wood and composites.

American Tree Farm System (ATFS) http://www.treefarmsystem.org

The ATFS certifies the operations and forestry of small, family-owned forests in the United States. It is recognized by the Programme for the Endorsement of Forest Certification (PEFC) and the Sustainable Forestry Initiative (SFI) as suppliers of forest products.

California Air Resource Board Airborne Toxic Control Measure http://www .arb.ca.gov/toxics/compwood/compwood.htm

CARB released its Airborne Toxic Control Measure (ATCM) to reduce formaldehyde emissions from composite wood products: hardwood, plywood, particleboard, and medium density fiberboard, or MDF. Products that meet its standard are known as "California 93120 compliant." California continues to be the industry leader in regulations that protect the environment, and ATCM's phase 2 emission limits are becoming the norm for composite woods. The regulation limits formaldehyde emissions for plywood to .05 parts per million.

If a manufacturer of hardwood plywood, particleboard, and medium density fiberboard uses no-added formaldehyde (NAF) based resins or ultra-low-emitting formaldehyde (ULEF) resins, it is exempted from some of the testing requirements, when regularly below applicable phase 2 emission standards.

Canada Standards Association CAN/CSA-Z809–02 Sustainable Forest Standard   http://www.csagroup.org/documents/testing-and-certification/ product_areas/forest_products_marking/CAN_CSA_Z809–02O_English.pdf

This Canadian national standard sets the criteria for sustainable forest management. It is endorsed by both government and industry as a third-party certification, although it is not as stringent as that of the Forest Stewardship Council (see below).

Eco-Certified Composite Sustainability Standard http://www.decorative surfaces.org/cpa-green/go-ecc-green.html

The Composite Panel Association (CPA) developed a standard for green composite wood panel products. The certification takes life cycle aspects into consideration, including carbon footprint, recycled content, renewable resources, sustainably sourced wood, and low-emissions. Their ECC certified products must comply with the California Air Resources Board (CARB) formaldehyde emissions regulation.

Forest Stewardship Council (FSC) http://www.fsc.org/

FSC sets the bar when it comes to third-party certification for environmentally and socially responsible forestry practices and their related wood products. Established in 1993, FSC is one of the most well-known and

respected certifications due to its rigor and promotion of environmentally appropriate, socially beneficial, and economically viable management of the world's forests.

They offer two types of certifications. The first is FSC Certification for Forest Management, which recognizes vigilant, long-term forest management. Certification is voluntary. It involves an inspection of the forest management by an independent organization to ensure that it passes the internationally agreed upon FSC principles and criteria of good forest management. The second is Chain-of-Custody, which applies to manufacturers of FSC-certified forest products. To put the FSC logo on products made with materials from an FSC-certified forest, a forest manager must achieve FSC chain-of-custody certification. The FSC label shows that it comes from a well-managed forest and enables you to pass along the benefits of that certification to your customers. FSC Forest Management certification is verified annually by independent auditors, and producers maintain FSC Chain of Custody certification.

The Programme for the Endorsement of Forest Certification (PEFC) http://www.pefc.org

The PEFC system is an international nonprofit program that promotes sustainable forest management (SFM) through independent third-party certification. The certification takes the entire forest supply chain into account, ensuring that at all stages it upholds forest stewardship and that timber and other forest products are produced ecologically and ethically. As an umbrella organization, PEFC endorses national forest certifications from Sustainable Forestry Initiative (SFI) to the American Tree Farm System.

Rainforest Alliance http://www.rainforest-alliance.org/certification-verification

The Rainforest Alliance works to conserve biodiversity and improve the livelihoods of communities by promoting and evaluating the implementation of sustainability standards. Through RA-Cert, the Rainforest Alliance's auditing division, it provides forestry, agriculture, and carbon/climate clients with independent and transparent verification, validation, and certification services based on these standards, which are designed to generate ecological, social, and economic benefits.

When a forestry operation meets certification or verification standards, it earns the right to display the appropriate mark of the FSC logo coupled with the Rainforest Alliance Certified seal on products and packaging. This confirms rigorous standards for protecting forestlands, communities, and wildlife have been met.

SCS Legal Harvest Verification http://www.scsglobalservices.com

This program provides third-party verification of forest products for forest managers, sawmills, pulp mills, manufacturers, distributors, and retailers, ensuring that the wood is from legal and non-endangered sources.

Sustainable Forestry Initiative (SFI) http://www.sfiprogram.org

SFI is a third-party forestry certification system with significant ties to the forestry industry. SFI certification includes chain-of-custody certificates for forests, paper products, and wood products. SFI is a viable alternative for certified domestic woods if FSC certification is not attainable. Product labeling includes three SFI chain-of-custody labels and one SFI-certified sourcing label. The usage of SFI labels and claims funnels directly through SFI requirements to ensure quality and metrics control.

OPENINGS: DOORS AND WINDOWS

American Architectural Manufacturers Association (AAMA) Gold Label http://www.aamanet.org/

As a second-party certification, AAMA applies to windows, doors, and skylights. Products are specifically tested for resistance to air leakage, water penetration, and wind pressure; the certification focuses on performance and quality.

Green Seal Standard GS-13 Windows http://www.greenseal.org/Green Business/Standards.aspx?vid=ViewStandardDetail&cid=1&sid=5

Green Seal has many sustainability standards that correspond to the Green Seal Certification Program. This standard applies specifically to windows, skylights, glazed exterior doors, and storm doors. The standard evaluates performance, environmental, and health requirements, including energy efficiency, reduced toxicity, and reduced packaging.

National Fenestration Rating Council Label http://www.nfrc.org/WindowRatings/

This third-party certification is ISO type 2 and assesses the thermal performance of windows as well as wind resistance and condensation.

FINISHES

Floorscore Indoor Air Quality Certification www.rfci.com

A third-party certification addressing emissions for resilient and hard-surface flooring and adhesives. The Resilient Floor Covering Institute (RFCI) and Scientific Certification Systems (SCS) created this flooring certification program specifically to address emissions, IAQ, and VOCs. The products certified meet California Section 01350 standards emissions criteria. These products are recognized by many green building rating systems, including LEED for Homes.

Carpet and Rug Institute (CRI) Green Label http://www.carpet-rug.org/commercial-customers/green-building-and-the-environment/green-label-plus/

A second-party certification from the Carpet and Rug Institute (CRI). CRI Green Label is for carpet cushioning and CRI Green Label Plus for carpet and adhesives with low-VOC emissions. Certified products adhere to the California Section 01350 standard emissions criteria. Adhering to this third-party emissions testing lends credibility to CRI's programs even though they have not been certified by a third-party organization.

Green Squared, SCS Certified http://greensquaredcertified.com/

The first multi-attribute standard developed for tiles and tile installation materials, Green Squared uses the transparency and consensus of the ANSI process and provides a third-party certification from several organizations. This validation covers product characteristics, manufacturing, end of product life management, progressive corporate governance, and innovation in an effort to establish sustainability criteria for products throughout their entire life cycle. This tile certification was established by the Tile Council of North America (TCNA) and includes ceramic and glass tiles plus a wide range of tile installation materials. Database search for certified products is available through approved Green Squared certification bodies that currently include NSF, SCS Global, and UL Environment.

Green Seal GS-11 Paints and Coatings http://www.greenseal.org/Green Business/Standards.aspx?vid=StandardCategory&cid=1

GS-11 establishes requirements for environmental and health standards and product performance for paints and coatings, including wall, anti-corrosive, and reflective coatings; floor paints and primers; and undercoats. It addresses the reduction of hazardous substances and requires low-VOC content.

This standard does not pertain to stains, clear finishes, recycled (consolidated or reprocessed) latex paint, specialty (industrial, marine, or automotive) coatings, or paint sold in aerosol cans.

Green Seal GS-36 Commercial Adhesives http://www.greenseal.org/GreenBusiness/Standards.aspx?vid=ViewStandardDetail&cid=0&sid=22

GS-36 establishes environmental, health, and performance standards for commercial adhesives applied onto substrates and aerosol adhesives. It addresses reduction of toxicity, hazardous ingredients, and VOC content.

Green Seal GS-43 Recycled Content Latex Paint http://www.greenseal.org/GreenBusiness/Standards.aspx?vid=StandardCategory&cid=1

GS-43 institutes environmental requirements for recycled-content consolidated and reprocessed interior and exterior latex paint. The standard includes product performance requirements and environmental and health requirements such as reduced toxicity and recycled postconsumer content.

Green Seal GS-47 Stains and Finishes http://www.greenseal.org/GreenBusiness/Standards.aspx?vid=StandardCategory&cid=1

GS-47 requirements pertain to stains and finishes intended for products generally applied to metal and wood substrates. It includes sealers but not paints, floor polishes, specialty (industrial, marine, or automotive) coatings, or products sold in aerosol cans. The primary focus is on stains and finishes used with water-borne, solvent-borne, semitransparent, or opaque stains, varnishes, shellacs, water-based finishes, polyurethane, lacquer, oil finishes, and clear metal lacquers. The standard includes product performance and environmental and health requirements with the aim of reducing hazardous substances and requirements for low-VOC content.

Greenwise Paint http://www.greenwisepaint.com

Coatings and paints with the "Greenwise" paint label are second-party certified and have been tested by the Coatings Research Group. The information is proprietary and only available to members. It strives to meet South Coast Air Quality Management District (SCAQMD) VOC emissions limits for interior and exterior paint as well as for wood and other surface coatings.

Master Painter's Institute Extreme Green http://www.specifygreen.com/

This is a third-party standard for paint that requires durability, low-emissions, and the typical 50 grams per liter or less of VOC contents. Look for products that meet the more rigorous Extreme(X)-Green certification, which demonstrates third-party testing for VOC content and emissions. The X-Green standard meets requirements for California Section 01350 standard emissions criteria, rigorous third-party chamber tests for VOCs, formaldehyde, and other chemicals of concern.

NSF/ANSI 140 Sustainability Assessment for Carpet http://www.nsf.org/ business/sustainability/product_carpet.asp?program=Sustainability

Sustainability-certified multi-attribute, third-party certifications for carpet with established performance requirements and quantifiable metrics throughout the supply chain. Protocols cover or address public health and environment; energy and energy efficiency; biobased, recycled content materials; environmentally preferable materials; manufacturing; and reclamation and end-of-life management.

NSF/ANSI 332 Sustainability Assessment for Resilient Floor Coverings http://www.nsf.org/business/sustainability/product_flooring.asp? program=Sustainability

A multi-attribute framework with third-party certification for evaluating and certifying the sustainability of resilient flooring products across their entire product life cycle. NSF/ANSI 332 employs a point system to evaluate resilient flooring against established prerequisite requirements, performance criteria, and quantifiable metrics in the areas of product design, product manufacturing, long-term value, end-of-life management, corporate governance, and innovation. Certification is based on point totals to achieve a conformant, silver, gold, or platinum level.

NSF/ANSI 342 Sustainability Assessment for Wall Covering Products http://www.nsf.org/business/sustainability/product_wallcovering.asp?program=Sustainability

A multi-attribute, third-party certification, this standard evaluates the sustainability of wall-coverings across their entire product life cycle. Based on life-cycle assessment principles, NSF/ANSI 342 employs a point system to evaluate wall coverings against established requirements, performance criteria and quantifiable metrics in the areas of product design, product manufacturing, long-term value, end-of-life management, corporate governance, and innovation.

SCAQMD 1113 Standard www.aqmd.gov

This is a government standard from the SCAQMD that addresses smog VOC emissions from interior and exterior architectural coatings, including roof coatings, concrete sealers, and aerosol coatings. It is a strict standard, but it is important to confirm that the product contents are compliant as well. Search out "supercompliant" paints, some with less than 10 grams per liter of VOC content. There is a listing of compliant products on SCAQMD's website.

SCAQMD 1168 Standard www.aqmd.gov

The purpose of this government standard is to reduce emissions of VOCs and eliminate emissions of chloroform, ethylene dichloride, methylene chloride, perchloroethylene, and trichloroethylene from the application of commercial and industrial adhesives, adhesive bonding primers, adhesive primers, sealants, sealant primers, and all other primers unless otherwise specifically exempted by this rule. There is a listing of compliant products on SCAQMD's website.

SCS Sustainable Carpet http://www.scsglobalservices.com/sustainable-carpet-certification

A multi-attribute, third-party certified carpet program that meets measurable environmental performance and social responsibility criteria. The certification is based on NSF/ANSI 140 Sustainable Carpet Assessment Standard Qualification for the SCS Certified mark. Assessment of product conformance includes the following criteria categories: manufacturing processes; reclamation and end-of-life management; energy usage and energy efficiency, use of bio-based, recycled, or environmentally preferable materials; and steps to minimize adverse public health, environmental, and community impacts. Products can achieve one of three levels of certification, depending on the number of points achieved. Silver is an entry-level certification tier, gold is a middle-tier certification, and platinum indicates the highest level of performance.

UL 100 Standard for Sustainability for Gypsum Boards and Panels http:// www.ul.com/global/eng/pages/solutions/standards/accessstandards/ catalogofstandards/standard/?id=100_1

This consensus standard establishes multi-attribute sustainability requirements for gypsum board and panel products for a third-party certification. The criteria are based on the life-cycle stages of gypsum boards and panels. Sustainability factors considered include materials, energy, manufacturing and operations, health and environment, product performance, and product stewardship.

SPECIALTIES

At this time there are no applicable environmental, social, or health standards, certifications, or claims specific to specialties.

EQUIPMENT/APPLIANCES

Energy Star http://www.energystar.gov/

Energy Star is a voluntary government program developed by the U.S. Environmental Protection Agency (EPA) and the U.S. Department of Energy. The Energy Star mark is the national symbol for energy efficiency, making it easy for consumers and businesses to identify high-quality, energy-efficient products, homes, and commercial and industrial buildings. Energy Star addresses energy efficiencies without sacrificing features or performance. Products that earn the Energy Star mark prevent greenhouse gas emissions by meeting strict energy-efficiency guidelines set by the EPA.

EnerGuide http://oee.nrcan.gc.ca/equipment/appliance/1799?attr=4#household

This program was created by the Canadian government to educate consumers about their appliance and equipment purchases. The EnerGuide labels indicate how much energy appliances consume in a year of normal service and make it possible to compare the energy efficiency from one model to another of the same size and class. All new major appliances sold in Canada are now required to have the EnerGuide label designating that the appliance meets Canada's minimum energy performance levels.

Hazardous Substance–Free Mark http://www.hsf.us/

This label assures consumers that the products they are buying do not contain unsafe components and materials that could harm their families. The mark applies to appliances, equipment, and lighting and addresses toxic ingredients that pose health risks. The seven main substances to avoid when purchasing products include lead, cadmium, mercury, polybrominated biphenyl (PBB), polybrominated diphenyl ether (PBDE), hexavalent chromium, and phthalates. Companies that comply with industry standards and are validated by ongoing third-party testing are licensed to use the HSF mark or logo for demonstrating leadership in corporate social and environmental stewardship.

MECHANICAL/PLUMBING

WaterSense http://www.epa.gov/watersense

The WaterSense program allows consumers to choose products that use less water without sacrificing quality or performance. WaterSense is a government-sponsored labeling program based on third-party testing for water-efficient products. Products that can achieve the WaterSense mark include showerheads, toilets, faucets, urinal fixtures, valves, and irrigation professionals. At a minimum, WaterSense products are generally 20 percent more water-efficient than similar products and are independently certified before qualifying for the label.

International Association of Plumbing and Mechanical Officials Research and Testing Green Mark of Conformity www.iapmort.org

IAPMO R&T is a plumbing and mechanical product certification agency. It provides certification for Energy Star, WaterSense, and solar products. IAPMO R&T has its own sustainability label called the "mark of conformity" to designate a sustainable product it has certified.

Since the program's inception, IAPMO R&T has been an approved certification body for the U.S. EPA's WaterSense program, working with manufacturers to certify their products' compliance with the efficiency standards. IAPMO R&T was also among the first certification bodies to be ANSI-accredited as an EPA WaterSense third-party certification body. ANSI accreditation adds value to the certification process, ensuring that certification bodies demonstrate compliance with the WaterSense product certification system and are capable and competent to carry out their responsibilities.

ELECTRICAL/LIGHTING

Electronic Product Environmental Assessment Tool (EPEAT) http://www.epeat.net/

EPEAT is a system that helps purchasers evaluate, compare and select electronic products based on their environmental attributes. EPEAT-registered electronic products meet environmental criteria are based on ANSI-approved public standards that provide technical details for every criterion and specify how a manufacturer must demonstrate compliance.

Desktops, laptops, and monitors that meet 23 required environmental performance criteria may be registered in EPEAT by manufacturers in 40 countries. Registered products are rated gold, silver, or bronze depending on the percentage of 28 optional criteria they meet beyond the 23 baseline criteria. Products meeting 50 percent or more receive a silver rating; those meeting 75 percent or higher receive gold.

EPEAT operates an ongoing verification program to ensure the registry's credibility. Products in the EPEAT registry are subject to unannounced audits, the results of which are publicly reported to ensure that all environmental claims are accurate.

Green Seal Standard GS-05 Compact Fluorescent Lamps (CFLs) http://www.greenseal.org/GreenBusiness/Standards.aspx?vid=StandardCategory&cid=1

Green Seal has many sustainability standards that correspond to the Green Seal Certification Program. This standard applies specifically to energy-efficient lighting and product performance and includes lamps used for general illumination purposes, special purposes, screw-based and pin-based lamps, and lamps with both integrated and nonintegrated ballasts.

International Dark Sky Association Dark-Sky-Friendly Fixture Seal of Approval http://www.darksky.org/outdoorlighting/about-fsa

This is a third-party certification for addressing light pollution that aims to minimize glare and reduce light levels in the night sky. The seal of approval provides third-party certification for luminaires that minimize glare, and reduce light trespass and other forms of light pollution.

Restriction of Hazardous Substances (RoHS) Standard http://www.rohscompliancedefinition.com

This standard is compliant with the European Union's RoHS Directive, which prevents the usage of hazardous materials in electronics. The directive restricts certain dangerous substances commonly used in electronic and electronic equipment. Any RoHS-compliant component is tested for the presence of lead, cadmium, mercury, hexavalent chromium, PBBs, and PBDEs.

FURNISHINGS

Business and Institutional Furniture Manufacturers Association (BIFMA) Level Sustainability Certification http://www.levelcertified.org/

SCS Global Services is the independent third-party certifier for the Level sustainability furniture certification program, which identifies products that have been evaluated to the multi-attribute ANSI/BIFMA e3 Furniture Sustainability Standard via three conformance thresholds or "levels."

Level delivers an open and holistic way of evaluating and communicating the environmental and social impacts of furniture products in the built environment. The program addresses a company's social actions, energy usage, material selection, and human and ecosystem health impacts. The program focuses on commercial furniture including case goods, seating, storage, systems furniture, tables, and work surfaces.

Global Organic Textile Standard (GOTS) http://www.global-standard.org/

GOTS aims to unify various existing standards for eco-textile processing and define requirements that ensure the organic status of textiles. GOTS standard specifically applies to organic textiles, ensuring that the certified products have a minimum of 70 percent organic fibers and that the material's organic status is validated from harvesting to manufacturing and then on to labeling.

Kitchen Cabinet Manufacturers Association (KCMA) Environmental Stewardship Program http://www.greencabinetsource.org

A second-party certification for cabinet labeling indicating that manufacturers meet its program requirements. Companies are rated on air quality, product and process resource management, environmental stewardship, and community relations. The program requires that 100 percent of the particleboard, medium density fiberboard, and plywood used in the cabinets meet the formaldehyde emission level of the CARB ATCM and must be third-party certified to meet low-formaldehyde emission standards and a written policy stating a firm commitment to environmental quality. ESP participants agree to report to KCMA within sixty days of any local, state, or federal citation in excess of $50,000 per violation to explain the circumstances surrounding the citation or violation; such a violation can potentially lead to termination from the program.

OEKO-TEX Standards 1000, 100, and 100plus https://www.oeko-tex.com

Oeko-Tex Standard 1000 is a testing, auditing, and certification system for environmentally friendly production sites throughout the textile processing chain. To qualify for certification for the Oeko-Tex Standard 1000, companies must meet environmentally friendly manufacturing processes criteria and provide evidence that at least 30 percent of total production is already certified under Oeko-Tex Standard 100. In addition, companies must prove that the social standards demanded by Oeko-Tex 1000 are fulfilled.

Certification criteria prohibit the use of environmentally damaging chemicals, auxiliaries, and dyestuffs and require compliance with standard values for wastewater and exhaust air, the optimization of energy consumption. Certified companies must avoid noise and dust pollution to ensure workplace safety. The use of child labor is prohibited. Manufacturers must also have basic environmental management and quality management systems in place.

Oeko-Tex Standard 100 is a globally uniform testing and certification system for textile raw materials, intermediate, and end products. The certification covers multiple human and ecological attributes, including the prohibition of harmful substances sanctioned or regulated by law and chemicals known to be harmful to health but are not officially forbidden as well as adherence to precautionary parameters. Textile products may be certified according to Oeko-Tex Standard 100 only if all components meet the required criteria. A tested textile product is allocated to one of the four Oeko-Tex product classes based on its intended use. The more intensively a product comes into contact with the skin, the stricter the human ecological requirements it must fulfill.

Oeko-Tex Standard 100plus is a product label that allows textile and clothing manufacturers to highlight the ways their products function to support human health and the environment. This standard certifies manufactured, domestic, and household textiles to ensure they do not contain harmful substances and chemicals that could off-gas. The closer a product comes in contact with children or human skin, the more stringent the testing.

The certification is awarded to manufacturers whose products have been successfully certified according to Oeko-Tex Standard 100 and also comply with the requirmenets of Oeko-Tex Standard 1000 throughout their production chain. Certain social standards set by Oeko-Tex Standard 1000 must also be met.

Scientific Certification Systems (SCS) Indoor Advantage http://www .scsglobalservices.com/certified-indoor-air-quality?scscertified=1

SCS is a third-party sustainability certifier offering Indoor Advantage and Indoor Advantage Gold for the certification of office furniture, paints and coatings, adhesives and sealants, insulation, wall coverings, furnishings, and other interior products.

SCS Indoor Advantage certifications demonstrate that products meet indoor air quality standards pertaining to emissions that may be harmful to human health and the environment.

Indoor Advantage Gold standards are more rigorous and comply with California Section 01350 standard emissions criteria.

TRANSPARENCY HORIZON

Corporations have begun standardizing their reporting for environmental, social, and health impacts, and building product manufacturers are working with life-cycle assessment tools to invent techniques that provide comprehensive, streamlined information for both the industry and consumers.

Currently, environmental product declarations (EPDs) and health product declarations (HPDs) offer some degree of transparency. As an industry, we need to encourage manufacturers to further provide user-friendly reporting for EPDs and HPDs comprised of consistent, manageable, reliable, and comparable product information.

Environmental Product Declaration http://www.environdec.com/en/What-is-an-EPD/#.Uc9X7L_7V0o

To meet the rigorous requirements for an EPD, companies must first fully reveal what is typically confidential information about how their products are made. Next, they perform a comprehensive life-cycle assessment according to ISO 14040 and 14044 standards. The life-cycle assessment information is then used to develop an EPD based on ISO 14025 standards. Both the EPD and the LCA then go through third-party verification to become certified as quantified environmental data for a product with preset categories of parameters. Communicating through an EPD ensures that the product's impacts are relevant, verified, and provide comparable information within product category rulings (PCRs). New categories continue to emerge to identify the type of information released as well as testing and calculation protocols based on various product sectors.

LCAs typically focus on data pertaining to environmental impacts, only sporadically addressing social, human health, and ecological concerns.

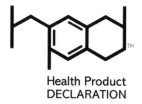

Health Product
DECLARATION

Health Product Declaration http://www.hpdcollaborative.org

The Health Product Declaration Collaborative is a customer-led organization for companies and individuals committed to the continuous improvement of the building industry's environmental and health performance through transparency and innovation in the building product supply chain.

The Health Product Declaration Open Standard is a format that systematizes reporting language to enable transparent disclosure of information regarding building product content and associated health information by defining the critical information needed by building designers, specifiers, owners, and users. The pilot version of the program was released in 2012 by a collaborative of design, construction, and building management firms.

The HPD Collaborative's aim is to provide product ingredient details that reveal the health implications of potentially hazardous chemicals and compounds. The platform assessing the health implications of products is the Pharos Project. It offers a product and chemical database and campaigns for transparency in the building materials market. The Pharos platform demonstrates to manufacturers the existence of a market for products manufactured according to the best environmental, health, and social equity practices. Pharos assesses a product's holistic health impacts, including ingredient-detailed examination of VOCs, toxic content, manufacturing toxins, renewable materials, and renewable energy. The detailed reporting options from Pharos include the following filters: manufacturer's level of participation in providing full-disclosure on ingredients and chemicals; restricted substance lists from EPA chemicals of concern, the Living Building Challenge's Red List, and LEED v4; and chemical attributes including bisphenol-A, formaldehyde, phthalates, halongenated flame retardants, perfluorocarbons, antimicrobials, and nanotech materials.

2030 Challenge for Products http://architecture2030.org/2030_challenge/products

Buildings are the major source of demand for energy and materials that produce by-product greenhouse gases (GHG). The raw resource extraction, manufacturing, transportation, construction, usage, and end-of-life stages of building products all generate significant GHG emissions. Slowing the growth rate of GHG emissions, and then reversing, is the key to addressing climate change and keeping global average temperature below 2°C above preindustrial levels.

To accomplish this, Architecture 2030 issued the 2030 Challenge for Products, asking the global architecture, planning, design, and building communities to adopt these two targets:

1. Products for new buildings, developments, and renovations shall immediately be specified to meet a maximum carbon-equivalent footprint of 30 percent below the product category average.

2. The embodied carbon-equivalent footprint reduction shall be increased incrementally from 35 percent or better in 2015 to 50 percent or better in 2030.

The industry requires the tools and resources necessary establishing LCA baselines for a product's environmental, social, and health impacts. EPDs, HPDs and other product assessments, like the 2030 Challenge for Products are the result of our demands of manufacturers for full disclosure and transparency of their products' ingredients. Our efforts as a community will help shape the health and environmental implications of future generations.

Resources

Building Green, Inc.: *Green Building Product Certifications: Getting What You Need*. 2011. "Toxic Chemicals Lurk in Unfinished Wood Floors." Blog, April 2012.

"The Sins of Greenwashing: Home and Family Edition, 2010." TerraChoice. http://sinsofgreenwashing.org/index35c6.pdf, UL Environment.

Guide to Eco-Labels. ASID. Washington, DC, 2011. http://www.asid.org/content/asid-guide-ecolabels

LCA for Mere Mortals: A Primer on Environmental Life Cycle Assessment. Rita C. Schenck. Institute for Environmental Research and Education, 2000

"The Product Transparency Movement: Peeking Behind the Corporate Veil." *Environmental Building News* 21, no. 1 (January 2012).

Sustainable Design: A Critical Guide. David Bergman. New York: Princeton Architectural Press, 2012.

concrete

Figure 9.1 A graceful, locally manufactured concrete countertop and concrete slab stained floor. The photo also captures recycled steel bar framework and cabinet, LED lights, and zero-VOC paints.

Design: Annette Stelmack, www.associates3.com. Photo by David O. Marlow.

When it comes to building products, reducing the carbon footprint from concrete is one of the most significant actions that the building sector can take.
—Ed Mazria, Architecture 2030, quoted in Setting Carbon Footprint Rules for Concrete, EBN, Nov 1, 2012

Concrete, in its simplest form, has been around since ancient civilizations first combined lime, chalk, oyster shells, and gypsum to make a substance that hardened and formed a permanent bond. The Romans developed a type of concrete made from ground volcanic rock, lime, and aggregates called *pozzolana*; the Greek Parthenon, one of many structures built with that material, still stands today. We began using Portland cement in this country in the 1800s (see the sidebar, "Cement or Concrete?"). Modern-day concrete is the most widely used building material—with a carbon footprint to match. Notably, world cement production now contributes 5 percent of annual global CO_2 production.

Concrete's superior longevity and indestructibility give it an eco-advantage over shorter-lifespan treatments for walls, floors, fireplaces, and countertops. It's also thrifty: New homes already feature a concrete slab floor, so by using the concrete structure as the visible finish, the need for carpet, wood, or linoleum on top of a subfloor is eliminated. The client will never need to replace the floor covering (since there is none), further improving its ecological value.

Even though concrete is manufactured, the material has rocklike properties: It doesn't off-gas, rust, mold, rot, or otherwise wear out. It has inherent thermal mass; light-colored concrete is naturally cool and perfect for hot climates, and darker colors collect passive solar or radiant heat well in cold-weather locations. A home with a high structural concrete content may actually allow for lesser-capacity heating and cooling equipment. Concrete may be poured and molded to fit almost any specification. It can be recycled indefinitely into more concrete by crushing it into aggregate.

Cement or Concrete?

Although the two words are often used interchangeably, technically, cement and concrete are not the same substance. Joseph Aspdin invented Portland cement in 1824, when he ground up a mixture of limestone and clay, then cooked it on his stove. Cement is just one ingredient in concrete. Concrete, on the other hand, is made up of four basic elements: sand, gravel, cement, and water.

And cement's connection to Portland? It's neither from Maine nor Oregon. Rather, Aspdin named his creation for its resemblance, when set, to limestone found on the tiny isle of Portland in the English Channel. Portland is now the most common type of cement, and there are many others made of widely varying mineral and synthetic components.

Basic concrete is nondescript, although mineral pigments, stains, texture treatments, and polishing make it shine. Concrete is also an excellent matrix for aggregates like recycled glass, forming a beautiful, terrazzo-like finish for floors and countertops. By incorporating a high percentage of recycled materials, concrete's environmental value increases. And when postindustrial waste replaces some of the aggregate or cement in concrete, the result is increased product strength and conservation of raw materials (see the sidebar, "Recipe: Recycled").

Although it has many positive environmental attributes, concrete is made primarily of nonrenewable resources. Aggregates such as sand and gravel make up 60 to 80 percent of the mixture. Portland cement, a mix of calcium (lime) and silicon (silica), along with aluminum, iron, and gypsum, comprise 10 to 15 percent of the mixture, which is the complex key ingredient that holds concrete together. To obtain the minerals to make Portland cement, a variety of sources are mined, including limestone, chalk, seashells, marl (loose, earthy deposits), shale, clay, slate, and silica sand. The collective minerals and by-products are then ground and fired at extremely high temperatures, so the resulting embodied energy is very high.

Other ingredients, especially postindustrial waste, may figure prominently in the mix. While many postindustrial compounds are quite safe, there has been concern about the risk of contaminants from fly ash, which contains trace amounts of heavy metals including arsenic, cadmium, chromium, mercury, and selenium plus compounds from hydrocarbons, sulfur, and other toxins. Preliminary testing by various organizations indicates that leaching of heavy-metal contaminants from fly ash is minimal, with trace amounts ranging from 1 to 3 percent.

If you are working with chemically sensitive clients, take the precautionary route and avoid concrete ingredients that may be toxic. That said, general consensus is that the toxins from postindustrial additives are minuscule, bound up in the concrete, and unlikely to leach or outgas once the concrete hardens. The verdict about relative safety is still out, but using fly ash and other recycled materials in concrete greatly reduces both the amount of waste going to landfills and the need for energy-intensive cement (see the sidebar, "Recipe: Recycled"). Admixtures—chemical "enhancements" that may slow the dry time or improve the flow, bond, finish, or look—are also common in concrete mixes. They are more important when building or designing outdoor applications, where the elements are harsher and greatly affect proper curing and the life span of concrete. For interiors, admixtures are rarely needed if optimal temperatures and conditions for pouring and curing are specified.

Cement production takes a heavy toll on the environment. High CO_2 emissions—5 to 10 percent of the U.S. total—are generated at these plants. Concrete production also requires large amounts of water, and the wastewater from the process is highly alkaline, posing a serious problem for disposal or neutralization. Cement dust exposure puts workers at a high risk for silicosis, an occupational lung disease. Add these factors to the embodied energy in concrete from the mining, transport to factory, firing, transport to retailer, then transport again to the site, and the strikes against concrete are numerous.

Concrete, however, pays off some of its environmental debts by virtue of its durability, longevity, and low maintenance. It will outlast some interior finishes by two to three times or even more. And if the client has chemical sensitivities, concrete (as long as it contains no questionable aggregates or admixtures) offers an inert, easy-to-keep-clean surface that will not become a sink for allergens and irritants.

Concrete is a relatively permanent interior design element, although a concrete floor or countertop can be easily covered with another finish. Weigh pros and cons carefully with the client. All in all, concrete offers longevity that is hard to beat—albeit at an environmental price.

Recipe: Recycled

Scientists and manufacturers have found that a variety of by-products otherwise headed for the landfill may be incorporated into concrete. The practice reduces waste, and the addition of some recycled content actually enhances the strength, plasticity, and imperviousness of concrete. Also, the percentage of cement needed in the concrete may be reduced significantly if fly ash, silica fume, blast furnace slag, or rice husk slag is added. The following are common postindustrial ingredients used in concrete.

- *Blast furnace slag* is the residual left over from the manufacturing of pig iron or other metal ores.
- *Cement kiln dust (CKD)* is collected from cement firing, then reused as raw material.
- *Fly ash* is a by-product of coal-fired power plants containing trace amounts of heavy metals including arsenic, cadmium, chromium, mercury, and selenium. The compounds in fly ash are shaped by the chemical composition of the coal that was burned. It strengthens concrete, decreases absorbency, and uses less water in production.
- *Foundry sand* is a by-product from metal casting.
- *Lime sludge* is generated when recycling paper. This paper sludge behaves like cement because of the silica and magnesium properties.
- *Rice hull ash* is left over from rice milling. Rice husks are used to fuel the parboiling process, and the resulting ash is roughly 85 to 90 percent amorphous silica.
- *Silica fume* is postindustrial waste from the production of silicon alloys. It was discharged into the atmosphere prior to the 1970s, but air-quality controls necessitated its capture.

Where Does It Come From?

- Concrete is a mixture of sand, gravel, water, and cement.
- Cement is manufactured mostly from limestone and a combination of minerals (calcium, silicon, aluminum, iron), which are fired at high temperatures then ground and combined with gypsum.
- Concrete may incorporate postindustrial waste as a substitute for part of the cement or some of the aggregate.
- Aggregates may also include decorative recycled glass, stones, or other manufactured or natural materials.
- A variety of chemical admixtures may be present, although it is possible to make concrete without them.
- Natural or synthetic pigments may be added to wet concrete.
- Concrete can be left unfinished, or it can be finished with epoxy, polyurethane, or other chemical sealants.
- Linseed oil and beeswax can be used as a finish.
- Concrete can be acid-stained with water-based, acidic liquids that contain metallic salts.

Installation

CONCRETE SUBSTRATE FINISHING

Structural concrete that is already in place can deliver a finished surface, creating attractive flooring that mitigates multiple life-cycle impacts. If the client wants the concrete substrate to become the finished floor or surface, there are several factors to consider. While it is certainly possible to remove a finish such as carpet or wood to reveal the concrete underneath, decorative or protective finishes may not adhere successfully to the previously covered substrate. Prior use of adhesives, oils, cleaners, or finishes potentially prevent the bonding of a new finish. Solvent-based cleaners or acid strippers are not recommended; the off-gassing, VOCs, and harsh chemicals are not eco-friendly.

Existing floors will necessitate preparation of the surface to remove dirt, grease, coatings, or blemishes. In some cases, power-washing may be adequate to remove light soil. Work with an experienced contractor to decide if an

Figure 9.2 Concrete floors used to capture solar mass for radiant heating. The space also features zero-VOC paints, formaldehyde-free trim, insulated window blinds, and wheat board cabinets, and takes advantage of south-facing windows and overhangs.

Photo by Michael Mathers. Project team: Robertson, Merryman, Barnes Architects, Inc.

existing substrate will be viable as a finished floor. If the concrete surface is irregular, porous, or needs patching, it may not be satisfactory for a finished surface.

Lastly, make sure that the floor is insulated from beneath. Otherwise the concrete slab floor may allow significant heat loss from the home, reducing the radiant temperature of the space. The subfloor must be insulated to ensure thermal comfort for homeowners and guests.

PRECAST CONCRETE

Some concrete applications, such as countertops, tubs, sinks, and furnishings may be precast off-site. The installation process for these is simpler, usually requiring nothing more than placement, fastening, and/or low/zero-VOC adhesives. Precast pieces are excellent options for clients with chemical sensitivities, as they can also be finished by the supplier before installation and allowed to outgas, if needed. Outgassing will still affect the environment and air quality overall, but if done outdoors it is easier on a chemically sensitive client.

CAST-ON-SITE CONCRETE

If new concrete is to be poured, specify that the content of the cement and/or concrete are completely safe for use in residential interiors. Rarely, the aggregate or cement will emit radon gas, which is present in natural stone. Specify radon testing before purchase or installation if it is a concern.

For maximum strength and durability in cast floors, walls, fireplace surrounds, countertops, and similar applications, concrete must be properly cured (hardened); it must achieve maximum hydration at optimum temperature (not lower than 50°F/10°C). This will take anywhere from five days to a month, depending on the project, material specifications, and weather conditions.

Specify that potable water be used for curing so as not to introduce any contaminants. Highly alkaline wastewater from the work site should not be allowed to drain onto landscaping.

If the pouring won't be completed in one day, consider specifying (in advance) the use of safe sucrose-based retardants so that the unused wet concrete can be kept for use later and not wasted. Alert contractors and workers that the concrete design element will not be covered with another finish such as wood flooring or a composite countertop. The slab must be protected at all times from dust, chemicals, nails, and other construction debris with a tarp or similar covering, and all tradespeople should take precautions to avoid marring it. Even the tiniest amount of dust or debris will adversely affect the final outcome of a finished concrete surface.

When casting concrete on-site, there are numerous available treatments for adding color, shine, and durability. Some products are detrimental to the environment and/or human health. Mineral pigments and polishing are generally benign. Rely on companies that manufacture low-VOC, low-solvent, water-based materials and finishes and on products that meet stricter air quality standards. Consult the material safety data sheets (MSDSs) to learn about health scores, worker-safety precautions, residual odors, and potential outgassing.

ADMIXTURES

Although most admixtures are negative contributions environmentally, those that slow the drying time, called retarders, may be marginally environmentally beneficial because they reduce waste. Normally, wet concrete must be used immediately, but with retarders (mostly sucrose-based and innocuous), the remaining material may be saved and used the following day. Preferably, use no admixtures or, if needed, go with low-VOC, low-solvent, biobased and/or water-based products.

Super-plasticizers usually contain various forms of hazardous formaldehyde. There are a host of other chemicals that can be added to "improve" concrete, but many outgas or pose a known health risk. Potentially toxic additives can include semivolatile organic compounds (SVOCs) like benzene and diethanolamine plus biocides, including fungicides, germicides, and insecticides.

Various chemicals are generally added to concrete to control setting time, strength, plasticity, water content, and freeze/thaw resiliency as well as color. Most additives, like retarders, are sucrose-based chemicals that are relatively mild and added in miniscule proportions (0.15%). If your client has chemical sensitivities, work closely with the contractor and specify minimal use, if any, of chemical additives. Finally, to preclude off-gassing, end with a water-based concrete sealer.

PIGMENTS, STAINS, AND PAINTS

Pigment can be added directly to wet concrete mix for a wide range of colors and patterns. Across the board, look to low-VOC and low-odor concrete colorants. Concrete can be colored and sealed using biobased, semitransparent penetrating concrete stains from soybeans, corn, and sunflowers that are combined with a water-based acrylic that penetrates with a sealing finish. Additionally, consider recycled materials and postindustrial mineral by-products, concrete stains from a blend of acrylic polymers and pigments, or inorganic, mineral-based pigments that become inert when dry.

Stains and paints (see "Acid Staining or Etching," below) that are specifically designed for concrete and masonry may also introduce permanent color to the surface. Although some are water-based, they still rely on petroleum-based polymers and chemical colorants; therefore, specify that dyes do not contain aniline, chromium, or other heavy metals.

AGGREGATES AND SEEDING

When aggregates are added for visual effect, the process is called "seeding." Terrazzo-like recycled glass is probably the most popular aggregate; seashells, rocks, and pieces of hardware are also used. The client can personalize the results by featuring artifacts or a special stone from the property. Computer components are showing up as aggregate seeding in some countertops and flooring; they are not recommended, as they may contain toxic heavy metals, unless the electronics are third-party certified by the European Union's Restriction of Hazardous Substances Directive (RoHS).

FINISHING

For texture, concrete may be molded, stamped with designs, scored, or saw-cut into "tiles" or grids. These earth-friendly techniques usually require only simple power or hand tools. Specify adequate ventilation and worker protection from dust when cutting dry concrete.

Polishing

Concrete can be polished to a high sheen using progressively finer diamond stones and silicate chemicals; this technique is common for countertops and floors. Specify worker protection from dust. For new concrete products, manufacturers suggest waiting at least twenty-eight days before polishing to ensure adequate curing time. The polishing process creates a colorful, highly durable, inherently sealed and practically maintenance-free surface without the need for VOC-based finishes, waxes, or coatings. Ensure that all auxiliary products are water-based and zero-VOC.

Acid Staining or Etching

Acid staining isn't really a stain, in that there's no true pigment. The products used to color or "etch" concrete are usually corrosive, toxic liquids such as hydrochloric acid and metallic salts that together react with calcium compounds to form permanent blues, greens, and browns on the surface. Once the "staining" is finished, the concrete may continue to react with water in the air or on the surface, so a waterproof sealant is recommended. The process is very unhealthy and time-consuming—it can take up to a month for the chemicals to complete their reactions. Hydrochloric acid, if it is inhaled or comes in contact with the skin, is harmful to workers and residents, and it is a known carcinogen.

Although the final product is beautiful, inert, and will last indefinitely with regular sealing, acid staining is controversial among those who are environmentally conscious. Disposal of acid stain is toxic to the environment. If color is desired, there are less harmful, more eco-friendly methods, such as adding pigment or recycled glass.

Paint

On walls, ceilings, fireplaces, and similar concrete applications, silicate dispersion paint forms a permanent inert chemical bond. It's popular in Europe for exteriors, but is effective for interiors as well. The surface becomes breathable, and is non-toxic, zero-VOC, noncombustible, and moldproof.

Sealants and Finishes

Because concrete is porous, reacts with certain compounds, and stains easily, all horizontal surfaces should be sealed or finished with polyurethane or epoxy. The best alternative, rather than leave the concrete prone to damage, is to specify water-based or water-reducible, low-VOC, formaldehyde-free sealants. Linseed oil and beeswax seal concrete surfaces easily. A diamond-polished concrete provides an inherently sealed finish as the sealers are impregnated prior to polishing.

Studies indicate that concrete flooring exceeds OSHA and Americans with Disabilities Act (ADA) requirements for slip resistance, even when highly polished.

Maintenance

Concrete, once sealed, is a breeze to keep clean with a bit of mild detergent and water. Unsealed concrete should be dusted or lightly scrubbed with a nonmetallic brush and water. Advise the client to avoid the use of cleansers or detergent on either sealed or unsealed concrete.

Sealants and finishes, and eventually the concrete underneath, are prone to scratches or abrasion from dirt, shoes, cutlery (on countertops); it may be necessary to reseal the concrete every few years, depending on the particular sealant and the amount of wear on the concrete surface.

Where Does It Go?

Concrete's durability guarantees a decades-long life span under optimum conditions. However, concrete continues to be the primary component of construction and demolition (C&D) debris. The American Institute of Architects' *Environmental Resource Guide* indicates that concrete can account for 67 percent (by weight) of C&D waste. Only about 5 percent is currently being recycled; fortunately, concrete can be ground up and recycled as aggregate for new projects such as clean fill and road base. The good news, according to the Construction and Demolition Recycling Association (CDRA), is that nearly

Figure 9.3 This gallery has radiant-heated concrete floors with a natural color pigment added and has been sealed with linseed oil. The space also features recycled-content Masonite walls with integral color added, also sealed with linseed oil.

Photo by Greg Hursley. Architect: Eric Logan, Carney Architects.

140 million tons of concrete are recycled annually in the United States alone. Even though the cost to recycle concrete is high due to its weight and solid mass, recycling efforts continue to grow because of concrete's high disposal costs and regulations limiting how much can be added to landfills. Recycling concrete makes sense; it is an emerging, nonhazardous best practice.

Spec List

Request and engage manufacturers in providing environmental product declarations (EPDs), which consider baseline carbon footprint and the reduction of environmental impacts. Develop life-cycle assessment guidelines that assist in comparing various concrete suppliers (not products) and provide third-party verification addressing environmental impacts from embodied carbon, energy, and water. Look to suppliers that provide multi-attribute environmental certifications.

Specify:

- Concrete (and cement mix) made without admixtures and toxic chemicals
- Aggregates (or "seeding") and cement from all-natural materials or from verified-safe recycled materials
- Natural mineral pigments (if any)
- Potable water for curing
- Factory-finished slabs (for countertops and small applications)
- Biobased, low-VOC, water-based or water-reducible, low-solvent, formaldehyde-free stains, sealants, and finishes
- Silicate dispersion paint

Avoid:

- Aggregates or recycled ingredients that may introduce environmental contaminants or health hazards
- Admixtures (with the possible exception of sucrose-based retardants)
- Chemical pigments or paints with chromium, aniline, or heavy metals
- Acid stains
- Seeding with manufactured, possibly hazardous materials such as computer chips

Resources

"Special Report: Reducing Environmental Impacts of Cement and Concrete." BuildingGreen, Inc., 2012
The Concrete Conundrum. James Mitchell Crow. *Chemistry World*, 2008
The Concrete Network. www.concretenetwork.com
Portland Cement Associaion. www.cement.org

CHAPTER 10

masonry

Figure 10.1 The focal point of the living space, this locally sourced stone fireplace provides thermal mass.

Photo by Tim Murphy. Project Team: Annette K. Stelmack, www.associates3.com.

The definition of masonry is broad—it's any work a mason performs. For interiors, a mason's materials might include rock, brick, stone, tile, and veneer. The project may be dry stack (no mortar), mortar bed, grouted, glued in place, or simply cut to fit.

Stone, literally building block of all masonry, is formed through millions of years of volcanic eruptions (igneous rock), sifting and settling of sediment (sedimentary rock), and powerful geologic change (metamorphic rock). Masonry work is as old as mankind; it began when our ancestors began to create homes by stacking stones to build shelters. Mortar was first made from clay. Then primitive forms of concrete were devised to grip the masonry, and bricks were made by baking or drying clay in the hot sun. Eventually, masonry became more than just structure; it developed into an art form. Ancient temples, pyramids, monuments, and other symbolic edifices were constructed from rock and clay to give them permanence and authority.

Masonry is an obvious choice if a structure is to last for centuries. The Great Wall of China, possibly the most impressive structural feat of all time, stretches for more than 4,000 miles and is composed of millions of individual blocks of stone and brick. Most of the world's great government, cultural, and religious buildings, as well as most of its monuments, are made of stone and brick. And Chicago, Denver, and London—cities that were all devastated by disastrous fires in earlier centuries—rebuilt with stone and brick, then added requirements for masonry to their building codes.

For homes, natural masonry is a traditional, long-lasting, time-honored, classic design. Stone and brick don't emit volatile organic compounds (VOCs), will outlast many other materials such as wood or bamboo, and are water-resistant, fireproof, insect-proof, and moldproof. Most stone or brick applications require only simple dusting or cleaning with soap and water, although occasional sealing may improve stain- and scratch-resistance. The materials can also be reused or recycled.

Both stone and brick are excellent choices where thermal qualities are critical, such as for fireplaces, flooring over radiant heat, or walls and floors that collect passive solar radiation. The masonry stores up warmth and releases it slowly. The same masonry will stay cool if kept out of direct sunlight or away from sources of heat. Well-designed placement of stone or brick actually decreases heating and cooling costs.

If stone for interior design purposes is gathered from the site or found locally rather than mined, there are few ecological downsides to using it. Stone that is reclaimed from deconstruction is another superb green choice. The environmental value of new masonry decreases when the tally includes quarrying, mining, manufacturing, firing, or long-distance transportation.

Quarried stone, by definition, is that which is cut or shoveled. There is usually less waste from quarrying than from mining. Still, the United States alone produces almost 1.5 million metric tons of quarried and cut stone, most of which is used in construction applications. And that figure increases every year. Some U.S.-quarried stone is exported, but Americans import even more than they ship out.[1]

Mining, on the other hand, acquires relatively small amounts of ore from larger beds of rock. Methods include blasting and stripping, open pits, underground mines, or the use of hydraulics or augers. Once mined, the mineral must be extracted from the ore. Although mined rock has far more embodied energy than quarried rock, both methods leave permanent scars on the land and upset ecosystems. They affect runoff and water downstream, soil composition, and the plants and animals who live in the area. In addition, changes in slope or soil affect the absorption of rain, sometimes further damaging the landscape through erosion, landslides, toppled trees, and flooding.

---

[1]United States Geological Survey. http://minerals.usgs.gov/

Fact Check

■ Houses, buildings, cars, telephones, countertops, driveways, computers—even laundry detergent and salt—they are all made from minerals. Each person in the United States uses an average of 47,000 pounds of newly mined materials every year. Notably, there are more than 60 identifiable minerals in the typical computer.*

■ Thirteen million of the world's poorest people work in mining, and one million of the labor force in small-scale mines and quarries are children, many unprotected by labor laws and working long hours without proper training or tools, risking their health and unable to attend school.†

■ Eighty percent of Nauru, a tiny, independently governed island in the South Pacific, is now uninhabitable and completely devastated after decades of phosphate mining.**

*National Mining Association: www.nma.org.
†Global March Against Child Labor: www.globalmarch.org.
**American University: http://www.american.edu/ted/NAURU.htm.

Mining also negatively affects human health. Both quarrying and mining workers are subjected to many risks, such as dust inhalation, poor air quality, exposure to chemicals, injury, and repetitive motion disabilities, especially in developing countries where labor standards are lax.

Most stone used in residential settings is quarried, not mined. If the design application will last for generations and then be recycled or reused, or if the stone is locally acquired, it may be a wise, all-natural choice.

Brick has one distinct advantage over stone: It's made from common clay that is easily dug from local pits. Yet to become brick, the clay must be processed, pressed, and then fired at high temperatures, significantly raising the embodied energy, the energy its production requires, and the pollution its production generates.

Salvaged brick is readily available in many locations, and its use conserves natural resources and raw materials. Salvaged or reclaimed stone from deconstruction is less available. Research local land resources such as properties where field stones or flagstone are easily gathered. Obtaining stone from a quarry in the same region as the construction site also makes sense ecologically. Relying on local sources whenever possible greatly reduces embodied energy.

Bricks made during the eighteenth and nineteenth centuries were soft and porous, absorbing 20 to 25 percent of their weight in water. By the end of the nineteenth century, 10 percent or less became the accepted maximum. And soft, underburned bricks may absorb as much as 35 percent of their weight in water; their absorbency factor is important to know when comparing modern bricks with historic ones.[2]

Conversely, specifying a scarce stone that is shipped from abroad is more difficult to justify environmentally, especially if the main reason for its selection is aesthetic. Weigh all of the options and find the best masonry design element that is durable and easy on the environment.

The Risks of Radon

Some types of stone may emit radon gas, which is tasteless, odorless, and colorless, and are believed to be responsible for more cases of lung cancer than anything else except smoking. Radon can enter a home environment through well water and the foundation, where lower air pressure pulls the gas in from the surrounding soil. It's less common, although still dangerous, to find radon emissions from concrete or stone (usually granite) used in construction or design applications.

Fortunately, radon exposure in the home can be prevented because the gas is detectable. To lower the risks of radon exposure, the whole house should be tested for it, or individual building materials should be checked before use. If a very small surface is the culprit, then a water-based, low-VOC sealer may help prevent gas emissions. If there are dangerous radon levels within the home, pursue mitigation, which involves installation of abatement systems or, in rare cases, removal of the offending material. The requirements for mitigation licensing vary from state to state; contact the local public health department or visit this EPA website: www.epa.gov/iaq/whereyoulive.html.

---

[2] U.S. General Services Adminitration. http://www.gsa.gov/portal/content/112570

Where Does It Come From?

- Stone is mined, quarried, or simply collected from various landscapes.
- Brick is made from clay that is processed, pressed, and fired.
- Some stone or brick may be reclaimed from old roads, buildings, and fences.

Installation

Dry-stack masonry—where brick or stones are fit together with minimal cementitious-based mortar or adhesives is by far the most eco-friendly. For home interiors, dry-stack applications are typically veneer installations for walls, fireplaces, or special effects.

Specify darker colors of stone and brick and nonreflective sealants to maximize thermal absorption and release. Specify lighter colors in hot climates, where cooling is the main concern.

Some masonry dust, such as that from soapstone, is hazardous if inhaled. Cut stone outdoors with proper worker protections; wet-cutting methods are preferable. Consult the contractor or fabricator for other recommended precautions specific to the particular type of masonry.

Specify that underlayments are made from FSC-certified wood, gypsum, or agricultural by-products and free of formaldehydes, biocides and isocyanates. Specify all-natural cement (see page 244), mortar, and grout whenever possible. If all-natural is not available or appropriate for the particular job, go with the least-toxic, low-VOC, zero-solvent, minimal-additive material available.

Mastic or other adhesives may be necessary to secure masonry veneer or stone tiles, although they may outgas VOCs or contain hazardous materials. If an adhesive is needed for the particular application, consult the material safety data sheet, and specify one that is water-based, low-VOC, is not petroleum-based, and contains no toluene, hexane, benzene, or other solvents.

Sealants prolong the beauty and even the life span of masonry—but use them with caution. Many sealants for masonry are solvent-based. Specify those that are low-solvent, low-VOC, formaldehyde-free, and water-based. Avoid drying agents containing heavy metals. Also avoid

Figure 10.2 Everything in this home was carefully scrutinized to ensure selections of healthy and environmentally friendly materials, including the locally sourced structural stone walls and wood certified by the Forest Stewardship Council (FSC) for the stairs.

Photo by Ben Trempe. Project Team: Annette Stelmack, Rachael Morton, and Cassandra Coombe, www.associates3.com.

spray-on sealants, which release molecules more readily into the air than wipe-on types and expose occupants and workers to more VOCs and odors.

As with any natural material, plan carefully to avoid unnecessary waste. Unused stone or brick can be saved for future use or recycled to a construction exchange or salvage operation. Inexpensive filler stone or small pieces that can't be salvaged can be crushed on-site and mixed into the topsoil or used in landscaping.

Lastly, masonry typically lacks insulative properties. If you are working with a load-bearing exterior wall and the client wants to insulate from the inside out to address energy conservation, work closely with the contractor and a building science consultant. Proceed thoughtfully; there are no steadfast rules when it comes to insulating an existing load-bearing masonry wall. Generally, if the home is in a cold and/or rainy climate, there is greater risk and potential damage from the freeze/thaw cycle. Also, insulating an existing brick building modifies the drying potential of wall assemblies within the envelope, which can rot the ends of joists and beams. The precautionary approach is best practice; bring a building science expert in to determine how to proceed.

Figure 10.3 Set high in the Sierra Nevada Mountains near Lake Tahoe, this outdoor living room uses dry-stack stone veneer for both the fireplace surround and structural columns, providing visual support, texture, and color that contrast with the surrounding native alpine forest. The use of matching natural stone material for site-retaining walls and pathway edging aided in providing a visual transition from the developed living spaces to the undeveloped natural landscaping. Native flagstone flows in and between the various covered and uncovered outdoor living areas.

Photo by Tim Stone. Project team: Kelly & Stone Architects.

Maintenance

Masonry design elements require minimal maintenance, and some masonry installations can be left without any protective finish at all. Countertops and floors may need regular reapplication of sealants to maintain stain- and scratch-resistance or to protect the grout between tiles; consult the supplier or installer about how often this must be done. Advise the client to avoid spray-on sealants if future applications are needed.

Where Does It Go?

Brick and stone can be reused or salvaged for new purposes. If the masonry application has been damaged beyond use in its original purpose, it can be downcycled into roadbed, landscaping, or even tile or terrazzo. Eventually, all types of masonry decompose and again become part of the greater geological process. Masonry is truly a cradle-to-cradle resource.

Natural grouts and mortars, such as those with lime or sand, will also follow the cycle of deterioration. Synthetic grout, adhesives, and mortar will not break down as easily.

Spec List

Specify:

- Reclaimed, salvaged, or recycled brick and stone
- Stone or brick from local sources
- Radon testing of materials before installation
- Natural mortars and grouts
- Low-VOC, low-solvent, water-based, formaldehyde-free sealants and adhesives
- Wipe-on or brush-on sealants

Avoid:

- Imported stone or brick
- Adhesives, grout, mortar, or sealants with solvents, additives, or toxic chemicals like formaldehyde, biocides and isocyanates
- Spray-on sealants

Resources

Brick Industry Association (BIA). www.gobrick.com.
"Consumer's Guide to Radon Reduction." www.epa.gov/radon/pubs/consguid.html.
"Insulating Old Brick Buildings." Martin Holladay. *Green Building Advisor*, August 2011.
U.S. Environmental Protection Agency (tel. 800-438-4318).

CHAPTER 11

metals

Figure 11.1 Stainless steel staircase railing, stringers, crossbars, and structural-support columns and beams.

Design: Annette Stelmack, www.associates3.com. Photo by David O. Marlow.

According to the *Encyclopedia Britannica*, the term "metal" includes all of those elements and alloys that are "characterized by high electrical and thermal conductivity as well as by malleability, ductility, and high reflectivity of light."[1] The category includes copper, aluminum, iron, and gold, as well as many alloys such as steel and bronze. (Calcium, sodium, and potassium are metallic elements in the scientific sense, but for design purposes, this discussion will be limited to the common definition.)

Metals are so important to human civilization that historical eras, such as the Bronze Age and Iron Age, get their names from the "discovery" and first known uses of those materials. Many metals and alloys are practically impervious to abuse. This characteristic, combined with their universally valued beauty, has made them the material of choice for coins around the globe.

Modern residential construction relies on various metals for their superb strength, especially in joists, supports, flashing, shields, plumbing, and essential hardware. Metals can be stamped, poured, hammered, and extruded. Railings, fireplace surrounds, and castings are often made from metal, as are decorative hardware, appliances, kitchen hoods, and countertops. Metals are more than utilitarian; they are beautiful, possessing unique lusters and textures. Additionally, they can be used in the form of delicate powders or leaf, perfect for faux finishes and fine detailing.

From an ecological standpoint, the use of metal in the home has significant advantages. It won't outgas in its unfinished state or irritate chemical sensitivities; depending on the particular metal, it may outlast the house itself. It's pestproof, fireproof, and moldproof. Many metals need little upkeep. And metal can be recycled over and over and over. Although recycled metal has yet to become a mainstay in residential design products, some factory-made hardware may already contain it, and many custom fabricators rely on it for their craft.

Before they are manufactured into usable products, metals must be mined, and mining takes a heavy toll on the environment, no matter how it's done. Mining scars the land, contaminates the water, uses vast amounts of fossil fuel for the machinery, and contributes to poor air quality. As an example, approximately 220 tons of earth are excavated for each ton of copper.[2] Mining causes an enormous loss of plant and animal habitats and upsets an area's ecology permanently.

Once removed from the earth, the actual metal, sometimes only a fraction of the total ore, must be extracted. Going from earth to mine to smelter to ore requires huge amounts of energy in the form of transportation, mechanization, power, and heat. And that's only the raw material; the metal must go to the fabricator, then possibly to a factory for assembly or to a retailer or dealer. It's an arduous trip, resulting in

---

[1] *Encyclopedia Brittanica:* www.britannica.com

[2] Payat Samppat, *From Rio to Johannesburg: Mining Less in a Sustainable* World, Worldwatch Institute, www.worldwatch.org

Heavy or Not?

There's an important distinction to be made between those metals that contribute positively to interiors and those that are toxic—specifically, heavy metals. Scientifically, the term "heavy metals" refers to those metals with high specific gravity. But in common parlance it has come to mean metals with toxic properties. Lead, chromium, cadmium, mercury, and beryllium, along with other less common metals, are categorized as heavy.

Lead, the heavy metal that was used as the primary whitening pigment and drying agent in house paint until such paint was banned in 1978, is the greatest environmental offender in residential applications. According to the Occupational Safety and Health Administration (OSHA), lead poisoning is still the most prevalent environmental illness in children.* Chromium is found in pigments, textile dyes, and chrome plating and used in wood preservation, tanning, and anticorrosion coatings. Cadmium shows up in some pigments and batteries. All three of these elements, along with others such as mercury and beryllium, are a serious risk to workers who use them regularly or manufacture products that contain them.

According to the Centers for Disease Control and Prevention (CDC), children living in more than four million households are being exposed to lead.† There are approximately half a million U.S. children between ages one and five with blood lead levels above 5 micrograms per deciliter (μg/dL), the reference level at which the CDC recommends public health actions be initiated. Lead exposure can affect nearly every system in the body; because there are often no obvious symptoms, it frequently goes unrecognized.

People are exposed to heavy metals on a daily basis through industrial emissions, fertilizers, pesticides, and even natural sources such as the food we eat and water we drink—all the more reason to avoid them when specifying materials for a healthy, green home. There is a direct relationship between a host of serious illnesses and prolonged or constant inhalation, ingestion, or contact with these metals.**

* Occupational Safety and Health Administration: www.osha.gov.
† Centers for Disease Control and PreventionL www.cdc.gov/nceh/lead.
** For more information on heavy metals and other toxins, see *National Report on Human Exposure to Environmental Chemicals*. www.cdc.gov/exposurereport/ and Safety and Health Topics, Toxic Metals www.osha.gov/SLTC/metalsheavy.

possibly the highest cost of embodied energy of any natural resource, certainly ahead of wood, tile, or stone.

Once elemental metals have been removed from the earth, they can't be put back. Unlike wood or straw, which biodegrade back into the earth, the massive geological forces that created these metallic elements take millennia. And some metals are quite rare. Although aluminum and iron are relatively abundant in the earth's crust, other metals, such as zinc, tin, nickel, and manganese, are scarce. For these reasons, designers must ask themselves: Will the longevity of an application make it worth the environmental cost?

Recycle metal to minimize its heavy ecological impacts. Scout architectural salvage shops and metalworks, especially for metal to be used primarily for interior design rather than protection or structure. By reusing what's already in circulation, the only added embodied energy is from transportation, or possibly for modifications.

Most common metals can be reused and recycled over and over again. In the United States alone, 68.8 million metric tons of selected metals were recycled in 2011—62 percent of the overall supply of metals that were mined that year; 90 percent of structural metals like heavy-gauge structural steel framing were recycled. Metals are significant, reusable resources within the industry and recycled metal contributes to their sustainable character. In fact, more steel is recycled annually than aluminum, paper, glass, and plastic combined. By specifying recycled metal content, we support energy consumption and reduce waste, in addition to avoiding the environmental impacts of mining. Specify recycled metal, and the ramifications are much improved.

Recycling steel saves energy and natural resources. In a year, the steel industry saves enough energy to power about 18 million households for a year. Every ton of recycled steel utilized saves 2,500 pounds of iron ore, 1,400 pounds of coal, and 120 pounds of limestone.[3] Economically, old steel scrap can be made into new steel in steelmaking furnaces specifically designed for recycling. The steel recycling industry is an established network of thousands of scrap processors. The maturation of steel recycling is meeting market demand, exceeding past years. Each year, over 70 percent of the steel produced domestically is recycled. And recycled aluminum reduces the amount of energy needed to produce it by 95 percent over production from virgin bauxite ore.

Look for products that contain a high percentage of recycled metal, such as steel, aluminum, and copper, and look to third-party certifications to confirm the recycled content.

Also consider the coatings, finish or paints used on a metal, either in the factory or on-site. Whenever possible, specify a type of metal like stainless

---

[3] Steel Recycling Institute: www.recycle-steel.org

steel that requires no finish or chemical cleaning solutions to prevent rust or oxidation or to maintain the sheen.

Sometimes an "unfinished" metal element such as a kitchen hood will be shipped with a protective coat of natural or synthetic oil that should be removed before installation (synthetic oils may aggravate chemical sensitivities). Check with the manufacturer or dealer to determine whether the coating is standard or if a synthetic oil can be avoided, and find out whether simple soap and water will remove it. For a finished or painted piece of metal, it's best to let the manufacturer or fabricator remove it, especially if a client's chemical sensitivities are an issue. Most paints and permanent finishes for metals are solvent-based and emit a large amount VOCs, especially when wet. Manufacturers control the application conditions, and the surface will have the opportunity to outgas before arriving in the home. Outgassing will still be harmful to the environment, but it will affect a sensitive client less if it is done outdoors.

Avoid chromium, cadmium, brass, and nickel plating, which produce toxic emissions and by-products and put workers at significant risk for environmental illnesses. Galvanized metals have zinc coatings, and though the factories produce relatively low emissions, they use large amounts of energy. Galvanizing zinc may also produce discharge harmful to aquatic life. Zinc is also relatively scarce, although some is recovered for use in other industries. Plastic polymer or powder coatings are extremely durable, comparable to or better than plating, and applied through a heat-fusion process that outgasses very little after the initial drying.

Figure 11.2 The focal point for this home's kitchen is the copper hood, which was handcrafted regionally. The cabinetry was made locally from Forest Stewardship Council (FSC)-certified walnut with water-based and low-VOC adhesives and finishes. The mosaic backsplash was crafted from recycled stone; all substrates were free of added urea-formaldehyde, the walnut flooring is FSC-certified, and the appliances are Energy Star and International Organization for Standardization–compliant.

Design: Annette Stelmack, Rachael Morton, Cassandra Coombe, www.associates3.com. Photo by Ben Tremper.

Inquire about the finishes and patinas a manufacturer or artisan uses, as many are created with acidic or caustic toxic chemicals. Instead, request benign methods that use low/zero-VOCs. Certain metals are predisposed to rust or discolor when handled or exposed to the elements. Understand the natural tendency of each metal, and specify a patina created through less toxic methods. Inquire about the waste or wastewater that is produced, as this may be an indicator of a method's toxicity.

When contemplating metal for decorative or structural pieces in the home, ask whether there's a better, less environmentally taxing material that might be used instead. That said, when the design element is permanent, such as stairs and railings, the advantage of metal may be its superior durability and structural integrity. Then, by adding recycled content, the eco-value improves, and if the piece is 100 percent recycled, raw materials haven't been squandered.

Where Does It Come From?

- Metal is mined from various locations around the globe.
- Some metals are extracted from ore through intensive manufacturing processes. Other metals, like silver and gold, are found in veins, so separating them from the ore is slightly less energy-intensive.
- Metals are often combined into alloys to increase their strength, sheen, or resistance to natural oxidation.
- Various factory coatings and finishes may be applied to metal, including paint, powder coating, protective (natural or chemical) oils, metal platings, and zinc galvanizations.
- Metal can be easily recovered from recycling and fabricated into new products.

Installation

Metal pieces may create thermal bridges or be highly reflective, bringing heat or cold from another source into the location. This may be either advantageous—for example, with a metal fireplace surround—or problematic, as with aluminum-clad windows that collect condensation or ice in a cold climate. Scrutinize the location of a potentially significant metal design element before specifying it, and factor in the probable amount of solar radiation, hot or cold thermal bridging, and condensation that will occur.

Metal may affect both the length and direction of electromagnetic waves within a room or building. Any substantial piece of metal, especially that which has significant conductivity (such as copper or steel), should not be installed in the vicinity of electronic equipment, electrical wires, or microwave ovens. Although the effects of electromagnetic radiation are debatable, the risk from exposure within the home has not been well-established for ornamental metals. The precautionary principle is the best guide; consult with the electrician and the general contractor before adding a large metal design element.

Recycle all metal scrap. The recycling rate for steel is the highest of any construction and demolition material due to its high demand and good price, and steel recycling now costs less than disposal.

Figure 11.3 A local artist designed and crafted the front door from recycled bronze, creating a grounding portal for the home.

Photo by Tim Murphy. Designer: Wayne Brungard, Architectural Elements, with Annette Stelmack, Associates III.

Maintenance

It's important to know the client's expectations for the appearance and maintenance routines of any metal design element. Many metal types require special cleansers, polishing, or coatings to remain pristine. Copper and silver oxidize rapidly; iron and some types of steel will rust. Commercial polishes and cleaning solutions often contain highly toxic or outgassing chemicals such as kerosene, naphtha, perchloroethylene, chromic acid, silver nitrate, and solvents: Substitute vinegar and food-grade oils, along with good old-fashioned elbow grease instead.

Fact Check

- Copper is a commodity. In the United States, nearly as much copper is recovered from recycled material as is created from newly mined ore.*
- Each year, steel recycling saves enough energy to power about 18 million homes—one-fifth of the households in the United States—for one year.[†]
- In 2010, 96 percent of aluminum cans were recycled in Germany and 50 percent in the United States.**

*Copper Development Association. www.copper.org.
[†]Steel Recycling Institute. www.recycle-steel.org.
**Container Recycling Institute. www.container-recycling.org

Whenever possible, specify a type of metal that allows for minimal upkeep. Patination, such as a naturally occurring verdigris on copper or bronze, can occur as an object ages. If it works design-wise, there's no need to polish or clean it.

Where Does It Go?

The majority of metals can be continually recycled. As with all materials, the consumer is primarily responsible for the amount actually recycled, and unfortunately much is still sent to landfills. In theory, metal debris will eventually become part of the earth's crust again through millennia of geomorphological processes.

Spec List

Specify:

- Salvaged architectural metal pieces
- One hundred percent recycled content, or the highest percentage possible with third-party verification
- Local fabricators to eliminate transportation
- Metal that develops a natural patina or verdigris
- Metal that needs minimal or no upkeep with cleansers and polishes
- Natural, protective oil coatings that don't outgas, or none at all
- No paint or finishes
- Factory-finished powder coating, galvanization, or paint
- Silicate dispersion paint
- Recycling of all scrap

Avoid:

- Pieces made with virgin metal
- Synthetic oil coatings
- Imported fabrications
- Painting or finishing metal on-site
- Chemical polishes, treatments, or cleansers
- Unwanted thermal bridging, reflectivity, condensation, or electromagnetic field disturbances as a result of poor placement of the metal design element

Resources

Copper Development Association. www.copper.org.
Specialty Steel Industry of North America. www.ssina.com.

CHAPTER 12

wood and composites

Figure 12.1 Certified cherry wood staircase in a timeless home entry.

Design: Kari Foster, www
.associates3.com. Photo: David O.
Marlow.

From the stick-and-hide lean-tos of primitive humans to the massive timber frames of European cathedrals, and from early American log homes to modern Western houses, much of our world has been built from wood. It is a fundamental construction material, used since ancient times and still the primary building resource in many regions today. Wood has the tensile strength of mild steel and the strength-to-weight ratio of reinforced concrete. Yet wood gives, adjusting to fluctuations in temperature and humidity, balancing static electricity, flexing slightly with exerted pressure, and absorbing sound.

Wood is also durable—a wooden monument in the Horyu-ji area of Japan, still standing tall after more than 1,300 years, is listed as a World Heritage Site.[1] It is also renewable—that is, if proper measures are taken to sustain the supply and to control demand. Sadly, as is well documented today, forests are rapidly disappearing, especially the largest trees. Half of the world's forests have already been cut and, at the current rate, the last expanses of undisturbed tropical forest will vanish in the next fifty years.[2] The culprits? Booming commercial and residential construction, the expansion of mining, and the need for fuel and cropland, among others.

It isn't just about clear-cutting. A single oak might take a couple of centuries to reach maturity, but a complete forest ecosystem requires thousands of years to fully develop. Fell a few trees carelessly and the complex biodiversity surrounding them is destroyed. Unquestionably, clear-cutting is disastrous in most settings, but selective logging that chooses only the biggest and best trees is also harmful. The remaining trees may be vulnerable to erosion, soil compaction, and high winds. Removal of even a small percent of the trees may damage or destroy those that remain.

As is true for damage to any ecosystem, the effects are not just local, but global as well. Trees, like all plants, are critical to Earth's "breathing." Trees take in carbon dioxide (CO_2) as they grow and capture the carbon, then emit only oxygen (O_2). Human beings obviously need oxygen to live. Concentration of carbon dioxide in our atmosphere is also a major component of climate change, and the cumulative effect from deforestation over the decades and centuries has been enormous.

Although some countries, including the United States, have planted millions of saplings to replace the cut timber—some estimates even say forest losses have stabilized—this secondary growth will not likely sustain such diverse ecosystems nor achieve the stature of its forested forbearers. Growth-augmentation agents are often added to the soil, promoting taller stands in lesser time—and of lesser quality. Tree farms can't replace or even successfully replicate nature. Sadly, various sources indicate a range of only 1 to 6 percent of the original old-growth forests now remain in the United States.

---

[1] www.worldheritagesite.org

[2] Environmental Defense Fund, www.edf.org

Once trees have been harvested, the wood can't be recycled in the same sense as metal, which can be melted down and reformed into a different product without losing the material's integrity. Most wood is downcycled when no longer useful; it's cut up, chopped up, or ground into sawdust to make a lower-grade material. Wood posts become particleboard, board becomes paper, paper is shredded for insulation, and so on. The good news is that the cycle may continue for decades and even centuries, and that wood and paper will ultimately biodegrade and hopefully remain benign as long as toxic binders, adhesives, and glues are not part of the manufacturing process.

Cutting down trees comes with serious costs—but few materials are better suited for many aspects of home construction and design. Wood is ultimately renewable in far fewer years than alternatives such as stone or metal. It biodegrades simply, quickly, and completely into the earth, where new soil is formed that will provide for the growth of more trees so that the cycle can continue. And when carefully protected, the life cycle of cut timber can outlast the life span of its still-standing relatives. If grown, harvested, and used sustainably, wood can truly be a green choice.

Sustainable Wood Choices

Although framing is the largest wood consumer in home construction, casework, paneling, trim, flooring, cabinetry, and additional interior design elements make up a

Figure 12.2 This handcrafted millwork was made from trees on the site that were killed by a fire.

Photo by Emily Hagopian, www .essentialimages.us. Designer: San Luis Sustainability Group.

large portion of the total. Design teams should be judicious in selection and acutely aware of wood consumption, setting an example for both contractors and clients. Specify reclaimed wood, sustainable species, locally available sources, and third-party-certified products, then carefully calculate the dimensions to optimize efficiency and minimize waste. These simple decisions will limit the detrimental effects on our fragile forests, encourage the production and certification of sustainable wood, and provide the client with a truly renewable, beautiful, and durable material.

RECLAIMED WOOD

Wood is a favorite for reclaiming, and using it for a second or third purpose. It's disassembled from old buildings like warehouses, barns, and homes, and from railroad ties and snow fences. Timbers are also collected from standing submerged trees, from the bottoms of lakes, rivers, and other bodies of water, left there from previous forestry operations or sunken with wreckage. Submerged-wood reclamation yields excellent quality wood, as the resins have been washed away and the wood density thereby increased. There is a downside to reclaiming wood from natural bodies of water; doing so may disturb established ecosystems for decades, making the ecology of reclamation debatable. Look to the Rainforest Alliance, which maintains a standard and lists businesses that hold active "rediscovered wood" certificates attesting to its responsible salvage from bodies of water.

Reclaimed wood is the best ecological choice for many interior wood applications, especially if acquired locally. If the reclaimed wood is being shipped in from overseas, consider that it requires long-distance transportation, raising its embodied energy. By opting for local "used" wood, trees are spared from the ax, long-distance transportation becomes unnecessary, and the used wood product doesn't wind up in a landfill.

Locally reclaimed wood varieties are often the species that grow—or used to grow—in the region, making them well suited for use there. Decades of acclimatization may prevent further warping, shrinking, or expansion in the home. The

Remanufactured Wood

In relation to wood flooring, "remanufactured" usually means reclaimed wood from various sources that is remilled to fit the intended purpose. But it can also designate recycled wood chips, planks, or even sawdust slated to be pressed into flooring (usually called "engineered" wood). The distinction is significant, so always specify reclaimed or remilled wood and be cautious when analyzing a product labeled "remanufactured."

quality of reclaimed wood is typically higher than new wood. While no one advocates chopping down old-growth trees as our ancestors did, reclaimed wood may have been harvested from such trees, and thus have wider planks and tighter grain than new wood.

Reclaimed wood offers one more aesthetic advantage: There's a special joy in seeing and touching a "historic" product that will soon be custom-fit to a home.

Sourcing reclaimed wood is especially important for indoor applications. Look to The Forest Stewardship Council (FSC), which defines reclaimed wood as recycled material, and carries either the "FSC Recycled" or "FSC Mixed" label. Additionally, "rediscovered wood" and "underwater salvage" certification from the Rainforest Alliance verifies the sourcing of reclaimed wood obtained using measures that preserve environmental integrity along with welfare and health of workers and the community.

Without these certifications, it can be difficult to track the origin of reclaimed wood. Ask for details about where the wood came from. Confirm that the reclaimed wood is free of arsenic (used to treat lumber) and lead (in older, chipped paint), both known human carcinogens. Also verify the safety of wood originating from an industrial or agricultural site, as it could be tainted with chemicals.

With limited availability of certified reclaimed wood, noncertified doesn't necessarily have to be avoided. Many rediscovered wood operators (RWOs) both recover and sell wood locally, know the source well, and may have deconstructed the site themselves. They may be able to supply details about the species, origin, and safety of the product for indoor use.

Figure 12.3 Reclaimed wood cabinets were crafted from rescued black walnut trees that had been blown down in a storm. The interior cabinet box is made from furniture board with no added urea-formaldehyde, and water-based glues were used to fasten the wood together and attach the veneer. The finish is a water-based, low-VOC material that lets the wood's beautiful natural color shine through.

Photo courtesy of Audrey Hall. Project Team: Associates III.

Antique Wood

It's fairly common to refer to reclaimed wood as "antique," but that's a misnomer. The source may be two-hundred years old, or only just a few. Although old wood may have its feel-good charms, ecologically, reusable wood of any age is better than new.

CERTIFIED WOOD

The Forest Stewardship Council (FSC) was established as an independent nonprofit in the mid-1990s to "promote environmentally appropriate, socially beneficial, and economically viable management of the world's forests"[3]; its logo is recognized worldwide. The FSC is the world leader in third-party chain-of-custody certification, meticulously requiring verifications of the source(s) and ensuring quality and environmental controls along the way to the consumer. It also embraces fair labor and responsible tree farming.

Choosing FSC-certified wood products ensures that the particular tree species is not endangered, that eco-friendly forestry practices have been monitored, and that the processing or manufacturing meets stringent guidelines. When specifying FSC-certified wood products, there are several options from which to choose (see table 12.1).

All the wood used in the product must meet the FSC guidelines in order to qualify for one of these labels. The program now provides certification for almost any product made from wood: underlayments, furniture, paneling, trim, and decking, in addition to lumber.

Table 12.1. FSC Certication Requirements Summary

Label	Requirements	
FSC Forest Management (FM)	Awarded to a forest by an accredited certier, indicating that FSC requirements as prescribed in the applicable Regional Standard were followed	
FSC Chain of Custody (CoC)	Follows the path of the wood product from forest to consumer, ensuring that it was indeed FSC wood that made it into product	
FSC Pure	All of the wood or wood ber in a product comes from an FSC-certied forest	
FSC Mixed	100% of the wood ber is either FSC-certied or post-consumer recycled, OR At least 70% of a product's wood ber is FSC-certied, OR 70% of the wood ber is either FSC-certied or post-consumer recycled, with at least 10% FSC-certied.	All wood ber in the product that is not either FSC-certied or post-consumer recycled must be either "reclaimed" (essentially pre-consumer recycled) or FSC Controlled wood (a lower-threshold certication requirement that seeks only to exclude wood from certain problematic sources).
FSC Recycled	Indicates the product's wood ber is 100% recycled, with minimum 85% post-consumer recycled (maximum 15% from post-industrial sources)	

Source: "Green Certifications Report," BuildingGreen. www.buildinggreen.com

---

[3] FSC, www.fsc.org

Suppressed wood—small undergrowth trees that are thinned and culled to aid in forest fire prevention on public lands—is not yet certified. Nevertheless, this type of wood, if the source can be verified, may be another environmentally positive choice.

The FSC certification system is not flawless, but their strict approach is the best available. The agency continues to raise its standards and to represent the interests of diverse parties, from loggers and indigenous peoples to consumers and conservation groups.

There are other third-party certifications that carry eco-labels for wood and forestry products. Some are regionally based or not recognized outside of a particular country. Others are affiliated with forestry, wood, or paper industries. For wood certifications and standards specific to interiors, refer to chapter 8, page 227.

SPECIES

When it comes to choosing wood products, knowing the best one for the job and the one least likely to be endangered is key. As designers, we do both ourselves and the environment a favor when we dispel desires for a threatened species by presenting this knowledge at the beginning of a project.

Either softwood or hardwood may be appropriate, depending on the intended purpose. Hardwood includes deciduous trees in nontropical regions such as oak, maple, ebony, walnut, hickory, beech, and mahogany. As the name implies, most hardwood varieties are more durable than softwoods, with finer grain that typically accepts stains more evenly—making them the frequent choice for flooring, fine furniture, exposed casework elements, and trim.

The high desirability and slow growth of many hardwoods make them especially vulnerable to deforestation. With the current focus on rain forest depletion, it's easy to not specify hardwoods. But some so-called tropical species might be acceptable choices if they are plantation-grown regionally. Moreover, some hardwoods are softer and some softwoods are harder; the casual designations are not reliably descriptive. So don't rely upon these arbitrary definitions for specifications; be particular about the species. It helps to have a an up-to-date chart of those species most at risk in order to avoid specifying them (see table 12.2).

Knowing what to use is as important as knowing what to avoid. Responsible forestry and lumber companies have worked diligently to discover and "farm" trees that grow quickly yet provide a high strength-to-weight ratio. Lyptus, a hybrid of two eucalyptus species, is an example. Grown primarily on formerly deforested land in Brazil, the species can be harvested at fifteen years rather than every sixty to eighty years for comparable mahogany. Still, there is high embodied energy in any imported wood, and questions of equity arise where trees are farmed on deforested land in socially underprivileged regions. And faster-growing hybrid trees, like intensive agriculture, deplete soil and water more quickly, take the place of naturally diverse ecosystems, and compete with nonhybrids.

Table 12.2. Selected Endangered, Threatened, and Vulnerable Tree Species Traded Internationally

Common Name(s)	Scientific Name	Threats and Uses	Distribution	Listings
African ash: koto, kyereye, oporoporo	Pterygota macrocarpa	Major international trade. Used in joinery, furniture.	West Africa	IUCN* Red List: vulnerable
African mahogany	Khaya grandi-foliola, Khaya senegalensis	Major international trade. Overexploitation of mature trees; Illegal logging.	Central and Northern Africa	IUCN Red List: vulnerable
African teak	Pericopsis elata	Commercial use, clear-felling habitat. Used in joinery, furniture, boatbuilding.	Central and Western Africa	IUCN Red List: and FAO**: endangered
Afzelia: aja, doussie, odo niyan	Afzelia bipindensis	Major international timber trade; heavy commercial exploitation; few remaining seed trees.	Western and Central Africa	IUCN Red List: vulnerable
Alcerce	Fitzroya cupressoides	Clear-felling of habitat, increased human settlement. Alcerce forests have been reduced to 15% of their original size, and many of the remaining populations are small fragments. Illegal logging still occurs. Traded internationally as furniture, cladding, and joinery.	Argentina, Chile	CITES†: Appendix III; IUCN Red List: Endangered
Almaciga	Agathis philip-pinensis, Agathis spp.	Clear-felling habitat; rare. Used in cabinet work, joinery, boat masts, moldings.	Philippines, Indonesia	IUCN Red List: vulnerable
Bintangor: damanu, beach calophyllum	Calophyllum insularum	Major international trade, human settlement, agriculture. Used for construction, flooring, and furniture.	Indonesia (Irian Jaya)	IUCN Red List: seriously endangered
Brazilian cherry (jatoba)	Hymenaea courbaril	Used for cabinetry, flooring, joinery. Threatened due to growing demand and overharvesting in certain regions. Non-endangered and FSC-certified varieties are, however, available.	Brazil and else-where in South America	
Bleedwood tree, mukwa kiaat	Pterocarpus angolensis	Commercial use, disease, local use. Major international trade. Small populations are heavily exploited by local people. Mature individuals suffer from a fungal disease. Some large pro-tected populations.	East and Southern Africa	IUCN Red List: near threatened
Honduras mahogany	Swietenia spp.	International trade. Seriously endangered. Possible extinction in the next 15 years. Often used as an alternative to other mahoganies but is itself becoming threatened.	Central and South America	IUCN Red List: vulnerable; CITES: Appendix III

Table 12.2. Selected Endangered, Threatened, and Vulnerable Tree Species Traded Internationally (*Continued*)

Common Name(s)	Scientific Name	Threats and Uses	Distribution	Listings
Ipe (a Brazilian rainforest hardwood, also called Brazilian walnut or diamond walnut or lapacho)	*Coriniana estrellenis*	Some FSC wood is available, but best to avoid. Used for hardwood flooring,	South America	
Kauri	*Agathis borneensis, Agathis* spp.	Clear-felling habitat.	Malayasia, Philippines, Borneo, Brunei, Papua New Guinea, Fiji	IUCN Red List: vulnerable
Lauan	*Shorea* spp., *Dipterocarpus* spp.	Clear-felling habitat.* Illegal logging.	Southeast Asia, Philippines	IUCN Red List: critically endangered; FAO: requires conservation action.
Meranti, batu	*Shorea* spp., *Parshorea* spp.	Clear-felling habitat. Major international trade for varieties of yellow, white, light and dark red meranti. Illegal logging.	Indonesia, Malaysia, India, China, Thailand, Singapore	IUCN Red List: critically endangered
Molave, vitex	*Vitex parviflora*	Clear-felling, overexploitation, minor international trade, illegal logging	Indonesia, Philippines, Malaysia	IUCN Red List: vulnerable
New Guinea walnut, paldao, dao	*Dracontomelum dao,* spp.	Clear-felling habitat.* Used in construction furniture, decking.	Southeast Asia	FAO: requires conservation action
Nyatoh	*Palaquium* spp., *Payena* spp.	Clear-felling habitat, extensive agriculture. Minor international trade in plywood, furniture, and moldings. Illegal logging.	Indonesia, Philippines	IUCN Red List: critically endangered
Parana pine; Brazilian pine, pino blanco	*Araucaria angustifolia, Araucaria* spp.	Major international timber trade. Logging has decreased Araucaria forests to less than 20% of their original range, and much of the remaining forest is small and fragmented. Few seed trees remain, but fruit and seeds are still collected for human consumption.	Argentina, Brazil, Peru	IUCN Red List: vulnerable
Parlatorei, red podocarp	*Podocarpus vitiensis, Decussocarpus vitiensis*	Clear-felling habitat; commercial use. Used in joinery and furniture.	Argentina, Bolivia, Peru	Included on list of Imported Timbers Whose Use Should Be Avoided
Pencil cedar, red nato	*Palaquium* spp.	Clear-felling habitat; International trade in plywood, joinery; illegal logging. Per USDA: Used in furniture, interior joinery, plywood; a general utility wood.	Indonesia, Philippines, Africa, India, Southeast Asia	IUCN Red List: low risk to critically endangered

Table 12.2. Selected Endangered, Threatened, and Vulnerable Tree Species Traded Internationally (*Continued*)

Common Name(s)	Scientific Name	Threats and Uses	Distribution	Listings
Ramin, merang	*Gonystylus bancanus*	Commercial use, clear-felling habitat.* Regeneration may decline due to overharvesting. Major international trade in furniture, moldings, picture frames, joinery. Illegal logging.	Indonesia, Malaysia, Brunei	CITES: Appendix II; IUCN Red List: vulnerable
Red sandalwood, algum, saunderswood	*Pterocarpus santalinus*	Commercial use, local use, clear-felling habitat. Valuable as timber, dye, medicine, cosmetics extracts. Plantations are being established.	India	CITES: Appendix II
Rosewood, tulipwood, Bahia/Brazilian/Rio rosewood	*Dalbergia nigra*	Commercial use, clear-felling habitat, seed predation. USDA[‡]: Used in decorative veneers, fine furniture and cabinets, parts of musical instruments, knives and other handles, fancy turnery, piano cases, marquetry. Also used for therapeutic purposes and deodorants and many body and skin care products.	Brazil	CITES: Appendix I IUCN Red List: vulnerable
Teak: Borneo teak, Moluccan ironwood	*Intsia bijuga*	USDA: Used in furniture components, floorings, back of plywood, boat framing, joinery.	Australia, Asia, Africa, and especially Southeast Asia, Oceania	IUCN Red List: endangered
Teak: Philippine teak	*Tectona philippinensis*	USDA: Used in furniture components, floorings, back of plywood, boat framing, joinery.	Philippines	IUCN Red List: endangered
Utile, African mahogany, sipo, sapele	*Entandrophragma utile, En. cylindricum*	Overharvesting, pests. Heavy exploitation, particularly of older trees. Major international trade as paneling and furniture. Slow growth rates. Insect predation. Some populations protected. USDA: Used in furniture and cabinetwork, joinery, decorative veneers, plywood, boat construction.	Central and Western Africa	IUCN Red List: vulnerable
Guatemalan fir	*Abies guatemalensis*	Extensive logging, timber.	Central America	CITES: Appendix I; IUCN Red List: vulnerable
Agarwood, aloewood, eaglewood, Malayan eaglewood tree	*Aquilaria malaccensis*	Type of core wood found in Aquilaria tree species. Used in the production of incense and perfume; threatened by extensive logging and growing demand.	South Asia, Southeast Asia	CITES: Appendix II; IUCN Red List: vulnerable
Ajo, garlic tree, Costus	*Caryocar costaricense*	Logged and harvested for timber, herbal, and medicinal uses.	Costa Rica, Panama, Colombia, Venezuela	CITES: Appendix II IUCN Red List: vulnerable

Table 12.2. Selected Endangered, Threatened, and Vulnerable Tree Species Traded Internationally (*Continued*)

Common Name(s)	Scientific Name	Threats and Uses	Distribution	Listings
King William pine, King Billy pine	*Athrotaxis selaginoides*	Vulnerable numbers due to extensive logging. Used for joinery, musical instruments, and building boats.	Australia	IUCN Red List: vulnerable
African teak, Afrormosia, assembla, ayin, egba	*Pericopsis elata*	USDA: Used for timber as an important alternative to teak. Used in boat building, joinery, flooring, furniture, decorative veneers.	West Africa	CITES: Appendix II, in the Democratic Republic of the Congo and Cameroon IUCN Red List: endangered
West Indian satinwood, yellow sanders, yellow-head, yellow heart	*Zanthoxylum flavum*	Highly sought for timber, cabinetry, and veneers.	Florida, West Indies	IUCN Red List: vulnerable
African cherry, kanda stick, red stinkwood	*Prunus africana*	Heavily exploited for medicinal uses (for prostate cancer) and cabinetry. USDA: Bark used, especially on European medicinal market.	Madagascar and elsewhere in Africa	CITES: Appendix II, in the Democratic Republic of the Congo and Cameroon; IUCN Red List: vulnerable
Cedar, Central American cedar, cedarwood, cigar-box cedar, cigar-box wood, red cedar, Spanish cedar, stinking mahogany, West Indian cedar	*Cedrela odorata*	Threatened by heavy logging and felling before trees reach maturity. Used in boat building and cabinetry. Also used as logs, sawn wood, and veneer sheets. USDA: Used in plywood and veneer. One of the world's most important timber species.	Most of Central and South America, and parts of Mexico	CITES: Appendix III in Colombia and Peru IUCN Red List: vulnerable
Walnut	*Juglans neotropica, Juglans* spp.	Decreased habitat, commercial use, food, construction. USDA: Timber used for decorative purposes.	South America	IUCN Red List: vulnerable

Other species to avoid and the names they are marketed under:

Kurupay (South American rosewood)

Lapacho (diamond walnut)

Yvyraro (crystal mahogany)

Guatambu (ivory wood)

Curuguay (South American cherry)

*IUCN: International Union for the Conservation of Nature

†CITES: Convention on International Trade in Endangered Species

**FAO: United Nations Food and Agriculture Organization

‡USDA: United States Department of Agriculture

Sources: Rainforest Action Network (http://readinglist.ran.org/es/node/1203); Forestworld.com 2001; World Conservation Monitoring Center (WCMC), 1992 Conservation Status Listing, Trees and Timbers of the World; WCMC, Plants Program, 1999; Tree Conservation Database; WCMC, Plants Program; Forests.org 2001; IUCN, 2004 IUCN Red List of Threatened Species (www.iucnredlist.org).

Environmentally Friendly Wood Alternatives

Two species that are more environmentally friendly than most tropical woods are bamboo and palmwood. Palmwood is usually culled from past-their-prime coconut "trees" that would be felled anyway, making it a new-wood option with reclaimed-wood characteristics. Bamboo is really a grass but compares favorably to wood, and it can be cut and regrown in less than a decade.

Some lumber and furniture industries specialize in the use of secondary-growth species and leave old-growth trees undisturbed. Neither fast-growth species nor secondary stands is an adequate answer to deforestation, but the benefits are undeniable, as ancient forests are preserved while the supply of wood products is increased.

WOOD-BASED SHEET GOODS

Cabinet boxes and faces, shelving, and furnishings are commonly made with wood-based sheet goods. Sheet goods—various forms of particleboard, engineered wood products, fiberboard, medium-density fiberboard (MDF), and plywood—are common components in the cores, backings, and nondecorative components of finish carpentry. Though they are usually specified by architects and/or contractors, designers can influence eco-friendly specifications.

Fortunately, smaller and younger trees, along with waste products such as sawdust, wood chips, and even old pallets, can sometimes be used instead of solid wood to make them. The environmentally advantageous result is that fewer older-growth trees are needed. If you do choose to use engineered wood, then specify formaldehyde- and isocyanate-free, FSC-certified, and 100 percent recycled content products.

The downside to engineered boards that are typically used in cabinetry, shelving, millwork, and anything with cores and veneers is that they can contain urea-formaldehyde binders and solvent-based finishes that outgas. These contaminants are of particular risk to those with chemical sensitivities. Imperfect but improved substitutes have been developed, such as methylenediphenyl isocyanate (MDI), a common particleboard binder that does not outgas yet still poses a known risk to factory workers. At a minimum, specify compliance with California 93120 Phase 2 emission standards, which limit formaldehyde emissions to .05 parts per million (ppm) for plywood. Additionally, specify formaldehyde-free and low-VOC adhesives, binders, finishes, and naturally derived, biobased adhesives.

Figure 12.5 Windfall Lumber specializes in building wall cladding, countertops, tabletops, and interior design products from reclaimed and FSC-certified wood from the Pacific Northwest. While the beauty of the wood is remarkable, there is also a compelling story about the heritage of each piece, adding an inspiring and historic feel to every design. www.windfalllumber.com

If a manufacturer of hardwood plywood, particleboard, and MDF uses no-added formaldehyde (NAF)–based resins or ultra-low-emitting formaldehyde (ULEF) resins, the products are exempted from some of the testing requirements, as they regularly fall within the California standards.

In addition, the wood content varies considerably from product to product, from recycled lumber-milling chips to cheap tropical species that were clear-cut. The FSC aids in determining the content and environmental responsibility of the manufacturer, as its certification programs have expanded to include engineered wood products. Specify FSC-certified whenever possible.

It may be possible to avoid wood altogether. Biocomposite boards made from renewable agricultural by-products are one alternative for cabinets, doors, trim, and even floors (see "Biocomposites," below). Biocomposites compare quite favorably with their wood counterparts and offer an earth-conscious solution.

Where Does It Come From?

- Wood products come from both domestic and exotic trees.
- Reclaimed wood is culled from residential, commercial, and agricultural floors, walls, and structures. It may also be removed from rivers, lakes, streams, and orchards, or from fallen trees.
- Some wood products are made from recycled (downcycled) wood scraps or sawdust, with added acrylics or resins.

- Wood sealants are usually polyurethane; resin-oil primers are a more environmental option.

- Wood finishes or stains may contain a variety of natural oils, resins, or pigments, solvents, chemical compounds, petroleum distillates, metal drying agents, formaldehyde, and sometimes water.

Installation

Emphasize the importance of careful measurements with the contractor, and request that they eliminate all but the tiniest fraction of potential waste.

Request that the installer or contractor do all cutting outdoors to keep sawdust out of the home, and specify protective masks for the workers. Sawdust from untreated or naturally treated wood can be bagged for use in mulch or compost or may be taken to a public drop-off that accepts it for such purposes.

Dovetailed, finger-jointed, or mortise-and-tenon joints may outlast those made with glue, staples, or nails alone and can cut down the amount of adhesives needed.

Veneer will contain adhesives; by design, the core, if not solid wood, may also contain binders. Both core and veneer can outgas or irritate sensitivities. Solid wood may be a better choice in many situations—and the client will never have to replace the woodwork because the laminate veneer has separated from the core.

Wood needs minimal protective treatments. Selecting finishes and stains that can be applied on-site give you greater control. Plant-based extracts offer the safest, most eco-friendly method for deepening or changing wood color. Avoid stains with heavy metals or chemical pigments—or specify no stain at all, the most ecological choice.

Fact Check

- Approximately three-quarters of an acre of forest goes into the average American home, and around one million new homes are built every year.*

- The most alarming number, perhaps, reflects a profound disregard for the environment: According to the National Resources Defense Council, one-sixth of the wood delivered to each construction site is never used and is finally thrown away.

*U.S. Census Bureau News Joint Release U.S. Department of Housing and Urban Development, August 2013. www.census.gov/construction/nrec/pdf/newresconst.pdf.

Toxic to Insects, Mold . . . and Humans

In general, manufacturers use fewer preservatives and pesticides for interior finish carpentry wood than for framing, decking, and other construction. For applications exposed to weather or pests, toxic wood treatments have been the norm—even on children's playground sets. The list of harmful substances used on wood includes creosote, pentachlorophenol, chromated copper arsenate (CCA), and ammoniacal copper arsenate (ACA). All should be avoided. Borate and natural penetrating oils are common earth-friendly alternatives.

Look for formaldehyde-free, solvent-free, or water-based zero- or low-VOC, and nontoxic treatments. Natural resins and oils are good alternatives to typical petroleum-based synthetics such as polyurethane. Choose food-safe varieties whenever possible, and check with the client for sensitivity to odors or natural VOCs that may be emitted.

Earth-friendly penetrating oils are usually less problematic for both the environment and the lungs, and they come from renewable sources such as linseed, tung, and beeswax. The treatments absorb into the wood rather than cover it with a hard finish, leaving a softer surface that stands up well to moderate use and moisture.

For a hard finish, specify one that is water-based and zero- or low-VOC as opposed to one with a solvent base. Water-based finishes and stains were once inferior to solvent-based ones when used for wood; they now compete favorably, dry quickly, and usually outgas far less. Specify no-formaldehyde preservatives. Avoid the use of metallic hardening or drying agents; for example, zinc is frequently used in floor finishes but is toxic to aquatic life. Consider products that meet more rigid air-quality standards (such as those accepted for use in California, schools, or health-care facilities). High-quality sealants are superprotective and may last for many years with proper care, thus eliminating the need for frequent refinishing or floor replacement due to damage.

Either way, with a water-based finish or penetrating oil, ventilate well when applying. If the client or installer suffers from chemical sensitivities or allergies, the smells and natural outgassing of all-natural or low-VOC treatments may be a problem until the surface fully dries and the air clears.

Specify factory-finished wood if the client has chemical sensitivities that might be aggravated by on-site application. If the wood has already been stained, finished, glued, or otherwise treated by the manufacturer or carpenter, air out the pieces before installation to allow for any residual VOCs to outgas. (Remember that the VOCs will nonetheless affect the atmosphere.)

Figure 12.6 The treads and stringer of this staircase were made from pine glulams, which were assembled by gluing smaller piece of wood together, thereby avoiding the need to cut down old-growth trees.

Photo by Ron Pollard Photography. Designer: Brady Lemae, Workshop 8.

Maintenance

Wood is simple to maintain, as long as it is treated with care. The softer the species, the more prone it will be to scratches, dents, stains, and other marks. Thus a harder finish might be in order if heavy wear is anticipated. For healthy indoor air and fewer wear issues discuss with the client a "no shoes" policy where there are wood floors and provide shoe storage at primary entry points into the home. Advise clients to use the mildest detergents and minimal water for cleanups.

If the client wants a more weathered patina, the wood can be distressed or patinated before installation or on-site with sanding and intentional marks, thus minimizing the need to maintain its appearances.

Where Does It Go?

The largest component of residential construction and demolition waste is usually wood, comprising more than 40 percent, according to the National Association of Home Builders (NAHB).

Work with contractors closely to ensure careful estimations, precise measurements, and thoughtful reuse of scraps—it's a simple way of reducing the volume of debris. Specify that all wood large enough for practical use is taken to a construction

Recycling Wood Makes Dollars and Sense

According to the Associated General Contractors of America (www.agc.org), wood recycling from construction pays off—literally. Nationwide, landfill tipping fees range from $20 to $105 per ton, and even higher near populated areas, with a average of $50 per ton. Tipping disposal fees have been steadily increasing—from approximately $1.25 to $1.95. Wood recycling costs only $40 to $60 per ton (this may vary even more by region).

Wood consists of the largest percentage of the residential construction and demolition (C&D) materials waste stream—approximately 40 to 50 percent of residential new construction materials—according to the NAHB Research Center. The Environmental Protection Agency (EPA) estimates that there are more than five hundred plants in the United States that accept wood for recycling. All of them accept clean, unpainted, or untreated wood, and a growing number have the technology to deal with paint. Nails or other bits of hardware are not an issue because they are easily sorted during the processing. The recycled wood goes into many new products such as particleboard, animal bedding, mulch, and paper.

exchange or saved for use on a future project. Smaller pieces might be donated to scouting programs, schools, or senior centers for crafts. Sawdust and very small bits, if free of contamination from hazards such as lead-based paint or chemicals (from deconstruction or demolition), can be incorporated into the soil.

When no longer useful in a particular application, the wood may be salvaged for a similar or different use or downcycled into a wood-based product. Permanently tainted wood, such as that which has been treated with chemicals or lead paint, may not be suitable for reuse.

Spec List

Specify wood that is:

- Fallen on or thinned from the property
- Reclaimed
- Locally harvested, third-party-certified, and of a nonthreatened species
- Suppressed (no certification available)
- Protected from moisture before and during the installation

Specify finishes and stains (either on prefinished wood or to be applied on-site) that are:

- Water-based
- Made of natural (sometimes called food-grade) oils, resins, pigments, and waxes
- Low- or zero-VOC
- Formaldehyde-free
- Isocyanate-free
- Free of metallic hardening or drying agents (such as zinc)
- Solvent-free

Avoid:

- Reclaimed wood of uncertain origin
- Chemically tainted wood (with lead, arsenic, factory chemicals)
- Uncertified wood
- Rare or threatened species
- Pentachlorophenol or creosote preservatives
- Solvent-based finishes
- Formaldehyde and other preservatives in the wood product or finish
- Diisocyanate binders (more commonly know as isocyanate)
- Metal-based drying agents in the finish
- Engineered wood, unless certified

Biobased Composites (Wood Alternatives)

The green building industry continues to advance technologically. As an alternative to wood, consider biobased composite boards, commonly referred to as wheat board, agricultural or "ag" board, crop board, or straw board. Pulp from crop residue is pressed with adhesive into sheets, then cut into boards, much like the manufacturing of wood-based particleboard, oriented-strand board (OSB) and medium-density fiberboard (MDF). Wheat straw is the most common fiber, but others are being used: sunflower hulls, rice, barley, and oat straw; bluegrass and rye grass stubble; cornhusks and sorghum stalks; hemp; soybean plants; and bagasse (sugar cane pulp).

Designers specify these agricultural-based composites for shelving, flooring, paneling, furniture, and cabinetry boxes, frames, and doors. While crop-based biocomposites are not yet widely used, they have good potential for both design and construction applications. The crops are harvested annually, making them a truly

Table 12.3. Biobased Sourcing Certifications*

Certification	Who's Behind it	What Gets Certified	Issues Covered	Applicable Products	Market Adoption
USDA BioPreferred	Government certification and label	Products	Percent of biobased material in the product based an ASTM D6868 lab test	Wide spectrum for "new" bio-based products	Established in 2011 and growing rapidly with government purchasing as driver.
Rainforest Alliance Certified according to Sustainable Agriculture Network Standards	Third-party certification following iSEAL best practices	Forms and products from those forms	Social and environmental management systems, ecosystem conservation, wafer conservation, worker safety, community relations, crop management, soil conservation, waste management, and more	Foodcfops— but virtually no crops relevant to building industry to date	Established in 2001, now over 200,000 operations certified, and recognition as a food product label. Referenced in LEED 2012 drafts.
Working Landscapes Certificates	Third-party Certification, a joint effort of the nonprofit Institute for Agriculture and Trade Policy lIATP] and Green Harvest Technologies	forms, by acreage	Based on Sustainable Biomaterials Collaborative's (SBC) Guidelines for Sustainable Bioplastics Requires a crop farm plan and compliance with prohibitions on continuous cropping, GMOs, and known human or animal carcinogens	Biopolymer feedstocks, such as corn	Established in 2010; program expanded with Stonyfield and Donnon purchasing WICs for Nature-Works PLA packaging.
International Federation of Organic Agriculture Movements (IFOAM)'s Organic Guarantee System (OGS) and related certifications	IFOAM is a worldwide umbrella organization for the organic movement. OGS is designed to provide international assurance.	Forms and products	Organic agriculture relies on ecological processes, biodiversity, and cycles adopted to local conditions lather rhan the use of inputs with adverse effects. GMOs are prohibited.	Broad spectrum of agricultural craps	Organic agriculture and labeling continues to grow rapidty, even in the economic downturn.
USDA Organic	Government certification and label	Process and products, chain of custody	Like other organic certification requirements, covers chemical inputs, and other farming practices and resutling agricultural crops.	Broad spectrum of agricultural crops	Most widely recognized organic label at this time.
Fairtrade labelling Organizations international (FLO)	FLO is a worldwide umbrella organization for Fairtrade labeling.	Products	Focused on social issues and ensuring a living wage for farmers. Prohibits GMOs.	Includes some building-industry-relevant crops like cotton	Widely recognized label for certain food, but still minor market overall.

*"Green Certifications Report," *Building Green.* www.buildinggreen.com.

Figure 12.7 The wall veneers in this stairwell are made of durable fiberboard that ensures longevity. The metal steps are made of 50 percent recycled content steel, and the wood ceiling joists are all reclaimed.

Photo Robert Meier © 2006. Architect: Locus Architecture.

renewable resource, whereas trees need decades of growth before they mature and can be used in construction. Instead of using almost an acre of forest, an entire home might be built with only 15 to 20 acres of wheat.[4]

Most manufacturers of ag boards are fundamentally eco-minded in their quest for wood substitutes, so low-VOC, formaldehyde-free binders are standard. MDI is a common formaldehyde substitute that bonds well with straw and similar crop residues. A few companies incorporate petrochemicals that outgas, so make the specifications similar to those for the equivalent wood products. Borate is also commonly used as a low-toxic preservative and pest preventative. Unfortunately, biocomposites labeled "pesticide-free" or "non-GMO" (genetically modified organism) can't yet be found, and standards for such have yet to be established. Some biocomposites are designed to take finishes, paints, stains, and hardware like their wooden counterparts, although results vary greatly from product to product. Therefore, consult the manufacturer for details and recommendations. Depending on the particular fibers incorporated, the board might have a smooth, consistent grain throughout, granite-looking speckles, or a dark-and-light, highly textural look. Also check for responsible sourcing for fiber content. Crop boards may also be lighter in weight than solid wood options, yet be similar in strength. They are not recommended for places where constant moisture is present, as they lack long-term water resistance and may warp.

In the end, confirm performance metrics with biobased materials to meet the projects needs, thoroughly vet the durability and maintenance measures, ensure that toxic content is minimal (certainly less than their petroleum-based counterparts, which contain fillers and binders), and ask for certifications toward sustainably sourcing products while driving change and, ultimately, transparency in the marketplace.

It would seem that ag-based boards would be the answer to the imperiled forests worldwide, but the removal of some types of chaff or straw directly from cropland may leave topsoil precariously exposed to erosion—a negative for both

---

[4]HUD, 2003.

the earth and the farmer. Some crop-board materials, however, such as sunflower hulls or bagasse, are not chaff but are by-products from processing and so pose few ecological drawbacks.

Where Does It Come From?

- Biocomposite boards are made from a variety of crop residues and agricultural by-products that may include wheat, rice, barley, or oat straw; sunflower hulls, bluegrass or rye grass stubble; cornhusks and sorghum stalks; hemp; soybean plants; or bagasse (sugar cane pulp).
- Biocomposite adhesives and binders may include low-VOC glues, outgassing solvents, formaldehyde, soy-based products, and natural or synthetic resins.
- Borate may be used as a pesticide, especially in the manufacturing plant. Other residual pesticides may be present from the use of cropland.
- Finished biocomposite boards may use water- or solvent-based polyurethanes.
- Formaldehyde may or may not be present in boards, as a preservative, or in the finish.

Installation

In general, biobased composites are not as water-repellent as wood and are more prone to warping. Countertops and backsplashes made of composites are not usually recommended, although a few water-resistant biocomposites have emerged on the market. Low- or zero-VOC, water-based adhesives and sealants should be specified in all applications.

Biobased boards, depending on their composition, may or may not take stains and finishes easily and evenly, depending on the species of wood. The unique characteristics of these wood substitutes is in their unusual grains and textures, which may best be highlighted with a clear finish. Test all stains and finishes on a sample before installation.

Consult with the manufacturer for the best stains, finishes, and adhesives for the particular fiberboard used, or have the contractor do a spot test to check for suitability.

Maintenance

Biobased composites are relatively new to the market. Their long-term suitability for particular design applications, along with specific needs for future maintenance, have not been well established. Consult with the manufacturer for recommendations.

Where Does It Go?

Like wood, biocomposite boards decompose back into soil naturally. Binders, resins, stains, and finishes used within or on the board will do so much more slowly and may contain toxic chemicals.

Spec List

Specify:

- Boards made from 100 percent renewable crop residue or agricultural by-product (no plastics added, for example).
- Formaldehyde- and isocyanate-free, low-VOC, water-based binders, sealants, adhesives, and stains.
- Borate (if necessary) for preservative qualities or pest resistance.

Avoid:

- Formaldehyde and/or isocyanate in the binder or finish
- Preservatives or pesticides (other than borate)

RESOURCES

"Biobased Materials: Not Always Greener," *Building Green*, 2012.
Forest Stewardship Council. www.FSCUS.org.
Green Seal Floor Care Products: Finishes and Strippers. www.greenseal.org/recommendations
    .htm.
Rainforest Alliance Certification (formerly known as SmartWood). www.rainforest-alliance
    .org/forestry/certification.

CHAPTER 13

openings: doors and windows

Figure 13.1 Handcrafted, reclaimed barnwood vestibule doors invite you into the living space.

Design: Kari Foster, Annette Stelmack, www.associates3.com. Photo: David O. Marlow.

Figure 13.2 A locally crafted pivot door and curved wall of sustainably certified beech enhance the entry to this powder room.

Photo by David O. Marlow. Design: Annette K. Stelmack, www.associates3.com.

Originally, the main function of a door was to provide access to a home while protecting its occupants from the elements. A door was also a barrier against unwanted intruders, both human and animal. In today's homes, exterior doors still offer security, but they also provide notable and significant design features, establishing the aesthetics of the home. Interior doors define spaces, control noise, provide privacy, and allow or impede airflow through the home.

Windows, too, served a utilitarian purpose in the days before electricity: to allow daylight into an otherwise dark structure. Openings in the walls provided ventilation as well, especially in hot climates. The Romans, one of the first civilizations to use glass extensively, put windows in their bathhouses, recognizing the function that glass panes played in illumination while keeping warmth and vapors in and cold temperatures out. Yet windows are more than just daylit openings: They've become works of art, gracing the world's cathedrals and architectural wonders with awe-inspiring color and geometrics.

People living in developed countries spend the majority of their lives indoors, so natural sunlight and connection to nature through a window is vital to their physiological and emotional health. Windows in a home permit visual

Fact Check

- Glass has high emissivity. One pane of clear glass will transfer 84 percent of the infrared energy from a warm indoor room to the outside on a cold day.

- Daylighting may save 30 to 60 percent of the energy used for lighting purposes in a building.

- The windows in a home may be responsible for more than a third of the heat gain or loss within, depending on their size, location, construction, and mechanics.

- A poorly insulated window in a cooler climate may cost the equivalent of a gallon of heating oil per square foot per year.

Source: National Fenestration Rating Council, "Windows: Looking through the Options," www.nfrc.org; BuildingGreen. www.buildinggreen.com.

communication between occupants and nature. A well-placed and well-designed opening connects a person emotionally to the outdoors, nurturing a thoughtfulness for the environment while maintaining control of indoor climate and comfort, no matter the external forces.

Designers most often specify interior doors, some exterior doors, and, less frequently, windows. As with any element of green home design, the materials from which these are made are an important consideration. They need to be renewable or recyclable, free of toxins, and durable.

Exterior doors and windows consume large amounts of energy by directly determining residential energy on a daily and annual basis. A cold, drafty door or a windowpane that lets in the hot sun can shift the temperature and thermal comfort level of a room or even the entire house, and the heating or air conditioning systems compensate. Well-designed and well-placed windows and exterior doors will ultimately conserve energy.

Specify interior doors distinctly from exterior doors and windows, vetting them primarily for the natural resources consumed in their construction. Windows and exterior doors are specified for their impact on overall home energy use.

Interior Doors

Evaluating interior doors for eco-friendliness is quite different from doing so for exterior doors and windows. Materials and composition are the most important consideration when selecting interior doors for their sustainable characteristics.

Reclaimed or salvaged doors are excellent choices for interior applications. Most older door styles are made from solid wood, whereas those made more recently—within the last fifty years—may vary greatly in material content and construction. Plywood cores with a better-quality wood veneer are common, as are hollow doors made from steel, vinyl, or aluminum, with or without wood, mineral, or synthetic cores. It may be difficult to determine the content of salvaged doors; take the same considerations into account as for wood and composites (see chapter 12). Also double-check paint for lead, even if the door is to be refinished (see "Getting the Lead Out Safely," page 386).

Opt for locally harvested species of wood, reclaimed wood, culled deadwood, or third-party-certified wood. Specify plant- and animal-based glues, mechanical fastening, and low- or zero-volatile organic compound (VOC), low-odor, water-based, formaldehyde-free finishes.

New doors manufactured from solid wood, veneer, and/or engineered wood are eco-friendly if the forest products are Forest Stewardship Council (FSC)–certified. Avoid all imports and threatened wood species, and look for locally crafted woods. Unfinished solid wood or veneer allows the team to select an eco-friendly stain or sheen. For all on-site finishing, specify all-natural or nontoxic, formaldehyde-free, low-VOC, solvent-free stains, finishes, and oils.

If engineered wood is preferred for interior doors, specify recycled content, and avoid formaldehyde in the binder. Cellulose cores made from recycled paper are another option in wood-veneer doors.

Biobased composites are also an alternative to wood, offering annually renewable agricultural products. Solid doors and veneers made from biobased composites are available; wheat board is a popular core for interior doors. Specify a formaldehyde-free binder and look for FSC-certified wood veneers. Almost all biobased composite doors are factory-finished.

Vinyl doors are not eco-friendly. Polyvinyl chlorides (PVCs) are a hazard for the Earth and its inhabitants (see "Wall Coverings," page 363) and should never be used in a home.

Some interior doors are made from lightweight aluminum or steel over foam cores. There are pros and cons to each of these materials. The metal, especially if recycled, is very durable and can be recycled, but the core may be hazardous if it contains isocyanate foam insulation.

Fiberglass doors are lightweight, durable, and can be painted if the surface needs refreshing or a change of color is desired. Fiberglass can't be recycled like beverage glass, but it is basically eco-friendly in that it's mostly made from simple silicon dioxide. The door's foam core material may be polystyrene, however, a material that is hazardous to humans and a challenge to dispose of or recycle.

Where Does It Come From?

- Interior doors are commonly made from wood and wood composites, vinyl, lightweight metals such as aluminum and steel (with foam cores), or fiberglass.

Installation

An interior door that's the entrance to a room usually requires an undercut (a small gap between the floor and door) to allow for air circulation in order to balance the heating and cooling systems. It's important that a door fit tightly if its purpose is to confine odors from a basement or storage area, maintain the temperature in a sauna or vestibule, provide acoustic separation, or protect belongings in a closet from dust or moisture. Using weather stripping may be desirable as long as airflow is not an issue.

Maintenance

Interior doors require little maintenance: Regular dusting or wiping with a damp cloth is usually sufficient. Oil or wax finishes on wood doors require periodic reapplication.

Where Does It Go?

Interior doors are frequently salvaged and reused. Wood, biobased composites, and cellulose break down easily at the ends of their life cycles; synthetic binders or glues used may not perform as well and can contain contaminants. Metal is regularly recyclable, although the core material, usually polystyrene, is not. Some recycling facilities may not accept metal doors because they don't have the capability to separate the components. Fiberglass is exceedingly durable and will eventually break down like glass, but it is not (yet) easily recyclable. Vinyl has little potential for reuse, and it contaminates landfills, soil, and water.

Spec List

Specify:

- Wood doors (solid, engineered, reclaimed, veneer, custom-made, or prefabricated)
- High-recycled or reclaimed wood content or FSC-certified wood content
- Biobased composite doors
- Low- or zero-VOCs, low-toxic, formaldehyde-free binders, stains, finishes, and glues
- Tight fit and weather stripping for closets, unheated spaces, odorous storage spaces, or wherever strict climate control is desired (such as in a sauna or vestibule)

Avoid:

- PVC vinyl
- Synthetic foam cores

Windows and Exterior Doors

Ideally, any thermal exchange that occurs through windows and exterior doors should be intentional. Windows and doors provide natural ventilation, allowing for desirable breezes but not unwanted drafts. Solar radiation is a positive in cold weather, but protection from it is necessary where summers are hot and sunny.

Specify climate-appropriate, high-performance products. For windows, look to the following performance properties: U-factor (thermal conductivity or the amount of heat that conducts through a material), solar heat gain coefficient (SHGC equals how much of the sun's heat energy is transmitted through the glazing), and visual transmittance (VT is the percentage of visible light transmitted through the glazing).

Figure 13.3 Passive house standards were utilized in the remodel of this San Francisco Bay home. While the home does not have a third-party certification, it does feature a high level of insulation and airtightness. Spray-foam insulation, high-thermal-mass and high-performance window units from German manufacturer Zola Windows, and heat-recovery ventilation all contribute to the home's overall tight envelope.

Design by Zeitgeist Design.

To find these properties, the National Fenestration Research Council (NFRC) provides reporting based on the standardized testing procedures.

The Efficient Windows Collaborative (www.efficientwindows.org) provides energy-performance comparisons with climate-specific guidance of various types of windows or skylights, including code, energy, durability, and installation issues. The impact of orientation, window area, and shading should also be taken into account so appropriate glazings—those that invite in or control solar radiation—are chosen.

Whenever possible, work with the client, the architect, and the contractor to ensure optimal placement of windows and doors to take advantage of features like the location of shade trees, seasonal changes in sun angle, and directional breezes. Operable windows or doors will allow for natural ventilation. Skylights will decrease the need for electrical lighting but, conversely, may increase the need for cooling in the summer, so thoughtful placement and insulating blinds or reflective coatings are important. South-facing windows under wide overhangs welcome low-angle winter sunlight but will be shaded from high-angle summer solar radiation.

Carefully consider window frames and exterior doors for their material composition; it can significantly impact the insulating value the ecological assets, and the indoor air quality within a house. Reuse is a green choice, and reclaimed wood windows and doors are available at many construction exchanges and salvage shops. Salvaged doors are most often made from higher-quality solid wood. There is a trade-off, however: Older pieces, especially single-glazed windows, may be less energy-efficient. If there is paint on a old window or door, test for lead before any stripping or sanding. Finding a good fit is also critical for replacements or if the openings have already been constructed; old windows and doors may need additional weather stripping for insulation.

Traditional wood-frame windows and doors are an excellent choice for their solid construction and insulating properties; for their resistance to condensation when used with double or triple glazings; and because they are made primarily from renewable, natural materials (wood and glass). New windows and doors may be made from solid wood, engineered wood, or have veneers; look for FSC-certified wood content for each option. Avoid formaldehyde-based binders and outgassing adhesives in engineered wood and laminates.

Factory-finished wood windows are usually best because they'll have time to outgas; specify low-VOC finishes. Window finishes are tricky to apply, and protecting them from the elements is imperative to avoid rot, warping, and cracking over the years. Outgassing affects air quality, but if the process is allowed to occur outdoors, it will be easier on a sensitive client. On the other hand, doors are easily finished on-site, and the interior side might be done with a healthful, natural oil or wax. Be certain to specify an earth-friendly finish on the exterior that will stand up to the weather.

Specify locally harvested species of wood and request reclaimed planks or deadwood from a nearby forest. Although these choices will lack FSC certification, the carpenter should be able to verify the source. Local work also ensures there will be minimal transportation, further conserving fossil fuels. Specify glues and finishes that are low- or zero-VOC, low-odor, water-based, and formaldehyde-free.

There are many other options for windows and exterior door materials, but most have environmental shortcomings. Solid vinyl, vinyl-core, or vinyl-clad frames are not eco-friendly; the perils of vinyl manufacturing and exposure to PVC phthalates are many. Aluminum windows are inexpensive, and recycled aluminum is being used in some window and door manufacturing, but even double-paned aluminum-clad windows lack insulating properties and encourage condensation problems.

Another option is fiberglass with an insulated core. Fiberglass is basically made from glass, so it's easier on the environment. But neither the core nor the fiberglass is readily recyclable, and the core may be mostly unfriendly polystyrene.

Steel is used for exterior doors (but not usually windows) because it is very durable and makes a house more secure; recycled steel is sometimes used. However, most residential applications are made with a polystyrene core; solid metal is too heavy. Without the synthetic insulation (of a not-so-natural origin and even more uncertain environmental future), the metal door would also be prone to condensation, and because it would transfer heat and cold too readily, is not energy-efficient. Steel doors are most eco-friendly if reclaimed or if made from 100 percent recycled steel over a natural core material such as wood or bio-composite board.

The glass in doors and windows is made from common sand and its manufacturing is gentle on the earth, but single-pane windows are not energy-conserving. Adding storm windows is the simplest method of improving them, and the extra cost will likely be recovered in lower utility bills. Double or triple glazing (two or three panes of glass sandwiched together) greatly improves on the storm window by trapping air between tightly sealed, closely set panes, forming insulated glass units (IG units). Glass is reassuringly green as well. Although its manufacturing does require high temperatures, it can be recycled indefinitely, and it introduces no toxins to the home or the environment.

Low-emissivity (low-e) coatings such as silver oxide let in as much as 95 percent of the visible light while reducing ultraviolet light penetration that can fade fabrics and furnishings. Low-e coatings also control heat loss by reflecting infrared energy back inside, keeping the house cooler in summer and warmer in winter. "Superinsulator" argon and krypton gases are nontoxic and have no odor; they are sometimes pumped in between insulating glass panes. The client might also be interested in electrochromic windows that tint and shade automatically, or windows that contain blinds between the panes (no dusting necessary). Assessing whether such chemical engineering and manufacturing advances are good or bad for the environment is complicated. A small amount of not-so-green coatings, for instance, might drastically reduce heating and cooling needs, energy consumption, and thus

Figure 13.4 The Zinc House features LaCantina Doors' contemporary aluminum folding door system. The seven-panel operable glass wall spans nearly 23 feet in width.

Photo by Ryan Kurz. Designer: Jose Garcia.

fossil fuel use for decades, but the effect on air quality and the chemical risks are still unknown.

Two independent rating systems remove much of the guesswork about the energy efficiency of any given window or door:

- A third-party nonprofit, the National Fenestration Ratings Council (NFRC), certifies, rates, and labels window products for thermal properties, how well solar radiation is blocked, how much light shines through, the rate of air leakage, and condensation resistance. Some states now require that windows be NFRC-labeled.

- Energy Star, a U.S. government–sponsored energy-efficiency initiative, goes a step further by identifying windows and doors that are both well-suited for a particular climate zone and have been labeled by the NFRC. Its logo appears on approved products.

Another helpful guide is the Window Selection Tool, an online energy-costs calculator (www.efficientwindows.org) that allows for comparing energy costs and savings between window types. It's maintained by the Efficient Windows Collaborative, whose members include educational institutions, research organizations, and industry representatives. The calculation takes into consideration the regional location of the house, average public utility rates, window frame and fenestration specifics, Energy Star certification, and whether the home is new construction or a remodel. In addition, state-by-state fact sheets are available that recommend NFRC ratings for the particular region and that list any mandated labeling or certifications.

Where Does It Come From?

- Windows are primarily made from glass, which is manufactured through the melting of common sand (silicon dioxide).

- Sealed double or triple glazings may have argon or krypton gas between the panes.

- Glass may be treated with a variety of low-e coatings (often made from silver oxide) or synthetic tints.

- Exterior door and window frames may be made from a wide variety of materials, including wood, PVC vinyl, steel, aluminum, fiberglass, and polystyrene.

- Doors and windows are usually factory-finished.

- Reclaimed doors and windows, especially older ones, are usually made from wood.

- Older painted doors and windows may be covered with lead-based paint.

Installation

Specify insulation around every window and door frame, since these are often the areas of greatest heating and cooling losses. Magnetic seals, good hardware, and adequate weather stripping on exterior doors will ensure tight seals all around.

Maintenance

Exterior doors and windows need little maintenance except to keep the finishes and weather stripping in good condition. Advise the client to do an annual check of airtightness around all windows and doors; many electric and gas utilities offer energy audits that include this service for free or at little cost.

Where Does It Go?

Glass can be recycled indefinitely and will eventually become sand again through erosion. Wood, steel, and aluminum frames may be recycled or even reused. Mesh from screens can be recycled if made from metal; fiberglass recycling may become more accessible in the near future. PVC and plastic may or may not be recycled, do not decompose well, and leach toxins.

Spec List

Specify:

- Optimal window position and orientation to benefit from solar gain, natural light and natural ventilation
- Low-emissivity glass
- Krypton- or argon- filled panes, especially in colder climates
- Double- or triple-glazed windows
- Various window types and glazings for different directional orientations and placements
- FSC-certified wood doors and frames
- Factory finishing or on-site finishing with all-natural or low- or zero-VOC, formaldehyde-free, water-based products that are free from heavy metals
- High-quality insulation around all window frames and doors
- Tight seals around all windows and exterior doors
- Casement, awning, or tilt/turn windows rather than double-hung or sliding windows, for tighter seals

Avoid:

- PVC or vinyl, either solid or clad
- Aluminum or steel windows
- Synthetic foam cores
- Doors and windows with lead-based paint

Hardware

Almost all door and window hardware is made from metal (often steel or brass) because it can be formed to any configuration, is incredibly durable, and provides a tight closure mechanism that provides security against intrusion and weather (see "Metals," page 259). Window hardware is most often supplied by the window manufacturer and may already be installed on the components. This preinstallation ensures a perfectly tight fit, a prerequisite for energy efficiency and high fenestration ratings. Specify recycled metal content in the preinstalled hardware whenever possible.

Door hardware, in contrast, is almost always purchased separately from the door itself. A few companies specialize in manufacturing door hardware from recycled metal, especially steel from minimills. These manufacturers are often smaller and may do more customized, decorative pieces. Whenever possible, look for door hardware that has high recycled content.

Salvage shops often feature door hardware. This is a terrific option for replacements and remodelings, especially if the client appreciates reuse. Sometimes it is difficult to find enough matching pieces for an entire job, but with careful design, an eclectic combination may be appealing.

Some doorknobs are made from decorative glass, crystal, or ceramic (porcelain), especially vintage ones. Glass is a safe, eco-friendly, cradle-to-cradle material. Ceramic also has green properties: It is made mostly from common clay, is inert once fired, and breaks down into minerals at the end of its life cycle. Crystal knobs pose no known risk to occupants since they don't deteriorate like flaking paint and can't be ingested or inhaled. On the other hand, crystal is made with lead oxide, and lead contamination is a serious risk for those who ingest or inhale it and for those who work with it in factories. If the existing knobs are crystal, there's no need to replace them, but the beauty of new crystal is hard to justify

Figure 13.5 A local blacksmith crafted this recycled-content metal-door hardware.

Photo by David O. Marlow. Designer: Annette Stelmack, Donna Barta-Winfield, www.associates3.com.

in a green home because of the hazards for workers. Nontoxic glass imitates the look of crystal well, and it is much safer.

Where Does It Come From?

- Window and door hardware is made primarily from metal such as steel.
- Doorknobs may be made from glass, crystal, metals, wood, or ceramic (porcelain).
- Lead crystal contains lead oxide, a known toxin to humans.

Where Does It Go?

The hardware on windows and doors frequently outlasts the life span of the house, and hardware is often salvaged. Steel and glass can be recycled indefinitely, and a strong market exists for both. Crystal has a very long life span, but the hazards of its disposal are undefined, and the lead may eventually leach into water or soil.

Spec List

Specify:

- Window and door hardware that has high recycled-metal content
- Decorative parts made from glass, ceramic, wood, or metal
- Antique or salvaged or reclaimed hardware

Avoid:

- Newly manufactured lead crystal

RESOURCES

Efficient Windows Collaborative. www.efficientwindows.org.
Home Energy Saver (home energy audit), Lawrence Berkeley Laboratories. http://homeenergysaver.lbl.gov/consumer/.
National Fenestration Rating Council. www.nfrc.org.

CHAPTER 14

finishes

Figure 14.1 Fireclay Tile's American-crafted 70 percent recycled content that is sourced within 220 miles of their sustainable manufacturing facility. Featuring over 80 natural, lead-free glazes and 24 standard sizes, the Debris Series is perfect for floors, wall, and countertop designs.

Photo courtesy of Fireclay Tile.

Finishes—treatments for walls, ceilings, and floors—are where we move from the infrastructure of a *house* into the realm of creating a detailed, carefully crafted, individually tailored *home*. As responsible designers, we want the design process to dovetail with the research and selection of materials that are healthy, high-performing, and have minimal environmental impact.

A respectful relationship with the contractor and architect will help to ensure the use and implementation of eco-friendly finishes, especially if the building envelope was not planned to strict green standards. Fortunately, high-performing, healthy building standards are being adopted across the country at the state and municipal level. There are numerous construction-related questions to be answered before the finishes can be specified, among them: Will you be determining the type of drywall and plaster used, or will the builder? If the client prefers recycled glass tile, will you be able to specify the substrate, or is it already in place? Will the structure become the finish—exposed wood beams, concrete floors, or unpainted plaster (a best practice and environmentally sound choice because it uses fewer resources altogether)?

When remodeling and redesigning, investigate the existing structure and the surrounding land with an eye toward minimal destruction and optimization of what exists. Consult ASID's Regreen Residential Remodeling Guidelines for in-depth assessment and green strategies for the site, including water and energy efficiency, material and resources, and indoor environmental quality; this resource guide will show you how to blend product selection, building systems integration, and proven technologies.

The beauty of most green finishes is that they are inherently adaptable to multiple applications. Reclaimed flooring becomes paneling; recycled glass bottles show up in countertops, floors, or shower surrounds; repurposed cardboard boxes are made into countertops. Since finishes can be used in countless ways, this chapter will cover the basics for floors, walls, and ceilings, and should be used as a launch pad into the ever-growing, transforming market of interior finishes.

Plaster and Gypsum Board

Plaster is a fundamental building and design material. Earth, gypsum, and lime have all been used for thousands of years to protect, finish, and enhance interiors and exteriors, and centuries-old plastered structures have survived brutal natural disasters on every continent. Plaster both contributes to the structure of the wall and provides a finished veneer or topcoat. It has terrific thermal properties, staying cool in extreme heat but also insulating against cold. As a bonus, plaster is fireproof, making it an ideal material for mountain and desert communities at high risk for fire.

Clients with chemical sensitivities will appreciate mineral-based plaster (without synthetic additives) because it's basically inert once dry. Walls made of plaster breathe and adapt marvelously to climate changes within a building by allowing water vapors in and out, improving indoor air quality. This same attractive feature also allows plaster to "exhale" chemicals, so it's important to specify nontoxic materials that don't outgas for the plaster mix as well as for the underlayments and substrates.

If the plaster is mixed on-site, there will be little waste to end up in the landfill. Depending on the type used, a plaster wall may lend itself to many environmentally friendly finish options: paint it, tint it, apply a clear-coat finish or beeswax, or just leave it as is. Consider specifying plaster that allows the structure to become the finish, as it is a waste-free, eco-friendly principle.

Gypsum board evolved from gypsum plaster and quickly gained preference in the late twentieth century for its preformed, ready-to-finish convenience. Gypsum board, or drywall, is the most common material used in new construction for walls. The smooth surface takes almost any finish well. That convenience, however, comes with an environmental price: On-site construction waste and postindustrial debris is piling up in landfills. Most gypsum board contains chemicals and additives intended to enhance particular properties, but this may cause unintended environmental and health repercussions as well. Nearly half of American-made drywall is now produced from synthetic gypsum. This wallboard is comprised of a waste product of air pollution control technology at coal-fired power plants or a by-product of other manufacturing processes.

Many wallboard manufacturers utilize scrap drywall, recycling it into the manufacturing of new drywall using their own postmanufacturing leftovers. Postconsumer gypsum wallboard is also recycled in several areas across the United States. However, due to the synthetic content in various drywall, recycling for postconsumer scrap drywall may be limited in your area.

While all mineral-based plasters and wallboards have some earth-friendly characteristics, they vary greatly in the amount of embodied energy and the waste they generate. The following will help determine the best options available.

GYPSUM PLASTER

Gypsum plaster is also known as plaster of Paris, named for the once-abundant Parisian gypsum beds. It was widely used in the twentieth century, but it has been around since ancient Egyptian times and is what most people think of as plaster.

The main component, hydrous calcium sulfate (also called calcium sulfate dehydrate) is an abundant mineral that is mined, dehydrated at about 300°F into a powdery substance (hemihydrate gypsum), then remixed with water for application to walls or for joint compound. This crude or "virgin" gypsum has some environmental drawbacks: It's nonrenewable, mined, and usually transported long distances.

Synthetic gypsum plaster, also called recycled or by-product gypsum, is recovered from legislation-mandated power plant "scrubbing" of fossil fuels and from production of titanium dioxide. Recovered gypsum fills an eco-niche by reducing waste and landscape destruction; however, these products are unregulated and may not be as durable, so always inquire as to the source material.

Both crude gypsum and synthetic gypsum need only be hydrated to be made into plaster. These plasters are suitable only for interiors because rain and weather will erode them. Gypsum plaster can be built up on a lath to become the structural wall element, or simply applied as a veneer on top of a structure such as gypsum board. The beauty is that natural mineral- or vegetable-based pigments can be added directly to the mix, so other finishes like paint aren't necessary. Gypsum is a superb surface for virtually every type of wall treatment; once set, it is basically inert. All are characteristics that lend longevity to the finish.

Fact Check

- Mineral gypsum is very safe for humans. It is used in orthopedic casts, food, and toothpaste.
- The average person will consume 28 pounds of mineral gypsum in a lifetime.

Source: National Gypsum: www.nationalgypsum.com.

Other minerals, such as lime, may be added to gypsum plaster to prevent shrinkage and cracks. Crystalline silica—a ground-up version of the most common mineral, quartz—also shows up on the ingredient lists as a drying agent. Although long-term, heavy, unprotected, and repeated exposure to the dust causes silicosis (a form of cancer), the risk to inhabitants of a plaster-walled home is miniscule. However, many gypsum plasters today also contain harmful fungicides, setting agents, and other chemicals, negating some of the eco-benefits. Specify natural gypsum plaster with no or low-VOC additives, if possible.

Where Does It Come From?

- Gypsum plaster is primarily made of powdered gypsum mixed with water in varying formulas.
- Synthetic gypsum may contain a form of coal ash produced by the scrubbing process that removes sulfur dioxide from the emissions of coal-fired power plants.
- Plaster may also contain chemical epoxies and/or plastics, fungicides, setting agents, drying agents, binders, and fillers.
- Quartz or crystalline silica is often used in gypsum plaster mixes as a drying agent.
- Lime and other inert minerals may be used in plaster to prevent shrinkage and cracking.

Installation

Specify that plaster be mixed on-site in the precise quantities needed to limit waste and additives like biocides and fungicides. There are two basic application methods, depending on the chosen substrate:

Figure 14.2 American Clay earth plasters are a nontoxic, natural, and environmentally friendly way to finish any interior.

Photo courtesy of American Clay Enterprises, LLC. Photo by Patrick Coolie.

- *Veneer plaster*. One or more thin layers of specially formulated veneer (also called thin-coat) plaster is applied, each approximately one-eighth-inch thick, over blue board drywall, a plaster based board or similar cementitious backing board intended for such a purpose (see "Gypsum Board," page 313).

- *Plaster over lath*. Two or more coats of gypsum plaster go over wooden, metal, or gypsum lath. The first coat is called the base coat or scratch coat, which is scratched to rough up the surface in preparation for the next one; the second is called the brown coat; the third, the finish coat. A simpler two-coat system may also work and will use less product—fewer less natural resources. The final depth of the plaster varies. Eco-friendly choices for lath include Forest Stewardship Council (FSC)–certified wood, recycled steel, or possibly blueboard that is made of synthetic or recycled gypsum.

Traditional wooden lath may expand and contract due to moisture within the wall and plaster, so metal lath may be a more durable choice. Another alternative is gypsum lath with an absorbent-paper face. Specify high recycled-paper content when using gypsum lath.

The plaster, if free of volatile organic compounds (VOCs) and additives, may be left unfinished—the best option for those with chemical sensitivities. The final coat may also be sanded or polished.

Maintenance

Take care to keep the walls dry and clean, as they will deteriorate if wet, or "chalk" if scuffed. Fortunately, plaster can be easily patched or sanded to fix damage. Overall, natural or low-VOC gypsum plaster is a good long-term, highly adaptable choice for a home that is eco-friendly, as it promotes good indoor air quality.

Where Does It Go?

Leftover plaster mix can be used on another application or taken to a construction salvage exchange. The mineral gypsum in the plaster is not considered harmful to the environment; however, any chemical additives within it could leach into land or water upon disposal.

Paint and wallcoverings are difficult to separate from plaster, and plaster is difficult to separate from the wall, so plaster deconstruction and recycling isn't yet feasible. Deconstructed plastered walls at best are challenging to recycle. The lath may be recycled through a wood or steel recycling resource. The plaster could be compostable as long as arsenic, often found in older plaster, is not a component (see "Gypsum Board," page 313).

Spec List

Specify:

- Natural gypsum plaster mix or recycled/synthetic/by-product gypsum mix with no additives
- Wooden lath, preferably reclaimed or FSC-certified, recycled steel or metal lath
- Natural gypsum or recycled gypsum lath with recycled paper face
- Low-VOC additives, if any
- Adequate dry time between coats

Avoid:

- Remodeling, sanding, demolition, or cutting existing plaster without first testing for hazards (arsenic, vermiculite, lead paint)
- Fungicides, chemical agents, or synthetic additives
- Water or high humidity in direct contact with walls

RESOURCE

The Natural Plaster Book: Earth Lime and Gypsum Plasters for Natural Homes. Cedar Rose Guelberth and Dan Chiras. Gabriola, BC: New Society Publishers, 2003.

PORTLAND CEMENT PLASTER

Cement plaster is made from Portland cement, sand, lime, and water. The most likely places to use cement plaster indoors are basements, fireplaces, and masonry walls. Concrete or masonry can be covered with cement plaster if clean and free of debris, and the cement plaster can then be painted or sealed. It is, however, uncommon to see large expanses of cement plaster indoors. The relatively cool temperature of the cement plaster, especially in warm, humid environments, may cause condensation and moisture problems indoors that lead to mold and compromised indoor air quality.

LIME PLASTER

Lime plaster is an ancient building material, dating back several thousand years; it is perhaps older than all other plasters except earthen types. It's distinct from cement plaster or stucco; treatments are usually reserved for exteriors that include Portland cement as an ingredient.

Lime itself is not a naturally occurring substance. It is derived from mined limestone (calcium carbonate), which is found in abundance worldwide. The rock is then crushed and fired in a kiln at a very high temperature between 1,600°F to 2,100°F. The product is then labeled "quicklime" (calcium oxide). Quicklime in turn becomes lime putty through the addition of water; the hydration process is referred to as "slaking."

Lime putty is the main ingredient in lime plaster; once the putty has achieved the right consistency, it's dehydrated to form a mix, then again combined with sand and water to form the plaster. It may also be thinned with water alone to produce a wash.

The process for making lime plaster is lengthy and quite energy-intensive. What may tip the eco-scales in its favor, however, is how lime plaster reverts back to being calcium carbonate when it dries. It starts out as limestone and it will return back to the earth as the same substance.

Lime plaster is basically rock solid and may last for centuries with regular upkeep. The inert nature of lime plaster, along with its purity (no chemical additives are needed) makes it a healthy option for a green home. Like earthen plaster, lime plaster is also vapor-permeable, but it resists cracking and eroding better. It is the hardest and most durable of all interior finishes and can be used in very humid indoor climates. Lime plaster can be applied directly on earth walls or masonry of all types, added as a final coat over earthen plaster, or applied on traditional drywall as a topcoat. If color is desired, natural mineral or vegetable pigments may be added to limewash or plaster. If marble dust is added to plaster and the finish is polished, it's called Venetian plaster (see page 310).

Figure 14.3 These straw-bale walls were finished with earthen plaster; the house-fused glass decorative windowpanes were by a local artisan.

Photo courtesy of Kelly Lerner, www.one-world-design.com.

Where Does It Come From?

- Lime and lime plaster are made from mined limestone that is crushed, fired, and rehydrated (slaked).
- Limewash is a water-thinned version of lime plaster.
- Crushed or powdered marble may be added for hardness and sheen.
- Natural pigments add subtle color to limewash.

Installation

Lime putty powder, when rehydrated, "boils" and is extremely caustic. The plastering process, from start to finish, may be lengthy. After an extended period of carefully guarded slaking—days or sometimes weeks, depending on the plasterer's preference—sand is added to the lime putty. Marble can be mixed in for sheen, or mineral pigment for color. The plaster is then troweled or harled (see the sidebar, "The Art of Plastering") onto the walls, smoothed or textured, and left to dry. Daily misting, especially in dry climates, ensures proper curing; weather may greatly affect the outcome and time needed to set.

Maintenance

A lime plaster finish is practically eternal, especially if a new topcoat or wash is added when the surface starts to show minor signs of deterioration. Once hardened, it would be a chore to effectively deconstruct. And the beauty in a fresco or similar plaster treatment is timeless—Michelangelo himself used it; few would ever attempt to destroy it. An experienced artisan may perform touch-ups if needed. Wallcoverings or paint over lime plaster are not recommended, as the alkalinity of lime may leach through and cause spotting.

Where Does It Go?

Lime plaster, like limestone, will eventually disintegrate naturally back into the earth.

Spec List

Specify:

- Lime without synthetic additives
- Natural/mineral pigments

Avoid:

- Wallcoverings or traditional paint on lime plaster

RESOURCE

The Natural Plaster Book: Earth Lime and Gypsum Plasters for Natural Homes. Cedar Rose Guelberth and Dan Chiras. Gabriola, BC: New Society Publishers, 2003.

The Art of Plastering

Lime plaster lends itself readily to eco-friendly interiors with simple mineral pigments and sculptural detailing. Expert plasterers are considered nothing less than artists in many parts of the world. Some use a Scottish method called "harling" in which the lime plaster and pebbles are "thrown" with a special tool. In the Mediterranean region, experienced artisans developed the fresco technique where pigment is ground into water then painted directly onto fresh, damp lime plaster. The English word "cartoon" comes from the ink-on-paper outline that is first traced onto the wall for guidance prior to painting; "graffiti" is derived from the Italian term meaning a carved or scratched plaster design on the wall. Any or all of these methods may be employed for a highly decorative touch in the home that won't compromise the environment. Limewash, a thin mixture of lime putty and water, is an excellent topcoat; adding mineral pigments will give it a soft color.

VENETIAN PLASTER

Venetian plaster, also called Italian plaster or Venetian stucco, was developed on its namesake island in the 1500s. Artisans developed the technique and materials to imitate the polished beauty of marble. Venetian plaster is made of lime (see "Lime Plaster," above) and marble dust, applied in several thin layers, then burnished, sanded, or polished. In this way, the beauty of natural stone, without the weight or expense of real marble, was achieved.

Traditional Venetian plaster is an earth-friendly, mineral-based option that dries to an inert, no-VOC, nonallergenic surface. The lime and marble or mineral content varies by blend. Synthetic acrylic resins or pigments are often added, but all-natural products are preferred for green homes. Check with the manufacturer for details regarding the content of the plaster mix. Specify low-VOC finishes for bathrooms, kitchens, or high-use areas to protect the finish from stains.

Where Does It Come From?

- Venetian plaster is made from a mixture of lime and marble.
- Sometimes pigments and synthetic resins are added.

Installation

Venetian plaster application is similar to that of lime plaster (see "Lime Plaster" in previous section). As the final coat is being applied, before the first sections are completely dry, the surface is burnished by hand or with power tools.

Maintenance

Venetian plaster may be patched by an expert, but the surface ages gracefully and requires virtually no upkeep.

Where Does It Go?

Lime and marble will break down naturally in the environment.

Spec List

Specify:
- Venetian plaster with natural lime, marble, or mineral content
- Cementitious resin

- Low-VOC binders and adhesives
- Natural mineral pigment

Avoid:

- Binders that outgas high levels of VOCs

Resource

The Natural Plaster Book: Earth Lime and Gypsum Plasters for Natural Homes. Cedar Rose Guelberth and Dan Chiras. Gabriola, BC: New Society Publishers, 2003.

EARTHEN PLASTER

Earthen or "mud" plaster is as ancient as humankind; it has the permanence of rock yet has the modern look and feel of suede. Although traditionally used on homes built from straw bale, cob, adobe, or rammed earth, mud plaster can also be applied over drywall. It provides a natural, breathable, no-VOC surface that adapts to humidity and adds thermal insulation.

Earthen plaster has the least embodied energy of any building material. The best recipe for durability lies in the regional soil, which is already adapted to the home's particular environment. And it's literally dirt-cheap if the home site has suitable clay available and the earthen plaster can be made with it. But before proceeding, specify that the soil be tested for contaminants from nearby sites, if there is any doubt as to its healthfulness and suitability for the project.

Traditional earth plaster recipes include some or all of the following ingredients, all available at little or no charge: clay dirt, sand, straw, and cooked flour paste or manure. Commercial clay plaster mixes can be purchased, along with sanded primers and special sealants, for application as a veneer over existing paint, wallboard, gypsum plaster, or even wallpaper. The primary ingredients in the purchased clay plasters are earth (clay) mineral pigments and borax. Primers and sealants, available from the clay mix suppliers, are specially designed for eco-friendly homes and will usually be nontoxic, solvent-free, and low- or no-VOC. Although clay mixes are essentially all-natural choices for a green home, they require off-site excavation and shipping and, therefore, add embodied energy through transportation.

Unfinished earth plaster is best suited for dry ecosystems and well-ventilated home environments, as constant moisture or humidity will compromise the plaster integrity. Commercial sealants solve most moisture-related problems for the purchased clay plaster veneers.

Where Does It Come From?

- "Homemade" earthen plaster is made from clay earth and natural additives such as sand, straw, and cooked flour paste or manure.

- Commercially made earthen plaster mixes usually include borax, derived from naturally occurring borate.

- Sometimes synthetic resins are added to commercial mixes.

- Mineral pigments may be added to "homemade" or commercial earthen plaster.

Installation

Seek out expert installers to find just the right blend of ingredients, savvy application techniques, and expertise to determine time of year or weather that is best for plastering in the region. The best approach will also depend on the particular substrate:

Figure 14.4 This bathroom used integral color earthen plaster on the walls and ceiling. It also features locally crafted recycled glass sink and cabinet doors, Energy Star compact fluorescent lamp (CFL) sconces, recycled content wall tile, and WaterSense plumbing fixtures and fittings.

Designed by Annette Stelmack, Rachael Morton, and Cassandra Coombe, www.associates3.com. Photo by Ben Tremper.

- Dry and clean cement stucco, unsealed lime or earth plaster, and unsealed masonry are ideal for earth plaster or clay mix.

- Unfinished walls of earth, straw, building-form blocks, concrete, or rough-surface masonry require a base coat or brown coat of lime plaster, fibered cement, drywall, or plaster.

- Sealed, finished, or painted surfaces; smooth plasters; blueboard; or smooth stone work best with a primer.

Earthen plasters may be mixed up to a day in advance to maximize the water absorption into the clay particles. Specify a minimum of two coats: one as a base (it may be slightly thicker depending on the surface underneath) and the second as a topcoat. The clay may also be used in place of traditional joint compound on drywall or blueboard. The final coat may be smooth or rough, depending on client preference, then left natural in color or washed with a clay slip or alis (clay and sand in equal proportions mixed to the consistency of yogurt), with or without pigment.

Purchased clay mix must be allowed to dry completely between each coat. It will not require a finish to protect it from water except in humid or moist environments. If a sheen to the topcoat is preferred, casein or milk paint works over the walls to finish it, as do beeswax, clay wall paints, or commercial, all-natural wax-oil treatments.

Maintenance

Excellent ventilation and air circulation are the keys to sustaining earth plaster, especially if the room is occasionally humid. Exhaust fans or windows that open should be specified if not already present in the home design. Minor plaster cracks and blemishes that develop are easily patched with more clay plaster mix or earth and water.

Where Does It Go?

Earthen plaster is one of the best examples of a cradle-to-cradle building material. From the dirt to the house and back into dirt again, the plaster will naturally decompose.

Spec List

Specify:

- Earthen plaster made from locally acquired soil
- Purchased earthen plaster mixes made from clay
- Primers made with all-natural ingredients (clay, sand, borax)
- Sealants made from beeswax or all-natural oils
- Natural mineral or vegetable pigments
- Fair weather for application, excellent ventilation, and adequate drying time between coats

Avoid:

- Excavation that may cause drainage problems or damaging scars on the landscape (if soil is acquired locally)
- Water in direct contact with the walls

RESOURCE

The Natural Plaster Book: Earth Lime and Gypsum Plasters for Natural Homes. Cedar Rose Guelberth and Dan Chiras. Gabriola, BC: New Society Publishers, 2003.

GYPSUM BOARD: DRYWALL, WALLBOARD

Soon after World War II, labor-intensive gypsum plaster fell out of favor and was replaced by prefabricated wallboard—plaster sandwiched between paper—that is cut to fit. Gypsum wallboard is now the overwhelming choice for the vast majority of American homes and offices. Typically, the architect or builder specifies this material, so if the client and contractors are willing, select the most eco-friendly type.

Gypsum board is generic for drywall, wallboard, plasterboard, or sheetrock (depending on its purpose and, sometimes, the regional dialect). As the most common wall and ceiling material, gypsum board is made by compressing gypsum plaster to create rigid sheets. The standard sheet size for these panel products is a 4-by-8-foot sheet with custom lengths up to 16 feet. Specify a sheet size that will minimize seams and waste. The gypsum core is noncombustible, with a paper surface on the face, back, and long edges typically made of recycled newsprint; it provides a solid, uniform surface and is installed using screws and fasteners plus tape for the joints.

There is a range of treated boards available, which are usually color-coded for identification. Specific varieties have more than one quality like moisture- and fire-resistance, and all are available with square or tapered edges. For interior gypsum board applications, specify by their technical names as follows:

- *Gypsum wallboard* is primarily used as an interior surfacing material with a manila-colored face paper. It is available in a range of thicknesses with both regular- and fire-resistant core material.

- *Gypsum ceiling board* is specifically used for interior ceiling boards with the same characteristics as wallboard. The ceiling board material is ½-inch thick, designed for a water-based, textured finish with sag resistance equal to ⅝-inch-thick gypsum wallboard.

- *Predecorated gypsum board* provides a prefinished surface such as painted, textured, printed or wallcovering that is preapplied; it is available in a variety of thicknesses with core material that is standard- and fire-resistant.

- *Water-resistant gypsum board* is designed for use on walls primarily as a base for the application of ceramic or plastic tile. It is known as "greenboard" due to its green-tinted face paper. It has a water-resistant core, water-repellent face, and back paper that is breathable to support drying.

- *Gypsum base for veneer plaster* has a blue-tinted face paper treated so the thin coats of plaster adhere and bond to the gypsum board. It is available in standard sheet sizes and a fire-resistive core.

- *Sound board* provides a reduction in noise transmission, adding viscoelastic polymers to conventional gypsum cores.

- *Cement board* is technically not a drywall, but it is included here because it has comparable uses and characteristics. Cementitious-based board is a strong, moisture-resistant product used for subflooring and tile substrate, especially in wet areas that are prone to mold and mildew. Various sizes and thicknesses are available.

While gypsum itself is an abundant natural material, wallboard not only loses the plaster artisan's touch but many of the environmental benefits. Gypsum board scrap is piling up in landfills, and the chemical additives leach into the earth (see the sidebar, "Addressing Wallboard Waste").

In the United States, recycled or synthetic gypsum wallboard is usually made from postindustrial by-products such as from gypsum wallboard manufacturing and from "scrubbers" in power plants that run on fossil fuels. Nearly half of U.S.-made drywall is from synthetic product, commonly known as flue gas desulfurized gypsum (or FGD gypsum) products. Gypsum reclamation may actually consume less energy than the mining and transportation of the mineral, especially if the gypsum reclamation plant is located near the power plant.

Reports from Building Green and the Consumer Product Safety Commission indicate concerns with the level of toxins found in drywall products. Initially, the issues were with foreign products, but research has found that U.S.-made products also contain these toxic chemicals, which are used to disperse the gypsum slurry. These plasticizer formulas used in the process have been found to exceed more than the allowable emission levels according to California Section 01350. The California testing and Environmental Protection Agency (EPA) testing in 2009 found that the material core of gypsum boards manufactured in the United States contain sulfonated naphthalene, listed by the EPA as a persistent bioaccumulative toxicant and formaldehyde, and by the Occupational Safety and Health Administration (OSHA) as a carcinogen. The Pharos team, a project of The Healthy Building Network, also notes that these ingredients are of concern.

Additionally, strategic source reduction of drywall will contribute to lowering greenhouse gas emissions. According to the EPA, the benefits of source-reducing drywall primarily comes from fewer manufacturing and transportation emissions, with a minor advantage deriving from decreased raw material extraction.

Where Does It Come From?

- Gypsum board, manufactured from mined calcium sulfate, usually has a paper face.
- Gypsum board may contain chemical additives such as fungicides, adhesives, vinyl, naphthalene, or formaldehyde.
- "Recycled" or "synthetic" gypsum board is made from industrial by-product gypsum, flue gas desulfurized gypsum, or other industrial by-products.

Addressing Wallboard Waste

Drywall is the material of choice for American homes, mostly because it is versatile and easy to use. It can be cut to fit, and no drying is needed, as it is for plaster. Herein lies the problem: Prefabricated slabs aren't one size fits all, and the wallboard waste generated by residential construction is staggering.

- The United States produces approximately 15 million tons of new drywall per year.

- Approximately 12 percent of new construction drywall is wasted during installation.

- Most drywall waste is generated from new construction (64 percent), followed by demolition (14 percent), manufacturing (12 percent), and renovation (10 percent).

- More than 95 percent of U.S. building interiors use some form of gypsum-based wallboard.

- The most common markets for recycled gypsum drywall are in the manufacture of new drywall, an ingredient in Portland cement manufacturing, a soil amendment, and in compost.

- The Michigan Department of Environmental Quality estimates that drywall comprises 26 percent of all new home construction waste, or 1.5 tons for each 2,000-square-foot home.

- Resources vary from state to state, and despite its successful use in many locations, most drywall in North America is still disposed of in landfills. Challenges to widespread recycling include collection and separation, low landfill disposal fees, and the need for more education of potential end users of the recycled material.

Sources: CalRecycle: http://www.calrecycle.ca.gov/condemo/Wallboard/default .htm; Construction and Demolition Recycling Association: http://www.cdrecycling .org/drywall-recycling; Scott Gibson, "Job-Site Recycling: Gypsum Wallboard," *Green Building Advisor*, 2011: www.greenbuildingadvisor.com/blogs/dept/ green-building-blog/job-site-recycling-gypsum-wallboard.

Installation

The paper on wallboard has been known to attract mold that compromises indoor air quality, human safety, and structure, especially if vapors become trapped. Most gypsum board manufacturers add fungicides and similar chemicals to control this. Fungicides are not desirable, either for human health or for the environment, but the risk of mold in the home is much greater without them. It may be in the client's best interest, especially if the climate or home site is damp, to allow for some fungicides. Better yet, work with a building science expert addressing the assemblies of the walls, floor, and ceiling to ensure that mold and mildew strategies are adopted. Gypsum board can be specified without the paper sheath, but doing so usually necessitates the use of chemical binders in the gypsum. Review the manufacturer's material safety data sheets (MSDSs), consult with the manufacturer for details as to the chemical content of the fungicides, and then discuss the options and risks with the client.

The best medicine for mold control, especially if gypsum board without fungicides is used, is prevention. Work with the contractor to ensure that quality construction materials, drainage, and structure breathability are employed so that water and humidity are not trapped underneath surfaces or against the walls. Understand the vapor profiles of all the wall assembly products, including the interior finishes, to ensure the building is allowed to dry out.

Waste management is critical when using drywall (see sidebar, "Addressing Wallboard Waste"), and careful measuring and planning will eliminate as much scrap as possible. Design wall heights to work with gypsum board sizes, if possible, and use leftover pieces in closets, basement stairwells, or other places where joints will be less visible, or leave inside interior wall assemblies rather than sending to the landfill.

Specify recycled-content paper tape for joints and low-VOC or natural gypsum joint compound to bridge the gaps. Hypoallergenic drywall finishing products are available for chemically sensitive clients. Consider the trade-offs: Plaster may involve more human energy and craftsmanship to achieve the desired results and provide a healthier, high-performing end result. Paint may be the most cost-effective but not last as long as plaster. Coverings may provide a desired aesthetic and ensure eco-friendly and healthy products and installation. High humidity will cause gypsum-based surfaces to deteriorate, so a water-repellent finish such as tile or paint is typically used in bathrooms, laundry areas, and kitchen sink backsplashes.

Maintenance

Drywall is never left without a finish because of the unsightly joints and the susceptibility to moisture. The boards will warp or degrade if exposed to standing water, high moisture, or constant humidity, so the most important maintenance consideration is a quality finish. Almost any drywall texture, plaster, paint, or wall-covering may be applied over wallboard to protect it.

Minor damage can easily be patched with taping and more plaster or joint compound, but moldy sections of drywall should be replaced immediately.

Where Does It Go?

In some locations, where soil conditions allow, crushed gypsum can be used as a soil conditioner. If no construction waste recycling for wallboard is available in the region, talk to the contractor about pulverizing leftovers into pieces smaller than one-half inch (by hand or with power tools), then mixing them into the topsoil.

Currently, wallboard is challenging to recycle once it has been used in the home, but the burden on landfills may drive the demand for more wallboard recycling options in the future. In the landfill, gypsum board and the paper envelope will break down, but paint, chemical adhesives, and other manufactured materials may introduce potentially toxic off-gassing and contamination.

Spec List

Specify:

- Wallboard purchases in precisely measured amounts, the same as room height, to eliminate waste
- High gypsum content (natural or synthetic/recycled)
- High natural material content in addition to gypsum (sand, quartz, etc.)
- Recycled paper sheathing or no paper sheathing with minimal additives
- Hypoallergenic or zero- to low-VOC joint compound, preferably gypsum-based plaster
- Recycled content paper for joint tape and/or acoustical sealant
- Reuse of construction scrap on-site
- Small amounts of ground scrap be incorporated into topsoil if allowable by code
- Scrap recycling (look for wallboard recycling programs in your region).

Avoid:

- Powdered joint compounds with antifreeze, vinyls, preservatives, biocides, or those that outgas VOCs
- Chemical additives to wallboard, especially those that may give off VOCs
- Wasteful drywall purchases or installation methods

RESOURCES

Construction & Demolition Recycling Association. www.cdrecycling.org.
Drywall Recycling. www.drywallrecycling.org.
Gypsum Association: www.gypsum.org.
Gypsum and Sustainability. www.gypsumsustainability.org.
USG Corporation (USG). www.usg.com
See also "Gypsum Plaster," page 313.

Tile

The definition of tile covers a broad spectrum of materials that are installed in geometric shapes or flat pieces. Tile may be made of ceramic, porcelain, terra-cotta, or earthenware (all of which are types of fired clay); new or recycled glass; cement; stone; or a mix of minerals and/or reclaimed components in a resin-based conglomerate called terrazzo.

Tile is specified for flooring, shower surrounds, walls, ceilings, and backsplashes because it is very durable and needs to be replaced infrequently. Tile can be maintained by washing it with water, and its essentially inert properties that promote healthful indoor air quality. Most tile will resist mold and stains, is fireproof, won't outgas, and doesn't break down in water.

Tile does have some drawbacks environmentally. Though it's usually made from widely available natural materials such as clay, sand, or stone, these are

Figure 14.5 This rectangular kitchen mimics the long, narrow, rectangular shape of this open-plan living, dining, and kitchen area. The simple color scheme incorporates white quartzite countertops, stainless steel, neutral recycled content glass back splash, and gray laminate cabinetry. The floors have large-format 24-inch square commercial porcelain tiles with tight grout joints that provide a clean, neutral backdrop and high-traffic durability with slip resistance.

Designed by Anne Grice, www .annegrice.com. Photo by Brands & Kribbs Photography.

nonrenewable. Tile may contain a number of less desirable materials such as synthetics, recycled postindustrial or postconsumer compounds of questionable origin, or rare minerals. Even simple clay excavation can cause water quality issues and scar the landscape. The raw materials might be quarried at a distant location then transported to a tile factory for manufacturing and firing. Many types of tile are fired or baked at very high temperatures. All of this occurs before it is shipped to the retailer or distributor, then again to the site. The whole tile-making process results in high embodied energy.

The glazing process for tiles, which are inert once fired, may contain toxic chemicals that are risky to the factory workers, the earth, or the atmosphere. Historically, tile glazes were composed of radioactive materials, asbestos, or lead; fortunately, these are now banned in the United States, although they may still be found abroad. (If the tile has an MSDS, it has been approved for import.)

All negatives considered, tile still makes sense for use in an ecologically oriented home for two reasons. First, it's healthy for the occupant and is neither a source of contaminants that outgas (if installed with healthy materials) nor a sink where they will collect. Second, tile is extremely durable and could easily outlast the house.

Look to third-party certification for tile products. Green Squared–certified products raise the sustainability bar with a transparent, multiattribute product certification process. This certification covers product characteristics, manufacturing, end-of-product-life management, progressive corporate governance, and manufacturing innovation in an effort to establish sustainability criteria for products throughout their full life cycle and for the specification and installation of systems for tile products.

Additionally, look for tiles that are manufactured regionally and whose raw materials have been extracted nearby. If no such option exists, broaden the search. Specify natural materials or those with positive environmental impact, such as recycled glass. Then consider the underlayment in the equation, as well as the mortar, mastic, grout, and sealants; any or all may contain unhealthy chemicals. The best choice for the client and the environment will involve carefully weighing of many factors: the tile content, the manufacturing processes used, the distance shipped, and the methods and substances needed for installation.

To support the health and safety of your clients, specify the appropriate coefficient of friction for the application. The coefficient of friction measures a tile's frictional resistance as it relates to traction and slipperiness. The Americans with Disabilities Act (ADA) recommends a static coefficient of friction SCOF value of 0.60 for accessible commercial areas and 0.80 for ramps. For residential installation, it's equally important to consider slip resistance when researching tile options. Also verify the relative hardness of glazed tile. Look to the method of hardness (MOH) rating scale, which performs a scratch test with different minerals and subjectively assigns an MOH rating number. Values of five or greater are suitable for most residential floor applications. Address both abrasion resistance and glaze hardness when considering glazed tiles, especially for floors and counter products.

CERAMIC AND QUARRY TILE

The terms "ceramic," and "quarry" loosely refer to almost any type of tile that is made of clay and is fired. The definitions were once distinct: porcelain and ceramic were made from finer clay that was glazed; quarry tile (glazed or unglazed) was larger than 6 inches square; and terra-cotta was unglazed and reddish in color. Now almost any tile made from fired clay is called "ceramic." In addition to clay, the tile might contain materials reclaimed from the tile manufacturer, glass, stone, or other natural and manufactured substances.

Conventional ceramic or quarry tile provides a durable, water-resistant, low-maintenance surface. It's fireproof, bugproof, and moldproof. In its unsealed state, it won't outgas VOCs, and glazed tile won't absorb contaminants and reemit them. It's also effective for energy-efficient passive solar storage or radiant heat systems. Tile can outlast multiple installations of other materials. As testament to their longevity, mosaics installed on walls, fountains, and domes by Islamic and Roman artists more than a thousand years ago still showcase vivid color and pattern today.

For most residential applications, a sealant will be needed on the unglazed surfaces to protect it from dirt and stains. The tile will also absorb tiny amounts of contaminants, depending on the porosity.

If the client has chemical sensitivities, choose factory-glazed tile. A glaze becomes inert when fired, so it won't outgas and it provides a waterproof, impervious surface that is easy to keep clean. The drawback to the glazed tiles, however, is that many are manufactured in developing countries, where workers might have few protections against the highly toxic chemicals and metals used in standard glazes. Lead, cadmium, and radioactive metals are all hazardous to consumers as well and are banned from use in the United States, most of Europe, and many other countries. These substances are occasionally found in the glazes on handmade tiles and cookware from nonregulated countries. Although all regulated imports and domestic tiles will come with an MSDS that will help you determine the properties of the tile itself, it may be difficult or impossible to know a specific manufacturer's environmental practices.

Clay: The Main Ingredient

Humble, seemingly abundant (albeit nonrenewable), clay is the primary ingredient in most ceramic tile. In fact, 650 million square feet of ceramic tile is produced in the United States each year—enough to pave the entire island of Manhattan.

Source: Ecology Action. www.ecoact.org.

Figure 14.6 This bathroom features recycled glass tile flooring and tub surround.

Photo courtesy of Oceanside Glasstile, Christopher Ray Photography.

In general, it's difficult, if not impossible, for a designer to know the exact content of most ceramic tile, other than the hazardous components listed on the MSDS. All other ingredients and processes are proprietary. For this reason, specify tile from manufacturers or dealers with good environmental policies. Look online for published company guidelines that set internal standards for lowering factory emissions and waste, improving recycling rates for raw and scrap materials, and protecting human safety.

GLASS TILE

Glass, made primarily from limitlessly abundant sand (silicon dioxide) is terrific for making tile and provides an inert, easy-to-clean surface. Recycled glass tile is currently popular. It is made from postconsumer and postindustrial waste bottles, windshields, and windowpanes. The amount of recycled glass content varies considerably, from incidental to 100 percent.

It's easy to appreciate the concept of recycled glass tile: It takes briefly used beverage containers, along with other types of glass, out of the waste stream and makes them into semipermanent design materials (see sidebar, "Bottleneck," page 465). The manufacturing for glass tiles is straightforward: ground-up glass, called cullet, is poured into molds (sometimes mixed with metallic oxides for color), then fired or melted and shaped. No glaze is needed; glass is impervious without it. Subtle variations in color only add to the charm. Pure glass tile is generally less energy-intensive to manufacture than ceramic, as the glass is melted or heated at an even lower temperature ("sintered"), not fired. Glass is also popular in terrazzo-like tiles that use concrete as the matrix (see "Terrazzo," section, page 354).

STONE TILE

See "Masonry," chapter 10.

METAL TILE

See "Metals," chapter 11.

TERRAZZO TILE

See "Terrazzo," page 354.

Where Does It Come From?

- Traditional ceramic tile is usually made of fired clay.
- Talc, cement, or other minerals may be added when making ceramic.
- Manufactured or recycled materials such as fly ash or glass may also be added.
- Tile may be glazed or unglazed; glazes consist of metals, pigments, and various chemicals along with simple silicon dioxide—sand—that become inert when fired.
- Glass tiles are made mostly from silicon dioxide (sand). Glass for recycled glass tile generally comes from postconsumer waste such as bottles and windshields.
- The recycled glass content varies greatly by manufacturer and product, even between particular colors of tile.
- Small amounts of metals and chemicals may be added to glass for color and texture.

Figure 14.7 This wet bar came from a "found" space under the stairs during a client project walk-through while the home was under construction. The team created a cozy service bar for one with all the requested amenities. The mosaic wall tile is from recycled content glass and stone, used low-VOC installation methods, and features FSC-certified walnut cabinetry and stair treads, slate flooring, and LED lighting.

Designed by Annette Stelmack, Rachael Morton, Cassandra Coombe, www.associates3.com. Photo by Ben Tremper.

Installation

The general methods for installing ceramic, glass, terrazzo, and other kinds of tile are similar. Manufacturer specifications will differ according to the design application and the particular tile, as will recommended underlayments, mortars, adhesives, grouts, and sealants. Aim for all-natural materials and products with third-party certification to ensure healthy indoor air quality and performance. If they are unavailable, go with the least toxic, low-VOC, zero-solvent, minimal-additive material possible. Urge the installer to measure carefully, as well; it's easy to be wasteful and buy more tile than is needed. The tiles should be cut outdoors or in an open area such as a garage or deck, preferably with a wet saw; the superfine ceramic or glass dust can be hazardous. Dry installation conditions are vital to give the tile a good defense against mildew or cracking.

- *Underlayment*. The weight and strength of the underlayment needed will be determined by the purpose and location of the tile surface: wall, shower stall, floor, or countertop. FSC-certified formaldehyde-free medium-density fiberboard (MDF) or exterior-grade plywood are the greenest choices. Cementitious board or cured-and-dried concrete are other possibilities.

- *Mortar*. Thickset mortar (greater than one inch deep) is ideal because the mortar itself provides the "grip" and so obviates the need for synthetic adhesives and mastics. Thickset can be done with simple Portland cement, sand, and lime. Thin-set mortar is more fragile and prone to cracking, so chemicals and latex are usually added for flexibility. If thin-set is the preferred method for the particular tile, opt for a water-based, additive-free, low-VOC variety with third-party certification.

- *Adhesives/mastics*. Mastic (a particular type of ceramic adhesive) and other tile adhesives are popular because they are cheap and make for quick installation: The tile is glued to the flat substrate and the grout filled in, but no mortar is needed. In general, mastics and adhesives are not the best choice for eco-friendly tile applications because they are manufactured from toxic ingredients and may outgas VOCs. Mastic also has limited applications; it can't be used in damp areas, with glass tiles, or on even slightly uneven surfaces. If an adhesive or mastic is required for the particular application, specify a water-based, low-VOC type that has no petroleum base; no toluene, hexane, benzene, or other solvents; and is third-party certified.

- *Grout*. Simple grout made of Portland cement, sand, and water (lime is optional) works very well in many residential applications, and mineral pigments may be added for color. Unsanded grout should be specified if the tile might be easily scratched (glass) or will have very narrow grout joints.

> ### Giving Grout a Good Name
>
> Some of the most common complaints about grout are easy to address. Stains, for example, are much less obvious if a dark-colored grout is used. Dime-thin grout joints and bigger tiles will fend off mold by reducing the surface area of grout available to fungal growth. Either strategy will result in less cleaning and fewer grout repairs.

Specify additive-free grout. Be aware that commercial grout blends may contain a host of questionable ingredients and outgassing components, so look for those without synthetic latex or polymer additives, and third-party certification.

Maintenance

Tile, especially if glazed, is wonderfully durable and needs little more than soap-and-water cleaning. Unfortunately, the tiny cracks and holes in grout are prone to expansion and contraction by water and heat, leading to deterioration. Mold and mildew will move in and take up permanent residence in grout if the tile and the room are not kept dry. Good ventilation through windows and via exhaust fans is a must, as is regular cleaning of the tiled surface.

Unglazed ceramic, terra-cotta, frosted glass, or other more porous tiles are more susceptible to damage from stains, scratches, and general abuse (underfoot or on a countertop). In addition, the porous unglazed surface provides a sink for contaminants and bacteria. Glazed tile, on the other hand, is resistant to just about everything.

The grout around both glazed and unglazed tile, however, is more vulnerable and should always be sealed on-site after installation to prevent mold and stains. Specify a zero- or low-VOC, water-based, wipe-on sealant rather than a spray-on variety, as it will have fewer negative repercussions on indoor air quality.

It may be tempting to avoid the use of sealants, but the grout, and then the tile, will deteriorate much more quickly and need replacement. Ultimately, if the tile falls apart and must be disposed of in a landfill, it's worse for the environment than the use of sealants. Sealants also prevent mold, a sanitary-health and indoor air-quality concern. To prevent tile degradation, apply a sealant immediately after the tile is laid, then reapply as recommended by the manufacturer.

Figure 14.8 The backsplash tile is 100-percent recycled glass manufactured and sourced from base materials through finish goods within 30 miles of the project. The round raised table is Vetrazzo in charisma blue and patina color, while the rectangular portion is Paperstone in evergreen color. The cabinetry is FSC-certified, sustainably harvested cherry wood on formaldehyde-free plywood. The upper cabinet doors have 3form panels with a seaweed pattern in lieu of glass, with real seaweed sandwiched between high-recycled content acrylic panels. The cabinetry finish is OSMO Polyx-Oil, is a penetrating, plant-based finish that leaves the wood silky smooth but not shiny. The flooring is a floating cork floor from Nova Distinctive Floors in the Comprido style and sand color. The paint on the walls is a zero-VOC acrylic paint tinted with zero-VOC colorants from Yolo Colorhouse. All the lighting in the kitchen is LED.

Designed by Lydia Corser, www.greenspacecompany.com. Photo by Bernardo Grijalvo.

Advise clients that they need not replace tile or employ toxic cleansers just because the grout has become stained or dirty. Simple cleansers such as vinegar and water, borax, or baking soda, used with a stiff brush, work just as well. For persistent mold, professional steam cleaning may help. Grout can be carefully removed and redone without removing the tile as well.

Where Does It Go?

Broken pieces of tile can be used in mosaics, underneath soil in potted plants for drainage, or tossed into the garden. Extra tiles may be saved as replacements for future repairs and breakage or taken to a construction recycling or exchange site. Consider using leftover tiles as decorative accents in other applications such as tabletops or trim, or donating them for crafts to youth groups, schools, or senior citizen centers.

Fired clay, mortar, and grout are similar to metamorphosed rock and will eventually break up into inert rocklike pieces at the end of the tile's life cycle. (The glaze is inert, too.) In some localities, porcelain and ceramic recycling exists for old toilets and bathroom fixtures; tile may be accepted there as well.

Glass tiles have the most promising future of all. Those that are 100 percent glass can theoretically be recycled over and over, eventually becoming sand again.

Spec List

Specify:

- Tile made with third-party certifications and full life-cycle assessments
- Unprocessed, all-natural tile from clays or safe recycled materials such as glass
- Domestic tile, especially locally made tile
- Factory-glazed ceramic
- One-hundred-percent recycled glass tile or high recycled-glass content
- Natural backerboard, MDF, or underlayment (FSC-certified wood, plaster, gypsum, or concrete)
- Simple mortar from cement, sand, water, and possibly lime (no additives) with third-party certification
- Grout without added fungicides and with third-party certification
- Low-VOC, water-based, wipe-on sealant
- Low-VOC, low-solvent, additive-free, latex-free mortar and grout

Avoid:

- Unregulated import tile
- High amounts of new glass added to glass tiles
- VOCs, solvents, fungicides, vinyls, or latex additives in mortar, grout, and sealants

Resources

Green Squared Certified. http://greensquaredcertified.com.
National Terrazzo & Mosaic Association. www.ntma.com.
The Tile Council of North America. www.tcnatile.com.

Flooring

BAMBOO FLOORING

Bamboo continues to be a popular green option for flooring as well as for cabinets, wall paneling, and furniture. Some types of bamboo are harder than oak or maple, have the tension of steel, and are as versatile as wood. High-density versions work best for underfloor radiant heat systems. Unlike wood, which takes decades to replenish itself in forests, bamboo can be cut and regrown every five to ten years; it is a true rapidly renewable resource.

All bamboo products are not created equal. Some may have been coated with pesticides, fungicides, biocides, and fireproofing chemicals, and many manufacturers employ urea-formaldehyde as the binder, acknowledged by the EPA as a known carcinogen to humans. Some bamboo flooring will exceed OSHA and Leadership in Energy and Environmental Design (LEED) recommendations for allowable formaldehyde, while others fall well within acceptable levels. Formaldehyde-free is by far the best option; check the MSDS for details and consult the manufacturer for proprietary contents when working with chemically sensitive clients.

Bamboo flooring types are almost as variable as wood; solid or 100 percent bamboo, engineered, veneer, or strand products are available. Strand bamboo products take individual fibers—or strands—and binds them with pressure, heat, and a resin. The

A man can sit in a bamboo house under a bamboo roof, on a bamboo chair at a bamboo table, with a bamboo hat on his head and bamboo sandals on his feet. He can at the same time hold in one hand a bamboo bowl, in the other hand bamboo chopsticks and eat bamboo sprouts. When through with his meal, which has been cooked over a bamboo fire, the table may be washed with a bamboo cloth, and he can fan himself with a bamboo fan, take a siesta on a bamboo bed, lying on a bamboo mat with his head resting on a bamboo pillow. His child might be lying in a bamboo cradle, playing with a bamboo toy. On rising he would smoke a bamboo pipe and taking a bamboo pen, write on a bamboo paper, or carry his articles in bamboo baskets suspended from a bamboo pole, with a bamboo umbrella over his head. He might then take a walk over a bamboo suspension bridge, drink water from a bamboo ladle, and scrape himself with a bamboo scraper (handkerchief).

Source: William Edgar Geil, *A Yankee on the Yangtze* (London: Hodder and Stoughton, 1904); World Agroforestry Centre: www.worldagroforestry.org.

resins usually contain a form of formaldehyde. Engineered and veneer bamboo flooring contains a core wood, which may or may not have been harvested from a certified sustainable forest. Rubberwood, which is harvested when the latex-producing tree is no longer viable, is popular as a bamboo core. Look to FSC-certified bamboo products including the wood cores (see chapter 12, "Wood and Composites") and compliance with California Section 01350 (see chapter 8, "Certifications and Standards").

One of the limitations of bamboo is that high moisture and humidity can cause it to warp or weaken. It's therefore a poor choice for bathrooms or applications in very wet climates. (Manufacturers recommend it not be installed where humidity levels exceed 60 percent.) Another is that color choices are limited, as bamboo does not take stain easily, but some manufacturers who use water-based stains have had more success of late, and this may continue to improve. One existing alternative is carbonized bamboo. When bamboo is formed into building products, manufacturers steam the fibers to straighten them. If they prolong the steaming period, fibers darken, leading to carbonization. The extended steaming period also softens the fibers, making carbonized bamboo about 20 percent less durable than natural products. Carbonizing creates a caramel to dark-brown color, changing the color of the fibers themselves, so if the surface is scratched, it won't expose lighter-color material underneath.

Domestic bamboo production is not yet reliable, and the need to transport the raw materials from overseas is a red mark on bamboo's report card. Although it is grown in many developing countries and may provide opportunities for sustainable, economically viable commerce, as yet there are no certifying agencies that ensure quality control or that workers are treated justly. The best guideline is to specify from a manufacturer meeting third-party certifications for other products. But bamboo is in demand; we can expect domestic sources to appear in the future.

Where Does It Come From?

- Bamboo is technically a grass with a woody stalk; there are more than a thousand species worldwide. Most bamboo is grown in Asia, although U.S. sources are emerging as demand increases.

In Demand as Food, Too

Bamboo is the sole source of food for giant pandas; each panda consumes 22 pounds a day. No wonder they grow so fast—the bamboo stalks, that is. Fortunately, commercial bamboo flooring is not the same species as the type favored by the endangered panda.

- Flooring, wallcoverings, and other residential applications may be made from solid or from engineered bamboo.
- Plantation practices vary greatly in their sustainability and ethics; no certification from the FSC or a third-party is yet available.
- Engineered bamboo is layered like a laminate and may have rubberwood or another wood as the core; look for FSC-certified core wood.
- DDT or harmful pesticides are sometimes used on bamboo farms in countries where pesticide use is not as well regulated as it is in the United States. Borate, a pest-inhibiting treatment considered safe around humans, is also employed.
- Urea-formaldehyde is frequently used in bonding agents for flooring planks. Formaldehyde-free bonding agents are less common.
- Other chemicals are sometimes added for mildew control, fireproofing, and pest resistance.
- Aluminum oxide and polyurethane are in standard factory finishes.
- Water-based acrylic stain may be added in standard factory finishes.

Installation

Bamboo must be allowed to acclimate to the home environment for several days prior to installation. While bamboo is touted to be more moisture-resistant than some hardwoods, humidity or water trapped underneath may compromise the

Delicious Coconut

Durapalm is made from reclaimed plantation-grown coconut or sugar palms that are past their fruit-bearing years. Because they are no longer productive, the trees will die or be cut down to plant productive palms. Manufacturing products from the old palms gives them a new life!

In fact, Alex Wilson, executive editor of *Environmental Building News* and the founder of BuildingGreen, has said, "Durapalm could almost be considered an agricultural waste product. It is a great example of a company recognizing an opportunity."

Colors include dark- to medium-red, mahogany (coconut palms), and light tan to golden brown (sugar palms). These durable and uniquely beautiful products can be used in both commercial and residential environments for flooring and paneling products. Durapalm products can be found with no added formaldehyde.

integrity of the floor over time, so specify that the substrate be tested for moisture content beforehand; there should be no more than a 3 percentage point difference between it and the bamboo itself. Manufacturers recommend bamboo be installed at a relative air humidity of below 60 percent; some will even void the warranty if that condition is not met.

To use concrete slabs as the substrate under bamboo, they must be cured for at least sixty days, allowed to dry completely, and then tested for moisture content. It may then be necessary to specify a vapor film to protect the flooring from seepage.

Depending on the particular flooring system selected, bamboo can be nailed, stapled, floated, or glued in the same manner as wood—over tile, wood, underlayments, concrete, and many other surfaces. A high-water-content adhesive is not recommended; specify a low-VOC alternative.

Bamboo does not take stain well, so any staining should be done during manufacturing. If specifying solid bamboo flooring with on-site finishing, specify a low-VOC, water-based finish as well.

Maintenance

Bamboo can discolor in direct sunlight, especially at high altitudes where the solar radiation is intense. Window coverings or UV-coated window treatments will minimize the effect. Occasional use of mild, nonabrasive, environmentally friendly cleaners, in addition to regular vacuuming and/or sweeping, will keep the floor looking bright. Oil soaps and damp mopping are not recommended.

Where Does It Go?

Bamboo with minimal amounts of binding adhesives, contaminants in the topcoat, or chemical treatments will biodegrade safely and quickly, much like wood. Engineered bamboo, with chemical binders, will not do as well. Bamboo can also be reclaimed, refinished, and reused in other applications.

Figure 14.9 This stairwell is constructed of bamboo stair treads, risers, and nosings. This space also features a railing made from unpainted steel with a low-VOC clear sealer and walls finished with no paint "tinted gypsum plaster."

Sanger Residence. Architect: Bruce Millard. Photo by Bruce Millard.

Fact Check

- An acre of bamboo absorbs 33 percent more carbon dioxide and releases 35 percent more oxygen than hardwood trees. Forests of bamboo—which can thrive at subtropical sea level and on 12,000-foot mountains—can significantly boost the oxygen content of the surrounding atmosphere.

- Depending on the species, a bamboo "forest" can completely regenerate every five to ten years. Some species grow more than a foot a day.

- Bamboo houses have survived floods, landslides, earthquakes, and cyclones. The stalk's flexibility is well known, but they're also so strong they've been used instead of rebar in Asia to reinforce concrete. In 1992, during a magnitude 7.5 earthquake in Costa Rica, all of the buildings surrounding a development of twenty bamboo houses collapsed, but the bamboo structures remained standing; the government subsequently decided to subsidize the construction of a thousand new bamboo houses.

Source: The World Future Society. www.wfs.org.

Spec List

Specify:

- Formaldehyde-free bamboo
- Third-party certifications like FSC
- California Section 01350 compliance
- Low-VOC finish (factory-finished is preferable)
- Low-VOC underlayment, adhesives, and binder
- Minimal use of adhesives
- Perfectly dry subflooring

Avoid:

- Formaldehyde in the underlayment, binder, or finish
- High-humidity weather for installation
- Chemicals added for mildew control, fireproofing, and pest resistance, and in finishes

American Bamboo Society. www.bamboo.org.

LEATHER FLOORING

Durable animal skins were probably one of the original flooring materials, along with grasses and dirt. Today, with the exception of vegan purists, leather flooring provides a soft, cushioned surface with terrific sound absorption, durability, and warmth. The surface breathes and gives with fluctuations in indoor temperatures and humidity.

Most animal skins are acquired by leather tanneries as a secondary product of the meat industry. Consultation with a sustainable/organic meat producer may provide leads to the tanneries that purchase from them. This will ensure that the skins were obtained from a pesticide-free, all-natural environment.

The modern production and tanning of hides uses a large amount of water, some of it to wash chemicals from the skins. And those chemicals, especially chromium sulfate and certain dyes, are poisonous. In developing countries, which are the largest producers of leather, there are few controls to protect the safety of the workers or regulate the quality of the discharged wastewater. In addition, the chemicals used may cause clients with sensitivities to react to large swaths of new leather, which will continue to outgas for a time (think of that new-shoe smell—amplified).

A few companies employ vegetable-based tanning processes, which rely upon natural tannins from rhubarb, tree bark, tare (a weed also known as vetch seed), and valonea (the beard of the acorn from an oak tree that grows in Greece). Natural vegetable and mineral dyes are popular with these tanneries. Specify leather from a company that specializes in these Old World methods. Local artisan leatherworkers might also be able to custom-make the flooring to specifications, thus providing a locally produced, more eco-sensitive product.

Recycled leather, which is obtained primarily from clothing and upholstery scraps, is an alternative for use as flooring. The leather will have already finished outgassing. (The VOCs will still be a problem no matter where they outgas, but using recycled leather will minimize the effect on a chemically sensitive client.) The leather will have already stretched as well. However, recycled leather flooring is not widely available; look for specialty artisans and producers.

Installation

Leather flooring is available in tiles or sheets. Leather is sensitive to humidity and temperature, so it should be acclimated for several days, then installed when the temperature is moderate. Leather is not recommended for damp areas. It can be laid over concrete or underlayment like any other resilient flooring, then glued, smoothed with a weighted roller, and tacked or covered with trim at the edges. Adhesive is necessary to prevent the leather from stretching or moving against the subflooring. Always specify low-VOC, solvent-free glues that work with the natural porosity of leather.

Manufacturers recommend several applications of carnauba or other naturally penetrating waxes or oils immediately after installation.

Maintenance

Light use enhances the patina of leather. Touch-ups with colored wax will hide some markings, but leather will not stand up to heavy abuse from heel marks or pet claws. To maintain the finish and protect the leather, wax or oil it frequently.

Where Does It Go?

Although leather and animal skins, by their nature, resist deterioration from the elements, they will eventually decompose. Certain tannery chemicals, however, present an ecological dilemma. Although the chemicals are only barely present in the finished product, their use creates water quality hazards that have not yet been fully measured.

Spec List

Specify:

- Vegetable tanning and dyeing processes that rely on tare, rhubarb, valonea, and tree bark
- Locally tanned leather with minimal chemical processing or dyes
- Third-party certifications
- Low-VOC, water-based glues

Avoid:

- Leather tanned with chromium
- Chemically dyed leather
- Solvent-based adhesives

CORK FLOORING

Cork is one of the best examples of a cradle-to-cradle resource. It originates as the bark of the cork oak tree, *quercus suber*, a species that grows primarily in Portugal and six other Mediterranean countries—Algeria, Spain, Morocco, France,

Figure 14.10 This kitchen has natural cork flooring.

© 2006 David Bergman

Italy, and Tunisia. There are approximately 6.6 million acres of cork forests in the Mediterranean region. These forests support the second highest levels of forest biodiversity in the world, second only to the Amazon rainforest. And there is an abundance of cork oak trees.

To make cork, the bark is harvested within a decade (every nine to ten years) after trees mature to an average age of fifteen to twenty years. Healthy trees live to a ripe young age of two hundred years.

The bark removal process dates back three thousand years. Regular extraction does not harm the oaks and actually ensures top-quality cork. The World Wildlife Fund proclaims cork harvesting a prime example of harmonious interaction between humans and nature.[1] With the demand for eco-friendly products expanding, many cork producers are moving toward FSC certification, ensuring that sustainable yields and sound environmental practices continue.

The environmental impact of shipping lightweight cork from Europe is slightly less than that of shipping heavier ceramic tile or stone. The processing for cork is simple and green: Slabs of bark from the tree are cleaned and boiled. In the cutting room, the production of wine corks usually gets priority, while the remaining scraps are collected for other uses, such as flooring and wallcoverings (see "Wallcoverings," page 363). There's virtually no waste.

Binder is added, and the cork is baked into a sheet. The composition of the binder depends on the manufacturer. While urea-formaldehyde was once common, some companies now opt for polyurethane or (supposedly) greener protein-based compounds; the specifics are proprietary and therefore difficult to judge. Avoid cork with vinyl or styrene butadiene backings or blends—they are not environmentally friendly.

Cork's cellular structure, consisting of polyhedral (14-sided) hollow walls, gives cork its buoyancy in water and makes it comfortable underfoot. Cork has the pliability of linoleum, outstanding sound absorption qualities, and bounce-back

---

[1] World Wildlife Fund. www.wwf.panda.org.

resiliency—up to 94 percent of the initial dimension—along with superb flaw-disguising qualities. And it's not a new flooring option—it's been used for over a century.

There's more. Suberin, a natural fatty acid intrinsic to cork, provides water resistance, has antimicrobial properties, deters pests (even termites), and is fire-retardant. Cork won't mold or rot like wood. It's antistatic and provides a nonslip surface especially appropriate for children or the elderly. The material is ideal for those with chemical sensitivities, as it does not outgas or shed potentially irritating microfibers.

Rumors of a cork shortage may be unfounded (see sidebar, "Cork Quandary"). And cork recycling—for everything from cork wine stoppers to postmanufacturing cork remnants—is now more widely accessible in the United States; it is yielding unique products like footwear, watchbands, fishing bobbers, and flooring (see the Fact Check sidebar, page 337).

Cork is sometimes blended with synthetic latex (styrene butadiene). Synthetic latex is often just called "latex," or even "rubber," but it is not the natural substance derived from rubber trees (see page 520). Avoid cork flooring blends for this reason.

Cork Quandary

For cork, the quandary of long-distance shipping is counterbalanced by the need to preserve cork oak forests. Nora Berrahmouni, Mediterranean forest unit director at the environmental nonprofit World Wildlife Fund (WWF), says that cork forest ecosystems are being endangered by population growth and forest clearing. Most of the cork in the world comes from a delicate, biodiverse ecosystem in southern Portugal called the Montado, home to the largest number of cork oak trees on the Earth. But with the loss of viable Montados, "There could be intensification in forest fires, a loss of irreplaceable biodiversity and an accelerated desertification process," she says.

"The cork forest loss is coming from the decline of the global cork market," Berrahmouni says, explaining that conventional wine corks are being replaced by aluminum screw tops and petroleum-dependent plastic stoppers. The decreased demand for cork has devalued the forests, leading to the sale—even the abandonment—of the once-priceless land.

Cork products such as flooring, on the other hand, will keep Montados intact and support a sustainable form of agroforestry, Berrahmouni says. "We encourage consumers to buy cork flooring materials."

Source: *Mother Earth News*. http://www.motherearthnews.com/green-homes/benefits-cork-flooring.aspx#axzz2gt1ffrUP.

Cork Is Tops

■ A French monk from the eighteenth century discovered the special ability of cork to stop up a bottle. Dom Perignon is famous not only for his champagne, but for the top that's fun to pop. Cork was widely used for bottling beverages before it was recognized as suitable for flooring, wallcoverings, and other applications.

■ Wine cork is readily recycled in Europe and Australia, and now in the United States, too!

■ Guides Australia, a girl's club, has collected more than seventy-five million bottle corks for recycling into floor tile, sporting goods, and boat decking. Girl Guides in Canada is following suit.

Source: www.guidesvic.org.au.

Where Does It Come From?

■ Cork is harvested from the bark of the cork oak tree, found exclusively in the Mediterranean region.

■ Cork flooring is made from sheets of bark pressed from scrap and/or recycled pieces.

■ Binders may contain urea-formaldehyde or polyurethane, or may be protein-based.

■ Cork flooring can be stained or left unstained. If finished in the factory, it may have an acrylic topcoat.

■ If needed, low-VOC, water-based adhesives are preferable.

■ Cork/rubber flooring blends are usually a mix of recycled styrene butadiene (synthetic) rubber and cork granules.

Installation

Cork flooring comes in large sheets, square or geometric tiles, planks, or mosaics. Some have interlocking systems and backings that make it unnecessary to use adhesives, except perhaps in high-traffic areas or around the edges. The color spectrum available is comparable to that of wood flooring, and natural stains can be used to enhance or change the hue of unfinished cork. Tiles come in varying shapes and sizes, making it easier to fit sloping floors and odd angles.

Cork will expand in high-humidity locations and will contract or become slightly brittle in arid environments, so specify acclimation to the particular home space before installation—most manufacturers recommend at least seventy-two hours.

The suberin in cork makes it unnecessary to treat the floor with finishes or chemicals, but the life span and stain resistance may be increased by doing so. Specify that the finishing be delayed until five days or more after installation to further allow for acclimatization. Inconsistencies may then be sanded out. Specify a beeswax-based finish or a low-VOC, water-based polyurethane. Any factory finish should also be low-VOC and formaldehyde-free.

Maintenance

Cork is basically maintenance-free: Vacuuming and sweeping are all that is necessary. Occasionally, it can be lightly damp-mopped; cork can be damaged by standing water, however, so advise the client to use a well-squeezed mop, never to allow the water to pool on the floor, and to put a towel under the bucket.

A cork floor can also be refinished with 00-grade steel wool on a floor sander.

Where Does It Go?

Except for any added finishes or adhesives, cork is fully biodegradable. Although cork from bottles can be recycled, the technology for recycling cork flooring has not yet been developed.

Spec List

Specify:

- Formaldehyde-free binders in the cork
- Minimal low-VOC adhesive backing or adhesive applied to the subfloor

Historical Cork

The use of cork in home design is timeless. Frank Lloyd Wright, eco-builder extraordinaire, used cork flooring in Fallingwater, the home that is now a historic landmark and museum in western Pennsylvania.

Source: http://www.paconserve.org/43/fallingwater

- Interlocking tiles that need very little adhesive
- Unfinished or factory-finished surfaces with low-VOC polyurethane
- Resin-oil primer and/or beeswax-based finish
- Natural pigment-based stains
- Reharvested or recycled content

Avoid:

- PVC (polyvinyl chloride)/vinyl blends or backings
- VOCs and solvents in adhesives and finishes
- Synthetic rubber (styrene butadiene) blended into cork flooring

RESOURCES

Cork Forest Conservation Alliance. www.corkforest.org.
Forest Stewardship Council. www.fsc.org.
Recork. www.recork.org.

BIOCOMPOSITE FLOORING

The popularity of biocomposites—especially boards made from agricultural by-products—is expanding exponentially in popularity for home construction and design (see chapter 12, "Wood and Composites"). They are manufactured from wheat or sorghum chaff, bagasse (sugar cane pulp), sunflower hulls, and a number of other leftovers from harvesting and processing. Biocomposites are most commonly specified as substitutes for plywood, medium-density fiberboard (MDF), oriented strand board (OSB), paneling, cabinet bodies and faces, and veneer. Agriculture-based biocomposites offer an annually renewable resource from crop by-products available from crops being grown anyway.

While not all ag boards possess the hardness or water resistance of solid wood, most varieties compare favorably to their respective engineered wood equivalents for purposes such as millwork, underlayments, backings, and casework. Where used as finish materials, the inherent grains, speckles, and color striations of the boards add unique beauty to an environmentally conscientious home.

Biocomposites can be used for flooring, cabinetry, or wall paneling applications. They are somewhat experimental, as the products' track record is not established, and the long-term results of their use are not yet unknown. Boards made from sorghum waste fiber are being marketed as durable enough for flooring. The sorghum crops, which are drought-tolerant and require little fertilizer or pesticide, are mostly harvested in northern China. The potential for a U.S. supply has not yet been exploited; sorghum, however, is already grown worldwide for ethanol, for sweeteners, and as a feed enhancer for livestock.

Ag board manufacturers are strategically oriented to please the eco-minded market, meeting California Air Resources Board (CARB) II compliance (see chapter 8,

Table 14.1. Biobased Materials

Category	Biobased Content	Key Questions
BASIC BUILDING MATERIALS Sourcing concerns are paramount with unprocessed materials, but performance can hold the trump card.		
Structure and Frame	Wood, bamboo, straw	Ensure responsible sourcing, such as with FSC certification
Insulation	Cellulose insulation Spray polyurethane foam with biobased polyols and binders Cotton and wool	Energy performance and indoor air emissions are key. Sourcing concerns are secondary.
Composites	Myriad types of fiber from sawdust to variety of agricultural wastes Vegetable-oil-based epoxies Binder of PLA or other biopolymers	Check performance benefits or concerns. Particularly with fibers, look for responsible sourcing, such as waste material. For binders, are they less toxic than the alternatives?
FINISHES AND FURNISHINGS Consider how the product compares with alternatives on a toxicity and life-cycle-impact basis. Sourcing may be a secondary concern, particularly if only a small proportion of the total product is biobased.		
Hard Surface Flooring	Wood, bamboo, laminates, and VCT alternatives from PLA	Look for responsible sourcing; for VCT alternatives, seek reduced hazardous content.
Resilient Flooring	Linoleum, cork, biobased polymers, natural rubber	Meet durability needs, and minimize indoor emissions. Then look for responsible sourcing.
Carpet	Wool, PLA, soy foam backing	Embodied energy and greenhouse gas emissions of raw materials are significant, but overall impact depends also on low indoor emissions, durability, and effective recycling.

(Continued)

Category	Biobased Content	Key Questions
Textiles	Cotton, sisal, leather, wool, silk, hemp, and other natural fibers along with PLA	Reducing both sourcing and processing impacts is important.
Wall Coverings and Wall Protection	PLA	Effective alternatives to PVC may reduce overall hazard profile.
Furniture	Wood, soy-based foams, biobased fabrics	Biobased matters, but don't let it distract from issues like emissions testing and multi-attribute certification of environmental performance.
WET-APPLIED PRODUCTS		
Does the product have lower toxicity and emissions than alternative?		
Paints and Coatings	Soy-based polyols\n\nOther biobased sugars and oils as ingredients to meet a variety of performance needs	What are the hazard profile and performance of the product? Are biobased ingredients facilitating phase-out of hazardous and fossil-fuel based ingredients?
Binders, Adhesives, and Sealants		
Concrete Curing Agents, Form-Release Agents, etc.		
FACILITIES MANAGEMENT		
Ensure the product is safer during and after use.		
Cleaners, De-icers, Fuels, and Lubricants	Predominantly vegetable oils, including soy	Ensure product is biodegradable and safe for people and the environment during use and after disposal.
Food Service	PLA plastic. Note some "compostable" plastics may not be biobased.	End-of-life strategy is key. Will it end up in recycling or industrial compost, and can it be made clear to the user and waste operator what to do with it?

Source: Jennifer Atlee, "Bio-based Materials: Not Always Greener," *BuildingGreen,* May 2012.

"Certifications and Standards") and using low-VOC, formaldehyde-free binders. Some manufacturers are even experimenting with soy-based substitutes for methylene diphenyl diisocyanate (MDI) (see chapter 12, "Wood and Composites"). Keep specifications for stains and finishes similar to those for equivalent wood products. In general, sorghum-based or other types of biocomposites are not recommended for bathrooms or laundry areas, as they are not waterproof and may warp easily.

There are trade-offs with using biocomposites, from its embodied CO_2 to the oversimplifications pertaining to material criteria to ensuring sustainable farming and harvesting. Although a renewable resource, its manufacturing process can have negative health and environmental impacts. Additionally, there are currently no third-party certifications for bio-based building products. A few standards lend themselves to beginning to set such criteria, but only a small percentage of bio-based products would actually be addressed. Quoting Jennifer Atlee of BuildingGreen, "They hold great promise, and many specific products are environmentally superior to the status quo, but there are no guarantees that being bio-based makes them safer or more environmentally friendly than their nonrenewable counterparts. We need to scrutinize such products carefully, particularly as we create incentives to encourage their further development."[2]

Where Does It Come From?

- Biocomposite boards are made from a variety of crop residues and agricultural by-products that include wheat, rice, barley, or oat straw; sunflower hulls; bluegrass or rye grass stubble; cornhusks and sorghum stalks; hemp; soybean plants; and bagasse (sugar cane pulp).
- Adhesives and binders may include low-VOC glues, outgassing solvents, formaldehyde, soy-based products, and natural or synthetic resins.
- Borate is sometimes used as a pesticide, especially in manufacturing. Other residual pesticides may be present from the cropland.
- Finished biocomposite boards may have water-based finishes or solvent-based polyurethanes.
- Formaldehyde may be used in manufacturing as a preservative or in the finish.

Installation

Biocomposite flooring can be stained, finished, installed, and maintained much like wood; check with the manufacturer for recommendations. Specify zero- to low-VOC water-based adhesives and sealants in all applications. Unfinished biocomposite sawdust may be disposed of as mulch or tilled into soil. Scraps should be treated like wood construction waste and taken to an exchange. No biocomposite recycling for building products has been developed yet.

---

[2] Jennifer Atlee, "Bio-based Materials: Not Always Greener," *BuildingGreen,* May 2012.

Maintenance

Maintenance of biocomposites varies by the content. Consult with the manufacturer for suggestions as to periodic resealing. Otherwise, the material should be cared for much like wood. Where there's heavy traffic from shoes or pets, rugs may greatly prolong the life of the floor.

Where Does It Go?

Like wood, biocomposite boards decompose naturally, back into soil. Small amounts of binders, resins, stains, and finishes used within or on the board may also decompose, but will do so much more slowly. Confirm toxic content to ensure these chemicals don't end up back in the soil.

Spec List

Specify:

- Boards made from 100 percent renewable grain (no plastics added, for example)
- Formaldehyde-free, zero- to low-VOC, water-based binders, sealants, adhesives, and stains
- Borate (if necessary), added for preservative or pest resistance

Avoid:

- Formaldehyde in the binder or finish
- Preservatives or pesticides (other than borate)

WOOD FLOORING

When thinking of natural elements in a home, the first that probably comes to mind is wood. It's a logical choice for homes with children, pets, or people with allergies because unlike carpet, which may collect mold, dust, and pet hair, wood is simple to keep clean. If properly maintained and occasionally refinished, it can last the lifetime of a home and will be a superb long-term investment.

Wood has less embodied energy than nonrenewable mined material such as stone or tile, and it requires only cutting and finishing to be suitable for home flooring. Unfortunately, most wood grows slowly over many decades, making it a slowly

Figure 14.11 This home has recycled oak flooring that was removed from a demolition project in Kansas City, Kansas. This space also features recycled metal stairs and railings and ample daylighting.

Photo courtesy of Rockhill and Associates. Designed by Rockhill and Associates.

renewable resource—a fact that was largely ignored by previous generations, who felled old-growth trees at alarming rates.

Although there have been improvements in recent years, forestry practices remain highly controversial and problematic. Single-species tree plantations are one way that forest products companies have tried to meet consumer demand for wood, but they lack the vital biodiversity necessary to sustain a complex, healthy ecosystem. And the destruction of the tropical rain forests, at the rate of an area equal to six football fields per minute, according to Greenpeace, is frightening.[3]

To counteract traditional forestry practices that meet market demand at the expense of the environment, the Forest Stewardship Council (FSC) has developed

---

[3] www.greenpeace.org.

Standing Tall

It has taken more than 2,000 years—and a lot of luck avoiding fire, disease, lightning, and saws—to become the tallest tree in the United States. The Coast Redwood in Jedediah Smith Redwoods National Park soars over 300 feet tall and is close to 80 feet in girth.

Source: "National Register of Big Trees," American Forests. www.americanforests.org.

chain-of-custody certification and environmentally friendly standards for the industry. Look for the FSC symbol on new wood flooring (see chapter 8, "Certifications and Standards," and chapter 12, "Wood and Composites").

Reclaimed Wood Flooring

For truly eco-friendly wood flooring, specify reclaimed wood from a local resource, construction salvage yard, dealer, or from a building planned for remodeling, deconstruction, or demolition. Locally found repurposed wood prevents new logging, obviates long-distance transportation, and saves wood from disposal. Better yet, specify SmartWood-certified types to ensure the species, the logging methods, and the remanufacturing are all earth-friendly.

Confirm the source of the reclaimed wood to make certain the company is not soliciting homeowners to dismantle historical structures. Look for responsibly salvaged products with a third-party certification like the "rediscovered wood" and "underwater salvage" certifications from the Rainforest Alliance to verify the wood's sourcing. These programs consider procedures that preserve the integrity of the environment as well as the health and welfare of workers and the community.

Investigate the source of the reclaimed wood to determine whether it is suitable for indoor use. If the flooring has been exposed to industrial chemicals or agricultural pesticides, for example, it's unsafe for residential applications. Reclaimed residential flooring from older homes is widely available and usually ideal. Also, all sorts of unique woods are now being reused from wine and whiskey barrels, to old fishing boats, to pallets for flooring.

New Wood Flooring

New wood flooring can be an ecological choice if the species isn't endangered and the forestry practices are sustainable. Review the project's sustainable objectives to direct the research and specifications for wood flooring. For example, it may appear more ecologically prudent to specify domestic wood because it requires less energy for transportation, but the species might be endangered, making exotic or foreign wood a better choice. Look to the FSC for guidance. Its certification ensures the wood has been forested sustainably and did not deplete endangered ecosystems. The FSC considers the availability of the tree species, monitors a company's conservation efforts as well as those along the chain of custody, and prohibits the use of genetically modified organism (GMO) species and certain pesticides. Other reputable and credible certification organizations exist, but none have the FSC's reputation for thorough, unbiased methods (see chapter 8, "Certifications and Standards").

There are three basic types of new wood flooring: solid, engineered, and acrylic-impregnated.

- *Solid wood flooring* can be purchased prefinished or unfinished. If specifying FSC-certified and an eco-friendly finish, solid wood is an excellent green choice. Suppressed wood—small undergrowth trees that are thinned and culled to aid in forest fire prevention on public lands—may not yet be certified (due to technicalities), but they are another wise selection.
- *Engineered wood* uses a variety of chemicals in the manufacturing, and it's made of pressed layers (usually three-ply or five-ply) that run in different directions, which gives it added dimensional stability in humid conditions such as near bathtubs or sinks. Look for formaldehyde-free, FSC-certified products.
- *Acrylic-impregnated wood* is a popular choice for commercial installations such as gym floors, but it's not considered an ideal green choice for homes because synthetics are a major component. There are a few manufacturers of acrylic-impregnated products, however, that use FSC-certified wood.

The industry trend is to use solid or engineered wood flooring with minimal or no carpeting. "New homes had more solid- and engineered-wood floors in 2011 than in 2004," said Ed Hudson, market research director for Home Innovation Research Labs (formerly the National Association of Home Builders Research Center). "And buyers chose wood flooring more often in every major room but the upstairs bathrooms."[4]

Where Does It Come From?

- Wood flooring is made from both domestic and exotic trees.
- Reclaimed wood is culled from residential, commercial, and agricultural floors, walls, and structures and also from rivers, lakes, streams, and fallen trees.

---

[4] http://articles.chicagotribune.com/2013–05–17/classified/sc-cons-0516-wood-flooring-20130517_1_solid-wood-engineered-wood-flooring

- Sometimes wood floors are made from recycled (downcycled) wood scraps or sawdust with added acrylics or resins.

- Sealants are usually polyurethane. Resin-oil primers are also an option.

- Floor finishes or stains may contain a variety of natural oils, resins, or pigments, solvents, chemical compounds, petroleum distillates, metal drying agents, formaldehyde, and sometimes water.

Installation

Wear spots, uneven edges, and inconsistent widths and lengths in reclaimed wood are all part of its beauty but can make it tricky to install. The job is best done by a professional with expertise in reclaimed wood floor installation.

Specify that the installer do the cutting outdoors to keep sawdust down. There are three basic installation methods; the flooring choice and the "bones" of the house will determine which might work best.

Figure 14.12 This home features two-hundred-year-old reclaimed barnwood flooring with water-based sealer and low-toxic finishes.

Photo by David O. Marlow. Designer: Maggie Tandysh, www.associates3.com.

- *Nailed.* Each piece is nailed, at an angle, to a subflooring, in a process often called "blind nailing." This is the most traditional way, and it needs virtually no adhesives, so VOC emissions will be minimal.

- *Floating.* Engineered flooring or subflooring can be designed to attach to and support itself through interlocking pieces. This is the best choice for use over a radiant heat system.

- *Glued.* The flooring (usually engineered) is glued to a subflooring, usually concrete or plywood. The adhesives chosen should be low-VOC to minimize health concerns.

Factory staining and finishing of wood flooring avoids VOC outgassing in the home. (The VOCs will outgas anyway, but this will minimize the effect on indoor air quality and will protect chemically sensitive clients.) However, finishing on-site gives you greater control over the products used. Consider skipping the finish altogether if the house is in an arid climate, there are dry conditions in the home, there will be minimal foot traffic, or if the client desires a wood species that will develop a smooth patina with use.

Addressing Sawdust Concerns

Conventional floor sanding stirs up huge volumes of hazardous wood dust and particulate from the existing finish. Container systems attached to the sander must be manually emptied and are an improvement over the conventional method of floor sanding, but the best method is to rely on a professional floor refinishing company that uses a sanding system with a hose that extends out of the house, usually to a collection unit inside a vehicle.

Alternatively, if the existing finish is in reasonably good condition, there are some low-VOC, eco-friendly finishes that can be applied without sanding the floor first.

Maintenance

Preserving the beauty and integrity of a wood floor is simple. Apply penetrating oils and waxes occasionally, and follow by a thorough buffing. Stripping is a last resort if layers of grime have developed. Hard finishes, on the other hand, will last indefinitely if given a bit of TLC.

For both reclaimed and new wood flooring, advise the client to:

- Prevent scratches and marks by putting felt or floor protectors under all furniture, rugs, and appliances.
- Remove their shoes in the house.
- Put rugs down in high-traffic or play areas (secure with nonslip backing or padding for safety).
- Sweep with a soft broom or vacuum regularly (turn the rotating bristles off to avoid scratches).
- Use a bit of soap designed for use on wood floors and minimal water when a more thorough cleaning is necessary.
- Never allow water to pool on the floor; use a mop for spills, placing a towel under the mop bucket.

If one piece of flooring has been damaged, it should be replaced before the damage spreads. If it becomes necessary to refinish the entire floor and the existing finish is compatible, specify an eco-friendly product that adheres with minimal or no sanding. Stripping the floor bare not only creates a mess, but the resulting debris can be hazardous to both the health of the worker and the client.

Where Does It Go?

A wood floor may be deconstructed and then salvaged for a similar or different use, or downcycled into a wood-based product. Only wood that is rotten or has been permanently tainted with toxic substances is unsuitable for reuse.

Spec List

Specify wood that is:

- Fallen on or thinned from the property
- Reclaimed
- Locally or domestically harvested, FSC-certified, and a nonthreatened species
- Suppressed (no certification is available)
- Rapidly renewable

Specify finishes and stains (either on prefinished wood or to be applied on-site) that are:

- Water-based
- Made of natural (sometimes called food-grade) oils, resins, pigments, and waxes
- Low-VOC
- Formaldehyde-free
- Free of metallic hardening or drying agents (such as zinc)
- Solvent-free
- Protected from moisture before and during the installation

Avoid:

- Reclaimed wood of uncertain origin
- Wood tainted with lead, arsenic, factory chemicals, or fungicides
- Uncertified wood
- Rare or threatened species
- Solvent-based finishes
- Formaldehyde and other preservatives in the wood or finish
- Metal-based drying agents in the finish
- Engineered wood, unless certified

RESOURCES

Forest Stewardship Council U.S. www.fscus.org
Green Seal Floor Care Products. Finishes and Strippers: www.greenseal.org/recommendations. htm
Rainforest Alliance. www.rainforestalliance.org
See also chapter 12, "Wood and Composites."

LINOLEUM

"Linoleum" is both a brand name and a widely used term that is not brand-specific. In general terms, linoleum is made from linseed oil (from the flax plant), pine resin (or tall oil, a by-product of pine pulp processing), sawdust or wood flour, cork, and limestone. It is also used on desks, countertops, or walls. The material is available with or without an adhesive backing and comes in sheets and tiles.

Linoleum is not vinyl, although in vernacular English, the terms are often used—mistakenly—interchangeably. Resilient flooring is often made from PVC-vinyl as well as a host of chemicals and petroleum-based compounds. The confusion began after World War II when a vinyl floor craze overtook the industry: both linoleum and vinyl were sold in rolled sheets or tiles, and the distinction was blurred and persists to this day. Similarities between the two end there.

For a time, linoleum wasn't manufactured in the United States (adding to the embodied energy from transport), but that is changing; the raw materials are available here, and the demand for this healthy, environmentally friendly flooring is flourishing. A leading manufacturer reported in 2004 that linoleum sales growth outpaced the overall floor covering market by more than double in five years.[5]

History Check

An explanation of the confusion between linoleum and vinyl:

Frederick Walton invented linoleum in the early 1860s, and shortly thereafter there was a patent war over the name. Walton lost, and now the word is used for all brands of the product. (A similar fate befell Kleenex and Formica.) That's why you'll see similar names for manufacturers' own brands of linoleum. The generic term "linoleum" is often confused with vinyl composite tiles (VCT) as well.

---

[5] *Healthy Building News*, May 17, 2004. www.healthybuilding.net.

Linoleum is basically manufactured through mixing, pressing, and a curing or drying process that takes several weeks—like a slow baking process. Linoleum is made from mostly renewable resources in an ecologically gentle process. Look to third-party certification for stringent emissions protocols like FloorScore and/or at minimum, compliance with California Section 01350.

There are few drawbacks to using this material. Linoleic acid oxidizes naturally, releasing a VOC that is rarely irritating, but the slight odor can irritate a client with chemical sensitivities. The VOCs will, however, dissipate over time. Are the fumes harmful? It's unlikely, but the verdict is still out. On the flip side, linoleum's natural oxidation process is useful for preventing and eliminating bacterial growth, making linoleum the flooring choice of many health-care facilities.

The flooring can last thirty years in high-trafficked areas, or decades longer with less wear and tear. Linoleum underfoot has comfortable resiliency. The dyed-through color hides minor blemishes and damage, and a sort of self-healing repairs tiny cracks because of the give in the material. Kits with accurate color are available to patch small blemishes.

Where Does It Come From?

- Linoleum is mostly made from linseed oil, pine resin, sawdust or wood flour, cork, small amounts of pigment, and limestone.
- Linoleum usually has a burlap-type backing made of jute or sometimes hemp.
- The finish, if there is one, is usually ultrathin acrylic.
- Linoleum adhesives are chemical compounds; some are low-VOC, water-based, and formaldehyde-free.

Installation

Some manufacturers recommend linoleum not be used below grade or in bathrooms where moisture can stain it. FSC-certified wood-based underlayment or

---

Unique Tribute of Linoleum

Are bright sunlight and fading an issue for the client in selecting a floor finish? Linoleum has a unique property that will counteract this problem. When kept in the dark, linoleum may experience natural yellowing, but the colors will brighten again when exposed to daylight.

concrete are both acceptable subfloors. All subflooring cracks should be filled and bumps completely smoothed out, as the softer surface of linoleum shows imperfections. Specify that the floor must be perfectly dry before installation, according to manufacturer recommendations for moisture content. This is critical to avoid trapping water that will degrade the integrity of the flooring.

The adhesives recommended for linoleum are not interchangeable with those for vinyl, so follow the manufacturer's specs precisely. A low-VOC, water- or resin-based type is best. The small amount used may have an odor, but it is not a skin or eye irritant, and the MSDS for most linoleum adhesives is labeled "no hazardous ingredients." Linoleum seam adhesives, however, may outgas and the MSDS does include cautions for eyes and skin. Plan for proper ventilation both during and after installation.

Because linoleum usually comes in rolls or boxes of tiles, there will undoubtedly be extra, even after measuring carefully. Advise the client to keep some extra tiles for replacing small damaged or worn-out sections. Leftover pieces might also be put to use in a bathroom or closet. Thin strips can be safely shredded for garden mulch, as linoleum is completely biodegradable, or they can be donated to a school or senior citizen art program.

Maintenance

Linoleum is best vacuumed or swept or cleaned occasionally with a barely damp mop. No chemical cleansers or finishes are needed. For cracks or tiny holes, matching patch kits made from nontoxic glue and ground-up linoleum solids are available. Very light sanding will also improve a damaged linoleum surface.

Where Does It Go?

With the exception of its thin acrylic coating and adhesive, linoleum is fully biodegradable.

Spec List

Specify:

- True linoleum, not vinyl, made from linseed oil and other natural materials that meets third-party certification
- Smooth, dry subfloor or underlayment
- Low-VOC, water-based, formaldehyde-free adhesives

Avoid:

- Vinyl flooring mistakenly called linoleum
- Seam adhesives

"RUBBER" FLOORING

The verdict is still out on whether recycled "rubber" flooring—made not from rubber trees but from synthetic, petroleum-based latex recycled from tires—is truly safe for residential applications. Most companies that market the products to homeowners claim low-VOC levels that meet indoor air quality specifications, but as with automobile tires, this flooring has a distinct odor. Additionally, the source latex, which is rather spongy by nature, has been exposed to enormous amounts of toxins while rolling down the highways under someone's car. It seems unlikely that all dangerous compounds can be removed.

Although there is inherent value in recycling, and this product is frequently marketed as eco-friendly, specify recycled rubber flooring with care, especially if you are apprehensive about emissions, as the rubber, binders and additives may off-gas, contain heavy metals, or compromise indoor air quality.

Where Does It Come From?

- Recycled rubber/latex flooring is not made from natural rubber or latex (from rubber trees); it's made from recycled tire chips.
- Tires are largely manufactured from synthetic rubber, a petroleum-based product.
- Some recycled-rubber flooring has as little as 5 percent recycled tire rubber content.
- Rubber flooring may contain traces of heavy metals, chemicals, petroleum-based compounds, and other elements from its former life on the road. This is difficult to quantify because the content varies with supply.

Where Does It Go?

It may be possible to recycle this rubberlike compound, but it will not break down in a landfill for many years. The incineration of tires is highly controversial and can pose a serious human health hazard.

Spec List

- Because of its questionable content, recycled tire "rubber" is not a healthy choice for a home, even if it does prevent landfilling.

Fact Check

The Rubber Manufacturers Association notes that in 2009, U.S. scrap tire disposition broke down as follows: 40 percent tire-derived fuel, 26 percent ground rubber, 12.5 percent land disposal, 7 percent used tires, 5.5 percent civil engineering, and 8 percent other.

Source: Rubber Manufacturers Association. www.rma.org.

RESOURCE

Rubber Manufacturers Association. www.rma.org.

CONCRETE FLOORING

See "Concrete," chapter 9.

TERRAZZO

Traditionally, terrazzo refers to flooring made from small pieces of mineral (especially marble) in aggregate and cement or resin, often polished to a high sheen. Originally, the technique was designed to make use of waste marble and other rock chips from quarries, turning them into a product that mimicked expensive stone at a more affordable price. The Italians perfected the terrazzo technique and gave it the name we still use in English. And they discovered that goat's milk intensified the beautiful color of the marble, making it the first all-natural terrazzo finish.

Modern terrazzo can be poured on-site, prefabricated into slabs, or manufactured into tiles that are laid in mortarlike ceramic or stone. It is made from chipped, ground, or sorted mineral or manufactured aggregate. The pieces are then bound together in a cement matrix, a modified cement matrix that contains acrylic additives, or a resinous matrix. Sometimes brass, metal, or manufactured forms are inlaid to produce beautiful patterns. The color and design possibilities are endless, and the final product can be specified to fall below the most rigid standards for VOC emissions.

Terrazzo is more common in commercial settings than residential ones, yet it offers many benefits for a healthy eco-home. It's superdurable and will easily last the life span of the house. It doesn't collect substances that aggravate chemical sensitivities, and it's simple to sweep, vacuum, or damp-mop. If the terrazzo is made from postconsumer recycled glass then the aggregate is nontoxic, zero-VOC, and stain-resistant. Another ecological plus is that the use of "waste" rock keeps valuable mineral-based material out of the waste stream.

If you are considering terrazzo with recycled glass, note that the alkali-silica reaction between the recycled glass and the cementitious base can weaken the product and lead to fractures in the cement. Some manufacturers coat the glass with an epoxy binder to address this issue. Epoxy binders contain bisphenol-A, a potential developmental and reproductive hazard on the EPA's chemicals of concern list.

Look to third-party certifications – FloorScore, C2C, Greenguard – coupled with careful specifications will ensure that the aggregates, base materials and binders in the terrazzo are environmentally sound. Recycled glass is an earth-friendly aggregate choice. Quarried rocks like marble or granite, especially if imported or rare, are less green because they are nonrenewable and have higher embodied energy from mining and transportation. Be wary of aggregates of other manufactured or recycled materials, as they may contain undesirable petrochemicals, vinyls, heavy metals, or other toxic or outgassing substances. Pigments that occur naturally in the aggregate stone, minerals, or recycled glass are better for home and earth than chemical colorants.

Cement and concrete are energy-intensive "binders" but are very long-lasting and made from relatively abundant natural resources. If admixture-free concrete is used, the hardened substance will be inert and not outgas. Cement terrazzo will need to be sealed, however, because it is porous and absorbs stains and dirt.

The resinous matrix for the aggregate is often made with epoxy, latex, polyester and acrylic, or a combination. This type of terrazzo will not need to be sealed, as the surface is basically impermeable. The complex composition of these resins, usually proprietary and not readily available to consumers or contractors, can be difficult to analyze for nontoxic properties or eco-friendliness and might contain chemicals that are harmful to the workers or emit VOCs after application. Careful investigation into ingredients and methods is warranted. Look for low-VOC, formaldehyde-free, water-based, or low-solvent binders.

Where Does It Come From?

- The agglomerate, also called matrix or conglomerate, may consist of stones, mineral chips, glass, metal, or any number of manufactured or natural materials.
- Minerals are often gleaned from postindustrial waste.
- Glass is usually postconsumer bottles and windshields.
- The binder may be cement, modified cement with acrylic additives, or a polyester/epoxy system.

Installation

Poured terrazzo flooring systems require a heavy-duty, perfectly level, flat substrate, preferably made of concrete. Additional sand and cement underneath, in a metal grid system, are needed for cementitious terrazzos. Resin-based, thinset terrazzo systems do not require a sand-cement underbed.

Once the aggregate and resin are poured, it is polished on-site with power or (rarely) hand tools. Because polishing creates airborne particulates that are inhaled, it's critical that the resin matrix be nontoxic. Specify that all furnishings be removed from adjacent areas and that proper ventilation or vacuum systems be used to prevent contamination of other living areas.

Terrazzo tile may be laid like ceramic or stone; specify FSC-certified wood or agricultural fiber underlayment. (see "Tile," page 319). Tile or cementitious terrazzo will need to be sealed. Specify a low-VOC, water-based type, preferably wipe-on (as opposed to spray).

Maintenance

How you maintain terrazzo depends on the materials it's made from. Consult with the manufacturer for specifics. However, terrazzo flooring should never be cleaned with chemicals, harsh detergents, or abrasives. Advise the client to damp-mop with water and mild detergent, or simply vacuum or dust-mop. Cementitious terrazzo may eventually need to be resealed.

Where Does It Go?

The natural terrazzo tile content will break down—ceramic, stone chips, and glass deteriorate into minerals. The binders, epoxies, acrylics, and other manufactured compounds may complicate the biodegrading of the terrazzo, slowing the process as a whole or by leaching contaminants.

Spec List

Specify:

- Products that meet third-party certifications
- High recycled-glass content
- High (waste) mineral content, preferably not rare or imported types
- Cement matrix without admixtures
- Low-VOC, water-based, no-odor resin or modified cement binder
- Low-VOC, water-based, wipe-on sealer

Avoid:

- Manufactured aggregate content that may contain contaminants, epoxy binders, or harmful chemicals
- Outgassing binders or sealants

RESOURCES

Marble Institute of America. www.marble-institute.com.
National Terrazzo and Mosaic Association. www.ntma.com.

CARPET

"Where does it come from and where does it go?" are the questions to answer when considering the environmental impact of carpet, as most conventional carpet is not made from natural materials and won't easily decompose or biodegrade at the end of its relatively short useful life. Historically, natural animal and plant fibers were knotted or woven for floor coverings; large carpets were reserved for the wealthy. Along with cheap petroleum and post–World War II scientific "advancements" came the advent of 100 percent manufactured fibers. The price of carpet plunged, making it affordable and immensely popular.

The carpet industry was implicated when people began to complain of multiple chemical sensitivities (MCS) or sick building syndrome (SBS), then pointed at the floor. The suspects? The outgassing of an array of chemical carpet treatments (individually or in combination)—even the primary materials. In lab tests on mice, the mice got sick and died from exposure to these chemicals.

The Carpet and Rug Institute (CRI) implemented a voluntary-compliance Green Label program that tests for—and verifies the absence of—many potentially harmful substances in certain brands of carpet, padding, and adhesives, especially as they affect indoor air quality. Green Label Plus meets the strict guidelines for low-VOC emissions compliant with California Section 01350. Note that both these programs are second-party certifications through the CRI association. Although other, VOC-emitting chemical substances may be substituted for the ones that are found to emit even higher levels of VOCs, the improvement is a step in the right direction for the conventional carpet industry.

For deeper green products, NSF-140 is a third-party, multi-attribute standard for sustainable carpet that takes a life-cycle approach to its assessments. This voluntary, point-based standard looks at the entire life cycle of carpet, from material selection to carpet recycling and certifies three levels: silver, gold, and platinum. Platinum carpet products must contain 10 percent postconsumer recycled content, be certified by the CRI's Green Label Plus program or California Section 01350 for indoor air quality, be free of polybrominated diphenyl ether (PBDE) flame retardants, and meet Carpet America Recovery Effort (CARE) recycling goals.

Figure 14.13 This home has natural wool carpet with natural jute backing.

Designed by Annette Stelmack and Beth Scott, www.associates3.com. Photo by David O. Marlow.

Most carpet is still made with nonrenewable petroleum by-products, and most types can't be recycled. Natural fibers are a much more eco-friendly choice. Unfortunately, for those with environmental preferences, all-natural carpet is an oddity in the mainstream marketplace. Even those touted as 100 percent wool, the natural fiber of choice, are often chemically treated with mold and moth inhibitors. Natural backings and paddings are even less common. Grasses and plant fibers such as jute, hemp, coir, sisal, and sea grass are more likely to be found in area rugs rather than wall-to-wall carpet.

In greening a carpeted home, go with all-natural types (no chemicals or synthetics) made from wool, ideally with organic certifications. Specify domestically made, if possible, to avoid transportation and the pesticides that are mandated for imports. Wool is already stain-repellent, fire-resistant, and extremely durable without any treatments. Jute, coir, and plant materials do not last as long as wool and stain more easily, but they are completely biodegradable.

After all-natural carpets with no additives, all-wool carpet with minimal chemical treatments is the second-best choice. Avoid synthetic dyes. Because conventional carpet dyes are chemicals, the color choices for an eco-friendly home will be limited to nature's palette of subtle hues. Look for the

Fact Check

- Formaldehyde is no longer used in carpet manufacturing. The formaldehyde that outgasses from old carpet may come from other sources—for example, when home and garden chemicals are tracked in on the soles of shoes.

- The latex used in most carpet backing and padding is synthetic and will have no effect on someone with a true latex allergy.

Carpet Recycling

Carpet comprises up to one percent of landfills in the United States. That's almost 5 billion pounds total; and a huge proportion of it is nonbiodegradable nylon.

California's AB 2398 carpet recycling law is facilitated by CARE. In 2011, the first year CARE served as the stewardship organization, CARE reports that during the reporting period of July 1 through December 31 in California:

■ 80 carpet manufacturers participated in the CARE Stewardship Plan.

■ 385 million pounds of postconsumer carpet were discarded; of that amount, 60 million pounds were diverted from landfill and 36 million pounds were recycled.

■ The diversion rate for carpet was 15 percent, 4 percent higher than in 2010.

Carpet manufacturers have also committed to closing the loop in a different way. They've designed carpet squares that need little adhesive, so that only one tile—and not the whole carpet—can be pulled up and replaced if damaged. A handful of companies even offer to take back the carpet for recycling at any point in the future—a truly valiant step toward environmental responsibility.

To locate a carpet recycler, contact the manufacturer, Carpet America Recovery Effort (CARE) (www.carpetrecovery.org) or check out Earth 911 (www.earth911.org).

Sources: Carpet and Rug Institute. www.carpet-rug.com; CARE. www.carpetrecovery.org.

NSF-140 and Green Label Plus certifications, then avoid additional stain repellents or mothproofing.

Though carpet tiles made from natural fibers are available, they aren't always 100 percent natural; they will nonetheless be made predominantly from wool, coir, hemp, and even corn sugar fiber in some of the blends.

Who would ever imagine that the film on a glass windshield might someday be downcycled into carpet? Spurred on by the need for PVC-free carpet and by the burgeoning supply of recyclables, carpet is being made from (polyvinyl butyral (PVB), or nonchlorinated vinyl. No microbial agents are needed, the carpet won't mildew, and the PVB doesn't outgas or cause health problems. Carpets are also being made from downcycled polyethylene terephthalate (PET) plastic bottles or carpet manufacturing scraps. While all of these certainly merit as landfill-reduction strategies, they only stall the inevitable.

Don't forget to consider the carpet backing. Jute and natural latex are found on the underside of natural carpet fibers, while cotton and hemp are also used. Conventional synthetic carpets will typically have synthetic backings.

Where Does It Come From?

- All-natural carpet is made from natural fibers such as wool, silk, jute, coir, sisal, and sea grass.

- Synthetic carpet or synthetic/natural blends contain artificial fibers such as nylon, olefin, and acrylic.

- Carpet backing is often made from synthetic latex (called styrene-butadiene, SB latex, or styrene butadiene rubber SBR); natural-fiber backings such as jute are less common.

- Padding may be made from PVCs or vinyls, recycled carpet fibers, wool, jute, camel hair, or mohair.

- Carpet, padding and backing may contain potentially toxic substances such as benzene, styrene, toluene, vinyl acetate, PVC, fungicides, mothproofing, stain-proofing, mildew inhibitors, and antistatics.

The Truth about Carpets and Allergies

You'll probably want to specify another floor covering if anyone in the client's household suffers from allergies or MCS. Carpet's cushy surface is a superabsorbent sink for all kinds of airborne and footborne irritants: dirt, allergens, pet hair, dust mites and insects, water, even toxins on shoes carried in from the workplace or street. There is a small body of research that indicates carpet collects some irritants, thereby removing them from indoor air so that air quality is improved, but the offensive substances presumably still end up between the occupants' toes. Even the most fastidious housekeeping can't remove it all; recent studies showed that considerable dust could still being extracted from carpet after forty minutes of vacuuming.

Source: *Environmental Building News*, May 2003. www.buildinggreen.com.

Installation

Before removing old carpet, request that it be vacuumed thoroughly to eliminate as much dust as possible so it doesn't escape into indoor air. Specify that new carpet be installed in good weather so it can be aired out in the sun for a day before bringing it into the house. Sunshine and good air circulation will speed up any remaining outgassing.

- *Underlayment.* Specify FSC-certified, CARB II-compliant, low-VOC, plywood or gypsum substrate with no-added urea formaldehyde (NAUF).
- *Padding.* To enhance a carpet's life span, don't skimp on the padding. The padding makes up half of the total weight or volume of some carpet installations, thereby providing a buffer against the hard floor underneath. Specify natural padding made from wool, jute, horsehair, or similar materials. Specify that it be formaldehyde- and free of butylated hydroxy anisole (BHA).
- *Adhesives.* Use little or no adhesives to support optimal indoor air quality; opt instead for wooden tack strip or "tackless" strips along the walls. If adhesive is needed, specify a low-VOC, solvent-free, or water-based variety.

Removable tiles with adhesive backings or corners and carpet held in place through a hook-and-loop (Velcro) tape are two other alternatives; the client will be able to lift the sections for easier cleaning, repairs, or replacement.

Maintenance

Avoid topical stain treatments that can outgas or flake harmful contaminants, and talk to the client about avoiding do-it-yourself stain treatments.

Excellent care will extend carpet's lifetime. Dust and other heavier-than-air toxins settle into the carpet, degrading the quality of both carpet and the indoor air. The secret to maintaining carpet, especially an all-natural one, is simple: keep it clean and dry. Encourage the client to vacuum thoroughly at least once a week with a HEPA-filtered model. Natural products such as club soda or a tiny amount of mildly soapy water can be employed for stain removal. Cornstarch can be used as a blotter; sprinkling baking soda will help remove odors. Natural wool, especially, is prone to mold, so avoid wet-extraction cleaning methods.

Where Does It Go?

Nylon can be recycled; check your local area for the availability of carpet recycling programs through CARE. Wool, jute, coir, sisal, sea grass, corn, cotton, and silk carpet will all biodegrade. Some manufacturers have committed to allowing customers to return their carpet—one square to a whole houseful—for recycling. Urge the homeowner to keep the warranty and product information for future recycling and disposal options.

Spec List

Specify:

- Products that meet multi-attribute, life-cycle assessment certifications, CA 01350, or CRI Green Label Plus
- 100 percent wool carpet, domestically produced, free of dyes, additives, and all chemical treatments
- 100 percent plant-fiber carpets (jute, coir, sisal, sea grass), free of chemical additives and dyes
- Carpet content that is recyclable and/or returnable to the manufacturer, especially if made from natural fibers
- Carpet tiles for easy cleaning and replacement
- Jute backing
- FSC-certified wood underlayment or gypsum substrate
- Tackless strip, tack strip, or Velcro-type fastening systems
- Low-VOC adhesive backing
- Small amounts of water-based yellow or white glue, or low-VOC adhesives, applied to perimeters only
- Formaldehyde-free
- BHA-free
- Brominated flame retardant (BFR)-free
- Pesticide-free
- Recycled-content carpet
- Recycling of replaced carpet

Avoid:

- Manufactured fibers such as nylon
- Stain repellents
- Synthetic dyes
- Benzene, styrene, toluene, vinyl acetate, and similar chemicals
- PVC-vinyl, especially in the backing or padding
- Fungicides, mothproofing, stain-proofing, mildew inhibitors, antistatics, BFR, or other chemical treatments

RESOURCES

CARE. www.carpetrecovery.org.
Carpet and Rug Institute. www.carpet-rug.org.

Wall Treatments

WALLCOVERINGS

If it's flat and can be hung vertically, it can be made into a wallcovering. Traditional paper is just one green option; there's also sisal, bamboo, linen (made from flax), hemp, jute, wood, fabric, cork, and more. That's a great environmentally friendly option for covering old paint or blemished walls or for simply adding texture and color to a living space.

The practice of finishing walls with rice paper may have begun in the Orient over 2,000 years ago, but the concept of decorative wallpaper made its debut in Europe in the fifteenth century. Those with limited financial means used painted wallcoverings to mimic the luxurious tapestries, paneling, molding, and scrollwork that embellished the homes of the very rich. By the late 1700s, fashionable wallpaper was being printed onto rolls in mass quantity.

In the mid-twentieth century, PVC-vinyl became the wall "paper" of choice. Soft, pliable vinyl offered durability, could be scrubbed and stripped off the wall, and offered other practical and affordable characteristics. It also had some frightening ones:

- PVC-producing factories poison the air, water, and soil—as well as the factory workers—with dioxins.
- Products made with vinyl outgas hazardous VOCs during manufacture, immediately after installation, during fires, and if incinerated improperly.
- PVC and its softening agent, phthalate, have been implicated in causing a host of illnesses ranging from respiratory irritation to cancer.[6]

There's another downside to vinyl that directly affects the indoor environment: it lacks breathability. Moisture trapped between it and the wall creates a breeding ground for mold and prevents a wall from drying into the interior of the home. Open-weave wallcoverings are much more vapor-permeable, and plant- and animal-based materials are inherently more porous. Needless to say, there are few applications in eco-friendly home design where vinyl should be considered.

Nevertheless, vinyl is still prominent in the "fabric" of most conventional wallcoverings and their backings and coatings. The growing public awareness of PVC toxicity and hazards is, however, quickly decreasing its popularity on walls—the

[6]*Environmental Building News*. www.buildinggreen.com.

Figure 14.14 This scalable wallcovering is manufactured from rapidly renewable material. The design, demonstrating the movement of synthetic neural systems, was created by Casey Reas for Maharam.

Designed by Annette Stelmack, www.inspirit-llc.com. Photo courtesy of Zocalo Development.

market share has dropped more than 25 percent in recent years.[7] In an effort to camouflage PVC content, the word "acrylic" is often used instead of "vinyl"; though it sounds more benign, the substance is usually one and the same.

Some manufacturers have switched to other synthetics. It's a step in the right direction for human health, but still reliant upon petrochemicals and nonrenewable resources. Still others are offering new, greener options made from all-natural and recycled fibers.

Careful research into both the manufacturer and the materials is warranted before introducing a client to any wallcovering option. Some companies offer natural fibers in a particular line of wallcovering but add vinyl to those products. Others feature a line of all-natural wallcoverings, but use synthetics and vinyl in all their other offerings. Specify coverings that are absolutely vinyl-free, not just made with a percentage of all-natural materials in the total composition.

Next look at the potential life span of the product. Will the treatment last in the particular environment? Can it be wiped clean? Can a single section be replaced if soiled? If it's removed, will it biodegrade?

Once you've found an eco-friendly wallcovering that suits the client's needs and aesthetic, consider any additives used on the paper or covering, along with the methods and products that will be used during installation. Water-based inks or dyes are best; heavy metals should be excluded in the manufacturer's specs. Look

---

[7] Carole Beeldens, "Green by Selection," *Environmental Design and Construction*, March 7, 2005. www.edcmag.com.

for vinyl-free, low-VOC, no-formaldehyde, solvent-free products, and apply these same specs to strippers, lining papers, pastes, coatings, sizings, and backings. Avoid chemical additives such as stain repellents, biocides, fireproofing, and pesticides. (Borate is an acceptable mineral treatment that both repels insects and resists fire.)

Look into products that carry the multi-attribute, third-party certification from the National Sanitation Foundation—NSF-342. To evaluate the sustainability of wall-covering products across their entire product life cycle, this certification employs a point system that compares products to established requirements, performance criteria, and quantifiable metrics in the areas of product design, product manufacturing, long-term value, end-of-life management, corporate governance, and innovation.

Designers beware! The team at the Pharos Project recently found that researchers from Healthy Stuff (www.HealthyStuff.org) tested a wide range of wallpaper products. They learned that some national and local brands contain lead, phthalates, brominated flame retardants, and an assortment of other chemicals connected to human health complications, from asthma and liver damage to reproductive problems, birth defects, and autism. (For more details, visit www.pharosproject. net/blog/detail/id/79#sthash.9OKwqrX2.dpuf.)

Paper and Nonwovens

Wallpaper is often affordable, and the selection of colors and patterns is nearly infinite. The term "wallpaper" is used generically to describe many kinds of wall-coverings, including those made with no paper at all. The term is also often used to describe vinyl sheeting that contains no wood-fiber content.

That said, conventional wallpaper is often made from wood, but other all-natural, fiber-based paper coverings can be produced from rice, bark, cotton, linen (flax), straw, or parchment (animal skin). A truly green wallcovering would be derived from organically grown, pesticide-free, non-GMO crops, but such wallpaper has yet to be developed. Focus on specifying natural content with a minimum of processing or additives. Wallpaper with postconsumer and postindustrial stock may also meet the client's preferences and green objectives; look for a high percent of recycled content, such as paper or sawdust. When specifying, be precise in your request for paper content.

Sometimes minerals figure into the content of wallcoverings, including clay, sand, and powdered stone, which add texture or color. Ceramic beads and glass fibers, although manufactured, have mineral-like qualities. They add durability and "scrubability" to the wallcovering, give off no VOCs, and cause no harm to the environment when disposed of, and so are considered eco-friendly.

Embossed wallcovering—Lincrusta or Anaglypta—was invented by Frederick Walton, the inventor of linoleum, using many of the same ingredients used to formulate the flooring—sawdust, linseed oil, plant resin, colored dye, and zinc oxide. This essentially bio-based wall coveirng gets tougher with time; many examples still exist in buildings more than one hundred years old. A primary concern is that a lining containing a fungicide is required.

Value in Tradition

Zuber has been manufacturing wallpaper in France since 1797 using a traditional system that is quite eco-friendly. Every panel is painstakingly printed by hand using carved woodblocks and natural pigments, chalk, and sizing. The most elaborate wallcoverings require more than a thousand separate blocks and hundreds of colors. Many older residences and historical sites throughout the United States that feature Zubers have hired restoration specialists to preserve their extraordinary beauty. The wallpaper has tremendous cultural value, as well; in 1995, the French government declared the blocks "nationally valuable historic monuments."

Other manufactured substances such as polyester, rayon, and polyvinyl alcohol (PVA) may be blended into the natural mix. Though they might add slightly greater durability, they subtract nonrenewable petroleum from the earth and are made through intensive manufacturing processes. Avoid synthetics in general. Lastly, specify water-based inks (or none at all) to avoid solvents and VOC emissions.

Wovens

Eco-friendly woven wallcoverings are made from a wide variety of fabrics (see "Furnishings," page 449), grasses, and fibers such as sisal, silk, raffia, linen, hemp, and cotton. Grass cloth is a traditional type of woven wallcovering made from ramie (a member of the nettle family), although imitations and those with vinyl backings are also common, so be sure to double-check the specifications. All natural-fiber wovens are intrinsically breathable, but not all are suitable in high-humidity locations or near tubs and sinks, where water stains can be an issue.

Glass "yarns" made from sand and treated with a modified starch, are the latest wallcovering innovation. These glass-based wallcoverings, which can be wiped clean, meet stringent low-VOC requirements and are far more durable than traditional papers or fabrics. The surface can be painted over if it becomes badly soiled, eliminating the need for future removal. While the fabric is not all-natural, glass is inert and will eventually revert back to silicon dioxide (sand) when it disintegrates after the end of the wallcovering's useful life cycle.

As with wallpaper, woven wallcovering backings are sometimes made from vinyl. Search for products with no PVCs or vinyl, added fire retardants, pesticide inhibitors (except borate), waterproofing, or other synthetics. Water-based dyes and inks—or none at all—are preferable.

Cork

Cork wallcovering adds superb sound absorption to any room. It has natural microbial qualities, needs only occasional dusting or light spot-cleaning, and is available unfinished or factory-finished with low-VOC waxes or polyurethane. In addition, cork has great thermal qualities, retaining heat or staying cool as needed. The only place that this wallcovering might not be ideal is in a kitchen or other area that gets wet or soiled easily, as cork can't be scrubbed, and it absorbs oils and stains. (See also "Cork Flooring," page 334.)

Leather

It might not be the first thing that comes to mind to use as a wallcovering, but leather is extremely durable and can be applied in tiles or sheets. However, leather is usually processed with toxic chemicals in developing countries with few worker protections; some clients will also be opposed to the use of animal products.

Leather wallcoverings should be allowed to outgas the tanning substances outside of the home. Look into recycled or locally made leather, or leather processed with minimal dyes and chemicals, and look to third-party certifications like Greenguard that address emissions. It may be necessary to reapply natural oils, waxes, or sealants to protect the finish and maintain the desired patina.

Leather stretches over the years as it succumbs to gravity, so a combination of fasteners and low-VOC adhesives are recommended when it's applied to walls.

See also "Leather Flooring," page 333.

Wood, Bamboo, or Biocomposite Paneling

Wood paneling is a popular wallcovering that also shows up in wainscoting and beadboard. Bamboo and agricultural-waste biocomposites are catching on as well because they are more quickly renewable and have many of the same qualities as wood.

See also "Biocomposite Flooring," page 339; "Biocomposites," page 284; and "Bamboo Flooring," page 328.

Installation

Depending on the particular material, installing wallcovering may require sizing; priming the walls; adhesives, glues, or pastes, stapling or tacking; and seam or edge treatments such as extra adhesive or trim.

Specify natural glues and pastes whenever possible, or a low-VOC, low-odor, water-based type of synthetic adhesive if the former will not provide an adequate bond. Similarly, specify low-odor, low-VOC, water-based primers. Avoid all products that contain formaldehyde or vinyl.

Maintenance

With proper care, fine wallcoverings made from quality materials can last for decades. Gentle dusting or occasional spot-cleaning is all that is required. Consult with the manufacturer for specific recommendations.

Wood, leather, and cork will last longer than most fabrics or papers, and paneling may endure the full life span of a house. Although unsealed cork and leather may develop water spots, they can be spot-cleaned with mild detergent and water if they have been sealed. Depending on the type of material, the adhesive, and the substrate, wallcoverings can sometimes be removed easily and replaced with a different wall finish.

Where Does It Go?

If made with 100 percent natural fibers or material, wallpaper will decompose so easily that it could be shredded and used as garden mulch. Cork, leather, wood, and bamboo have potential for reuse or recycling and will also break down quickly when disposed of.

Spec List

Specify:

- Products that meet third-party, multi-attribute certifications
- Wallcoverings made from all-natural fibers such as grasses and reeds
- Wallpaper made from all-natural paper (wood, rice, or other pulp)
- All-natural cork wallcoverings
- Leather wallcoverings that have been minimally processed with the use of natural tannins
- Wallpaper or wallcoverings made from high recycled-paper or fiber content
- Water-based inks or dyes
- Nontoxic, low-VOC wallpaper paste

Avoid:

- PVC-vinyl
- Heavy metals in the inks or dyes
- Formaldehyde
- Solvents in strippers

- Stain repellents
- Biocides
- Fireproofing
- Pesticides

Paint and Coatings

Wall color is one of the design changes homeowners request most often; half of them will paint soon after moving in. As designers, we understand that paint color is more than just embellishment; there is psychological energy in a well-chosen hue. In addition to aesthetics, the inhabitants' health is the top priority to be balanced with performance. To support a healthy indoor air quality (IAQ), specify products that have zero- to low-VOC content (under 50 grams per liter), are compliant with California Section 01350 emission standards, and meet the higher standards of the Master Painters Institutes Extreme Green (MPI X-Green) standard which, like GreenSeal standard, includes performance metrics.

Paint was designed to preserve and protect the home's surface and structure. Architectural coatings, the most common of which are paints, effectively seal out moisture and mildew, prevent abrasion and damage, repel dust, and provide a surface that can be washed or cleaned occasionally. Paint can last years with only minimal maintenance. These are sound ecological characteristics that also increase the longevity of a home.

Evaluating paint for its environmental pluses and minuses is complex. The same chemical components that boost the durability of conventional paint may also outgas VOCs, irritate chemically sensitive individuals, pollute the air (both indoors and out), smell bad, or eventually chip or flake toxins. Because paint will cover a large surface area, it can have a significant effect on the health of clients and on the environment.

Figure 14.15 Whimsical and vivid hues that awaken your inner child, the Sweet & Hot Beans collection from Divine Color is biocide free, delivers a zero-VOC interior paint that is easy to apply, and has a fabric-like finish enhanced with light-enhancing pigments.

Courtesy of Gretchen Schauffler, www.divinecolor.com.

The Culture of Color

There's more to hue than meets the eye. As designers we understand the powerful meanings and cultural interpretations possible when selecting the perfect color to pair with furnishings. Yellow may be sunny and upbeat to Westerners, but it signifies mourning in Egypt and Burma. Red is the color of weddings, prosperity, and good luck for most Asians. And in some parts of China, blue signifies little girls while black is reserved for little boys. The paint colors the client prefers may have subtle or strong spiritual and personal significance.

The push for cleaner air, both indoors and out, has motivated paint manufacturers to scrutinize the safety and health of their products, at least regarding VOC outgassing level (see "VOCs," page 381). The volatile organic compounds in paint present a special risk when indoors, where ventilation is limited and soft surfaces such as furniture can be a sink where they collect. (All furnishings should be removed for any interior paint job). VOCs also react with the atmosphere to form ozone. To deal with these problems, new architectural coatings that have lower-than-ever VOCs and less odor are constantly being introduced to the market. But eliminating VOCs is not the end-all answer to improving paint ingredients.

Standard architectural coatings may contain hundreds of other chemicals—preservatives, fungicides, biocides, drying agents, suspension agents, and more—so deciphering labels and MSDS warnings for the pros and cons can be challenging. Unless the quantities of certain hazardous compounds exceed a certain level, the manufacturer is often not required to put a warning on the label or MSDS for them. And the risks when different chemicals are combined are not always predetermined. Worse still, a label will carry some warnings of known hazards, but the paint's "recipe" is considered proprietary, and the rest of the contents remain a mystery to designers, contractors, and architects.

Furthermore, precisely measuring the indoor emissions and toxic content from paints and coatings is challenging at best. The various product certifications address varying criteria without providing a clear guideline for comparisons. Some consider the total volatile organic compound (TVOC) content and emissions in their testing, while only a few address the VOCs in pigments and tints. South Coast Air Quality Management District (SCAQMD) Rule #1113 looks through the lens of smog-based requirements. Emissions testing, TVOC, toxic content, smog-based impacts, tints, and pigments—including SVOC, formaldehyde, and other chemicals of concern passing third-party chamber testing protocols—must all be part of the sustainable product assessment and certifications moving toward a full life-cycle assessment.

There are alternatives to conventional paint made from naturally occurring substances. Some have outstanding ecological characteristics and have been in use for decades or even centuries. But paints touted as made from all-natural or organic ingredients are not necessarily benign in their effects on the environment and human health. Unlike organic produce, no labeling standards exist for coatings. Natural-ingredient paints may contain as many or more irritants and odors as conventional types and may pose their own health or environmental risks. Evaluate any paint, even those marketed as natural or organic, before selecting it, and then try it out in a smaller area before using it for an entire job.

And remember, painting is not always essential. The materials used in wall construction or an existing finish will determine, at least to some degree, whether options besides conventional paint might be preferable from an environmental standpoint. If the walls have not yet been constructed, forgo paint altogether and specify no finish, a natural finish over plaster or wallboard, or a pigment added to the plaster. These choices have fewer VOCs and negative repercussions than conventional paint.

Faux Finishes

Faux finishes are an alternate decorative treatment, usually painted, that simulate another material. Stone, metal, Venetian plaster, brick, and panoramic views can all be imitated with the use of other materials. Sometimes faux finishes are intended to replicate something more costly or rare, such as marble tabletops or gilded trim. Other times the intent is purely whimsical, such as a landscape painted on the dining room walls.

There are benefits to using faux finishes in a green home if they replace the use of a resource that would be less ecologically prudent. Instead of using a rare wood for trim, for example, a skilled artisan might be able to paint or stain a sustainably grown variety to look the part.

On the other hand, the faux-finishing techniques might require the use of paints or other compounds that are not earth-friendly (see "Artist Paints," page 383). It might make more sense to apply a non-toxic mineral-based plaster, for instance, than to mimic the look with layers of conventional paint.

Weigh the options before deciding on a faux finish for a green home.

Paint Composition Basics

All paints—the conventional type and alternative varieties—contain three basic elements:

- The liquid, called the vehicle, carrier, or solvent
- The pigment(s) and solids
- The binder, which keeps it all flowing together in liquid form

In addition, many paints contain additives to improve drying time, flow, mildew resistance, scrubability, coverage, and fade prevention.

The *liquid carrier* is what gets the paint from can to wall; it then evaporates, leaving only the pigments and binder. In latex paints, water is the liquid. In oil-based paints, a variety of oils, alone or in combination, are used. Alcohol is also used as a carrier in specialty paints.

Pigments do the hiding or covering and the coloring. Titanium dioxide is the most common pigment used; it provides a bright white base with excellent coverage. Filler pigments such as clay, calcium carbonate (chalk), or other powdered minerals may be added to provide bulk at less cost. Other pigments may include simple mineral compounds (like iron oxide), organic (plant-based) compounds, or synthetically derived substances. When combined with a liquid dispersion agent so they can be added to paint, they are called "colorants" or "tints." Pigments and covering agents together are called solids.

Binders enable the pigment to float in the liquid and be applied to a surface. The content of the binder varies greatly among products, from simple casein in milk paint to highly complex mixes of chemicals. The pigment and the binder—what's left after the liquid evaporates and the paint dries—are together called the "solids."

Typically, the solids comprise 25 to 45 percent of the paint; glossy paints have the lowest percent. "Dead flat" paints may have a pigment-to-volume ratio (see the sidebar, "Come to Terms," page 385) of as much as 80 percent, but 40 to 50 percent is more common. Better-quality paint has a higher percentage of solids and will cover in fewer coats and last longer, making it the environmentally responsible choice. In most cases, the more expensive the line of paint (within a particular brand), the higher the solids content and the longer the warranty.

Source: Paint Quality Institute: www.paintquality.com.

Still, there will be many times when paint is the preferred finish, either because of economics (it's inexpensive), practicality (there is already a coat of paint on the wall), or client preference (the zero-VOC types may contain the least irritating compounds). And quality paint does have some ecologically positive characteristics. Paint provides a cost-effective wall treatment that is easily "repaired" or covered with more paint if the décor—or the homeowner—should change. No demolition or deconstruction is needed—just a few gallons of paint and a brush. It will last for decades if the surface was prepped well and the finished paint job is kept clean. When evaluating conventional paint options, steer toward those with the lowest amounts of harmful chemicals, especially VOCs that are a risk to homeowners, workers, and air quality. Whenever possible, specify zero- to low-VOC, water-based coatings without preservatives, biocides, or solvents. Avoid the chemicals listed in this chapter as particularly risky.

Careful surface preparation will ensure the longest life span for the product. Prudent sampling and estimating the quantities needed precisely will avoid waste, and leftover paint can be reused or recycled to avoid sending it to the landfill.

This information is a starting point for evaluating the seemingly infinite choices and combinations of paints and primers. As designers, we can continually educate ourselves about the technological changes so that we can guide the client, the contractor, the architect, and the crew to selecting—and disposing of—architectural coatings in an environmentally friendly way.

CASEIN OR MILK PAINT

Casein, the protein in milk, has been used since prehistoric times as a coating or binding agent. Cave drawings were done with a mixture of pigments, milk, clay, and lime. Similar paint is very common on early American furniture and walls. Today's milk paints are made of the same ancient materials but usually come in a powder form that is mixed with water on-site.

Milk paint (or casein paint, as it is sometimes called) is an ecological hero to many designers. Individuals who are sensitive to odors might find the wet-paint smell problematic, but milk paint dries quickly to an odorless, food-safe, completely nontoxic, biodegradable, durable, zero-VOC finish. Remove all furnishings before painting to lower the risk of VOCs settling into the upholstery and porous surfaces. (Otherwise, the VOCs and odors can reemit later.) There's virtually no waste because the precise amount needed can be mixed, and the leftover powder may be kept indefinitely in an airtight container for touch-ups or other projects.

Casein paint dries to a hard, flat finish that is easy to maintain. And the slight variations in color from the natural mineral pigments are aesthetically desirable. Although small amounts of nonrenewable minerals and energy-intensive lime figure into its composition, this drawback is certainly outweighed by its excellent preserving, beautifying finish that will potentially last for centuries.

A few companies offer premixed, liquid-form milk paint. However, like the milk we drink, casein-based conventional paint spoils rapidly, so the ecological positives are diminished by the preservatives that are required. There are also so-called milk or casein paints that are actually oil-based or formulated like latex paint that nevertheless include casein as an ingredient, but these are more akin to conventional paints (see "Conventional Paints," page 380).

Where Does It Come From?

- The liquid is water.
- The binder is the casein naturally found in milk.
- Pigments include naturally occurring metal oxides, salts, and clays.
- Lime is also added.

Installation

Remove all furnishings before painting to lower the risk of VOCs settling into the upholstery, textiles, and porous surfaces. Otherwise, the VOCs and odors will reemit later as SVOCs as they attach themselves to particulates.

Milk paint may be used on unfinished, uniformly porous surfaces such as gypsum plaster and wood. Previously painted surfaces and unfinished drywall with joints will need a surface prep coat as recommended by the milk paint manufacturer. The prep coat or primer will diminish the ecological characteristics overall but might be a good option if a milk paint finish is desired.

Mix the paint fresh on-site as needed so there will be minimal waste and spoilage. Leftovers may be covered tightly and refrigerated, but the paint will spoil in a matter of days.

Milk paint may be brushed, rolled, or sprayed on. It must be stirred several times per hour to keep the solids suspended. Clients should expect subtle color variations, even within a single batch. Although rigorous color standards are kept by most milk paint companies, the mineral pigments themselves will have natural, subtle differences reflected on the painted surface. Multiple coats will diminish these variations but not eliminate them.

Because it is porous, unfinished milk paint is susceptible to stains and water spots. If the milk paint is applied near a tub or sink, a traditional water-based acrylic topcoat (per the manufacturer's recommendations) will prevent damage but will lessen the environmental benefits of using milk paint. Natural penetrating oils or waxes may also be used as finishes; however, they will darken the color.

Small amounts of wet milk paint can be safely disposed of by pouring it out in the yard or down the drain. There is no need for disposal of the powdered form; it may be saved indefinitely for touch-ups or used on other projects. If the paint is likely to become soiled from water, dirt, or oils from the skin, manufacturers recommend a protective sealant or topcoat be applied after the paint dries.

Maintenance

Milk paint is porous and thus prone to water-spotting and stains. The colors and surface will remain vivid and durable over many years, but the flat surface can't be washed.

Simple touch-ups may be done with more milk paint. Milk paint will not chip or flake like traditional paint, and age only enhances its rustic, natural beauty.

Where Does It Go?

Natural milk paint—in dry powder, with water added, or as a finish—is completely biodegradable. The painted surface is considered food-safe and has no known harmful effects during deconstruction or disposal, or as it deteriorates.

Spec List

Specify:

- Dry milk paint powder made from casein, lime, clay, and natural pigments.
- Mix fresh paint daily on-site; small quantities of leftovers may be saved in a refrigerator overnight and used the next day.
- All leftover powdered base be saved for touch-ups or future projects.
- If milk paint becomes soiled, finish with a natural penetrating oil, beeswax, or water-based, low-VOC topcoat as recommended by the manufacturer.

Avoid:

- Latex, oil-based, or premixed paints labeled as containing casein.

SILICATE DISPERSION PAINT

Silicate dispersion paint is made from liquefied potassium silicate, which reacts and binds with calcium salts, silica, ceramics, and some metals to form a permanent coating on a variety of surfaces. (Liquefied potassium silicate is sometimes called "water glass," or "inorganic mineral paint.") Many materials will accept silicate paints and form an insoluble, crystalline, rocklike finish, including Portland cement, limestone, marble, mortars, concrete, brick, terra-cotta, and iron, among others.

Although it is most commonly used on exteriors because of its high durability, it's suitable for use on interiors as well. Paint made with this substance has been around for more than a century and has recently caught on in Europe, where walls made of lime plaster and rock are more prevalent than in North America.

Silicate dispersion paint is not suitable for wood or plastic, but with the correct primer (as recommended by the paint manufacturer), it may be used over paper-faced drywall. It is both permeable and durable, allowing air and moisture to breathe through the surface, and water will not damage it. The paint is completely noncombustible, odorless, VOC-free, and nontoxic, and the mineral-based colors are virtually fade-proof. It also has inherent antifungal properties. It's perfect for a green home, especially for clients with chemical sensitivities.

The major drawback to silicate paints is its energy-intensive manufacturing. Potassium carbonate (also historically called potash), the chief ingredient in potassium silicate, is commercially prepared by a process of electrolysis and carbonation sequentially applied to mineral compounds. The potassium carbonate is then fused with silica at high temperatures. The resulting potassium silicate compound is water-soluble and is blended with mineral pigments to form the paint.

Where Does It Come From?

- Mineral pigments are the primary coloring agents.
- Potassium silicate is derived from a complicated process involving electrolysis, carbonation, and high temperatures applied to mineral compounds.
- Water is the liquid carrier.

Installation

Silicate dispersion paint can be applied with brushes or rollers in the same manner as conventional paint. The surface should be clean and free from oils or substances that might interfere with the natural bonding process. Because the paint is VOC-free, it poses no known risks to workers or inhabitants. One word of caution: Glass surfaces such as windows need to be protected to prevent permanent etching through a chemical interaction with the paint.

Maintenance

The dried and hardened silicate surface is less statically charged than traditional paint, so it repels dirt better. It is also water-resistant. Little upkeep is needed, and the surface may last for generations. Touch-ups and additional coats of silicate dispersion paint can be done on top of the preexisting silicate paint with no preparation beyond a simple cleaning.

Where Does It Go?

Silicate dispersion paints bond chemically with the substrates. If the surface underneath the paint is limestone (calcium carbonate), for example, together they form a benign mineral compound that is also a carbonate. Any metal in the substrate and the minerals used as pigments will also safely decompose at the end of their life cycles. There are no known risks to the environment.

Spec List

Specify:

■ Silicate dispersion paint

■ Low-VOC primer, if needed

■ Removal of all furnishings before painting the area to avoid contaminating them with VOCs and odors

Avoid:

■ Primers or paint additives that outgas

"NATURAL" OR "ORGANIC" PAINTS

There are many companies that promote their products as "natural," although there are no firm labeling standards for paints that use ingredients found in nature. So-called natural or organic paints, which are often oil-based, usually contain natural oils, mineral or plant pigments, and plant resins. Some companies adhere strictly to an all-natural policy, whereas others use fossil-fuel solvents and chemicals as needed, although in smaller quantities than in conventional paint. A few companies ride the proverbial fence, combining natural oils with traditional paint technology to produce conventional latex or oil-based paints that have slightly more eco-friendly characteristics (see "Conventional Paint," page 380).

If the manufacturer chooses to rely on truly natural ingredients, the contents might include dammar resin, turpentine, natural-rubber latex, carnauba wax, or tung oil (all derived from trees). Shellac (made from insect secretions), citrus extracts such as d-limonene, vegetable oils, and beeswax may also figure into the compositions. Heavy-metal pigments are excluded from the formulations. Calcium carbonate (chalk) or talc is often preferred over titanium dioxide as the covering agents for natural paints.

Natural paints may seem like a natural choice for the environment and the client. Although simpler, naturally derived substances seem like they'd be benign, that's not always the case. Lead, for example, is a metal found in nature, but it can be lethal to humans. In the same respect, not all natural paint ingredients are nontoxic or have fewer VOCs and less odor. Oils such as d-limonene (known to cause skin rashes) and turpentine have significant odors that can be irritating to those with sensitivities. Like their manufactured counterparts, these organic compounds will outgas, although it hasn't been determined whether natural VOCs are less harmful than manufactured ones. Some naturally derived oils and resins are under scrutiny for other more serious health risks as well. Still, common vegetable oils such as castor (also called ricinus), soybean, canola, and safflower have virtually no smell and are obviously less problematic, so they are the safest choices. If the natural paint contains compounds not easily recognized, spend the time to investigate them and understand the potential risks.

There is one more distinct advantage to specifying natural or organic paints. The manufacturers are more forthright in revealing the ingredients, as these substances are their source of pride. For the most part, conventional paint companies keep their paint compositions secret unless they are required by law to reveal a particular risk.

When specifying an oil-based natural paint, a sniff test on a painted patch within the home is prudent. Bear in mind that different colors will have different smells because of the chemical reactions between ingredients and different color blends used to keep the mineral pigments in suspension.

Improved Paint Sampling

The choice of an interior paint color depends on numerous factors: paint luster, interior lighting, daylight (or lack of it), adjacent furnishings and flooring, surface texture, and the size of the space. Sampling in the location to be painted is optimal for accurate selection and is especially important if odor or chemical sensitivity needs to be tested. Until recently, paint colors were chosen using small paint chips as a starting point; a few brushstrokes from quart- or gallon-sized "sample" cans were then applied to the wall. The amount of paint wasted through trial and error was significant.

In their effort to make painting easier and more cost-effective for consumers, manufacturers have been developing more user-friendly sampling media. The resulting decrease in waste generated is good news for the environment as well. Paint chips have graduated to paint sheets, large "painted" papers, some of which are poster-size and even stick to the wall. Smaller cans and pouches of paint colors are another recent innovation that make it simpler and less expensive to try them out with far less waste. It's a win-win situation for the designer, the client, and the Earth.

One advantage over conventional paint is that the manufacturing of natural or organic paints is usually less intensive, with fewer chemicals and manufactured compounds and generally less processing. The risks listed on the MSDS may also be more straightforward, there's likely to be fewer of them. Natural or organic paints may have the upper hand over their conventional counterparts in another way: Because the substances are derived directly from plants and minerals, they usually break down better at the end of their life cycles.

Where Does It Come From?

- Plant-based oils are the primary carrier for natural paints, including but not limited to turpentine, tung oil, d-limonene, safflower oil, and castor oil.
- Resins and binders are usually plant-derived as well, and may include dammar, shellac, carnauba wax, and beeswax.
- Pigments are mineral-based and plant-based.
- Calcium carbonate is a common covering agent.
- Some companies use petrochemicals or synthetics in combination with the natural ingredients.

Installation

Remove all furnishings before painting to lower the risk of VOCs settling into the upholstery and porous surfaces. Otherwise, the VOCs and odors will reemit later.

Natural, oil-based paints may be used wherever conventional paint might be applied: on wood, drywall, metal, and plaster, among other surfaces. A test spot will determine suitability. Because the paints are made with mineral pigments and oils, they will not yield a perfectly consistent color; rather, the paint will display variations that add to the earthy quality of the finish. Cleanup will require a compatible solvent, which may negate some of the environmental positives; consult with the manufacturer for specifics (see "Conventional Paint, Installation," page 386.)

Maintenance

Natural paints need little maintenance or upkeep, similar to their conventional paint counterparts, although their scrubability is limited. Future touch-ups may be tricky because some natural paints don't store well, and good color-matching technology may be limited.

Where Does It Go?

The oils, pigments, and resins found in many minimally processed natural paints will break down much faster and more safely than complex chemicals found in conventional paint. Leftovers should never be dumped down the drain or thrown out with regular trash, as the solvents and oils may be flammable and therefore should be treated as hazards.

Spec List

Specify:

- All-natural plant-based or mineral-based oils and pigments—food-grade, when possible
- Zero- to low-VOC additives
- Removal of all furnishings before painting the area, to avoid contaminating them with VOCs and odors
- Proper disposal of leftovers as hazardous waste at cleanup and completion

Avoid:

- D-limonene or odorous paints if client is sensitive to them

CONVENTIONAL PAINT

There are several factors to consider when judging a conventional paint: the VOCs, the chemical additives, and the choice between latex and oil, among others. For healthy IAQ, research and specify products that have zero- to low-VOC content (under 50 grams per liter), are compliant with California Section 01350 emission standards, and meet the higher standards of the MPI X-Green standard, which includes performance metrics.

At first glance, it would seem the choice of liquid vehicle is obvious. Water is better than oil, right? Well, mostly so. Water certainly provides an earth-friendly base for paint that is natural, renewable, and that cleans up with more water. Although quantities of paint should never be dumped down the drain, the small amount left on a brush may be rinsed at the sink.

There's another reason for the preference for latex over oil. Latex paints—almost all of them water-based—generally outgas far less than solvent-based paints. The water carrier naturally evaporates without giving off VOCs. Solvent-borne paints, commonly called oil-based, are made with natural or manufactured solvents. They also dry when exposed to air, but in the process, give off VOCs (see "VOCs," page 381).

VOC Labeling for Paint

Cleaner air indoors and out, along with ease of use, are behind the popularity of today's latex paints. This popularity is reinforced by legislation. Some governing agencies, such as the State of California and the European Union, have put limits on the VOCs allowed in paint, and have strict labeling requirements.

The standards for labeling paint as "low-VOC" vary according to locale and type of paint. While "low-VOC" and "low-odor" are often used interchangeably, they are not equivalent. Low-VOC paints emit less VOCs, but there still may be components in the paint that give off objectionable odors. And don't assume that because a paint is labeled "low-odor" that it is low in VOCs; it may simply have less odor than a different type or line of paint.

"Zero-VOC" is another common claim by paint manufacturers, but it doesn't always mean what it appears to. The method used to measure VOCs (EPA Reference Test Method 24) is only accurate above 5 grams per liter; below that, the compounds can't be accurately assessed. So zero-VOC or no-VOC paint may actually outgas, albeit in miniscule amounts. And keep in mind that these standards were meant to measure the VOCs' effect on ozone and low-level smog; toxic chemicals that outgas but do not contribute to ozone are not considered in the VOC total, so there still may be odors or vapors from dangerous substances in low-VOC paints. Be certain to ventilate well, whatever product is used.

In addition, oil-based types require yet another outgassing solvent for cleanup. Latex has fast become the preference over oil-based, both for its simpler cleanup and its less-noxious odor.

The drawback to latex? To enable water-based paints to dry effectively and to keep them from spoiling and mildewing, the manufacturers add drying agents, preservatives, fungicides, suspension agents, and a host of other chemicals. So while oils outgas as a result of their solvents, latex paints introduce other chemical issues. Both types will emit the most VOCs immediately after application, then taper off. However, VOCs can settle in fabrics and carpet, and the effects may be longer term. If a client has a sensitivity to a particular chemical, check the labels scrupulously, even for water-based and low-VOC paints.

Figure 14.16 Interior view of unit kitchen in Eco Modern Flats features low-VOC paint complemented by a custom-fabricated steel bar, solid wood millwork, concrete countertops, and polished concrete floors, creating a durable, clean, and sustainable finish palette.

Designed by Chris M. Baribeau, www.modusstudio.com. Photo by Brandon Horner of Adaptive Creative.

Other Considerations

Whatever the variety—oil-based or latex—there are other factors to consider. In general, the higher-gloss paints contain elements that raise the VOC level; conversely, so-called dead flat paints almost always have the lowest levels. If the colorant is solvent-based, deep colors will increase the VOC emissions slightly. Specify natural food-grade or mineral-based pigments.

The typical binder for conventional paint is an acrylic such as polyvinyl acetate (PVA). Acrylics are petroleum-based, energy-intensive, and generally nonrenewable. Their complex chemical makeup also breaks down very poorly upon disposal. The production of acrylics creates an abundance of waste and by-products as well.

Titanium dioxide production is yet another downside to conventional paint. The compound has replaced lead, a known toxin and significant health threat, as the number one choice for covering power and whitening pigment. Titanium is the fourth most common element on Earth, yet the manufacturing process for it is anything but environmentally friendly. Synthetic and natural rutile (a titanium compound) are combined with the titanium-rich slag from pig iron smelting. The complex manufacturing is best understood by a chemist, as it involves high temperatures, chemical washes, and reductions. The process contributes to pollution and is hazardous to workers. Other pigments, like chalk and clay, are usually considered secondary fillers because they don't cover as well nor last as long, but they are occasionally used as primary pigments. Yet the mining of clay and chalk also has drawbacks and health risks for workers. The decision

Artist Paints

Artist paints, lacquers, and thinners are commonly used for faux finishes and murals. Generally speaking, artist paints are highly concentrated and may contain a wide variety of toxins such as petrochemicals, heavy metal pigments, and VOC-emitting solvents. These paints and associated chemicals have limited applications within a green home.

There may be occasions where a faux finish is a better choice than the rare or nonrenewable natural material that the client desires (see "Faux Finishes," page 371). To minimize these negative effects, encourage the use of nontoxic paints or finishes such as plaster, mineral pigments, lime washes, or milk paints. Specify water-based products whenever possible. Avoid all sprays, as the airborne particulates are especially harmful to air quality. If the client is sensitive to odors, the artist may be able to paint a mural on canvas elsewhere and then transfer it to the home after it has had time to dry and air out.

for or against titanium dioxide in paint, from an environmental standpoint, is a complicated one.

Heavy metals are hazardous additions to paint, too, usually showing up as pigments or in colorants. Lead was banned from use in architectural coatings in 1978; mercury was banned from interior paints in 1992. Artist paints and colorants (see the sidebar, "Artist Paints") may contain cadmium and chromium hexavalent (also called chromium VI). Specify that all paints be free of these, and use extreme caution when removing old paint that could be contaminated with lead or other toxins.

Formaldehyde-based resin is still found in some paints and should be avoided. Formaldehyde also appears as a biocide, along with copper, arsenic, phenol, and ammonium compounds. While such additives are intended to prevent mold, mildew, and wet-paint spoilage, they are associated with numerous health risks and can trigger reactions in those with chemical sensitivities. Specify paint that is mixed "fresh" and biocide-free.

Remanufactured Paint

Leftover paint that would otherwise end up in hazardous waste disposal sites is now being collected by manufacturers and remade into useable new product. It's a noble effort on behalf of the environment. The companies sort the used paint by type (oil or latex, interior or exterior), test it to determine its particular properties, then mix it with compatible products. Some locations add the recycled paint to new paint for even better quality remanufactured blends.

The final product is usually tested for VOCs and is suitable for many uses, even though the color choices are limited to gray, beige, or other muted colors. Because the chemical content is still unclear, remanufactured paint is best used forstorage areas, garages, or exteriors in order to minimize its affects on someone with chemical sensitivities. As remanufacturing technology improves, more low-VOC and specialty paints will become available.

Recycled Paint

Many communities have drop-offs that divert leftover paint from the landfills; some are then made available to the public through "swaps." The rest of the collected paint is usually sorted (interior or exterior, water or oil-base) and then mixed with similar types. The resulting unpredictable shade of gray is often used for graffiti abatement, community restoration projects—even park shelter finishes.

A few locations make the remixed paint available to consumers at a nominal charge. Unlike remanufactured paint that undergoes testing, meets certain safety standards, and whose VOCs and basic chemical content are disclosed on its labeling, VOC emissions and other details about these recycled paints are not known. While the community recycling program certainly prevents waste, the remixed paint is a poor selection for a healthful interior and is best left to lower-risk exterior projects.

The Yes List

With so many things on the no list, what's left for a project team to choose from if conventional paint is the client's preference? Fortunately, there are companies that strive to manufacture quality products and leave the hazards out of their formulas.

To support a healthy IAQ, research and specify products that have zero- to low-VOC content (under 50 grams per liter), are compliant with California Section 01350 emission standards (Greenguard, Indoor Advantage Gold), and meet the higher standards of the MPI X-Green standard (available at www.specifygreen.com) which, along with Green Seal, includes performance metrics. For requirements related specifically to smog, meet the South Coast Air Quality Management District (SCAQMD) rulings for 2012 and newer limits for 2014 (available at www.aqmd.gov).

Start by evaluating the MSDS carefully for each brand or style of paint being considered, and consult with the manufacturer on chemicals of concern and/or proprietary blends. Then consult with the client to avoid known allergens or chemical sensitivities. Specify the paints and primers best suited to the project that have the least amount of known hazards and the highest performance. Specify the highest quality of paint possible; repainting less often saves money and is environmentally friendlier.

Educate the client about effective maintenance and cleaning of painted surfaces. Help the client establish optimal storage solutions for leftover paint, along with earth-friendly disposal methods when leftovers kept for touch-ups are no longer usable. Finally show clients how to get a good paint match in the future so they can avoid a complete repainting.

Come to Terms

Here are clarifications for a few confusing paint terms.

- *Latex.* Although it once referred only to the material derived from the rubber tree, the term is now used to describe a wide variety of synthetic resins that remain elastic or pliable. "Latex" paint, however, is not made from rubber. (For more information, visit the National Paint and Coatings Association website: www. paint.org.)
- *Enamel.* Enamel paint once referred to the glossy, oil-based variety. Because it implied durability, "enamel" came to be used by manufacturers to describe almost every paint: water-based, oil-based, glossy, or even flat. "Enamel" now basically means "paint."
- *PVC.* This abbreviation usually refers to PVC-vinyl, but PVC-vinyl is almost never used in architectural coatings (although vinyl-acrylics are). And these initials mean something quite different to someone in the paint industry. PVC is "pigment-volume concentration," the relative volume of pigment as compared to binder. A high-PVC ratio will usually be lower in VOCs, at least in conventional paint. See the Rohm and Haas Paint Quality Institute website: www .paintquality.com.)

Where Does It Come From?

- Conventional paint, with few exceptions, is made from hundreds of petrochemicals and synthetic oils, resins, and binders. The exact composition is usually proprietary and not completely revealed on the label.
- Energy-intensive manufacturing is common.
- Water-based paint uses water as the carrier; oil-based paint uses manufactured solvents.
- Water-based paint, often called latex, is not made with natural rubber but rather manufactured, flexible synthetic latex compounds.
- Colorants contain a mixture of mineral pigments and solvents.
- Other chemical additives may include those that serve as drying, flow, and suspension agents, and preservatives and biocides.

Installation

The first step to keeping a home safe and green is to remove all furniture, rugs, and décor from the area before a paintbrush is lifted or can opened. (Drop cloths will protect from spills but not VOCs). Paint will emit VOCs, and they will permeate the surfaces of these items. Soft goods collect airborne molecules (and can even react with them chemically), then outgas for an indefinite period. Be certain the paint is completely dry and odorless before returning the furnishings to their places.

Primer is the key (and often overlooked) step to adequately prepping an area for paint, especially if the surface has never been painted before (new drywall or wood, for example). Professionals agree that it greatly improves adhesion of the finish coat and thus the paint's life span—an ecologically wise move because it obviates the need to reapply paint in the future. Color changes and deep hues require fewer coats of paint with a primer, and using one can prevent stains, odors, mold, uneven texture, cracking, and peeling. Primers also improve water-, stain-, and mold-resistance.

A primer must be used over unsealed surfaces such as masonry or concrete, or if covering a nonporous surface. Lead-based paint and outgassing surfaces may successfully be covered with primer as well. If you're changing from oil-based paint

Getting the Lead Out Safely

Lead was banned from use in architectural coatings in 1978; before then, it was a popular drying agent and white pigment. Microscopic amounts of lead in the bloodstream, from simple sources such as paint chips and dust, can be toxic and cause illness or even death.

If a house was built before 1978, there is a chance that renovations such as sanding, scraping, deconstruction, or demolition will expose both the workers and the occupants to this serious hazard. Approximately 7.7 million repairs or renovations occur each year in older housing containing lead-based paint. Professional testing should be done before any such work is undertaken, and all necessary precautions and protection used if lead is found. Where large amounts of lead are present, professional abatement is recommended.

For more information on lead hazards and abatement, go to the Environmental Protection Agency's website, www.epa.gov/lead, or call the National Lead Information Center (NLIC) at 800-424-5323.

Source: Environmental Protection Agency. www.epa.gov.

Fact Check

- The amount of paint sold in the United States annually is equivalent to approximately two gallons per person.
- The sheer volume of paint manufactured is staggering: Roughly three-quarters of a billion gallons of architectural coatings are sold annually in the United States, and more than half is for interiors.

Source: American Coatings Association. www.paint.org.

to a new water-based latex paint, a primer will help make the transition go more smoothly.

Unfortunately, typical primers often contain some of the most noxious chemicals and are the worst culprits for outgassing VOCs, so it's imperative to seek out the least toxic primer—and one that outgases the least—for the specific surface or problem to be addressed. Rely on reputable manufacturers that formulate low-VOC, formaldehyde-free, water-based products (when possible), with minimal additives. If the priming step is not within the scope of the interior design specifications, then be certain to present these healthier primer options to architects and contractors beforehand.

Specify brush or roller applications. Sprays only aggravate air quality issues, both indoors and out. Specify that conventional paint be applied in good weather so it will dry faster, and when windows and doors can be left open to improve ventilation. The workers and homeowners will thereby be exposed to fewer VOCs and less odor, and the offending substances will be able to dissipate.

Maintenance

Water-based paint cleans up with water. Measurable leftovers should be poured back in the cans or containers and kept for touch-ups, and stored at a constant, cool temperature away from living areas. Record the date and location on the lid.

If leftover paint will not be used, encourage donation to a graffiti-abatement program, a community restoration project, a local nonprofit, or a theater program. There may also be recycling or remanufacturing options in the area. If a paint container is virtually empty, the residue should be allowed to air-dry completely outdoors, away from pets and children. Steel paint cans are recyclable in some places; others may require them to be disposed as hazardous waste.

Where Does It Go?

Conventional paint is a complex substance designed to resist deterioration within the home. Those same chemical enhancements that make it last also keep it from biodegrading, and it is usually treated as hazardous waste. The water and solvents will evaporate and the solvents will outgas VOCs that contribute to ground-level ozone. Most other ingredients will remain in landfills or on painted surfaces for years, decades—perhaps even centuries—and the future chemical hazards are largely unknown.

Spec List

Specify:

- Products compliant with California Section 01350 and low-VOC levels of 50 grams per liter or less
- Compliance with MPI X-Green standard
- Third-party certifications
- Conventional paint if other paint or finish options are not possible
- Water-based or natural plant-based oils in the base
- Zero- or no-VOC paint
- Low-VOC paint
- Formaldehyde-free
- Preservative-free (paint mixed fresh, if possible) free of biocides and fungicides
- Low-VOC, formaldehyde-free, water-based, minimal-additives primer for surface problems, prep, deep colors, or color changes
- Conservative paint sampling
- Recycling of leftover paint, or proper storage for potential touch-ups

Avoid:

- Preservatives
- Biocides, fungicides, mildew preventatives
- Formaldehyde
- Lead and other heavy metal pigments or drying agents, especially chromium hexavalent, cobalt, cadmium, and mercury
- Recycled or remanufactured paint for projects indoors

RESOURCES

BuildingGreen. www.buildinggreen.com.
Master Painters Institute Specify Green. www.specifygreen.com.
National Coatings and Paint Association. www.paint.org.
The Natural Paint Book. Lynn Edwards and Julia Lawless. New York: Rodale, 2003.
Rohm and Haas Paint Quality Institute. www.paintquality.com.

Overview: Stains, Finishes, and Adhesives

As designers with ecological sensibilities, our duty is to find the best possible products for the tasks at hand while causing the least amount of harm to the client, the construction team, and to the Earth. It's impossible, within the scope of this book or any other, to discuss and adequately analyze every substance used to tint, glue, or coat materials used in residential interiors.

The world of chemicals available for design and construction is both astounding and frightening. It would be easy to blame the manufacturers for the undesirable aspects of these highly complex compounds. But as consumers, we continually demand "better" compounds that adhere under every condition, color every surface consistently, and finish every material with eternal durability—often to the eventual destruction of our health and our world.

Yet it's not all gloom and doom. Many companies are committed to providing quality products that balance consumer needs with those of the Earth. And there are still simple, eco-friendly choices for many applications.

Whenever a stain, colorant, finish, adhesive, or stripping agent is to be used, research the contents of the proposed product thoroughly. Request the MSDS from the manufacturer, distributor, or retailer, or go to the company website and print it out. Look for simple compounds with few ingredients, as multiple chemicals might interact and cause hazards that haven't yet been evaluated. Also look for products that have the fewest known health risks or recommended precautions and contain no phthalates, heavy metals, or aromatic solvents. If the product is listed as having carcinogenic ingredients, reproductive toxins, or other serious health risks, seek out a more benign product. Stay well below the SCAQMD standards for VOCs (available at www.aqmd.gov). In general, risks to human health are also risks to environmental health, as well; apply the precautionary principal and specify natural products with less environmental and minimal health burden.

Request a sample if the client is sensitive to chemicals or odors. After selection, specify that every precaution for use is precisely followed by workers, including recommendations for disposal. Finally, provide the client with instructions for maintenance.

The following is an overview and spec list to guide you when specifying stains, finishes, and adhesives. For more information on the best products to use with a material such as wood, metal, or concrete, consult the chapter in this book that covers that material.

Stains, Colorants, and Tints

Most synthetic colorants are solvent-based, made from petroleum-based compounds that evaporate when drying. Even though the amount of colorant, stain, or dye used might be miniscule, the solvents and other chemicals may contribute to outgassing, VOCs, toxicity levels, and odors (see "VOCS," page 381). Although a product such as paint may be advertised as zero-VOC, when a colorant or another additive is added, the level of VOCs can change, often for the worse. Deeper hues, if made with solvent-based colorants, may outgas more than lighter ones.

The greenest choice, by far, is to specify that the material be left in its natural state without any added color. The next best choice is to specify natural mineral pigments, natural penetrating oils, or water-based vegetable dyes. Food-grade or mineral-based colorants are safe at any concentration level.

Avoid heavy metals such as chromium, lead, and uranium (the latter was once commonplace in yellowish colorants). Because other countries may lack restrictions against the use of known harmful substances in dyes, paints, and glazes, avoid painted objects such as souvenir tiles that have not been imported through regulated channels.

Finishes, Sealants, and Topcoats

As with colorants, the safest, greenest choice is to use no finishes, sealants, or topcoats at all. Many natural materials need no assistance to maintain their durability and beauty. Others, however, will deteriorate rapidly if not protected against moisture, dirt, stains, mold, or insects. It's ecologically prudent, for example, to seal grout rather than risk having to replace an entire section of tile. Sometimes the finish protects the client as well. Mold, VOCs, and odors can be controlled through the application of effective, nonporous sealants.

Factory-finished products keep many offending odors and harmful VOCs out of the home because the material will have extra time to outgas before being installed. (Although the outgassing will still be harmful to the environment, this minimizes the harm to the home's occupants.) But specifying on-site finishing or sealing allows for greater control over the application method and the substances used, possibly improving the ecological balance and the health of the home.

All-natural waxes and oils provide porous, breathable protection for many surfaces. They'll likely need regular reapplication, however. Some finishes, such as silicate dispersion paint, chemically bond with the substrate (usually mineral-based products) and become completely inert and safe when dry. Borate, a mineral, can be added to a finish or treatment to provide resistance against pests and fire.

If a nonporous or hard finish is desired, specify the least toxic product that contains no formaldehyde, low amounts of solvents and VOCs, and is water-based. Avoid chemical biocides. Zinc was once popular as a hardening agent in floor finishes, but its use has been found to be toxic to aquatic life, so it should also be avoided.

The method of application may be as important as the ingredients in the finish. Do not use spray-on sealants unless they can be applied within a spray booth by the manufacturer. Alternatives can be wiped, brushed, rolled, or poured on. The use of sprays will directly affect air quality and may be particularly irritating to a chemically sensitive client.

Adhesives and Glues

In the world of adhesives, there are particular distinctions made by manufacturers that work as guidelines for specifying more eco-friendly products.

- *Paste* is usually made from a base of flour and water.
- *Glue* is usually made from animal products (casein, hide) and plant sources (natural rubber, cellulose, paste).
- *Adhesives* may be made from any number of synthetics: epoxy, cyanoacrylate, contact cement, hot melt, polyurethane, polyvinyl acetate (PVA), resin, resorcinol, silicone, or urea formaldehyde.

Although the terms are often used interchangeably, these definitions are a place to start when looking for earth-friendly products. In general, paste and glue will be the more benign and can be used with many porous natural materials such as unfinished wood, wallpaper, or cork. Adhesives, on the other hand, grip to nonporous surfaces or more difficult applications such as stone, tile, or finished bamboo. Start with reviewing the MSDS to ascertain the content of pastes, glues, and adhesives. Then specify products that are well below SCAQMD Rule #1168 for limitations on VOC content and meet California Section 01350 emission standards. And find products that meet certifications with strict testing for emissions rulings, such as Greenguard Gold.

Some interior design materials have peel-and-stick backings. The factory-applied, extremely thin coat of adhesive, especially if found only on the material's perimeter or in small spots, may need considerably less adhesive than would an on-site application. This may be helpful to a client with sensitivities to odors or chemicals. Choosing the adhesive, however, allows for greater control over the product content, and it may be possible to find one that has less odor than the preapplied backing does.

If glue or paste won't provide a bond that's durable enough, specify low-odor synthetic adhesives with low VOC levels. Look for companies that specialize in manufacturing low-toxic, environmentally safe compounds, especially if the products meet more rigid air quality standards and specifications for schools or health-care facilities. Tack strips, staples, decorative studs, nails, trim pieces, or screws may reduce the amount of adhesive needed as well.

Spec List

Specify:

- Products compliant with California Section 01350
- VOC levels lower than SCAQMD Rule #1168
- Third-party certifications with emissions testing
- No colorant, tints, or dyes added
- Light colors if synthetic colorants are to be used
- No finish if material integrity or durability will not be sacrificed
- Low- or zero-VOC
- Low-odor
- Factory-finished materials if client sensitivity to odors or on-site outgassing is an issue
- Nails, staples, tacks, trim pieces, and so on to reduce the amount of adhesive needed
- Solvent-free, water-based, or natural-oil-based
- Natural plant-based, animal-based, or mineral-based dyes, oils, waxes, and finishes
- Animal- or plant-based pastes or glues (as opposed to chemical adhesives)
- Formaldehyde-free
- Natural borate preservatives or pest controls
- Brush-on, wipe-on, or pour-on substances

Avoid:

- Heavy metals such as chromium, lead, cadmium, or mercury
- Metallic hardening or drying agents such as zinc
- Sprays
- Solvent-based formulas
- Biocides
- Compounds that require chemical solvents or thinners
- Factory finishes of unknown content

Resources

BuildingGreen: Adhesives and Sealants
"Choose Green Report: Wood and Stains." Green Seal. www.greenseal.org.

CHAPTER 15

specialties

Figure 15.1 Custom shower door enclosure in guest bath for healthy home with nontoxic tile substrates.

Design: Rowland + Broughton Architecture and Urban Design, Wendy Silverman Interior Design. Photo by Brent Moss Photography.

Figure 15.2 This bathroom has a shower door of frosted, frameless glass. The space also features a green slate countertop, recycled glass tile in the shower, anigre wood cabinetry, a wood ceiling from a reforested area, fluorescent lighting, and low-VOC paint.

Used by permission of My House Magazine. Photos by Mikel Covey. Designer: Gail Madison Goodhue.

Shower Enclosures

When it comes to shower enclosures, the greenest choice is to have none at all. Citizens in many parts of the world do not have enclosed shower stalls, leaving at least one side open instead. In some places, the shower is defined by nothing more than the bathroom or bathing area walls, a drain on the floor, and the showerhead on the wall. For added privacy, the shower might be designed with a partial wall or be situated behind a visual barrier. Eliminating the enclosure simplifies the design and uses fewer materials. The open-sided design is also functional for those in wheelchairs or with limited mobility.

Tempered glass, which is specially heated and cooled, or annealed, to resist breakage and five times stronger than typical glass, is common for shower stall walls. The edges are often defined and protected by metal trim with metal towel bars attached; frameless glass is also available and a more environmentally friendly choice because it can be easily disassembled for recycling. Powder-coated, recycled steel, or recycled aluminum are the best green choices for frames.

Where Does It Come From?

- Tempered glass is made from common sand (silicon dioxide).
- Metal frames are made from mined metals or alloys and are often powder-coated.

Where Does It Go?

Tempered glass cannot be cut, fabricated, or manipulated in any way because it splinters. Nor can tempered glass be recycled with beverage glass or in the same manner, posing a special challenge for the recycling industry.

Even though recycling tempered glass is tricky, it is possible. The glass can be melted and remanufactured into Fiberglas. Ground glass can be incorporated into "glassphalt," a glass and asphalt blend, or stirred into the reflective yellow and white paint used on roads. Products that use a cold-cast process, such as recycled glass and concrete countertops, may incorporate recycled tempered glass from shower surrounds, windshields, and other sources.

Fortunately, creative industry professionals are finding diverse uses for tempered glass. With careful harvesting of unwanted tempered glass, artisans recycle discarded glass transforming it into useful items, reducing the amount of glass in the landfills and creating glass products for interior décor, landscaping, and many other solutions.

Installation

The contractor must provide a level finish surface where the door is being installed. To seal against leaking, a slightly concave bead of caulking is normally used. Specify a water resistant, nontoxic caulk to seal the installation against the finished surface; this will provide an excellent initial and permanent adhesion. Also request that masking tape be used to prevent the caulk from trickling into the grout joints.

Maintenance

Shower doors typically do not encourage the development of mold and mildew, which is more prone to occur on shower curtains. Daily use of a squeegee and adequate air circulation will deter mold, and the shower will dry faster. Utilize a nontoxic glass cleaner and address potential buildup with a solution of half water and half distilled white vinegar or a nontoxic spray made for this purpose.

Spec List

Specify:

- No shower enclosure or frameless glass
- Metal frames with powder coating or no finish at all (if the metal won't rust)

Closets and Shelving

See "Cabinetry," page 472.

Fireplaces and Stoves

Humans first relied on fire for existence; it provided security, warmth, light, and the ability to cook food. Today, a fireplace or stove can serve as a primary or supplemental source of heat for the home, or even as the primary one, especially where utilities are costly; some types have a cooking surface or oven. More often than not, the modern hearth is valued for its aesthetics and for "psychological warming."

EPA Certification

In 1988, regulations governing wood stoves went into effect. All those sold in the United States must have certified emissions below 7.5 grams of smoke per hour, and many newer stoves and inserts have even lower emission rates. Catalytic stoves must have emissions less than 4.1 grams per hour. The regulation does not govern fireplaces.

Fireplaces and stoves are usually built from a combination of some of the following materials: all-natural stone, cast iron, enameled steel, brick, clay, cement or concrete, tempered glass, or ceramic. Intrinsic to stove and fireplace design is that the materials must be noncombustible, not outgas, and be extremely durable. Some fireplaces and stoves are made from cast iron or steel that may incorporate recycled metal. Soapstone is another desirable material, preferred for many stoves because of its high thermal efficiency and radiant qualities.

Older stoves or cheaply manufactured ones will burn fuel inefficiently, causing air pollution and wasting valuable natural resources. In addition, the poor combustion creates carbon monoxide, nitrous oxides, and particulate matter, among other health hazards. Many municipalities have strict ordinances that forbid woodburning on days when the air quality is predicted to exceed federally regulated standards unless the home has no other source for heat or cooking.

The fuel choice for the stove might be dictated by local availability, air quality restrictions, or the client's desire for innovation and super energy efficiency. Will the fire be a primary heat source in an off-the-grid home, or just be used as a secondary heat source on cold winter days? Or will it be used only occasionally for ambience? The client may desire an oven or a cooktop as a feature. There are even stove designs that may include hot water heating units.

FIREPLACES

Used as the primary source for indoor heat and for cooking until the twentieth century, fireplaces were found in almost every home. Today, many are built for ambience alone. In terms of green design, they are rarely effective—a typical fireplace actually draws heat *out*, up to 24,000 cubic feet of warm air to the outdoors—increasing energy consumption and heating bills in the winter.[1] Installing a conventional wood-burning fireplace is therefore never the best environmental choice; however, a stove, masonry heater, or fireplace insert greatly improves

[1] Energy Efficiency and Renewable Energy, "Energy Savers." http://www.eere.energy.gov/.

energy efficiency and still provides a warm, inviting focal point. If the client has an existing fireplace, consider retrofitting it with an insert. It will warm the immediate area efficiently in the winter, lower utility bills, and ultimately save energy.

To improve energy efficiency in an existing home, upgrade to an insert. Have tempered glass doors along with a heat-exchange system or blower. Specify caulking around the hearth—use a noncombustible, low-VOC caulk designed for this purpose. Check the damper for a tight fit and replace it or the seal if needed.

FIREPLACE INSERTS

Fireplace inserts are usually made of cast iron or stone for added radiant heat and thermal properties. Inserts are designed to be retrofitted to existing fireplace openings, with a damper that will control airflow and a special box design that will maximize thermal properties. An insert will drastically improve the energy efficiency of the existing fireplace. A chimney liner or slight modifications to the firebox may be necessary to accommodate an insert.

MASONRY STOVES OR HEATERS

A masonry heater or stove is made of stone, brick, and ceramic with some cast iron, is often assembled on-site, and is usually freestanding. It works by burning a very hot fire for a short time with the doors closed. The design of the heat-exchange channel and chimney causes most gases to be completely consumed before exhausting through the chimney. The high temperatures absorb into the masonry, which in turn releases radiant heat into the home for many hours. The whole process is super-efficient, using very little fuel. Masonry heaters produce almost no ashes, smoke, or creosote. Because the burning is enclosed, these heaters won't dry out the air, skin, or sinuses, as fireplaces and conventional stoves do.

BTU Defined

A British thermal unit, or BTU, equals approximately as much heat as is given off by burning a match. Technically, it's the amount of heat needed to raise the temperature of one pound of water one degree Fahrenheit. The more BTUs, the warmer the output.

They may be small, but they add up: A single U.S. house consumes about 100 million BTUs a year, and about half of that is for heating.

Source: Home Energy Saver: http://homeenergysaver.lbl.gov/consumer.

Masonry heaters are designed to fit, and these customized designs have higher price tags. But if the unit is well situated in a moderately sized home with an open floor plan, the entire space may be heated with one stove. Small baking ovens, cooktops, water heaters, and warmed benches can be added.

VENT-FREE BURNERS

Unlike traditional fireplaces, ventless burners are modular units that do not require permanent flues for ventilation or a permanent connection for fuel delivery. They generate heat quickly through an open flame fueled by denatured alcohol, which is produced through the fermentation of sugars originating from agricultural and forestry products, including sugarcane, potatoes, bananas, beetroot, and recently, from wheat cereals.

The thermal output is efficient: Over 90 percent of the energy used is transformed into heat and kept inside the room rather than up a traditional flue. Typically, the units are available in burner kits, zero-clearance fireboxes, portable pieces, and grate inserts.

The burner housings are usually stainless steel, including the burner chassis. It is simple to control the intensity of the flame through built-in regulatory mechanisms, including simple on/off switches.

To ensure safety, look for rigorous product testing, including for CO/CO_2 consumption ratios, flame stability, wind temperament, ignition safety, heat output, combustion characteristics, and fuel consumption and efficiency. Product certification and approvals should include the following:

- Quality Management System Standard AS/NZS ISO 9001:2000 Certification, whose objective is to safeguard life, property, and the environment. The certification covers the research, development, design, manufacture, production, and distribution of environmentally friendly, flueless fireplaces.
- Underwriters Laboratories (UL), which establishes a testing platform for this product type.

FUEL

Each stove is designed for only one type of fuel. Fuel type, cost, availability, and ease of use are especially important considerations if the client intends to reduce their reliance on public utilities. If the main purpose of the stove is to serve as backup heat, avoid those dependent upon electric controls or blowers, as they won't function during a winter power outage.

If the client wants the occasional ambience of a fire and has a standard fireplace that is rarely used, or lives in a municipality with wood-burning restrictions, natural gas may be an option. Natural gas and propane are accessible and reliable sources: Just flip a switch, and the ceramic "logs" ignite. But they are not the best fuel choices for most situations, ecologically speaking, as they are nonrenewable resources.

Biomass fuel is a superb option if it's locally available. The pellets are made from corn and other agricultural by-products, or sawdust and waste wood from sources such as furniture-making and construction, all held together with a natural, safe-to-burn resin. Because biomass is new to the green marketplace, it's not readily available everywhere. Some environmentally conscientious consumers have formed local biomass co-ops and built storage silos, enabling them to buy in bulk and guarantee a steady supply.

The major drawback with pellet stoves is that almost all are dependent upon electricity and won't be usable during a power outage (a rare few have battery backups). Still, the stoves are incredibly energy-efficient—so much so that the Environmental Protection Agency (EPA) doesn't regulate them. And the fuel is made from annually renewable or recycled sources.

Another agricultural by-product can be used in a specially designed fireplace: denatured alcohol, also called methylated alcohol. Crops such as corn, beets, and bananas can be used to manufacture the fuel, which is a denatured version of 100 percent ethanol alcohol. A fireplace burner using this fuel requires no hookup to gas or electric lines, no chimney or flue, and doesn't necessarily require a permanent fixture. The consumer simply purchases the fuel, decants it into the special burner, and ignites it. The fire produces a warmth and aesthetic similar to natural gas. It burns clean, and no special ventilation is required since the only by-products are heat, steam, and carbon dioxide. Alcohol-burning fire is a patented technology not widely available, and the fireplace and equipment designed for it must be purchased and shipped from the supplier, thereby raising the embodied energy.

Emerging variations for the alcohol stoves rely on small canisters of fuel, much like fondue pots or food warmers. Sugarcane or corn is commonly used to make the alcohol-based gel fuels. While these stoves are usually much smaller than conventional fireplaces, they may be an eco-friendly alternative for a client who desires the ambience, heat, and flickering light.

Where Does It Come From?

- Fireplaces, stoves, and inserts are made from a variety of noncombustible materials such as all-natural stone, cast iron, enameled steel, brick, clay, cement or concrete, tempered glass, and ceramic.
- The fuel may be wood, pellets made from agricultural and wood by-products, natural gas, propane, denatured alcohol, or alcohol-based gels.

Installation

The installation and specification of an EPA-approved energy-efficient stove, masonry heater, or insert is best handled by a certified technician. The technician

Figure 15.3 This Tulikivi masonry soapstone oven provides heat for the entire home. The space also features solid wood furniture and natural clay plaster.

Photo by Laurie E. Dickson. Architect: Baker Laporte & Associates.

will ensure proper clearance between the venting system and fuel, protection of the floor and surrounding spaces, and assembly of the appliance. The technician will also be aware of codes regulating the placement of the stove or insert, restrictions on burning, and air-quality requirements.

Maintenance

If the client already has a fireplace, make certain they know to keep the damper closed when it's not in use. Leaving a damper open in the winter is like forgetting to shut a window.

The most important component of fireplace and stove maintenance is chimney inspection and sweeping, which should be done annually. Proper wood selection also enables the stove to burn efficiently with the least amount of creosote buildup. Scrap wood should not be used if its origin is unknown; it may have been treated with or exposed to chemicals. Advise the client to avoid painted or treated wood of all kinds.

Although uncommon, some newer stoves have catalytic converters much like those in cars to keep the emissions cleaner. These stoves require a more rigorous cleaning schedule and will need replacement of the converter every few years.

Where Does It Go?

The materials in stove construction are made to last for generations. Almost all components—steel, iron, stone, brick, clay, ceramic, and glass—can be recycled, reused, or will eventually decompose.

Clean Sweep

Creosote is an oily, tarlike substance that's left over in the chimney after burning wood, and the buildup can ignite. Some wood species produce much more creosote than others, so careful fuel selection is important. Efficient burning reduces creosote, too. Annual inspection and cleaning by a certified sweep will further eliminate the risk of a chimney fire.

Natural gas burning produces methane, but no particulate matter. Wood and biomass fuels produce carbon monoxide, nitrogen oxides, particulates (ashes and smoke), and other substances. Efficient burning improves air quality through more complete combustion of gasses and particulates.

Spec List

Specify:

- EPA-certified wood-burning stove or insert
- A masonry heater, a fireplace insert, or a freestanding stove
- UL-listed ventless burners
- Wood or biomass fuel

Avoid:

- Conventional fireplace installations without efficient inserts
- Poor-quality wood that burns inefficiently or contributes to creosote buildup
- Wood that has been treated or painted in any way, or scrap wood of unknown origin

RESOURCES

Chimney Safety Institute of America. www.csia.org.
Hearth Education Foundation. www.heartheducation.org.
Hearth, Patio, and Barbecue Association. www.hpba.org.
Masonry Heater Association of North America. www.mha-net.org.
National Fireplace Institute. www.nficertified.org.

equipment: appliances and office equipment

Figure 16.1 In this LEED-H Platinum home, the designers created a single integrated family social space. The family room flows to the kitchen and breakfast nook, enabling even large families or large groups of friends to congregate in a single space. The kitchen incorporates Shaker-style inset cabinets made with VOC-free plywood and FSC-certified wide-plank oak floors for a classic look. Fireclay Tile's Debris Series field tile adds a splash of color; it is comprised of more than 60 percent recycled material and uses nontoxic glazes. Caesarstone counters offer the look of Carrera marble with a more sustainable material. Low-VOC chalkboard paint creates a fun family message and art space in the desk area to the left. Luxury features include a walk-in pantry, double ovens, a 48-inch cooktop, and period-style faucet and pot filler. Appliances are all Energy Star–rated with the highest level of energy efficiency.

Design by eco+historica and Feldman Architecture, San Francisco. Photos by Paul Dyer.

Appliances

Energy efficiency and water usage are important criteria for determining the environmental impact of appliances. And conserving natural resources by selecting appliances will translate into decreased monthly utility bills. High-performance homes that rely on alternative energy sources lower electrical loads by using energy-conserving appliances.

Washers, dryers, refrigerators, and freezers are responsible for a significant percent of the average home's energy bills. They are the principal consumers after the heating and cooling systems and the water heater. An individual product draws relatively little standby power, but a typical American home has forty products constantly drawing power, and together these amount to almost 10 percent of residential electricity use. Lawrence Berkeley National Laboratory's standby power calculator is at http://standby.lbl.gov/.

Newer model appliances use far fewer natural resources than those made just ten years ago. There may be local or national incentives to purchase more efficient equipment, as well. Some states and municipalities require front-loading washers, which use far less water than top-loaders. Public utilities are struggling to keep up with the ever-burgeoning demand for power and water and issue tax breaks and rebates as incentives for replacing old refrigerators or other appliances. The U.S. Department of Energy (DOE), in collaboration with North Carolina Solar Center at North Carolina State University and with support from the Interstate Renewable Energy Council, created a comprehensive platform capturing incentives and policies that address and reward renewables and energy efficiencies. The Database of Statewide Incentives for Renewables and Efficiency (DSIRE) was established in 1995 and is an invaluable resource for finding rebates, loans, and grants along with guidelines, regulations, and policies for energy-efficient initiatives.

Two common labeling programs make it easier to distinguish the most energy-efficient appliances. Since 1980, all washers, dryers, refrigerators, dishwashers, and freezers in the United States display the required yellow-and-black EnergyGuide label, enabling consumers to compare energy efficiency among brands and models by indicating the estimated operating cost and energy use of that mode. There's no special designation, however, for those appliances ranked best, nor does EnergyGuide judge appliances for water usage or other factors besides energy use. EnergyGuide labels are also required for televisions, water heaters, room air conditioners, central air conditioners, furnaces, boilers, heat pumps, and pool heaters.

The Energy Star label picks up where EnergyGuide leaves off. Energy Star is a partnership between industry and the U.S. government (through the Environmental Protection Agency) that labels and promotes energy-efficient products that use less energy and typically save money. The program began in 1992, and the blue star logo appears on most energy-efficient products. The first products to be labeled with Energy Star were computers; now Energy Star

Energy Star's stamp of approval is also applicable to new homes that are designed and built to above-average energy-efficiency standards when compared to most homes on the market. A new home with an Energy Star label has been inspected, tested, and verified to meet strict requirements set by the U.S. Environmental Protection Agency (EPA). To receive an Energy Star label for a new home, work with an independent third-party that can verify all guidelines have been met. Home Energy Raters (HERs) are trained to evaluate construction techniques, take key measurements, and perform inspections. Raters verify the presence of energy-efficient features appropriate to the climatic region as well as the critical assembly details throughout the building process; they also certify that the systems are performing as designed and constructed to deliver greater efficiency, durability, and comfort.

qualifies heating and cooling equipment, major home appliances, lighting, fans, home electronics, office equipment, roofing products, and windows, doors, and skylights, all of which are independently certified to save energy without sacrificing features or functionality. Utilize both labeling systems to compare brands and models, as they will differ dramatically.

Figure 16.2 This kitchen features Energy Star appliances and Forest Stewardship Council – certified cherry flooring.

Photo by Emily Hagoplian, www.essentialimages.us. Architect: Michael Heacock.

In spite of the measurable advantages of purchasing new, resource-efficient appliances to replace older models, there is an environmental trade-off: Appliances consume great amounts of raw materials during manufacturing, transportation, and even packaging, which adds up to a large amount of embodied energy. Not all parts of all appliances can be recycled. Studies indicate that nearly nine million refrigerators end up in landfills every year. Carefully evaluate whether immediate appliance replacement makes economic and environmental sense, or if waiting might be more prudent.

Also remember to assess an appliance's acoustical qualities; they can be a source of unwelcome noise. Look for the noise ratings on appliances, typically noted by the logarithmic decibel-A scale (dBA); anything below 45 dBA is unobtrusive in a home environment. Consumer Reports is a good resource for dBA ratings, as this information sometimes has to be requested from the manufacturer.

REFRIGERATORS AND FREEZERS

The refrigerator was designed to keep food from spoiling, and it was a substantial improvement on cellars stacked with snow and iceboxes that required regular ice deliveries. Although invented in the 1920s, the refrigerator didn't gain popularity until after World War II. Now it's arguably the most important appliance we have and can be found in every American household and a large percentage of homes worldwide.

Refrigerators are available with many specialty features: icemakers, sparkling or filtered water dispensers—even television screens, and touch screens. Refrigerators are already the greatest electricity consumers in most households, and all these extra features increase their energy usage. The sheer size of a refrigerator necessitates the use of large amounts of steel, plastic, glass, and metal in their manufacture. Refrigerators are challenging to recycle because of the coolants that by law must first be extracted.

There are ways to improve a refrigerator's environmental performance. New models may need less than a third of the electricity of those built 30 years ago. To receive the Energy Star label, full-size refrigerators must exceed the federal standard set for energy efficiency by at least 15 percent, freezers by 10 percent, and compact models by 20 percent. In general, models with the freezer on the bottom use 15 percent less energy—and freezer-on-top models use 13 percent less energy—than side-by-side models. Icemakers raise energy use by about 10 to 20 percent and reduce the usable cubic footage.

Evaluate how many cubic feet are actually needed for daily use. Many people want a second refrigerator or an additional freezer. But a large refrigerator will be more efficient than two smaller ones. If a second freezer is needed, a chest freezer is slightly more efficient than an upright one. But will the second appliance be used only occasionally? Efficiency measures only matter if the extra appliances are indeed needed and are used wisely.

Fact Check

- In the United States, nearly nine million refrigerators end up in landfills each year.
- Four million pounds of ozone-depleting chemicals escape from appliances at disposal, annually. The harmful gasses may survive for as long as 150 years in the stratosphere.

Source: EPA, www.epa.gov.

Proper disposal of an old refrigerator or freezer is an environmental imperative because of the hazardous coolants within. Refrigerators originally used more toxic coolant gases—ammonia, methyl chloride, and sulfur dioxide—than they use now. Then, in 1929, Freon, the trade name for chlorofluorocarbon (CFC) gas was first put to use. We now know that Freon destroys the ozone layer. Laws effective since 1992 require all ozone-depleting refrigerants to be recovered by a certified agency during the service, maintenance, or disposal of any refrigeration or air conditioning equipment. When replacing a refrigerator or freezer, locate a certified refrigerator service company to recover the coolant and make certain they will have the remaining steel and materials recycled.

RANGES, COOKTOPS, AND OVENS

Gas or electric? It used to be the only question a person needed to answer when purchasing a kitchen range. Now, simple four-burner stoves are no longer the standard in the modern American home. Down-vented grills, built-in slow cookers or fryers, convection ovens, induction cooktops, smooth cooktops, and sophisticated temperature controls are just a few of the options available.

Because the United States has no minimum efficiency standards for cooking ranges, manufacturers have not been challenged to come up with better resource-conserving technology. EnergyGuide does not label kitchen ranges, and Energy Star does not rate them. The selection of gas or electric, therefore, is usually based on a personal preference. Both gas and public electricity are, unfortunately, reliant on non-renewable fossil fuels. Gas (natural or propane) will use less energy overall because it is delivered directly to the home; electricity must be produced at power plants and then routed to the home. A gas range requires that the house be equipped for it; it's imperative that there be ample ventilation through an electricity-powered duct to the outside. If the client's home has a renewable alternative energy source such as solar, an electric range might be a better idea.

Figure 16.3 The backsplash tile is 100 percent recycled glass from Fireclay's Crush series, manufactured and sourced from base materials through finish goods within 30 miles of the project. Appliances all meet Energy Star as applicable to product type.

Photo by Bernardo Grijalva. Designed by Lydia Corser, www.greenspacecompany.com.

Generally, gas ovens are less energy-efficient than electric ovens because more airflow is required throughout the oven and the operating safety feature uses considerable electricity. Gas ranges with electronic ignitions eliminate the need for an ever-burning pilot light. While this results in gas conservation, a small amount of standby electricity is used. Electric ranges, either smooth-top or exposed-coil, heat up slowly compared to other range types, but electric ovens are sometimes chosen because they cook more evenly and are more energy-efficient. Hybrid ranges that combine a gas stovetop with an electric oven are an alternate solution for those who want the best of both worlds.

Convection ovens are an energy-efficient choice, as they speed up the cooking process consume less energy, by circulating hot air throughout. Self-cleaning ovens are generally more efficient because they have higher insulative properties and better seals on the oven doors. The self-cleaning feature itself, however, is energy-intensive, so advise the client not to use it more often than is really needed. Also, clients with sensitivities need to be careful when using the self-cleaning feature and ensure that fresh air exchange is at the highest setting to avoid any potentially aggravating fumes.

Induction cooktops are the most efficient option; they work by transmitting electromagnetic energy directly to ferrous metal cooking pans. Induction responds quickly—as rapidly as gas cooktops—and the surface remains cool throughout cooking. Cast-iron solid disk elements on rangetops are slower to heat up and use more energy, so they are less than ideal for an eco-friendly kitchen. Another option is halogen-bulb cooktops with glass-ceramic surfaces. Halogen cooktops are about 80 percent more energy-efficient than most conventional ranges and induction stoves are 70 percent more energy-efficient, but both are typically more expensive than electric or gas models.

To maximize energy conservation, consider if there is a more efficient way to cook. Ovens are especially consumptive energy users, as a large amount of space and steel must be heated up, even for a small meal. And when the oven or stove releases heat into the kitchen air, the air conditioning needs to work harder. In general, a smaller appliance will concentrate the heat where it's needed and lose less of it to get the job done. Pressure cookers speed up the process on the stovetop, reducing energy use by 50 to 75 percent. Slow cookers, toaster ovens, and even microwaves offer significant energy savings, especially when cooking a small meal. For cooking small portions of food, toaster ovens are more energy-efficient than full-size ovens. In the end, the choice of appliance and method for a particular cooking task has the greatest environmental impact.

RANGE HOODS AND DOWNDRAFT VENTILATION

Proper kitchen ventilation, especially with a gas range, is required by building code. Range hood fans need to be directly exhausted to the outdoors to adhere with combustion safety requirements for gas appliances. This ventilation also helps to control indoor odors and manage and support healthy indoor air quality. An Energy Star–rated fan is the best place to start, ensuring energy efficiency of at least 2.8 cubic feet per minute of airflow per watt of power (cfm/watt) consumed by the motor and controls, a maximum sound level of 2.0 sones, and fluorescent lighting for products with integral lights. Again, acoustics are important, to ensure that the noise from the ventilation doesn't discourage its use.

Range hoods that simply circulate air through a charcoal filter are common in conventionally built houses. For home and occupant health, a hood that vents to the outside and rids the air of the cooking and combustion by-products such as carbon monoxide, carbon dioxide, moisture, and volatile organic compounds (VOCs), is the best strategy. Specify the right fan for the range size to optimize airflow, but do not provide more than necessary. Updraft vents are much more energy-efficient than downdraft types, although advancements in technology continue to improve the latter.

MICROWAVES AND SMALL APPLIANCES

Large families were once the norm; today there are cookbooks devoted to meal preparation for one person. When the quantity of food to be cooked is small, choosing to use a smaller appliance instead of a larger oven or the stovetop can save energy, time, and even cleanup. But it's not an exact science, as the temperature of a stove burner or the setting on a microwave affects the energy consumed.

Microwaves can be especially effective at reducing energy consumption, as they are oriented toward speedy reheating and small-meal cooking, and they don't radiate heat as they heat the food directly. In addition, the food may be cooked on a plate or in a bowl that doubles as the serving dish, eliminating hot water and power needed for dishwashing. Slow cookers, pressure cookers, toaster ovens, and electric teakettles are also energy-saving appliances.

As always, there are ecological and health-related trade-offs: A small appliance that is rarely used or a luxury item is a waste of raw materials. Small appliances are often thrown away when components break because repairs cost more than a new appliance or parts are difficult to secure. Few small appliances are recycled, as they have numerous small plastic and metal parts that are difficult to disassemble. For microwaves, electromagnetic fields can impact sensitive individuals.

Determine which small appliances might be best suited to the household needs and also have the least impact on the environment. Factor in the frequency at which they are likely to be used, the typical energy consumption per use, and the life span of the appliance.

DISHWASHERS

Most American homes now have a dishwasher. Newer models save considerable water over washing by hand, often cutting the amount in half. Yet water conservation is only part of the total picture when it comes to resource consumption. Dishwashers also rely on electricity to run the motor and more energy to heat the water (gas or electric); the appliance accounts for 1 to 2 percent of home energy use. With an average life span of only nine to twelve years, the amount of metal and plastic used to make the appliance is also a serious consideration, as not all of it will likely be recycled.[1]

When selecting a dishwasher, focus on features and specifications that will optimize energy and water efficiency. Booster heaters within a dishwasher allow the consumer to set the home water heater temperature lower but still use a sanitizing rinse in the dishwasher. "Light wash" or "energy-saver" features usually reduce the wash time and dry time and are sufficient for most loads. Air drying cuts out the heater, and those that use the fewest gallons of water per load are usually the most energy-efficient. Energy Star–labeled dishwashers ensure top performance in energy conservation. If there is a solar hot water heater or solar power in the home, it will reduce the overall effect on the environment as well.

GARBAGE DISPOSALS

Although standard in almost every kitchen today, the garbage disposal unit is not a green addition. Contrary to what most people believe, conventional disposals (also called "disposers") don't return organic waste to nature. The bits of food must first go through the sewage system, adding to the ever-growing burden on water treatment plants. (For septic systems, garbage disposals may also create undue organic loads.) What might otherwise be "nutrients" if they were composted actually contribute to algae bloom and other undesirable conditions in our wastewater systems, which must therefore be chemically and biologically managed. The end result, when food is washed down the drain, is that the organic matter never really

---

[1]Consortium for Energy Efficiency, www.cee1.org.

Table 16.1 Typical Appliance Energy Consumption*

Appliance	Watts[†]	Energy Use	Use Time	kWh per Month**	Monthly Cost ($, based on $.12 per kWh)
Blender	400	0007 kWh/min.	Twice a week for 1 minute each	—	—
Bread machine (single-loaf)	400 (while baking)	.4 kWh/hr. (one loaf)	Twice a week	3.2	.29
Coffeemaker (drip, brewing)	1,000	.25 kWh/use (15 min.)	Every day	7.5	.68
Coffeemaker, warming	70	.07 kWh/hr	Every day for 2 hours	.4	3.60
Deep fryer, small	600	.6 kWh/hr	4 times a month for a half hour each	1.2	.11
Dishwasher (not including water heating)	1,200	1 kWh/load	4 loads/week	16	1.44
Dishwasher, high energy-efficiency (including electric hot water heating)	1,500	2 kWh/load	4 loads/week	32	2.88
Electric skillet	1,200	1.2 kWh/hr	Once a week for 30 minutes	2.4	.22
Food processor	350	.35 kWh/hr	Twice a week for 3 minutes each	.14	.01
Freezer, chest (15 cu ft)	350	1.3 kWh/day	—	39	3.51
Freezer, upright, frost-free	450	2.8 kWh/day	—	84	7.56
Microwave (.7 cu ft)	700	.7 kWh/hr (at high power)	Every day for 15 minutes	5.3	.48
Oven, 350 degrees	5,000	5 kWh/hr	4 times a week for 30 minutes	40	3.60
Refrigerator/freezer, frost-free (17 cu ft)	500	.57 kWh/day	—	17	1.53
Slow cooker	200	1.8 kWh per use (9 hours)	Twice a month	3.6	.32
Toaster	1,100	.055 kWh/use	Every day	1.7	.15
Toaster oven, broiling	800	.57 kWh/hour	Once a week for 10 minutes	2.3	.96

Source: Misty M. Lees, "The Kitchen, Unplugged," *Natural Home,* September/October 2004.

*Although appliances and home equipment vary greatly in the amount of electricity they use, this chart helps analyze the best places to cut back. The wattages listed were taken from the nameplates on various appliances.

†A watt is a unit of energy: a kilowatt is 1,000 watts. Multiply the kilowatt times the hours of operation to get the kilowatt hours used.

**kWh = kilowatt hour

Figure 16.4 This kitchen has Energy Star appliances and features sustainably grown mahogany cabinets and bamboo flooring.

Photo by David O. Marlow. Designed by Poss Architecture.

gets back to the earth. Moreover, a garbage disposal unit requires the use of water and electricity to function and is made of numerous metal and plastic parts that can't be easily separated for recycling.

Alternatively, there are some disposal units that are propelled by water pressure, not electricity. While these certainly cut down on energy use and are therefore more eco-friendly than conventional disposals, increased organic waste in the water remains an issue.

The optimal way to handle kitchen food waste is to develop a compost system. Urban dwellers might not have the garden to implement composting, so many waste management districts are taking a new approach: They collect kitchen scraps and food-soiled paper with yard debris, all of which is recycled into compost. In some places, a special collection bucket with a tight-fitting lid is supplied to each household. The resulting compost is sanitized and may even be resold.

Garbage disposals may be required by code and are standard in modern construction. If there's an existing disposal unit, there's no need to get rid of it, but there are better ways to deal with food scraps.

WASHERS

The washer may be the consumer of the largest amount of water in the home. Fortunately, new technology can reduce the amount of water needed to do the job well. Conventional top-loading (vertical-axis) washers that fill completely with water are being supplanted by front-loading (horizontal-axis) models that use a minimum of water, tumbling the clothes rather than agitating them. Top-loaders use about 40 to 50 gallons of water in order to saturate and cleanse properly, but front-loaders need only about a third to half as much.

Energy Star has devised a system by which it rates washers for modified energy factor (MEF), a figure that evaluates washer tub capacity along with the energy consumption for both the washer and the dryer (i.e., time needed to remove the remaining water from the clothes and then dry them). The higher the MEF, the more efficient the washer. Start with an Energy Star clothes washer, which requires an MEF of 1.72 and a maximum water factor (WF) of 8.0. Look to the Consortium for Energy Efficiency

---

Fact Check

■ The water saved by front-loaders is so substantial that the "thirsty" state of California has mandated strict regulations for residential washers: Since 2007, all new models must be horizontal-axis types. Other states are following suit.

Source: California Energy Commission, www.energy.ca.gov.

(www.cee1.org), which identifies different tiers for clothes washers relative to the maximum MEFs and minimum WFs, and choose the highest tier possible to minimize water and energy use. Specify Energy Star qualification for all washers.

Front-loaders are typically more expensive, but they save an average American household 7,000 gallons of water a year.[2]

Approximately 95 percent of the energy used to wash clothes is for heating the water, and front-loaders reduce that need substantially. In addition, the front-loader's improved spin cycle removes more water from the clothes and thus cuts the amount of energy consumed by the dryer—or the time on the clothesline. A study of 204 families that switched to front-loaders found they lowered energy use by 56 percent.[3]

DRYERS

Specifying a dryer is not as straightforward as specifying a washer. Dryers are not required to display an EnergyGuide label, nor are they certified by Energy Star. Most dryer models use similar amounts of energy to get the heating and tumbling done. In fact, the truly eco-friendly way to dry clothes is not to use a dryer at all, but to hang them out (see the sidebar, "On the Line"). Next to that, removing as much water as possible in the washer's spin cycle will cut dryer time; using front-loading washers will also help.

The choice of gas or electric will be influenced by the client's preference, the available public utilities, the cost, and whichever dryer system is already in place (i.e., if there is a 220V outlet or a gas hookup). In general, gas dryers are slightly more efficient, although the availability of alternative electrical power might sway the decision in favor of an electric dryer. Good controls on the dryer will help energy conservation efforts; look for automatic shutoffs and moisture sensors. Timers are the poorest controls, as they may overdry clothes before shutting off. Thermostats that sense air temperature do a fair job of determining when clothes

---

[2] Consumer Energy Center, www.consumerenergycenter.org.
[3] Department of Energy, www.energy.gov.

On the Line

Clotheslines were once the only way to dry clothes, and they are still the most environmental way. Ironically, in many communities that are otherwise quite progressive, clotheslines have been banned as unsightly. Nationwide, more than a quarter million homeowner associations (HOAs) govern upward of sixty million people. It's estimated that at least half of HOAs restrict or ban the use of a clothesline. Fortunately, nearly twenty states, including densely inhabited ones such as California, Florida, and Texas, have right-to-dry laws.

It's estimated that 30 million tons of coal could be saved every year if every American switched to hang-drying their clothes. Project Laundry List, an environmental coalition, calls the idea a "revolution." Best of all, it only costs a few dollars for the equipment, which will last for years. Even by using a clothesline part of the time—when the weather is favorable or the humidity low—the energy savings—along with personal satisfaction—is high.

Source: Project Laundry List: www.laundrylist.org.

are dry, improving on timer efficiency by about 10 percent, but moisture sensors excel at about 15 percent over timers.[4]

Confirm that the dryer's exhaust ducting has a minimum number of turns, is the shortest length possible, and that smooth, rigid metal ducting is used. To support healthy indoor air quality, clothes dryer exhaust should be vented directly to the outside.

Lastly, ensure that the vent used to exhaust the hot moist air from drying clothes has a vent cap. This helps to protect air infiltration when the dryer is not being used. Also make sure that the dryer vent cap doesn't restrict exhaust air flow; otherwise, lint can collect, decreasing drying performance and increasing energy use.

Where Does It Come From?

- Appliances are manufactured from a wide array of materials, including stainless steel, plastic, cast iron, copper, ceramic, and glass.
- The energy supplied to run appliances comes from a variety of sources, including burning of coal and fossil fuels, nuclear power, hydroelectricity, solar energy, and wind power.

---

[4] ACEEE, www.aceee.org.

- The heat source for some appliances may be fueled by natural gas, propane, kerosene, heating oil, or wood.
- Many appliances also consume water and create wastewater.

Installation

Make certain that all appliances have the proper clearances for air circulation, secure hookups suggested by the manufacturer, and ample ventilation vented directly to the outdoors. Position refrigerators and freezers away from heat ducts, bright sunlight, and warm appliances such as stoves and dishwashers.

Maintenance

Replacing an appliance is a major decision that directly impacts the environment, especially if the existing appliance wastes water or energy but is still in a usable condition. Although most appliances can be recycled for the large amounts of steel, there will be many components that end up in the landfill. Simple replacement parts, such as refrigerator drawers or dishwasher door handles, can often be found online, through the original manufacturer, parts retailers, or even auction sites. If the appliance is otherwise in good condition and conserves water and energy even moderately, it might be best to wait to replace it. On the other hand, if energy or water use can be greatly improved and the appliance recycled, it's time for a better model.

Provide homeowners with maintenance manuals addressing the appropriate cleaning and maintenance of appliances. Instruct that all appliances be kept clean and free from dust that can hamper motors or moving parts. Refrigerators should be maintained by vacuuming the coils annually, or more frequently as needed; removing dust from the heat-exchange coils can significantly improve energy performance. If the client does not have a frost-free refrigerator or freezer, they will need to be defrosted to be most effective. To safeguard ovens and ensure efficient operation, clean off accumulated food prior to the next use. Using only biodegradable, eco-friendly, and safe detergents, soaps, and cleansers in or on appliances helps in three ways: The substances are less corrosive and abrasive to the appliances, they don't have toxic fumes or chemicals to harm humans, and they don't destroy the environment.

The following are general tips to help the client maintain their appliances and maximize energy and water efficiency.

Kitchen Appliances

- When cooking, use the smallest pan, the smallest burner, the smallest oven (if there are two), or the smallest and most energy-efficient appliance for the job. An appliance too big for the job will waste heat and, therefore, energy. Match the pan size to the burner to optimize efficiency. Flat-bottomed pans work much better with smooth surfaces and electric elements.

- Turn off the oven or the electric burner a few minutes before the cooking is complete; the radiant heat will continue to cook the food.
- Defrost foods in the refrigerator a day ahead rather than using an appliance such as the microwave or oven to defrost them.
- Keep preheating to a minimum.
- Keep the oven door closed; using the oven light to check the food prevents heat from escaping.
- Use the self-cleaning feature when the oven is already hot from cooking.
- If a part is loose or damaged, replace the seal on the refrigerator, freezer, or oven to maximize thermal efficiency.
- If the dishwasher has a heat booster, set the water heater temperature at 120°F, no higher.
- Avoid rinsing dishes unnecessarily before loading the dishwasher.
- Use the shortest dry cycle time on the dishwasher, or hand-dry the dishes.

Laundry Appliances

- Use the coolest water setting possible.
- Use the lowest water-use setting possible.
- Use the maximum spin cycle to lessen dry time.
- Wash only full loads.
- Hang-dry clothes whenever possible.

Where Does It Go?

Most of the energy expended to run appliances comes from nonrenewable sources such as coal and natural gas. Water used by appliances is somewhat renewable, although demand for water in the United States has outpaced supplies from sources such as aquifers and even natural rainfall. Anyone who has lived in the Western states knows well the struggle to obtain enough water to sustain a conventional American lifestyle.

One of the heaviest burdens on the environment, outside of energy and water consumption, is the "death" of an appliance. Most appliances are made from a variety of natural and manufactured materials, including some that can be recycled easily; the EPA says that 95 percent of refrigerator materials are eligible for recycling. Washers, dryers, and refrigerators all contain enough steel and other metals to make them worthwhile to scrap businesses, which shred the appliances and sort the debris magnetically. However, many smaller items, such as microwaves, get tossed out with the trash because the metal content is less than 50 percent.

In Europe and other places where landfill space is very limited, recycling is mandated in some jurisdictions, especially for equipment with toxic components such as coolants, heavy metals, and cathodes. Appliance manufacturers in these locations are required to build appliances so they last much longer and contain no banned hazardous materials or heavy metals. In some cases, manufacturers must establish an end-of-life plan for the equipment or take back the used appliances.

Until stricter manufacturing and recycling standards are established in the United States, the best ecological policy is to specify top-quality, recyclable household equipment that will last a long time and require few natural resources to operate it.

Spec List

Specify:

■ Energy Star appliances

■ Appliances with the best efficiency, according to EnergyGuide labels

■ Maximum water-conserving features

■ Front-loading washers

■ Dishwashers with hot water boosters and shorter wash and dry cycles

■ Recycling of all appliances that are being replaced

Avoid:

■ Unneeded or luxury features on appliances

■ Purchases of appliances that the client might not use fully or at all

■ New garbage disposal systems, unless required by code

Computers, Printers, and Office Equipment

Home offices are equipped with numerous electronic or computerized equipment and components; such electronics are part of daily life. Eighty percent of all American households have computers and use the Internet,[5] and that number continues to grow. Desktop computers and laptops, tablets and smart phones, printers, scanners, and other peripheral office equipment—all are practical necessities for homeowners whether they work full- or part-time from their homes. In our globally

---

[5]U.S. Census Bureau, 2012.

interconnected world, home office equipment is now the norm for professionals, students, and families of all sizes.

Telecommuting saves fuel that would be used by commuting. Today, people in more than thirty-three million households work from home.[6] Home offices allow for shared, more efficient use of space and equipment and enable parents to remain home with their children while "at work." The positives of home offices are exponential.

The flip side is that all this office equipment consumes vast quantities of nonrenewable materials, and improper or unprotected exposure to some of them can be toxic. A computer is made from more than sixty different minerals, and phones contain more than forty—lead, cadmium, and mercury among them.[7] Unfortunately, computers and electronics often become technological dinosaurs in just a few years, and replacement components, even batteries, are so difficult to obtain or so expensive that it's easier and cheaper to purchase new equipment. Many outdated computers, printers, phones, copiers, and scanners end up in the trash, where those hazardous materials leach into soil or groundwater. Electronics are a significant source of hazardous waste; the European Union estimates that electronics disposal is growing at a rate three times faster than that of regular municipal solid waste,[8] and those numbers may be even higher in the United States.

Office equipment and computers consume energy as well as natural materials. A desktop PC with a 20-inch flat-panel LCD monitor needs about 100 watts to power the computer and monitor. If these pieces are left on 24/7 for one year, the system will guzzle nearly 900 kilowatt hours of electricity. That would discharge approximately 750 pounds of carbon dioxide into the atmosphere, comparable to driving 820 miles in an average car. Most computer manufacturers have a power-down or "sleep" function—the only feature necessary for Energy Star qualification. The amount of energy conserved by using that feature is significant: An Energy Star computer will save an average of 70 percent energy over one that doesn't meet this criterion, and other office equipment with power-down modes may save as much as 90 percent.

Whenever possible, upgrade or repair office equipment rather than replacing it, or purchase a used or refurbished model (as long as it meets Energy Star criteria). By doing so, the need to recycle or dispose of it is delayed, and valuable raw materials are conserved. Specify products that meet standards like the European Union's Restriction of the Use of Certain Hazardous Substances in Electrical and Electronic Equipment (RoHS) Directive, which minimizes the use of hazardous substances, and the Electronic Product Environmental Assessment Tool (EPEAT), where you can find registered electronic products and an assessment of their environmental attributes.

---

[6]Energy Efficiency and Renewal Energy, www.eere.energy.gov.
[7]National Mining Association, www.nma.org.
[8]Environmental Protection Agency, www.epa.gov.

Fact Check

- 80 to 85 percent of electronic products were discarded in landfills or incinerators, which can release certain toxins into the air.

- E-waste represents 2 percent of America's trash in landfills, but it equals 70 percent of overall toxic waste; lead, for example, can cause damage to the central and peripheral nervous systems, the blood, and the kidneys.

- 20 to 50 million metric tons of "e-waste" are disposed worldwide every year.

- Cell phones and other electronic items contain high amounts of precious metals like gold or silver. Americans dump phones containing over $60 million in gold and silver every year.

- Only 12.5 percent of e-waste is currently recycled.

- For every one million cell phones that are recycled, 35,274 pounds of copper, 772 pounds of silver, 75 pounds of gold, and 33 pounds of palladium can be recovered.

- Recycling one million laptops saves the energy equivalent to the electricity used by 3,657 U.S. homes in a year.

- E-waste is still the fastest growing municipal waste stream in America, according to the EPA.

- A large number of what is labeled "e-waste" is actually not waste at all, but rather whole electronic equipment or parts that are readily marketable for reuse or can be recycled for materials recovery.

- It takes 539 pounds of fossil fuel, 48 pounds of chemicals, and 1.5 tons of water to manufacture one computer and monitor.

- Electronic items considered hazardous include televisions and computer monitors that contain cathode ray tubes; LCD desktop monitors; laptop computers with LCD displays; LCD televisions; plasma televisions; and portable DVD players with LCD screens.

Source: Eleven Facts About E-Waste: www.dosomething.org.

Figure 16.5 The stairs serve as an open, transitional space from the kitchen to the small upstairs home office that makes use of energy-efficient equipment. Also featured is an accent wall created out of Wall Flats made with 100 percent bamboo pulp. Wall Flats are biodegradable and recyclable at the end of their life cycle.

Photo by Jennifer M Koskinen/Merritt Design Photo. Design by RE.DZINE, Studio 2b, and Architectural Workshop. Contractor: Urban Green.

Where Does It Come From?

- Computers and office equipment are made from a wide variety of materials, the majority of which are metal, plastic, and glass.
- Computers and office equipment often contain hazardous materials such as heavy metals, vinyl, and toxic chemicals.
- Computers and office equipment rely on electricity for power.

Maintenance

Keep the computer, printer, and other office equipment turned off when not in use. Activate automatic shutdown and power-saver features on the computer; turn off the power strip or unplug the adapter as well. Clocks, power-indicator lights, and similar devices use standby energy, which can quickly add up to 1 percent or more of the residential total.

Rechargeable batteries are much more eco-friendly than disposables. Locate battery and printer cartridge recycling options.

Where Does It Go?

Ideally, home office equipment will be recycled. Approximately one billion computers were scrapped between 2007 and 2010.[9] But there has been little economic incentive to do so thus far. The thousands of different plastic components, benign by comparison to the toxic heavy metal components, are still the most challenging to recycle, according to the EPA. The process requires disassembling hazardous components, a job primarily relegated to the people at the lowest economic rungs of society, such as prisoners and citizens of developing countries—including children. Without protective gear or fair labor standards to protect them, they are at high risk for poisoning, cancer, and other work-related ailments.

Manufacturers, governments, and public-interest organizations are attempting to make electronics and computers greener and to make recycling an economically

---

[9] Consumer Reports Greener Choices, www.eco-labels.org.

feasible industry. Some states require retailers and manufacturers to take back used equipment for recycling, and there are new laws and incentives to reduce the amount of toxic lead, brominated flame retardants, and other toxic materials used to make electronics. New initiatives prevent the export of hazardous computer components to developing countries, the disposal of waste equipment in municipal landfills and incinerators not equipped to handle it, and the use of prison labor for dismantling hazardous components.

In addition, manufacturers are being pushed to make it easier for consumers to upgrade, fix, or replace parts. In the past, parts, batteries, printer cartridges, and similar components were expensive, model-specific, and difficult (if not impossible) to procure. The consumer had few motivations, other than eco-conscientiousness, to recycle broken or unusable components. Now, manufacturers are beginning to provide postage-paid recycling packages for consumers as well as making it easier to purchase replacement parts and components. Pursue electronics recycling whenever possible.

Spec List

Specify:

- Energy Star power-down features
- Equipment that meets RoHS and EPEAT standards
- Upgrades, if possible, rather than replacements of office equipment
- Recycling of all components

Avoid:

- Throwing any office equipment in the trash; many pieces contain hazardous materials

RESOURCES

American Council for an Energy-Efficient Economy. www.aceee.org
American Water Works Association. www.awwa.org
Earth911.org
EnergyGuide. www.eere.energy.gov/consumer/tips/energyguide.html
Energy Star. www.energystar.gov
EPEAT.net
GreenerChoices.org
H$_2$ouse.org
Lawrence Berkeley National Laboratory. www.lbl.gov
Project Laundry List. www.laundrylist.org
U.S. Department of Energy, Office of Energy Efficiency and Renewable Energy. www.eere
.energy.gov.
U.S. Environmental Protection Agency. "Water Efficiency Measures for Residences." www
.epa.gov/owm/water-efficiency/resitips.htm.

mechanical: plumbing

Figure 17.1 The sustainable design strategies for this kitchen included water-efficient faucets; Energy Star appliances; local, recycled glass backsplash tile; and eco-friendly cabinetry.

Photo by Bernardo Grijalva. Design by Lydia Corser, www.greenspacecompany.com.

In most cases, green interior design specifications are oriented toward the materials used for the production of a finish, furnishing, or fixture. Environmentally conscientious plumbing, on the other hand, focuses on the consumption of water. The toilets, sinks, showers, tubs, and faucets in our homes affect how much water we use—or waste—every day.

Water has gone from the most common substance on Earth to being, conceivably, the most valued one. The booming human demand for water, especially in regions where freshwater is precious, has stretched supplies to their limit.

While interior residential use is only a portion of the total—agricultural and industrial needs are far greater—every drop matters. Americans are especially thirsty, with residential use totaling 92 gallons (350 liters) per capita per day. That's compared with 52 gallons (200 liters) in Europe and only 5 gallons (20 liters) or less in sub-Saharan Africa, where it's barely enough for survival.[1] Only a small portion of U.S. residential consumption is for drinking water, however; 78 to 85 percent goes to our washing machines, showers, toilets, and dishwashers.

It's easy to make a big difference. Behavioral changes like turning off the water while brushing our teeth saves around 3,000 gallons of water per person annually. Residential water consumption could be decreased between 30 and 60 percent if every household in the United States installed water-saving fixtures and fittings. New faucets and showerheads use less water and provide the same perceived pressure (through aeration, which boosts the sensation of pressure) and cleansing ability. Improved toilet design has decreased each flush from as high as 7 gallons per flush (gpf) down to 1.28 gpf or less. Depending on the model being replaced and the model specified, homeowners can save between 20 and 60 percent, equivalent to nearly 13,000 gallons for every household annually.

There are larger-scale efforts as well. On-demand, recirculating, graywater, and solar hot water systems drastically cut the amount of energy used to heat water and they are relatively easy to retrofit to existing plumbing. On-demand water heaters replace conventional tank types by flash-heating water across a small system as it's needed rather than keeping gallons of hot water stored for occasional use. Recirculating systems can capture heat from shower and tap water as it drains, then redirect the warmth to hot water pipes on their way to the spigot. Solar-dependent hot water heaters conserve electricity. Graywater systems—installed by a plumber, or simply dependent on the client's habits—prevent waste by diverting wastewater directly into landscaping.

Fact Check

- Ninety-seven percent of the Earth's water is saltwater and 2 percent is frozen, leaving only 1 percent freshwater for human use.

- The United States has freshwater resources totaling about 660 trillion gallons, and Americans tap into about 341 billion gallons of those resources every day.

Source: American Water Works Association. www.awwa.org.

---

[1] World Water Council: www.worldwatercouncil.org.

Adding Up Savings

Interested to see what kind of savings a few changes in the plumbing might make? Water-budget calculators are available at www.saveourh2o .org and www.epa.gov to help determine what a client's water use and utility bill would be if toilets, showerheads, faucets, and the washing machine were replaced with high-efficiency options.

Water districts benefit too. Through individual conservation efforts, the infrastructure will last longer and won't need to be replaced as soon. To encourage residential water-use cutbacks, many districts offer rebates for replacement toilets and more efficient plumbing, great incentives to make water-conserving changes.

While it is always wise to replace an inefficient toilet or showerhead, the decision to replace or refinish damaged tubs and sinks is not as clear-cut. Many older fixtures with simple rust or small chips can be repaired or refinished, adding decades to their useful life. But there are significant drawbacks to refinishing. The chemicals used to etch the surface in preparation for the refinishing, such as hydrofluoric acid, are noxious and may also corrode existing pipes. The room in which the refinishing is done must be well ventilated for the safety of the worker, who should wear protective clothing and ventilators. The whole process is tough on indoor air quality and should not be attempted in a home where a client has chemical sensitivities. It is possible, although much less economical, to remove a fixture, refinish it off-site, and then replace it.

A great amount of resources and energy go into the manufacture of each fixture made from cast iron, ceramic, steel, acrylic, or fiberglass. And plumbing fixtures can be heavy burdens on landfills. The decision to replace or refinish a tub or a sink is a tough one. Both choices have a negative effect on the environment. If a fixture must be removed, look for salvage or recycling possibilities. Before refinishing a fixture, consult with subcontractors to find the least toxic, longest-lasting product and method (ask for the warranty specifics), then take every precaution to ensure the safety of workers and clients.

Toilets, Urinals, and Bidets

A number of technologies will cut water usage by toilets; most of them demand that we rethink the way we flush. The toilet is the single largest consumer of water: Residential toilet flushing accounts for up to 40 percent of water use alone. The simplest, most important way that Americans can conserve water is to replace old toilets, an initiative supported by national and local incentives.

All toilets manufactured for use in the United States must now flush with less than 1.6 gallons of water. These types, typically called ULFTs (for ultra-low-flush), were initially unpopular, as many needed double-flushing that counteracted the intended water savings. Thanks to performance testing, toilets today meet criteria standards and, in most cases, outperform their conventional, less efficient counterparts. (Check into the maximum performance testing of popular high-efficiency toilets at www.map-testing.com/about/maximum-performance/map-search.html.)

High-efficiency toilets (HETs) are designed to use less than 1.3 gpf despite superior flushing performance. HETs deliver at least a 20 percent savings over the current standard 1.6 gpf toilets and use less water than (ULFTs). Those toilets are now considered only standard efficiency toilets, meeting—rather than exceeding—current water-efficiency standards. HETs exceed these standards.

To discover the age of a toilet, look under the tank lid to find the date stamp. The older it is, the bigger the flush. Before 1992, when ULF models became a requirement in the United States (see table 14.1), toilets used anywhere from 3 to 7 gallons per flush. A new toilet (the marking on these should be behind the seat) will use only 1.6 gallons, or as little as half of that if it's a dual-flush model. Depending on the model used, homeowners can save 20 to 60 percent, equivalent to 13,000 gallons for every home annually.

If the client does not yet want to replace the toilet, either because it is used infrequently or has a flush capacity of just slightly more than 1.6 gallons, an add-on control will reduce water consumption. The mechanism allows the user to push the handle down for 1.5 gallons or up for the full flush. It can be retrofitted on most models that have the flush lever on the front.

Even better for water conservation are dual-flush toilets. On most dual-flush models, the handle can be levered or rotated by the user to provide more water or less, as needed; some models have two separate buttons. The lighter flush gets used about 80 percent of the time, consuming 25 to 50 percent less water, and most households with dual-flush toilets cut water used in toilet flushes by 50 percent.

Public restrooms have long since made use of toilets with pressure-assisted flushes, but their residential use is limited. Compressed air inside the tank provides 20 to 45 percent more efficiency than the ULFTs. The most often cited drawback of pressure-assisted flush models is the increased noise and added energy load.

Waterless urinals rely on an oil-and-alcohol mixture in the sanitary-chamber drain for cleansing, and to keep sewer gases from entering the home. The cartridge needs to be replaced after several thousand uses, and the bowl must be cleaned on a regular basis. Odor, however, is not an issue, as urine is odorless until it comes in contact with water. Almost all waterless urinals are for men; urinals for women do exist and are fairly common in some parts of the world, but they have never caught on in the United States.

There is also a type of hybrid sink-toilet bathroom fixture that routes the wastewater from the bathroom sink to the tank of the toilet. Because the sink use does not provide adequate water to keep the toilet tank full, supplemental freshwater is also plumbed in. The graywater is then recycled into the flush, with reported savings of another 5 gallons a day.

Although some municipalities formally exclude composting and incinerating toilets in their building code, the units are commonplace in remotely located cabins and homes where there are no sewer lines. They also eliminate the need for costly septic system construction and maintenance. Composting types turn human waste into usable compost, yet look like conventional toilets and are not unsanitary or necessarily more odorous. Self-contained composting units are the least expensive but must be emptied frequently; the price increases with a full composting system that has greater capacity or that serves multiple toilets. Composting systems need to be emptied only about once a year, and the compost removal is designed to be inoffensive, mostly odorless, and simple enough for the homeowner to do. The compost may then go directly into the landscaping.

High-tech toilets and bidets are available with heated seats, motion detectors, and other automatic sensors popular in some parts of the world. Few of these options do anything to conserve water, and almost all require electricity (although solar-powered toilet features are emerging) and more electronic parts. Unless the client has a family member with limited mobility and motion detectors or automatic sensors would be helpful, these "supertoilets" should be considered luxury items, as they offer no added environmental benefits.

Toilets and bidets are usually porcelain/ceramic, which is sanitary, weighty, and very durable. Fiberglass and acrylic models are also available but not as easily recycled. Stainless steel is a high-style, completely recyclable option.

Saving Paper or Water?

The production of tissue paper, which includes toilet paper and facial tissue, is a voracious consumer of wood pulp. And don't forget the cardboard rolls. Although a large percentage of toilet and tissue paper comes from recycled sources, Americans still have a long way to go to reduce their dependence upon trees for paper needs. If every household in this country replaced a single roll of virgin-fiber paper towels with one made from 100-percent recycled fiber, 544,000 trees would be saved

An alternative that is less popular in the United States but very popular in other parts of the world is the bidet. Although the bidet conserves paper, it increases water use substantially. The environmental victory is a toss-up: more trees and more paper manufacturing or more water and another fixture? The choice will be up to the client.

Source: National Resources Defense Council. www.nrdc.org.

Plastic, wooden, and vinyl seats and lids are available. Wood is difficult to keep clean, because the finish wears down and tiny cracks may develop. Plastic and vinyl are by far the most popular for their lightweight and sanitary properties. PVC-free seats and lids are commonplace for babies and nursing care facilities, but not yet standard for typical residential applications, so consult with manufacturers to see if they offer it.

When replacing an old toilet fixture, investigate recycling options for the old one. The porcelain can be recycled into road base; check with the local waste management or recycling authorities, which might even pick it up curbside. The Virginia Oyster Heritage Program has used recycled porcelain toilets and sinks to restore oyster beds (Virginia Department of Environmental Quality, www.deq. state.va.us).

Lavatories and Sinks

Lavatories and sinks are typically made from enameled cast iron or ceramic (also called porcelain or fireclay); stainless steel is also used for kitchen sinks. Bathroom basins are available in carved stone, cast concrete, copper, bronze, aluminum, enameled steel, glass, and a host of synthetic resins. With the exception of synthetic resins and acrylics, which are rarely good choices in an earth-friendly setting, all of the aforementioned materials have some eco-friendly characteristics. They can be recycled (although some will inevitably be down-cycled), all are nontoxic, and none will outgas. Sanitary characteristics are implicit in the design of any kitchen or bathroom sink, as they are in constant contact with hands, dishes, and food. All sinks have extremely long life spans and may outlast the house itself, although each type of material has its particular weakness.

Cast concrete is popular because it's easy to design with: It can be customized into any shape or configuration, often with integral sink in the countertop. Because concrete will patinate and develop hairline cracks over time, recommend sealing, finishing, or waxing; this is usually done off-site. Carefully weigh the pros and cons of particular finishing techniques and products, as some emit fewer VOCs but do not last as long. Specify low-VOC products whenever possible.

Copper requires constant maintenance if your client wants a new-penny shine, but scrubbing and polishing isn't necessary, as a desirable patina will develop over time. Enameled steel and cast iron may eventually crack, craze, and rust, yet they are durable and can be recycled. Porcelain or fireclay may also lose some of its sheen and glaze over time, especially if abrasives are used to clean it. Glass is a perfect choice for bathroom sink basins but not for kitchens, where contact with heavy cookware could crack or break the glass.

Consider installing an undersink collection system for graywater. The rinse water from the kitchen or bathroom sink can be harvested for use in the landscaping. There's even an innovation that combines the bathroom sink with a graywater catchment and filtration unit so that wastewater can be reused to flush the toilet.

Showers and Tubs

Next to outmoded toilets, showers are usually the biggest water consumers, accounting for about 17 percent of total indoor use.[2] Some older, conventional showerheads flow at a rate of 5 gallons per minute (gpm) or more—that's 50 gallons for a 10-minute scrub-down—which also exceeds many water heater capacities.

Most of the "enhanced" bath fixtures, which are the latest on the list of must-haves for many upscale homes, use inordinate amounts of water. A full-body spa-type shower tower with multiple nozzles can consume as much as 60 to 100 gpm, even though each nozzle outputs less than 2.5 gpm as mandated by the Energy Conservation Policy Act (table 17.1). "Rain" or "downpour" showerheads sold in the United States also comply with the 2.5 gpm law, but because there is only one nozzle, they may be the one luxury that is still water-conservative. Whirlpool and luxury baths have extralarge capacities—to fill one up, it might require 225 gallons of water instead of 10 to 25 gallons for a typical shower.

Encourage clients to select only water-savvy bath fixtures and fittings to maintain high environmental standards. WaterSense sets the maximum at 2.0 gpm for showerheads, and some are available from as little as 1.2 gpm. These standards cut the water usage by half or more while providing more than adequate water pressure. Some come with a shutoff knob that makes it easy to stop the flow while soaping up. To ensure safe water levels, specify a scald guard or a balance valve.

Tubs require significantly more water per use than does the typical shower. Reducing the tub size or the frequency of baths will save water. Specify a standard-size tub or bathrooms with only a shower.

Figure 17.2 This bathroom sink was handmade from pottery; the faucet came from a deconstructed house. The space also features strawbale wall plaster (an earthen mix of straw, sand, and clay), American Clay on the alternate wall, a mirror recycled from a deconstructed house, and low-VOC wheatboard cabinetry.

Design by Carney Architects. Photo by Greg Hursley.

---

[2] Environmental Protection Agency.

Table 17.1 Energy Policy Conservation Act

Faucets: The maximum water use allowed by any of the following faucets manufactured after January 1, 1994, when measured at a flowing water pressure of 80 pounds per square inch, is as follows.	
Faucet Type	**Maximum Flow Rate (gallons per minute or per cycle)**
Lavatory faucets	2.5 gpm
Lavatory replacement aerators	2.5 gpm
Kitchen faucets	2.5 gpm
Kitchen replacement aerators	2.5 gpm
Metering faucets	0.25 gpc
Showerheads: The maximum water use allowed for any showerhead manufactured after January 1, 1994, is 2.5 gallons per minute when measured at a flowing pressure of 80 pounds per square inch.	

Note: Water-efficiency standards established by the Energy Policy Act of 1992: www.epa.gov/owm/water-efficiency/wave0319/append_b.htm.

Figure 17.3 Reclaimed tub from Philadelphia, repurposed by using a Dornbracht wall-mounted faucet and handles. A new drain and stopper mechanism have been retrofitted. They are covered with basic poplar siding and have been stained. A crystal chandelier softens the atmosphere.

Designed by Liz Tiesi, Threshold Interiors. Photo by Randall Bye.

One-piece or complete-ensemble shower and bathtub combinations are commonly made from fiberglass or acrylic. Although they offer durability and an easy-to-clean surface, these materials are not eco-friendly because they are manufactured with large amounts of chemicals and energy and they can't be recycled. Some outgas and carry a significant odor when first installed. It's better to specify a tub from a material that can be recycled, such as cast iron or enameled steel. Consider a vintage tub, lavatory, or sink.

Fittings

In 1992, federal legislation was passed that required water-conserving features be included in all new faucets, showerheads, and toilets. Most kitchen faucets now have water flows of less than 2.5 gpm and bathroom sinks less than 1.5 gpm (see table 17.1). The latest, most water-efficient models save even more.

The technology behind many of these improvements is quite simple. Water flow is reduced by decreasing the supply or delivery pressure, either by installing flow restrictors (usually aerators) or controls. The easiest to improve water conservation is to install an aerator on the end of a sink faucet. The device mixes water with air, increasing the water pressure. Most faucets can be retrofitted, cutting water use at that point by half or more. For renovation projects, make certain all kitchen and bathroom faucets have aerators. This simple improvement costs only a few dollars but reduces water utility bills and water consumption significantly.

Directional or swivel spray heads on faucets function similar to aerators; they also allow water to be directed accurately, which saves water as well. Faucets that shut off when touched or tapped allow the user to turn off the water flow but maintain the temperature while brushing their teeth, rinsing the dishes, or other tasks that require both hands. Automatic and infrared sensors provide the same function, although they rely on electricity and require a few more electronic components. They may be particularly useful in households with small children or for those with limited mobility.

Faucets and other plumbing fittings are made from a variety of metals, including bronze, cast iron, aluminum, brass, chrome, steel, and copper. Many have recycled content; check with the manufacturer for specifics. Glass, ceramic, and acrylic are often used for handles; both glass and ceramic have earth-friendly characteristics but might not last as long as metal because they are prone to breakage.

Graywater

Although sewer lines are outside the realm of interior design, encourage the architect and contractor to rethink where the wastewater goes. A few alterations to typical plumbing will send graywater to the landscaping instead of the sewer, reclaiming water that is scarce in many regions. And graywater does more than nourish the flowers: It increases the longevity of home sewer and septic systems as well as that of the sewage treatment infrastructure by reducing the load. Graywater diversion will even decrease the energy consumption of wastewater treatment facilities. The client will also gain an increased awareness of and appreciation for the amount of water expended and conserved.

A graywater reuse system need not require plumbing alterations; at its simplest, it's a basic philosophy: "don't let it run down the drain." The homeowner can collect the kitchen sink or shower rinse water in a small bucket, then use it for outdoor or indoor plants. An integrated system requires the plumber to route all of the

Shades of Gray

Residential graywater is that which is left over after dishwashing, bathing, laundry, and light cleaning. (*Graywater* can have two meanings: it is sometimes used for reclaimed runoff from landscaping and roadsides.) Blackwater is waste from toilets, softeners, septic systems, and pools.

Figure 17.4 The powder room of this sustainable home includes a recycled-content metal sink, locally made bronze accent tiles, Forest Stewardship Council–certified walnut doors and trim, low-VOC substrates and adhesives, slate flooring, and compact fluorescent lamp (CFL) pendants.

Designed by Annette Stelmack, Rachael Morton, and Cassandra Coombe, www.associates3.com. Photo by Ben Tremper.

drains that capture graywater (sinks, washer, tubs, and showers) to a purchased or custom-designed filtration system, mulch, or leach field. The debris is captured; the graywater is then sent to the home's landscaping or to a holding tank for such use at a later time. It is also possible to send graywater to the toilet tank and use it to flush the toilet. Check with building codes to see if graywater plumbing systems are permitted.

Where Does It Come From?

- Water is obtained from a number of renewable and nonrenewable sources such as lakes, rivers, and aquifers.
- Some graywater may be collected for reuse from sink basins, washing machines, showers, and tubs.
- Plumbing fixtures can be made from concrete, stone, glass, ceramic, cast iron, steel, copper, acrylic or other plastics, and wood.
- Fittings are generally made from durable metals such as steel, cast iron, copper, and brass.

Installation

For new construction or a major remodel, recommend or specify the installation of systems that save water and energy such as solar water heaters or on-demand water-heating systems. Confirm that all architect and contractor specifications include hot water pipe insulation to minimize thermal loss. To meet Energy Star home requirements, heat-wrap the cold water pipes and do not spec pipes along the exterior walls.

Maintenance

Advise the client to choose paper products that disintegrate quickly, preferably with 100 percent postconsumer recycled content containing no virgin pulp: Paper that comes from virgin wood fiber destroys forests. Chlorine dioxide is typically used to bleach toilet paper during manufacturing, which releases dioxin, a known carcinogen, into the environment along with countless other chemicals. Recycled, chlorine-free products are better for the environment, sewer and septic systems, and the end user.

Flushing less often may be a difficult topic to discuss with a client, but it's an earth-wise concept worth mentioning. Other ways to save water include shutting off the flow while soaping up in the shower, brushing teeth, or shaving. And conserving water equals energy conservation too. The EPA notes that running water for five minutes uses as much energy as burning a 60-watt light bulb for fourteen hours.

Encourage the use of earth-sensitive, biodegradable, and healthy bathroom and kitchen cleansers such as vinegar, borax, and simple soap. Recommend that caustic bowl cleaners be avoided; they are ecologically hazardous, toxic, and can damage the tank and its parts, causing leaks as well as increasing the hazardous waste load on wastewater systems.

Water-Saving Tips

- Running the washing machine and dishwasher only when they are full can save 1,000 gallons a month.

- Use the garbage disposal sparingly. Compost instead and save gallons every time you don't use the disposal.

- When you shop for a new appliance, consider one offering cycle and load-size adjustments. They are more water- and energy-efficient than older appliances.

- Install a low-flow showerhead. They're inexpensive, easy to install, and can save your family more than 500 gallons a week.

- Turn off the water while you brush your teeth and save 4 gallons a minute. That's 200 gallons a week for a family of four.

- Install aerators on all faucets.

- Listen for dripping faucets and toilets that flush themselves. Fixing a leak can save 500 gallons each month.

- If you accidentally drop ice cubes when filling your glass from the freezer, don't throw them in the sink. Drop them in a houseplant instead.

Source: http://www.wateruseitwisely.com/index.shtml.

---

[3] Saving Water Partnership, www.savingwater.org.

Timely repairs will save money and conserve water. According to various industry guesstimates, up to a quarter of all households have running toilets or dripping faucets. In fact, up to 8 percent of all residential water consumption may be accidental, primarily from leaks.[3]

Where Does It Go?

Porcelain fixtures such as toilets and sink basins are sometimes recycled into road base; check with the waste management district to see if there is a porcelain recycling program.

Spec List

Specify:

- Third-party-certified WaterSense products
- Graywater recycling, whenever possible
- Recycling of old fixtures, if possible
- Smaller tubs
- Valve fittings with a lifetime warranty
- Fewer nozzles in showers and tubs to reduce the water consumption per use
- Cast iron, steel, glass, ceramic, or other recyclable materials for all tubs, toilets, sinks, and shower stalls
- Vintage tubs, lavatories, and sinks

Avoid:

- Larger tubs
- Full-body or multiple-nozzle shower systems
- Reusing fixtures that do not conserve water. (Don't send them to construction exchanges; instead, recycle the materials.)
- Acrylic or fiberglass tubs, sinks, shower stalls, and toilets that can't be recycled

RESOURCES

American Water Works Association. www.awwa.org.
Create an Oasis with Greywater: Your Complete Guide to Choosing, Building, and Using Greywater Systems. Art Ludwig. Self-published, 2002. www.oasisdesign.net.
EPA WaterSense. www.epa.gov/watersense.
Irrigation Association. http://www.irrigation.org.

CHAPTER 18

electrical: lighting and light fixtures

Figure 18.1 The chandelier in this rustic ranch game room was custom-crafted from recycled wrought iron, repurposed cowboy boots, and rawhide shades.

Designed by Annette Stelmack and Donna Barta-Winfield, www.associates3.com. Photo by David O. Marlow.

The advent of electricity in the home began a revolution. The flip of a switch and—voila!—a bulb comes to life. We no longer marvel at it. In fact, we expect nothing less.

The simple convenience that we now take for granted was developed out of sheer necessity, from the critical need to provide safe navigation in dim shelters and at nighttime. Primitive types of illumination once consisted of simple wicks in oil, candles, and lanterns. In the late 1800s, Thomas Alva Edison, building on the work of Englishman Joseph Wilson Swan, developed the light bulb. The rest is history. Today, 100 percent of U.S. homes rely on electricity for lighting.[1] In fact, residential lighting consumption was about 186 billion kilowatt hours (kWh) or 13 percent of all residential electricity consumption in 2011—and most energy dedicated to lighting is used inefficiently. Candles, oil lamps, and lanterns are still used in modern homes, but for their rustic or aesthetic qualities, not convenience or practicality.

As designers, we focus on specifying decorative, ambient, task, and accent lighting coupled with their controls systems, including switching, dimming, sensors, and timers. The remaining residential electrical systems are specified by the architect, mechanical/electrical (ME) consultant, or lighting consultant. To realize the highest energy efficiency, it is imperative to work closely with a qualified consultant. Lighting affects each room's mood, color, warmth, and safety as well as the arrangement of furnishings, so it's a critical element of the design. Illumination

Tubular Skylighting

They look like recessed electrical lighting, but they are narrow, tubular skylights with domed caps and highly reflective walls that focus and intensify the brightness of natural sunshine. Even though these tubes work only when there's daylight, they'll cut down on energy costs considerably, especially if a room or closet has no window. Want to control the ambience? These skylight tubes may be "dimmed" with butterfly baffles (flaps that open and close). And they have less impact on heating and cooling costs than traditional skylights. Although metals and manufactured coatings are used in their construction, the daylight systems are sustained by the renewable energy of the sun—no electricity needed—unless you decide to include day and night home lighting solutions or ventilation. A tubular skylight can cut up to 90 percent of lighting energy use and ultimately improve the overall levels of daylighting.

---

[1] Energy Information Administration, www.eia.doe.gov.

needs must be carefully planned to maximize the placement and efficiency of the fixtures and underlying electrical systems.

The materials used in manufacturing light fixtures affect the environment, but choices are somewhat limited by technology. Yes, all fixtures must have electrical conductivity (wires and metal) and a protective, transparent surround (glass) that can withstand certain temperatures. But more important than the materials for the light fixture, lighting must be energy-efficient in order to be eco-friendly.

Electric lights consume vast amounts of fossil fuel. Residential lighting (indoors and out) accounts for approximately 3 percent of all U.S. electricity consumption and approximately 9 percent within the home. Seventy percent of our electrical energy comes from nonrenewable resources such as coal, gas, and oil, and another 20 percent is nuclear.[2] The need for residential energy conservation is clear.

Figure 18.2 The chandelier, a find on Etsy.com, was crafted from old silverware and offers a playful solution for lighting the nook. The space of this LEED Platinum home also features transitional trim and a classic footed cabinet style, while the bright and rich blue recycled-content field tile backsplash by Fireclay Tile adds a splash of color and richness to the space. A bill-paying or homework desk sits in the kitchen and breakfast nook because the kitchen, as the center of the home, is used for more than just eating and cooking.

Designer: eco+historical, inc. and Feldman Architecture. Photo by Paul Dyer.

---

[2] Ibid.

Well-designed rooms emphasize natural and reflective light sources. After you evaluate the available natural light and assess the daylight models, determine the amount, placement, and orientation of artificial lighting needed—or not needed—to determine potential energy consumption and savings.

Types of Bulbs

Before selecting light fixtures, specify the bulb type (sometimes called the lamp), as the most energy-efficient bulb for the job may not fit a particular light fixture's configuration and programming. Incandescent bulbs have long been the most popular choice, but fluorescents and light emitting diodes (LED) use far less electricity and last significantly longer. In addition, bulb choice affects the color rendering index (CRI), color perception, comfort, and health.

In 2007, the Energy Independence and Security Act (EISA) was passed. Manufacturers had until 2012 to produce more energy-efficient light bulbs. As an energy-efficiency standard, EISA requires all screw-in light bulbs to use 25 to 30 percent less power beginning with 100-watt bulbs in 2012, followed by 75-watt bulbs in 2013 and 60-watt and 40-watt lamps by 2014. Additionally, by 2020, the standard requires all bulbs to use 65 percent less energy. Ironically, if a manufacturer could produce an incandescent bulb that used less power today, the maker could sell it. Manufacturers are unable to make a bulb that meets these specifications; in essence, the EISA standard bans certain types of inefficient, energy-guzzling incandescent lamps.

It's unfortunate that there are exemptions written into the standard for specialty bulbs. These bulbs include the Edison, three-way, silver-bottomed, candelabra/chandelier, and countless more.

With the 2012 law in effect and 2020 not far away, designers now have three selections: halogen incandescent bulbs, compact fluorescent lamps (CFLs), and light-emitting diodes (LEDs).

INCANDESCENT BULBS

Incandescent bulbs use a tungsten filament, halogen gas filling, and quartz-glass bulb. They've long been the standard, and at first cost they are the cheapest. But their environmental impact is enormous. Their color rendering index, or color accuracy when compared to daylight, is almost 100 (see the sidebar, "Color by Number"). Soft white coatings eliminate much of the characteristic incandescent glare. But their inefficiency will cost the client and the environment more in the long-term.

Incandescents last only 750 to 2,000 hours on average, a fraction of the life span for CFLs and LEDs. Moreover, some 90 percent of the electricity in an incandescent bulb used is wasted as heat, and these bulbs pose a fire danger if placed

Color by Number

The color rendering index, or CRI, is a mathematical system for comparing different light sources for color perception accuracy using eight pastel colors. Daylight is assigned a CRI of 100; the scale measures a light source's similarity to natural daylight. An incandescent bulb of 100 watts comes close to rendering the same color value as daylight, and CFL and LED technology can now achieve a CRI of 85 or higher. (The lower a CRI number, the less natural a color will look.)

CRI isn't a perfect indicator, however. Some bulbs render certain color spectrums better than others. To be absolutely accurate, only bulbs with the same color temperature should be compared. Color temperature is the color bulb of light the bulb produces expressed on the Kelvin scale. "Warm white" or "daylight" compact fluorescent light bulbs (CFLs) have color temperatures similar to incandescents.

Use CRI and color temperature as guides when selecting bulbs. After installation, help the client maintain ambience *and* energy efficiency by supplying specification sheets or detailed notes on the selected bulbs for future purchases.

too close to fabric or paper shades. A room lit brightly by incandescent bulbs in the summertime may require extra cooling, pressing the energy-efficiency issue further.

Halogen bulbs are a type of incandescent that also uses a tungsten filament enclosed inside a smaller quartz envelope. The bulbs are filled with a halogen gas that combines with the tungsten, which first evaporates and then redeposits itself on the filament. This recycling process allows for a longer-lasting filament, relative to conventional incandescents, and the bulbs also run hotter, delivering more light per unit of energy. However, these gains may be negated by the extra energy needed to cool a room lit by halogen bulbs. Although a low-voltage halogen bulb is slightly more efficient than a conventional incandescent, the energy savings is negligible because of the energy requirements of the voltage transformer.

FLUORESCENT BULBS

Fluorescent bulbs cost more initially, but over the life of the bulb can save money. Because they give off approximately only 30 percent of their energy as heat, they are much more energy-efficient than incandescents. They last an average of 20,000 hours each, 10 times longer than their standard incandescent counterparts. The newest compact fluorescent light bulbs fit most standard fixtures and lamps.

Figure 18.3 This powder room cube features fluorescent lighting inside the walls. The space also features a 50 percent recycled content steel door and fiberboard walls.

Photo © 2006 Robert Meier. Designed by Locus Architecture.

Best practice now replaces incandescent light bulbs with CFLs, thereby lowering a home's electric consumption: CFLs use one-quarter to one-third as much electricity as incandescents. Because they generate significantly less heat, CFLs help to reduce air-conditioning loads.

A fluorescent bulb is a sealed glass tube (straight, twisted, and folded) that has electrodes at each end and is filled with a very small amount of mercury. The synthetic fluorescent coatings on the inside surface of the glass are absorbed and illuminated when the mercury is vaporized by the electric current running through.

Electronic ballasts in CFLs has eliminated the flicker and hum of older fluorescents, and minimized the time delay before they light. A variety of advances has also improved the quality of light, durability of the lamp, and provided three-way switching and dimming capabilities. Nonetheless, there are still a few drawbacks. Fluorescents do not have perfectly accurate color rendering. Because the light given off is a different color from that of incandescents, CFLs may be perceived as less bright. A slightly higher wattage will compensate for the difference and still save energy.

Be sure to specify the correct bulb for the application and fixture. CFLs should not be used in enclosed, recessed locations because the wattage necessary to generate adequate light within is so high that it can overheat. Adaptation fixtures have been designed to modify recessed lighting to accept them. Dimmer switches require special fluorescent bulbs; electronic timers and photocells may not function properly or at all. That said, CFLs are terrific choices for kitchens, bedrooms, and most living and play areas, and their average life span is eight to ten times that of incandescent bulbs.

Defining Rated Lifetime

Manufacturers report lamp life, called "rated life," usually in hours, on the packaging of various light sources. However, the definition of "rated lifetime" varies from lamp type to lamp type. The use patterns and conditions under which the lamp is used has an impact on its overall service life. To complicate matters, the standard testing conditions used to measure lamp life seldom correspond to real-life conditions. Even with these limitations, the rated life provides important information for calculating the economic cost and impact of a lighting solution.

Specify CFL bulbs with low mercury levels significantly below the average. Mercury is a known toxin, so fluorescents require special disposal; check with the local waste management authorities for specifics or work with the manufacturer to ensure they reclaim the toxic mercury in the lamps. The largest source of mercury pollution, however, is from coal-burning power plants, and fluorescents reduce the energy needed from them. To further diminish the environmental impact and home health risks, specify low-mercury bulbs, which are distinguished by green end caps.

For the highest level of energy efficiency and performance, look to Energy Star requirements for CFL light bulbs. Criteria address the efficiency (efficacy) of light bulbs measured through the light output (lumens) compared to the energy (watts) needed to power the bulb. CFLs must provide at least three times more lumens per watt than incandescent bulbs to earn an Energy Star rating.

All light bulbs grow dim over time, but Energy Star–qualified CFLs must maintain 80 percent of the initial light output for 40 percent of their rated lifetime. This means that to qualify for Energy Star, an 8,000-hour CFL has to give off 80 percent of the light it gave off during its first 100 hours of operation after 3,200 hours of use and have a rated lifetime of 6,000 hours or greater. The current average rated lifetime for Energy Star–qualified CFLs is 10,000 hours. The typical use of 3 hours per day yields an average lifetime of 9 years.

Energy Star light bulbs must also start in less than one second and reach full brightness in less than one minute when using mercury vapor; bulbs with amalgam mercury must reach full brightness in under three minutes. They must have a CRI of 8; all indoor reflector lamps must pass a high-heat test for recessed applications. Energy Star bulbs always come with a manufacturer-backed warranty; manufacturers must file a commitment form with the National Equipment Manufacturers Association Voluntary Industry Commitment to Limit Mercury Content in Self-Ballasted CFLs sold in the U.S. And they are subject to random, independent third-party testing during their manufacture.

Bulb Conversion

This is a basic conversion chart comparing incandescents and CFL. The bulb box's labels will also have this information.

- 60 watts incandescent = 15 watts compact fluorescent
- 75 watts incandescent = 20 watts compact fluorescent
- 100 watts incandescent = 26 to 29 watts compact fluorescent
- 150 watts incandescent = 38 to 42 watts compact fluorescent

Source: General Electric, www.gelighting.com.

LIGHT-EMITTING DIODE BULBS

Light-emitting diodes, or LEDs, work differently than other light bulbs—they ignite a tiny semiconductor microchip that produces infrared light. LEDs consume very little energy and can last 30,000 to 50,000 hours.

Producing quality white light with desirable CRI levels has always been challenging. The creators of LEDs devised methods to combine a variety of LED colors or phosphor coatings to produce white light improving the light quality; most LEDs have a CRI of 90 or more.

LED lighting is more efficient than incandescent and CFL bulbs, and contain no toxic mercury. Dimmable bulbs are available for most LED fixtures.

The initial cost of an LED lamp and lighting fixture is higher than that of incandescent and fluorescent products. The good news: Their cost is coming down, and their performance is improving. For the best return-on-investment, specify quality products rather than those that are the least expensive. Cheaper LED products do not manage heat buildup as well, thereby shortening the lifespan.

In order to meet Energy Star requirements, LED light bulbs must meet the following criteria: color quality must remain consistent over the bulb's entire life span; the output must meet minimum levels for replacement claims and be maintained through the end of its rated life; it must demonstrate 75 percent or more efficacy (light output divided by the total power input, expressed in lumens per watt); and it must carry a three-year minimum warranty. Energy Star requires a minimum power factor of 0.7, but you should use LED luminaires with a power factor higher than this standard. Power factor is the active power divided by the apparent power.

Bulb Efficacy

Let's dive more deeply into the efficiency differences between LEDs, CFLs, and incandescents by looking at a significant study conducted by the U.S. Department of Energy's Energy Efficiency and Renewable Energy division. In August 2013, it issued a report demonstrating that LED lighting uses less energy and provides better lighting quality and performance than conventional lighting technologies. The study estimated the life-cycle energy consumption of three technologies—LED, CFL, and incandescent—based on existing life-cycle assessment (LCA) studies.

The study revealed that the average life-cycle energy consumption of LED lamps and CFLs is similar and about one quarter that of incandescent lamps. As compared to EISA 2007–compliant halogen lamps, however, the energy savings of LED and CFLs is not as great; their life-cycle energy consumption is about three-quarters that of halogens.

This is the first installment of a multitiered DOE project that will continue to assess the life-cycle environmental and resource costs in the manufacture, use, and disposal of LED lighting products in relation to comparable traditional technologies. (More detailed and subsequent studies can be found at http://www1.eere.energy .gov/buildings/ssl/tech_reports.html.)

For other energy-efficiency measures, look to federal, state, and local resources for incentives and rebates. The DOE's Database of State Incentive for Renewables and Efficiency (DSIRE) is a solid source for incentives and policies that support renewables and energy efficiency in the United States. Established in 1995, DSIRE is currently operated by the North Carolina Solar Center at North Carolina State University, with support from the Interstate Renewable Energy Council, Inc. It can be found at www.dsireusa.org.

Residential electrical lighting consumes 3 percent of total energy in the United States,[3] but that amount could be reduced by about 66 percent if all incandescent bulbs were replaced with CFLs.[4]

Lighting Controls

Additional strategies to reduce electricity use include dimmers, automatic daylight shutoffs, occupancy sensors, and timers.

- *Dimmers* work in two different ways: manually or self-adjusting. The latter can be counterproductive because they automatically brighten when there is

---

[3] Ibid.
[4] Energy Star, www.energystar.gov.

less daylighting even when the additional light isn't needed. When used with incandescent lamps, dimmers allow for a gradual start-up that may lengthen the life of bulbs. Any incandescent bulb can be controlled by a dimmer, but only special fluorescent bulbs can be dimmed.

- *Occupancy sensors* "know" when a person has entered a room, making them practical for those with disabilities, for small children who can't reach switches, and for people with their hands full of packages. They also detect when there is no movement in the room, so that (working in tandem with a timer) after a preprogrammed length of time they will automatically dim or shut off.

- *Automatic daylight shutoffs* prevent lights from coming on during the day. However, some automatic controls turn lights on, which may provide light when it's not really needed.

- *Timers* on interior lighting will reduce energy consumption only when the occupant is unavailable (or has forgotten) to turn the lights off. They are most useful for controlling lights in greenhouses, pet areas, or for spotlights on artwork. (Timers and occupancy sensors are often used with exterior lighting to heighten security.)

Fixtures

Energy Star fixtures use one-fourth of the energy of traditional lighting. The fixtures are "nonregressive": they are designed to fit only CFLs. They also distribute light more efficiently and evenly.

Energy Star fixtures are available in countless styles, including table, desk, and floor lamps, plus hard-wired fixtures for ceilings and walls. Typically they carry a three-year warranty. The fixture light lasts between 10,000 and 50,000 hours on average; if the fixture is used for 3.5 hours a day, the bulb won't need changing for approximately seven years. Used throughout the home, the savings can add up to hundreds of dollars.

Where Does It Come From?

- Most electricity is generated by burning of fossil fuels at power plants. Smaller amounts are created through nuclear fission and renewable wind, water (hydroelectric), and solar sources.

- Residential lighting consumes approximately 3 percent of total U.S. electricity and 9 percent of the electricity in a home.

- Residential light fixtures rely on metal and glass for integral components; other pieces may be made of plastic, wood, or other materials.

■ Bulbs are made primarily of glass with metal electrodes and fittings. They also may contain various types of gas or mercury.

Installation

Work closely with the lighting consultant and/or electrical contractors to determine the best placement, controls, and fixtures for providing the desired aesthetics, and color rendition, temperature, and perception while maximizing energy efficiency. Infrequently, the infrared light emitted by a fluorescent bulb can interfere with electronic equipment that uses infrared technology (e.g., remote controls and wireless telephones). Consult with the electrician to avoid this problem.

Specify the most energy-efficient bulb and fixture for the job. A balanced combination of CFL and LED bulbs will reap long-term savings for the client while protecting the environment.

Light Pollution

Light pollution is misdirected, too-bright, and sometimes unnecessary light that spills into the surrounding environment. While planned lighting installations improve security and safety, too many fixtures, excessive light levels, glare, and poor location can create a nuisance. Light pollution disturbs natural aesthetics, as well as the diurnal rhythms of birds, plants, and animals, and makes seeing the stars and natural landscape impossible. Unwanted light in sleeping areas may aggravate sleep disorders or negatively affect health in other ways. Light pollution can actually *decrease* visibility if the source is too bright or focused incorrectly, impeding safety on roads, sidewalks, front steps, and yards.

While most light pollution is caused by exterior fixtures, interior fixtures can also contribute to environmental and physical malaise. Carefully evaluate designs and plans to ensure that the light is directed correctly, that it's not too bright, and that it doesn't trespass into areas where it's undesirable or unnecessary.

Look for fixtures that are "dark sky compliant," a standard of the International Dark Sky Association (http://www.darksky.org/) aimed at eliminating glare and minimizing the adverse effects of poor-quality lighting.

Maintenance

Help maintain energy efficiency by providing the client with a list of ideal bulb types and optimal wattage for each fixture. The following are common misperceptions.

- Turning fluorescent lights off for short periods wastes energy. This is untrue: Turning fluorescent lights off, even for short periods, saves energy.

- Turning a light off does not lengthen bulb life. This is also not true: Leaving a bulb on when it's not in use causes it to burn out faster.[5]

Where Does It Go?

A fluorescent light tube in your dumpster is a violation of hazardous waste laws in California and other parts of the country. It can result in fines and criminal prosecution. Fluorescent tubes contain mercury and are considered hazardous waste.

Recycle nonworking CFLs through an authorized recycling firm or the manufacturer or by working closely with the waste management disposal agency rather than discarding them. Though the amount of mercury in an individual bulb is tiny, the cumulative effect on discarding CFLs in landfills is undeniable. In 2004, 142 million fluorescent bulbs entered the waste stream, but only 2 percent were recycled.[6]

Consult with the waste management district to learn if recycling or better disposal options for bulbs exist. Some districts collect them at hazardous waste or recycling sites. Recycling containers, mostly intended for places such as schools, hospitals, and commercial buildings that dispose of bulbs frequently, may soon become more available to individual homeowners. To participate, the consumer must purchase a bulb-collection box that has prepaid postage; when it's full, it's sent to the recycling facility.

For household recycling, look for participants in the Take it Back Partnership. They will take away fluorescent tubes and/or bulbs at no cost, depending on the project's location. Check out Earth911 (www.earth911.org) for disposal options for fluorescent tubes and bulbs as well as other universal wastes that get them to a responsible recycler.

---

[5] *Energy User News*, www.energyusernews.com.
[6] LampRecycle.org.

Spec List

Specify:

- Compact fluorescent lamps and light emitting diode bulbs whenever possible
- Controls such as dimmers, occupancy sensors, daylight shutoffs, and timers if they will reduce lighting use
- Energy Star fixtures and bulbs

Avoid:

- Incandescent bulbs; use them only when other options are inadequate or can't be adapted to current fixtures
- Light pollution, by overlighting a location or misdirecting light
- Landfill disposal of fluorescent bulbs; encourage the homeowner to recycle

RESOURCES

Bulb Recycling. www.lamprecycle.org.
Earth 911. www.earth911.org.
Energy Star. www.energystar.gov.
U.S. Department of Energy. www.energy.gov.

CHAPTER 19

furnishings

Figure 19.1 Furnishings in this living room were created by local artisans, upholstery was produced using nontoxic glues and domestic woods, and the coffee table was crafted from blown-down cedar.

Designed by Associates III, www.associates3.com. Photo by David O. Marlow.

The residential furnishings market is successfully following the lead of the commercial industry by providing products and materials that meet sustainable, healthy, and eco-friendly criteria. That said, it is easier to locate and specify green architectural materials, because the market for those has largely been driven by the Occupational Safety and Health Administration (OSHA) and Leadership in Energy and Environmental Design (LEED) rating systems and the benefits of compliance with them. Fortunately, many manufacturers work in both industries, and others recognize the benefits of adopting healthy, sustainable market initiatives and strategies that boost the availability of green residential building materials. Unfortunately, no rigorous system for interior furnishings has yet been established.

NB: Unlike chapters 9 through 18, which follow the Construction Specifications Institute (CSI) MasterFormat divisions, this chapter is organized to follow the order in which a designer would likely research and specify residential furnishings.

Countertops

Countertops are horizontal work surfaces. For kitchens and baths they need to be both sanitary and durable. They must withstand rigorous daily use, frequent exposure to water, and make a fitting design statement. Solid-surface or laminate countertops traditionally made from petrochemical-based synthetics have, until recently, been the top choices. Green design avoids these synthetics, because they may contain questionable content, are made from nonrenewable resources, can't be easily recycled or reclaimed, and don't break down well in landfills.

The growing market for earth-sensitive and healthier products has encouraged the development of numerous countertop options that still meet aesthetic and durability criteria. Countertops can now be made from a number of beautiful, eco-friendly materials, including pressed recycled paper, recycled glass-concrete terrazzo, traditional wood butcher block, and linoleum.

There are all-natural products and materials with high recycled content; a countertop's location and use will determine which materials are most appropriate. Some are better suited to abuse from cutlery or water from sinks, for example, while other types are easier to fit to a particular configuration or require no sealants. Selecting a material that resists stains, cutlery marks, scrubbing, and frequent use is wise from an eco-perspective, as it will delay future replacement.

When remodeling, consider refinishing or repairing the existing countertop, or covering a damaged or outdated countertop with a new surface rather than removing the existing one (confirm that there will still be adequate room to house appliances underneath the cupboards after the profile is raised). Overlayment of an existing countertop surface obviates sending the original materials to the landfill. It is also a savvy way to avoid debris, volatile organic compounds (VOCs), and dust from a deconstruction that might irritate the client's allergies or sensitivities.

Before settling on a particular countertop, consider the installation methods and materials needed for it. They vary widely, and some will introduce more VOCs and toxic content or irritating odors than others. Steer away from countertops that rely heavily on adhesives or mastics for installation, and instead select products that are environmentally benign. Some countertops will also require regular oiling or sealing with chemically formulated products; others require only cleaning with a damp, soapy cloth.

CONCRETE COUNTERTOPS

Concrete, a traditional construction material with tremendous design possibilities, is a popular choice for countertop material. It's extremely durable and long-lasting. Concrete counters can be cast off-site to keep indoor air quality clean, or on-site if the design must be customized.

Some concrete countertops, especially precast composites, incorporate recycled material such as fly ash that reduces the overall weight and increases the compressive strength. Fly ash typically consists of mineral elements from coal power plants that often contain harmful heavy metals such as arsenic, cadmium, mercury, and lead. At this time, the industry assumes that these metal substances will not leach out of concrete during use, but disposing of concrete with fly ash might be difficult because of their presence. They might also contain other recycled material of questionable composition: polypropylene, recycled carpet fibers, or plastics. Request the material safety data sheet (MSDS) and full ingredient disclosure from the manufacturer. And carefully research the use of synthetics in composites for health and environmental risks.

Aggregates and seeding can add color and texture to concrete countertops, as well as strength and scratch resistance. Recycled glass is a particularly wise aggregate choice, as it rescues a nontoxic, reusable, mineral-based material from disposal. It also comes in spectacular colors. Stones, antique hardware, seashells, and botanical imprints may also embellish the concrete. Be wary, however, of synthetic aggregates such as computer chips or plastics that may contain hazardous or toxic metals or chemicals.

The drawbacks of concrete countertops include heavy energy consumption and water pollution during manufacturing. Concrete has a porous surface that must be sealed regularly to avoid staining.

Where Does It Come From?

- Concrete is a mixture of sand, gravel, water, and cement.

- Cement is manufactured from a combination of minerals (calcium, silicon, aluminum, iron) that are fired at high temperatures and then ground and combined with gypsum.

- Concrete may use postindustrial waste as a substitute for part of the cement or some of the aggregate.

- Aggregates may include decorative recycled glass, stones, or other manufactured or natural materials.
- A variety of chemical admixtures may be present, although it is possible to make concrete without them.
- Natural or synthetic pigments may be added to wet concrete.
- Concrete may be left unfinished, or it may be finished with epoxy, polyurethane, or other chemical sealants.
- Concrete may be acid-stained with water-based, acidic liquids that contain metallic salts.

Installation

Inquire as to the type of cement and avoid synthetic enhancers called admixtures. Surface tints or acid stains are extremely caustic and outgas considerably when applied, putting workers and occupants at risk, so specify that colorants or tints be mineral-based and mixed into wet concrete.

As concrete is quite porous, the countertops usually require a sealant to protect the surface from stains and water damage. Specify a low-VOC, water-based, food-safe sealant or wax. A wipe-on sealant will affect air quality less than a spray-on type.

Maintenance

Regular protection with a wipe-on sealant is recommended. Advise the client as to the most eco-friendly types—those that are low-VOC, water-based, and food-safe.

Where Does It Go?

A concrete countertop is basically a permanent design addition to a residence, as the material is difficult to remove or deconstruct and may well outlast the house itself. Although concrete recycling exists, it primarily serves large concrete consumers such as commercial construction and road maintenance, so smaller residential design applications of concrete may not be accepted.

Should the concrete be disposed of, the cement, lime, natural minerals, natural aggregates, and mineral colorants will eventually disintegrate in a manner similar to stone. Synthetic admixtures, fly ash, aggregates, and colorants have a more uncertain future and may contaminate the environment.

Spec List

Specify:

- Concrete (and cement mix) made without admixtures
- Aggregates (or "seeding") and cement from all-natural minerals
- Aggregates from safe, recycled materials
- Food-safe aggregates, sealants, colorants, or admixtures for kitchen applications
- Natural mineral pigments (for color)
- Potable water for curing
- Precast or factory-finished slabs
- Low-VOC, water-based, or water-reducible low-solvent, no-formaldehyde stains, sealants, and finishes

Avoid:

- Aggregates or recycled ingredients that may introduce contaminants
- Chemical pigments or paints with chromium, aniline, or heavy metals
- Acid stains
- Seeding with synthetic, possibly hazardous materials such as computer chips

Resources

ConcreteNetwork.com.
Portland Cement Association. www.cement.org.
See also "Concrete," page 241.

STONE COUNTERTOPS

Solid stone, such as granite, marble, or soapstone, provides a durable surface that is literally rock-hard. A stone countertop can be cut from a solid slab or installed as tiles. The stone itself is 100 percent natural and won't outgas (with the possible exception of radon; see sidebar, page 254). It is heat-resistant, sanitary, and may never need replacing. If and when deconstruction occurs, the stone can potentially be reused, recycled, or simply returned to the earth.

Figure 19.2 The sandstone in this powder room was quarried and manufactured locally, reducing the embodied energy of the stone and provides a durable, long-lasting, and easy-care finish.

Designed by Associates III, www.associates3.com. Photo by David O. Marlow.

All stones are porous and must be sealed. Solid granite is the strongest of all stone building materials and as such a durable option for kitchen countertops. Soapstone and slate are other possibilities for countertops. They don't react with acids such as vinegar, wine, and lemon juice, which are problematic for granite and marble. Marble and limestone are more porous and prone to stains.

Salvaged slate tiles from rooftops have emerged as an eco-friendly choice. They are scoured thoroughly prior to installation, providing a countertop that is both natural and reclaimed.

Lava stone, a volcanic rock, is crushed, glazed, and fired much in the same way as ceramic tile, making it a stone-tile hybrid with the characteristics of both. It doesn't need sealing, is very hard, and will never outgas VOCs. The downside to lava stone is the large amount of embodied energy inherent in the firing. The glazes, while inert after firing, may be hazardous to factory workers in the liquid stage.

Stone is ultimately a nonrenewable resource, and a stone countertop isn't easily or cheaply removed or replaced. The environmental impact from mining stone is especially severe and permanently scars ecosystems. In addition, stone is difficult to transport, and some of the most popular types are shipped from overseas.

SIMULATED/CULTURED STONE COUNTERTOPS

The terms "simulated stone" and "cultured stone" usually refer to a composite countertop made with both natural rock and a synthetic binder or cement. Typically, they contain at least 90 percent quartz or other common minerals. The ground-up minerals are then pressed and superheated with a resin to form a surface that may be more impervious to stains and water than natural stone. Composite stone countertops usually don't need to be sealed like natural stone. According to the manufacturers, they outgas only minimally, primarily before installation. The synthetic resins used and the energy needed for manufacturing are downsides, although some are made with cement binders.

Ask about antimicrobial treatments, as most contain heavy metals or hazardous chemicals.

Where Does It Come From?

- Stone is mined or quarried.
- Some stone can be reclaimed from rooftops, deconstruction, and other sources.

Installation

Although the risk of significant radon exposure (enough to cause illness) from a countertop is unlikely because of the small amount of stone used in residential

Antimicrobials

The manufacturing processes associated with antimicrobials release metals into our water, soil, and air—the same metals that, ironically, may contribute to antibiotic resistance. Silver, in particular, has been linked with bacterial resistance. Antimicrobials can also lead to what is known as cross-resistance, whereby bacteria become resistant to the antimicrobial itself.

And questions are being raised about whether antimicrobials serve a measurably useful function in interior flooring and finishes for health-care setting; their efficacy has been called into question by several independent studies. The Centers for Disease Control and Prevention (CDC) concluded a 2003 comprehensive study of infection control practice with the statement that "no evidence is available to suggest that use of these [antimicrobial] products will make consumers and patients healthier or prevent disease. No data support the use of these items as part of a sound infection control strategy."

Kaiser Permanente (KP) similarly concluded in a December 2006 position statement that "we do not recommend environmental surface finishes or fabrics that contain antimicrobials for the purpose of greater infection control and the subsequent prevention of hospital acquired infections." KP states that there is "no evidence that environmental surface finishes or fabrics containing antimicrobials assist in preventing infections." Rather, the organization recommends strict hand hygiene and environmental surface cleaning and disinfection.

Source: http://www.healthybuilding.net/healthcare/Toxic%20Chemicals%20in%20Building%20Materials.pdf.

applications, radon testing may be prudent. Have the testing done before the countertop slab is purchased.

Stone tiles or veneers, which are generally more economical than solid stone, will require more adhesive, grout, or mastic for installation; specify low- or no-VOC, additive-free products whenever possible. When the supporting structure isn't strong enough to support solid stone, stone tiles or veneers may be preferred for their lighter weight.

Request that all cutting and mechanical polishing be done outdoors or off-site to prevent dust from entering the home.

Maintenance

If left unsealed, stone is prone to stains and scratches. Use low-solvent, low-VOC, formaldehyde-free, water-based sealants that don't contain drying agents made from heavy metals. Spray-on sealants may affect indoor air quality or pose hazards to the workers, so wipe-on varieties are preferred.

Where Does It Go?

Natural stone will eventually decompose when disposed of. It can also be reused, reclaimed for another purpose, or ground up and recycled into a different product. Unfortunately, cultured stone does not biodegrade; it can be repurposed and possibly reground for use in other products.

Spec List

Specify:

- Reclaimed, salvaged, or recycled stone
- Stone from local or regional sources
- Radon testing of materials before installation
- Low-VOC, low-solvent, water-based, formaldehyde-free sealants and adhesives
- Wipe-on or brush-on sealants

Avoid:

- Imported stone
- Adhesives, grout, mortar or sealants with solvents, additives or formaldehyde
- Spray-on sealants
- Antimicrobials

RESOURCES

"Consumer's Guide to Radon Reduction." Environmental Protection Agency. 800–438–4318. www.epa.gov/radon/pubs/consguid.html.
"Toxic Chemicals in Building Materials: An Overview for Health Care Organizations." Healthy Building Network. www.healthybuilding.net.
See also "Masonry," page 251.

METAL COUNTERTOPS

Stainless steel, aluminum, zinc, and copper can be used in countertop applications. Although copper is used infrequently, stainless steel is common in commercial and institutional applications because it is sanitary, long-lasting, extremely durable, and easy to clean. More and more residential design applications are following suit. Commercial stainless steel shelving and counters are easily obtained from restaurant suppliers, and used ones can be purchased at equipment auctions. Aluminum looks similar to stainless steel and uses up to 60 percent recycled material; however, it is softer than stainless steel. Zinc is a living metal that patinizes over time. It has antibacterial qualities and is nonporous. It scratches easily, has a low level of heat resistance, and reacts to acidic foods and moisture, causing discolorations that blend together over time.

Metal is hygienic and suitable for use in kitchens or baths. It is nonporous, won't outgas, and can be kept clean with simple soap and water—no sealants required.

Most types of metal can be recycled into other metal products. All types of metal, however, are nonrenewable resources obtained through mining operations that permanently alter the geology and landscape, thereby incurring a heavy environmental price. Look for high recycled metal content, especially in steel and copper.

Figure 19.3 This bathroom has a countertop of recycled 1/8-inch aluminum. The space also features natural concrete flooring with integral color and radiant heat, and cabinets made of raw medium-density fiberboard (MDF) with a clear, water-based sealer.

Photo by Greg Hursley. Design by Eric Logan, Carney Architects.

Fact Check

■ Stainless steel products contain an average of 65 to 80 percent recycled content.

Source: Specialty Steel Industry of North America, www.ssina.com.

Where Does It Come From?

■ Metal is mined from various locations around the globe.

■ Metal for countertop applications is usually extracted from ore through intensive manufacturing processes.

■ Metals are often combined into alloys to increase their strength, sheen, or resistance to natural oxidation.

■ Various factory coatings and finishes may be applied to metal, including paint, powder coating, protective oils (natural or chemical), metal platings, and zinc galvanizations.

■ Metal can be easily recovered from recycling and fabricated into new products.

Installation

Chemical coatings or wax are sometimes applied to countertops and backsplashes to protect the finish while in transit. Request that the coating be omitted, whenever possible, to eliminate odors and potential VOCs within the home, or request removal of the coating before it is brought on-site. Alternatively, specify that a food-grade wax or oil be used.

Metal should not be used where there is a high incidence of electromagnetic waves, such as near microwave ovens or induction cooktops, as this could impact individuals with electromagnetic hypersensitivity (EHS). Consult with the homeowner, electrician, and general contractor before adding a metal countertop in the kitchen. (See "Electromagnetic Fields," page 22).

Specify that all scrap metal from the installation be recycled.

Maintenance

Avoid commercial polishes and cleaning solutions that contain chemicals such as kerosene, naphtha, perchloroethylene, chromic acid, silver nitrate, or solvents. Simple soap and water will suffice for cleaning most metal countertops (see the sidebar "Pretty as a Penny").

Pretty as a Penny

Concerned that a copper countertop or backsplash will turn green with age? It won't, unless it comes in contact with acids, as it does outdoors when exposed to the elements. For a new-penny sheen, clean at least once monthly with a rubbing of salt and lemon wedges—or ketchup!—then rinse thoroughly. Using only soap and water will allow the copper to develop a caramel luster. The countertop will be beautiful either way.

Source: Copper Development Corporation, www.copper.org.

Where Does It Go?

Countertop metals can be recycled over and over, and their value is high enough that most types are sought after by salvage operations. Disposing of metal in landfills is a last resort, although most types of metal will simply deteriorate over time and pose little risk to the environment.

Spec List

Specify:

- Salvaged metal countertops and shelving
- One hundred percent recycled material, or the highest percentage possible
- Local fabricators to eliminate transportation
- Metal that develops a natural, pleasing patina or verdigris without the need for polishing
- No paint or finish
- Careful location of large metal design applications to avoid electromagnetic fields from microwaves
- Recycling of all scrap

Avoid:

- Pieces made with virgin metal
- Synthetic oil coatings
- Chemical polishes, treatments, or cleansers

RESOURCES

Copper Development Association. www.copper.org.
Specialty Steel Industry of North America. www.ssina.com.
See also "Metals," page 259.

WOOD COUNTERTOPS

Wood chopping blocks are used worldwide for food preparation, and many modern kitchens feature a section of wood built into the countertop or food preparation area. A section of wooden countertop is far less demanding on the slowly renewable supply of trees than the construction of an entire house, but similar ecological considerations apply. Consider whether the wooden object will outlast the tree needed to produce it. Wood countertops will last for decades, although wear and stains may eventually warrant replacement. A slightly damaged section can be sanded to restore its appearance.

Reclaimed wood is ideal for many residential applications and is a wonderful green choice, although it may not be the safest for a kitchen or bath countertop. The porous surface might have been exposed to bacteria or toxins in its prior application as flooring or as a door. Therefore, specify reclaimed wood for a countertop only if the source can be verified as food-safe and the surface is completely free of harmful finishes.

Certain species such as maple, cherry, walnut, and mahogany are hard, tightly grained, and won't damage cutlery. To ensure that the desired species is not endangered and that the forest management is sustainable, specify third-party certification of new-wood products such as approval by the Forest Stewardship Council (see page 227). Specify locally or regionally harvested wood to limit transportation and shipping and keep the embodied energy low.

A countertop made from a nonaromatic wood species can be left unfinished or be treated with natural oils. When specifying wood countertops formed with multiple segments (of end-grain or butcher block) to counteract possible warping, specify food-safe wood glues with no formaldehyde or VOCs. Because wood warps easily, protective sealants such as healthful oils or waxes or a permanent water-resistant finish are necessary to use it near sinks.

Sanitize for Safety

The small cuts and gouges on a wooden cutting board or other porous countertop surface can harbor bacteria. Wood and acid-resistant surfaces may be cleaned with a spritz of half-vinegar and half-water mix, followed by a mist of hydrogen peroxide. Simple soap and water isn't as effective, but might be used on countertops that would be stained or marred by vinegar or peroxide. Advise the client of these natural sanitation methods to ensure a safe, healthy countertop.

Where Does It Come From?

- Wood products come from both domestic and exotic trees.
- Reclaimed wood is culled from residential, commercial, and agricultural floors, walls, and structures. It may also be culled from rivers, lakes, streams, orchards or fallen trees.
- Some wood products are made from down-cycled wood scraps or sawdust, with acrylics or resins added.
- Wood sealants are usually polyurethane; natural resin-oil primers are a more healthful and environmentally positive option.
- Wood finishes or stains may contain a variety of natural oils, resins, or pigments, as well as solvents, chemical compounds, petroleum distillates, metal-drying agents, formaldehyde, and sometimes water.

Installation

For all kitchen applications, specify food-grade finishes and treatments. Also specify formaldehyde-free, low-odor, low-VOC glues, adhesives, and finishes that contain minimal or no solvents.

Maintenance

Regular light oiling or waxing with food-safe, all-natural vegetable oils or beeswax will help prevent water damage and stains to the wood. To remove stubborn stains or to even out a rough surface, wood countertops can be lightly sanded.

Where Does It Go?

Wood biodegrades. A used, clean section of countertop can be reused for another application such as a tabletop, be recycled into mulch, or even be burned (if unfinished) in a wood stove.

Spec List

Specify wood that is:

- Reclaimed, if the source can be verified as safe for a countertop
- Locally or domestically harvested, FSC-certified, or a nonthreatened species
- End-grain or butcher block made with food-safe glues

Specify finishes and stains (either on prefinished wood or to be applied on-site) that are:

- Food-safe (for all kitchen installations)
- Water-based
- Made of natural (sometimes called food-grade) oils, resins, pigments, and waxes
- Low-VOC
- Formaldehyde-free
- Solvent-free

Avoid:

- Reclaimed wood of uncertain origin
- Chemically tainted wood (lead, arsenic, factory chemicals)
- Uncertified wood
- Rare or threatened species
- Solvent-based finishes
- Formaldehyde and other preservatives in the wood or finish

RESOURCES

Forest Stewardship Council. www.us.fsc.org.
Rainforest Alliance (formerly SmartWood). www.rainforest-alliance.org.

CERAMIC TILE COUNTERTOPS

Ceramic tile is a perennial favorite for kitchen and bath applications because it is resistant to abuse from knives, staining or acidic compounds found in foods and personal care products. Glazed tile is especially stain-resistant. Unglazed tile should be protected with a sealant. Large-format porcelain panels are great for counter-tops, as significantly less grouting materials are needed. Look to mainstream U.S. tile manufacturers for this application.

Specify tile with third-party certifications from Green Squared, offered through several bodies of certification (see chapter 8). Simple ceramic is made primarily from abundant clay, although some styles now incorporate recycled tile, stone, or glass. The glazes are inert once fired, providing a zero-VOC, sanitary, superdurable surface. (Although lead-based and heavy-metal glazes are still a concern in less-developed parts of the world, the glazes on all tiles made for sale in the United States are free from these hazardous metals.) Tile's long life span tips the scales in favor of its use, despite its high embodied energy from its intensive manufacturing process.

Tile remnants are available at many construction exchange sites, and it's always ecological to use materials that might otherwise end up in a landfill. If there are not enough remnant tiles to complete the entire job, consider using them as accents.

Where Does It Come From?

- Traditional ceramic tile is usually made of fired clay.
- Talc, cement, synthetic or recycled materials such as fly ash or glass, and other minerals may be added.
- Tile may be glazed or unglazed; glazes consist of metals, pigments, and various chemicals, along with simple silicon dioxide—sand—that become inert when fired.

Installation

Cut tile outdoors, off-site, or in an open area with a wet saw to prevent dust within the home. Recycle tile remnants through a construction exchange or similar venue.

- *Underlayment.* Specify third-party-certified (FSC) wood underlayment or that made from recycled wood or biocomposites with ultra-low-emitting formaldehyde levels.
- *Mortar.* The use of thickset mortar (greater than one-inch deep) reduces the need for synthetic adhesives and mastics. Thick-set mortar can be done with simple Portland cement, sand, and lime. Thin-set mortar, more fragile and prone to cracking, usually relies on chemical and latex additives for flexibility; it is used, opt for a water-based, additive-free, low-VOC variety.
- *Adhesives/mastics.* Choose mortars, adhesives, grouts, and sealants with the least toxic, low-VOC, zero-solvent, minimal-additive ingredients possible. Specify those with no petroleum, toluene, hexane, benzene, or other solvents.
- *Grout.* Whenever possible, specify third-party-certified (Green Squared) simple grout made of Portland cement, sand, and water. Mineral pigments can be added for color (they also hide eventual staining). When using commercial grout blends, specify that they be additive-free, without synthetics. Specify unsanded grout when the joints between tiles are very thin.
- *Sealants.* The best way to avoid grout problems and ensure tiles remain stable and beautiful is to apply a sealant, which closes the pores in the grout. Specify a low-VOC, water-based, wipe-on variety to minimize the negative effect on indoor air quality.

Maintenance

Glazed ceramic tile needs little more than regular soap-and-water cleaning, but grout is prone to discoloration and deterioration from mold, mildew, and stains.

In moist bath and kitchen areas, ventilation through windows and via exhaust fans will slow the growth of mold. Regular resealing with a low-VOC, water-based, wipe-on sealant will also discourage mold and grout discoloration.

Advise clients to avoid toxic cleansers should the grout become discolored with mildew or dirt. Instead, recommend using vinegar and water, borax, or baking soda and scrubbing with a stiff brush. Professional steam cleaning is also helpful. As a last resort, rather than replace the tile, grout lines between tiles can be removed and then filled in with new grout.

Where Does It Go?

Fired clay, mortar, and grout are much like rock and will eventually break up into inert pieces; the glaze will also be inert. Tile remnants are popular at construction exchanges. Used tile may be recycled with other porcelain such as toilets, which are usually crushed and added to roadbed.

Spec List

Specify:

- Third-party certification from Green Squared
- Tile made with unprocessed, all-natural clays or with safe, recycled materials such as glass
- Factory-glazed ceramic
- Natural wood underlayment, preferably made from FSC-certified wood
- Simple mortar from cement, sand, water, and possibly lime (no additives)
- Grout with no added fungicides or biocides
- Low-VOC, water-based, wipe-on sealant
- Low-VOC, low-solvent, additive-free, mortar and grout

Avoid:

- Unregulated import tile
- VOCs, solvents, fungicides, vinyls, or latex additives in mortar, grout, and sealants

RESOURCES

National Terrazzo & Mosaic Association. www.ntma.com
Tile Council of America. www.tcnatile.com

GLASS AND GLASS TILE COUNTERTOPS

Recycled glass from bottles, windshields, and other sources (see the sidebar, "Bottleneck") provides a rich source for countertop tiles or glass backsplashes. Glass itself is manufactured from abundant sand, and the tiles or plates are simply made by melting or sintering (a melting process done at an even lower temperature) recycled glass and adding color. Glass is completely inert, emits no VOCs, won't stain, and won't absorb other VOCs and toxins because it has no "pores." It's one of the most sanitary surfaces available, appropriate for both kitchens and baths. Like ceramic tiles, glass tiles wipe clean with simple soap and water or vinegar and need no chemical upkeep. Recycled glass can be a wonderful choice for an eco-friendly home.

Ask the manufacturer about the specific recycled glass content, as it varies considerably between products. Choose the highest percentage postconsumer recycled content available.

Where Does It Come From?

- Glass is made mostly from silicon dioxide (sand).
- Glass for recycled glass tile generally comes from postconsumer waste such as bottles and windshields.
- The recycled content of glass tiles varies greatly by manufacturer and product, even between particular colors of tile.
- Small amounts of metals and chemicals may be added to glass for color and texture.

Installation

Specify FSC-certified wood, high recycled wood content or biocomposite underlayment, both with California Air Resources Board (CARB)-compliant ultra-low-emitting formaldehyde levels (ULEFs).

Specify Green Squared–certified unsanded grout, as sanded grout will scratch glass tiles. Specify low-VOC mastic and additive-free grout whenever possible. (Outgassing may still be harmful to air quality and the environment, but it will be less problematic for a sensitive client when it is done outdoors.)

Bottleneck

- Since the first Earth Day in 1970, Americans have thrown away 600 billion glass beverage bottles, weighing approximately 166 million tons, according to the Container Recycling Institute.

- In 2009, 12 million tons of glass were generated in the United States, and 3 million tons were recovered.

- In 2009, Americans threw away almost 9 million tons of glass. That amount could fill enough tractor trailers to stretch from New York to Los Angeles and back!

- Over a ton of natural resources are conserved for every ton of glass recycled, including 1,300 pounds of sand, 410 pounds of soda ash, 380 pounds of limestone, and 160 pounds of feldspar.

- That means that Americans wasted around 11 million pounds of sand with the glass bottles discarded in 2009. That amount could fill every room in the White House with sand 12 feet deep!

- Glass container manufacturers use up to 70 percent recycled glass, or cullet. A glass container can go from a recycling bin to a store shelf in as few as 30 days.

- Recycling one glass bottle saves enough energy to light a 100-watt light bulb for 4 hours, power a computer for 30 minutes or a television for 20 minutes.

- The use of cullet in place of raw material saves energy because it melts at a lower temperature. That means it also emits less carbon dioxide and nitrogen oxide, two greenhouse gasses.

Source: Keep America Beautiful, Recycling Facts, www.kab.org.

Maintenance

As with ceramic tile (see page 321), use a sealant to protect the grout from eventual deterioration and discoloring. Specify a low-VOC, low-solvent, wipe-on type to minimize odors and the release of VOCs in the home.

Glass needs no special upkeep, only soap-and-water cleansing. Abrasives should be avoided. Regular reapplications of sealant may be necessary to protect the grout, so advise the client as to the most eco-friendly types.

Where Does It Go?

Glass can be recycled from bottles to tiles to something else, over and over and over, but only if it doesn't end up in the trash or on the roadside. Currently, only ten U.S. states require bottle recycling. Many of those states are considering updating and expanding those laws, while there is similar legislation pending in other states. The bottle bills require refundable deposits on beverage containers, which motivates customers to return or recycle. The growing glass tile industry, thankfully, encourages the growth of bottle bills and curbside recycling initiatives by creating a market for recycled glass.

Spec List

Specify:

- One hundred percent recycled glass tile or high recycled glass content
- Natural backerboard, MDF, or underlayment (FSC-certified wood; CARB ULEF high recycled wood; or biocomposite, plaster, or gypsum)
- Low-VOC, water-based, wipe-on sealant
- Low-VOC, low-solvent, additive-free, mortar, mastics, and grout
- Certified Green Squared unsanded grout

Avoid:

- VOCs, solvents, fungicides, vinyls, or latex additives in mortar, mastics, grout, sealants

See also "Glass Tile," page 322.

SOLID SURFACE, COMPOSITE, AND LAMINATE COUNTERTOPS

Laminate countertops made from melamine, a crystalline substance made from a synthetic resin (see the sidebar, "Melamine," page 476), were once all the rage. They were easy to install and easy to clean, and they could be peeled up and replaced when they wore out. Then along came composite, solid-surface, and acrylic countertops that could be cut to fit the specifications of the kitchen or bath, were practically impervious to abuse, and were far more durable than laminates. Both laminates and composites, unfortunately, are manufactured primarily from synthetics and chemicals. The countertops are energy-intensive to make, contain toxic substances, and don't biodegrade.

Solid or laminate composite countertops have become more eco-friendly. Manufacturers have devised ways to incorporate a host of relatively eco-friendly ingredients into long-lasting, cut-to-fit surfaces. Hemp, recycled paper, sustainable-forest paper products, soy resins, and agricultural wastes (called bio-composites) are now found in the composition of these new materials. Some composites also feature mineral content such as fly ash, quartz, and sand. They feature the necessary water resistance for use in baths and kitchens, and most of the companies that make these greener products strive to incorporate binders that are low- or zero-VOC. Look for products that contain 100 percent postconsumer recycled or FSC-certified content.

In the typical laminate manufacturing process, several sheets of cellulose-based paper are treated with phenol formaldehyde. Under high heat and pressure, materials are bonded to a decorative and/or melamine formaldehyde-treated cellulose layer. The binding resins in these high-pressure laminates (HPLs) typically make up 25 to 45 percent of the total weight of the product. The laminate is adhered to particleboard or MDF panels. Specify products with FSC-certified content and ensure they meet California Department of Public Health emissions requirements (CA 01350). Additionally, there are some bio-based products without added formaldehyde.

Distinct from those with a plant fiber or pulp base are composite countertops, whose primary ingredients are minerals or concrete. Recycled materials often figure into the composition, as well (see "Concrete Countertops," page 451, and "Cultured Stone Countertops," page 454). Precast concrete countertops frequently contain postindustrial fly ash or recycled glass as a means of strengthening the surface and reducing the weight. Some precast concrete types may include ingredients such as plastics, carpet fibers, and other synthetics, which are all generally undesirable in a green home.

Composites with high recycled plastic/acrylic content are making an appearance on the market as well. If the client has a preference for keeping recyclable materials such as plastic out of the landfill, this might be an option. However, it's important that a home be both environmentally responsible and healthy. The material content and resin base of many recycled plastic composites is difficult to ascertain, and the potential for outgassing or ill health from such a countertop is undetermined, at best.

Each composite, laminate, or solid-surface countertop, whether bio-based or mineral-based, is quite distinct in its composition. Check with the supplier or manufacturer for details, and inquire specifically as to use of formaldehyde, synthetics and VOC-producing compounds, as well as potential odors that could be a problem for sensitive clients. Specify products with high percentage of post-consumer recycled content and for optimal indoor air quality, double check that they meet CDPH (CA 01350) emissions requirements. In addition, performance characteristics such as scratch, stain and water resistance will vary for each particular brand, making some less appropriate for use in a kitchen or bath.

Recycled glass and/or porcelain composites use pre- and post-consumer waste typically with a Portland cement-based binder. Take care to ask about the resins in these products; bio-based resins are typically sound, but epoxy based resins may contain bisphenol-A, a known endocrine disruptor.

The environmental benefits and drawbacks to these composite and laminate surfaces have not been fully established. Some are more green and feature natural, renewable, or recyclable materials, and some are less so because they are made from nonrenewable resources or synthetics. Before committing to a composite or laminate countertop material, carefully consider the origin, use, installation, maintenance, and eventual disposal or recycling potential.

Where Does It Come From?

- Composite or solid-surface countertops may be made from any variety of natural or manufactured components, including (but not limited to) hemp, recycled paper, sustainable-forest paper products, soy resins, wood pulp, agricultural wastes (biocomposites), quartz, other minerals, concrete, fly ash and polymers or plastics.
- The resin binder may be natural, synthetic or bio-based.
- The countertop may be manufactured through heating, pressing, rolling or other processes.

Installation

Because of the variability of the materials, each countertop selection should be evaluated carefully for the installation materials and processes that will be required. Inquire as to the types of adhesives or glues required, all finishes or sealants that are recommended and specify the most eco-friendly materials (low-VOC, low-solvent, water-based and formaldehyde-free) that meet the manufacturer's performance standards and the project's environmental goals.

All cutting should be done off-site or outside to eliminate residential exposure to VOCs, particulates and/or dust. (The environment and air quality will still be affected by the outgassing of VOCs, but the process will be less problematic for a sensitive client when it is done outdoors.)

Maintenance

Maintenance will depend on the specific surface. Inquire as to the most benign methods and materials, then supply the client with a complete list of recommendations.

Some composite or solid surface countertops can be lightly sanded to restore a new appearance.

Where Does It Go?

The composition of solid surface countertops varies greatly and may be so complex that it's difficult to determine how well they will break down. Reuse of a countertop is unlikely because each is cut to spec, but may be possible if it can be successfully removed, then recut or refinished. The higher percentage of natural materials it contains, the more likely it can be recycled or disposed of safely. Synthetic content will make biodegrading slower or impossible.

Spec List

Specify:
- A high percentage of all-natural, bio-based materials in the countertop material
- A high percentage of safe recycled materials
- Bio-based binders (such as soy)
- Low-VOC, formaldehyde-free binders, resins, adhesives, and finishes
- Certification that meets CDPH residential VOC emissions test

Avoid:
- Synthetic ingredients or binders like epoxy
- Formaldehyde, VOCs, solvents, or odorous adhesives, finishes, or binders
- Melamine

LINOLEUM COUNTERTOPS

"Linoleum" is both a brand name and a widely used term that is not brand-specific. It can be successfully used on countertop applications such as furniture tops and utility surfaces where it is not constantly exposed to water, as excessive moisture can stain it or cause the surface to deteriorate. Although naturally antimicrobial and easy to maintain, linoleum can be scratched or gouged easily with cutlery, so it may not be suitable for all kitchen installations.

Figure 19.4 The cabinets in this remodeled ranch house kitchen are locally produced and made of wheatboard, a very low VOC and formaldehyde free alternative, with light gray melamine finish. The countertops are Durat, a solid surface material with 35 percent recycled content. The horizontal wall cabinet doors, as well as the back of the peninsula, have panels of 3-form capiz shell ecoresin (with 40 percent recycled content). The backsplash tiles behind the range and the vent hood are unglazed porcelain tiles, also with high recycled content.

Photo by Tim Murphy. Design by Ulla Lange, Workshop8

Natural linoleum (not to be confused with vinyl) is made from linseed oil, tall oil (from pine resin), sawdust or wood flour, cork, and limestone. It usually has a burlap backing, sometimes with a preapplied adhesive. Linoleum outgasses little, if any, and the VOCs emitted are part of a naturally occurring process. Linoleum has been shown to possess natural antimicrobial properties that discourage the growth of bacteria. Small marks or indentations in the countertop can easily be patched with a matching linoleum compound (available from the manufacturer), or sections can be replaced. Finally, linoleum will successfully biodegrade when no longer usable.

Where Does It Come From?

- Linoleum is mostly made from linseed oil, pine resin, sawdust or wood flour, cork, small amounts of pigment, and limestone.
- Linoleum usually has a burlap-type backing made of jute or, sometimes, hemp.
- The finish, if there is one, is usually ultrathin acrylic.
- Linoleum adhesives are chemical compounds; some are low-VOC, water-based, and formaldehyde free.

Installation

Specify FSC- or third-party-certified wood underlayment or a biocomposite. A low-VOC, water-based type is best.

A small amount of adhesive is necessary for installation. Specify low-VOC types whenever possible. Plan for good ventilation both during and after installation.

Maintenance

No chemical cleansers or finishes are necessary; simple soap and water will suffice. Patch kits, made from simple nontoxic glue and ground-up linoleum solids, can be purchased to repair small holes or gouges. Very light sanding will also restore the countertop.

Where Does It Go?

Linoleum, with the exception of the thin acrylic coating and adhesive, is fully biodegradable.

Spec List

Specify:

- Linoleum made from linseed oil and other natural materials
- Low-VOC, water-based, formaldehyde-free adhesives

Avoid:

- Using linoleum where it is exposed to constant moisture, standing water, or cutlery
- Linoleum blends that contain synthetics

See also "Linoleum Flooring," page 350.

Cabinetry

Wood is the main component for residential finish cabinetry. Solid wood is preferred for door and drawer fronts because of its beautiful grain, but less-expensive particleboard and MDF are commonly used to make drawer boxes, bodies, and

Figure 19.5 Kitchen cabinets built from reclaimed American wormy chestnut.

Photo by Joel Wilson. Design by Ben Riddering and John Brigham.

frames because the components are less visible. Bamboo, agricultural biocomposites, metal, and particleboard are also used for faces and frames, along with glass shelves and doors. Many homes feature a combination of materials for the cabinetry throughout.

Wood, by far the most popular choice for cabinetry applications, is natural, durable, biodegradable, and renewable—albeit slowly. It's a good option for casework in an earth-friendly residence. Fortunately, the use of forest products is under the keen scrutiny of environmentalists, as large stands of old-growth trees and wide expanses of rainforest continue to disappear. Booming construction and the desire for cleared land are the driving forces behind the losses worldwide, as is the demand for specialty or rare woods for finish carpentry and furnishings. The ecosystems are uprooted, the soil eroded, and the natural balance of life is severely disturbed when a stand of trees is cut down and destroyed. The long-term prognosis is also grim: Species are lost, greenhouse gases increase, and global warming increases.

To counteract these harmful forestry practices, specify wood for casework that has been grown and cut with minimal environmental impact. Third-party certification of the chain of custody, where eco-standards are followed and documented through every step of forestry, milling, and distribution, is the surest way to maintain healthy forests for the future. The FSC sets the standards for third-party certification that are accepted worldwide (see "FSC," page 227).

Avoid selection of wood species that are endangered (see table 12.2, p. 274) or that come from unknown or uncertified sources. In particular, avoid tropical woods unless they have been certified as sustainable through the FSC. Encourage the client to select from locally available or domestic wood species in order to reduce long-distance transportation.

If the client has sensitivities or allergies, consider whether the tree species has an inherent odor. Although much of the cabinetry can be finished or sealed, some odor may still be present in the home after installation.

Instead of purchasing all-new cabinetry, reclaimed or salvaged cabinets make excellent alternatives for a green home. If remodeling, consider whether a simple change in the existing cabinet faces might be enough to customize or update the look. Or consider shelving instead of upper cabinets to use fewer resources. New drawer pulls and handles or a coat of eco-friendly paint on the boxes or faces will change the look without replacing the existing casework.

Specifying reclaimed wood that can be crafted into cabinetry is another eco-minded choice. Scout for local sources of reclaimed wood and for local cabinet-makers to minimize the embodied energy added with transportation. Verify the reclaimed wood's source—kitchen applications, especially, should be free of peeling paint, chemically treated wood, or wood that may have been exposed to contaminants from a previous application in an industrial setting. These contaminants or toxins could come in contact with food, cutlery, or dishes.

Many reclaimed wood operations (sometimes called RWOs) are small local businesses that may not participate in a third-party certification program but recover and sell the wood locally, know the source well, and may have deconstructed the materials themselves. These sources are generally reliable if they adhere to strict internal environmental policies. The Rainforest Alliance provides certification for rediscovered wood and underwater salvage wood products. Its program stamps its seal of approval on reclaimed wood procured using procedures that preserve the integrity of the environment as well as the health and welfare of workers and the community. As the call for forest products grows, so does the burden on virgin forests. Products with rediscovered wood and underwater salvage certification are a sound choice for saving forests.

Solid wood is only one option for cabinets. The boxes, frames, and shelving are often made with less expensive wood-based sheet goods such as particleboard, engineered wood products, fiberboard, MDF, or plywood. Sheet goods are often manufactured from mill by-products, wood chips, and other waste materials. These products are economical and eco-friendly because they replace the need for wide planks of solid wood from old-growth trees.

Specify FSC or third-party certification of all engineered wood products. This ensures that the wood content was sustainably grown and not culled from endangered tropical rain forests or poorly managed tree farms. Look for sheet goods that are made from a high percentage of recycled wood.

Figure 19.6 The materials for this shoreside cottage were chosen for their sustainability and low-maintenance features. The fireplace surround and the kitchen cabinetry were crafted from reclaimed oak. Along with being a sustainable and renewable material, the reclaimed wood has a rustic yet sophisticated appearance. The cottage also features 12" x 24" natural slate floor, low-VOC paint on walls, painted steel beams and railings.

Photo by Sam Orberter. Designed by Richard Bubnowski Design, www.richardbubnowskidesign.com.

The drawback to using sheet goods is that standard cores and veneers usually contain formaldehyde-based binders or solvent-based finishes that outgas. Methylenediphenyl isocyanate (MDI) is a alternative binder that outgasses less but may still pose risks and is noted on the EPA's "Chemicals of Concern" list. Find a custom cabinetmaker who will work with only formaldehyde-free and low-VOC adhesives, binders, and finishes.

Biocomposite boards are another alternative for cabinetry (see "Biocomposites," page 284). They are an excellent substitute for wood-based sheet goods because they are made from quickly renewable agricultural by-products, and some types are durable and attractive enough to be used for cabinet faces. In addition, biocomposite boards were developed to meet the need for renewable wood substitutes, so many manufacturers are ecologically minded and avoid the use of unhealthy chemicals in their products. Give preference to low-VOC, formaldehyde-free binders, as well as low-toxic borate preservatives or pest repellants; it's difficult, however, to

Melamine

Melamine is a crystalline substance that is used as a resinous laminating agent in wood products, in paper and textile production, and in leather tanning. It was once popular for making dishes (as in vintage Melmac). Melamine-coated particleboard—often just called "melamine"—is used for countertops. Most varieties of melamine are inert and insoluble once hardened. The shiny surface is easily wiped clean, and it's an inexpensive way to boost the appearance of particleboard.

There is concern that the manufacturing process, which is reliant on a chemical reaction with formaldehyde, is harmful to workers and to the environment. At the very least, it can irritate the skin, eyes, and the throat, but it may cause kidney damage and is suspected to cause other serious health problems. Melamine is neither biodegradable nor recyclable. The verdict? Although few formalized studies have established the risks from melamine to humans and to the earth, it's best to steer away from melamine in an eco-minded home. Consider using particleboard without melamine coating for closet shelving, where no moisture is present. It can be stained or painted with nontoxic products, is quite attractive, and often inexpensive.

establish a baseline for biocomposites, as standards and performance are inconsistent. Also look into what farming standards were followed, as organic farming practices for biocomposite suppliers are not yet required.

Rapidly renewable plants like bamboo and palmwood (from coconut trees) are an eco-friendly alternative to wood. They regenerate more quickly than trees, are as hard as many tree species, and are easily manufactured into sheet goods, cabinet faces, and frames. Bamboo growers have been slower to adopt third-party certification standards; a limited number of products meeting FSC certification are available. If certification is not available, verify the sustainability of the plantations or working conditions. When specifying bamboo, look for companies that set high environmental standards for themselves and can verify the working conditions at their sources.

Less common alternatives to traditional wooden cabinetry include metal or glass cabinetry and shelving (see "Metals," page 259). Although metal is exceedingly durable, the environmental cost of mining, extracting the ore, and long-distance transportation is very high. Metal cabinets and shelves, however, can easily be salvaged from commercial settings such as restaurants or older homes. Salvaging the shelves eliminates additional mining and reuses a valuable natural resource.

Glass shelving and glass for cabinet doors can be manufactured from recycled glass or made new from common sand (see "Glass Tile," page 322). Both glass and metal are inert and can be recycled over and over or reused. The materials are ideal in homes for clients who have allergies or chemical sensitivities. Cabinet hardware is made primarily from metal (usually steel or brass) and is almost always purchased separately from the cabinets themselves. Salvaged hardware is particularly eco-friendly, as is metal or steel hardware that features high recycled content. Glass, wood, or ceramic pulls and knobs are other green options.

When researching and specifying cabinetry, inquire about the glues, adhesives, paints, stains, and finishes that are used. This is particularly important if the client is sensitive to chemicals or odors. Request low-VOC adhesives or water-based wood glues ("white" or "yellow" glues) whenever possible. To seal particleboard or seams that might outgas, specify a water-based, low-VOC finish be applied before installation.

Most cabinets are finished as part of the assembly at the factory, which avoids introducing VOCs and odors into the home (although they will still outgas and affect the environment). It is possible, however, to order unfinished cabinets that can be left as they are or finished on-site. Unfinished cabinets are not ideal if they'll be exposed to high humidity, water, or stains (in a kitchen or bath, or in a very humid climate).

On-site finishing allows for more control in the exact type of finish, paint, or stain that is used. When finishing on-site, specify low-VOC, water-based products, or those made with natural oils or waxes.

Where Does It Come From?

- Solid wood cabinetry comes from trees.
- Some wood products are made from recycled wood scraps or sawdust, with acrylics or resins added.
- Sheet-good binders may incorporate low-VOC glues, outgassing solvents, formaldehyde, soy-based products, or natural or synthetic resins.
- Reclaimed wood is culled from residential, commercial, and agricultural floors, walls, and structures. Cabinets can be made from reclaimed wood, and complete units can be salvaged.
- Wood finishes or stains may contain a variety of natural oils and resins, pigments, solvents, chemical compounds, petroleum distillates, metal drying agents, formaldehyde, or water.
- Biocomposite boards are made from a variety of agricultural by-products from wheat, rice, barley or oat straw, sunflower hulls, bluegrass or rye grass stubble, cornhusks and sorghum stalks, hemp, soybean plants, and bagasse (sugar cane pulp).

Figure 19.7 This bathroom has locally manufactured, reclaimed-wood cabinetry. The space also features locally sourced wall sconces, an antique rug, and locally sourced mirrors wrapped with vegetable-dyed natural leather.

Photo by David O. Marlow. Designer: Associates III, www.associates3.com.

- Biocomposites may contain residual pesticides or chemicals from crops, although the amount of such or frequency of use is unknown.
- Bamboo is technically a grass, grown for ten years before harvest.
- Metal cabinetry can be made from all-new or recycled metal.
- Glass shelves and cabinet fronts are made from common sand or recycled glass.
- Hardware is usually made from steel, brass or another metal, but it may also include components of glass, ceramic, or wood.

Installation

Cabinetry is bulky. To reduce embodied energy from shipping, employ a local cabinetmaker. When ordering stock or custom pieces, request that they be shipped in cardboard, kraft paper, or barrier cloth instead of plastics or bulky, nonrecyclable (and possibly hazardous) foam. Specify that all shipping materials have recycled content and that they be recycled.

If the cabinets must be preassembled or finished on-site, specify that this be done outside. Request that the installer or contractor do all cutting outdoors as well, to keep particulates and dust out of the living spaces.

If the cabinets are finished on-site, there is a higher risk of outgassing, odors, and irritants. Factory-finished pieces, on the other hand, have had a longer time to outgas prior to installation. Allow as much time as possible, before installation, for outgassing of the finish, paint, or adhesives (VOCs will still affect the environment but will not pose a direct risk to the occupants).

Weigh the finishing options carefully with the client. Whatever the final decision—unfinished, factory-finished, or finished on-site—specify the least toxic, lowest-VOC finish, paint, or stain available, preferably water-based or made with natural oils and extracts. Avoid finishes that contain chemical solvents, formaldehyde, or metallic drying agents.

Request that no finish or oils be applied to the hardware as a protective coating, or specify that natural waxes or oils be used instead. Specify that any oily residue on the metal from stock parts be removed with warm soapy water before installation.

Maintenance

Most casework requires little maintenance other than occasional dusting and cleaning with a damp cloth. Natural oil or wax finishes on wood or biocomposites require regular reapplications.

Where Does It Go?

Cabinets in good condition may be salvaged and reused or down-cycled into another wood-based product. Wood or biocomposite boards will decompose easily; binders, resins, stains, adhesives, and finishes used on the cabinets will break down much more slowly. Metal and glass components can usually be recycled. Usable cabinet hardware such as pulls, hinges, and knobs should be taken to a construction exchange or salvage yard.

Spec List

Specify:

- Locally or domestically harvested, FSC-certified nonthreatened wood species
- Salvaged cabinetry or reuse or renovate of existing cabinetry

- Glass shelving or cabinet door accents that are made from recycled glass
- Biocomposite boards, particleboard, or plywood that is third-party certified, or particleboard that contains a high percentage of recycled wood
- Metal that has a high percentage of recycled material
- Hardware that is salvaged or contains a high percentage of recycled material
- Removal of any oil finishes before installation
- Formaldehyde-free, low-VOC, water-based binders, sealants, adhesives, glues, and stains
- A minimum of shipping and handling with recycled-content, all-recyclable paper, cloth, and cardboard

Specify finishes and stains that are:

- Water-based
- Made of natural (sometimes called food-grade) oils, resins, pigments, and waxes
- Low-VOC
- Formaldehyde-free
- Free of metallic drying agents
- Solvent-free

Avoid:

- Reclaimed wood of uncertain origin in kitchen applications or where the its use might be unsafe
- Uncertified wood
- Rare or threatened tree species
- Solvent-based finishes
- Melamine
- Formaldehyde and other preservatives in the wood product or finish
- Metal-based drying agents in the finish
- Engineered wood, unless certified
- Formaldehyde in the binder or finish
- Preservatives or pesticides (other than borate)
- Foam, "peanuts," or plastic shipping materials

Resources

Forest Stewardship Council. www.US.FSC.org
Rainforest Alliance (formerly SmartWood). www.rainforest-alliance.org

Textiles

Textiles serve many purposes in residential design, some purely utilitarian, some aesthetic. They protect surfaces from wear, provide softness to the touch, filter light, and wrap us in warmth. To the client, however, the greatest function textiles may serve is to add beauty, color, texture, and pattern to the home. Residential fabrics in all their manifestations—bedding, upholstery, rugs, window treatments, accessories, and even art—personalize a home and make it more comfortable.

Textiles technically include every type of cloth, from natural knits and wovens to synthetics spun from petroleum or fiberglass filaments. When designing a healthful home that treads softly on the Earth, emphasize natural materials. Fibers derived from plants and animals come from renewable resources, and they can be harvested annually, or at least regularly enough to keep replenishing the supply. When a natural fiber has worn out or needs to be discarded, it will biodegrade.

The majority of synthetic fibers are derived from petroleum, a nonrenewable resource that is then liquefied and extruded into a filament or yarn. A chemical dye is usually introduced when the liquid is blended, as most synthetic fabrics do not accept dyes well once they are made. Ultimately, the finished products won't easily biodegrade, and synthetic residential textiles are not often recycled.

Newer synthetics are made from renewable materials such as soy or perpetually recyclable polyester. Some of these are biodegradable or can be easily recycled or down-cycled; check with the manufacturer or supplier for specifics. The manufacture of any synthetic fabric, however, requires more energy than that which is spun from natural fibers or handmade.

Fully greening your selection of residential textiles requires committing to more than just the basic fiber type. It is easy to find cloth made from natural materials, such as cotton, silk, hemp, flax, or wool; it's more challenging to find fibers that haven't been dyed with synthetic colorants, treated with chemicals to enhance fabric performance, or farmed or produced with the use of pesticides. Textiles made from raw materials that are organically grown or raised by sustainable methods make up only a small fraction of the market. Organic cotton, for example, makes

Figure 19.8 Opulent yet organic, sensuous yet sustainable, O Ecotextiles creates ethical and exceptional textiles, as shown here in the fabric folds.

Photo courtesy of O Ecotextiles, www.oecotextiles.com.

Textile Terminology

The word "textile" is derived from the Latin *textilis*, meaning "woven fabric." Today the term is used for any fabrics, threads, or yarns that are woven, knitted, felted, or braided together.

Textiles through Time

Prehistory	Human beings weave grasses and skins to make clothing and durable coverings for rooftops.
5000 BCE	Flax (linen), possibly the oldest spun fiber, is used to make burial shrouds for the Egyptians.
5000 to 3000 BCE	Cotton and wool are spun into fibers and used for clothing.
1725 BCE	Silk-spinning becomes an "industry" in China.
1793	Eli Whitney invents the cotton gin, which is more efficient than human labor for picking and separating cotton.
1884	The power loom is invented and mechanizes weaving.
1910	Rayon, the first manufactured fiber, is introduced and mass-produced.
Twentieth century	Acetate, polyester, polypropylene, nylon, and other manufactured fibers are introduced.
2004	The Organic Trade Association (OTA) establishes standards for the processing and certification of textile fibers.

up only about .03 percent of the cotton supply.[1] It will take some scouting to find all-organic textile sources.

Textile factories, where most textiles are produced, are not immune to the problems common to other large industries: wastewater pollution, hazardous by-products, questionable working conditions, and air-quality issues. In addition, any number of harsh or hazardous chemicals might be used to wash, dye, weave, and finish them; the specific chemicals won't be revealed on the labels but will remain on the fabric. Common chemicals used in textile production include chlorine compounds, heavy metals, azo dyes, halogenated solvents, and polybrominated diphenyl ethers (PBDEs), and decabrominated flame retardants.

To avoid these pitfalls, look for products made with natural dyes, fibers, processes, and fabric treatments. Work with companies that have the highest

---

[1] Organic Trade Association: www.ota.com.

environmental standards for each aspect of fabric production, from agricultural impacts, mill processes, to labor practices. Look for production processes that use biodegradable surfactants, detergents, and degreasers.

An ideal textile manufacturer would use a fabric mill powered by renewable energy, treat its wastewater on-site, and be free of pollutants; it would avoid the use of harmful, hazardous, chemicals throughout the production and qualify for third-party certification. Fabrics would have zero-emissions and come from bio-based and sustainably harvested resources; fibers would be bleached with ozone instead of chlorine; and dyes and colorants would be tested to meet third-party standards. It would adopt best practice fair trade and engage in socially responsible labor practices. Now that's what you call intelligent style!

PLANT AND ANIMAL FIBERS (INCLUDING LEATHER)

Surrounding ourselves with natural fibers is like eating comfort food. All natural fibers—cotton, wool, soy silk, flax/linen, ramie, bamboo, lyocell, corn, jute, hemp—have less embodied energy than their petroleum-based counterparts. All are made from natural plant and animal fibers—and there are many more. Natural fibers are always preferable; they come from renewable sources that are replenished in a matter of months or years, far less time than the usual life span of the fabric. They offer breathability rarely found in synthetics, and they will biodegrade easily.

Natural fibers tend to require minimal processing prior to manufacturing, reducing their environmental impact. Eco-characteristics include minimal use of chemicals and pesticides, responsible land management and sustainable ranching/farming practices, certifications, and fair trade practices. Nonetheless, always look into the raw material selection, production, dye process, usage, and disposal, in addition to the consumption of energy, water, and chemicals.

Not all fiber farming, harvesting, and acquisition methods are alike. Some respect the Earth and its inhabitants more than others. Traditional cotton crops, for example, are notoriously heavy on pesticide and fertilizer use (see "The Truth about Cotton," page 485), and the majority of animal farms rely on chemical pest control methods. Although it is unlikely that pesticide residual will directly harm the client after the extensive washing and processing fibers and fabrics undergo in mills, the chemicals are fundamentally bad for the environment and extremely toxic to our water, air, and soil.

Wool and silk—animal products typically imported from overseas sources—are often treated with chemicals to ward off moth infestation and microbial growth. Hemp and jute, also primarily from overseas sources, are fairly resistant to pests, both as plants and after being manufactured into fabrics.

Organic or sustainable farming, on the other hand, uses natural methods for enriching soil and preventing pest damage and disease. Instead of relying on chemicals, it uses natural controls such as beneficial insects, compost as a fertilizer, and crop rotation to maintain soil productivity. Sustainable agriculture may also focus on providing the animals with an open range for grazing, natural foods, and respectful and humane treatment. While initially more expensive for the farmer, and thus the consumer, the long-term yields from sustainable agriculture include less erosion, more fertile soil, healthier ecosystems, and a quality product that harms neither the earth nor the consumer.

Finished or processed textile products that are certified as organic must meet the Global Organic Textile Standard (GOTS), a rigorous, voluntary international standard for the processing of organic fiber products, that addresses all the postharvest processing stages, including spinning, knitting, weaving, dyeing, and manufacturing. GOTS includes environmental and social provisions for post-farm to retail shelf management. Key requirements include a ban on child labor, genetically modified engineering, heavy metals, and highly hazardous chemicals such as formaldehyde. It also requires fair living wages and strict wastewater treatment practices. Specify natural-fiber textiles from companies that subscribe to this global standard certification process or follow eco-friendly farming practices.

Artisans are often excellent sources for all-natural textiles, as many eschew high-tech methods in favor of weaving or spinning by hand, dyeing with local plants, and even raising their own crops or animals. Selecting a local artisan's textiles also reduces the energy consumed by lessening shipping demands. Cooperatives are excellent resources for locating artisans; consult with local indigenous tribes, the county extension office, or artist guilds.

If the textile comes from abroad, check into whether environmental and fair trade standards have been adhered to. Reasonable pay and good working conditions may not seem to impact the environment at first glance, but indirectly, they almost always do (see sidebar, page 537). Companies that value workers and their families will also value health and environmental well-being and are unlikely to utilize highly toxic chemicals or destroy the ecosystem for the sake of a profit. Fair trade maximizes the assets that a region already possesses, both human and environmental. Specify fair trade or cooperative-made textiles if purchasing them from a developing region.

Next to its origin, the suitability of a fiber to a particular application or environment is the most important factor to consider. If it deteriorates from typical use, washed in water, or exposed to sunlight, it may not be the best choice. Textiles should be durable enough for their intended purpose and require little upkeep. They should also be easy to wash or clean, as chemical dry cleaning and stain repellents negate the green attributes of natural fabrics.

Consider the following natural fibers when specifying textiles. This list is not comprehensive, and there are many, many combinations and blends; these are some of the most popular eco-friendly choices.

Organic Cotton

Organic cotton is grown without pesticides, herbicides, insecticides, or chemical fertilizers. By using sustainable agricultural methods it reduces or eliminates pests, enhances growth, maintains soil quality, and protects cotton harvesters, and the fiber is actually stronger because it's not processed with chemicals.

On the flip side, organic cotton uses large amounts of water; when possible, look for crops that come from fields that irrigate the crops with rainfall. It grows naturally in shades of green, brown, and natural, and is fade-resistant, is rapidly renewable, minimally processed, moisture absorbent, reusable, recyclable, and biodegradable.

Specify organic cotton with certification that addresses processing and growing issues, such as GOTS or the Oeko-Tex Standard 1000.

Conventional Cotton

Cotton is comfortable against the skin and can absorb twenty times its weight in water. The cotton fiber is harvested from the cottonseed pod. Cotton usually has a white or cream color but can be grown with other natural color variations such as rust, tan, gray, and even with a bluish hue. It readily accepts dye and stands up to very hot water and sanitization, making it an ideal fiber for clients with allergies or health issues. Conventional cotton fabric, however, is typically farmed using large amounts of water as well as chemical pesticides and fertilizers. Most cotton has been genetically engineered. Look for unbleached or naturally dyed fibers. Avoid wrinkle-resistance or sizing treatments and flame retardants.

The Truth about Cotton

- Cotton farming uses more than 25 percent of all the pesticides in the world.
- Seven times more chemical fertilizer than pesticides is used to grow cotton.
- The cotton for one T-shirt has been grown with a third of a pound of chemicals.
- The EPA has declared 7 of the top 15 pesticides used by cotton growers as potential or known carcinogens.
- Cotton is also a food crop. U.S. residents eat and drink more cotton, usually in the form of cottonseed oil (found in such foods as coffee creamer, salad dressings, and candy bars) than they wear or sleep on.

Sources: Organic Trade Association, www.ota.com; Organic Consumer Association, www.organicconsumers.org.

Organic Wool

Organic wool is rapidly renewable, minimally processed, moisture absorbent, inherently fire retardant, stain resistant, reusable, recyclable and, ultimately, biodegradable. Ensure that the wool is unbleached or bleached with ozone-based products and dyed with responsible, eco-friendly methods rather than with dyes containing heavy metals.

Wool harvested by sustainable ranchers is a strong, beautiful fiber with few limitations and amazing longevity and durability. (Naysayers maintain that sheep create high levels of carbon dioxide and abuse the land.) Wool also needs to be scoured, which uses significant amounts of water and leads to polluted wastewater.

Specify organic wool that is woven according to GOTS. Also look for sustainable farming practices that adopt responsible care of animals according to organic or holistic management principles. Ensure that raw wool processing is avoids the typical scouring and descaling chemicals. Also specify no dyes, or that natural dyeing processes are used.

Wool

Wool is a favorite for warmth and durability and will literally last for centuries with proper care. Various species of animals produce distinct types of wool: sheep, goat, vicuña, alpaca, llama, angora, and camel. Wool is usually acquired from shearing of animals, which for some species is actually beneficial. Some animals are bred for their different coat colorations that produce subtle, natural hues. Look for firms that practice good animal husbandry, which sequesters carbon and reduces the level of greenhouse gasses in the atmosphere while replenishing and renewing grassland soils.

Wool absorbs approximately thirty times its weight in moisture before actually feeling wet; conversely, the natural lanolin and oils present in wool help it to shed water. Wool can improve air quality by absorbing and retaining VOCs. Wool also breathes and helps regulate humidity, is a rapidly renewable, sustainable resource, and absorbs VOCs.

Some people dislike wool because the curly fibers are itchy, although a true allergy to wool is very rare. Certain species, such as merino, are less troublesome for those with such sensitivities.

The particular "scales" of the wool fiber strands enable them to stick together when abraded, producing a dense felt that is popular for making rugs, blankets, and clothing.

Wool washing and processing is often chemical- and water-intensive. While fire-retardant chemicals are generally unnecessary due to wool's natural flame resistance, chemical treatment for other reasons, such as to repel moths, is not uncommon. In addition, sheep emit methane, a potent greenhouse gas that can be problematic from a climate perspective. However, wool's natural durability gives it an environmental advantage.

Figure 19.9 This settee uses a 100 percent virgin eco-wool sateen made from non-mulesed sheep without any harmful chemicals. The fiber is crafted into a durable, hard working fabric that can withstand even the rigors of commercial applications. 100 percent non-mulesed Australian Eco wool, certified by Australian Certified Organic (ACO) to EU2092/91 organic standards and dyestuffs are compliant with Oeco Tex 100.

Photo courtesy of O Ecotextiles, www.oecotextiles.com.

Silk

Silk is derived from the natural protein fibers of the silkworm cocoon, which are then spun into filaments. Silk is very durable—a strand of steel will break before a strand of silk of the same diameter. Don't confuse that with abrasion resistance, as silk does not stand up to heavy wear. It is lustrous and accepts dye well; it is warm in the winter and cool in the summer, absorbent, shrinkproof. Bright sunlight or high heat will damage silk.

Chemicals have become an integral component of conventional textile and clothing manufacturing, and chemical treatments are often added to silk to control static, repel water and oil and make the fabric flame-retardant, and more stabile. Ask what chemical treatments have been added to understand potential health hazards.

Organic methods of cultivating silk are becoming more common; the cocoons are harvested after the butterfly has left rather than by boiling the cocoons to remove the larvae.

The issue of child labor has arisen in some Asian countries where silk is produced. Look for silk producers that prohibit child labor, as well as those that promote sustainable, organic production.

Linen (Flax)

Linen is probably the oldest textile in the world. It is made from the stalk of the flax plant and obtains its luster from the plant's natural waxes. After harvesting, the fibers must be released from the stalk. This process is called "retting": The plant's woody bark is rotted away to expose the resin that attaches the fiber to the stem. Retting uses chemicals that must be neutralized before being released into water supplies to lower the environmental impact.

Although linen has poor elasticity (the fabric can actually fray along creases), the fiber itself is several times stronger than cotton. It can also be sanitized in hot water. The natural color is a light tan or cream; linen readily accepts dye, is color-fast, and nonallergenic. Linen is rapidly renewable, absorbent, reusable, recyclable, biodegradable, and requires little water or fertilizers.

Hemp

Hemp, or cannabis, when cultivated not as a drug but to make into fabric, is strong, durable, and absorbent—a multitalented natural fiber with remarkable benefits and attributes. Its long strands of fiber are suitable for spinning with minimal processing, creating the strongest of the natural fibers. Hemp has gained popularity as an environmentally friendly alternative with a beautiful hand, feel, and drape. It grows quickly and densely, eliminating the need for herbicides, pesticides, and artificial fertilizers, and is drought-tolerant, usually growing well without irrigation. It is biodegradable, recyclable, and resists fading, rotting, mildew and mold; this is why it has been used as for twine, rope, and ship riggings for centuries. Hemp is rapidly renewable, minimally processed, absorbent, and reusable.

Hemp is a subspecies of a more controversial plant commonly known as marijuana. Hemp textiles are made from the stems, not the narcotic flowers, seeds, or leaves. Hemp comes in an assortment of textures and weights—woven or knit fabrics, ropes, belts, area rugs, and carpets are all made from this versatile, inherently insect- and mildew-resistant plant.

In the farming industry, hemp is considered a "closed-loop" product because it yields high volume using minimal land resources, and its waste and end products can be recycled over and over.

Ramie, Jute, Coir, and Sisal

China grass, a member of the nettle family, is a flowering plant native to Asia; it is better known as ramie. It is one of the strongest fibers, highly absorbent and naturally resists stains. Ramie is often blended with other fibers, such as cotton and hemp, to produce very durable fabrics. It is similar to linen, though it may be prone to shrinkage or become rough when washed. Ramie is rapidly renewable, minimally processed, absorbent, reusable, recyclable, and biodegradable. It grows with little water and fertilizers.

Fiber Production

Average fiber production, in pounds per acre

Conventional Cotton	Organic Cotton	Flax (Linen)	Wool	Hemp
121–445	80–102	323–465	62	485–809

Source: UK-government funded project at University of London, "Demi: design for sustainability" (www.demi.org.uk), © Kate Fletcher, 1999.

Jute comes from the stalk of a flowering vegetable plant that grows to 10 feet tall; historically, the fiber has been used to make rope, twine, carpet, and rugs. Inherently strong, jute is also one of the cheapest natural fibers available. It has also been used to make paper, geotextile (a Fiberglas alternative) and particleboard. Jute improves soil quality, grows with little water and fertilizers, and is rapidly renewable, carbon-neutral, minimally processed, absorbent, reusable, recyclable, and biodegradable.

Coir and sisal are similar fibers. They are very durable but rough in texture, hence also used for rope, twine, rugs, and backings. Sisal is also acquired from the stalks of plants, whereas coir is made from coconut husks.

Bamboo

Bamboo is a renewable grass. It has natural antibacterial properties and is hypoallergenic. It drapes like silk but is more durable and less expensive. It is rapidly renewable, grows with little water and fertilizers, absorbent, reusable, recyclable, and biodegradable. Bamboo is typically farmed in China; if planted in nonindigenous areas, it can become invasive.

"Panda-friendly" bamboo plants are a must as they sustain China's endangered panda species. Bamboo plants grow quickly without fertilizers or pesticides and require minimal amounts of water. The grasses also release 35 percent more oxygen into the air than an equivalent stand of trees. Bamboo fabric is created from the pulp of the stalk, readily accepts dyes, and needs no chlorine bleach.

The negative aspect of the process comes from the sulfuric acid used in the processing of the pulp. This contributes minimally to air pollution and the wastewater must be neutralized with bacteria before it is returned to the ecosystem.

Tencel

A newer fabric made from wood pulp cellulose, Tencel is a branded lyocell fiber that comes from eucalyptus trees that yield a high-quality fiber with less water than a fast-growing tree requires. For an even greener product, look for eucalyptus trees certified by the Forest Stewardship Council. Tencel is rapidly renewable, requires little water and fertilizers, reusable, recyclable, and biodegradable.

A nontoxic organic solvent is created from the wood pulp that is then reclaimed and recycled in a closed-loop spinning process to conserve energy and water. Statistics show that up to 95 percent of the solvent is recovered and reused. Look for Tencel that does not utilize harmful chemicals (like formaldehyde) to treat the fibrillation of the fibers.

One of the drawbacks of Tencel- and lyocell-based fabrics is that that they don't take dyes well; as a result, chemical-based dyes or other treatments that are not eco-friendly are sometimes used.

Ingeo Corn Fiber

Ingeo is a manmade fiber made out of corn. After the starch and sugars are extracted from corn, they are processed into a fiber that is spun into yarn or woven into fabric—an innovative, eco-friendly material The fabric is stain- and fade-resistant, odor-absorbent, and hypoallergenic, but doesn't retain moisture.

It is a trademark of Natureworks (www.natureworksllc.com), which claims Ingeo is the world's first manmade fiber derived from 100 percent renewable resources. They describe the fabric as follows: "Ingeo fiber combines the qualities of natural and synthetic fibers in a new way. Strength and resilience are balanced with comfort, softness, and drape in textiles. In addition, Ingeo fiber has good moisture-management characteristics. This means that Ingeo fiber is ideally suited to fabrics from fashion to furnishings."

Leather and Skins

Leather and skins, although not traditionally categorized as textiles, are used for many of the same purposes: upholstery, accessories, and rugs. Leather breathes, is soft and pliable, and is very durable.

In many cultures, the use of animal skins for shelter, clothing, and ornament is considered fundamental—even sacred—as no part of the animal is wasted after slaughter. However, some individuals object to the use of animal products for ethical reasons; others for religious reasons. Always consult with the client when contemplating the use of animal products.

The primary criterion for incorporating leather or skins into a green home is whether the processing is natural or chemical. Modern tanning of leather relies on toxic chromium and chemical baths and an enormous amount of water for rinsing and processing those chemicals. These baths are a health risk for workers. The chemicals may also be odorous. Opt instead for leather or skins from companies that feature vegetable-based tanning processes that rely on natural tannins from rhubarb, tree bark, tare, and valonea. These same companies feature natural vegetable and mineral dyes, reducing the leather's environmental footprint, although not completely.

Vegetable tanning simply replaces the chromium for bark or plant tannins—all other steps, unfortunately, remain the same. About 250 chemicals are used in tanning hides. The other chemicals normally used in tanning may include alcohol, coal tar, sodium sulfate, sulfuric acid, chlorinated phenols (e.g., 3,5-dichlorophenol), azo dyes, cadmium, cobalt, copper, antimony, cyanide, barium, lead, selenium, mercury, zinc, polychlorinated biphenyls (PCBs), nickel, formaldehyde, and pesticide residues.

The manufacturing process also impacts the environment; it is the environmental stewardship practice of tanners coupled with the chemicals they use that determine how eco-friendly a leather is. The following areas of leather manufacture have the most significant potential impact: management of restricted substances, energy and water consumption, air emissions, waste management (hazardous and nonhazardous), environmental management systems, control of manufacturing processes, effluent treatment, chrome management, and how easily the materials can be traced back to their source.

Certain materials or ingredients that lend themselves to an improved eco-profile for leather include biodegradable wetting agents for soaking, reduced sulfide processing, nonsynthetic or polymeric re-tannage systems, optimized dyestuffs, vegetable oil–based fat liquors, optimized finishing systems to reduce waste, and whether it biodegrades in less than a year.

These are the key determinants for "eco-leather":

1. Control of leather manufacturing processes
2. Clean technology and transparent chemical selection process
3. Effective management of restricted substances in the leather
4. A measure of the end-of-life impact[2]

Leather and skins are often a secondary product of the meat industry. Tanneries with a focus on sustainable, natural methods may acquire their materials from organic ranches that provide a pesticide-free, all-natural environment for the animals. Inquire as to the source; if seeking a natural tannery, check with an organic ranch.

Although leather is by nature resilient to deterioration from the elements, it will eventually decompose. Tannery chemicals and synthetic fabric treatments, usually considered hazardous waste in quantity, pose serious risks to water and soil when landfilled.

BIO-BASED SYNTHETICS

Rayon was the first synthetic textile. It is produced through the chemical treatment of wood pulp (cellulose), which is liquefied and then extruded as a filament. It's not an all-natural fiber, but the incorporation of renewable materials has its ecological

---

[2] O ecotextiles: www.oecotextiles.com

merits. In a drive to lessen our dependence on nonrenewable resources such as petroleum, manufacturers have been developing other bio-based synthetic textiles derived from sustainable sources such as corn, soybeans, sugar beets, rice, and wood pulp. Some of these textiles are designed to improve particular characteristics difficult to find in all-natural materials that make them appropriate for surgical applications or institutional settings.

The development of new textile fibers is commendable, especially if the raw material is renewable and the final product biodegrades or can be recycled. However, the intensive manufacturing process adds considerable embodied energy compared with that of a plant or animal fiber that is simply spun or woven. For most residential applications, the benefits of bio-based synthetics are negligible.

SYNTHETICS

Synthetics represent 65 percent of the world's fiber production; the remaining 35 percent are natural fibers. The big names in synthetic fabrics and fibers include acetate, acrylic, nylon, and polyester. Polyester is the most popular synthetic, representing 70 percent of all synthetics manufactured. It is made of polyethylene terephthalate (PET). Polyesters are more commonly specified for commercial projects, as they are cost effective and flame-resistant. Traditionally, synthetic fabrics are made of virgin polymers that use toxic substances or additives, and, therefore, are not recyclable. The majority are derived from chemicals or petroleum.

In a few cases, synthetics have characteristics difficult to duplicate in nature, such as the elasticity of nylon. In general, they are less breathable and don't absorb moisture well (either an asset or a drawback, depending on the application). Most synthetics are dyed with artificial colorants then treated with more chemical finishes. Limit the use of these conventional synthetic textiles. If you must specify them, look for alternatives that lower their environmental impact—low-emitting, reduced chemical toxins, recycled content, no hazardous ingredients, recyclable, bio-based, compostable, sustainably sourced, and third-party certified.

There has been a concerted effort among textile manufacturers to develop synthetics that are not harmful to the consumers and that biodegrade or be recycled. These new synthetics may even improve on natural materials, with longer life cycles, greater durability, or specialized applications, such as medical settings. Some are made from consumer and commercial waste, further diverting materials from the landfill; others are hybrids made from natural materials in a synthetic process. A few manufacturers accept their synthetic textiles back for recycling into new fibers or fabric, thereby creating a closed loop.

The majority of these new synthetics have been developed for commercial use, but a few have entered the residential market. While natural materials are still the top choice for most applications in green residential design, there will be more environmentally friendly synthetic textiles in the future.

RECYCLED TEXTILES

Before the era of industrialization, fabric scraps were seldom wasted because textile-making required preparing the fibers, spinning, knitting, and weaving—all very effortful activities. One of the best examples of this frugal use of fabric is the patchwork quilt. By extension, the most innovative eco-strategy of all might be to use what the client already has. Antique or vintage quilts, tea towels, and other linens that have been relegated to a drawer might be ready for a new life as pillowcases, window coverings, tablecloths, or slipcovers.

In a nod to environmental concerns, everyone from large manufacturers to individual artisans are using textile waste to create anew. Scraps from the mill floors, yarn ends, and even recycled denim jeans are used to produce new fabrics or other products, such as insulation. Sometimes the processes require little additional energy, such as when rags are hand-sewn into patchworks or hand-woven into rugs. Others are more energy-intensive

Figure 19.10 These pillows are made from reused French linen tablecloths. Heiberg Cummings Design, Southampton Design Project, www.Hcd3.com.

methods performed in factories, such as turning the fibers into pulp, or respinning them, then weaving or pressing them into new textiles. To reclaim materials that might otherwise be landfilled, mills now recycle polyester, carpet fibers, or other synthetics into new textiles. Some synthetics or natural-fiber textiles may be continually recycled, and a few manufacturers will take back their own textiles at the end of the life cycle.

If the client is interested in recycled materials, these options may be appealing. Check with the manufacturer or artisan for details about the content, processing, and health and environmental impacts for specific recycled textiles.

DYES

Best practice is using natural, undyed fabrics, but who wants to live in a colorless world?

Look for natural dyes from plants, animals, and minerals or low-impact reactive dyes that do not contain heavy metals. Berries, bark, insects, spices, and many common plants can be used to tint the dye bath, and simple vinegar or pickling alum is often used to set the dye. Natural dyes are unlikely to be problematic for sensitive individuals, but if chronic allergies are an issue, it may be advisable to specify no dye.

The entire spectrum of color is available from natural dyes, although they are generally a bit more muted than the brightest chemical dyes. Naturally dyed textiles will require gentle washing (cold water, little agitation, mild soap) to retain the vivid hues.

Chlorine bleach is frequently used to whiten cotton and other fibers; but it is highly caustic and toxic. In addition, bleach removes some of the natural finish of cotton, making its texture rougher. Rather than using chlorine bleach look for "next-to-skin' comfort by choosing oxidizing chemicals such as ozone and hydrogen peroxide, which break down into oxygen and water.

Chemical dyes and colorants are frequently used on both natural fibers and synthetics, especially those that are commercially made. Most synthetic dyes and colorants are made from petroleum based chemicals, contain toxic hazards like aniline, and do not biodegrade. The textile label is not required to list the type of dyes used, but those who specialize in natural textiles frequently supply this information. Request information on the dyes to avoid all synthetic substances, or specify no dye.

FABRIC TREATMENTS

Textile mills employ the use of hundreds of different chemicals for stiffening, softening, wrinkle-proofing, and stain- and water-resistance, and make textiles shiny and colorfast. The treatments of interest to the consumer—special stain resistors, for example—are usually listed on the label, but there's no requirement to do so. Some of these chemical agents are under scrutiny as health hazards (see "PBDEs," page 512), and others may be problematic for those who are chemically sensitive. To avoid chemical treatments altogether, seek out specialty textile producers such as artisans or small mills that make all-natural fabrics.

Work with companies that restrict the use of flame retardants, manmade chemicals made from polybrominated diphenyl ethers (PBDEs) and other brominated chemicals. PBDEs are often added to foam padding, plastics, and fabrics so they won't catch on fire or burn as easily when exposed to flame or high heat. They do not breakdown quickly and remain in the environment for an indefinite period. If flame retardants are necessary, specify that they be free of hazardous chemicals.

Some fibers are inherently stain- and water-resistant. Wool, for example, contains lanolin, an oily substance so effective at waterproofing that it's used in furniture polish and hand creams. The best method for preventing textile damage and ensuring longevity is careful selection of the most appropriate fabric for the intended purpose.

A few specialty retailers and distributors catering to environmentally friendly interiors offer prewashed textiles that have been cleansed of all finishes and fabric treatments. These companies may provide this service even for textiles they haven't manufactured. If the client has chemical sensitivities, this may be especially valuable.

Lastly, ask for fabric finishes made of beeswax, aloe vera, and vitamin A often offered by cutting-edge boutique fabric houses like O Ecotextiles (www.oecotextiles.com) that specialize in healthy, eco-friendly textiles.

TEXTILE LABELING

Although not all textile products are required by law to carry labels, many companies provide them voluntarily. They may be attached to the product on the end of a bolt or on a separate tag. The content of the label is strictly governed by the Textile Fiber Products Identification Act of 1960, which prohibits misrepresentation of the textile's content. When purchasing off-the-shelf textiles or those from a standard retailer, such labels can be helpful in determining whether a product possesses eco-friendly qualities.

What the labels must include:

- Generic fiber name (wool, cotton, etc.)
- Percentage, by weight, of each kind of fiber
- The manufacturer, by name or registered number (the Federal Trade Commission has a list; see www.ftc.gov)
- Where the textile was made or assembled

What they typically don't include:

- How the fabric was made (woven, braided, etc.)
- Dye content
- Finishes or fabric treatments

Wool and cotton are governed under separate labeling acts that require more specific information. Wool labels tell whether the fibers are virgin (new) or recycled, and the species of animal (merino, vicuna). If the fiber content is 100 percent wool or 100 percent cotton, the textile label will display a special mark.

Care labels, which are optional on items other than clothing and fabrics (leather and fur, for example), indicate the best cleaning and pressing methods. The manufacturer always recommends the most gentle cleaning technique least likely to change the quality of the textile in any way, but it is often possible to clean the textile using another method. Avoid textiles that are labeled "dry clean only" unless you're reasonably certain they can be washed instead. Wool, silk, and even cotton, for example, are so labeled, but, after taking careful precautions or using a test swatch, are often washable.

Where Does It Come From?

- Textiles come from all-natural plant or animal fibers; recycled fabrics and yarns; petroleum-based or chemical synthetics, extruded fibers; and bio-based synthetics.
- Bio-synthetic fabrics are made from renewable raw materials such as paper or wood pulp, soy, corn, or bamboo.

- Plant-based fibers such as cotton, jute, hemp, and ramie may be organically grown or by conventional farming methods.

- Animal products such as wool and leather may come from sustainably managed or "humane" ranches or from conventional ranch facilities.

- Dyes are derived from natural sources, such as plants and minerals, and are also made from chemicals.

- Most common fabric treatments are chemical-based, but there are all-natural options made from plants and minerals.

- Leather may be tanned with chromium and countless other chemicals or, less commonly, with natural bark and vegetable agents replacing the chromium.

Maintenance

The best way to maintain textiles is to select materials appropriate to the setting and for their intended use. If the client has children or animals and the textile will be used daily or will be subjected to regular washing or sunlight, then delicate fabrics with special care requirements would not be good choices. Poorly chosen fibers may wear out, fade, or need special chemical cleaning methods to restore their appearance.

Simple soap and water, dusting, or vacuuming are the preferred cleaning methods for residential textiles. Borax or borate, a mineral found in nature, can be added to the wash cycle as a whitening agent. For deodorizing, baking soda is still the champion, either dissolved in water or sprinkled on the textile (such as a rug) and vacuumed. Natural stain removal tricks may work even better than commercial, eco-unfriendly solvents. Visit the Internet for healthy cleaning tips, or give the client a book on the subject. The county extension office is another valuable source for helpful hints on textile care.

Fabrics that need dry cleaning are less desirable because they must be transported to a dry cleaner and because dry cleaning requires special equipment uses chemicals and solvents. Healthier dry cleaning methods—carbon dioxide (CO_2), the "fizzy" gas in soda pop—are being used successfully. Employ businesses that rely on CO_2 methods if dry cleaning is necessary.

Where Does It Go?

Natural plant-fiber textiles can be shredded for compost. Certain types of synthetic fabrics can be recycled, down-cycled, or reprocessed into new textiles or other polymers. Most synthetics, however, end up in landfills and biodegrade slowly, if at all.

Textile Maintenance Tips

There are dozens of commercial detergents, stain removers, bleaches, and fabric softeners on the market; most are made from chemical compounds unsafe for the environment or human health. Traditional, natural, nontoxic methods are best for keeping textiles clean.

- Use water temperature and proper care as recommended on the label; use cold water if there is no label or instructions.
- Purchase biodegradable laundry soap.
- If the client is sensitive to odors, avoid scented soaps.
- Avoid chlorine bleach.
- To boost cleaning power, add baking soda or borax to the wash water.
- To brighten their appearance, hang all-cotton whites in direct sunlight to dry.
- Avoid hanging darker colors or brights in direct sunlight.
- Choose a medium-temperature dryer setting instead of a hotter one to reduce wear and keep fabrics soft. A low dryer temperature also conserves energy.
- Hang or fold textiles immediately when after they dry to obviate ironing, which is hard on fabrics.

Spec List

Specify:

- Certified organic natural fibers
- Third-party certifications for textiles
- Natural plant- or animal-based fibers
- Rapidly renewable and sustainable sources
- Sustainably farmed products with minimal ecological footprint on the land, energy, water, resources, waste, etc.
- Textiles made in a closed-loop cycle
- Reusable, recyclable, and biodegradable fabrics

- Minimal processing without added chemicals or dyes
- Natural dyes from plant, animal, or mineral sources
- Environmentally sound mill practices (e.g., water treatment for pH)
- Benign chemical and biological impacts
- Fair-trade and socially responsible mills
- Textiles that can be cleaned with natural or benign methods such as dusting, soap and water, or vacuuming
- Ozone or hydrogen peroxide oxidization
- Natural stain and water repellants (tightest weave, lanolin in wool, etc.)
- Biosynthetic fabrics, preferably recyclable or biodegradable, made from a high percentage of renewable, natural products such as paper, wood pulp, soy, corn, or bamboo
- Vegetable tanning and dyeing processes for leather that rely on natural elements such as tare (vetch seed), rhubarb, valonea (oak tree acorn "beard" from Turkey or Greece), and tree bark rather than on chromium
- Locally tanned leather with minimal chemical processing or dyes
- Locally made artisanal textiles, especially by nonmechanized methods
- Recycled-content textiles
- Reuse of textiles

Avoid:

- Synthetic fibers made from petroleum products or hazardous chemicals of concern
- Acrylic and polyvinyl chloride (PVC) yarns and backings
- Fibers from farms or suppliers that use pesticides, biocides, or herbicides
- Chlorine bleach
- Chemical deodorizers, detergents, or dry cleaning agents
- Fireproofing treatments
- Chemical dyes
- Synthetic waterproofing and stain-proofing treatments
- Leather tanned with chromium
- Chemically dyed or treated leather

RESOURCES

Hemp Industries. Association: www.thehia.org.
International Federation of Organic Agriculture Movements. www.ifoam.org.
O Ecotextiles: www.oecotextiles.com.
Organic Trade Association. www.ota.com.
Sustainable Cotton. Association: www.sustainablecotton.org.

Case Pieces

Strive to make every case piece eco-friendly. Is the piece really needed? Can it be adaptable and serve another purpose in the future? Will it be a new piece, or can a collectible be repurposed?

If a specialty or custom-made furniture piece must be ordered, ensure that detailed green specifications are followed. Most big-box retailers or large furniture manufacturers generally don't have items that meet these standards, but this too is changing with the adoption of corporate sustainability reporting. Look for all-natural materials, those made with recycled components, and those finished with nontoxic, low-VOC substances (see "Stains, Finishes, and Adhesives," page 389).

Whether restoring an antique or purchasing new furnishings, evaluate each component for its effect on the earth and home. Select a furniture company with established environmental guidelines that uses all-natural and/or third-party-certified materials or those with a high percentage of recycled or salvaged materials. Look for furniture manufacturers who maintain a manufacturing floor free of toxins and VOCs; ship the pieces with a minimum of packaging made from recycled content and recyclable or reusable materials; and have an eco-friendly waste management program for scraps.

Figure 19.11 Fitted as a humidor, this armoire is FSC-certified for being crafted primarily of wood harvested in a sustainable manner from a well-managed forest.

Photo by John Glos. Designer: John Wiggers.

RECYCLED AND SALVAGED CASE PIECES

Before purchasing new furnishings, consider what the client already owns or has access to. Eco-friendly furnishings start with salvaged frames and case goods. Residential furnishings are major contributors to landfills—so much so that many landfills charge fees for the disposal of large items such as chairs, sofas, desks, and dressers. A high percentage of what gets tossed is still perfectly usable or could be restored. Ask the client if there are pieces that might be reupholstered, antiques that could be refinished, or furnishings that need only touch-ups or repairs to be revitalized. In addition to being environmentally thrifty, the client might appreciate the TLC given to a worn-out but cherished furnishing. (Unused old furnishing should be donated to a local charity.)

The older the furniture, the more likely it is to be made from solid wood and steel, iron, or brass components—materials that may last for many more decades. Case pieces constructed after 1960 were frequently made with cheaper plywood, particleboard, or aluminum and may not be salvageable if damaged. Sometimes, however, a component of the old furnishing can be adapted for a new use. For instance, if the tabletop is damaged but the legs are still good, brainstorm with a furniture restorer for how it can be reused. Can the piece be renovated without

Flexibility Is Eco-Friendly

Modular case pieces are eco-smart choices because they are versatile. As children grow up, as design tastes change, or if the client moves to a new home, the components can be put together in new configurations or rearranged. No new furniture need be purchased and no more resources need be consumed.

Request modular case pieces made from certified solid wood or recycled metal such as steel. Many modular components are made from particleboard; be sure to specify formaldehyde-free, low-VOC binders and finishes and request certified wood or biocomposite wood substitutes.

Freecycling

"Think globally, recycle locally." That's the mantra of a loosely organized, web-based nonprofit initiative called Freecycle that diverts millions of items from landfills around the globe by putting them into the hands of those who can use them. The idea is simple: List still-usable items you have to give away on the Freecycle website. Those seeking such items scout the listings, then respond and arrange for pickup. Even items that others have set out to be picked up by the trash collectors can be listed.

There are millions of Freecycle participants worldwide, in thousands of communities (it's organized by region or city); "membership" is free. It's a great way to look for furniture or to give away that bunk bed that the kids outgrew. And by extending the life span of items and diverting them from the landfills, this grassroots effort is helping to save the environment one piece of furniture at a time.

For more information, or to find a Freecycle online group, visit www.freecycle.org.

using harsh chemicals? Conventional furniture restoration relies on toxic solvents to strip the finish or paint. Consult with a restoration specialist to determine whether minor touch-ups, a new coat of zero-VOC paint, or a thorough cleaning and conditioning with all-natural oils or waxes might suffice.

Figure 19.12 This bench is made of felled, torched fir.

© 2006 Johngranen.com. Designer: John Wells.

There are a few furniture stripping products derived from soy or natural resins, rather than petrochemicals. Although these are an improvement, as they rely on a renewable resource and are usually lower in VOC emissions, they can still pose health risks and should be used with caution.

Another advantage to using older furnishings is that the longer the life span of the piece, the more sustainable the resources become. A century-old rocker, for example, may have survived longer than the tree from which it was made. It may cost a bit more to restore a piece of such furniture, but it saves our natural resources.

WOOD CASE PIECES AND WOOD SUBSTITUTES

The majority of furnishings as the main component. Solid wood has a beautiful grain and is very durable. It's natural, recyclable, biodegradable, and renewable as long as the furnishing outlasts the tree from which it was made. On the other hand, cheaply made pieces that don't last and are quickly disposed of only contribute to deforestation and ecosystem loss. Selecting and specifying wood case pieces that will last through several generations is essential ecologically.

Figure 19.13 These pieces have a past life and were transformed by an artist into functional pieces. Terra Amico designs and builds all of their residential and commercial furnishings from salvaged and reclaimed materials. High-performing finishes are low- and zero- VOC. "Terra Amico" means "earth-friend" in Italian, and it is their goal to treat the Earth with respect and dignity in each of their designs.

Photo © Terra Amico Salvaged Wood Furniture, www.terraamico.com.

Kiln-dried wood is desirable for furniture that must bear weight because the process strengthens the frame and keeps it from warping or splitting. By thoroughly eliminating all but a small percentage of moisture through kiln drying, the wood becomes less vulnerable to changes in humidity and temperature. The method does increase embodied energy, but the improved longevity makes it a good trade-off. Most quality furniture makers use kiln-dried wood.

Whenever possible, specify third-party-certified wood (to ensure environment stewardship and ecofriendly forestry, milling, and distribution practices. Also specify wood species that are not endangered (see table 12.2, p. 274), avoiding those that come from unknown or uncertified sources. Favor local or domestic wood sources over tropical species and those that are shipped long distances, in order to lower the embodied energy.

Turning reclaimed or salvaged wood into new furnishings is another worthy approach. The Rainforest Alliance provides a certification program for rediscovered wood operations (RWOs) that sell reclaimed wood products, as well as those that sell new wood (see chapter 12); nonetheless, many RWOs remain uncertified. Whenever specifying wood for interior use, inquire about the source. Avoid reclaimed wood that has been treated for outdoor use or that may have been exposed to contaminants from industry or agriculture.

Particleboard, MDF, and other engineered, wood-based sheet goods are commonly used in less expensive furnishings. The eco-advantage to engineered wood is that it avoids using wide planks of solid wood from old growth trees and uses scrap instead. Look for engineered wood and sheet goods manufactured with a high percent of content from mill by-products, wood chips, and other waste materials. Specify FSC- or other third-party certification to ensure that the wood content was sustainably grown.

Unfortunately, sheet goods often contain formaldehyde binders or solvent-based finishes, so they outgas harmful emissions. Specify formaldehyde-free and ultra-low-emitting formaldehyde levels with zero- or low-VOC adhesives, binders, and finishes in all engineered wood products.

OTHER CASE PIECE MATERIALS

Biocomposites are sheet goods made from renewable agricultural by-products such as wheat, sunflowers, soybeans, and rice (see "Biocomposites," page 284). They are enjoying increasing popularity as a wood substitute in furniture case pieces. Each type of biocomposite has a distinctive textural grain or look.

Binders are necessary to hold the fibers together, so specify that they be low-VOC, formaldehyde-free, and solvent-free. Also specify low-VOC, formaldehyde-free finishes and stains.

Bamboo is a grass that regenerates quickly and has the hardness of wood. It is often used as a veneer over a wood core. Sometimes, solid bamboo is used for furniture legs or in decorative pieces. Some manufacturers of bamboo case pieces rely on urea formaldehyde binders, so specify formaldehyde-free binders. Also specify water-based or low-VOC finishes.

Third-party certification of bamboo plantations or products is available; look to FSC for the highest level of forestry stewardship.

Metal frames, legs, tabletops, and even chair seats are popular because they are extremely sturdy, need little upkeep, and can support a great deal of weight. The disadvantages to using newly mined and fabricated metal include the high embodied energy from the mining and smelting and the depletion of

Figure 19.14 This clerestory end table is made from found chestnut and with a steel top.

© 2006 Johngranen.com. Designer: John Wells.

nonrenewable resources (see "Metals," page 259). On the other hand, metal is perpetually recyclable,. Look for new metal furniture that has been fabricated from a high percentage of recycled steel, aluminum, or other metal.

Because metal furnishings and frames are so durable, they are often available for salvage. If the metal is in good condition, simply cleaning the piece may make it usable. Consider reusing the client's existing metal case pieces or salvage from a second-hand source.

If the metal won't rust or corrode, specify it be left unfinished. Request that any synthetic oil protectant used on the metal be removed before installation (soap and warm water usually suffices), or specify no oil or natural oils instead. (Synthetic oils may aggravate chemical sensitivities.)

Recycled Plastic: To Use or Not to Use?

Recycled plastic is showing up in a variety of home furnishings. Outdoor furniture, children's play sets, folding tables and chairs, and bathroom accessories often incorporate plastic because it is waterproof, stainproof, and impervious to abuse. And plastic recycling saves the environment.

Or does it?

At its best, plastic is easy to clean, can be molded into any shape, and is sanitary and hence indispensable in hospitals and health care settings. At its worst, plastic manufacturing uses nonrenewable petroleum and a variety of chemical ingredients, many of which are toxic to humans. PVC, probably the most notorious example, is known to outgas considerably, giving off a distinct smell characteristic of soft plastics and vinyl. It is now considered a health risk to workers and consumers alike. And it doesn't biodegrade.

Recycling plastic is, fundamentally, a good idea. Americans generate more than 26 million tons of plastic waste every year, much of it from food and beverage containers and retail packaging (e.g., "clamshells" and polystyrene foam). The plastic recycling process takes plastic objects of the same type (they're sorted by the numbers on the containers), melts them down, and re-forms them into new objects such as decking, plastic "lumber," picnic tables, and toddler-size chairs. But the question remains: Is this the best use?

Although some plastic in the home is inevitable, natural materials should still be your first choice. In particular, avoid plastics where they might cause the most harm through accidental ingestion or constant exposure—especially in children's furnishings and kitchens.

Sources: Healthy Building Network, www.healthybuilding.net; Greenpeace, http://archive.greenpeace.org/toxics/pvcdatabase; Grassroots Recycling Network, http://www.grrn.org/pvc/; Healthcare Without Harm, http://www.noharm.org/us/pvcDehp/issue); Environmental Protection Agency, www.epa.gov.

Factory-finished metal is better than metal that must be painted or finished on-site, especially when client chemical sensitivities are an issue, as paint or finishes for metal are solvent-based and emit VOCs. Manufacturers can control the conditions for application, and the piece will be able to outgas before it is in the home. Avoid plating, which is environmentally hazardous and dangerous to factory workers. Powder coatings outgas very little after drying and are virtually inert when dry, making them the best paint choice for metal in a green home.

Where Does It Come From?

- Solid wood case pieces and furnishings come from trees.
- Some wood products are made from recycled wood scraps or sawdust with added acrylics or resins.
- Reclaimed wood is culled from residential, commercial, and agricultural floors, walls, and structures and can be made into beautiful furniture.
- Biocomposite boards are made from a variety of crops, residues, and grains, including wheat, rice, barley, and oat straw; sunflower hulls; bluegrass or rye grass stubble; cornhusks and sorghum stalks; hemp; soybean plants; and bagasse (sugar cane pulp).
- Biocomposites may contain residual pesticides or chemicals from crops, although the amount or frequency of such is unknown.
- Bamboo is technically a grass, grown for several years before harvest.
- Sheet-good binders may include low-VOC glues, outgassing solvents, formaldehyde, soy-based products, and natural or synthetic resins.
- Metal is mined from various locations around the world, smelted at high temperatures, then fabricated into furnishings. Some metal is recycled from used metal products.
- Finishes, paints, or stains may contain natural oils, resins or pigments, solvents, chemical compounds, petroleum distillates, metal drying agents, formaldehyde, and sometimes water.
- Plastics are made from petroleum by-products.

Installation

When ordering, request that all case pieces be shipped in cardboard, kraft paper, or barrier cloth instead of plastics or bulky, nonrecyclable (and possibly hazardous) synthetic foam "peanuts" or pieces. Specify that all shipping materials be made with recycled content and that they be recycled after use.

If the case pieces will be factory assembled and finished, specify the use of zero- or low-VOC adhesives or water-based wood glues ("white" or "yellow" glues) whenever possible. Factory-finished pieces will be able to outgas prior to installation, which is helpful for those with chemical sensitivities—although the outgassing still negatively affects the environment.

If the furniture is finished on-site, there is a higher risk of odors and irritants from outgassing. Specify the least toxic, lowest-VOC finish, paint, or stain available, preferably one that's water-based or made with natural oils and extracts. Avoid finishes that contain solvents, formaldehyde, or metals as drying agents. Allow as much time as possible for the finish, paint, or adhesives to outgas and for them to cure before bringing the case piece into the home.

Maintenance

Most case pieces require little maintenance other than occasional dusting and cleaning with a damp cloth. Natural oil or wax finishes on wood require regular reapplications. Check with the artisan or manufacturer for their recommended cleaning methods. Healthy, benign cleaning products are available from organic grocers furniture artisans, and online. Think about the height of the furniture and whether the client will be able to clean the top periodically.

Figure 19.15 The integral color natural earthen plaster in this bedroom is nontoxic, zero-VOC, and made in the United States. It is a perfect backdrop for farmed teak shelving with natural finishes and natural bedding textiles of silk, cotton, wool, and chenille. The carpet is 100 percent wool and contains no dyes or fireproofing chemicals.

Photo by David O. Marlow. Design by Associates III, www.associates3.com.

Where Does It Go?

Furniture may be salvaged for a similar or different use. Wood or biocomposite boards will decompose easily, or they can be down-cycled into other wood or pulp products. Binders, resins, stains, and finishes will break down much more slowly—if at all.

Spec List

Specify:

- Locally or domestically harvested, third-party-certified (Forest Stewardship Council, Cradle 2 Cradle), nonthreatened wood species
- Reclaimed wood, third-party certified
- Salvaged furnishings or the reuse or renovation of existing case pieces
- Biocomposite boards or third-party-certified particleboard or plywood or particleboard with a high percentage of recycled wood
- Oil-free finish on hardware, or its removal prior to installation
- Formaldehyde-free, low-VOC, water-based binders, sealants, adhesives, glues, and stains

Specify finishes and stains (either on prefinished wood or to be applied on-site) that are:

- Water-based
- Made of natural (sometimes called food-grade) oils, resins, pigments, and waxes
- Zero- to low-VOC
- Formaldehyde-free
- Free of metallic drying agents
- Solvent-free

Avoid:

- Reclaimed wood of uncertain origin where its use might be unsafe (especially in children's rooms)
- Uncertified wood
- Rare or threatened species
- Solvent-based finishes
- Formaldehyde in the binder or finish
- Plastics

RESOURCES

Cradle-to-Cradle Certified. www.c2ccertified.org
Forest Stewardship Council U.S. www.US.FSC.org

Upholstery

Soft goods, such as sofa cushions or an upholstered chair, provide comfort and warmth. Upholstery adds softness and personality, manages acoustics, and adds color and texture to a home.

When researching, specifying, and purchasing upholstery, consider all of the components—frame, legs, batting, backing, webbing, springs, cushion fill and wrap, fabric and trim, dye, and fabric treatments—for their green characteristics. Specify each element to minimize environmental impact and maximize home health. It's best to work with a custom upholsterer or local artisan or track down the various larger furniture distributors who offer eco-friendly options.

Figure 19.16 Healthy furnishings represented by el: Furniture include the Pyxis Dining Chair and Pava Bistro Table. Upholstered pieces use natural latex, organic wool batting, and wool barrier cloth as well as other natural materials. Woods are reclaimed or sustainably harvested, and structural elements are made from FSC-certified core material. el also uses stainless steel, which can be recycled and reused. The finishes are naturally derived and nontoxic.

Photo courtesy of Jill Salisbury / el: FURNITURE, http://el.xblu.com.

The upholstery, pillows, and batting have a profound effect on the health of the client and the indoor environment. Soft goods, because of their porous nature, collect airborne particulates such as dust, mold, allergens, and environmental toxins, and are therefore called "sinks": Unlike a countertop, plumbing fixture, or wall, upholstered goods can't be wiped clean, and small particles can "sink" into the fabric and filling and then be re-released.

At its most benign, a sink may collect dust, pet hair, or mold, contributing to allergic reactions. At its worst, soft goods function as a reservoir for toxins: chemicals from the pavement carried in on shoes and clothing, SVOCs from drying paint or adhesives that have attached themselves to the dust particulates, or fabric stain-proofing that flakes away. The particulates settle until disturbed, residing in the foam in a sofa or the down of a pillow for weeks, years, or even decades. The risks from constant or repeated exposure through the re-release of toxins from soft goods has not yet been established.

The conditions in the furniture-making facility can contribute significantly to the sink phenomenon. Cigarette smoke, fumes from paint or finishes, or odors can contaminate the piece before it ever reaches the client's home. Know the manufacturer and request clean, odor-free conditions and excellent ventilation for all upholstered pieces, especially if the client is chemically sensitive. When in doubt, allow time for outgassing in a well-ventilated, protected environment or have the upholstery cleaned in the most benign manner possible before use. (The outgassing will still affect the environment, but the health of the home will be improved.)

While salvaged furnishings are a sound environmental choice because the items are diverted from the landfill, the pieces should always be thoroughly cleaned before reuse. The battings and fabrics, especially if vintage or antique, may harbor dust mites, mold, or toxins such as cigarette smoke or cleaning solutions. Unless the piece is in superb condition, reupholster all salvaged items to eliminate any chemical irritants or allergens, especially if the client has sensitivities.

UPHOLSTERY FABRICS AND TRIMS

All-natural textiles have the least environmental impact overall and the highest degree of health benefits for the client. Plant and animal fibers come from rapidly renewable resources and they also biodegrade easily enough that they can be used as compost. Leather and skins, if they have been prepared with eco-friendly methods, are very durable choices that also biodegrade, although some clients may be opposed to the use of animal products.

Other ecologically minded options are synthetic fibers derived from all-natural, recyclable, biodegradable materials; cloth made from recycled fibers, especially natural sources like cotton or wool; and reclaimed, recycled, or salvaged textiles.

Figure 19.17 This living room features sustainably crafted furnishings, including upholstery with vegetable-dyed leather frame and cotton chenille cushions, repurposed console cabinet, reclaimed copper coffee table top with FSC-certified wood base, and solid coconut wood lamps. It also features local stone, reclaimed oak floors, integral color earthen plaster walls, and LED lighting.

Photo by Tim Murphy. Designed by Annette Stelmack, www.associates3.com.

Avoid synthetic upholstery, especially petroleum-based fabrics, as well as chemical dyes, stain resistors, and waterproofing and other chemical treatments. Most synthetic fabrics can't be recycled and require energy-intensive manufacturing methods. Common chemical textile treatments should be avoided as well, as they pose health risks for factory workers and consumers. Even those with no known risks may create problems for a client with chemical sensitivities.

BATTINGS, FILLERS, AND FOAM

There are just a few basic options for selecting battings, foams, and fillers. Traditionally, cotton, wool, sisal, straw, horsehair, rags, moss, feathers, and fur were used as stuffings, and many are still available. The modern versions are usually thoroughly cleaned and sanitized to eliminate mold and insects.

Wool is available in a loose form (stuffing), in felted sheets, and in thicker pads. Wool is naturally flame-retardant and antimicrobial. It absorbs water and does not dry quickly, so avoid using wool in very humid environments. Look for wool that is obtained from sustainable, organic, and humane resources.

Cotton batting comes in sheets and in loose form. It compresses easily, so it is often combined with other materials for support. It also absorbs moisture, so avoid using cotton in very humid environments unless the upholstery can be easily removed for thorough drying. Because traditional cotton farming relies heavily on pesticides and fertilizers, specify organically grown cotton.

Grasses and plant fibers such as straw, jute, hemp, or sisal are rougher to the touch and are usually surrounded with a softer batting or cloth encapsulation. They provide durable, breathable loft. Some are water-repellent and therefore ideal for use in baths or outdoor furniture. Sisal and similar plant fibers are often precoated in (synthetic) latex foam or rubberized for use in upholstery, so specify all-natural fibers without coatings.

Natural down is still prized for pillows and upholstery; it is often applied around a firmer core as the final layer of batting. It is very soft and easily fluffed to regain loft. Allergies are usually reactions to dust and dander, not the down itself, and will be lessened if the product is thoroughly sanitized by the manufacturer before use, encapsulated in appropriate cushion wrap, and then regularly laundered. Down soaks up water and doesn't dry quickly, so avoid using it in moist or humid locations.

Animal hair is only occasionally used today, mainly by artisans and specialty upholsterers as stuffing, although it is frequently found in antiques. It lasts indefinitely but must be thoroughly washed and sanitized and may be attractive to pests.

All-natural latex foam is derived from rubber trees, but it should not be confused with synthetic latex derived from chemical processes. The term "latex" is used for both and for blends of the two. All-natural latex foam is durable, breathable, waterproof, biodegradeable, inherently antimicrobial, and resilient. Consult with the manufacturer to ensure the foam is 100 percent naturally derived.

Most big-name furniture makers today rely on synthetic paddings because of their predictable, durable results. These foams and battings are made by blowing gases into petroleum-based polymers. The end product is long-lasting—so much so that it won't biodegrade and can't usually be recycled. In addition, synthetic foams are suspected of releasing some of their chemicals over time as SVOCs or, worse, as hazardous particulates or molecules that collect in the environment and human tissue (see sidebar, "PBDEs," page 512).

Since the 1960s, the most popular filler in the market has been polyurethane foam, or polyfoam, because it is economical and readily available. Every year, 2.1 billion pounds of flexible polyurethane foam is produced in the United States. As a by-product of the petroleum industry, polyfoam contains polyols and diisocyanates, which give the foam flexibility. The EPA notes that foam production is an apparent source of several hazardous air pollutants: methylene chloride, toluene diisocyanate (TDI), and hydrogen cyanide.

Bio-based cushions made from soy provide another alternative. Unfortunately, the highest soy content available is between 30 and 35 percent—the rest of the filler is petroleum based: any greater percentage of soy and the cushion would degrade quickly. A large percentage of soy crops are genetically modified organisms (GMOs)—over 90 percent in the United States and nearly 60 percent globally, according to the U.S. Department of Agriculture—and the industrial farming of soy uses pesticides and herbicides. Because of the high percentage of petroleum in soy foam, the soy fill is not biodegradable.

Avoid synthetic foam and battings and the chemical compounds that are associated with them: chlorofluorocarbons (CFCs), polystyrene, and formaldehyde. Specify no bleaches, no synthetic dyes, and no chemical treatments to the batting or filler.

WEBBINGS, BACKINGS, AND BARRIER CLOTHS

As with upholstery and batting, all webbings, barrier cloths, backings, and functional fabrics should be made from all-natural plant or animal textiles. Jute, natural (rubber) latex, organic cotton, and wool are durable materials for these utilitarian purposes. Avoid the use of synthetics such as plastic, nylon, polyester, synthetic latex, and acrylic.

Where Does It Come From?

- Upholstery, webbings, backings, and barrier cloths may come from all-natural plant or animal fibers; from recycled fabrics and yarns; from petroleum- or chemical-based synthetic, extruded fibers; synthetic or natural rubber latex; or from bio-based synthetics.

PBDEs

What are PBDEs? Chemical fire retardants are common in consumer products, particularly in highly flammable synthetic materials. Some of the most common are brominated fire retardants (BFRs), including polybrominated diphenyl ethers (PBDEs).

PBDEs are most likely to be found in polyurethane foam products manufactured before 2005 such as upholstered furniture, mattresses, pillows—and electronics. You'll probably find them in dozens of products in your home and office, from the padding below your carpet, to your bed, couch, cell phone, and television. They are no longer used in children's sleepwear and have been phased out of mattresses sold in the United States.

PBDEs are found in the bodies of nearly every American. How the chemical enters the bodies of humans and animals is still unknown, but it is most likely through dust, airborne particulates, and possibly food. Laboratory studies show that exposure to even minute doses of PBDEs at critical points in development can damage reproductive systems and cause deficits in motor skills, learning, memory, and hearing, as well as behaviorial changes, slowed brain development, and thyroid problems. In addition, they persist in the environment and therefore bioaccumulate in people.

Studies have indicated that PBDEs build up in the food chain, soil, and air. They've been discovered in human breast milk, as they tend to collect in fat, and may thereby be transferred to infants. Traces have even been found in remote and sparsely populated places like the Arctic Circle. It's no longer just a problem in industrialized areas, but one that threatens the whole planet.

The sole U.S. producer of two types of PBDEs has agreed to discontinue their production, but the chemical is used throughout the world. The most reliable way to avoid PBDEs is to select textiles from companies that have strict policies against its use. Two of the main commercial grades of PBDEs were banned by the California Legislature in 2006. The European Union has followed suit.

The form of PBDEs used in foam furniture was withdrawn from the U.S. market in 2005 after widespread reports of PBDE contamination in people, households, wildlife, and common foods.

New foam items do not likely contain PBDEs. However, mattresses, mattress pads, couches, easy chairs, foam pillows (including breast-feeding pillows), carpet padding, and other foam items purchased before 2005 are likely to contain them. PBDEs were also used in vehicle seating, car seats, and office furniture.

Take these steps to avoid contact with items containing PBDEs that remain in your homes, offices, and vehicles.

1. *Inspect foam items*. Replace anything with a ripped cover or foam that is misshapen and breaking down. If you cannot replace these items, try to keep the covers intact. Beware of older items like car seats and mattress pads if the foam is not completely encased in a protective fabric.

2. *Use a vacuum fitted with a HEPA filter*. These vacuums are more efficient at trapping small particles and will likely remove more contaminants and other allergens from your home. HEPA-filter air cleaners may also reduce particle-bound contaminants in your house.

3. *Do not reupholster foam furniture.* Even those items without PBDEs might contain poorly studied fire retardants with potentially harmful effects.

4. *Be careful when removing old carpet.* The padding may contain PBDEs. Keep your work area isolated from the rest of your home. Clean up with a HEPA-filter vacuum and mop to pick up as many of the small particles as possible.

5. *Ask manufacturers what type of fire retardants they use.* Avoid products with brominated fire retardants and opt for less flammable fabrics and materials like leather, wool, and cotton. Be aware that "natural" or latex foam and natural cotton are flammable and require a fire retardant method that may contain toxic fire retardants.

Sources: Washington State Department of Ecology, www.ecy.wa.gov; California Air Resources Board, www.arb.ca.gov/toxics/pbde.html; Environmental Working Group, www.ewg.org.

- Plant-based fibers such as cotton, jute, hemp, and ramie may be organically grown or grown by traditional farming methods.
- Animal products such as wool and leather may come from sustainably managed or humane ranches, or from traditional ranch facilities.

Installation

Whenever possible, test wash a sample, then wash or air out the fabrics that are not labeled "all-natural" before use in upholstery. This will help rid the fabric of chemical treatments, dust, particulates, VOCs, and odors.

Maintenance

Because an upholstered piece can become a sink where toxins, mold, dust, and allergens accumulate, dust, vacuum, or launder them regularly. Rotating the cushions, slipcovers, and pillows will avoid soiling in the places where they are used most often.

When possible, specify fabrics that can be laundered or spot-cleaned with soap and water. Recommend natural spot-cleaning methods; avoid solvent-based treatments. If dry cleaning is recommended by the textile manufacturer, look for dry cleaners that employ carbon dioxide in an environmentally safe process.

Where Does It Go?

Natural textiles and upholstery will decompose; the plant-based types can be shredded for compost. Some synthetic fabrics can be recycled or reprocessed into new textiles or other polymers. Most synthetics break down slowly, if at all, after disposal.

Spec List

Specify:

■ Locally or domestically harvested, third-party-certified (FSC, C2C), nonthreatened wood species

■ Third-party-certified reclaimed wood

■ Battings, fillers, and foams from plant fibers that are all natural, organically grown, sustainably farmed, or obtained using humane methods

Avoid:

■ Synthetic, petroleum-based foams or padding

■ Chemical treatments to batting or fillers

RESOURCES

International Federation of Organic Agriculture Movements. www.ifoam.org

Organic Trade Association. www.ota.com

Sustainable Cotton Association. www.sustainablecotton.org
See also "Textiles," page XX.

Lighting

Hardwired light fixtures are specified during the design phase in preparation for the construction and/or remodeling stage. Freestanding floor and table lamps are specified as furnishings to highlight finishes, furnishings, and art; provide optimal lighting for tasks such as reading, entertaining, and crafts; and set the mood in a room. The goal: maximum energy efficiency.

Figure 19.18 Whimsical pendant from recycled glass pebbles and salvaged bicycle wheel with LED bulbs.

Photo by David Bergman. Designed by Fire & Water, www.cyberg .com/fw/cycLED.htm.

Chapter 18 covers the basic principles of eco-friendly lighting design that minimizes energy usage. When selecting lighting, consider the natural light in a room and fixture placement in relation to furnishings and windows. Try various Energy Star light bulbs with different wattages and color renditions, using a light fixture similar to the one that might be purchased for that precise location. Then specify the bulb with the lowest electrical demand.

With the 2012 law in effect and 2020 not far away, designers now have three basic bulb selections: halogen incandescent bulbs, compact fluorescent lamps (CFLs) or light-emitting diodes (LEDs). Refer to chapter 18 for detailed information on lamping options.

Controls such as motion detectors, light sensors, and timers are often used to improve safety by turning lights on automatically in dark rooms. These controls can improve energy savings by shutting off lights automatically when a room is empty or when the natural light is sufficient. They can also increase energy use, however, by turning lights on when they aren't needed, so consider all such applications carefully.

Lamp bases and fixtures can be made from practically anything—coconut shells, recycled aluminum cans, pottery, bicycle parts—as long as the material is safe to use near electrical wiring and the heat generated by light bulbs. Shades can also be made from a large variety of materials, as long as they filter light adequately. When specifying materials for the light fixture itself, the greenest choice will always be the most easily renewable, longest-lasting, natural material. Next on the list might be recycled or salvaged materials, to keep them out of landfills.

Avoid potential health hazards, especially materials that might outgas, disintegrate, or emit odors when affected by the warmth of a light bulb. Plastics, oils, and synthetic fabrics are all undesirable. If the client has allergies or chemical sensitivities, these are especially important considerations. Essentially we want to avoid the new car smell, which is the offgassing of chemicals. Unstable paints and finishes are not intended for use on light fixtures; metal light fixtures that have been factory-finished with a powder coat are acceptable. Wood and other porous surfaces should be left unfinished or have a heat-tolerant, water-based, low-VOC finish, preferably applied at the factory.

Textiles, skins, and papers may be used as shades if they have not been chemically treated and don't emit VOCs. Dyes—even those made with all-natural substances—may be affected by the bright light and heat, so avoid their use in shades. Also avoid fire retardants that might contain PBDEs (see sidebar, "PBDEs," page 512) and opt instead for cool-temperature bulbs (compact fluorescent lamps or CFLs) and leave an appropriate distance between the shade and bulb.

Bulbs and light fixtures are fragile, requiring the use of special packaging and shipping materials that can present environmental dilemmas. Request that all boxes and packaging be made from recyclable paper, cardboard, or similar material. Avoid "peanuts," plastic "clamshells," plastic bags, and other synthetics; not only are they difficult to recycle, they can taint the contents with outgassed odors and chemicals.

Where Does It Come From?

- Most electricity for residential lighting is generated by burning fossil fuels at power plants. Smaller portions are created through nuclear fission and renewable wind, water (hydroelectric), and solar power.
- Residential light fixtures rely on metal and glass for integral components; the decorative parts can be made from any material that is not flammable or won't melt when in close contact with wiring and light bulbs.
- Lamp shades are most often constructed from materials that filter light, such as textiles, paper, or skins, but can be made from a wide variety of materials.

Maintenance

Provide a list of preferred bulb types and wattages for the client once the fixture selections are complete to help them find replacement bulbs; this will also maximize energy efficiency in the long run.

Lamp shades and light fixtures should be dusted or lightly vacuumed.

Where Does It Go?

Once spent, electricity from nonrenewable sources can never be recovered. There are, however, recycling options for bulbs:

- There may be a local program for recycling fluorescent bulbs. Consult with the municipality or waste management district to see if they are collected at hazardous waste or recycling sites.
- Mail-in boxes are another recycling method. The consumer must purchase a bulb-collection box that has prepaid postage, then send it off to the recycling facility when full. These programs are currently oriented toward businesses but may become more available to individual consumers.

Light fixtures should be disassembled and the components recycled, if possible. Natural paper or fiber shades (without finishes or chemical treatments) can be composted or mulched.

Spec List

Specify:
- Energy Star bulbs with the lowest energy use that still meet the client's needs
- Controls such as dimmers, occupancy sensors, and timers if they will reduce lighting use

- Energy Star fixtures
- Recyclable shipping and packing materials for new bulbs and light fixtures

Avoid:

- Incandescent bulbs, using them only when all other options are not adequate or adaptable to current fixtures
- Light pollution by overlighting a location or misdirecting light
- Landfill disposal of fluorescent bulbs; encourage the homeowner to recycle responsibly
- Packing materials for bulbs and fixtures made of nonrecyclable materials and synthetics such as plastic or foam

RESOURCES

Bulb Recycling. www.lamprecycle.org.
Earth911. www.earth911.org.
Energy Star: www.energystar.gov.

Mattresses and Bedding

We spend approximately a third of our lives asleep. And most of us, at least in the Western world, sleep on manufactured mattresses and pillows. Once upon a time, people slept on simple mats or frames, or mattresses stuffed with straw, feathers, or moss. The sleep systems were certainly earth-friendly, and the materials easily biodegraded. But mold, insects, rodents, and general discomfort kept us searching for a better place to sleep.

Today, mass-produced mattresses are made with steel springs, polyurethane foam, polyester encasings, typically with box springs and a second base below. But in trying to assure ourselves a good night's rest, we have, by ridding mattresses and pillows of natural materials and replacing them with petroleum-derived fibers, vinyl, flame retardants, and other synthetics, disturbed something much more important than our sleep. These modern-day mattresses are also made from non-renewable materials that fill up landfills with nonbiodegradable materials. And we haven't been all that successful in solving the initial problem: many individuals suffer from a host of allergies and chemical sensitivities, some of which are aggravated by the six to eight hours per night spent lying on a not-so-natural bed. Even some all-natural materials may be allergens or irritants for particular clients.

Test swatches of bedding and mattress materials are helpful for determining which environmentally safe options are also the most comfortable. Replacing the mattress, frame, and bedding may be one of the most significant and positive changes in the greening of a home. Take care to specify materials that are not only eco-friendly, but that promote the client's health and sense of well-being.

Anatomy of a Bed

pillows
comforters
linens
mattress pads
barrier cloths
mattresses
foundations/box springs
frames

Figure 19.19 There are several components to a bed; terminology varies from region to region. This is a diagram of all the possible components of a sleep system. The bed starts with a frame, which can be made of wood or metal and is the support for the box spring or foundation. The foundation can be a box with wood slats or a box with spring support. The mattress goes either on a foundation or on a platform bed frame. The barrier cloth is of tightly woven cotton that zips around the whole mattress and protects against dust mites. The mattress pad is like a fitted sheet, which is made with layers of cotton to protect the pad from spills and body oils. The linens are the sheets and blankets on the bed. A comforter, also called a duvet, can be filled with wool, polyester, or down. Pillows can be filled with wool, cotton, down, or fill.

© Suite Sleep, www.suitesleep.com. Used with permission.

BED FRAMES

If the client wishes to purchase a new, all-natural sleep system, begin with the frame. Select a wood frame with finishes that are low-VOC, water-based, and formaldehyde-free. Also specify third-party-certified wood.

California's New Flammability Standard

California's new furniture flammability standard—TB117–2103—was released February 8, 2013, and the public comment period ended March 26, 2013. The Bureau of Home Furnishings and Thermal Insulation is evaluating and responding to comments, and then the regulation needs to be approved.

Manufacturers can begin to make products under the new regulation as soon as it is officially adopted, targeted for January 2014. The mandatory compliance date will likely be about a year after official adoption.

Flame retardants are not needed to meet the new standard, so once it is implemented it should be possible to buy furniture that does not contain such retardants.

Source: Green Science Policy Institute, www.greensciencepolicy.org/node/529#10.

A metal frame is slightly less eco-friendly because metals are nonrenewable. Look for a steel frame that has been made with high recycled material content. Avoid metal platings (see "Metals," page 259) on the frame and decorative headboard and footboard, as they create toxic hazards for factory workers. Look instead for alloys that are rustproof, or for powder-coated, factory-applied finishes that don't outgas.

Adaptability is an eco-friendly principle, as one piece of furniture with multiple functions conserves natural resources that would be otherwise used to manufacture another piece. Fold-up beds also conserve valuable floor space, convenient for a smaller residence.

MATTRESSES

There are several different materials that are commonly used in natural sleep systems for fillers, casings, and frames and/or springs. Look for these materials in a new mattress:

- *Latex*. All-natural latex made from rubber trees is an eco-friendly and healthful choice. It is resistant to mold, bacteria, dust mites, and other allergens and comes in different levels of firmness. Some natural latex beds have interchangeable plates of rubber that permit the creation of variable degrees of firmness. Natural latex should not be confused with synthetic latex, although both are called simply "latex" on labels and are often blended. The definition of "100 percent natural latex" is not strictly defined by labeling laws, so it may include synthetic content. Request specific content information from the manufacturer, and specify all-natural rubber latex without synthetic content.

- *Wool*. Tufted wool is another common choice for eco-friendly, healthy sleep. It breathes and allows moisture exchange, making it comfortable in all temperatures. Wool mattresses are usually only a few inches thick, so a natural latex layer added underneath may be more comfortable than wool alone. Wool also provides an excellent encasement or barrier cloth for wool-filled or latex mattresses. Look for wool that comes from sustainably managed ranches that use no pesticides or that is certified through the Organic Trade Association. Avoid wool that has been chemically treated or bleached.

- *Cotton*. Cotton is rarely used as the primary mattress core because it will flatten and lose its loft, but it is occasionally used for filler in pillows. Cotton is, however, commonly used in the mattress encasement or barrier cloth, and it is the number-one choice for pillow ticking. It breathes and is particularly comfortable in warmer climates. Cotton is also easy to spot-clean or launder with soap and water. Specify cotton that is organically grown, unbleached, and undyed, and has not been treated with any chemicals. Cotton fiber may be certified through the Organic Trade Association, as with wool.

Mattresses are best if they come with zippered or removable covers that can be aired, laundered, or taken to earth-friendly dry cleaners. This will keep the mattress clean and reduce allergens and irritants.

Steel springs within the mattress are called "innersprings"; springs underneath the mattress are called "box springs." Visit showrooms with your client to try out several mattress types, including those with and without springs, before making a purchase. A few manufacturers offer mail-order swatches of their mattress materials specifically for consumers with allergies or sensitivities. If your client is sensitive to electromagnetic fields, metal springs may be an issue (see chapter 4, "Healthy Interiors").

In the event that the client does not wish to replace their existing mattress, a wool mattress topper is an excellent addition. It puts a layer of natural, healthy materials between the person and the conventional mattress. A topper is easy to wash or air regularly, making it ideal for anyone with allergies, whether used on top of a conventional or all-natural mattress.

FILLERS FOR PILLOWS, COMFORTERS, BATTINGS, AND MATTRESS PADS

In addition to wool, cotton, and latex, pillows, comforters, and mattress pads may include a number of other filler materials. Look for 100 percent natural fillers that are unbleached and not chemically treated. Specify certified organic, sustainably farmed materials, and request third-party certification of organic fiber content.

- *Buckwheat, spelt, millet, and other grains*. These feel similar to a soft bag of sand, and hold contours to support the neck and spine. Look for organically grown, naturally cleaned and sifted grain that has not been fumigated. Some grain pillows can be heated in the microwave for therapeutic use.

- *Down and feathers*. For many, down is the only material for pillows. Goose down is loftier and softer than feathers and is sometimes combined with synthetic fillers or less desirable duck down. Specify 100 percent goose down from sustainably managed or organic farms that has been collected after the animals molt naturally. Chemical washings and treatments may exacerbate sensitivities, so specify down that has been cleansed with turbid water (a process that agitates the dirt free from the fibers).

- *Kapok*. Kapok is taken from the pods of the ceiba tree, found in the rain forests of Java. It was so commonly used in lifejackets before World War II that soldiers called the preservers "kapoks." Although the long-distance importation of kapok reduces its eco-friendliness, it may be a viable, all-natural option for those with allergies or ethical objections to wool or down.

Fact Check

Allergic Responses: Healing Effects

■ Allergies—to all manner of things—are the sixth leading cause of chronic disease in the United States, costing $18 billion in health care annually.

■ *Latex.* Relatively unknown before 1990, allergies to latex are becoming increasingly common for reasons that are unclear. It is now estimated that up to 6 percent of the population may be allergic to latex.

One hundred percent pure, natural latex is inherently hypoallergenic, antimicrobial and resistant to dust mites. Although rare, latex allergy can cause an anaphylactic response; this usually develops through repeated exposure to products such as surgical gloves.

See MedlinePlus for more information (www.nlm.nih.gov/medlineplus); a booklet on latex allergies is available from 1–800–7ASTHMA.

■ *Wool.* Because wool resists mold and mildew, it can be a good choice for people with allergies. "Wool itch" is not usually a true allergy, but a reaction to the fiber's shape and length, the allergic reaction to wool comes from contact with lanolin in the wool.

Merino wool is the least scratchy. Wool also helps to reduce dust mites, the biggest source of airborne allergies in the United States.

■ *Healing.* Synthetic materials are disconnecting from nature's own healing properties. Studies conducted at both the Polytechnic Institute of Wales and the Hohenstein Institute in Germany have shown that "sleeping with untreated natural fibers actually slows the heart rate and helps regulate body temperature."

Sources: American Lung Association, www.lung.org; American Academy of Allergy Asthma & Immunology, www.aaaai.org; Green Home Environmental Store, www.greenhome.com/info/articles/sleep_well/91/; National Institute of Allergy and Infectious Diseases, www.niaid.nih.gov.

- *Milkweed or syriaca*. The fluffy stuff from milkweed pods is being cultivated for use in bedding and other natural products. Syriaca, the scientific name for milkweed, is reputed to be allergen-free. It is usually mixed with wool or down.

- *Hemp*. One of its many uses, hemp can be spun into pillow filling. Hemp pillows are firm, with a soft feel that gets softer over time, providing a medium-loft pillow with inherent mold resistant and durability. Like with most pillows, placing them in the sun for a few hours refreshes. One hundred percent organic hemp pillows are available.

Many environmentally conscientious pillow and bedding makers go one step further to cater to those with allergies, by providing samples to potential customers. Request samples of pillows and bedding, whenever possible, so the client can test the products before committing to purchase them.

Because the mattress and pillows are in such close contact with human airways and skin, it is advisable to avoid synthetics because they can be hazardous to health. They are also bad for the environment, as most are made from nonrenewable resources and won't biodegrade. Unfortunately, synthetics are used widely by mattress and bedding manufacturers.

Avoid the following materials:

Figure 19.20 This master bedroom is open like a tree house complemented by natural earthen plaster walls, wool carpet, and natural textiles that reflect the adjacent colors from nature.

Photo by Pat Sudmeier. Design by Associates III, www.associates3.com.

- *Polystyrene foam and foam beads*. Polystyrene contains the chemical styrene, which has been linked to nervous system disorders. In addition, the small foam beads are a choking hazard for children. Several states have prohibited their use in children's clothing, toys, and other items and also require the beads to be double-bagged within pillows and other products as a preventative measure.

- *Memory foam*. This popular mattress and pillow material is also known as viscoelastic polyurethane or urethane foam. It is manufactured from derivatives of petroleum and won't biodegrade. It is supposedly inert and won't outgas VOCs, but it is often made with other chemicals or treatments that give off odors and may be especially problematic for chemically sensitive individuals.

- *PBDE*. Synthetic pillow foam is a flammable material because of its open cell structure and chemical makeup, so it is often treated with the fire retardant

Slumber Laws

The content of a mattress or pillows from a conventional retailer is disclosed on a "law label," or large affixed tag, in many states; some laws cover car seats, stuffed toys, sofas, sleeping bags, and beanbag chairs as well.

Developed by the Association of Bedding and Furniture Law Officials (www.ABFLO.org) and the International Sleep Products Association (www.SleepProducts.org), the tags specify the filler content, chambered bedding, and various other information. Example disclosures include "all new material," "secondhand," "80 percent goose down," or "polyurethane foam filler." Unfortunately, some states have opted out of this system, although most manufacturers apply the labels to all products to ensure compliance in the states that do require them.

The International Sleep Products Association (ISPA)(http://www.sleepproducts.org/ispa-earth/) provides disposal resources for mattresses and are encouraging the development of mattress recycling legislation. ISPA works diligently to support efficient industry- and consumer-friendly mattress recycling alternatives and initiatives alongside state-level legislation.

In 2013, Connecticut launched a mattress recycling law, the first of its kind in the United States.

Source: www.ct.gov/deep/cwp/view.asp?a=2714&q=482160&depNav_GID=1645.

PBDE (see sidebar, "PBDEs," page 512). The substance has been implicated in a number of serious health issues, and California is leading the way in phasing out its use in mattresses. Avoid the use of fire retardants altogether.

- *Polylactide acid (PLA).* This biosynthetic fiber is engineered from corn; there are many similar compounds in development. It eventually biodegrades and is made from a renewable resource—both ecological positives—and it's being used in everything from disposable plates to bedding. PLA holds promise as a replacement for petroleum-based synthetics, which don't biodegrade. The use of such bio-based synthetics for sleep products is hard to justify, however, when so many other natural, renewable materials are already available.

Toxic Phthalates

Phthalates (pronounced *tha*-lates) are used in soft plastic teething rings and toys, and should be avoided to protect a baby's health. These hazardous chemicals, which are regulated as pollutants in air and water, are essentially unregulated in children's toys, cosmetics, and many other consumer products. Although some types of phthalates have been shown to be toxic to developmental, reproductive, and other organ systems and their use therefore discontinued, they are still used for teethers and other toys. Avoid all soft plastic teethers and food containers until manufacturers prove they are safe. Harder plastic toys are probably phthalate-free, but wooden teethers and toys are the best alternative.

On February 10, 2009, a federal ban on phthalates, a toxic plasticizer, went into effect; they can no longer be used in children's toys or childcare items, including mattresses.

Source: Environmental Working Group, www.ewg.org.

SHEETS, PILLOWCASES, AND OTHER BEDDING

When selecting sheets, pillowcases, and other bedding items, follow the general guidelines for specifying healthier, earth-friendly textiles. Optimally, all bedding types should be washable, especially if the client has allergies. As with any textile, avoid fabric treatments, stain repellents, waterproofing compounds, fire retardants, or any other chemicals, and specify natural dyes if color is desired.

Figure 19.21 The master suite was created as a serene retreat that supports the client's holistic health. The designers used all-natural textiles throughout as well as organic bedding and mattress assembly. It also features FSC-certified walnut floors, doors, trim, and case pieces, a 100 percent wool area rug, stained bamboo furnishings, CFL table and floor lamps, and locally crafted fireplace surround.

Photo by Ben Tremper. Designed by Annette Stelmack, Rachael Morton, Cassandra Coombe, www.associates3.com.

Cotton is the most popular and affordable fiber for sheets, pillowcases, and comforters. Pillow ticking (encasings) is almost always made of cotton, as it can be tightly woven with a high thread count to enclose the battings. Certified organic cotton is no longer difficult to obtain, so specify it for all cotton bedding.

If a client with allergies prefers natural fibers like silk, wool, linen, bamboo, and Tencel (see "Textiles," page 481) a double pillowcase with a high thread count will provide a barrier against dust and other particulates.

Where Does It Come From?

- Frames are usually made from metal or wood.
- Mattresses may be filled with wool, natural (rubber) latex, synthetic latex, synthetic fibers, or a blend.
- Mattress casings and barrier cloths are commonly made from wool, synthetics, or cotton.
- Mattresses may also feature innersprings or box springs made from steel.
- Pillows may be filled with wool, cotton, synthetic battings, latex, or sometimes grains, kapok, milkweed/syriaca, down, or feathers.
- Sheets, pillowcases, and bedding are made from a wide variety of textiles, including cotton, wool, linen, silk, hemp, synthetics, and bio-based synthetics.

Maintenance

Mattresses should be flipped and rotated regularly to ensure good ventilation and to redistribute fillers for maximum support and comfort. Advise the client to spot-clean with soap and water or natural cleansers when necessary. Avoid solvent-based cleaning solutions. Launder mattress covers and vacuum or air out toppers.

Follow manufacturer directions carefully for cleaning pillows that contain down, grains, or specialty fibers. Specify that all sheets, pillowcases, and bedding be washable. If the client has health concerns or allergies, specify unbleached and undyed bedding because it can be washed in hot water. Encourage the use of eco-friendly, biodegradable laundry products. Air-dry pillows, quilts, and similar items that contain batting, then fluff them by hand so the batting doesn't clump.

Where Does It Go?

Mattresses take up a lot of space in landfills with materials that slowly—or never—disintegrate or biodegrade. Conventional mattresses can't be sanitized easily and eventually lose their loft, so reuse is not a healthful option. Do not dispose of any mattress, whether synthetic or all-natural, before consulting with the local waste management authority to determine if there are restrictions on mattress disposal. At least one bed manufacturer accepts mattresses and frames for recycling, and salvage yards will also accept the steel frames. (See sidebar, "Slumber Laws," page XX, for more mattress disposal resources.)

Other bedding, such as sheets and pillows, will last for many years if carefully maintained. All-natural bedding can be reused as rags, or even composted.

Spec List

Specify:

- Bed frames made from natural materials such as certified wood or metal, with nontoxic, low-VOC finishes
- Mattresses made from all-natural materials such as latex (natural rubber), wool, and cotton
- Mattress toppers for clients with allergies or sensitivities made from all-natural materials
- Pillows made with all-natural wool, cotton, latex, down, grains, kapok, hemp, or milkweed/syriaca
- Bedding made from all-natural cotton, wool, silk, linen, hemp, or other textiles
- All-natural dyes or no dyes

Avoid:

- Chemical bleaching
- Natural latex if the client has a latex allergy
- Synthetic latex
- Synthetic fabrics and fillers
- Foam, especially memory foam and polystyrene beads or pieces
- Fire retardants, especially PBDEs and brominated
- Chlorine or chemical bleaches
- Synthetic dyes
- Fabric treatments such as stain and water repellents, sizing, and fire retardants

RESOURCES

Association of Bedding and Furniture Law Officials. www.ABFLO.org.
International Federation of Organic Agriculture Movements. www.ifoam.org.
International Sleep Products Association. www.SleepProducts.org.
Organic Trade Association. www.ota.com.
Sustainable Cotton Association. www.sustainablecotton.org.

Area Rugs

Area rugs may be as small as a breadbox or as large as a room. The fibers that support a rug may be delicate and made from cotton rags, chenille, or even paper. There are many more eco-friendly area rug choices than there are eco-friendly wall-to-wall carpet options.

Small rugs are easily laundered at home with detergent and water, and larger ones can be taken to an eco-friendly cleaner—a distinct advantage over large expanses of carpet that must be cleaned in place. Off-site cleaning is of particular value to a client with allergies or sensitivities.

In addition, many rugs have lower embodied energy than carpets While most carpet is manufactured on large looms in factories, many types of rugs are woven on small hand-looms, often from local specialty fibers obtained from indigenous sheep or native grasses. Rug-makers and weavers sometimes do their own dyeing, as well. All-natural colorants can usually be specified when working with an artisan.

GoodWeave: Putting an End to Child Labor

The GoodWeave label is the best assurance that no child labor was used to make your rug. In order to earn the GoodWeave label, rug exporters and importers must be licensed under the GoodWeave certification program and sign a legally binding contract to adhere to the no-child-labor standard and not employ any person under age fourteen; allow unannounced random visits by local inspectors; and pay a licensing fee that helps support GoodWeave's monitoring, inspections, and education programs.

To ensure compliance, independent GoodWeave inspectors make unannounced inspections of each loom. If inspectors find children working, they offer them the opportunity to go to school instead, and the producers lose their status with GoodWeave. To protect against counterfeit labeling, each label is numbered so its origin can be traced.

GoodWeave also sets contractual standards for companies that import certified rugs. Importers agree to source only from GoodWeave-certified exporters in India, Nepal, and any other country where GoodWeave rugs are available. In the United States and other rug-importing countries, only licensed importers are legally permitted to sell carpets carrying the GoodWeave label.

Look for the GoodWeave label on all rugs—and avoid those without it.

Source: GoodWeave, www.goodweave.org.

Almost anything that can be made into a textile (see "Textiles," page 481) can be woven, knotted, or knit into a rug. Natural fibers are the obvious choice. Area rugs are made from a wide variety of plant and animal fibers, another distinct advantage over wall-to-wall carpet, which is usually made from synthetics. The possibilities for rugs include, but are not limited to: wool, cotton, silk, jute, hemp, coir, sisal, and sea grass. Select the fiber or blend that best fits the intended purpose and that will last the longest.

Whenever possible, choose fibers that are organically grown or farmed according to sustainable methods. Wool and cotton growers may subscribe to third-party certification, but it is uncommon for most other fiber producers to do so. Look for manufacturers that have strict standards for environmentally friendly production practices, waste management and recycling, and worker safety programs. Or purchase from local artisans who take pride in working with all-natural materials, and thus eliminate the wasted energy inherent in long-distance transportation.

Specify all-natural dyes or none at all. Avoid chlorine bleaching and chemical colorants.

Avoid petroleum-based synthetic materials such as polyester, olefin, nylon, acrylic, or acetate. Some synthetic rug fibers outgas or carry odors that can be irritating, as well.

Avoid stain repellants, waterproofing, and other chemical treatments; they may not be listed on the label, so request details from the manufacturer. If working with a local artisan or specialty rug-maker, request that only natural dyes be used. Specify no dye if the client suffers from sensitivities or allergies that might be triggered by it.

Area rugs are also made from a wide variety of recycled materials. Old denim jeans, T-shirts, and other clothing items or fabrics—even paper—can be torn into rags and woven, braided, or sewn into rugs. Such materials are both thrifty and ecological: no new materials or natural resources are used in their creation. Because the fabrics' content will be varied and its origins unknown, it may not be a good option for chemically sensitive clients.

Felted Wool

Wool has a unique property: If it is washed in detergent and abraded (rubbed and agitated) when wet, the fibers will cling together. The final product, a densely matted, soft, thick wool, has been "felted." The process can be used to create beautiful, durable rugs and paddings.

When specifying felted wool, request that only mild soap or detergent be used in the process.

RUG PADS

The padding underneath a rug, whether part of the rug itself or a separate layer, provides more than just comfort and safety. It protects the floor from abrasion by dust particles trapped underneath the rug or rough backings. It also extends the life of the rug.

There are two basic types of rug pads: those that cushion, and those that also grip the floor to prevent slipping. Cushioning pads can be made from all-natural wool. Synthetic pads are the most common type available, but not desirable in a green room. The gripping pads are usually made from latex; specify all-natural rubber latex. (The term "latex" is used for both the natural type and synthetic, so make precise inquiries when purchasing the pad.) Never use pads made from PVC, also called vinyl, which carries a distinct odor and outgasses harmful substances.

Where Does It Come From?

- Rugs can be made from all-natural fibers such as wool, silk, jute, coir, sisal, sea grass, and cotton, or from artificial fibers such as nylon, olefin, and acrylic.
- Rug pads can be made from PVC or vinyls, synthetic or natural latex, recycled carpet fibers, wool, jute, camel hair, or mohair.

Maintenance

Regularly vacuuming both sides of a rug will extend the life of the fibers and prevent particles underneath from scratching the floor. If the fiber content allows, small rugs should be laundered regularly with mild detergent and water. Larger rugs may be cleaned by a service that uses only water or by dry cleaners that use carbon dioxide processes. Advise the client to avoid solvent-based stain treatments, chemical dry cleaners, and stain repellents.

Where Does It Go?

Wool, cotton, jute, coir, sisal, sea grass, cotton, paper, and silk rugs, along with natural backings and pads, will biodegrade easily. Rugs made from recycled clothing or rags may be problematic if they contain a high percentage of synthetics, although it is possible to recycle synthetic-fiber rugs. A few rug manufacturers accept products back at the end of their life cycle, but the effort is primarily targeted at commercial wall-to-wall carpet. Otherwise, synthetic fibers simply add to landfill waste and environmental problems.

Spec List

Specify:

- One hundred percent natural-fiber carpets (wool, cotton, silk, jute, coir, sisal, sea grass, paper)
- All-natural dyes, or no dye at all
- Recycled-content rag rugs
- Locally made or artisan-produced rugs
- GoodWeave certification
- Rug pads made from all-natural rubber latex, wool, or other natural materials.

Avoid:

- Manufactured fibers such as nylon, polyester, olefin, and acetate
- Stain repellents, waterproofing, or other chemical treatments
- Synthetic dyes
- Synthetic rug pads, especially those made with PVC-vinyl

RESOURCES

Carpet and Rug Institute. www.carpet-rug.org.
Good Weave. www.GoodWeave.org.

Window Treatments

Before specifying window treatments for an eco-friendly home, consult with the client to determine whether the treatment is functional, decorative, or even necessary. Window treatments can serve a variety of purposes: They regulate sunlight through the opening and keep weather extremes at bay—both important for energy conservation—in addition to framing the view of the outdoors, providing privacy, and enhancing a room's ambience.

In new construction windows should be located to maximize

Figure 19.22 The honeycomb fabric of these cellular shades trap air, providing an insulating barrier from cold drafts or oppressive heat coming through the window while protecting against damaging UV rays.

Photo courtesy of Comfortex Window Fashions.

Fact Check

- Heating and cooling your home uses more energy and costs more money than any other system in your home—typically making up about 54 percent of your utility bill. A third of all heat loss occurs through windows and doors.

Source: www.energy.gov/energysaver/articles/tips-heating-and-cooling.

solar gain and minimize heat loss, but it isn't practical to change the orientation of the windows once the house is built. When a home is located in a climate with large temperature fluctuations, appropriate window coverings boost energy efficiency by keeping the house warm in winter and blocking hot sun in the summer. They should also prevent drafts. Insulating, reflective, or blackout window treatments may make a noticeable difference in both comfort level and utility bills, as well as in the overall consumption of nonrenewable fuel for heating and air conditioning.

Most homes need additional window insulation and/or light regulation. If the windows are both the centerpiece of a room and highly efficient, the client may want window treatments that highlight the view or improve the ambience.

DRAPERIES AND WINDOW TEXTILES

Focus on long-lasting textiles and materials that will need little maintenance and won't deplete the environment. Organically grown cotton, hemp, flax (linen), ramie, wool, or silk from sustainably managed operations are ideal choices for window coverings. They might also be made from a variety of grasses, bamboo, or wood. Look for products that have been third-party certified as sustainable or organic.

The client may request that no dyes be added; if color is desired, specify that all dyes be natural, not chemical. Then specify low-impact finishes and no additional fabric treatments such as stain repellents or flame retardants (see "Textiles," page 481).

Avoid specialty coatings on textiles that contain vinyl, plastic, synthetic rubber, or other manufactured polymers. Tight weave and fabrics are both washable and stain-resistant. Synthetic waterproofing treatments may actually encourage condensation on the window or fabric, defeating the intended purpose. For moisture control, specify highly breathable textiles with natural resistance to mold, such as wool.

SHUTTERS

Shutters on the inside of a window provide control over light, privacy, and to a lesser degree, temperature, if they cover the window completely and fit snugly. Wood shutters can be ordered unfinished and left as is or finished at the site with low-VOC, low-odor paint, all-natural waxes, or oils. The wood is long-lasting and the shutters can eventually be salvaged and reused or repurposed, or they will decompose naturally over time. Specify FSC- or other third-party-certified wood.

Factory-finished wood shutters are a good choice for clients with sensitivities, as they will outgas off-site. (The outgassing will still affect the environment and air quality, however.) Specify low-VOC, formaldehyde-free finishes, and look for Greenguard Gold certifications to address indoor air quality goals.

Wood shutters are often the most expensive but are a far better choice than outgassing and potentially hazardous vinyl shutters. Vinyl and polymer shutters are sometimes called "satinwood," "faux wood," or "composite," so request specific composition details from the manufacturer whenever the description is ambiguous. With the exception of shutters manufactured from a certified recycled wood product, these composites are basically plastics made from petroleum and other chemicals. They are not acceptable in a green home and may be irritants to those who are chemically sensitive.

BLINDS

Blinds, made from a variety of materials, are primarily intended to block out sunlight and provide privacy. Conventional venetian blinds are usually made from PVC-vinyl or metal. PVC-vinyl outgasses and poses significant health risks for workers and consumers. PVC-free alternative materials that meet third-party certifications like Greenguard Gold and C2C are available. Metal blinds can be troublesome because they may be statically charged and collect dust, which is irksome for those with allergies. Moreover, blinds made of metal are energy-inefficient because they conduct heat and cold, and collect moisture.

Bamboo, wood, and natural textiles are terrific choices for all types of blinds. Look for unfinished slats or those with low-VOC, no-odor finishes. Natural materials that are certified by the FSC or another third party are not commonly used in window blinds; the search is worth the extra effort if they can be found.

INSULATING, REFLECTIVE, AND BLACKOUT WINDOW TREATMENTS

In hot climates or where little shade exists, consider using a reflective textile or backing. The most environmentally benign and healthy options include natural textiles that are light-colored or have a reflective sheen. Less eco-friendly are reflective synthetics, such as Mylar, that are used as backings or liners. While they keep the heat and sun out of the house, they are manufactured from petroleum and other chemicals, negating some of the energy benefits overall. In addition, they are not at all breathable and will trap moisture.

Reflective textiles can be sandwiched between insulating layers in blinds or heavy draperies but may not be necessary if the fabrics are carefully chosen and specified to fit. Batting or heavy textiles are particularly effective in home temperature regulation, especially if the window treatment seals to the frame with the help of magnets, weights, or fasteners. Natural cotton, wool felt, and suede are more breathable and trap less moisture than synthetic backings while still providing a barrier to drafts, light, and harsh weather.

Other offerings that decrease the energy deficit are usually made with synthetic textiles—the environmental pros and cons should be evaluated with the client and weighed against the need for comfort and privacy. If home comfort is a serious issue and window replacement is not an option, synthetics may aid in lowering utility bills and improving the temperature within. Cellular or honeycomb shades trap air between the cells, controlling heat loss in the winter and solar gain in the summer. Triple-cell types offer the greatest barrier for heat and light, but double- and single- cell varieties are also available. Solar screens, another specialty window textile, allow for maximum visibility to the outside and diffuse harsh sunlight. Solar screens are available with PVC-free products, so specify them accordingly.

CONTROLS

The most environmentally sound way to regulate light and darkness, privacy, and heating and cooling is via manual controls. Window treatments should be adjustable so they can be opened and closed easily and maneuvered for subtle changes in light and glare control. This can be achieved through a multiple-layer system of sheer curtains, shades, and heavy draperies; with horizontal blinds that adjust manually; or by mechanical pulleys, levers, drawstrings, or sashes. The client will have eco-friendly, energy-efficient, all-natural window coverings that lower utility bills while keeping the temperature and light levels comfortable.

Consider the total impact of the manufacturing needed to make these specialty controls, built-in window shades, and electrical systems, along with the energy involved in shipping them and the electricity needed to run them. Then ask whether a manual curtain pull or control rod makes more sense.

HARDWARE

Consider the ease with which window treatments can be removed for cleaning before specifying the hardware for them. Some rods, rings, blind mechanisms, and drawstrings are difficult—or impossible—to detach and reattach.

Hardware for window treatments is usually made of metal (see "Metals," page 259), but may incorporate glass, ceramic, bamboo, wood, or other materials in the structure or decorative accents. Whenever possible, specify all-natural materials (such as wood or bamboo) or a high percentage of recycled content (as in metal or glass).

Local fabricators or metalworkers may be able to custom-make hardware to specifications and incorporate recycled steel from a minimill or other recycled metals. Specialty artisans might also make finials from salvaged items, recycled glass, or hand-thrown pottery.

Avoid finishes that emit VOCs as well as platings on metal. Specify low-toxic, durable finishes such as powder-coating on steel or natural beeswax on wood.

Where Does It Come From?

■ Window treatments and hardware are made from wood, bamboo, grasses and reeds, natural textiles, synthetic textiles, metal, vinyl, and other materials.

Maintenance

If made from porous textiles, the window covering may collect allergens, dust, and possible toxins. Ideally, the textiles should be easy to dust or vacuum, wipe clean, or launder with soap and water.

Reflective and specialty textiles are not usually washable; if they're part of a thermal system or blind, they may eventually inhibit the laundering of the other layers.

If the textiles require dry cleaning, they should be compatible with carbon dioxide methods that are easy on the environment; advise the client about any local eco-friendly dry cleaning outlets.

Where Does It Go?

Window treatments are rarely recycled into other materials, but you can often find used components at thrift stores. All-natural textiles, bamboo, and wood are biodegradable and, if the finishes are natural as well, can be composted or shredded. Synthetic window treatments, however, will remain in landfills indefinitely.

Spec List

Specify:
- Third-party certifications for wood products, organic content, and indoor air quality
- Window treatments that minimize heating and cooling needs
- Window treatments that can be manually opened, closed, and adjusted as the needs for privacy, lighting, and thermal comfort change
- All-natural materials and textiles such as wool, cotton, wood, bamboo, and grasses, preferably from sustainable or organic enterprises
- Window treatments that can be easily cleaned or laundered
- No dye or natural dyes on all textiles

- Inert, low-VOC metal finishes such as powder coating
- No finish or low-VOC, all-natural finishes on wood, bamboo, and reeds

Avoid:
- Synthetic materials
- Metal blinds
- PVC-vinyl
- Electronic controls, unless the window treatment is difficult to reach or too large to open manually
- Textile finishes such as stain repellents, waterproofing, and sizing
- Finishes on rods or blinds that emit VOCs or odors

RESOURCE

Window Coverings and Attachments. www.efficientwindowcoverings.org.

Accessories and Art

Accessories and art individualize a home. Because art and accessories are very personal, it's difficult to ensure they'll be eco-friendly. Try to guide the client in making

Figure 19.23 Living art piece provides a connection to nature, color, texture, and fresh air.

Photo and design by Debora Carl Landscape Design.

wise decisions about what to keep and what to purchase so that their life is enriched and the environment is not unduly harmed.

Artwork is chosen for its aesthetic appeal. We may think of art as an oil painting on the wall or a sculpture that graces the entryway. But the category of art can include a blanket, hand-thrown pottery, a particularly cherished photograph, or even a collage of vintage license plates. Like beauty, the value of art and accessories is in the eye of the beholder.

If these design elements are so personal, how can we as designers guide a client toward wise decisions about the accessories and art in an environmentally friendly home? The answer lies in values and guidelines, not specifications. By focusing on what is most important to the client, and by suggesting that frivolous or environmentally harmful purchases be rethought, the designer can help enhance the life of the client while improving the living space and tending the earth.

NEW ACCESSORIES AND ART

Ideally, an accessory or new work of art should be made from all-natural materials such as wood, clay, bone, rock, or another readily available resource. It's best if the resource is renewable, but if not, evaluate whether it might be recycled or reused at the end of its useful life. The piece should not emit VOCs or odors or otherwise be harmful to the occupants. Locally or domestically made objects lower the embodied energy by reducing on the shipping. These green basics apply equally to counter-tops and artworks.

Controversy With Trading Fairly: Two Perspectives

The World Fair Trade Organization (www.wfto.com) envisions a world in which trade structures and practices have been transformed to work in favor of the poor and promote sustainable development and justice.

Their mission is to enable producers to improve their livelihoods and communities through fair trade. WFTO will be the global network and advocate for fair trade, ensuring producer voices are heard. The interests of producers, especially small farmers and artisans, should be the main focus in all the policies, governance, structures, and decision making within the WFTO.

WFTO members are organizations differentiated by their 100 percent commitment to fair trade in an effort to eradicate poverty through sustainable economic development, pioneering social and environmental policy and practice, and continual reinvestment in marginalized artisans, farmers, and producer communities in some of the most fragile places on earth.

The goal of the WFTO is to enable small producers to improve their communities and make a better living through sustainable fair trade practices. It does this by delivering market access through policy, advocacy, campaigning, marketing, and monitoring

Fundamentally, the WFTO is a global community of pioneering and passionate change-makers responsible for the development of a sustainable fair trade economy for the good of us all.

Fair trade is for small farmers and small producers who are democratically organized. If you take the democracy out, you have traditional aid or world bank development, or what the TransFair USA and the European certifiers are now trying to call "fair trade". . . . If you want the fastest supply chain that produces the most tea or coffee or bananas at commercial terms you have entered into some socially responsible product world of which there are many examples. It just ain't fair trade, and it won't have the same positive benefits.

Rink Dickinson, Equal Exchange co-founder and co-director, during a speech he gave at a conference in October 2011 of the InterReligious Task Force on Central America.

Deep divisions in the fair trade movement have been simmering for a decade. The situation has at last reached a boiling point; without immediate action, we risk losing everything we have collectively built.

Fair trade is a way of doing business that aims to allow small farmers to remain an active part of the world marketplace and to empower consumers to make purchases that support their values. Fair Trade is a set of business practices voluntarily adopted by the producers and buyers of agricultural commodities and hand-made crafts designed to advance many economic, social, and environmental goals.

Ultimately, we need to decide for ourselves which organization and model to promote. Check out their principles at their websites.

Sources: World Fair Trade Organization, www.wfto.org; Equal Exchange, Fairly Traded, http://www.equalexchange.coop/fair-trade.

Frequently, foreign-made objects are desirable for their uniqueness and for the cultural messages they convey. Exercise caution when selecting them: In their quest to offer the best price, some companies in developing countries pay poverty wages or even enslave workers and force them to live and work in inhumane conditions. And when high output at the lowest cost is the ultimate goal, resources are stripped from the earth with little or no attention to environmental stewardship.

One way to counteract these alarming trends is to support fair trade organizations. The fair trade movement attempts to ensure decent working conditions and adequate pay for artisans and workers, especially in underdeveloped areas. These principles are especially important when considering the purchase of art and accessories, since many of these interior design elements are made abroad and where working conditions are difficult to determine.

Consider whether materials are eco-friendly and safe, whether their extraction or harvest has consumed natural resources (such as electricity or water) conservatively, whether they will have a long life span, and whether they will ultimately improve the client's home and lifestyle.

Rather than selecting a piece simply because it matches the décor, discuss its value with the client. Is it needed? Will it be used every day, or is it just for appearances? Will it still be beautiful and usable in five years? Ten? Are the materials all-natural? Is it made from components that can be recycled, or from materials that are fundamentally healthy? Where was it made? Were the workers treated fairly? Where does it come from and where will it go?

Many artists are devoted to the environment's well-being and choose mediums that are all-natural and least toxic and/or work with salvaged materials; approach your client with examples of such artists' work.

Finally, ensure that all accessories and art will be of enduring value. Avoid fads that quickly become outdated, and focus on things the client has always found beautiful and interesting. What inspires the client? What draws his eye or stimulates her mind? Are there materials, colors, or textures that bring the client a deeper appreciation of the earth? Determining what's most important to your client will ensure their enduring satisfaction with a piece of beautiful—and eco-friendly—art.

EXISTING ACCESSORIES AND ART

A client's possessions may not have been acquired with ecological sensibilities in mind. When evaluating a client's existing accessories and artwork, the environmental mantra, "Where does it come from and where does it go?" cannot be the only criteria. Value and function are key. Does the piece have a function or purpose in the home? Does it have lasting value? If the client can answer yes to either of these questions, then the accessory or art has a place. There's no need to consider getting rid of antiques, collectibles, useful accessories, or precious artwork if they are being used or enjoyed. Ultimately, it is environmentally friendly to appreciate what we already have.

Figure 19.24 *This kitchen features recycled glass tableware resting on solid cherry shelving. Also featured are unfinished honed-slate countertops.*

Photo by Laurie E. Dickson. Architect: Baker Laporte & Associates.

On the other hand, if the client owns things that have lived beyond their usefulness, either practically or aesthetically—especially if they are taking up valuable storage space or need ongoing resource-intensive maintenance—discuss where they might be donated, sold, or disposed of.

Thankfully, there is always a better place for an item than a crowded attic, basement, garage, or closet. Charitable organizations, thrift stores, garage sales,

> *Have nothing in your houses that you do not know to*
> *be useful or believe to be beautiful.*
> —WILLIAM MORRIS, 1882

and online auctions are all splendid places to find homes for still-usable household items. It is a sound ecological principle to find uses for unused things and homes for items where they will be appreciated. If the objects in question are beyond repair, encourage the client to disassemble all the parts and recycle as many as possible.

Where Does It Come From?

- Art and accessories can be made from virtually any material.
- Ideally, a green home should focus on art and accessories that are natural, healthy, environmentally sustaining, and biodegradable—or, at the very least, so valuable and beautiful that they will never be thrown away.
- Articles purchased from abroad should have been made under the umbrella of fair trade guidelines.

Installation and Maintenance

Assist in finding ways to best display possessions such as collectibles, heirlooms, and art that will conserve and preserve them. Protect paintings, antiques, textiles, delicate collections, and similar items to last indefinitely. This will provide years of satisfaction to the client and even to future generations and, ultimately, prevent waste.

Figure 19.25 These pillows were made from reclaimed flour sacks.

Photo courtesy of Heiberg Cummings Design, www.Hcd3.com.

Choose proper framing, display, and conservation techniques appropriate to the needs of a piece or collection. For old photos, framed art, and other two-dimensional objects, specify protective frames and matting that are acid-free (often called "conservation grade" or "museum grade"). If the piece is especially fragile or valuable, specify that all components that touch it be dye-free; even natural dyes or colorants that come in contact with paper can cause deterioration over time. Some frames and mattings may contain recycled paper or wood. If the criteria for preservation can be met, then using these recycled-content materials is a bonus for the environment.

It might be best to display some collections, antiques, sculpture, or two-dimensional art under glass, where they will be safe from dust and grime. Specify UV-protective glass to minimize fading from sunshine and artificial light.

Textiles and paper usually require very specific methods of conservation. If the art or accessory needs care beyond the scope of interior design, consult an art or history museum to find conservation specialists who can be of assistance.

Where Does It Go?

Where will this accessory or piece of art be in a few years, a decade, or even a century? Items that have short life spans—a trend that will soon be outdated, components that will wear out, or collections that will be outgrown—are not fundamentally wise choices for the environment. Select items whose value will endure.

Figure 19.26 This bedroom features several antiques, including a wooden bowl and spurs. The rug is made of naturally dyed wool; its design is based on a traditional Navajo design. The bed's headboard, footboard, and side rails were handcrafted by a local artisan.

Photo by David O. Marlow. Designed by Associates III, www.associates3.com.

Whenever possible, specify all-natural materials that biodegrade or that can be recycled, especially for accessories with shorter life cycles.

Spec List

For existing accessories and art

Specify:

- Accessories that are regularly appreciated and used
- Collectibles, heirlooms, memorabilia, and art that are appreciated or cherished

Avoid

- Accessories that are never used
- Accessories or art that are not appreciated or cherished (i.e., they are in storage and will continue to be) or that might be better appreciated by someone else
- Items that take up valuable space in the home that is needed for another purpose
- Objects that require maintenance or cleaning beyond their value to the client

For new accessories and art

Specify:

- All-natural materials
- Recycled materials
- Materials that are safe, not harmful
- Materials that won't harm the environment
- Accessories that are long-lasting and durable
- Art and accessories that will still be valuable to the client many years from now

Avoid:

- Manufactured, synthetic, or chemically derived materials
- Materials that outgas VOCs, emit odors, or are unsafe for use within a home
- Materials that harm the environment, either through manufacturing or upon disposal
- Trends, fashions, and impulses

green business development

Business is the only mechanism on the planet today powerful enough to produce the changes necessary to reverse global environmental and social degradation.

—Paul Hawken

An effective marketing effort incorporates relationship-building, networking, speaking, writing, and sharing successful projects, along with focusing on specific target markets and value-bonding with clients. These efforts are no different as you move into the realm of marketing sustainable design services.

The commitment to healthy, high-performing, and intelligent design, both individually and as a firm, provides even greater potential to serve clients and establishes you as a leading-edge interior designer. Consider this: Who doesn't want a healthy environment in which to live and work while contributing to the well-being of the planet and its future generations? Hold this thought uppermost in your mind while greening your marketing efforts.

Jerry Yudelson, PE, LEED Fellow, writing in *Marketing Green Building Services: Strategies for Success* (Burlington, MA: Architectural Press, 2008) outlines how sustainable design and construction firms should think about green marketing. He notes that many firms now have the experience of successful projects to back up their marketing claims for sustainable design and construction.

What Should Be the Green Marketing Strategy for Leading Firms?

Budgets. Building is still about meeting budgets *and* expectations for high-performance sustainable design outcomes. Now you need to prove that you can design such projects on a conventional budget. The new normal is "frugal green": clients expect high-performance outcomes on conventional budgets.

Performance. Do your projects actually perform as predicted? Is there a high level of occupant satisfaction? Does the project's energy modeling actually come close to predicting energy use?

Innovation. How readily have your project innovations become mainstream applications? Do you have a signature approach to design you can readily articulate that actually brings innovation to a project and makes it work?

Beyond green. There's obviously more to buildings than just the Leadership in Energy and Environmental Design (LEED) or sustainable elements. How well does daylighting facilitate the building's purposes, for example? Do your projects incorporate new ways to work so that they minimize building area (and thus cost)?

Regenerative buildings. Are you designing and building with an eye to the future, a time when all buildings will have to meet Living

Relationship Building

Your internal team is vital to success on the road to sustainability. This is a journey, not a destination; by building a strong company commitment to responsible design and business practices, you can grow into a sustainable firm. It is important to garner support and buy-in from your internal team—make a major commitment to sustainability at all levels of your business.

Nurture, encourage and support your team to learn all they can about sustainable principles and practices, as they are among your greatest environmental advocates. Take time for training; complement professional continuing education with a consistent in-house program focused on learning objectives that address healthy, sustainable interiors. Provide the resources to attend green conferences and promote professional advancement, including LEED Green Associate and LEED Accredited Professional designations. Encourage your environmental champions to share their knowledge with both internal and external teams. If your team feels

Building Challenge (LBC) prerequisites and Architecture 2030 requirements? How many projects have you completed that are zero-net-energy, LBC or "max green" in all respects?

Indoor environmental quality. Ultimately, buildings are for users. How well are you documenting avoidance of Red List and Chemicals of Concern materials?

Talk is cheap (but essential). Are you and your key firm members active, regular, and forceful champions of sustainable design and construction? Are you recognized as someone who knows more than the rest of the firms about these topics? What is your publishing, speaking, social media and Facebook exposure, for the firm and for each project? Have you written a book about your firm's approach, especially if you're *not* an architect?

Existing buildings. Clearly the action in green buildings has shifted to the existing building market. Renovation and reconstruction present radically different challenges than new construction. What are you doing to burnish your credentials in this rapidly growing market? Do you have a marketing plan for addressing high-level green renovation, refurbishment, and remodeling projects?

Source: Jerry Yudelson, http://www.triplepundit.com/2012/07/10-marketing-tips-address-green-buildings-new-expectations/.

confident and understands that green building adds value to their projects, they will enthusiastically embrace helpful tools in moving forward.

With clients, architects, and contractors, reinforce these principles and strategies so that your passion for, and expertise in, sustainable design become the firm's key identifiable characteristics. Seek out like-minded team players who share a sustainable vision. The prospect of professionals coming together with a common vision opens doors to work on projects that are innovative and exciting—the basis of relationship-building.

Center your initial efforts on past, current, and potential project team members. As you begin to solicit work, identify those who also care about the environment. Together, you can seek out collaborative opportunities and engage well-trained and knowledgeable people for your project teams.

Designers who already have close working relationships with clients, architects, contractors, and other project professionals will have more success in greening their projects. Being an integral member of the team will ensure that your designs will get built on budget and on time, utilizing appropriate technology and meeting project goals.

Positioned as thoughtful environmental leaders within the industry, our clients will regard us, in our role as their interior design consultants, as trusted business professionals. You can tangibly demonstrate the ways that home environments impact health and quality of life by meeting their basic needs and exceeding their expectations. As your company's culture matures and each firm member more fully embodies sustainable values, external branding will further demonstrate your commitment to the health, safety, and welfare of your clients. Through gained expertise and a growing passion, and by creating a composed and credible presence, clients will want to connect with you and forge deeper and more productive relationships.

Networking

What is networking all about? Networking refers to an extended group of people with similar interests or concerns who interact and remain in informal contact for mutual assistance or support. Build these relationships authentically; by engaging with your community genuinely—whether through projects, volunteerism, or sharing knowledge—you build long-lasting relationships.

Networking is inherent to life. We meet people daily at work, home, school, events—even when commuting. We are constantly interacting with and helping each other. Networking opens the doors to amazing connections, opportunities, and experiences. Consider the inspiring and passionate individuals you've met at events, volunteering, on projects, or through social media. Whether you are seeking clients, a mentor, professional development, diversity, or promoting a cause, nurture this social capital. Think about your network as a set of circular connections—your family and friends, professional colleagues, fellow volunteers, alumni associations, event and conference attendees, and project team members, to name a few.

By being a resource to your network you support your community, giving without expectation. Ask "What can I do to help you?" first. Listen attentively to others' needs and stories, and respond accordingly. This will build your reputation as a good listener, adding greater integrity to your personal brand. Good karma returns to you when you help others sincerely.

Recognize the value you provide through your professional and personal brand and fully understand what you bring to the table. Think about the three e's—your energy, enthusiasm, and experience—and how they show others who you are. Consider how you engage in conversations—approach with a warm, grounded presence, and speak clearly. What are the open-ended questions you plan to ask to engage the listener? As the conversation wraps up, communicate your next steps and repeat back actionable items. From there, take action and follow up on the commitments you've made.

Follow-up is critical to effective networking and making a lasting impression. When you exchange business cards, be the one to send a personalized "It was great to meet you!" note or e-mail. This will enhance your relationship and leave the door open for future business.

- Approach your connections with a respectful, genuine, positive, and reciprocal approach.
- Take time to connect at educational and social events, then meet one-on-one to share information.
- Follow your passion and volunteer for an organization that aligns with your values and goals—a wonderful way to meet like-minded people.
- Participate in professional social media platforms by asking and answering questions and sharing thought-provoking dialogue to spark interest in you and your business.
- Enjoy meaningful interactions and focus first on what you can offer to others.

Think about how you can quickly communicate your specific value, what you offer, and the ultimate outcome you are looking for. Tailor your message to your audience—be aware of your terminology and delivery style, and communicate the benefits of working with you. Be authentic, using your emotional intelligence to make a positive impression. By paying attention to nonverbal cues, you can gauge the needs of the audience and adjust accordingly—Should I keep chatting? Is it time to make a graceful exit?

What opportunities do you have to pay it forward? Pay attention and be helpful. Sending thank-you cards to those who helped you with your new opportunity reminds them that you continue to be a resource for them. Form partnerships and collaborate with members of your network, and ask to be introduced to new people.

Next, begin sharing and exhibiting your commitment and passion for the welfare of others and for the environment. Network by joining organizations with aligned values. The American Society of Interior Designers (ASID), the International Interior Design Association (IIDA), the American Institute of Architects (AIA), the U.S. Green Building Council (USGBC), and Architects/Designers/Planners for Social Responsibility (ADPSR) are professional organizations in the building industry that incorporate sustainability into their core values. Our role as environmental stewards within the building industry has become paramount to a growing number of organizations where ecological accountability is a primary tenet of their mission.

ASID has a sustainable design section in the knowledge center on its website where you can find information on sustainability and green design. You will also find links to other online resources (www.asid.org).

IIDA established the foundation's Sustainable Design Education (SDE) Fund to offer IIDA members an opportunity to apply for financial support to further their knowledge of and to increase environmental awareness about the importance and effects of sustainable design in everyday life. IIDA members who

Emotional Intelligence (EQ)

Emotional intelligence is the capacity to be aware of, control, and express one's emotions, and the ability to handle interpersonal relationships judiciously and empathetically. Emotional intelligence (EQ) is the ability to identify, use, understand, and manage emotions in positive ways to relieve stress, communicate effectively, empathize with others, overcome challenges, and defuse conflict. Emotional intelligence impacts many different aspects of your daily life, such as the way you behave and the way you interact with others.

If you have high emotional intelligence, you are able to recognize your own emotional state and the emotional states of others and engage with others in a way that draws them to you. You can use this understanding of emotions to relate better to other people, form healthier relationships, achieve greater success at work, and lead a more fulfilling life.

Emotional intelligence consists of four attributes:

1. Self-awareness. You recognize your own emotions and how they affect your thoughts and behavior; you know your strengths and weaknesses; and you are self-confident.

2. Self-management. You're able to control impulsive feelings and behaviors, manage your emotions in healthy ways, take initiative, follow through on commitments, and adapt to changing circumstances.

3. Social awareness. You can understand the emotions, needs, and concerns of others, pick up on emotional cues, feel comfortable socially, and recognize the power dynamics in a group or organization.

4. Relationship management. You know how to develop and maintain good relationships, communicate clearly, inspire and influence others, work well in a team, and manage conflict.

Why is EQ so important? As we know, it's not the smartest people who are the most successful or the most fulfilled in life. You probably know people who are academically brilliant but socially inept and unsuccessful at work or in their personal relationships. Intellectual intelligence (IQ) on its own isn't enough to be successful in life. Yes, your IQ can help you get into college, but it's your EQ that will help you manage the stress and emotions when facing your final exams.

Source: www.helpguide.org/mental/eq5_raising_emotional_intelligence.htm.

pass the LEED Accredited Professional Exam can apply for tuition reimbursement from the SDE Fund.

The AIA Committee on the Environment (AIA-COTE) works to advance, disseminate, and advocate to the architectural profession, the building industry, the academy, and the public those design practices that integrate built and natural systems and enhance both the design quality and environmental performance of the built environment. In September 2013, the AIA board announced four sustainability priorities; these include two issues central to architecture and two emerging areas where architects can contribute to a better environment for current and future generations[1]:

Core issues

Energy. Drive building energy efficiency and the use of renewable energy toward meeting the AIA 2030 goals of achieving net-zero energy in buildings.

Materials. Equip architects to make informed decisions about material selections based on full life-cycle and health-related criteria.

Emerging issues

Design and health. Play an active role in improving human health and wellness through the design of the built environment.

Resilience. Promote design that adapts to changing conditions and that maintains or regains functionality and vitality in the face of natural and man-made disturbances.

The USGBC is the nation's foremost coalition of leaders from across the building industry working to promote buildings that are environmentally responsible, profitable, and healthy places to live and work, thereby producing a new generation of high-performance buildings inside and out. Through its LEED products and resources, its annual Greenbuild International Conference and Expo, policy guidance, and educational and marketing tools that support the adoption of sustainable building, USGBC forges strategic alliances with key industry and research organizations and federal, state, and local government agencies to transform the built environment.

ADPSR works for peace, environmental protection, ecological building, social justice, and the development of healthy communities. Its members believe that design practitioners have a significant role to play in the well-being of our communities.

The goals of ADPSR's programs are to:

- Raise professional and public awareness of critical social and environmental issues.

- Further responsive design and planning.

- Honor persons and organizations whose work exemplifies social responsibility.

---

[1] http://www.aia.org/aiaucmp/groups/aia/documents/pdf/aiab100279.pdf.

Many of the building industry organizations and design associations recognize the importance of educating design professionals in the theory and practice of sustainable design. They are committed to promoting informed environmental responsibility throughout the industry. We are living in a world with limited natural resources that are being squandered. By committing to environmental responsibility and viewing their practices through an environmental filter, credible organizations have dedicated themselves to making a positive difference.

In addition, there are countless citizen organizations, among them the National Resources Defense Council (NRDC), the Sierra Club, and Friends of the Earth, that provide knowledge, resources, inspiration, and relevant information on environmental issues.

- Get to know other professionals in your area with a similar vision and passion for green design.
- Contact manufacturers and encourage them to share information on their environmentally friendly products with you.
- Align yourself with similarly focused architects and contractors, exchange experiences over brown-bag lunches, and invite them to join a green training program.

This is a way to rally potential project players *before* a project goes live. Work together to design ecologically oriented architecture and interiors that celebrate your region's vernacular.

Target Markets

Aligning yourself with like-minded professionals is a launching pad for attracting clients. Your commitment to sustainability, critical thinking skills, foundation of knowledge, research strategies, and technological savvy will enable you to market yourself and to meet the sustainability needs of your future clients.

You have become confident that your design solutions will contribute to a sustainable future. By incorporating designs that reduce waste and by using products that are environmentally friendly, your work will begin to show the results and benefits of ecologically appropriate design solutions. See yourself as an expert educated and trained to safeguard the health and welfare of people and the planet in the life-supporting environments you design. Take on the responsibility of green design leadership and embrace the societal need for safer materials, and your design solutions will contribute to a sustainable future.

As interior designers, we bring to fruition the interface between people and buildings; we play a vital role in creating quality indoor environments. Building on your qualifications, project experience, and passion for the work, carve out your area of specialization and capitalize on the importance of your role within the building industry.

To fine-tune your target markets, focus on your potential clients' expressed and unexpressed needs. Define who your customers are in order to effectively focus your marketing efforts. Once you have identified your market focus, craft your message to include what you have to offer and your value proposition.

Maybe you are aiming for a specific niche of the market. For residential interiors, there are many such markets: project location or community; age, gender, education and income level; new or renovated homes; health and/or eco-conscious values; current networks and past clients. The various channels to reach your target markets vary and may include contractors, architects, real estate agents, landlords, and others in the home building industry.

Increased market competition necessitates differentiation and innovation and demands a specific and strategic course of action. There is no one competitive response to the green building market that rings true for every firm; your marketing must instead focus on the intention of your mission, your specific and special capabilities, and the culture of your firm.

Market Differentiation

Offering green design services will encourage potential clients to think about the broader environment and can bring you clients already aligned with your message. Emphasize that green does not necessarily cost more and can often save money in the long run. Marketing green provides unique opportunities by distinguishing your company from others and can establish it as expert in a new arena.

Create a distinction by building on your unique qualities, thereby differentiating yourself from others. Think of yourself as the leading-edge firm in your area specializing in green design. This may initially limit your market, but it will sharply delineate you to buyers seeking that essential quality when searching for an interior designer for their projects.

Or focus on healthy, sustainable design solutions. If you mention health benefits to potential clients, they will almost always express interest in hearing more. Who does not want a healthy, eco-friendly home for their family and future generations, one that saves energy and uses resources responsibly? This will encourage discussion about the client's wants and needs and reframe his or her thinking regarding return on investment.

Authenticity is imperative in marketing your services; it preserves the integrity of the design industry and honors firms who invest in sustainability through education, by achieving professional designations, and by meeting testing protocols. Represent your abilities credibly and avoid greenwashing, or making false claims about being environmentally responsible solely to bolster your brand rather than by the honest practice of sustainable design.

Innovation Benefits

Innovation is a key component to any thriving design practice. Clients hire you for your unique vision, so identify and communicate your originality in your marketing tools and messaging. Green concepts—such as energy efficiency, improved indoor air quality, environmentally preferable products, higher durability and lower maintenance materials, and resource conservation—while easy to describe, do not necessarily address all of your clients' needs. Assemble a story linking these concepts with the core values and needs of your target market.

What can you give to your clients to provide a positive experience throughout the process? Design is an unfolding journey, and ultimately, your job is to reflect the clients' wishes. Creating a home is a deeply satisfying, emotional experience, that when successful bonds together everyone involved and provides lasting memories. By slowly unveiling itself, a story materializes and unfolds.

Your greatest resource for building a sustaining business practice is success with your past clients. They hold the key to your future—they spread the word about you and return with new projects. Your creativity is your value, in particular when the home integrates healthy and environmentally responsible solutions.

Strategic Action Plan

Differentiate yourself clearly. Choose strategically which markets to compete in, which to stay away from, and which clients you desire.

When sharing your brand, consider the following strategies to grow your firm, embracing sustainability as a core value and demonstrating how it permeates each level of the design process:

- Create specialized marketing materials.
- Craft a new division.
- Hire outside experts.
- Be the green expert in your region.
- Target regional versus national clients, or vice versa.
- Define ideal client types and projects.
- Seek out clients who value sustainability.
- Commit to improving indoor air quality on all projects.
- Develop a cost-competitive approach.
- Consider giving a discount to truly green clients.

Incorporate sustainable solutions in your standard design procedures so that the client need not pay higher fees for sustainable design. Keeping operational costs low will give a firm pricing flexibility. Budgets are tight; the ability to compete on price is essential. A firm that is good at managing the process of integrated design is able to design a green home at the same fee as a conventional project. Lowering costs might be even more important than branding for competing in the marketplace, although it does take commitment and discipline to manage a project within tight budgets.

Outline the techniques necessary to successfully complete green projects without additional design fees. Take time to attend training sessions and seminars and acquire new information as you stay current with design trends. Consider absorbing the extra time that it may take to become a knowledgeable green designer; it will be worth the investment. Despite the up-front costs and learning curve, it will benefit you and your firm in the long term.

Clients respond to:

- *Energy cost savings*. Clients want to save energy, save money, save resources.
- *Health of the planet*. Clients want to do their part to restore the health of the planet.
- *Healthier environment*. Clients want better quality of light, improved ventilation, and healthier indoor air quality to improve their quality of life and rejuvenate themselves and their families.
- *Increased property values*. Clients are interested in a green home that adds value to their home.

Outreach

Sharing your expertise in sustainability is an effective way to establish a strong presence in the marketplace. Speaking, lecturing, networking, writing articles, getting publicity, and winning awards for successful projects enhance the firm's visibility, reaffirming and highlighting your green message.

The green building community brings together a diverse group of professionals who are both passionate and inclusive, often willing to give of their time and to share their ideas. Sharing successes and supporting one another through the challenges related to eco-friendly design is good for business.

Teach other project professionals about the need for sustainable solutions. Get to know and recommend green experts in related fields, such as mechanical, electrical, and lighting consultants. Offer to share knowledge and experiences with contractors and subcontractors. Discuss how to improve health conditions on the job site by using low-emitting products. Encourage environmentally friendly practices in the field.

Trusted experts who share their knowledge with others transform our market. Both word of mouth and photos in publications spur interest in sustainable design.

As with the fashion industry, the tipping point for green buildings will happen more quickly through the combined actions of well-respected design industry professionals. Such individuals, who have the ability, influence, and experience to inspire through compelling success stories will spread their vision of a sustaining building industry.

Establish yourself as a credible resource within the interior design community and beyond by communicating your knowledge, practices, and values to others. Question conventional processes, methods, and products and encourage the application of environmental principles and practices on all projects, using guiding tools such as LEED for Homes, the trademarked Green Building Rating System developed by the U.S. Green Building Council, and comparable sustainable homebuilding programs.

Promote responsible design in the building industry. Inspire and engage others in green design conversations, establishing a lasting green image of your firm. By modeling and educating the external team on sustaining practices and materials, you can become the sought-after expert in your area.

LEED for Homes

According to the U.S. Green Building Council (www.usgbc.org), the LEED for Homes rating systems provides the following benefits to homeowners:

- *Health*. LEED-certified homes are designed to maximize fresh air indoors and minimize exposure to airborne toxins and pollutants.

- *Savings*. They are designed to save costly resources—energy and water. On average, LEED-certified homes use 20 to 30 percent less, with some homes reporting up to 60 percent less energy use than a home merely built to code. *Trusted*. They are third-party inspected, performance-tested, and certified to perform better than a conventional home.

- *Value*. Green homes can be built for the same cost as conventional homes, and they resell for more money in less time than traditional homes.

Making this happen for your project just takes proper planning.

Source: USGBC LEED for Homes Rating System, http://www.usgbc.org/leed/rating-systems/homes.

Sharing Successful Projects

If you do good work, you'll establish yourself in the marketplace. As part of your approach, consider developing internal tools that measure sustainability. Refer to our several checklists for help in developing your own metrics for quantifying the success of your green projects.

Sharing success stories about your projects is one of the best vehicles to promote and celebrate your firm's commitment to sustainability. Stories about what worked—and what didn't work—capture people's attention. By sharing this information, your credibility will grow with both current and potential clients. Every time the story of a project is published or showcased, the industry becomes more aware not only of the latest green developments but also of your expertise, demonstrating to clients that you can be trusted with their next project.

Provide case study information by presenting your projects at design conferences and publishing articles in trade magazines. Submit projects to sustainable design competitions now being held by most design organizations and eco-magazines. Your efforts will further influence market transformation and provide additional credibility for your firm.

Green Building Outlook Strong

Green building is a bright spot in a still uncertain economy. Green designs and renovations made up 20 percent of the residential market in 2012 and that market share is predicted to increase to 38 percent by 2016. Green commercial and institutional construction is expected to represent 55 percent of the entire market by 2016. In 2013, a 22 to 25 percent market share by value in the residential market was expected; this equates to a $34 to $38 billion opportunity within the industry. By 2016, this share by value is expected to increase to 29 to 38 percent—an estimated $89-$116 billion—based on the current single-family residential construction forecast. The value of green building grew from $10 billion in 2005 to $78 billion in 2011. In 2013, overall new green building was projected to rise to between $98 billion and $106 billion. By 2016, this number is expected to reach $204 billion to $248 billion.

In addition:

- Health-related green building labels are taking precedence in construction specifications, growing more rapidly than any other aspect of green.

- One third of all homebuilders in the United States expect to be fully dedicated to building green by 2016.

- Green construction jobs are following the green building market; 35 percent of those who work in that industry have green jobs today.

- Eighty-one percent of executive leaders in corporate America believe the public expects them to adopt and implement sustainability—one of the key forces driving corporations to institutionalize green philosophies. Thirty percent of senior executive officers report that they are greening two-thirds of the buildings in their portfolio—with 47 percent expecting to do so by 2015.

A green building is defined as one built to LEED or an equivalent standard, or one that is energy- and water-efficient that also addresses improved indoor environmental quality and/or resource efficiency.

Source: McGraw-Hill Construction's "2013 Dodge Construction Green Outlook," www.construction.com/about-us/press/green-building-outlook-strong-for-both-non-residential-and-residential.asp.

Cost Considerations

Clients may resist green projects because they believe that green projects cost more. Having clear, accessible information that demonstrates otherwise is essential.

Although some costs may be higher for more energy-efficient HVAC systems and appliances, energy- and water-conserving construction, and healthier, non-toxic, and environmentally friendly building materials, studies in the commercial sector are available to prove that an integrated design approach can minimize any increases—and that often there are none to minimize.

Find out whether the project is in an area where local or state agencies are giving significant tax rebates and credits for going green. These incentives encourage development and construction of smarter, more sustainable homes and communities, help conserve undeveloped land, reduce air and water pollution, improve public health, reduce traffic congestion, ensure more efficient water usage, and reduce energy bills and transportation costs.

Remind the client that green building and environmental benefits will add value to their home in the long run. Green or energy-efficient homes generally command a higher selling price, a tangible return on investment. Incorporating green features such as long-lasting materials, energy savings, and lower maintenance and costs of operation also saves money year by year over the lifetime of the home. Concerns

Commitment to Green

Here are some of the advantages to green design that will help convince a client that green is the right way to go:

- Save money and resources by saving energy.
- Be energy-independent.
- Use your home as a net energy exporter (producing more energy than the home demands).
- Build to last with low maintenance.
- Save money and resources by using fewer building materials.
- Drive the market for green building.
- Create healthy living environments for your family.
- Reduce your personal impact on the community and planet.
- Be a good neighbor.
- Become more self-sufficient.
- Live in harmony with your beliefs.
- Set an example for others.
- Use local materials and labor to support local economy.

Source: Angela Dean, AIA, LEED AP, *Green by Design* (Salt Lake City, UT: Gibbs Smith, 2003).

about health and well-being are still the best way to connect with clients about green design. Remind them that their family will benefit from a healthier home through improved ventilation and indoor air quality as well as less toxic finishes and materials—that good health is priceless.

Value Bonding

What motivates and interests your client? Interior designers have a responsibility to educate clients about the need to build responsibly. Meet the needs of your clients by understanding their personal values and principles. Tell them that sustainable design fundamentally makes better buildings by improving performance, saving money, and improving health. Better still, bond with your clients over mutual values. What are the reasons your client wants a green home? They might include one or more or all of the following:

- Meeting family's needs and desires
- Embracing or exemplifying environmental stewardship and responsibility
- Creating ambience and feeling of home
- Doing the right thing
- Saving water and energy
- Having healthy indoor air quality
- Using recycled, salvaged, renewable, and sustainable materials
- Protecting natural resources
- Ensuring a healthy home for the family
- Showing concern for climate change
- Desiring a green building certification
- Saving on operating costs
- Enhancing quality of life
- Accessing outdoor activities
- Addressing health issues or chemical sensitivities
- Protecting natural habitats.
- Saving money

In 2012, the Earth Advantage Institute assembled their top green building priorities for the residential market specific to homebuyers and owners:

- *Urban infill and density*. Both younger people and empty nesters are choosing urban dwellings with easy access to cultural activities, mass transit, more sustainable lifestyles, and other like-minded people.
- *Green multifamily homes*. There has been an increase in multifamily green building certifications nationally. Building owners and operators focus on energy-efficiency savings. In 2011 alone there was a 17 percent uptick in multifamily homes.[2]
- *Energy upgrades*. Priorities for home buyers include smaller homes and reduced energy use. Builders are capitalizing on energy upgrade work, providing energy audit and residential retrofit services.
- *Performance testing*. Universities and national labs are partnering with builders to research the performance of new energy systems, materials, and equipment.

---

[2] McGraw-Hill Construction, "2013 Dodge Construction Green Outlook." www.construction.com/about-us/press/green-building-outlook-strong-for-both-non-residential-and-residential.asp.

- *Energy tracking.* Energy-use monitors make it possible for homeowners to track the energy and water use of their appliances and systems. These easy-to-use devices are readily available, change behavior, and help save money.

- *Marketing transparency.* Consumers are more informed because they have access to information on the Internet that allows them to distinguish between greenwashing claims and green facts. *Accurate appraisals.* The industry is greening the multiple listing service (MLS), and appraisers' drive-by assessments are a thing of the past. Buyers and sellers can also request a green-certified appraiser (Certified Residential Green Appraiser) through their bank. Bringing lenders into the green conversation helps them understand the value-added benefits and return on investment offered by new green-certified homes and remodels.

- *Energy ratings.* Energy labeling systems provide an estimate of a home's energy consumption to homebuyers and homeowners. The U.S. Department of Energy's Home Energy Score and the Energy Performance Score are available in different climate zones across the United States to encourage homeowners to compare energy usage and undertake energy upgrade work.

Marketing demographers speak of "cultural creatives," a segment of the population that is educated, affluent, and ready to act on their social, environmental, and spiritual values. They care deeply about ecology, about saving the planet, about relationships, and about peace and social justice. They seek authenticity, are self-actualized, and genuinely mindful of spirituality and self-expression. Significantly, at least 60 percent of cultural creatives are women. (For more information, see Paul Ray and Sherry Andersons' *Cultural Creatives: How 50 Million People are Changing the World* [New York: Three Rivers, 2000]).

The cultural creatives market is bigger and stronger than many realize, comprising a quarter of the population of the United States and Europe. That's a lot of people interested in integrating core values into their purchasing and investment decisions. Thus, businesses incorporating social and environmental relevance into their values are uniquely positioned to cater to this sector.

The majority of cultural creatives, who range in age from eighteen to seventy, are not looking for absolutes; they are seeking sound alternatives that resonate with them and demonstrate their values. They are mainstream, grounded, reasonable individuals, both liberal and conservative, working class and affluent, and members of all ethnic groups.

They represent a vast market potential for companies that integrate sustainable design into their practices. The cultural creatives are ecology minded and eager to learn about environmentally conscious services and products. It will literally pay to align your firm with this sector of the marketplace that values a healthy, sustainable lifestyle.

The industry that serves these consumers has been identified in a research report by the Natural Marketing Institute, which designates it as "lifestyles of health and sustainability, or LOHAS—a market conservatively estimated at $290 billion in the United States, and growing. Areas of spending include:

- *Green building:* Certified homes, Energy Star appliances, green materials, valued at $100 billion.

- *Personal health:* Natural and organic foods, personal care, supplements, and so on, valued at $117 billion.

- Eco-tourism: Nature-seeking excursions valued at $42 billion.

- *Alternative transportation:* Hybrid cars, electric vehicles, and car sharing valued at $20 billion.

- *Natural lifestyles:* Natural home interior and exterior furnishings, fabrics, and apparel valued at $10 billion.

- *Alternative energy:* Renewable power valued at $709 million.

Marketing that incorporates social equality and environmentalism can win clients from among the cultural creatives by value bonding with individuals who are reframing their life and values and want to walk their talk. They are practical individuals looking for ways to integrate their core values into every purchasing decision they make—including decisions about home design. By embracing the tenets of sustainability, you will be aligning yourself with countless others whose values define their work and lifestyle, and you will come to fully appreciate how effective you can be as a driving force of change through your sustainable design services.

Resources

Built Green. www.builtgreen.net.

"Green Building, Remodeling, and Development." National Association of Home Builders. www.nahbgreen.org.

Green Home Guide. www.greenhomeguide.com.

Green MLS Toolkit. http://www.greenthemls.org/.

Green Resource Council. http://www.greenresourcecouncil.org/green-resource-council-info/greening-mls.

"LOHAS Market Size." Natural Marketing Institute. 2008. http://www.lohas.com/sites/default/files/lohasmarketsize.pdf.

Marketing Green Building Services: Strategies for Success. Jerry Yudelson. Burlington, MA: Architectural Press, 2008.

Think Progress/Climate Progress. http://thinkprogress.org/climate/2012/01/19/407379/top-10-residential-green-building-trends-to-watch-in-2012/.

CHAPTER 21

sustaining life

Figure 21.1 This truth window offers insight into a strawbale wall.

Photo by Doug Graybeal. Architect: Doug Graybeal.

We might peer into the future at the generations yet unborn and ask ourselves if we're really trustworthy custodians of their heritage. Do we have the right to tell them that they can never see a whale?
—DAVID R. BROWER

We are instinctively passionate about our beautiful blue planet, knowing that there is only one Earth that sustains all life. We can see that there is a gap between our values and the condition of the world, and that inspires us to action. The journey to narrow this gap between our values and the state of the environment begins to close as we become more involved in questioning the way we live and the way we work.

We have come full circle to the question we asked as we set out: Why be sustainable? Whether we realize it or not, the health of our planet is important to every one of us; how each of us responds to the challenges ahead will differ.

Questioning the Status Quo

The only real voyage of discovery exists, not in seeing new landscapes, but in having new eyes.

—Marcel Proust

How does change begin? Does it come from a longing and a willingness to reconcile something that is not making sense—from a deep desire to create, to look at a situation from a new, fresh perspective? We are continually inspired by extraordinary individuals who ask penetrating questions and cause real change. They reframe issues and provide fresh viewpoints, and their brilliance is that they challenge the assumptions of conventional thinking and the status quo. (For inspiration from cutting edge thought leaders, see chapter 22, "What's Next?")

What was Rachel Carson saying?

Keep pollution out of your backyard? No. She was saying that we were beginning to see the death of nature. Carson's *Silent Spring*, which in 1962 exposed the hazards of the pesticide DDT, eloquently questioned humanity's faith in technological progress and helped set the stage for the environmental movement.

What are Paul Hawken, Amory Lovins, and Hunter Lovins saying?

Bring an end to human economic activity because it is exceeding the planet's limits? No. Rather, in their groundbreaking book, *Natural Capitalism: Creating the Next Industrial Revolution* (New York: Back Bay, 2000), they reframed ways of doing business. This was the first book to explore the lucrative opportunities for businesses to transform themselves in an era of approaching our planet's environmental limits. Although we have been extending those limits with clever new technologies, living systems remain undeniably in decline.

These seemingly mutually exclusive trends need not be in conflict—in fact, there are opportunities and fortunes to be made in reconciling them. In their revolutionary blueprint for a new economy, these three business visionaries explain how the world is on the verge of a new industrial revolution—one that promises to transform our fundamental notions about commerce and its role in shaping our future. *Natural Capitalism* describes a future in which business and environmental interests increasingly overlap, and in which businesses can better satisfy their customers' needs, increase profits, and help solve environmental problems, all at the same time.

"Natural capital" refers to the natural resources and ecosystem services that make possible all economic activity—indeed, all life. These services are of immense economic value; some are literally priceless, as they have no known substitutes. Yet current business practices typically fail to take into account the value of these assets—which is rising with their scarcity. As a result, natural capital is being degraded and liquidated by the wasteful use of such resources as energy, materials, water, fiber, and topsoil.[1]

What are William McDonough and Michael Braungart saying?

Stop the accepted ways of the industrial world and the building industry? No. They are saying that we can transform industry with cradle-to-cradle design, the paradigm on which their firm, MBDC, models human industry on natural processes, creating safe and healthy prosperity. *Time* magazine called it "a unified philosophy that—in demonstrable and practical ways—is changing the design of the world."[2]

Instead of designing cradle-to-grave products that are dumped in landfills at the end of their "life," MBDC transforms industry by creating products for cradle-to-cradle cycles whose materials are circulated perpetually in closed loops. Maintaining materials in closed loops maximizes material value without damaging ecosystems.[3]

What was Ray Anderson saying?

Stop striving for financial prosperity? No. The soft-spoken CEO of Interface, Inc., an Atlanta-based commercial carpet company, shared his personal realization that businesses need to embrace principles of sustainability. Upon reading Paul Hawken's book *The Ecology of Commerce* (New York: Collins, 1994), Anderson said he felt "the spear in his chest." In an extraordinary moment of corporate leadership and responsibility, he decided to turn his nearly $1 billion company around and become zero-waste and energy-efficient (and then energy self-sufficient) and improve the working conditions for all seven thousand of his employees in forty cities worldwide.

In his book *Mid-Course Correction* (Atlanta, GA: Peregrinzilla, 1999), Anderson shares his (at times frustrating) efforts to apply these principles within a billion-dollar company. Today, Interface is an industry leader that exemplifies how that the

---

[1] See www.natcap.org.

[2] Charles P. Alexander, "Heroes for the Planet," *Time*, Apr. 26, 1999.

[3] See www.mbdc.com/c2c_home.htm.

principles of sustainability and financial success can coexist within a business and can lead to a new prosperity that includes environmental stewardship and social equity. Interface has cut its greenhouse gas emissions by 82 percent, and the goal is to reach zero environmental footprint by 2020. In his latest book, *Confessions of a Radical Industrialist* (New York: St. Martin's, 2009), Anderson shared how he revolutionized his company, meanwhile bringing down costs, improving quality, making Interface one of *Fortune* magazine's "100 Best Companies to Work For," and increasing profits.

"America's greenest CEO" and the hero of the award-winning documentary *The Corporation* inspires us by demonstrating a compelling case that sustainable business pays.[4]

What is Al Gore saying?

Change our politics to stop global warming? No. Al Gore's best-selling *An Inconvenient Truth* (New York: Rodale, 2006) warned us about a crisis that impacts us all: global warming.

Scientists agree that global warming is increasing. Carbon dioxide and other gases that warm the surface of the Earth trap solar heat in the atmosphere. But instead of protecting life on this planet as they should, the increase in temperature caused primarily by human activities and the use of fossil fuels is causing temperatures to rise at an unprecedented and detrimental rate.

Our actions directly affect global warming—it is not a natural occurrence. Al Gore asks us to look at the signs: Glacier icecaps are melting, plants and animals are being forced from their habitat, and the number of severe storms and droughts is increasing.

- What will the future hold if we allow this warming trend to continue? Extreme weather cost U.S. taxpayers $110 billion in economic losses in 2012 alone.
- Global sea levels could rise by more than 20 feet because of the loss of shelf ice in Greenland and Antarctica, devastating coastal areas worldwide.
- Heat waves will be more frequent and more intense.
- Droughts and wildfires will occur more often.
- The Arctic Ocean could be ice-free in summer by 2050.
- More than a million species worldwide could be driven to extinction by 2050.[5]

Further demonstrating that together we can "BE" part of the solution, below are historic developments following the release of the film:

- Over 106,000 tons of carbon were offset in the year following the film's release, which is equivalent to 225 million car miles.

---

[4] See http://sustainable.state.fl.us/fdi/fscc/news/world/9904/midcc.htm.

[5] www.climatecrisis.net; www.an-inconvenient-truth.com.

- 4,200+ tons of carbon were offset by people switching to compact fluorescent light bulbs.

- Over fifteen climate change bills have been introduced in Congress, with the historic Markey-Waxman bill passing the House in June 2009.

- Five countries—England, Scotland, the Czech Republic, New Zealand, and Germany, as well as the Canadian province of British Columbia—incorporated *An Inconvenient Truth* into their secondary schools' curricula.

- President Barack Obama created the new position of assistant to the president for climate and energy.

- The U.S. House of Representatives and the Senate both established a Select Committee on Energy Independence and Global Warming.

- Over 3,500 people worldwide have been trained to give the Climate Project presentation and former vice president Al Gore has trained over 4,000 "climate leaders" around the globe; subsequently, the issue of global warming was raised with more than a billion people worldwide, and public perceptions changed: 33 percent of people surveyed before the film's release believed global warming was real, versus 85 percent after the film's release.

Global warming is a moral issue, and we have a responsibility to act and to prevent or reverse these catastrophic events. There are many practical and worthwhile actions we can all take, and our choices today will influence whether our planet will support life in the future. Our collective action, even at the smallest level, can make a difference, and there is no doubt that together we can solve the problem of climate change.

What will you now be saying?

Begin by questioning the unspoken assumptions in your practice—your own best practices and procedures—and then begin to question those of others in the interior design industry. Questioning can give us courage as we venture into unfamiliar territory, expand our reality, and lead to new ways of thinking about environmental stewardship.

- Is it really okay to allow destruction of the environment? No!

- Is it really okay to pollute our waters with toxic chemicals? No!

- Is it really okay to allow pollution that is killing our forests and lakes with acid rain? No!

- Is it really okay to use pesticides that poison the land and the crops that we and our children eat? No!

- Is it really okay to use hazardous chemicals of concern on our projects? No!

As we reframe major concepts, two things begin to happen: The content of the questions change our viewpoint, and we grow comfortable with the process of questioning the unspoken assumptions of the old culture. This creates and sets us in a passionate new direction.

In a paper entitled "Leverage Points: Places to Intervene in a System," (Sustainability Institute, 1999) Donella (Dana) Meadows, the founder of the Sustainability Institute and a professor at Dartmouth College, concluded that the most effective, and most difficult, way to intervene in a system is to challenge the mind-set behind the system in the first place—the paradigms, the perceptions of reality, the mental model of how things are that underlie the system.

It is time for a paradigm shift based on an accurate view of reality. The life-support systems of the earth are clearly in decline. Many different species are disappearing at a faster rate than at any other time in the last sixty-five million years. Paul Hawken calls it "the death of birth."

During a sustainability conference, Chrisna du Plessis, an associate professor in the School for the Built Environment at the University of Pretoria in South Africa challenged the audience to think outside the box with a radical ecology statement: "The approach to sustainability is failing because it's reductionist methodologies cannot foresee unintended consequences. What is required is a quantum leap; society needs to change the paradigm within which it operates." Absolutely!

Each time we make a choice it affects the planet, either positively or negatively. With every positive action we take, we change the world. Our responsibility is to question, respond, and take action. Gather reliable information on how to apply healthy, high-performing, sustainable design principles and practices, and model change by respectfully yet tenaciously questioning the status quo.

Purposeful Living

Designers set the stage for creating memorable and inspirational environments, connecting with clients on an emotional level through our art—the art of design. We cultivate the spirit of a home through an intricate language that speaks of texture, color, scale, layer, tone, and style. We play a key role in incorporating a holistic approach to solving environmental problems and creating healthy, nurturing, zero-impact homes for our clients. Intention brings forth a relationship with core values and results in a deeper respect for nature, reconnecting us with all that is life-affirming.

Through design and personal growth intertwined with environmental advocacy, we become more deeply engaged in community and global concerns. As we become more involved in ecological issues and in our own personal growth, we are better able to achieve balance in our lives. This reframing process is a defining step. It compels us to question the status quo—the old opinions and beliefs that have dictated how we work and live. A new perspective and a new take on reality pave the way to redefining our moral concerns. And by paying close attention, we gain clarity in unexpected ways—ways that anchor our thinking.

At first this may feel a bit daunting: We realize there is much to tackle and many other areas to deal with. But as we learn to affirm our values and find new solutions to old problems, we become optimistic about the future. As we rede-fine the meaning of success, we begin to lead more passionate, purposeful lives; we accept responsibility for and become accountable to the environment and the community at large, ultimately creating a better future for everyone on the planet. What could be more personally fulfilling?

- ■ 'BE' part of the solution.
- ■ Walk the talk.
- ■ Adopt environmental principles and practices.
- ■ Develop your own personal vision and action plan.

In sum, we have a tremendous opportunity to integrate healthy, sustainable design into our projects. Move forward with energy-saving concepts, sustainable, zero-low impact materials, and healthy alternatives for both your client and your planet. Embrace sustainability through your passion for design, and stay committed. Invigorate your spirit, the work, the clients, and the project team; bring synergistic solutions to all proj-ects. The reward will be a profound connection to a sense of place.

Connection to a sustaining world inspires ingenious designs, so be courageous, spirited, and persistent in your practice. Enjoy and embrace the journey. Offer envi-ronmentally responsible designs that showcase your integrity—designs that are so beautiful that they bring out the best in people.

Inspirational Mentors

Over the last decade we have had the good fortune to find many inspiring mentors in the field of sustainable design. From William to Janine, Ray to Hunter, Paul to Paula, Daniel to Julia, David to Penny, Michael to Steve, these insightful teachers inspired us to think and act. Filled with intense commitment and enthusiastic inten-tion, we can, likewise, aspire to be responsible citizens of planet Earth.

With these motivational leaders and world-renowned environmental entre-preneurs as our guides, we can truly transform the practice of residential interior design. By continually seeking out advisors and mentors who inspire us, we reached out to industry thought-leaders to hear what they think are the next priorities (see chapter 22, "What's Next?"). To whom will you reach out to discuss what's next? Who are your role models? There is an abundance of information available to guide you on your intelligent, sustainable design journey. Read and research, attend sem-inars and conferences, and then read and research some more. We can integrate the language and spirit of sustainable design into our beings and advocate and implement its principles, strategies, and practices.

We regard Ray Anderson, the former chairman and founder of Interface, Inc., and former cochair of the President's Council on Sustainable Development, as a phenomenal role model. While serving on the President's Council on Sustainable Development, he addressed the Twenty-First Century Policy Project, a statewide initiative in California to divert waste from landfills, along with other interested parties involved in forming a new consensus for the future of solid waste management in California. We are highlighting parts of Ray's speech here because we believe wholeheartedly in his passionate and powerful message. We aim to honor his extraordinary legacy every day, and although he is no longer with us, he continues to inspire us to action.

> I am often asked to make the business case for sustainability, and here it is in my opinion. First, to provide the framework: The economy is the wholly owned subsidiary of the environment. Without a healthy parent, the child is doomed. Therefore, the first case for sustainability, in a pure business sense, is survival. If we don't get there, if we don't move there rapidly, our descendants will see markets, as well as society, disintegrate. We must do better than that by them.
>
> The second case is that it is really possible to do well by doing good, and we're seeing it in our business every day. I believe that is the paradigm for success in the next industrial revolution. In the twenty-first century, the companies that do well and do good will be recognized as successful. And it will not be possible to do well without doing it responsibly.
>
> The third case, I believe, is that there are new and noble fortunes to be made in bringing the technologies and the products of those technologies to market in the next industrial revolution. I think entrepreneurs everywhere should thank Rachel Carson for starting it all in 1962 with that wonderful book *Silent Spring*. In the next industrial revolution, the technophobes—the people who hate technology and say it's the problem—and the technophiles—the people who say it is the solution—will be reconciled, and [the resultant] technologies [will be] sustainable technologies. Technology and labor, so at odds throughout the whole industrial revolution, will be reconciled in the next industrial revolution.
>
> The interest of business, the interest of nature, so at odds in the first industrial revolution, will be reconciled—thesis, antithesis, synthesis, the Hegelian process of history again, but leading us toward a sustainable Earth.
>
> I think one more important characteristic of the next industrial revolution is the ascendancy of women in business, in government, in education, in all of our institutions. It is coming just in the nick of time. Women bring that right-brain nurturing instinct to the table, and any man who has been in a meeting where there was a woman present knows it's a better meeting, with a better outcome, because of a woman's presence . . .

A few days later, totally out of the blue, came a message from one of the people in that audience. It was one of the most encouraging moments of my life because it told me that at least one person in that audience really got it. It was an original poem composed after that Tuesday morning meeting and sent to me by e-mail from Glenn Thomas:

> Tomorrow's child,
> without a name,
> an unseen face
> and knowing not your time or place.
> Tomorrow's child though yet unborn,
> I met you first last Tuesday morn.
> A wise friend introduced us two,
> and through his shining point of view,
> I saw a day that you would see,
> a day for you,
> but not for me.
> Knowing you has changed my thinking,
> for I never had an inkling
> that perhaps the things I do
> might someday, somehow,
> threaten you.
> Tomorrow's child,
> my daughter, son,
> I'm afraid I've just begun
> to think of you
> and of your good,
> though always having known I should.
> Begin I will,
> to weigh the cost of what I squander,
> what is lost
> if ever I forget,
> that you will someday come and live here too.

"Tomorrow's Child" speaks to us across the generations with a message so simple yet so profound, reminding us that we are all part of the web of life—every last one of us. During our brief visit here to this beautiful blue planet, we have a simple but profound choice to make—to help that web of life or to hurt it. And it's your call how you live your life.[6]

---

[6]Reprinted with permission. www.ciwmb.ca. gov/2000Plus/Events/SummitJan99/keytext.htm.

Taking Action: David Suzuki

David Suzuki is leading the sustainable way in Canada through the David Suzuki Foundation, a science-based environmental organization working to protect the balance of nature and quality of life. To put Canada on a direct path to sustainability by the year 2030, the foundation has developed an action plan called Sustainability within a Generation: A New Vision for Canada. Written by leading environmental thinker David Boyd, the report outlines the solutions to Canada's environmental challenges.

> Sustainability is neither a lofty ideal nor an academic concept, but an urgent imperative for humanity. Sustainability means living within Earth's limits. In a sustainable future, no Canadian would think twice about drinking a glass of tap water. Food would be free from pesticide residues, antibiotics, and growth hormones. Air, water, and soil would be uncontaminated by toxic substances.
>
> In a sustainable future, it would be safe to swim in every Canadian river and lake and safe to eat fish wherever they were caught. Clean, renewable energy would be generated by harnessing the sun, wind, water, and heat of the earth.
>
> A sustainable future would mean a global climate undisturbed by human pollution. Canadians would no longer fear sunburn or cancer caused by damage to the ozone layer. No one would worry about nature's extraordinary diversity diminishing at human hands. Endangered ecosystems and species would recover and thrive. Canadians would be confident that future generations would enjoy the same spectacular natural heritage and quality of life that we enjoy today.

Source: The David Suzuki Foundation, www.davidsuzuki.org/.

Next Steps

What is the next step? Is it restorative design—or better yet, regenerative design that heals Mother Earth, the one and only source of all its living beings? Is it a deeper connection with nature through biophilic design? Is it advocating for and adopting cradle-to-cradle in every decision?

We must begin to think beyond ourselves. Let's consider not just our own species and living environment, but all species and all ecosystems and the impact of our brief time on this planet. Maintaining the health and the diversity of nature (which includes the entire world of living beings and the great outdoors) is crucial to sustaining the web of life.

Remain open and question what you care about, then seek answers to those questions, as this will move the sustainability conversation forward and further connect you with your values, your mission, and your life's purpose. Passionately share your questions, share your answers, share your knowledge, share your experiences, share your hopes and dreams, and share your spirit. Set your goals, engage your peers in the respectful exchange of ideas, and make things happen. Doing so is vital to honoring and celebrating life on our planet.

Discover what thought leaders and peers consider their next steps in the following chapter. Enjoy their visionary, thought-provoking, and heartwarming perspectives. We hope they further inspire you to 'BE' the change you want to see in the industry, in the world. They certainly inspire us.

> *Whatever you can do, or dream you can, begin it.*
> *Boldness has genius, power and magic in it.*
> —GOETHE

CHAPTER 22

what's next?

Figure 22.1 This home on the Long Island Sound takes the exterior location into consideration. There are three oil separators installed in the driveway to capture car oil from washing into stormwater runoff and snowmelt preventing contaminants from entering adjacent waterways.

Photo courtesy of Dujardin Design.

"It's not about what it is, it's about what it can become."
—DR. SEUSS, *THE LORAX*

With tremendous optimism, immense gratitude, and deep admiration we offer you essays, perspectives, and letters from industry thought-leaders, mentors, peers, and friends. Their collective voices embrace environmental stewardship as they discuss their priorities for the future and who inspires them. When we embrace the abundance the world offers us and take time to connect with one another and with nature, we're able to create healing interiors where we thrive for ourselves and for future generations. We hope these visionary contemplations empower you like they did us.

Abundance

WILLIAM MCDONOUGH

Advisor, designer, thought-leader, and author; founding principal, William McDonough + Partners; cofounder, McDonough Braungart Design Chemistry

Design is the first signal of human intention. It is about the future, and the central statement is: What's next is what's next.

But the real question is: Are we intentionally trying to poison people where they live and work?

If not, then why don't we think about what we put into our buildings? I wouldn't intentionally put a toxin in my home. Would you use lead paint where a child might chew on it?

We have a materials problem. The lead in a computer, as solder that is never intended to leave the technosphere of that product, is not a toxin—it's a solder. In this application, the lead is a technical nutrient, to cite terminology from the Cradle to Cradle design platform. But the moment it is no longer solder and gets into the biosphere, it becomes a neurotoxin. It is when the material ends up in the wrong place that it becomes a toxin.

It's up to us to understand if a material is good or bad. If a residential interior is a tool providing a service, is the service beneficial or detrimental? Human intention gives the tool value, as the tool does not know whether it is good or bad. Are you intentionally toxifying someone, or providing them with health?

In 1992, I wrote the Hannover Principles, and more than two decades later those principles remain a guide for our work. Consider how they relate to residential interiors:

1. Insist on rights of humanity and nature to coexist.
2. Recognize interdependence.
3. Respect relationships between spirit and matter.
4. Accept responsibility for the consequences of design.
5. Create safe objects of long-term value.
6. Eliminate the concept of waste.
7. Rely on natural energy flows.
8. Understand the limitations of design.
9. Seek constant improvement by the sharing of knowledge.

If you are asking "What's next?" look to these principles.

It's time to ask what's next for materials. They need to be designed into things in ways we've never done before. Look at materials and ask what happens when the building in which they're used burns down or gets repurposed. We don't think about that in our culture of planned obsolescence, where we constantly toss things away, as if "away" exists. Throwing things away needs to go away. There is no "away." We must understand what's next because we are not leaving: "Away" has arrived.

These practices date back from the 1800s, the dawn of the first Industrial Revolution, when we adopted fossil fuels. An emblematic moment: Ralph Waldo Emerson went to Europe on a handcrafted sailboat operated by artisans practicing an ancient skill out in the open air. But he cruised home in a steel rust-bucket, a steam-ship spewing smoke into the sky after shoving fossil fuels into its boilers and operated by people working in darkness. Was this design? Was this intention? It planted the seed for the cause and effect of the Industrial Revolution. Was it our intention to pollute the atmosphere and have people work in the dark? That's what we did.

The 1900s was the pollution century. Human production systems—industry—exploded, and fossil fuels enabled the explosion, but we polluted the rivers, the sky, the land in the process. Toward the end of the 1900s—and especially in 1992, at the Earth Summit—we started to talk about sustainable development, as if we want to sustain what we did. We talked about eco-efficiency and having less impact, being less bad—in other words, accepting the idea of being bad. And to this day, everyone still looks at reducing their ecological footprint. Reduce, avoid, minimize—reduce my carbon emissions by 2020, reduce my toxins in the building, with zero as our goal. If zero is our goal, that means we have nothing. Are we saying our goal is nothing?

That's so sad for the children.

What's next is a different goal. What's next is we are going to be more good, not just less bad. Instead of the current commerce, which seems only to ask "How much can I get for how little I give?" it is now time to transform the question: "How much can I give for all that I get?" That's the question I like to ask. This moves us into a spirit of generosity, into a world of abundance.

It's a fundamental, a philosophical understanding, that if it exists, it's possible. But for people like us—for designers—if it is possible, it exists. We have to ask ourselves what we want next. And by design, and with intention, move into it. We can't be held back by something ordinary. We have to manage it, rendering the possible real. Then if someone says, "That's impossible," you say to them, "Don't tell me things are impossible, tell me you can't do it."

Le Corbusier said a house is a machine for living in. What if we had living machines and used nature as a tool? A natural machine that understands biodiversity where buildings are like trees, making oxygen, sequestering carbon, distilling water, providing habitat for species, accruing energy, making fuel, complex sugars, and food, and creating microclimates. Then the question becomes quite different. The question is no longer, "Is the house a machine for living in?" The real question is, "When is the house alive?"

What does it mean to be a living thing? In 1962, Francis Crick, in his essay "Of Molecules and Men," called it the nature of vitalism, defining what it means to be a living thing. In his conclusion he noted three characteristics: you have growth; you have free energy from outside the system (in nature that's the sun); and you have open metabolism for chemicals operating for the benefit of the organism through reproduction. That is a tree—celebrating fecundity as the sun shines on the earth, we get growth, nature's plan, and the growth is safe, healthy and diverse.

So what does that mean to us now? For us, as designers, what is next? We recognize how critical the opportunities are for magnificent design with thoughtful intention by humankind. You know what it is? It's beautiful. When do humans become a tool of nature? We don't just use nature as a tool; we become tools for nature and we support its diversity.

The projects I work on give health in a positive way. The buildings have the potential of making 120 percent of their energy from renewables. I'm designing a building that restores butterflies to their habitat. The building has an office lobby where the walls are two layers of glass and as you go to work in the morning you'll see butterflies hatching on the other side of shells within the glass walls. On weekends children will come, lower the outside glass, and free the butterflies. Why should I use *ficus interruptus* in my design schemes for lobbies when I have butterflies hatching and children releasing them into the city? Then the children talk to the parks department asking, "Where are our butterflies?" They need their habitats to survive, so rather than weed-whacking the highway verges, they become butterfly gardens. The migrating birds are happy because the caterpillars are back. The butterflies thrive in their natural habitats

Fecundity, beauty happens: It's the butterfly effect.

I'm inspired by the ambition of people who go Cradle to Cradle. It is what's next. Cradle to Cradle is a deep, detailed scientific assessment combined with a large, optimistic design intentionality and ranges across human creativity from the scale of the molecule to the global—including residential interiors. When transparency is required by regulation, it's usually only about 5 percent of the content: superficial transparency. With the Cradle to Cradle platform, companies have to embrace transparency down to the molecule. If they have trade secrets in their formulations, they still have to report them to us, and agree to show us every fragment. Why? Because we must know now.

Insist upon Cradle to Cradle–certified products and materials, which are based on a defined system for safe and healthy protocols. That's what has to happen; that's why we gave the tool to the public—so we can say it's possible. And you don't have to become a chemist because we had an eco-toxicologist, genius Michael Braungart, do the work for us. With Cradle to Cradle in the public domain, design is indeed the first signal of human intention, because it does good. We did it; it's there. Use it!

That's exciting. We can open to the depth of the human and physical experience as we witness humanity rising to our occasion.

It is a joyful opportunity for everybody to make a place for everyone in the world. The time is now to seek a delightfully diverse, safe, healthy, and just world with clean air, soil, water, and power, economically, equitably, ecologically, and elegantly enjoyed. Period.

When are we going to positively define what we do? The exciting part for me is when the world gets better, not just less bad. The health, safety, and welfare of our clients are nonnegotiable. Don't poison people, tell the truth, and let them know you're telling them the truth. Don't tell me it's impossible to make a safe, healthy interior. Instead tell me you weren't able to do it because you aren't able to find materials and products to create a healthy space. And celebrate that there are so many of us here to help make this happen. Our community is growing. As Dean Kamen has said, "Don't tell me it is impossible. Tell me you can't do it." This book speaks to this notion. Let's all get to it together. A future of abundance is ahead.

Building Science

PETER YOST

LEED AP; vice president, technical services, Building Green

In my work on building performance and durability, building science remains the hub. As we build our buildings to perform at higher and higher levels, more and more building professionals must become proficient in basic building science principles.

You are probably thinking this: What in the heck does interior design have to do with building science? The main answer is: In order to understand how any exterior assembly manages heat and moisture flows (and particularly the latter), I need to know the hygrothermal properties (hygro = moisture, thermal = heat) of every layer of that assembly, including the most interior one—the finish. That is where you, the interior designer, come in. In your work specifying interior finishes, your choice of paint or paneling or wallpaper may determine in what direction that assembly—or even *if* that assembly—dries when it gets wet.

The work that Annette Stelmack and I did on the ASID/USGBC Regreen program, in which interior designers worked side by side with architects and remodeling professionals, is an example of the direction in which our industry needs to go. Interior designers can have real impact on the hygrothermal performance of the building enclosure, and their work significantly affects the overall beauty, and hence the durability, of buildings. We need all hands on deck if we are going to move our buildings to higher and higher levels of performance.

And one of the most significant factors that affect any buildings environmental footprint is size: The larger a building, the larger its footprint. Space planning is a green building skill that must become integral to every building project.

SPENSER VILLWOCK

MNM, LEED AP; CEO, IEC Rocky Mountain

I have been engaged with professional sustainability for over fifteen years. After college, I started a bicycle-powered curbside recycling business in my home state of Iowa. Since then I have worked on international sustainability initiatives for George Soros, run green building programs in Colorado, and sat on the local USGBC board of directors. I currently lead a trade association for electrical and renewable energy companies in the Mountain/Southwest region of the United States.

Priorities for the future are largely dependent on market maturity of sustainability practices and technologies. There still exist several barriers to adopting sustainability due to lengthy return on investment (ROI) and costly upfront expense. Until we reach economies of scale for several emerging products and sustainable solutions, many options will only be accessible to a small segment of the population.

Take, for example, solar photovoltaics (PVs). The PV market has been subsidized by government, manufacturers, and utilities for a number of years. This has resulted in a stronger demand for the technology, which has significantly driven down the market price per watt. The ROI remains relatively high for PVs when compared with traditional electricity that comes via power plant utility providers. This high ROI renders the technology unattainable for a large majority of the population.

A few things need to happen here. The most critical is a concerted push for further R&D on PV technologies that focuses on increasing the efficiency of electricity produced per PV panel, thereby hastening ROI. Much of this product development has taken place over the past few years, yet the efficiency must continue to increase before the market matures and there is widespread technology saturation.

I am inspired by visionary thought. In my opinion, we are all visionary beings. It is simply a matter of tapping into the right thought connections with each person in order to open up true vision and inspirational insight. We each possess this energy innately, but we must be calm, open, and cooperative with our very nature in order to unleash the creativity and visionary thoughts that are uniquely our own.

Education

HOLLEY HENDERSON

LEED fellow; author, speaker; consultant, H2 Ecodesign

A bit of background: In high school, I was voted "most creative" (translation: "We don't really get her").

Creativity has always come to me naturally. Early in my career, it was translated into art (painting) and interior design of large-scale civic work. In more recent years, with the founding of H2 Ecodesign, the inventive eco-gene manifests as vision, communication, and collaboration.

Priorities: Education, education, and more education is critical. With the launch of LEED v4, the opportunities to transform the market are enormous. But it will take some creative genius to reach the masses with a catalytic message while providing the support tools necessary for continued "in the trenches" learning.

Inspiration: My inspirers are my mom and John Mackey, CEO of Whole Foods.

JOHN "JAY" HALL

LEED AP Homes; principal, Jay Hall & Associates

My formal training is as a mechanical engineer. In my senior year of undergraduate engineering, I designed a passive home for the Canadian climate and realized that homes can perform so much better than the ones we typically build—and that technology is sometimes not ready for the marketplace. Generally, society believes that technology can and will solve their problems. So why is there such a large gap between our current homes and what we are capable of designing and building?

The answer came to me once I finished grad school and entered the workforce. For the first fifteen years of my career, I worked as a consultant to the U.S. Environmental Protection Agency and aided in the development of several of their Energy Star programs, which brand specific products as environmentally friendly. My real world education taught me all about market transformation and started to answer my questions: Why do consumers make the purchasing decisions they make? How can they be influenced to make different, better, more sustainable choices?

I learned that there is a very wide gap between what technologies are available, what they are capable of, and what consumers' basic awareness of these technologies is. Curiously, I saw that consumers tended to focus on a very small subset of technologies they perceived as valuable (or trendy) and were often completely unaware of the broader set of valuable technologies that could make their lives substantially better (i.e., healthier, more comfortable, more resource-efficient, less polluting, more sustainable).

We are capable of designing, building, and using (i.e., living in) buildings that perform substantially better than those currently available (both existing and new). Even better technologies are being developed and will be coming to market soon. The ongoing challenge is to get society to realize that they already have choices (both technological and behavioral) that will enhance their lives substantially.

One of the major obstacles to broader consumer awareness is a branding problem. Energy Star has helped consumers identify and select energy-efficient products from light bulbs to refrigerators. However, so far, we have not been as successful in branding the value of the broader sustainable options. The word "green" is commonly used to identify products that are sustainable. But there are so many types of green products. "Green" means so many different things to different people, including recycled materials, low-emission paint, xeriscaping, rain gardens, low-flow toilets, solar panels, geothermal, green cars, and so on. There is no one single brand to help consumers to identify these preferable sustainable products. Instead, there are hundreds of companies and labeling systems promoting a vast array of green products. Consumers are justifiably confused.

My own priorities come from three perspectives: the personal, the product level, and the whole-building level.

At the personal level, I try to use all resources wisely. Society is putting more and more pressure on our planet's precious resources. If we all use these resources as wisely as possible, we can keep them around for as long as possible. Every day we all can learn more new ways to do things. Living sustainably is all about continuous learning. If every day we try to do something new, different, better, we are living sustainably; we lift up those around us by living by example.

At the product level, the biggest challenge for consumers is to conquer the steep learning curve related to vast array of sustainable living practices and choices. As the planet's population grows and economic development advances, there is a growing need for humans to have a smaller footprint.

Societal changes can come about from either legal mandates or voluntary actions. Legal mandates are effective for taking small incremental steps. My professional interest and passion is to promote voluntary actions through voluntary market transformation (or consumer education) programs. From this perspective, the greatest priority for the future is to rebrand "green" as a national initiative that compellingly communicates the value of living and working in a safe, healthy, peaceful, and environmentally responsible manner. This brand may be singular and be applied to all sustainable products (like Energy Star), or there may be many new sustainable product brands (but the latter may perpetuate consumer confusion).

At the whole-building level, LEED and the National Green Building Standard (NGBS) have made some progress toward the branding of sustainable homes, albeit mostly new construction. NGBS has a new remodeling certification and a new small project (e.g., bath, kitchen) certificate. But the certification does not have much traction yet. The labeling of sustainable existing homes is the nation's biggest opportunity—and the most challenging one: over one hundred million existing homes that need upgrading. The challenge is to identify and promote the most cost-effective sustainable measures for homeowners with relatively tight budgets across a country of diverse climates. (Perhaps this needs to be addressed at a regional or even microclimate level.) The value of sustainable homes has not yet been effectively communicated to consumers, but when it is, the demand for comfortable, healthy, durable, and environmentally responsible homes will grow quickly. It is a foundational idea that people will be drawn to.

We must shift away from a technological focus toward an educational focus that promotes individual goals and actions. This is a big challenge, but the need is great and the time is right.

I strongly believe that there is a divine universal power (call it whatever you prefer—Nature, God, etc.) that influences the way each of us lives their life. I believe that we are all attracted to a joyful and peaceful existence. As I deepen my understanding of the principles of sustainability, they make more sense, and they fit with my universal sense of good and right.

For example I love the principles of biophilia. I suspect that we are all naturally attracted to the beauty and diversity of nature (whether it be nature's palate of blues, greens, and earth tones, plant life, wildlife, or a panoramic view of a natural area). Who would not want to feel more connected to nature while they are *inside* their home or workplace? Anything that connects us to our spiritual roots is a very powerful force in our lives. I strive to constantly renew myself by stepping out of the fast lane and quietly reconnecting with my deep spiritual roots. And of course, there is the hope that we all want the same thing—a healthy home, community, and planet.

ROWENA FINEGAN

BBEC; managing partner, Pine Street Natural Interiors

Our mission has always been to provide the next wave of green furniture and design, one that combines social responsibility and healthy habits with color and texture—and fun.

The idea for this particular combination hatched years ago when I visited countries across the globe, developing a design sense that is especially influenced by African and European pattern and style. Emigrating from Brighton, England, when I was in my early thirties, I started my business life in Jackson Hole, Wyoming, by building my own workroom in that resort town. I built a tiny shop handling ski clothing alterations into a very successful interior design concern that handled high-end clients and hotels in the area.

Though successful, I was not satisfied with my work, and eventually sold my business and enrolled in the Institute for Bau-Biologie and Ecology, which promotes the use of healthy building principles in homes. It teaches its students how to identify potentially dangerous elements like mold and volatile organic compounds released from materials as carpet and plastics. I earned a certification as a building biology environmental consultant (BBEC) and currently use the principles of bau-biologie in my work as managing partner and interior designer in Pine Street Natural Interiors, the boutique studio in Sausalito, California that I run with my business partner, Agnes Bourne.

Those of us who have been working in the arena of sustainable interiors for the past decade must continue to lead and educate not only our peers but also everyone who crosses our path. And those, too, who are sometimes ambivalent, sometimes skeptical, and sometimes downright mistrustful of what they fear may be just more greenwashing. We must continue to lead by example, to be passionate about what we do, and to work together in order to gain the necessary momentum that is required to turn this gigantic ship of greedy, uncaring, and unsustainable practices around.

We continue to be adamant about what will pass muster for our clients. Many of our customers come to us out of sheer desperation because they can no longer live in their homes bombarded constantly by the volatile organic compounds, electromagnetic fields, and radiation that are ubiquitous in our living spaces. We must encourage those businesses taking up the challenge—sometimes against great odds—to offer only those products that are healthy for ourselves, our environment, and our planet.

For inspiration, I look to Patty Grossman and Leigh Anne Van Dusen, who founded their company, O Ecotextiles "to make the whole world safer while making our personal environments more beautiful." Since 2004, they have been tirelessly working to find partners interested in a cradle-to-cradle process of creating no-impact, perfectly safe, incredibly luxurious fabrics.

Dr. Devra Davis, who is recognized internationally for her work on environmental health and disease prevention also inspires me. Devra is the author of such books as *When Smoke Ran Like Water* (New York: Basic Books, 2002), *The Secret History of the War on Cancer* (New York: Basic Books, 2007), and *Disconnect: The Truth about Cell Phone Radiation and Your Health, What the Industry Has Done to Hide It, and What You Can Do to Protect Your Family* (New York: Dutton, 2010). Her books have brought attention to the perils that go with our growing addiction to cell phones and other useful gadgets. She teaches us to question what makes us uncomfortable rather than just trusting that it's OK.

LISA FAY MATTHIESSEN

FAIA, LEED fellow; principal, Integral Group

I am an architect and sustainability consultant. I came to architecture through the back door: I was a residential-scale carpenter and cabinetmaker first. I have done extensive research on the cost implications of sustainable design; readers may be familiar with the "cost of green" studies.[1] I have also been closely involved with green metrics, beginning with LEED in the 1990s and more recently with the Living Building Challenge and the Delos Well Building Standard. I am currently the principal of the Los Angeles office of Integral Group, a deep-green engineering firm.

Sustainability needs to become old hat.

Right now, our industry is producing buildings that run the gamut from barely meeting code to being living buildings. Net-zero-energy buildings seemed a formidable challenge just a few years ago; now my firm alone is working on at least a dozen, and net zero will be the standard for California in just two code cycles. At the same time, the building industry churns out cookie-cutter houses paying little or no attention to green issues. And it is not that the technologies and expertise are not available. Nor is green building unaffordable. It is just new, and we are not good at new.

---

[1]See http://www.usgbc.org/resources/cost-green-revisited.

I am not sure what the answer is, but I think it has to do with politics, and with awareness and empowerment. We need to figure out how to make sustainability and resiliency the standard across the country, to divorce it from politics, because survival is not a political issue. Stewardship of our natural world should not be a political—read "divisive"—issue. Sustainability is a moral and philosophical issue, and it is immensely practical now that it is affordable and available.

And sustainable design needs not to be solely in the hands of the designers and builders. If our customers become savvy consumers willing and able to demand sustainability and to become part of the solution through their daily actions, then the industry will turn greener more quickly.

Global warming will not wait.

Kids inspire me. The young engineers that start at Integral Group, fresh from college, are incredibly smart and idealistic. They really do want to save the world, and they have the guts and the brains to do it.

Bob Berkebile also inspires me. An architect who has taken sustainability to heart, he and his colleagues at the architectural firm BNIM have taught themselves not only how to design green but how to reach into communities and bring the wisdom and power of the people in those communities into the design process. The results are transformative.

SUZAN GLOBUS

FASID, LEED AP; principal, Globus Design Associates

Sustainability is integral to my design practice; it is no longer an added value to my design solutions; it is ingrained in those solutions. I have stopped trying to convince clients to accept the pursuit of a sustainable solution and instead offer no other solution.

Designers must educate themselves about sustainability; to do otherwise is to practice irresponsibly, at best. To that end, I have started to teach Design for Sustainability at Kean University in New Jersey so that I can raise the awareness of future design and science students there. (On a personal note, I built the first active and passive solar house in Monmouth County, New Jersey, over forty years ago and am exploring designing and building a net-zero house for my next residence.)

Educating designers about the environmental, social, and long-range economic impacts of their design decisions is my priority. The future I envision is filled with responsible consumption of goods, local food, and shared services, all of which result from a massive behavioral shift. And all are issues that can be addressed through design.

There are so many who inspire me: People who don't use the automatic door opener and turn off the water when they brush their teeth, even when no one is looking. People who advocate for environmentally sound planning for our cities. In short, people who take action inspire me.

Future Generations

PAULINE SOUZA

LEED fellow, AIA, LEED AP BD+C; partner and director of sustainability, WRNS Studio

I have loved architecture for a long time. And I love the *practice* of architecture, despite its humbling process and endless appetite for all your time. I believe it can make a difference in people's lives by making a space that is joyful or peaceful or invigorating.

So I was stunned to learn in the 1990s that this wonderful thing I had devoted a lot of my life to was possibly making the world sick, and that climate change had already been a global topic for twenty years. This awareness coincided with becoming a new mom. Both things were powerful and life-changing. And I realized that people are moved to act when such issues become personal. Not graphs, not facts, and not charts.

I love charts and graphs, so much so that my colleagues tease me about it. And I thought the data they expressed would change the way we developed architecture and change the way clients invested in their buildings. Too many frustrating years later, I understand that people are moved to change their behavior by connecting to their values, and different types of people—students, corporate clients, educators, parents—need different ways to help them make that connection.

Books like *Switch* by Chip and Dan Heath (New York: Broadway Books, 2010), and *What Are People For?* by Wendell Berry (Berkely, CA: Counterpoint, 1990) remind me how powerful values are, and of the importance words like "gratitude," "thanks," and "love." We don't want green buildings just because they are efficient; we want them because they make us better, happier, healthier people. How sad it is to have to be reminded to be people-centric.

I am amazed and inspired by so many people every day, from practitioners to biologists to educators to family members. It is a wide circle, and I am ever grateful to a cast of thousands. A few special people keep me on track—Nadav Malin, Larry Strain, Katie Murphy, Linda Crouse, Olivia and Maria Gee. They are mentors, educators, friends, and daughters. They remind me that we can change the world by loving life first.

I am greatly inspired by Green Schools; nobody can argue with providing sustainable, healthy environments for young people.[2] It is stunning that the relative exposure limits for materials are tested for a 165-pound man. Imagine how the emission of a toxin might affect a preschooler who is just 30 pounds! Our challenge, our opportunity, is to remember, beyond energy efficiency, the importance of

---

[2] See http://www.centerforgreenschools.org/home.aspx.

healthy environments with improved air quality, and to provide good connections to the outdoors.

I recently participated in a Green Apple Day of service, an initiative tied to the Center for Green Schools. On this day, we performed audits on the school and talked about material resources, lighting, and water conservation. The students ranged from seven to fourteen, and all were inquisitive and educated: They know what kind of world they will inherit. They pushed us, the volunteers and professionals, to answer hard questions, and they inspired us to think of new ideas; they invigorated our group, and they reminded us of what we value.

RACHEL GUTTER

Director, Center for Green Schools, U.S. Green Building Council

Meet Paige. Paige is pursuing her masters in interior design. Paige wants to be a green interior designer. But when she goes online to register for classes, alas, there is but one offering on the topic of green building—to prepare students for the LEED Green Associate exam. While that's helpful for some, not so for Paige. She became a LEED Green Associate before she applied to grad school. So she does what any motivated young professional would do. She tracks down her dean.

Impressed by Paige's initiative, the dean tasks her with becoming the resident expert on sustainable interiors. A bona fide digital native, Paige opens up her laptop and types the keywords "LEED," "green," and "design" into the browser's search field, and she's magically whisked away to the U.S. Green Building Council (USGBC) website. Paige's elation quickly turns to despair as she wanders from page to page in pursuit of a course, a publication, or any other resource that will satisfy her thirst for knowledge.

After twenty minutes, it's time for class. Paige admits defeat and resolves to try a different search tomorrow.

What a missed opportunity. But what went wrong? Three things:

1. *The token sustainability course just doesn't cut it*. Sustainability has been on the radar of today's young professions for quite some time. In fact, the *Princeton Review* reports that approximately two-thirds of prospective college students factor a college or university's commitment to sustainability into their school selection process. Many of these students show up on campus with baseline knowledge about sustainability expecting that sustainability will be integrated across course offerings, not treated as an add-on.

   Colleges and universities must ensure that all their graduates are well-versed in environmentalism and sustainability, regardless of their course of study.

2. *The majority of green education focuses on test preparation, credential maintenance, and designing and constructing green buildings*. If you're an architect or an engineer, you can probably track down the courses you're

looking for. If, however, you're one of so many other professionals who also need green building education, you might not be so lucky. If advanced or highly-specialized education is what you're looking for, the market hasn't caught up to your needs.

Providers of green building education should utilize market research to develop products that are targeted, relevant, and timely.

3. *Green building and design education is hard to track down.* The onus is on the learner to seek out relevant content, and there's no way to gauge the quality of the handful of courses that are offered. Recently, the USGBC conducted more than 250 one-on-one interviews with education stakeholders. Interviewees responded overwhelming that USGBC needs to be the go-to place for green building education.

Based on this feedback, USGBC committed to a robust online marketplace that features a broad selection of LEED and green building educational offerings with a simple, user-friendly interface and powered by peer reviews and ratings. A new subscription model also makes green building education more affordable and accessible.

I'm happy to report that Paige's story has a happy ending. She did, in fact, go on to educate herself, her peers, and her faculty about green building and sustainability themes. After graduation, Paige got a job working for the USGBC at our national headquarters. Since then, she has gone on to start her own sustainable interiors practice.

Another green building fairytale come true.

SARAH SPENCER-WORKMAN

LEED AP; sustainability education specialist, Colorado State University-Pueblo; principal, Sedgwick Consulting Group

As a mother and sustainability professional, my career often, if not always, overlaps with my personal life. I have been working in sustainability for almost twenty years, but I have been drawn to it my entire life. To me, sustainability means finding balance and resilience in how we live, work, and play. For good or bad, I know my carbon footprint and consider it to a measure of my success.

Dear Daughter,

You are part of the "digital native" generation. As you make your way toward adulthood, I hope I can empower you to believe in who you are and to show you a path that remains true to the life goals I have worked hard to meet. May this letter begin to light your way.

The environmental movement was born in the early 1960s with the release of books like *Silent Spring* by Rachel Carson and the formation of President Nixon's Council on Environmental Quality. But many of us had

been practicing sustainability long before it was a trendy buzzword. We can trace sustainability practices back to the Roman aqueducts and the Native Americans of Colorado, who understood that we must use what we have, not overconsume, and divert waste from the communities in which we live for it will over the land we need to sustain us.

Fast forward to today. As I teach higher education students, governmental leaders, and members of the private sector to take what history shows us and improve upon it to find balance and resilience in our lives, I continue to see gaps in our understanding of sustainability. While death and taxes are certain, so is population growth. This will translate into an increased consumption and depletion of both natural and manmade resources if we do not take preventative ecological measures.

Simply spoken, we must practice "reduce, reuse, and recycle" in the way we live, work, and play. We can reduce the goods and services we consume, and we can recycle our waste using easily accessible commingled recycling containers; the most difficult part of this equation is "reuse." But that won't always be true.

I see the seamless integration of renewable energy in residential households through new construction and retrofitting. Whether it is solar, wind, or geothermal, renewable energy will not be a choice but a requirement, a necessity for residential living. Garages will be equipped to power electrical vehicles. Smart systems will automatically power down electricity when not in use and autonomously switch to an alternative fuel source such as propane or natural gas until renewable sources become available again. Fossil fuel use will be minimized much as renewable energy is today, with just a small share of the market. In essence, renewable energy will switch places with carbon-based fuels and become the primary, perhaps the only, energy choice.

The cost of electricity will be so great that no one will choose to install inefficient energy fixtures. Incandescent bulbs will cease to exist. Appliances and digital devices will efficiently use energy from a renewable source. The cost of energy will exceed that of a monthly household mortgage or rental payment.

Waste and used materials will become valued resources. Recycling and composting will become the primary means of household waste disposal. Trash receptacles will be replaced with recycling containers and compost bins for organic materials, including food and yard waste. Compostable waste will either be collected by a commercial service, like recycling waste, or reused in household gardens. Trash collection will be cut back drastically, and communities will sponsor regular waste collection days when households can dispose of nonrecyclable items. The cost of trash will outweigh the benefits of having waste hauled away. People will learn to divert materials and waste, or reuse what they have. Family items such as Grandmother's china cabinet, will be valued not just for the treasured memories, but for the savings from not hauling it away.

I see our society realizing the terrible consequences their daily actions and the way they live will have if they do not practice their new mantra, "reduce, reuse, recycle."

Daughter, may you take from this "what's next?" letter a way to achieve a life of balance and resilience. Living on this planet is a luxury. For as the Lorax says, "Unless someone like you cares a whole awful lot, nothing is going to get better. It's not."

SHARLYN THACKER

CID, ASID, LEED AP BD+C

Present and Grateful

My girlfriend texts me a crazy, hilarious yet sad, story about her family and follows it with her infamous "*life." I find myself thinking frequently—and gratefully—of her "*life" mind-set, breathing in deeply, and finding my way to gratefulness.

My journey to green started with a haunting presentation slide about chemicals found in mother's milk during a Natural Step presentation in Oregon.[3] I had embraced environmental choices in my day-to-day lifestyle—eating local and organic foods, composting, minimizing consumption, recycling, and using public transportation. Now I began to more closely examine the impact of my decisions as an interior designer on the environment. The thought of tons of furniture landfilled as a result of choices I had made sickened me.

Inspired and motivated by a William McDonough lecture, I jumped at the chance to work with his architecture firm and moved back East, closer to my family. At McDonough's firm, I dug in deep, exploring the chemical compositions of materials, researching material sources, compiling specifications to support my research, and conversing with like-minded people.

The mountains called to me, and I moved to Roanoke, Virginia, a city nestled in the Blue Ridge Mountains. Roanoke was not a hotbed of sustainable design when I arrived, so I had to forge my own path and spearheaded the formation of the local USGBC chapter. Over the next few years I was swallowed by a green tidal wave. I chaired the local USGBC chapter, administered a cradle-to-cradle design competition that went global, designed for a small, passionately green architecture firm, served on numerous committees, and consulted directly with the USGBC. Then the ocean calmed.

---

[3] See http://www.naturalstep.org/.

I gave birth to my son, and he refocused my life. Being present became a priority: present for my son, present for the limited hours available to work, and present for myself. Failing to maintain my health could be devastating to my son, who fully depends on me. A failure to set a good example of patience, peace, generosity, compassion, and connectivity could impact my son for his lifetime.

I was raising my son alone. But when given the opportunity to work a forty-plus-hour-a-week job with benefits, I chose to do otherwise. I work several part-time jobs from home and mirror my son's school schedule. The mornings start early, and most workdays are condensed and feverishly paced. But I am present. When the school bus comes in the afternoon, I'm at my son's bus stop. I focus on workaday details: Am I doing work that is meaningful to me and those impacted by it? Did I conserve fuel by consolidating errands into one trip? Did we eat healthy local, minimally processed food? Did my dog and I go for a walk and breathe in the outside? Did I hug my son and tell him I love him? Did I express gratitude to my coworkers, friends, family, and myself? I am present. I am grateful.

My days as an in-house university interior designer and an interior designer within an architecture firm are in the past. My work now encompasses green building consulting, administrative work, and commercial furniture sales. Through it all I see a common thread: community-building. As I continue on my life's path, my thoughts are of sharing, coming together to support, grow, and enrich other lives, and being grateful. Tired of consumerism, constant information overload, and marketing that frames us as always busy and always needing another thing, I'm striving not to think of myself as busy or needful. I am learning to slow down, and enjoy the peace that comes with sitting quietly. I stop to talk with my neighbors during the day. I lend a helping hand to an elderly person at the post office. I send a Facebook message to a grieving friend. I listen to my son's stories. It is these moments that community builds and on which our future depends.

Much as I started looking at the impact of my interior design decisions earlier in my career, I now find myself digging deeper into the companies that I support and promote—community-driven digging. Do they pay their employees fairly? Do they purchase their raw materials from a sustainable, well-managed source? Do they give back to the communities in which they operate? Do they provide some freedom to their employees to adapt their working hours to the their individual needs? Does the management stop and listen? Visionaries like Ray Anderson, Paul Hawken, and William McDonough and thought-leaders like E. O. Wilson and David Orr compelled me to where I am today. Now I find hope and joy in the individuals, families, and companies that have answered those questions compassionately *and* successfully and in those who share their joy with the communities in which they live or touch in some way: a potter, a banjo-maker, a budding gardener, a couple of folksingers, a brewer, a permaculture teacher, community-supported agriculture farmers, and a master craftsman woodworker.

Instead of resisting "*life," I am learning to embrace all that life entails.

With health, patience, peace, generosity, compassion, and connectivity at the core of all my decisions, my community will grow. This community-centered mindset gives me hope for tomorrow.

I am present. I am grateful.

Health

ALLISON BEER MCKENZIE

AIA, LEED AP; architect and director of sustainability, SHP Leading Design

After earning my master's degree in architecture from the University of Cincinnati in 2006 and receive my architects license in 2009, I settled in as an architect and my firm's director of sustainability. Occupying those roles simultaneously allows me to research and pursue strategic decisions for my firm's sustainability mission without losing sight of the realities of project budgets and client needs and expectations. My firm, SHP Leading Design, focuses on educational environments, but we also dabble in residential projects. My work on educational projects is fulfilling, but the residential projects become personal. There is something unique and powerful about shaping the environment that someone will live in, something urgent and important.

Whatever project I am working on, I strive to make it as sustainable as possible. For me, sustainability is not just about saving energy and picking green materials; it is about making the correct choices for the ongoing durability and health of the building and its occupants. Sustainable design has a giant arsenal of tools for positively impacting the lives of a building's users, and my goal is to use the right tools for each client and project.

Sustainable design is not static. New technologies and materials are invented or discovered constantly, as are new methods for evaluating our current practices. I try always to stay on top of these new developments and find ways to employ them on projects responsibly. Currently my firm is pursuing the AIA 2030 Commitment and the growing availability of environmental product declarations and how those can be incorporated into true life-cycle thinking about our projects.

Many architects have inspired me, but right now I am much more inspired by the startup culture pervading the United States and especially my own hometown, Cincinnati. This is the age of the agile thinking entrepreneur who sees a problem or a need and throws herself into addressing it, often at great risk and sometimes with huge rewards. The profession of architecture is changing, and I think we can learn a lot about risk and reward and catalyzing growth in our culture. Society and technology are moving much, much faster than they ever have before, and our profession of bricks and mortar must be a little nimbler if it is to be sustainable.

BETH SCOTT

Creator and owner, AD RescueWear, LLC

As a designer at Associates III, I gained experience in sustainable design and feel strongly about a sustainable approach to living. But when I became a mother of a child with asthma, allergies, and eczema, its importance really hit home. My son's illness not only strengthened my convictions about sustainable living, it also inspired me to start an eco-friendly medical device company with products that naturally treat childhood eczema. I'm now connected with many people who are searching for natural, simpler solutions to health issues, a desire that flows into all areas of their lives.

There seems to be a yearning for the past—or at least what people *perceive* to be simpler times—and people want to be inspired. Sustainable products and spaces designed to inspire will be in demand, and they will blend old and new, beauty and simplicity, and a greater connectedness to nature. The goal of the design process should be to reduce stress and make people happier by nurturing their spirit and mental health. I'm inspired by the essentials important to children and my aging friends and family alike: health, connection, nature, comfort, simplicity, and balance.

Figure 22.2 The Wrap-E-Soothe suit is a specialty medical garment for the treatment of atopic dermatitis or eczema. The suit is made from 94 percent Oeko-Tex fiber tencel, lyocell, and 6 percent spandex.

Photo: Beth Scott, courtesy of AD RescueWear, LLC.

CLAIRE E. TAMBURRO

ASID, LEED AP, ID+C

I was born at the end of the 1960s, and the recycling, antipollution, and fire prevention campaigns were popular and pervasive—in schools, on TV and radio, on billboards. In 1971, television ads such as the ones promoted by the United States Forest Service had a profound influence on me. In it, Woodsy Owl proclaimed, "Give a hoot—don't pollute," and Smokey the Bear told us, "Only *you* can prevent forest fires. That year also brought us the "Keep America Beautiful" public service announcements featuring actor Iron Eyes Cody portraying an Native American crying at the sight of Earth's natural beauty destroyed by thoughtless litter and pollution.

My Depression-era parents also modeled the benefits of recycling and reusing in our home. As the youngest of five children, our regular routine included collecting and separating green, clear, and brown glass and newspapers to bring to a recycling bin in a local church parking lot. My parents also reused many items to help our large family save money and conserve resources. Worn out bath and hand towels and bed sheets became rags for cleaning. Empty mayonnaise, peanut butter, and glass jars were used to refrigerate leftovers. Glass baby food jars held nails and screws that lined the shelves of my father's basement workbench. To this day, my family still uses old half-gallon glass orange juice bottles with metal lids for freshly made iced tea and lemonade.

In the future, there must be more collaboration among industries. Specifically, the medical, recycling, and manufacturing industries must envision, design, and produce new building materials and products that integrate recycled materials into all design projects. And architects and designers must listen to and collaborate with the medical community, because doctors are on the frontlines of how human beings react to the built environments we create and to the products we use in those environments.

After many consultations with doctors, naturopaths, allergists, and nutritionists about my own allergies and sensitivities, it became apparent that the cause of many illnesses begins with the decisions we designers make at the drawing board. These two industries working together could avoid or eliminate many chronic illnesses and end needless suffering. The advent of sustainability has produced myriad alternative building methods and materials whose manufacturers tout excellent performance difficult to judge without long-term empirical data. Medical insight into evaluating these new products would help both confirm those claims and avoid costly or harmful mistakes. Working as a team to refine our product designs and manufacturing processes, we can better address the health, safety, and welfare of the public for which we design.

To keep our country viable, sustainable, lean, and on the cutting edge of technology, we need large-scale, coordinated recycling efforts between businesses that will bring manufacturing back to the United States. By using the abundance of untapped resources already in circulation, we can prevent precious natural resources from being further depleted. This is especially true of companies in industries who may never have considered doing business with each other before.

This is where innovation lies. If the Japanese can build an imposing naval fleet from scrap metal they purchased from the United States in the 1930s, then surely we can reuse all of the materials, plastics, metals, glass, cardboard, paper, and textiles we throw away by the ton every day and turn them into useful products that don't require the use of any new resources. The production of goods that are useful, affordable, and safe and that also keep our land, air, and waterways clean will make the United States self-reliant and profitable. Add medical advisors for human well-being and interior designers to that mix of visionaries, and the new products will not only be functional and safe but also luxurious and beautiful. Interior designers will specify how to coordinate these efforts to make recycling a standard practice. If we request it, it will happen.

I admire my parents, as well as Dr. Sherry Rogers, Dr. Joseph Mercola, and Dr. Arlene Blum, who have inspired me to combine my education and life experiences into a focused practice of sustainable interior design.

My parents, Rose Marie and Bill Tamburro Sr., taught me to respect the earth by reusing and recycling materials to prevent buildup in landfills and to save money by reusing resources. My parents are also strong advocates of natural medicine and support alternative therapies that work *with* the body. They attribute illness prevention to good nutrition and a healthy lifestyle, practices I also embrace.

I am a life-long allergy sufferer. During her thirty-seven-year practice, my allergist, Dr. Sherry Rogers, has researched natural medicine and molecular biochemistry of the body to understand how it heals itself. After reading her book, *The E.I. Syndrome: An Rx for Environmental Illness*, I understood that working together, the design and medical communities can make a vast difference in the lives of our clients and patients by integrating our knowledge to eliminate toxins from our environments and perfecting the design of new and existing products marketed to the public.[4]

Dr. Joseph Mercola has helped me learn more about of the causes of environmental illness through his online newsletter.[5] Dr. Mercola is board-certified in family medicine. An osteopathic physician is trained in both traditional and natural medicine, he uses a holistic approach, treating the entire person rather than just symptoms. His focus is the prevention of illness through lifestyle changes rather than symptom management with medications. Dr. Mercola regularly comments on environmental illness caused by electromagnetic fields (EMFs); exposure to Mercury in water, dental amalgams, and lighting sources; fluoride toxicity in our water supplies; phthalates from vinyl flooring; and bisphenol-A (BPA) water bottles.

Dr. Arlene Blum is a biophysical chemist, an author, and a visiting scholar at the University of California-Berkeley's Department of Chemistry. She is the founder and executive director of the Green Science Policy Institute, whose mission is to promote the responsible use of chemicals and reduce the use of harsh, bioaccumulative chemicals with healthier ones. She is also known for her pioneering research into regulating the use of two cancer-causing chemicals in children's sleepwear in the 1970s.

Currently, Dr. Blum and her team have worked on Technical Bulletin CAL 117, specifically the updated standard TB 117-2013, which went into effect in January 2014. TB117-2013 seeks to protect public health and increase fire safety by addressing how and where fires start in the real world. Fires start on fabric, and cigarettes are the leading cause of furniture fires. TB117-2013 requires a smolder test for fabric, which was absent from the old standard. And flame retardant chemicals are not needed in order to meet TB117-2013. This means improved fire safety without toxic chemicals.

---

[4] http://organicconnectmag.com/sherry-rogers-md-god-designed-the-body-to-heal/#.UlnJO1Nuhg0.

[5] www.mercola.com.

CYNTHIA LEIBROCK

ASID, Hon. IIDA; Easy Access to Health LLC; author[6]

In my own house, I have integrated over 200 green and universal features.[7] For example, we use active solar panels and passive solar greenhouses to provide most of our heat.

Many older and disabled people have reduced circulation and need higher ambient temperatures (up to 78°F) but can't afford the higher heating costs. Our heating bills have averaged $69 per month in Colorado, and we are at an altitude of 7,500 feet with temperatures as low as −20°F.

We have insulation with high R-values, and we have tested for leaks using pressure and infrared techniques. We added door bottoms that drop down to seal, obviating thresholds, which are tripping hazards for older and disabled people. Our programmable thermostat reduces energy use and can be set from a laptop, a real advantage for wheelchair users and those who are bedridden. It can be operated from anywhere there is Internet access (including an airplane) in case you forget to turn down your heat or need to preheat your house to accommodate someone with reduced circulation.

In the summer, our evaporative cooler uses far less energy than air conditioning while making the house comfortable for older and disabled who cannot tolerate extremes of heat and cold. Our reversible ceiling fans also cool in the summer and draw heat up from the greenhouses in the winter.

But these ideas apply to all projects, not just those for older and disabled people. Universal and sustainable design is really just good design, not a special type of design for a special population.

MARY CORDARO

Bau-biologist specializing in healthy and sustainable building materials, interiors, and indoor air quality, Mary Cordaro, Inc.

There is no separation between my love for and connection with the earth and my deep passion for human health. For the last twenty-four years, I have worked with people who have been seriously injured by the effects of poorly designed and built homes and workspaces—by mold, chemicals, EMFs, and other contaminants—and I have learned that indoor environments dramatically and unquestionably affect human health.

Whether we're outdoors or indoors, we are designed to maintain a constant healing connection with nature. Our body's biology depends on that connection

---

[6]Cynthia A. Leibrock and Debra D. Harris. *Design Details for Health: Making the Most of Design's Healing Potential* (Hoboken, NJ: Wiley, 2011).

[7]www.AgingBeautifully.org/ranch.

and will be supported by buildings that connect us to the natural frequencies of the earth and contribute to lowering our body's burden of contaminants, thus helping us avoid serious illness. The indoor levels of any type of contaminant should be no higher than background levels found in clean, healthy, natural environments. Nature is not something "out there." During my career, I have aimed to bring healing nature indoors, to make the home a retreat and a healing environment, and to help bring the body back into balance.

The outer world is unhealthy for most of us: We are constantly bombarded by EMFs, smog, and other serious environmental contaminants; but if we can retreat to our own healthy homes, we can regenerate and heal and better deal with what we cannot control in our outdoor worlds.

Over twenty years ago, after completing a course in bau-biologie,[8] I wanted to find a career in natural building. I took hands-on natural building courses and experienced the feeling of being in nature while indoors. There was nothing like it: It spoke to a primal part of me. I fell in love with natural building in all its forms. And I was taught prudent avoidance, a harbinger of the current Precautionary Principle.[9] Consequently, I became suspicious of synthetic, petroleum-based product materials because so little good science existed to prove their long-term safety.

Unfortunately, a career in natural building in Los Angeles, was a long way off. Instead, I spent the next ten years learning all that is wrong with light-frame structures typically built in North America and how to remediate or improve them. I learned that light-frame buildings are inherently energy-intensive and often unhealthy, and I learned how to test, diagnose, and remediate homes for many types of pollutants, including mold, chemicals, and electromagnetic fields (EMFs). A far cry from creating buildings that connect us to nature, I was forced instead to focus on avoiding contaminants.

Working with colleagues in related, specialized fields, I now do the best possible job to bring down those contaminants to healthy bau-biologie standards, both for new or existing homes and workplaces. Given the usual toxic materials, building defects, moisture issues, unhealthy forced-air heating and cooling systems, and very complex building physics typical of light-frame buildings, this is not an easy or inexpensive task.

But the future of healthy building cannot simply be one of remediating the flaws inherent in our toxic structures. There's no longer any reason to be satisfied with "less toxic," and there's every reason to push the envelope farther, to use the healthiest

---

[8]Bau-biologie, a field of study that originated in Germany and Switzerland, is the study of the holistic interrelationships between humans and their living environment. http://www .baubiologie.de/site/english.php.

[9]The Precautionary Principle states that if an action or policy has a suspected risk of causing harm to the public or to the environment, in the absence of scientific proof that the action or policy is harmful, the burden of proof that it is not harmful falls on those taking the action. http://www.sehn.org/precaution.html.

materials and systems available, and to teach our clients to put health first—before the home's size and fixed ideas of aesthetics. Moreover, we must design and build for the most exquisitely sensitive of us all: the developing fetus. As scientist and author Sandra Steinberger so eloquently puts it, the benchmark for health must be safety for the developing fetus because the developing fetus is our future.

And yet, we have no standards of environmental safety for the developing fetus, despite studies proving that up to three hundred chemicals can be found in their umbilical cord blood. When exposed in utero to some contaminants, babies are much more likely to be born at lower birth weights, may display behavioral problems, and may later develop serious illnesses, including heart disease, diabetes, and cancer.

Environmental contaminants increased in magnitude and seriousness overall, and science has also been rapidly keeping pace with their toll on human health. Allergy, asthma, cancer, and autism rates for children are skyrocketing. We now know that even very low levels of some contaminants over the long term can be more dangerous than short-term acute exposures and that some exposures can cause transgenerational damage. There are many international databases full of studies and research on environmental health effects. The field of environmental medicine has uncovered the ugly truth that most of us walk around with a body burden of accumulated toxicity conducive to serious health effects, including cancer.

The focus of green design and green building is gradually moving toward biological health. This is appropriate, but "less toxic" environments are not the same as environments that actually support human health and the health of the developing fetus. We cannot send pregnant women to another planet, as one environmental physician so aptly noted. Health-supportive environments must be what drives all of us who are in the profession of building and design. That is my goal as I specify healthier building and interior materials and systems, help healthy and environmentally sensitive clients improve existing homes, and when I teach and write.

PENNY BONDA

FASID, LEED fellow, partner, Ecoimpact Consulting, LLC, author[10]

In 1996, as the national president of the American Society of Interior Designers, I attended a very early meeting of the U.S. Green Building Council. Walking in, I didn't even know what a green building was. As I listened to early green pioneers such as Rick Fedrizzi, David Gottfried, Rob Watson, Bill Reed and others, I learned that over the course of my thirty-year career as a commercial interior designer, I had been inadvertently harming the occupants of the spaces I designed. Designers are sometimes guilty of creating bad or even dehumanizing environments; I've likely contributed to untold health problems.

---

[10]Penny Bonda, Katie Sosnowchik, and Summer Minchew, *Sustainable Commercial Interiors*, 2nd ed. (Hoboken, NJ: Wiley, 2014).

My epiphany was followed by a gradual realization of the profound impact of my work and that of my professional colleagues on the quality of buildings and their effect on occupant health. Working with the very smartest people in our field, I've watched the green building movement mature, led by the development and adoption of LEED in multiple market segments. We are no longer wondering what to do or how to do it: We are challenged to take what we know and moving beyond sustainability into what my friend Bill Reed calls "regeneration." We must follow the USGBC and the Healthy Building Network into a new era of transparency that makes green building possible. Innovators are developing brilliant technologies for reducing water use and alternatives to the use of fossil fuels. Manufacturers introduce products with positive life-cycles and eliminate end-of-use waste. And Alex Wilson, founder and executive editor, BuildingGreen, is addressing our most pressing need with his advocacy of resiliency in the design of our buildings so they can keep us safe when the damages we've inflicted on our climate harm us.

Sustainability is not just a buzzword; it's a real issue. It's a concept that the all nations must vigorously embrace—right now. Sometimes we treat this planet as though we have a spare one in our pocket.

High Performance

ANN V. EDMINSTER

LEED AP, owner, Design Avenues, LLC, author[11]

After earning a bachelor's degree in architecture, I spent fifteen years doing residential remodeling design, with a parallel career in technical writing. I then got bitten by the green building bug (before the term "green building" had been coined), went back to school, and got my master's in architecture. My graduate work focused on energy efficiency and green materials, which have remained important to me throughout the twenty years since I earned the M.Arch. I'm now a green building consultant, educator, advocate, and author. I spent a big chunk of time bringing the LEED for Homes program to fruition and then, wanting to more directly address the climate crisis, wrote my most recent book, *Energy Free: Homes for a Small Planet*. *Energy Free* is a guidebook for those wishing to design and build zero-net-energy dwellings.

My current pursuits reflect my priorities for the future: zero net energy, integrated project delivery, and nurturing individuals' and organizations' capacity to deliver higher-performing buildings. Underlying all of these is my sense of urgency for transforming the processes by which we create, modify, and maintain our built environment to new approaches that produce climate-positive and life-affirming results.

---

[11] Ann V. Edminster and Peter Yost, *Energy Free: Homes for a Small Planet* (San Rafael, CA: Green Building Press, 2009).

I am inspired by my son Quinn, by the urge to mend the world he will inherit, and by what I learn from him as we grow together. The extraordinary community of green building practitioners is also a source of great inspiration, a cast of brilliant, dedicated, loving, and uplifting characters. I am particularly indebted to (in approximately the order I met them) Ray Cole, Peter Yost, Rob Watson, Nadav Malin, Betsy Pettit, Joe Lstiburek, Linda Wigington, Bill Reed, Alex Wilson, Kathleen O'Brien, Bruce King, Kirsten Ritchie, Danny Parker, and Ed Mazria.

CARL SEVILLE

Recovered contractor, green curmudgeon, consultant, educator, writer on residential green building, SK Collaborative

During my twenty-five years as a remodeler, I learned about green building, which ultimately led me to leave the construction industry and focus on education, writing, consulting, and the certification of green buildings. I've been involved in EarthCraft Homes, the LEED reference guide, Regreen Residential Remodeling Guidelines, and Green Building Advisor.

The priorities for the future should be: high-performing healthy and safe buildings for all. Green building must become the standard. Right now, so few buildings even meet basic codes and manufacturers' recommended installation instructions it makes green a stretch. In a competitive market, it is hard for contractors to charge more for high-quality work when competing against others who do substandard work.

I fear we will continue to see a large portion of the construction market improve quality too slowly, only as codes and enforcement become more stringent and incentives are offered. It will be a slow march to high-quality, high-performance construction. Consumers will be attracted by the bling—solar panels, tankless water heaters, "natural" materials—but may ignore the complex process that construction is.

The industry is sold individual products that must be carefully selected and assembled into a system for proper short- and long-term performance. Unfortunately, not enough industry professionals understand building systems to make the right decisions in selections and installation that ensure systems are properly designed and implemented. I would like to see manufacturers of non-competing but complementary products work together to educate the industry about how to do things right.

When I see a designer, builder, developer, or owner who makes the effort to do things right because it is the right thing to do, I am always impressed. Too many people build green for the wrong reasons—incentives and requirements—and often cut corners to meet minimum requirements. When buildings are planned green from the start, it makes me happy—too many projects are designed without considering overall sustainability; certification is an afterthought, and many of the high-performance features and systems are value-engineered out of the project in the process. I want to see design teams incorporate their consultants and certifiers from the very beginning of a project. They provide an understanding of the project that most others don't get from working in their individual silos. They can help evaluate mechanical and structural systems early in the design phase to make sure that buildings work as well as possible. Too many buildings are greened up as an afterthought. This must change.

DAVID BERGMAN

RA, LEED AP; principal, David Bergman Architect; Fire & Water Lighting; adjunct faculty, Parsons/The New School for Design; author[12]

Sustainable thinking tells us that we live in a world in which we have too much stuff (at least in some parts of the world) and that the ways we make all that stuff is harming the environment. That leaves eco-designers with a dilemma. We've all heard the statement "the only green product is nothing." What, then, are responsible designers to do? It isn't satisfying, let alone professionally or financially responsible, to design nothing. I've been tackling this question from my overlapping perspectives as an architect, sustainability advocate, author, and professor.

Designers are, by nature, optimists. (Indeed, it's one of the reasons my blog is titled *EcoOptimism*.) Designers look at a thing or a problem and immediately start imagining what could be.

One of the routes conflicted designers can take—and for which we're very well suited—is to employ our abilities as generalists spanning the disciplines of art, math, physics, sociology, psychology, economics, and, sometimes, for those designing private residences, couples counseling. This renaissance-like training uniquely qualifies us to look at complex, multidisciplinary issues as a system. And this makes us ideally suited to see—and communicate—the bigger picture inherent in environmentalism.

Designers must also be visionaries. How else to see possibilities amid the economic and ecological rubble? Or to envision potential utopias where others fear postapocalyptic dystopia? We have the ability (and responsibility) to devise solutions to some of the pressing problems of our built world. Doing this enables us to design without contributing further to the proliferation of consumerism, embodied in the justly pilloried McMansion and other types of conspicuous consumption. In short, we can still follow what led us to be designers—the desire to create—without contradicting our environmentalist role.

Two specific areas of design, both with implications for residential interiors, come to mind. While it's more fun and a lot sexier to ponder futuristic ideas (like cutting-edge, high-tech homes or one of my favorite concepts, organically growing

---

[12]David Bergman, *Sustainable Design: A Critical Guide* (New York: Princeton Architectural Press, 2012)

new buildings), the reality is that we have a huge stock of existing buildings, both in and out of our cities, that are terribly energy-inefficient and/or in danger of becoming obsolete as we demographically change from a suburban to a more urban population. Those buildings, including much of our current housing, represent a tremendous amount of existing materials and embodied energy. Tearing them down or abandoning them, as we could very well in auto-dependent suburbs, would be enormously wasteful.

Instead, we should be focusing our energy and imaginations on devising better or innovative ways to bring those buildings into the future by upgrading buildings in our cities to make them more energy-efficient and more responsive to twenty-first-century living and working styles and by rethinking our suburbs in the wake of both changing lifestyles and changing economics. Dying malls, foreclosed housing, and rising transportation costs have lead to predictions of the abandonment of the suburbs. But we can employ our designer's visionary optimism to devise solutions such as reusing malls and rethinking suburban bedroom communities.

This goes well beyond this book's topic of residential interiors, but that's part of the point. Architecture and interior design have tended to look at projects and goals in delimited terms rather than in more holistic, systems approaches. And we know that one of the tenets of sustainable design is to think in systems. Just as it is inadequate to call a house that is well-insulated but has poor indoor air quality sustainable, it is insufficient to deem a house or a building green if it throws away existing resources or if its location necessitates fossil fuel burning and congestion causing transportation.

None of this, mind you, competes with our designer's yearn for aesthetics, for the beauty, comfort, and function in kitchens, bathrooms, furniture, and cabinet knobs—what we tend to label "good design." Rather, it adds another layer, broadening both our responsibilities and possibilities.

MICHAEL LEHMAN

LC, MIES, LEED AP ID+C; Regreen-trained ASID educator; vice president of marketing and product management, ConTech Lighting

Over twenty years, I have been a lighting designer and energy professional on hundreds of projects for both architectural and theatrical environments as well as a lighting manufacturer executive, marketing vice president, new product developer, sustainability professional, energy code expert, and educator on all topics lighting from the latest lighting and computer technologies to lighting for human health and performance. I work with many industry organizations on standards and education, including the American Institute of Architect, the Illuminating Engineering Society of North America, the U.S. Green Building Council, the Green Building Certification Institute, the American Society of Interior Designers, and Healthy Child Healthy World. My continuing passion is to create and educate about the "lighting experience"—use nature and technology to design fixtures and environments that benefit people, their health and places, and our planet.

I see amazing opportunities for the future, provided our priorities are in order. But there are also opportunities for danger. Technology, education, and communication are the three priorities that will give us the brightest future. Illumination is an essential part of both human performance and sustainability, and always has been. Illumination has directly affected life on Earth from the beginning, letting us know when to sleep and wake. The evolution of artificial light has directly impacted human development throughout the ages. Think about it: subjects like medicine have been studied and practiced for thousands of years, while artificial illumination has been around for just over one hundred. As a discipline, lighting is in its infancy. Yet artificial light has literally changed our lives by giving us the opportunity to live and work at any time of day or night. Indeed, light affects us twenty-four hours a day. For the last hundred years, there have been lighting designers and an evolution of technology, but for the most part lighting has utilized standard sockets and standard practices. General complacency and lack of understanding in the late 1900s led many architects and engineers to simply overlight spaces with two-by-four fluorescent troffers just to make sure there was enough light. Unfortunately, this overlighting led not only to wasted energy and the introduction of toxic chemicals, but it also sometimes impacted human beings in a negative way.

Throughout those one hundred years, though, there were excellent lighting practitioners who created beautiful visions for spaces and the people who used them. Technological advances have given us the opportunity to create environments that benefit people, our places, and our planet. LED technologies as well as other new technology like organic light-emitting diodes (OLED), quantum dots, and bioluminescence, along with great new controls, occupancy sensors, and even daylight, are all great tools we can use if we understand them properly and apply them correctly. New technologies allow luminaires to produce the same quality and quantity of light that older sources produce while dramatically reducing energy consumption. For this to happen effectively, though, the quality has to be there as well, not just the quantity of light.

Light output will continue to increase, and the wattage will continue to go down. We can't identify sources by wattage as we have in the past because the wattage only measures energy consumption; to do this we need to add light output, shape, cutoff, glare control, and color accuracy. LED technology is allowing us to increase the quality of light in our spaces, as long as we specify the right fixtures, for all LEDs are not created equal. Glare, wattage, fixture appearance, beam appearance, and intensity are all criteria we can evaluate quickly, but many fixtures are specified based on erroneous claims or a misunderstanding of inaccurate information on specification sheets. Raw LED chip data, which is published by some manufacturers, is not delivered-fixture data. There is also the information many people cannot understand quickly and as a result take on faith, like thermal, color shift, and life data. Many five- or ten-year warranties really don't cover the complete fixture and are difficult to redeem, as most people don't keep receipts for ten years.

Newer manufacturing and materials give us the chance to make our light sources fully reusable or recyclable. Someday our light sources will be locally sourced and compliant with the cradle-to-cradle needs of our planet. Today, sustainability begins with reusing items where possible and recycling when it's not. Lighting today is more sustainable than ever, creating better lit environments that consume less energy than ever before—and we're just getting started.

These great tools offer many opportunities if they are properly understood and applied, which can be done only when we teach people about that technology and the solutions it provides. This education will give all users the tools to make their vision a reality. We have to look beyond the building industry requirements of lumens per watt to the actual delivered light and the appearance of the light itself. Glare is one of the primary problems with LED products today. Manufacturers just want to get the light out. But is it useable light? Usually not, but the product tests a high-efficacy rating anyway. And what are efficacy, glare, and lumens per watt anyway? First we must all speak the same language.

Let's think bigger. Why does an LED have to fit into a traditional E26 socket? Because there are millions out there to fill— and they should do so to save energy, provided the light is right. But do all LEDs have to fit the traditional sockets? No. LED technology is a completely different form factor than we have ever had; let's put it where we need it, not just for energy savings, but to enhance performance as well. The latest airliners are integrating LED technology not just to light up the cabin but also to shift to cooler colors to help the passengers relax. Why can't we do this in our homes? What if we integrated LEDs into our cabinetry as a flat panel, or illuminated a section of wall or ceiling or furniture? What if we integrated lighting technology into an architectural column so it self-illuminates? Can we send energy remotely to an illuminating light imbedded in a ceiling to avoid running power and controls through the wall? What if we just turned our lights on and off with sensors or with our phones?

Education about the technology may also help us create healthier spaces. Could current research into melatonin production and suppression allow us to create lights that help our bodies heal themselves and avoid disease? We are all part of nature. LED light can be tuned to provide the intensity and color of any place on earth, at any time of year—as nature intended. Perhaps we can eliminate seasonal affective disorder. I'm working on a source that mimics daylight throughout the day and year, so your circadian rhythm is consistently in balance. Why can't you get the same quality and quantity of light in northern Alaska that you would expect to get in Florida? You could even provide this natural-like light to astronauts in space so their circadian rhythm remains consistent and they stay healthy and perform better.

Color quality and tunable LEDs, just as daylight and natural views, can contribute to improved healing in hospitals. Lighting can also increase our comfort in residences, performance in offices, and sales in retail environments. Educating about how to approach design beyond sustainability to include not just *enough* light but a layered lighting approach that puts the right amount of light where and when you need it. Understanding general, accent, task, and decorative lighting on horizontal and vertical surfaces will create better environments for everyone while reducing energy load. Lighting design is no longer merely a nice-to-have service; it is evolving into a specialty that is needed in the construction and design industries. Education will also assist in research into and the understanding of other facets of lighting, like the impacts and reduction of harmonics, electromagnetic fields, phantom loads, and air transfer throughout.

We must also communicate this information in a way accessible to all users, from seasoned professionals, architects, and engineers to maintenance staff, students, and even household consumers. There are a lot of great products available today, and there are many manufacturers correctly communicating what they have. There are also a myriad of sources from which we are receiving unclear or just plain incorrect data. There are manufacturers that put one version of data on the front of their spec sheets and different info on the back. We also have codes and standards, both required and optional, at the international, national, state, and local level. Most of these focus on energy use and nothing else. The result is an ability to solve one part of the puzzle but not even looking at the rest. The information should be simplified so it can be communicated easily and explaining how it relates to energy, safety, light quality, and human health.

LEED v4 starts to do this with points for lighting quality. The Lighting Facts program is intended to be a benchmark. But how many consumers who have always purchased a 90-watt lamp know what a lumen is or what 3,000k measures? Some stores are now identifying lights based on wattage range as "bright" or "crisp." How does this help anyone? These terms are subjective and leave consumers confused. Effective communication requires clear, accurate, and understandable data.

Future possibilities are unlimited. New tools, new technology, and new collaborations can dramatically reduce our energy consumption, enhance the aesthetics of our built environment, and create healthier and better performing spaces for all of us. Through technology, education, and communication, we can realize these visions.

I find inspiration in a vision of the future and a better quality of light that results in a better quality of life for all people. I am also inspired by my family, nature, and past visionaries like Walt Disney, Robert Goddard, Leonardo da Vinci, and Michelangelo.

SAM KLEIN

LEED AP Homes; director of sustainability, Comfort Systems USA Energy Services

Energy efficiency is a cost-effective resource for limiting CO_2 emissions. Technology has outpaced energy codes, but banks do not require and even discourage increased upfront costs that could make building operations half as expensive; they evaluate payments, insurance, taxes, and interest (PITI) while ignoring E (energy), which is more than ITI combined. The typical homeowner pays $75,000 in energy costs over the lifetime of their mortgages. There are huge opportunities in building design, construction, legislation, and codes.

Building Design and Construction   Integrated design and energy models will allow project teams to evaluate the energy use. Building information modeling (BIM) can allow project teams to collaborate remotely in real time and see immediately the impact of different scenarios. In the past, energy models were expensive and difficult to manipulate. As the costs of BIM decreases and its accessibility improves, designs will allow more creativity in the pursuit of maximum efficiency.

Buildings are complex and expensive, yet much of the work on them is still done by hand and on the job site, which is rarely an ideal, controllable environment. Larger buildings are now constructed modularly and even robotically. Modular and factory construction not only eliminates waste, it allows the construction of more efficient wall systems that drive the reduction of heating and cooling costs. Heating and cooling loads account for more than half of residential building energy use. Often details like continuous insulation are much easier to build in the controlled environment of a factory.

Legislation and Codes   The SAVE Act will help banks understand the ramifications of bad first-cost decisions.[13] The bill requires homes to have the equivalent of a mile-per-gallon sticker and to factor energy costs into homebuyers' ability to purchase homes, just as banks do with PITI. As a result, builders and design teams will justify better but costlier designs with tangible cash flow evaluations of the downstream operating costs of buildings.

Maryland was the first state to adopt the International Energy Conservation Code (IECC) 2013. New construction in parts of the country consumes almost twice the energy that it would if it were built to IECC 2013. Homes built to IECC 2015 will consume nearly half of the energy of a home built to IECC 2006. As you can see from the map below, we still have a long way to go before the rest of the country follow suit.

---

[13] See http://www.imt.org/finance-and-leasing/save-act.

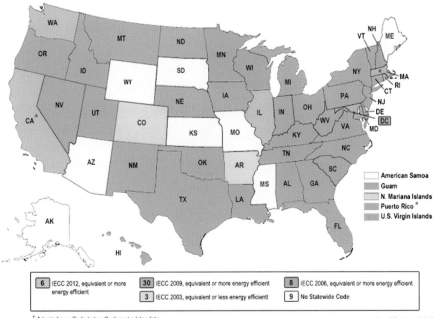

Figure 22.3 Status of state energy code adoption. The status displayed is for residential buildings in the United States and its territories.[14]

Source: U.S. Department of Energy.

The Future Europeans consume half the amount of energy per capita as Americans. They have stopped giving away their clean air for free to the utilities. This drives up the cost of energy, which allows for innovation in efficiency. In 1999, when I first showed my father a compact fluorescent light bulb that cost $25 he thought I was crazy. Now you can buy them for $4. The bulbs made economic sense at $25 fourteen years ago, and he still has a couple of those original bulbs in use. As codes and banking regulations converge on smart economic choices, investment in tools like modular construction and higher-efficiency systems will proliferate. If it can happen for light bulbs, imagine the possibilities for entire buildings.

DAVID HESLAM

Executive director, Earth Advantage Institute

I worked as a residential contractor in Portland, Oregon, for fifteen years, focusing on utilizing best practices in green design and construction methods. Since 2008, I have worked at Earth Advantage, a nonprofit that provides sustainability knowledge to professionals and building-performance information to consumers. A large amount

---

[14] http://www.energycodes.gov/status-state-energy-code-adoption.

of my work in recent years has been on the development of residential energy performance ratings. The goal is to establish systems that are cost-effective to implement, consistent through time, and deliver information that people can understand and use to make decisions about the operations and construction of their buildings.

In the future it is going to be very important to broaden the scope of building performance beyond just the energy required for operations, and we need to get those metrics right from the start. For instance, much attention paid to actual energy usage has not tracked what had been estimated in the design phase for green buildings. because our energy targets were measured in the wrong units. In the past we have strived for performance 15 or 30 percent better than code. But who knows what that means? Leading practitioners are now tracking energy budgets for buildings to make sure we hit our performance targets. Estimating performance against a theoretical design standard does not help people operate their buildings more efficiently. Let's get them the information they need. These targets will vary by climate zone, and that's fine: We also need to make sure our designs are regionally appropriate.

We need an equal level of transparency about the other impacts our buildings have on their occupants. For many years, green building certifications have all touted the same five pillars of sustainable building practice; energy, water, site, resources, and health. I've discussed the measurement of energy usage; now design and operations must address water usage. Much of the world is experiencing severe water shortages; the transparency we are developing around energy usage must now be applied to water.

Providing performance data on the health impacts of buildings is trickier. Environmental product declarations are a great step toward transparency; they tell us what chemicals are present within materials. But indoor air quality is also affected by many other factors, including relative humidity, cleaning habits, radon, outdoor air quality, filtration equipment, and ventilation strategies. In the past, testing the quality of indoor air has been relegated to expert technicians. In the future, low-cost sensors will be built into indoor environmental quality sensors that report on air quality in real time. There are already Wi-Fi-connected smoke detectors that measure carbon dioxide, relative humidity, and temperature, permitting those indicators to be tracked in every room in a building. This new generation of equipment will enable us to better manage our buildings for health *and* efficiency. It's the job of policy-makers and designers to determine what the target levels of performance should be and communicate them to occupants so they can make sure that performance is delivered.

I am inspired by every professional who tries to make a difference, who pushes beyond their comfort zones and recommends something new to a client. There's risk in every one of those actions. These actions require courage, but the future we face is going to require a great deal of courage. Once we start to track building performance, people will expect better performance. It's the work of design professionals to give it to them.

Restorative

AMANDA STURGEON

FAIA, LEED BD+C; vice president, Living Building Challenge, International Living Future Institute

The Living Building Challenge program inspires me. It sets out a vision for restoring our world through the buildings and communities that we create. Our priorities for the future must address the impacts of global climate change. Our world is changing rapidly; we need solutions that will restore our communities and ecosystems.

Every homeowner has the potential to enact those solutions through the choices they make with every purchase. Every homeowner can choose to restore their soul, place, and ecosystem through a series of small but powerful actions. Our world needs visionaries who can visualize a future that we currently think are impossible.

CARLIE BULLOCK-JONES

ASID, LEED fellow, LEED reviewer, Ecoworks Studio; sustainable design consultant; speaker

As a sustainability consultant with a background in commercial interior design, I've been actively engaged in green building since its infancy and have dedicated my entire career to bringing about a greener, healthier built environment.

Green building is finally becoming standard practice, but significant changes are still needed to address the growing concerns of global climate change: effective implementation of measurement and verification practices to understand how our buildings are performing, a reduction in potable water use in every aspect of building operations, rigorous third-party certification of the products and materials we specify, and overall life-cycle thinking are at the top of my list. We must take mainstream green building to the next level by embracing regenerative development practices, along with net-zero energy and living buildings.

Biomimetic architecture practices are truly inspiring. In my everyday work, it's the clients who start small but realize they're not doing enough and go on to make big impacts who also inspire me. Or the team members who continue to specify low-emitting materials and divert construction waste regardless of whether it's a LEED project or not. Playing a part in those decisions and making those long-term impacts feels good.

TRUDY DUJARDIN

ASID, LEED AP ID+C; educator; principal, Dujardin Design Associates

My longtime involvement with the Leadership Summit on Sustainable Design, hosted by the Design Futures Council, is one of the ways I work for a more sustainable Earth. This commitment encompasses both my green design work and teaching the public and new design students as well as my passion for protecting the environment. I am greatly concerned about climate change and global warming.

I believe that the architecture and design community must take the lead in transforming the way we live, work, and interact with the environment. That transformation will happen through improvements in water and air purification, food production, and carbon sequestration and through a reduction of fossil fuel use and the thousands of untested chemicals currently flooding our Earth. Our built environments must reflect a genuine concern for future generations and a willingness to engage with government, business leaders, and public policy to find the right balance.

I'm inspired by Ed Mazria, founder and CEO of Architecture 2030. An internationally recognized architect, energy expert, educator, and author, he has reshaped the international dialog on energy and climate change to incorporate building design. His focus is on dramatic reduction of the global demand for energy and materials that produce by-product greenhouse gases (GHG). Architecture 2030 recognizes that buildings are the major source of demand for energy and materials that produce greenhouse gases. Mr. Mazria's impassioned support for innovative sustainable design strategies is inspiring a new generation of concerned industry leaders to embrace his vision for the future.

Specifically, Mr. Mazria has emphasized the need to keep the global temperature increase below the 2°C threshold. Entire species disappear when the temperature changes only a fraction of a degree. The recently released Intergovernmental Panel on Climate Change's Fifth Assessment Report concludes that to keep the increase below that mark, global greenhouse gas emissions must peak by 2020 and then begin a rapid decline.

Mr. Mazria has focused on China, currently urbanizing at a rate unmatched in human history, as an opportunity to create healthy, resilient, and integrated regional infrastructures, cities, towns, and buildings that are models of economic and urban sustainability. With projections for its urban population to increase to one billion by 2030, China is leading the way to an urbanized future. Mr. Mazria and Architecture 2030 are working toward the Zero-Net-Energy (ZNE) Accord as an opportunity to plan and design sustainable, carbon neutral built environments that protect and enhance natural resources.

The ZNE Accord urges that cities, towns, urban developments, new buildings and major renovations in China be designed to be Zero Net Energy, or Zero Net Energy Capable. Architecture 2030 is organizing signatures from all those who have offices in China, or current or future plans for projects in China, to add their signatures and pledges to the Accord, to influence urban development in China and throughout the world. More information is available at architecture2030.org.

Regenerative

BILL REED

AIA, LEED AP; principal, Regenesis

The piecemeal mechanical, biological, and social sustainability fixes we have implemented since 1970 are an important and necessary means for slowing down the environmental damage. Yet we know this is insufficient.

My personal paradigm shift occurred when I saw that green buildings alone would not sustain life, because building more stuff sustainably would be a very slow way of ensuring life on the planet will thrive.

Why not use buildings as an opportunity to reframe our relationship with the way life works, allowing the processes of life in the unique place and watershed of the project—or life shed—to shape the nature of building and catalyzing a renewed and ongoing discovery of how the occupants or residents reengage with life so that humans and nature thrive together.

What then is required to build a coevolutionary relationship with the web of life? This is the basic question that has been driving my philosophic and professional journey.

What I see as priorities for the future:

The major problems of the world are the result of the difference between the way nature works and the way people think.
—GREGORY BATESON, *AN ECOLOGY OF MIND*

What we face as a culture is not a design problem; but the way we think. As designers, our design team, clients, and the communities we serve must reengage with life on its own terms, supporting the potential for healthy evolving life for all species.

Here are the kinds of changes in our thinking that will be required:

- Sustainability is not about the stuff, objects, or buildings, it is about life: the exchanges of energy and nutrients between living entities. To evolve we must understand what living entities need to be viable.
- Life consists of whole living systems nested within each other in each unique place.
- Think with nature. Whole systems and all living beings, including humans, can be understood by observing their patterns of living.
- Individual entities are unsustainable. Life requires relationships and exchanges.
- Observe the essential patterns that allow life to evolve.
- A place is the relationship between geology, soil, water, air, living beings, and the consciousness that connects them. Typically, a community and watershed

are the most useful and manageable scales of place for effective ecological design.

- Each place on the planet is unique and unlike any other. They are to be understood on their own terms.

- Thriving and sustainable interior designs, buildings, and master plans are outcomes based on understanding what is required for human and other living beings to coevolve in each unique place.

I'm deeply inspired by the founders of the Regenesis Group: Pamela Mang, Ben Haggard, Tim Murphy, and Joel Glanzberg. Equally, Carol Sanford a living systems thinker and author of *The Responsible Business* (San Francisco, CA: Josey-Bass, 2011); David Bohm, physicist; Fritjof Capra, author of *The Web of Life* (New York: Anchor, 1996); the permaculture movement, which assists people to become more self-reliant through the design and development of productive and sustainable gardens and farms, founded by Bill Mollison and David Holmgren; and many other philosophers, theologians, scientists, and designers who see life as a unified whole and a process of becoming.

LANCE HOSEY

Chief sustainability officer, RTKL

I'm an architect and author. I spent from 1999 to 2009 as a director at William McDonough + Partners, and in 2012 I joined RTKL, one of the largest firms in the world, as its first chief sustainability officer. My role is to develop and promote a strategy to improve the performance of all of our work. We call this strategy "performance-driven design" because we see it first and foremost as an effort to improve the value and quality of design. This builds on the theme of my book, *The Shape of Green: Aesthetics, Ecology, and Design* (Washington, DC: Island Press, 2012), in that we strive to bridge the gap between good design and good performance.

Look at the evolution of sustainable design over the past decade or more. We've moved from an agenda that relatively few people understood or embraced to an industrywide dialogue about how best to improve the entire built environment. Green has gone mainstream. Yet, as the dialogue becomes more popular, it also appears to become more narrowly focused. For many, "sustainability" appears to refer primarily or exclusively to energy and emissions. But imagine a day when everything we make is clean, harmless, and infinitely renewable. Is that enough? Is the goal to promote better life-support systems or better lives? The responsible consumption of resources is just the beginning. Our ambition should be nothing short of harnessing the greatest available intelligence at any given time to create the most sensitive and sensually fulfilling environments we can imagine. Design not just to survive; design to thrive.

I'm inspired by the Sierras and E. O. Wilson's *Consilience: The Unity of Knowledge* (New York: Knopf, 1998): "Until that fundamental divide [between the arts and sciences] is closed or at least reconciled in some congenial manner, the relation between man and the living world will remain problematic."

NANCY CLANTON

PE, FIES, IALD, LC, LEED fellow; president, Clanton & Associates

Reinventing Design For a long time, the building industries' emphasis has been on energy reduction. This may not have been the best decision, but it is where the industry has lived. Now, how do we quantify the scale of happiness to support the general knowledge that productivity increases in spaces with daylighting and a connection to nature.

Green design is inherently beautiful design. Fortunately, we are not living in the darkness of a cave. Instead we are embracing daylight, views, and fresh ventilation. Materials with fractural patterns—stone, brick, wood—are an extension of nature. Intentionally embrace nature in prominent, healthy ways to make built environments comfortable.

People are central to the design itself, not just the budget or sustainable strategies. But how do we quantify this? What is the metric of success? Design needs to be a circular process, from users' initial input to an expanding process that includes feedback once the building is occupied—after six months, one year, at least five years into the life of the project—to inform us at a deeper level.

Great designers understand and implement best practices in the built environment every day. They need to keep refining, constantly evaluating sustainable design strategies with regular feedback looped into the process. The building industry in general has embraced healthy, high-performing standards; now we need healthy, high-performing standards to become a household word for the general public.

It's time to move beyond the single-criterion, individualistic design approach—what I call "widgets." These widgets were important to get us started on the road to sustainability but are not serving people or the more holistic nature of regenerative design. What if we based the success of a building on the real energy it used? Or how healthy and happy the occupants are? Measuring the success of the built environment strictly on performance will move the industry to the next level. How cool would it be if we gave rebates to buildings that were net zero, or better yet, net positive? A holistic analysis of the building would also quantify pure happiness to assess levels of comfort, access to daylight and views, fresh ventilation, function, and aesthetics.

Natural disasters around the world have demonstrated that we need regenerative systems in place to function; water and energy demands are greatly impacted by these horrific events. On the other hand, human ingenuity kicks into high gear when we experience disasters, providing an opportunity to rethink ourselves and the systems we're accustomed to. We need to move away from those systems.

Communities now are looking at turbines, more complete applications of solar power, and central and diversified water systems, just to mention a few.

Reinventing ourselves is a fantastic opportunity to let go of the stuff we no longer need. It's a wake-up call for humanity. If we used solar or wind energy, even though it provides minimal power, we'd have power. If we had a greenhouse to grow our foods, we'd have fresh vegetables.

A colleague of mine in China has to take a completely different approach to engineering. He is responsible for caring for the design for five to ten years after the project is complete. This is an incredibly deep level of responsibility for the design, construction, operation, and management of a building. What an awesome feedback loop for the engineer and design team.

We have to have the guts to go back to past projects and ask what's not working. I'm excited about reinventing how we do design.

BILL BROWNING AND CATIE RYAN

Terrapin Bright Green; authors[15]

While indoor air quality, energy efficiency, and materials selection have been the leading drivers of sustainable interiors, many other aspects of personal well-being are also nurtured by the physical design and overall indoor environmental quality of a home. Science tells us that direct and indirect connections with nature foster resilience to chronic, discrete, or unanticipated personal, societal, and environmental stressors. A healthy home can affect our biological well-being, including respiratory health, sleeping patterns, and hormone balances, as well as our cognitive well-being: creativity, memory, and attention span.

Improving well-being in the home should be considered holistically, from the use of nontoxic and sustainably sourced materials to the practice of climate responsive and biophilic design—how the interior space connects and transitions to and from the outdoor space and nature. Biophilia is the study of how we can channel humanity's intrinsic connection to nature to improve the quality of our lives. From a design standpoint, biophilia can be understood as three pillar conditions:

Nature in the space	The presence of plants, water, animals, and other natural elements in the built environment.
Natural analogues	The presence of objects, materials, colors, and patterns in the built environment that evoke nature.
Nature of the space	The spatial conditions of the built environment that evoke psychophysiological responses similar to those experienced in corresponding conditions in nature.

---

[15] *The Economics of Biophilia* (New York: Terrapin Bright Green).

Since the 1980s, researchers have been measuring human physiological responses to nature. Research in the past decade has measured the effect of exposure to nature around the home and in other types of spaces on the general well-being. Some studies have isolated minute human reactions to biophilic experiences that can inform the way we design our built environment to enhance well-being.

Over the years, academics, researchers, and others have identified numerous patterns to articulate the science as implementable strategies for designers and planners. Seminal examples are Christopher Alexander's 253 patterns in *A Pattern Language* (New York: Oxford Univ. Press, 1977) and Stephen Kellert's seventy biophilic design attributes in *Biophilic Design* (Hoboken, NJ: Wiley, 2008).

As our understanding of how the built environment affects our well-being increases, the growing body of research and evidence has gradually been codified into a series of fourteen patterns of biophilic design that help designers achieve a desired user experience and potentially measureable health response. Adopting these patterns into sustainable residential interiors means thoughtfully incorporate nature and natural systems for the general well-being of a home and its occupants.

Fourteen Patterns of Biophilic Design

Nature in the Space

1. *Visual connection with nature*. A quality of content within a scene of living systems and natural processes.

2. *Nonvisual connection with nature*. Auditory, haptic, olfactory, or gustatory interactions with real or simulated stimuli that possess a positive reference to nature.

3. *Nonrhythmic sensory stimuli*. Elements of real or simulated nature with temporal properties that engage the sensory system with perceived spontaneity or randomness.

4. *Access to thermal and airflow variability*. The presence of thermal comfort conditions driven by a combination of air temperature, relative humidity, airflow across the skin, and the radiant temperature of surrounding surfaces.

5. *Dynamic and diffuse lighting*. Varying intensities of light and shadow that change over time and create conditions suitable for a range of user types and activities.

6. *Presence of water*. The presence of clean, reflective water that supports primarily visual, auditory, and haptic sensory experiences and enhances responses to other patterns of biophilia.

7. *Connection with natural systems*. The presence of processes in nature, primarily those perceptible to the human conscience such as climate and weather patterns, hydrological patterns and services, animal predation and feeding, habitation and migration, pollination, growth, and decomposition.

Natural Analogues

8. *Biomorphic forms and patterns*. The presence of shapes, forms, colors, and patterns that accurately, abstractly, or mathematically symbolize or imitate those found in natural environments.

9. *Material connection with nature*. The presence of elements from nature that, through minimal processing, reflect the local ecology or geology and create a distinct sense of place.

10. *Complexity and order*. The presence of rich sensory information that is configured with a coherent spatial hierarchy similar to that which can be found in natural environments.

Nature of the Space

11. *Prospect*. A spatial condition characterized by an unobstructed view that is focused upon a scene consisting of interesting, informative, or visually pleasing content.

12. *Refuge*. A spatial condition characterized by protection to the back and overhead.

13. *Mystery*. A spatial condition characterized by the promise of more information manifested by the presence of partially obscured views that fascinate and entice.

14. *Risk/peril*. A spatial condition characterized by the presence of an identifiable threat coupled with a reliable safeguard.

SUSAN SZENASY

Editor-in-chief, *Metropolis*

The Living Building Challenge is the most exciting idea: buildings that can support themselves through their design. No need to pump in electricity and water when a building functions as an organism. This way of thinking will change everything.

I believe in the human capacity for wanting to learn, understand, do good things, and pay attention to important issues. If we don't get derailed by the idiocy of pop culture and its emphasis on stardom and material gains, we may have a chance on this Earth.

People should work hard to understand the human condition and what a compromised environment does to our physical and emotional selves. Be alert to all kinds of information. Expand your knowledge in culture, science, and literature—all the time-honored creative activities that make us human and make us question ourselves.

Resiliency

ALEX WILSON

President, Resilient Design Institute; founder, BuildingGreen; publisher[16]

We continue to be reminded that the future holds surprises. Whether flooding from Hurricane Sandy's storm surge; Boulder, Colorado's torrential rains; wildfires in the parched Mountain West; or surprise October snowstorms in New England, a world with climate change promises more of the unexpected.

Our homes should therefore be designed and built to be resilient in the face of such disturbances.

A lot of that decision making involves issues outside the scope of interior design—things like where we build, the geometry and orientation of our homes, and land-use planning strategies that can reduce our dependence on automobiles.

But there are also many resilience strategies that fall under the realm of interior design. I'll address a few of those here.

- Use materials that can get wet and dry out without a loss in performance or creating hazards such as mold. In any locations where flooding is even a remote risk, avoid carpeting and cellulosic materials like paper-faced drywall and wood flooring. Instead, consider such options as polished-concrete flooring, tile flooring, and Fiberglas-faced drywall.

- Within code requirements, keep wiring runs and receptacles well above floor level in case of flooding.

- Create a highly insulated building envelope with some passive solar gain so that the home remains livable even without power or heating fuel.

- When remodeling, consider creating spaces that can be separated and kept comfortable during power outages and without heating fuel.

- In tornado-prone regions, add a safe room for sheltering in place.

- Avoid materials that contain toxins. In the event of flooding or structure fires, hazardous substances in our building materials can get into the environment or be inhaled by firefighters.

- Include photovoltaic systems that offer some islanding capability for when the grid goes down. Most grid-connected photovoltaic systems do not function during power outages, even when the sun is shining, but specialized inverters can deliver power during outages even without battery storage.

- Incorporate only the most water-conserving plumbing fixtures and appliances so that reasonable functionality can be maintained during water rationing or if stored water must be used.

---

[16] *Environmental Building News, GreenSpec*, and *LEEDuser*.

■ Consider rainwater harvesting to provide an on-site water supply for emergencies. For rural homes that rely on deep-well pumps, consider adding a new-generation hand pump that fits into the same well for use during power outages.

Technology

THOM BANKS

Former chief operating officer, American Society of Interior Designers

ASID planted its flag in the ground as a proponent of sustainable design a long time ago. Over the past fifteen years or so, ASID has made statements of support, issued sustainable design policy, created white papers, developed tools to help designers navigate an increasingly complex set of issues, and more. But that doesn't mean all our members were listening. In the beginning, as with most transformative change, there was just a small band of true believers (Annette Stelmack among them) intent upon making ASID members and the profession of interior design more cognizant of its responsibility for, and potential impact upon the planet. It's been exciting to see that small band grow: Issues of sustainability, at some level, are intertwined in the majority of design project conversations today.

While the broader acceptance of sustainable design principles is encouraging, one of the biggest remaining challenges is the overlay of available technology. We are now collecting massive amounts of data on people and environments in real time through a variety of means including that smart phone in your pocket. What are we going to do with it? The challenge comes in our capacity to effectively synthesize, distill, and apply that data in new and beneficial ways that provide added meaning and ease of use.

Recently, I had the opportunity to hear Mark Parker and John Hoke, CEO and VP of Global Design, respectively, for Nike, speak at the Fast Company Design Innovation conference. I was fascinated by their discussion of Nike's "Making" iPhone app. This app, available to the world on iTunes for free, catalogs the 75,000-plus items found in the company's materials library and scores them based on environmental impact and long-term sustainability. Thinking far beyond footwear, user-friendly interfaces like this one demystify the process of developing more sustainable solutions and enable the creative class to "plug and play" materials options in real-time and receive immediate feedback on the environmental impacts of their choices. This information may exist out there already, but the simplicity of this app and ones like it makes accessing and navigating this information much less intimidating, thus reducing another barrier to adoption.

The advances in sensor technology also present exciting opportunities for sustainability, particularly with what are referred to as "wearables." We've all seen the ubiquitous, rubber wristband activity trackers marketed under many brand names (FitBit, Up, FuelBand, etc.). They represent a new convergence of fashion and technology aimed at the personal health and wellness market. Sensor technology, in the form of what are essentially employee badges, is also being applied in the workplace to monitor not only patterns of physical movement but interaction and engagement patterns like conversational groupings, frequency, and dominance. These sensors get smaller and smaller while their capabilities only increase.

Spurred by this growing focus on personal wellness, people will move toward monitoring their own environments to track their exposure to environmental hazards (off-gassing, mold, etc.) One company, Lapka (www.mylapka.com), is already working in this space. As people are able to identify, quantify, and assess the threats around them for themselves and are no longer dependent upon the claims of others, they will be increasingly emboldened to demand environments that reduce and minimize those threats. I'm optimistic that putting the science in people's hands (or on their phones or around their wrists and necks) will be the missing piece of the puzzle and make considerations of environmental impact and concerns for sustainability a given rather than a nice-to-have.

CALEB LUDWICK

Principal, 26 Tools llc

For so long I believed that there were certain thresholds in the progress of sustainability that we'd be able to cross, as industries and markets, and as makers and users of things. Those thresholds always had to do with changing behavior, with reshaping a status quo so that changes that had once seemed great would now be a given. For example, that a certain percentage of recycled content in a flooring product would bump up demand and change behaviors all of the way upstream. Or that some renewable-energy source would shoulder forward and suddenly everyone would agree that there was one right way to do things. That threshold crossed, other improvements could become incremental.

Wishful thinking, certainly. But also hopeful thinking.

What's happened instead is a shift in thinking—call it the playlist generation, call it an "app approach"—but the result is that we all believe the next big thing will be a million little things. We look for brilliant little innovations and believe that we can cluster them around us so that our cumulative impact is reduced.

It's true, of course, but it's also not, because we judge everything purely on the basis of context and of relevance rather than because it is patently good or patently bad. So sustainability is constantly in a crisis of relevance. There's always a mitigating factor, there's always a caveat. Everything is seen as an iteration.

For solutions, this is a wise approach. We should never think that we've arrived—or even that we've crossed a threshold where change can be merely incremental going forward.

But for problems, it's not a wise approach. The problems that sustainability seeks to address aren't small changes of situational relevance. They're big and deep and wide. So they still call for big action, and deep values, and wide collaboration. We can't settle for small changes.

The future of sustainability will always rest with people who see this and act on it, people who want to do something big to make things better and who are willing to let it cost them something. Because real benefit always has a cost; real change always requires a sacrifice. Why not let it cost my company, my project, my wallet? That's the only way things will move forward.

The beautiful part of being where we are is that everyone is asking: "Dear Green, what you did ten years ago was great, but what have you done for me lately?" It's not about where we've been, or even where we're headed. It's about where we are right now, and how we can do better today. So we're perfectly positioned for big thinking once again.

Transparency

LORI J. TUGMAN

Allied ASID, LEED Green Associate; sustainability consultant, JTM & Associates

I was raised on a farm in a small Kentucky town. My family was rehabbing, recycling, and repurposing well before President Carter donned a sweater and asked us to turn down our thermostats. Sustainability was instilled in me at any early age. My siblings and I were taught to respect the resources we were given and never be wasteful. I proudly carry that legacy with me today and honor it by driving my 1997 Honda Accord until it dies and rinsing out my shampoo bottle for one more lather before tossing it into the recycling bin.

I started my professional career as a staffer on Capitol Hill, then lobbied for the Cast Metals Coalition, created the first job fair for spies (intelligence professionals with security clearances), and managed conferences for the defense industry. In 2007, I decided to follow my passion by getting my masters in interior design. During my last year at Marymount, I was honored to serve as the first student representative on ASID's Sustainable Design Council. After graduation, I parlayed that post into becoming the first interior designer/member to serve on ASID staff at national headquarters. As ASID's sustainability manager and subject-matter expert on ecological design, I developed initiatives and resources to help designers create healthier, environmentally preferable interiors. I created the "ASID Guide to Eco-Labels" and a business course called Sustainability Action Plan for the Interior Designer. The accomplishment I'm most proud of, though, is expanding Regreen, the comprehensive green residential remodeling program. I codeveloped the interiors-focused implementation workshop with Annette Stelmack and grew the Regreen Trained certificate program. It's gratifying to see how this program has transformed design professionals and their practices.

For the future, there are three important priorities:

> *Knowledge and transparency*. We feel empowered by the plethora of information readily available to us, but we don't always get the complete picture. Designers and homeowners should prioritize transparency and knowledge. Get to know your materials. Identify trusted sources of information, utilize third-party certifications, and demand health product declarations and environmental product declarations. Sustainability will continue to evolve at a rapid pace, and education is vital to keep up with it.
>
> *Choices and mindfulness*. Sustainability is never black and white; there are always trade-offs. Sometimes sustainability is as simple as being thoughtful. Our daily commute, food choices, and shopping habits have just as much impact on the environment as designing a LEED-certified building. We make hundreds of choices each day. Take for, example, paper receipts. Are they really necessary? Saying no to the "receipt?" question or opting for an electronic receipt saves trees and reduces waste. Strive to make good/better/best choices in both your design practice and personal life.
>
> *Empowerment and transformation*. In the past few years, entrenched habits and products have been transformed through grassroots efforts. Municipalities have banned plastic shopping bags; governments around the world have phased out incandescent lamps; noxious interior paint has been replaced by no-VOC options.

Not too long ago, sustainable materials were not readily available, cost-effective, or aesthetically pleasing. This has certainly turned around. I'm thrilled to see a resurgence of "Made in America" labels and the renaissance of hand-crafted furniture. I love that my closet company offers FSC-certified, no added urea form-aldehyde (NAUF) particleboard and West Elm sells Global Organic Textile Standard- (GOTS)-certified bed linens. I'm encouraged that carpet manufacturers are starting take-back programs and fabric houses are using nontoxic dyes. We can make a difference by patronizing vendors who offer benign materials that last, look, and perform as well as toxic ones. Help transform the marketplace by voting with your dollars.

Because of my diverse background, I tend to look at things from an outsider's perspective. One of the things that informs my work is questioning convention. Don't get me wrong: I'm a rule follower. But sometimes we acquiesce to conventionality too easily instead of exploring other— sometimes better—options. There should be sound reasoning or good science behind why we build a certain way or use specific resources. Questioning convention brought us Cradle-to-Cradle and Designtex compostable fabric. Just think how much more we can do.

MARTIN FLAHERTY

President/founder, Pencilbox, Inc.

Shifts are taking place in commercial and residential green product design. However, they are more akin to the slow change of a mini Ice Age than the seismic changes seen when tectonic plates shift. There hasn't been a massive revolution or protests for formulation changes to get bad stuff out of products, but if you look a little closer, the best brands in interiors are making huge changes. The real effects of massive change will likely be seen once retail behemoth Wal-Mart enacts its policy on sustainable chemistry in consumable products.

In the commercial building industry, the best-of-class product manufacturers are already out in front of eradicating chemicals of concern from their products. In the $12 billion commercial furniture sector, the industry association, the Business and Institutional Furniture Manufacturers Association (BIFMA), working with over 160 volunteers from member companies, developed a multi-attribute sustainability standard called "level" that looks at not just the product, but the corporation's behaviors and social impacts and the facilities their products are made in. And while the standard is only five years old, discussions are taking place to add new levels of transparency and environmental disclosure. While an industry-based standard, it's one that was crafted by companies like Herman Miller, Knoll, Haworth, Allsteel, and Steelcase, each of which has a long track record in environmental stewardship. While the process has been methodically developed, launched, and executed, in only a few years participating companies has grown from 4 to 52, with over 3,000 products meeting the sustainability standard.

Other building products manufacturers are aggressively promoting their products as beyond basic government requirements. Plumbing fixture manufacturer Toto has introduced material formulation changes to their porcelain finishes that include silver dioxide, a natural particulate repellant. What it means is that a single flush cleans the bowl entirely, reducing the need for cleaning chemicals. (I can testify that it works.) My household cleaning purchases no longer include any toilet cleaning products after having bought and installed two of their toilets. The company has also developed more efficient water management systems, drastically lowering water usage per flush.

Perhaps we'll see seismic change on the consumer side after all. On September 13, 2013, Wal-Mart released their Policy on Sustainable Chemistry in Consumables. In it they've announced that there are now ten (as yet undisclosed) chemical ingredients that will need "reduction, restriction, and elimination." By 2015, Wal-Mart will require suppliers to make online ingredient listings available to the public. And beginning in 2016, Wal-Mart will disclose its progress publicly. The impact of this announcement is already rippling through product supply chains. Both commercial and residential suppliers are preparing to move beyond exploration and actually implement product formulation changes that eradicate the chemical bad actors and exceeding today's product performance requirements.

PAUL FIRTH

Manager, UL Environment

There is a lot to be optimistic about. The pace of innovation and change, while not fast enough for many in the field, is still getting faster, even in a difficult economy. We are still developing new products, new construction methods, and better data to work with, and engendering more understanding by the broader community—the list could go on and on. Most inspiring is knowing that we are doing this for more than just a paycheck. As our beloved Ray Anderson used to remind us, it's all for tomorrow's child. I don't have to look to tomorrow, as I have four amazing kids today. Their adoring faces are enough inspiration to keep me going for lifetimes to come.

Conclusion

What will your legacy be?

Decide to be a catalyst, a positive force in transforming the market. By promoting change within the design industry, you will be doing your part in contributing to a healthy planet and the well-being of our children's children, and for all the generations to come.

Get motivated. Get informed. Reach out with courage and commitment. Embrace this purposeful journey of responsibility, education, accountability, power of choice, and passion. Help to create a better world. Be empowered and empower others.

If not you, who?

> *Unless someone like you cares a whole awful lot, nothing is going to get better. It's not.*
> —Dr. Seuss, The Lorax

Figure 22.4 Author Stelmack's inspiration for the future!

Photo courtesy of Annette K. Stelmack.

RESOURCES

Web Sites

Air Resources Board Airborne Toxic Control Measure: www.arb.ca.gov/toxics/compwood/compwood.htm

The California Air Resources Board released this Airborne Toxic Control Measure (ATCM) to reduce formaldehyde emissions from composite wood products—hardwood plywood, particleboard, and MDF This is also known as California 93120. ATCM's Phase 2 emission limits (.05 ppm for form-aldehyde emissions in plywood) are becoming the norm for composite woods industrywide. If a man-ufacturer of hardwood plywood, particleboard, and medium-density fiberboard (MDF) uses no-added formaldehyde (NAF)–based resins or ultra-low-emitting formaldehyde (ULEF) resins, they are exempt from some of the testing requirements, as they are regularly below applicable Phase 2 emission standards.

American Institute of Architects Committee on the Environment (AIA COTE): www.aia.org/cote

The Committee on the Environment works to advance, disseminate, and advocate—to the pro-fession, the building industry, the academy, and the public—design practices that integrate built and natural systems and enhance both the design quality and environmental performance of the built environment.

American Society of Interior Designer (ASID): www.asid.org

ASID is a community of people—designers, industry representatives, educators and students—committed to interior design. Through education, knowledge sharing, advocacy, community building,

and outreach, the Society strives to advance the interior design profession and, in the process, to demonstrate and celebrate the power of design to positively change people's lives. Its more than 38,000 members engage in a variety of professional programs and activities through a network of forty-eight chapters throughout the United States and Canada. They have a well-developed Sustainable Design Information Center on their website at http://www.asid.org/ resource/Sustainable+Design+Information+Center.htm.

American Tree Farm System (ATFS): www.tree farmsystem.org

The ATFS certifies small family-owned forests in the United States for their operations and forestry They are recognized by the Programme for the Endorsement of Forest Certification (PEFC) and Sustainable Forestry Initiative (SFI) as suppliers of forest products.

Architects/Designers/Planners for Social Responsibility (ADPSR): www.adpsr.org

Established in 1981, Architects/Designers/Planners for Social Responsibility works for peace, envi-ronmental protection, ecological building, social justice, and the development of healthy commu-nities. They believe that design practitioners have a significant role to play in the well-being of our communities.

Architecture Research Institute: www.architect .org/institute/programs/sustainable

Provides a comparative list of differences between conventional and sustainable design processes. Also includes a list of sustainable resources and of archi-tects who practice ecological design.

623

ASTM International: www.astm.org

One of the largest voluntary standards development organizations in the world, ASTM is a valuable source for technical standards for materials, products, systems, and services that are globally accepted and utilized.

Biodegradable Products Institute (BPI) Certified Compostable Program: www.bpiworld.org

BPI recognizes products that meet ASTM D6400 (for plastics) or ASTM D6868 (for fiber-based applications) and will compost satisfactorily in commercial composting facilities. In order for a product to be certified by this program, it must disintegrate quickly with no residue; convert to carbon dioxide, water, and biomass; support plant growth; and not introduce high levels of metals into the soil. The products include food service items, packaging, and compostable resins.

Blessed Unrest: www.blessedunrest.org

A leading environmentalist and social activist's examination of the worldwide movement for social and environmental change. Paul Hawken has spent over a decade researching organizations dedicated to restoring the environment and fostering social justice. A culmination of Hawken's many years of leadership in the environmental and social justice fields, it will inspire and delight any and all who despair of the world's fate, and its conclusions will surprise even those within the movement itself. Fundamentally, it is a description of humanity's collective genius, and the unstoppable movement to reimagine our relationship to the environment and one another.

Building Concerns: www.buildingconcerns.com

Directories (organized by geographic region) of organizations, businesses, and professionals working in the field of sustainable design, building, and development.

BuildingGreen: www.buildinggreen.com

A subscription-based online resource for environmentally sensitive design and construction. BuildingGreen Suite offers a range of information, from articles and product listings to project case studies.

Build It Green: http://builditgreen.org

Professional nonprofit organization whose focus is to transform the building industry so that buildings are remodeled and built using green practices and products. This website offers a diverse list of references and links for sustainable building.

Built Green: www.builtgreen.org

Located in Denver, Colorado, Built Green is one of the largest green building programs in the nation. A voluntary program, it encourages homebuilders to use technologies, products, and practices that will lessen the negative impacts of building on natural and indoor environments. On its "Other Related Sites" web page is a list of various websites that address many sustainable building options and questions.

Business and Institutional Furniture Manufacturers Association (BIFMA) "Level" Sustainability Certification: www.levelcertified.org/

SCS Global Services is the independent third-party certifier for the "level" sustainability furniture certification program, which identifies products that have been evaluated to the multi-attribute ANSI/BIFMA e3 Furniture Sustainability Standard. Products can be awarded a level 1, level 2, or level 3 conformance mark based on the combined score achieved in their sustainability evaluation. "level" was created to deliver an open and holistic means of evaluating and communicating the environmental and social impacts of furniture products in the built environment. The program addresses a company's social actions, energy usage, material selection, and human and ecosystem health impacts. The program focuses on commercial furniture and includes case goods, seating, storage, systems furniture, tables, and work surfaces.

CalRecycle Green Building: www.calrecycle.ca.gov/greenbuilding/

This California government site outlines the basics of green building, provides a tool kit, and reviews materials. It provides visitors with information to use resources efficiently, create healthier buildings, and save money through sustainable building practices. There are also resources including building specifications and case studies.

CarbonFree: www.carbonfund.org/

The National Science Foundation (NSF) established its CarbonFree product certification, which offers transparency in reporting the carbon neutrality of a product. It was driven by consumer demand for product information from companies that are being proactive in taking care of our environment. Corporate responsibility programs are addressing climate change and carbon reductions, responding to consumer demand for transparent, credible, and readily accessible information vital in the decision-making process. NSF's technical capabilities and third-party verification provide a reliable process to define a product's carbon footprint, decrease carbon impacts where possible, and offset lingering emissions.

Carbon Reduction Label: http://carbonreduction label.com.au/

The UK Carbon Trust launched this program in 2007 to help companies reduce greenhouse gas emissions during the production of their products. Planet Ark partnered with the UK Carbon Trust to bring this label to Australia as well. There are many certified products, ranging from food items, household goods, appliances, and the Dyson Airblade hand dryer.

Carpet America Recovery Effort (CARE): www.car petrecovery.org

CARE, a voluntary initiative of the carpet industry and the government to prevent carpet from burdening landfills, focuses on developing carpet reclamation and recycling methods.

Carpet and Rug Institute (CRI): www.carpet-rug.org

The national trade association representing the carpet and rug industry. Headquartered in Dalton, Georgia, the institute's membership consists of manufacturers representing over 90 percent of all carpet produced in the United States as well as suppliers of raw materials and services to the industry. The CRI Green Label Plus logo on carpet and adhesive samples informs customers that the product type has been tested and certified by an independent laboratory and has met stringent criteria for low emissions.

Centre for Design: www.cfd.rmit.edu.au

An Australian company that researches and documents options that support environmentally friendly design. Information, publications, and case studies detail sustainable products, buildings, and materials, as well as life-cycle assessment.

Climate Neutral Business Network (CNBN): www.climateneutral.com/index.html

CNBN offers a challenge toward measurable climate neutral assessment that aims for net-zero greenhouse gas (GHG) emissions associated with the entire life cycle of a product. By offsetting GHG emissions manufacturers work toward reducing their global warming potential serving to keep our atmosphere cooler. Interface has adopted this model as a leader striving for climate neutrality.

Cornell Cooperative Extension: www.cce.cornell .edu/schuyler/recycle/businesses.htm

A source of helpful information on recycling for businesses; also contains a reference list for further recycling research.

Cradle to Cradle (C2C) Certification: www.c2c certified.org

Developed by McDonough Braungart Design Chemistry (MBDC), Cradle to Cradle is a third-party certification that requires achievement across multiple attributes meeting government regulations: materials that are safe for human health and the environment through all use phases; product and system design for material reutilization; the use of renewable energy and carbon management; water stewardship, including efficient use of water and maximum water quality associated with production; and company strategies for social fairness. Cradle to Cradle certification is a four-tiered approach consisting of basic, silver, gold, and platinum levels.

Declare Products: www.declareproducts.com/product-database

At its core, Declare is an ingredients label for building products, with a growing database of products that are compliant with the Living Building Challenge (LBC) rating system. Manufacturers have been vetted by subject-matter experts that they are "red-list ready." The "red list" enumerates building materials that government agencies, such as the U.S. EPA, European Union Commission on Environment, and the State of California designate as harmful to living creatures, including humans. This is a key resource for project teams pursuing the LBC, providing them with a materials guide for product specification.

Decorative Surfaces: www.decorativesurfaces .org/cpa-green/go-ecc-green.html

This page explores the Composite Panel Association (CPA) standard for green composite wood panel products. The certification takes life-cycle aspects into consideration, including carbon footprint, recycled content, renewable resources, sustainably sourced wood, and low emissions. Their Eco-Certified Composite (ECC) Sustainability Standard certifies products that must comply with the California Air Resources Board (CARB) formaldehyde emissions regulation.

e-build: www.ebuild.com

An online directory of more than 300,000 building supplies, listed by category. A helpful overall guide for construction, but not necessarily for sustainable construction.

Ecological Building Network: www .ecobuildnetwork.org/general.htm

An international association of builders, engineers, architects, academics, and developers committed to promoting intelligent building methods and materials for a sustainable future. Contains an extensive list of resources for building green.

EcoLogo: www.ecologo.org/

The EcoLogo Program is a Type I eco-label as defined by ISO 14024. Companies comply with specific criteria that compare products and services with others in the same category. The criteria is rigorous and scientifically relevant, addressing the entire life cycle of the product. EcoLogo is third-party certified by Underwriters Laboratory, where an extensive variety of sustainable products meet stringent environmental standards.

Ecology Action: www.ecoact.org

The Green Building Program area of this site provides a Green Building Materials Guide, which explains in detail many of the pros and cons of a variety of sustainable building materials.

Economic Input-Output Life-Cycle Assessment: www.eiolca.net/

The Green Design Institute of Carnegie Mellon University created the Economic Input-Output Life-Cycle Assessment (EIO-LCA). This tool allows you to compare various environmental impacts, including greenhouse gases, toxicity, energy, and water use for a variety of products, estimating the resources required and the environmental emissions. This website takes the EIO-LCA method and transforms it into a user-friendly online tool to quickly and easily evaluate a commodity or service as well as its supply chain.

ecoScorecard: www.ecoscorecard.com

This is a website that provides the ability to search products, evaluate products against rating systems, and look at detailed manufacturer product documentation. There are also ecoScorecard plug-ins for BIM software, including Autodesk Revit and SketchUp, so that green decision making can be implemented at the point of design.

EnerGuide: http://oee.nrcan.gc.ca/equipment/appliance/1799?attr=4#household

This program was created by the Canadian government to educate consumers about their appliance and equipment purchases. The EnerGuide label indicates how much energy appliances consume in a year of normal service and makes it possible to compare the energy efficiency from one model to another of the same size and class. All new major appliances sold in Canada are now required to have the EnerGuide label designating that the appliance meets Canada's minimum energy performance levels.

Energy Star: www.energystar.gov

A partnership program between industry and the U.S. government (through the Environmental Protection Agency) that labels and promotes energy-efficient products. The program began in 1992, and now the blue star logo appears on those appliances that excel in energy efficiency. Energy Star qualifies computers, heating and cooling equipment, major home appliances, lighting, home electronics, office equipment, and even new homes built with the most energy-efficient appliances and equipment.

Environmental Home Center: www.environmental homecenter.com

An online store offering a large variety of home and building products that protect health, use energy and other resources sparingly, and are very well made.

Environmental Product Declaration (EPD): www.environdec.com/en/What-is-an-EPD/# .Uc9X7L_7V0o

This site discusses what it takes to be an EPD. An EPD will typically include a product description, material content with varied amounts of detail, product manufacturing flow charts, installation methods, product use and impacts, and end of life. All of this information is rolled up in the life-cycle assessment report.

Electronic Product Environmental Assessment Tool (EPEAT): www.epeat.net/

EPEAT is a system that helps purchasers evaluate, compare, and select electronic products based on their environmental attributes. EPEAT-registered electronic products meet environmental criteria. All of the criteria used in EPEAT are based on ANSI-approved public standards, which provide technical details for every criterion and specify how a manufacturer must demonstrate compliance.

Floorscore Indoor Air Quality Certification: www .rfci.com

A third-party certification addressing emissions for resilient and hard-surface flooring and adhesives. The Resilient Floor Covering Institute (RFCI) and Scientific Certification Systems (SCS) created this flooring certification program specifically to address emissions, indoor air quality, and volatile organic compounds. The products that are certified in this program meet California 01350 standard emissions criteria. These products are recognized by many green building rating systems, including LEED for Homes.

Forest Stewardship Council (FSC): www.fscus.org

An international nonprofit organization founded in 1993 to support environmentally appropriate, socially beneficial, and economically viable management of the world's forests. FSC administers a forestry certification program to assure that businesses supply trees and wood from a forest managed in an ecologically sustainable manner. Products bearing the FSC logo guarantee that the wood is from a certified well-managed forest, with wood and wood products available across the world from a variety of mills, manufacturers, and distributors.

Global Green USA: www.globalgreen.org

An American affiliate of Green Cross International, Global Green USA works with governments, industry, and individuals to create a global shift toward a sustainable and secure future.

Global Organic Textile Standard (GOTS): www .global-standard.org/

GOTS aims to unify various existing standards in the field of eco-textile processing and define worldwide acknowledged requirements that ensure the organic status of textiles. The GOTS standard specifically applies to organic textiles, ensuring that the certified products have a minimum of 70 percent organic fibers and that the organic status of the material is validated from harvesting to manufacturing and then to labeling.

Green2Green: www.green2green.org

Green2Green was started by GreenBlue, a nonprofit that provides resources to make projects more sustainable. Compare products side by side, get advice from green experts, and locate green products by source.

GreenBlue Institute: www.greenblue.org

A nonprofit institute inspiring transformation in the design of human industry and raising awareness on sustainable issues.

Green Building Advisor: www.greenbuilding advisor.com

This website provides information about designing, building, and remodeling sustainable, energy-efficient homes. It utilizes the Green Spec product directory and is specifically tailored to residential design. The site also provides CAD drawings/blocks for green residential projects, case studies, and in-depth blogs on building practices and strategies.

Green Building Pages: www.greenbuilding pages.com

A sustainable building materials database and design tool for the environmentally and socially responsible designer, builder, and client.

Greener Choices: www.greenerchoices.org/

The green version of *Consumer Reports* provides information on a variety of household products and identifies which choices are most environmentally sustainable.

Greener Product Certification Seal: www.greener product.com/default.aspx

The Greener Product Certification Seal demonstrates that a product has been vetted and complies with LEED for Homes and National Association of Home Builders (NAHB) green building standards. Building products are evaluated utilizing environmental qualifiers specific to energy conservation and renewables, regionally produced materials, air quality, certified wood, recycled content, and reused and renewable materials. Environmental claims are reviewed and verified through third-party certification and/or supporting documentation stating that products comply with LEED-H rating systems and NAHB building standards.

GreenFormat: www.csinet.org/Home-Page-Category/Formats/GF

The Construction Specification Institute (CSI) provides GreenFormat as a platform to compare sustainability attributes for multiple building products. When writing project specifications, GreenFormat lays out a sustainability information structure that works with CSI MasterFormat. As a voluntary program it aims to communicate the sustainability features of building materials, products, systems and technologies.

Greenguard Environmental Institute (GEI): www .greenguard.org

An industry-independent, nonprofit organization that oversees the Greenguard Certification Program. As an ANSI-Accredited Standards Developer, GEI establishes acceptable indoor air standards for indoor products, environments, and buildings. GEI's mission is to improve public health and quality of life through programs that improve indoor air.

Green Home Guide: www.greenhomeguide.com/ index.php

Offers unbiased views from professionals on a variety of home-related materials and products.

Green Squared, SCS Certified: http://green squaredcertified.com/

The first multi-attribute standard developed for tiles and tile installation materials, Green Squared uses the transparency and consensus of the ANSI process providing a third party certification from several organizations. The validation covers product characteristics, manufacturing, end-of-product-life management, progressive corporate governance, and innovation in an effort to establish sustainability criteria for products throughout their full life cycle. This tile certification was established by the Tile Council of North America (TCNA) and includes ceramic and glass tiles and a wide range of tile installation materials. Database search for certified products is available through approved Green Squared certification bodies that currently include NSF, SCS Global, and UL Environment.

Green Seal: www.greenseal.org

An eco-labeling group that works at certifying products, through a rigorous scientific process, that are ecologically responsible. Product evaluations are conducted using a life-cycle approach to ensure that all significant environmental impacts of a product are considered, from raw materials extraction through manufacturing to use and disposal. Green Seal works with manufacturers, industry sectors, purchasing groups, and governments at all levels to green the production and purchasing chain.

GreenTreks: www.greentreks.org

Offers entertaining programming about ordinary people doing extraordinary things for the environment. Educational links and resources as well.

Greenwise Paint: www.greenwisepaint.com

Coatings and paints that have the Greenwise paint label are second-party certified, with testing by the Coatings Research Group. The information is proprietary and only available to members, so they lack transparency for designers and consumers. They strive to meet California's South Coast Air Quality Management District (SCAQMD) volatile organic compounds (VOCs) emissions limits for interior and exterior paint as well as for wood and other surface coatings.

Green Wizard: www.greenwizard.com

Green Wizard's WORKflow Pro software helps designers and contractors define green goals, create and document a LEED checklist, evaluate project

energy use, and find products based on EPDs environmental product declarations (EPDs), health product declarations (HPDs), life-cycle analysis (LCA) and Cradle to Cradle.

Hazardous Substance Free (HSF) Mark: www.hsf.us/

This label assures consumers that the products they are buying do not contain harmful components and materials that could harm their families. The mark applies to appliances, equipment, and lighting. The seven main substances to avoid when purchasing products include lead, cadmium, mercury, polybrominated biphenyl (PBB), polybrominated diphenyl ethers (PBDEs), hexavalent chromium, and phthalates. Companies that comply with industry standards and validated by ongoing third-party testing are licensed to use the HSF mark or logo to demonstrate their leadership in corporate social and environmental stewardship.

Health Product Declaration (HPD) Collaborative: www.hpdcollaborative.org

The Health Product Declaration Collaborative is a customer-led organization for companies and individuals committed to the continuous improvement of the building industry's environmental and health performance through transparency and innovation in the building product supply chain.

Healthy House Institute (HHI): www.healthy houseinstitute.com

The Healthy House Institute is dedicated to helping consumers find information about green products and services to green their home. They look at the home as an entire ecosystem and take the entire indoor environmental quality into consideration. The consumer or designer can search for building products and services based on category and their local location.

HOK Sustainable Design: www.hoksustain abledesign.com

A design firm committed to sustainability practices and principles. Its website offers resources that include case studies and green design checklists as well as a list detailing the firm's Ten Keys to Sustainable Design process.

InformeDesign: www.informedesign.umn.edu

A research and communication tool developed by the University of Minnesota and sponsored by the Association of Interior Design (ASID) that offers extensive research on a number of products, including many building products.

Institute for Global Communications: www.igc.org

A source of news and informational articles on a wide variety of topics, including sustainability issues around the globe.

Institute for Market Transformation to Sustainability (MTS): www.mts.sustainableproducts.com

This organization creates standards to gauge the success of manufacturers in addressing three key areas of sustainable practices: environmental, social, and economic. The standards page of their website details many well-known product standards to look for in choosing products for projects.

Interface Sustainability: www.interfacesustainability.com

A leader in the commercial interiors market offering floor coverings and fabrics. The company is committed to sustainability and doing business in ways that minimize the impact on the environment. The website offers insight into the philosophy that is leading Interface in its vision to cause less of a negative impact by its manufacturing processes and to have an overall positive influence on the many facets of running the business.

Interior Design Magazine: www.interiordesign.net

A publication dedicated to the field of interior design. On the website is an area called the "Green Zone," which has links to articles and information on manufacturers that produce sustainable interiors products.

Interiors & Sources Magazine: www.isdesignet.com

Industry trade publication and website that offers articles and news on cutting-edge sustainability and interior design issues; also provides helpful information on products and associations.

International Association of Plumbing and Mechanical Officials (IAPMO) R&T Mark of Conformity: www.iapmort.org

IAPMO R&T is a plumbing and mechanical product certification agency. It provides certification for Energy Star, WaterSense, and Solar Products. IAPMO R&T has its own sustainability label or mark called the "mark of conformity" to designate a certified sustainable product.

International Council for Local Environmental Initiatives: www.iclei.org

An association of local governments and national and regional local government organizations that have made a commitment to sustainable development. Its focus is on programs and strategic planning that address local sustainability while protecting the global common good.

International Dark Sky Association (IDA) Dark-Sky Friendly Fixture Seal of Approval: www.darksky.org/outdoorlighting/about-fsa

This is a third-party certification for addressing light pollution to help minimize glare and reduce light levels in the night sky. The Fixture Seal of Approval provides third-party certification for luminaires that minimize glare, reduce light trespass, and don't pollute the night sky toward dark-sky compliance.

International Interior Design Association (IIDA): www.iida.org

The International Interior Design Association is a professional networking and educational association of more than 10,000 members in eight specialty forums, nine regions, and more than thirty chapters around the world. IIDA is committed to enhancing quality of life through excellence in interior design and advancing interior design through knowledge.

IIDA advocates for interior design excellence, provides superior industry information, nurtures a global interior design community, maintains educational standards, and responds to trends in business and design.

Kitchen Cabinet Manufacturers Association (KCMA) Environmental Stewardship Program (ESP): www.greencabinetsource.org

A second-party certification created by the KCMA, it offers a best-practice guideline with multi-attributes for cabinet labeling indicating that manufacturers meet their program requirements. Companies are rated on air quality, product and process resource management, environmental stewardship, and community relations. Mandatory program requirements include the following: 100 percent of particleboard, medium density fiber-board, and plywood used in the cabinets must meet the formaldehyde emission level of the California Air Resources Board Airborne Toxic Control Measure (CARB ATCM) and must be third-party certified to meet low formaldehyde emission standards; a written policy stating a firm commitment to environmental quality; and ESP participants must agree to report to KCMA with 60 days of any local, state or federal citation in excess of $50,000 per violation explaining the circumstances of the citation or violation, potentially leading to termination from the program.

Massachusetts Sustainable Design Roundtable Links to Research Studies and Websites: www.mass.gov/envir/Sustainable/initiatives/initiativesroundtablewgresearch.htm

An extensive list of online resources for sustainable design research and application.

Master Painters Institute (MPI): www.paintinfo.com

This site hosts information for designers, painters, and the general public. It features warnings, explains what can go wrong, and stresses the importance of standards. There are also guide specifications, formulas, and other relevant resources.

McDonough Braungart Design Chemistry (MBDC): www.mbdc.com

A product and process design firm dedicated to transforming the design of products, processes, and services worldwide. Founded by William McDonough and Michael Braungart, MBDC offers innovative support to businesses interested in implementing sustainable practices. The group supports the new design paradigm called cradle-to-cradle design and assists with the implementation of eco-effective design principles.

National Park Service Sustainability News: www.nature.nps.gov/SustainabilityNews

This online publication includes a searchable database of articles related to many aspects of sustainability.

National Resources Defense Council (NRDC): www.nrdc.org

A comprehensive website dealing with a multitude of local and global environmental and social issues. It includes articles on environmental impacts and links to related sites and resources. NRDC's mission is to safeguard the Earth, its people, its plants and animals, and the natural systems on which all life depends.

National Sanitation Foundation (NSF) International: The Public Health and Environmental Organization: www.nsf.org

The NSF is a nonprofit organization that act as an independent, third-party verification and certification company based on single-attribute claims. It ensures the safety of food, water, and household products and certifies green living/building products. The NSF provides a letter outlining the details of verification that is available to the public.

Natural Capitalism: www.naturalcapitalism.org

Natural Capitalism: Creating the Next Industrial Revolution by Paul Hawken, Amory Lovins, and L. Hunter Lovins (Boston: Back Bay Books, 2000) is the first book to explore the lucrative opportunities for businesses in an era of approaching environmental limits.

Natural Step: www.naturalstep.org

An international agency that focuses researches sustainable resource use and solution implementation worldwide. Its U.S. office, located in Oregon, can be accessed via www.ortns.org. This website offers sustainable building resources as well as guidelines for sustainable building processes.

Not So Big House: www.notsobighouse.com

This rich website with the same name of the book by Sarah Susanka, is full of inspiration on creating homes that are scaled to a size and serve the inhabitants as well as the planet. Many resources are listed here, along with the opportunity to purchase sustainable-size house plans.

OEKO-TEX: www.oeko-tex.com

This website outlines the OEKO-TEX Standard 100, which tests and certifies manufactured, domestic, and household textiles to ensure that they do not contain harmful substances and chemicals that could off-gas. The closer a product comes in contact with human skin or children, the more stringent the testing.

Oikos Green Building Source: www.oikos.com

Articles and products with a focus on sustainability. Oikos is also an independent bookseller offering sustainable book choices online.

OpenLCA: www.openlca.org/

OpenLCA is a professional life-cycle assessment and footprint software created by GreenDelta; it has a broad range of features and many available databases. Its goal is to provide a well designed, consistent, high-performance, modular framework for sustainability assessment and life-cycle modeling.

Pharos Project: www.pharosproject.net

From the nonprofit organization Healthy Building Network (HBN), Pharos is a tool for materials selection that relies on manufacturer participation and disclosure as well as the independent research the Pharos team. Its goal is to provide transparency in the building materials market. It reports scores on volatile organic compounds, toxic content, manufacturing toxics, renewable materials, renewable energy, and reflectance values. The tool allows you to evaluate and compare details on alternative products according to the projects needs or objectives and to identify health hazards relating to material contents.

Programme for the Endorsement of Forest Certification (PEFC): www.pefc.org

The PEFC system is an international nonprofit organization promoting sustainable forest management (SFM) through independent third-party certification. It takes the entire forest supply chain into account when certifying that timber and nontimber forest products are produced by ecological, social and ethical standards. As an umbrella organization, PEFC endorses national forest certifications from the Sustainable Forest Initiative (SFI) to American Tree Farm System (ATFS).

Rainforest Alliance Network (RAN): www.ran.org

The Rainforest Alliance protects ecosystems and the people and wildlife that depend on them by transforming land-use practices, business practices, and consumer behavior. Companies, cooperatives, and landowners that participate in their programs meet rigorous standards that conserve biodiversity and provide sustainable livelihoods. Based in New York City, with offices worldwide, RAN works with people whose livelihoods depend on the land, helping them transform the way they grow food, harvest wood, and host travelers. RAN has helped convince dozens of corporations, including Home Depot, Citigroup, Boise Cascade, and Goldman Sachs, to change their practices.

Rate It Green: www.rateitgreen.com

A relatively new user-based resource , this site has a growing database of green building products. It is a peer-reviewed directory where an individual or company can register and provide feedback about a green product. It's based on opinions and personal experience, and as it continues to grow, it will provide a helpful peer resource to designers and homeowners.

Restriction of Hazardous Substances–Compliant Standard: www.rohscompliancedefinition.com

This standard is compliant with the European Union's Restriction of Hazardous Substances (RoHS) Directive, which prevents the usage of hazardous materials commonly used in electronics. Any RoHS-compliant component is tested for the presence of lead (Pb), cadmium (Cd), mercury (Hg), hexavalent chromium (Hex-Cr), polybrominated biphenyls (PBBs), and polybrominated diphenyl ethers (PBDEs).

Rocky Mountain Institute (RMI): www.rmi.org

As described on its website, "Rocky Mountain Institute is an entrepreneurial nonprofit organization that fosters the efficient and restorative use of resources to make the world secure, just, prosperous, and life-sustaining. We do this by inspiring business, civil society, and government to design integrative solutions that create true wealth." This wonderful organization promotes research and conversation on many of the environmental issues and offers information to help people make environmentally responsible choices.

SCAQMD Rulings: www.aqmd.gov

This website provides an overview of a government standard from California's South Coast Air Quality Management District. The standard relates to smog VOC emissions of interior and exterior architectural coatings, which include roof coatings, concrete sealers, aerosol coatings and others. Although it is a strict standard, it's important to confirm that the contents of the products reviewed are healthy as well. Search out "super-compliant" paints, some with less than 10 grams per liter of VOC emissions. SCAQMD lists compliant products on its website.

Scientific Certification Systems (SCS): www.scs globalservices.com

SCS Global Services is an internationally recognized third-party certifier backed by rigorous scientific review. Its life-cycle assessment standard is currently undergoing public review under the ANSI process. It offers Indoor Advantage and Indoor Advantage Gold certifications of office furniture, paints and coatings, adhesives and sealants, insulation, wall coverings, furnishings, and other interior products. The products that meet Indoor Advantage Gold are also compliant with the California Section 01350 standard emissions criteria. SCS also offers other certifications, such as the Environmentally Preferred Product (EPP) certification for multi-attribute products based on life-cycle assessments, and the SCS Legal Harvest Verification that ensures that wood is from legal and nonendangered sources.

Sins of Greenwashing: sinsofgreenwashing.org/ index.html

This website outlines the major types of greenwashing in advertising and the harm they cause; it includes a resources page.

Slash the Trash/Wabash County Solid Waste Management District: www.slashthetrash.com/ grbld.htm#div9

Overview of a program initiated by Wabash County, IN, to reduce construction waste and diminish the waste that enters the landfill. The program supports green building measures as well.

Steel Recycling Institute: www.recycle-steel.org

Lists places to recycle steel, offers articles on steel construction recycling, and the location of steel recycling facilities.

Sustainable Architecture, Building, and Culture: www.sustainableabc.com

Helpful website listing sustainable products, events, and services in various categories.

Sustainable Builder: www.greenbuilder.com

This comprehensive site focuses on all aspects of sustainable building, including where to find resources and professional contacts. The sourcebook section was developed to foster the implementation of environmentally responsible practices in homebuilding.

**Sustainable Development websites: www.library
.gatech.edu/architect/CRP6233.htm#web**

Designed by students at Georgia Institute of
Technology, this site lists websites by several categories useful for gathering information on sustainable
building and design.

**Sustainable Forestry Initiative (SFI): www
.sfiprogram.org**

SFI is a third-party forestry certification system with
significant ties to the forestry industry. SFI certification
includes chain-of-custody certificates and SFI-certified
forests, paper products, and wood products. SFI is a
viable alternative for certified domestic woods. Product
labeling includes three SFI chain of custody labels and
one SFI-certified sourcing label.

**Sustainable Organizations Standard (LEO-1000):
www.leonardoacademy.org/services/standards.html**

The Leonardo Academy is a nonprofit organization
that develops sustainable standards and provides
third-party verification. It specializes in sustainability training, emissions, sustainable agriculture, and
sustainable buildings. This sustainable organization
standard is a new pilot standard designed to evaluate organizations in three main areas: environmental
stewardship, social equity, and economic prosperity.

Treehugger: www.treehugger.com

A web-based magazine that provides the latest
news, reviews, and information about green products and other environmentally responsible topics.

**UL Environment: www.ul.com/global/eng/pages/
aboutul/businesses/environment**

UL Environment supports the growth and development of sustainable products, services, and organizations in the global marketplace through standards,
development, education, and independent third-
party assessment and certification. It provides
services such as environmental claims validation,
product certification, energy-efficiency certification,
environmental product declarations, and advisory services. It also hosts a dynamic database for
researching sustainable products and verifying UL

Environment certification claims; documents life-
cycle assessment data; and helps develop product
category rules (PCRs). Two of their most widely recognized programs are EcoLogo and Greenguard.

**U.S. Department of Agriculture (USDA) Bio-Based
Program: www.biopreferred.gov/Labeling.aspx**

A government labeling program that promotes the
purchase and use of bio-based products. This is not
yet a rigorous product label, or a third-party certification; it is a federally administered label based on
the BioPreferred program created by the 2002 Farm
Bill to increase the purchase and use of bio-based
products in an effort to reduce petroleum consumption and carbon footprint and increase the use of
renewable resources.

U.S. Department of Energy: www.eere.energy.gov

Offers information, including articles and links, on
many energy-related topics, in particular on creating
energy-efficient buildings.

**U.S. Environmental Protection Agency (EPA):
www.epa.gov**

Website detailing current events in energy news. Also
provides sections dedicated to more specific environmental issues, such as mold, waste, and recycling.

**U.S. General Services Administration (GSA):
www.gsa.gov**

GSA's mission is to help other agencies better serve the
public by meeting their needs for products and services. This site simplifies citizen access to government
information and services. The building page details
laws that apply to many types of building use.

**U.S. Green Building Council (USGBC): www
.usgbc.org**

The mission of the USGBC is to be the nation's foremost coalition of leaders from across the building
industry who are working to promote buildings that
are environmentally responsible, profitable, and
healthy places to live and work. The website details
the LEED program, a revolutionary program aimed
at helping companies create sustainable structures.

Recommended Reading

BOOKS

Biomimicry: Innovation Inspired by Nature. Janine Benyus. London: Harper Perennial, 2002.

Build Green and Save: Protecting the Earth and Your Bottom Line. Matt Belcher. Washington, DC: Builder Books, 2009.

The Carbon Buster's Home Energy Handbook: Showing Climate Change and Saving Money. Godo Stoyke. Gabriola Island, BC: New Society, 2006.

Cradle to Cradle: Remaking the Way We Make Things. William McDonough and Michael Braungart. New York: North Point, 2002.

The Cultural Creatives: How 50 Million People Are Changing the World. Paul H. Ray and Sherry Ruth Anderson. Portland, OR: Broadway Books, 2001.

The Designers Atlas of Sustainability: Charting the Conceptual Landscape through Economy, Ecology and Culture. Ann Thorpe. Washington, DC: Island Press, 2007.

Design for Sustainability: A Sourcebook of Integrated, Eco-logical Solutions. Janis Birkeland. New York: Routledge, 2002.

Designing the Good Home. Dennis Wedlick. New York: Collins Design, 2003.

Design Like You Give a Damn: Architectural Responses to Humanitarian Crise: Architecture for Humanity. Washington, DC: U.S. Green Building Council, 2006.

Earth in Mind: On Education, Environment and Human Prospect. David W. Orr. Washington, DC: Island Press, 2004.

Eco. Elizabeth Wilhide. New York: Rizzoli, 2003.

EcoHome: A Healthy Home from A to Z. A. Krueger. New York: Avon, 1992.

Eco Interiors. Grazyna Pilatowicz. Hoboken, NJ: Wiley, 1994.

Ecological Design. Sim Van Der Ryn and Stuart Cowan. Washington, D.C.: Island Press, 1995.

The Ecology of Commerce. Rev. ed. Paul Hawken. New York: Harper, 2010.

Electromagnetic Fields: A Consumer's Guide to the Issues and How to Protect Ourselves. B. Blake Levitt. New York: Harcourt Brace, 1995.

Energy Free: Homes for a Small Planet. Ann V. Edminster. San Rafael, CA: Green Building, 2009

Environmentally Responsible Design: Green and Sustainable Design for Interior Designers Louise Jones. Hoboken, NJ: Wiley, 2008.

Every Breath You Take. B. P. Loughridge. New York: Collins Design, 1994.

Good Green Homes. Jennifer Roberts. Layton, UT: Gibbs Smith, 2003.

The Good House Book. Clarke Snell. Asheville, NC: Lark Books, 2004.

Green Architecture. James Wines. Cologne, Germany: Taschen, 2000.

Green Building Products: The GreenSpec Guide to Residential Building Materials. 3rd ed. Alex Wilson. Gabriola Island, BC : New Society, 2008.

Green by Design: Creating a Home for Sustainable Living. Angela M. Dean. Layton, UT: Gibbs Smith, 2003.

Greening My Life: A Green Building Pioneer Takes on His Most Challenging Project. David Gottfried. Berkeley, CA: Regenerative Publishing, 2010.

Green Remodeling: Changing the World One Room at a Time. David Johnston and Kim Master. Gabriola Island, BC: New Society, 2004.

Green Studio Handbook. Alison Kwok and Walter Grondzik. New York: Routledge, 2011.

Green to Gold: How Smart Companies Use Environmental Strategy to Innovate, Create Value and Build Competitive Advantage. Daniel C. Esty. Hoboken, NJ: Wiley, 2009.

Harmonious Environment: Beauty, Detoxify & Energize Your Life, Your Home and Your Planet. Norma Lehmeier Hartie. New York: Lingham, 2007.

Healing Environments. Carol Venolia. Berkeley, CA: Celestial Arts, 1988.

Healthy by Design. David Rousseau and James Wasley. Vancouver, BC: Hartley & Marks, 1999.

Healthy Child, Healthy World: Creating a Cleaner, Greener, Safer Home. Christopher Gavigan. New York: Plume, 2009.

The Healthy Home. Linda Mason Hunter. New York: Backprint, 2000.

The Healthy Home Kit. Ingrid Ritchie and Stephen J. Martin. Chicago: Dearborn Financial Press, 1994.

Healthy House Building: A Design & Construction Guide. John Bower: Bloomington, IN: Healthy House Institute, 1993.

Home Safe Home. Debra Lynn Dadd. Los Angeles: Tarcher, 2005.

Homes That Heal. Athena Thompson. Gabriola, BC: New Society, 2004.

The Household Environment and Chronic Illness: Guidelines for Constructing & Maintaining a Less Polluted Residence, Guy O. Pfeiffer and Casimer M. Nikel. Springfield, IL: Charles C. Thomas, 1980.

Indoor Air Quality and Human Health, Isaac Turiel. Palo Alto, CA: Stanford Univ. Press, 1985.

In Search of Natural Architecture, David Pearson. New York, NY: Abbeville Press, 2005.

Ishmael. Daniel Quinn. New York: Bantam: 1992.

Living Homes: Sustainable Architecture and Design. Suzi Moore McGregor. San Francisco: Chronicle, 2008.

Massive Change. Bruce Mau and Jennifer Leonard. London: Phaidon, 2004.

Mid-Course Correction. Ray C. Anderson. Atlanta: Peregrinzilla, 1999.

Natural Capitalism. Paul Hawken, Amory Lovins, and L. Hunter Lovins. Boston: Back Bay, 2000.

The Natural House Book. David Pearson. New York: Simon & Schuster, 1989.

The Natural Step Story. Karl-Henrik Robert. Gabriola, BC: New Society, 2002.

The Nature of Design: Ecology, Culture and Human Intention. David W. Orr. New York: Oxford Univ. Press, 2004.

The Non-Toxic Home & Office. Debra Lynn Dadd. New York: Tarcher/Putnam, 1992.

The Not So Big House. Sarah Susanka. Newton, CT: Taunton, 2001.

Places for the Soul. Christopher Day. Burlington, MA: Architectural Press, 2003.

Prescriptions for a Healthy House. Paula Baker Laporte. Gabriola, BC: New Society, 2001.

A Primer on Sustainable Building. Dianna Lopez Barnett and William D. Browning. Snowmass, CO: Rocky Mountain Institute, 1995.

Redux: Designs That Reuse, Recycle, and Reveal. Jennifer Roberts. Layton, UT: Gibbs Smith, 2005.

Rural Studio: Samuel Mockbee and Architecture of Decency. Andrea Oppenheimer Dean. New York: Princeton Architectural Press, 2002.

The Sick House Survival Guide: Simple Steps to Healthier Homes. Angela Hobbs. Gabriola Island, BC : New Society, 2003.

Silent Spring. Rachael Carson. New York: Mariner, 2002.

Starting Points for a Healthy Habitat. Carl E. Grimes. Denver: GMC Media, 1999.

State of the World: Is Sustainability Still Possible? Worldwatch Institute. Washington, DC: Worldwatch, 2013.

Stewardship: Choosing Service over Self-Interest. 2nd ed. Peter Block. San Francisco, CA: Berrett-Koehler, 2013.

Studio at Large: Architecture in Service of Global Communities. Sergio Palleroni and Christina Merkelbach. Seattle: Univ. of Washington Press, 2004.

The Sustainability Revolution: Portrait of a Paradigm Shift. Andres R. Edwards. Gabriola, BC: New Society, 2005.

Sustainable Commercial Interiors. 2nd ed. Penny Bonda and Katie Sosnowchik. Hoboken, NJ: Wiley & Sons, 2014.

Sustainable Design: A Critical Guide. David Bergman. New York: Princeton Architectural Press, 2012.

Sustainable Homes: Designs for Healthy Living. James Grayson Trulove. New York: Collins Designs, 2006.

Toward a Zero Energy Home: A Complete Guide to Energy Self-Sufficiency at Home. David Johnston and Scott Gibson. Newtown, CT: Taunton, 2010.

Toxic Free: How to Protect Your Health and Home from the Chemicals That are Making You Sick. Debra Lynn Dadd. Los Angeles: Tarcher, 2011.

Toxicology for Non-Toxicologists, Mark E. Stelljes. Lanham, MD: Government Institutes, 2007.

Women in Green: Voices in Sustainable Design. Kira Gould and Lance Hosey. Bainbridge Island, WA: Ecotone, 2007.

Worldchanging: A User's Guide for the 21st Century. Alex Steffen. New York: Abrams, 2008.

Your Green Home: A Guide to Planning a Healthy, Environmentally Friendly New Home. Alex Wilson. Gabriola, BC: New Society, 2006.

Your Health & the Indoor Environment. Randall Earl Dunford. Dallas: NuDawn, 1994.

Your Home, Your Health & Your Well-Being. David Rousseau. Berkeley, CA: Ten Speed, 1988.

Your Natural Home. Janet Marinelli and Paul Bierman-Lytle. London: Little Brown, 1995.

Zapped. Ann Louise Gittleman. New York: Harper One, 2005.

PERIODICALS

Conservation	www.conservationmag.org
Dwell	www.dwell.com
EcoBuilding Pulse	www.ecobuildingpulse.com
Ecological Home	www.ecologicalhomeideas.com
Eco-Structure	www.eco-structure.com
ED&C	www.EDCmag.com
The E Magazine	www.emagazine.com
Environmental Building News	www.buildinggreen.com
Green Building and Design	www.gbdmagazine.com
Green @ Work	www.greenatworkmag.com
GreenSource	www.greensourcemag.com
Interiors & Sources	www.interiorsandsources.com
LOHAS Journal	www.lohas.com
Metropolis	www.metropolismag.com
Mother Earth Living	www.motherearthliving.com
Plenty	www.plentymagazine.com
Sustainable Industries Journal	www.sijournal.com
Ultimate Home Design	www.UltimateHomeDesign.com
Worthwhile	www.worthwhilemag.com
Yes	www.yesmagazine.org

GLOSSARY

Acetone. A chemically derived solvent usually found in masonry, caulking, wallcoverings, strippers, adhesives, polyurethane, stains, and sealers.

Acidification. The process of becoming acid or the process of conversion into an acid.

Admixtures or additives (concrete). Minor ingredients mixed with concrete to impart particular properties such as color, decreased drying time, or improved workability.

Air-exchange rate. (1) The number of times that the outdoor air replaces the volume of air in a building per unit of time, typically expressed as air changes per hour. (2) The rate at which the ventilation system replaces the air within a room or building.

Air pollution. Airborne contaminants that adversely affect the environment or human health.

Allergen. Any substance capable of producing an allergic response. Some common allergens are proteins contained in pollens, grains, fungi, nuts, and seeds.

Anaphylactic. A severe and sometimes life-threatening immune system reaction to an antigen that a person has been previously exposed to. The reaction may include itchy skin, edema, collapsed blood vessels, fainting, and difficulty in breathing.

Aromatic hydrocarbons. A large family of chemicals characterized by the elements of hydrogen and carbon in ring-shaped molecules. Many aromatic hydrocarbons (e.g., toluene and xylene) evaporate readily and have strong odors. Many (e.g., benzene) are toxic or carcinogenic. All contaminate the air and groundwater.

Arsenic. Arsenic is a semi-metal element in the periodic table. It is odorless and tasteless. It enters drinking water supplies from natural deposits in the earth or from agricultural and industrial practices.

Asbestos. The Environmental Protection Agency's Substance Registry System defines asbestos as "a grayish, noncombustible fibrous material. It consists primarily of impure magnesium silicate minerals." The Agency for Toxic Substances and Disease Registry further defines asbestos as "a group of six different fibrous minerals (amosite, chrysotile, crocidolite, and the fibrous varieties of tremolite, actinolite, and anthophyllite) that occur naturally in the environment." Inhalation of asbestos fibers can lead to serious diseases of the lungs and other organs.

Barrier cloth. A special synthetic or cotton fabric that does not allow dust to penetrate. It has a very high thread count (300 per inch or greater) and is tightly woven.

Benzene. A carbon and hydrogen compound with a ring-shaped molecule made from petroleum and coal. Benzene is one of the most common building blocks for synthetic chemicals found in synthetic fibers and plastics. Highly toxic and carcinogenic, it was listed as a hazardous air pollutant under the 1990 Clean Air Act.

BHA or BHT. Butylated hydroxyl anisole (BHA) is a preservative listed as a carcinogen by state of California. BHT (butylated hydroxy toluene) serves as an ultraviolet inhibitor and an antioxidant. It was used through the years as a preservative in polypropylene yarn systems, carpet adhesives, some latex formulations, various backings and back coatings, and many other consumer products. Many rebond carpet padding products may contain BHT and has been attributed to numerous complaints about carpet yellowing. BHT is considered nontoxic and is even contained in many food items.

Biocide. An additive that will prevent growth of bacteria or fungi. Biocides are used in paints, floor coverings, and sometimes in fabrics. They are often toxic materials, safe only in very low concentrations.

Biodegradable. Able to decompose through the normal action of bacteria and fungi, without harmful effects to the environment. Typical examples of biodegradable materials are paper and wood products, natural fibers, and starches.

Biological. Of, relating to, caused by, or affecting life or living organisms.

Blackwater. Wastewater that is unfit for reuse because of sanitary concerns, such as that from toilets. *See also* Graywater.

Borax. A low-toxicity mineral with insecticidal, fungicidal, and herbicidal properties. It does not evaporate or volatilize into the air or pose the considerable health concerns associated with synthetic pesticides. Boric acid and borate salts are the refined forms of borax commonly used in structural pest control; these have been refined with low-grade acids and allowed to crystallize to form borates.

Building-related illness (BRI). Serious and diagnosable health condition, usually of the respiratory system, that can be attributed to specific air quality problems within a building.

Cadmium. A soft, easily molded heavy metal used in pigments and as heat stabilizers in the vinyl-making process. Cadmium is quite toxic, causing permanent kidney and liver damage, and accumulates in the environment.

Candela (candle power). A unit of luminous intensity equal to 1/60 of the luminous intensity per square centimeter of a blackbody radiating to the temperature of solidification of platinum (2046°K). Also called *candle*.

Carcinogen. Any naturally occurring or synthetic substance known to increase the risk of cancer.

Cementitious. Any material based on cement or cementlike products, i.e., inorganic, noncombustible, and hard-setting.

Certified wood. Wood that has been certified through a third party and supplied from sources that comply with sustainable forestry practices that protect trees, wildlife, habitat, streams, and soil.

Chain of custody. The path that a raw material follows, through harvesting, manufacturers, and retailers, to consumers. Verification of chain of custody is a key component to most eco-certifications.

Chemical sensitivity. A loosely defined condition experienced by some people who are affected by very small concentrations of chemicals in air, water, and food that would not have apparent effects on most people. Symptoms may be similar to minor allergies, although they may also include moderate to severe pains, muscle weakness, dizziness, confusion, and even seizures.

Chemical sensitization. Health problems caused to some people when they are exposed to chemicals, often characterized as dizziness, eye and throat irritation, chest tightness, and nasal congestion. Reactions may occur even to trace amounts of the chemicals when an individual has chemical sensitization.

Chlorinated polyethylene. A family of polymers produced by a chemical reaction of chlorine on polyethylene. The resulting thermoplastic elastomers contain 25 to 45 percent chlorine by weight and 0 to 25 percent crystallinity. These polymers are used in many thermoplastic and elastomer applications.

Chlorofluorocarbons (CFCs). A group of volatile gases manufactured from hydrocarbons such as methane, chlorine, fluorine, or bromine that can deplete or destroy the ozone layer of the Earth's stratosphere when released. These gases have been discontinued from use in refrigerants, solvents, and blowing agents in the making of foam. Most are being phased out by an international ozone treaty.

Chloroprene (Neoprene). A chemical intermediate used in the production of artificial rubber.

Chromated copper arsenate (CCA). A chemical wood preservative containing chromium, copper, and arsenic used in pressure-treated wood to protect it from rotting due to insects and microbial agents. The EPA has classified CCA as a restricted-use product, for use only by certified pesticide applicators. CCA has been used to treat lumber since the 1940s; after the 1970s, the majority of the wood used in outdoor residential settings was CCA-treated wood. However, pressure-treated wood containing CCA is no longer being produced for use in most residential settings, particularly decking or playsets.

Clean Air Act of 1972. Groundbreaking legislation administered by the EPA that mandates specific measures to protect the air quality and respiratory health of U.S. inhabitants.

Climate change. Any significant change in the measures of climate lasting for an extended period of time. Climate change includes major changes in temperature, precipitation, or wind patterns, among others, that occur over several decades or longer.

Closed-loop recycling. A production process in which post-consumer waste is collected, recycled, and used to make new products.

Comfort criteria. Specific original design conditions that include temperature (air, radiant, and surface), humidity, air speed, outdoor temperature design conditions, outdoor humidity design conditions, clothing (seasonal), and expected activity (ASHRAE 55–2004).

Compact fluorescent lightbulb (CFL). A fluorescent light bulb designed for use in fixtures that take standard-size incandescent bulbs. CFLs are many times more energy-efficient than incandescent bulbs.

Composite wood. Composite wood is made from several materials. It is used in door cores, panel substrates, particleboard, medium-density fiberboard (MDF), plywood, oriented-strand board (OSB), wheatboard, and strawboard.

Composting toilet systems. Toilets that treat human waste with microbiological processes. They are considered dry plumbing fixtures.

Construction IAQ management plan. A plan comprised of the steps to be taken to minimize contamination in a project building during construction and the procedures to flush the building of contaminants prior to occupancy.

Construction Specifications Institute (CSI). A national professional association that provides format standards for the organization and presentation of specification documents (specs).

Construction waste management plan (CWMP). A plan that diverts construction and demolition debris from landfills through conscientious plans to recycle, salvage, and reuse. Optimally, this type of plan also eliminates packaging materials and is carefully monitored or audited by the contractor on a construction site.

Cradle-to-cradle. A concept introduced by architect William McDonough and chemist Michael Braungart that describes a product that, at the end of its useful life, will decompose entirely with no negative environmental impact or otherwise be used again when recycled into a new product.

Cradle-to-cradle design protocol. A scientifically based, peer-reviewed process used to assess and optimize materials used in products and production processes to maximize health, safety, effectiveness, and high-quality reutilization over many product life cycles.

Cradle-to-grave. Introduced by architect William McDonough, a term that describes a product that is used for a period of time and then discarded.

Creosote. A dark brown oil derivative of the process of high-temperature distillation of coal tar containing a number of phenols, cresols, and other organic compounds. Used in various applications as a means to protect and preserve wood. It is applied by pressure methods.

Curing. The process and time period for a finish to achieve its final state of hardness and color. A chemical reaction is usually involved.

Daylighting. Natural daylight introduced into interior spaces and controlled specifically to reduce levels of electric lighting, to minimize glare, and to optimize lighting quality. Daylighting reduces the need for artificial light during the day. Common strategies for daylighting include proper orientation of windows and use of skylights, clerestory windows, and reflective surfaces.

Daylight factor. The ratio of exterior illumination to interior illumination. It is expressed as a percentage. Variables used to determine the illumination include floor and window area, window geometry, visible transmittance (Tvis), and window height.

Deciduous. Deciduous means "temporary" or "tending to fall off." Deciduous trees lose all of their foliage for part of the year. In some cases, the foliage loss coincides with the incidence of winter in temperate or polar climates, while others lose their leaves during the dry season in climates with seasonal variation in rainfall. The converse of deciduous is evergreen.

Design for disassembly. Designing so that a product may be dismantled for easier maintenance, repair, recovery, and reuse of components and materials.

Development footprint. The area impacted by project activity. The footprint includes hardscapes, access roads, parking lots, nonbuilding facilities, and the building itself.

Dichloromethane. A solvent found in paint remover, adhesives, paints, and aerosols. It may cause cancer and heart attacks and is a known water pollutant.

Diethylhexyl phthalate (DEHP). A known carcinogen found in plasticizers, used to keep vinyl flexible in products such as wall and floor coverings, furniture, upholstery, and shower curtains. DEHP is a colorless liquid with almost no odor.

Dioxin. A highly toxic chemical found in PVC products. Low levels cause cancer and endocrine disruption.

Down-cycling. The practice of recycling a material in such a way that much of its inherent value is lost.

Ecologically sustainable forestry. Dictates the management of a productive forest that supports a healthy ecosystem. *See also* Sustainable yield forestry.

Embodied energy. The sum of the energy used to grow, extract, and manufacture a product, including the amount of energy needed to transport it to the job site and complete the installation. For example, aluminum embodies four times as much energy as steel and about twelve times as much as wood.

Endocrine disruptors. Chemicals that mimic natural hormones, they may disrupt the body's endocrine system and produce adverse health effects in both humans and animals. Negative health effects include developmental, reproductive, neurological, and immune issues. Know endocrine disruptors include diethylstilbestrol (the drug DES), phthalate plasticizers used in PVC plastic , dioxin, PCBs, DDT, and some other pesticides.

Energy audit. Identifies total energy used in a building and for what purposes, and then identifies opportunities for improving efficiency and reducing costs. ASHRAE conducts three levels of energy audits: (I) walk-through analysis, (II) energy survey and analysis, and (III) detailed analysis of capital-intensive modifications (investment-grade audit).

Energy Star rating. A label developed by the EPA and the U.S. Department of Energy to identify appliances and products that exceed established energy-efficiency standards. This label helps consumers identify products that will save energy and money. Energy Star–labeled equipment and appliances often exceed the efficiency levels of other new products.

Environmentally friendly. Designed not to harm the environment, whether the biosphere, soil, water, or air.

Environmental tobacco smoke (ETS). Tobacco smoke producing airborne, cancer-causing particles that are exhaled by smokers and inhaled by all.

Ethylene glycol. A synthetic solvent often used in water- and oil-based paints, lacquers, and stains. It is a nasal irritant and a neurotoxin, highly toxic when ingested or inhaled, and may cause damage to blood and bone marrow. It is also the main ingredient in automotive antifreeze. Ethylene glycol is listed as a hazardous pollutant under the 1990 Clean Air Act.

Eutrophication. The process by which bodies of water are starved of oxygen and light by algae and other plants that multiply due to excessive concentrations of nutrients such as nitrogen and phosphorous. Typical sources include fertilizer runoff and poorly managed wastewater treatment systems, including home septic systems.

Exhaust air. Air removed from an area and discharged outside the area by means of mechanical or natural systems.

Fair trade. A system that allows workers and artisans to receive a fair wage for their products or at least the minimum wage established for their country. Since the minimum wage is often not enough for basic survival, whenever feasible, workers are paid a living wage, which enables them to cover basic needs, including food, shelter, education, and health care for their families. Fair trade does not necessarily cost the consumer more, as middle agents are often bypassed, cutting costs and returning a greater percentage of the retail price to the producers.

Feldspar. A natural silica mineral used in glassmaking and ceramic glazes.

Fiberboards. Construction panels made from compressed fibers, including wood, paper, straw, or other plant fibers. Three common types of fiberboards are high-, medium-, and low-density. *High-density* (low-toxicity) is highly compressed fiber, usually made with no added adhesive; it may also be tempered to provide an even harder surface. It is commonly used for furniture backs, interior doors, industrial flooring, and pegboard. *Medium-density* (MDF) is moderately compressed fiber held together with glue or binder and commonly used for cabinet and furniture frames, carpet underlayment, and as a core for decorative laminate paneling. Toxicity depends upon adhesive.

Low-density (low-toxicity) is slightly compressed fiber, usually with no added adhesive, and is commonly used for installation sheathing, acoustic panels, and tack boards.

Fire or flame retardant. A substance added to a flammable material to reduce its flammability. Fire retardants, used in fabrics, carpet, bedding, upholstery, and foamed plastics, only slow the spread of fire; they do not make flammable materials fireproof. Some, such as phosphates and chlorinated compounds, are irritating or hazardous.

Fly ash. A by-product of coal-fired electric generating plants. It is the finely divided residue resulting from the combustion of ground or powdered coal, which is then transported from the firebox through the boiler by flue gases. Fly ash improves the performance and quality of concrete, improving workability, reducing water demand, reducing segregation and bleeding, and lowering heat of hydration. Fly ash increases strength, reduces permeability, reduces corrosion of reinforcing steel, increases sulphate resistance, and reduces alkali-aggregate reaction. Fly ash reaches its maximum strength more slowly than concrete made with only Portland cement. Two classifications of fly ash are produced: Class C and Class F. Class C fly ash is preferable and is the main type offered for residential concrete applications from ready-mix suppliers.

Forest Stewardship Council (FSC). An international nonprofit organization founded in 1993 that supports environmentally appropriate, socially beneficial, and economically viable management of the world's forests. The FSC administers a third-party, chain-of-custody forestry certification program to assure that businesses supply trees and wood from forests managed in an ecologically sustainable manner.

Formaldehyde. Pungent and irritating, formaldehyde is a colorless gas compound used to bind together and preserve building materials and household products. It is an excellent resin and binding agent as well as very inexpensive, which contributes to its wide usage (approximately 6 billion pounds are produced each year). It is found virtually everywhere, indoors and out, and can be naturally occurring or manufactured. It can irritate eyes, mucous membranes, and the upper respiratory system, and can be inhaled or absorbed by the skin. Its use should be avoided whenever possible, as even at low levels, formaldehyde can cause serious health problems. Symptoms of low-level exposure include runny nose, sore throat, cough, dermatitis, sleeping difficulties, headache, fatigue, breathing difficulties, sinus irritation, chest pain, frequent nausea, bronchitis, and decreased lung capacity. Signs of acute exposure include abdominal pain, anxiety, coma, convulsions, diarrhea, and respiratory problems such as bronchitis, pneumonia, or pulmonary edema. In 2004, the World Health Organization (WHO) upgraded formaldehyde from a probable carcinogen to a known carcinogen after evidence showed that formaldehyde caused nasopharyngeal cancer.

Fossil fuels. Fuels such as coal, oil, and natural gas, that are extracted from beneath the earth's surface, often with significant environmental and political cost. These fuels are finite resources and are nonrenewable.

Fungi (molds, mildew, mushrooms). Plantlike organisms that do not require light for growth and survival because they do not produce chlorophyll. A few fungi are safe and edible, such as some species of mushrooms; most produce allergenic spores and odors.

Fungicide. Any substance added to inhibit the growth of fungus and consequent spoilage of a material. Paints, stucco, floor coverings, treated wood, and outdoor fabrics are commonly treated with fungicides. Many fungicides are compounds with hazardous metals or chlorine. Safer fungicides include those with boron or that are sulfate-based. *See also* Biocide.

Genetically modified organisms (GMOs). Plants and animals that have had their genetic makeup altered to exhibit traits that are not naturally theirs. In general, genes are taken (copied) from one organism that shows a desired trait and transferred into the genetic code of another organism.

Glazing factor. The ratio of interior illuminance to the exterior illuminance at a given point on a given plane, under known overcast sky conditions. Variables used to determine the daylight factor include floor area, window area, window geometry, visible transmittance (Tvis), and window height.

Glycols. A family of alcohols used as solvents in many paints, coatings, and the like. Some glycols are very safe while others are toxic. Examples of glycols are ethylene glycol and propylene glycol.

Graywater. Wastewater coming from sinks, showers and laundry that can be collected and treated for some reuse, such as that from sinks. *See also* Blackwater.

Green cleaning. Cleaning practices and products with less environmental impact than conventional practices and products.

Greenhouse gas (GHG). Gases that trap heat in the atmosphere, warming the earth. Greenhouse gases include, carbon dioxide, methane, nitrous oxide, ozone, chlorofluorocarbons, hydrochlorofluorocarbons, hydrofluorocarbons, perfluorocarbons, and sulfur hexafluoride.

Grout. A cementitious material used to fill the joints between tiles. Grout may contain acrylic or epoxy additives for greater durability.

Halogenated flame retardants (HFRs). Flame retardants with halogen in the chemical formula (generally chlorine or bromine). HFRs, or their breakdown products, tend to be persistent, bioaccumulative and toxic.

Hazardous waste. By-products with physical, chemical, or infectious characteristics that pose hazards to the environment and human health, especially when improperly handled.

Heavy metals. The elemental series of metals, which includes mercury, lead, cadmium, thallium, cobalt, nickel, and aluminum. Most are very toxic and persistent in the environment.

Hexane (n-hexane). A solvent derived from petroleum and used in adhesives and paints. Hexane is moderately hazardous in low concentrations, causing symptoms of nerve toxicity such as numbness, trembling, or disorientation.

High-efficiency particulate arrestance (HEPA). A HEPA filter removes at least 99.97 percent of contaminants from air that are 0.3 microns (.3 one-thousandths of a millimeter) in size or larger. Manufacturers of HEPA filters often advertise how many times per hour air would be cleaned, per square foot or per room; the greater the rate, the better.

High-performance green building. A building whose design includes features that conserve water and energy; use space, materials, and resources more efficiently; minimize construction waste; and have healthy indoor environments.

Hydrogenated chlorofluorocarbons (HCFCs or HFCs). Substitute refrigerants and solvents that do not have as much potential to destroy atmospheric ozone, if released, as CFCs. Most are less efficient as refrigerants than CFCs, and some are quite toxic. HCFCs are slated to be banned, along with CFCs, by 2030. *See also* Chlorofluorocarbons.

Indoor air quality (IAQ). The air quality within and around buildings and structures, especially as it relates to the health and comfort of building occupants. Indoor pollution sources that release gases or particles into the air are the primary cause of indoor air quality problems in homes.

Indoor environmental quality (IEQ). The quality of the air and environment inside buildings, based on pollutant concentrations and conditions that can affect the health, comfort, and performance of occupants. These include temperature, relative humidity, light, sound, and other factors. Improving IEQ involves designing, constructing, commissioning, operating, and maintaining buildings in ways that reduce pollution sources and remove indoor pollutants, while ensuring that fresh air is continually supplied and properly circulated.

Inorganic compound. Any compound that does not contain carbon atoms in its structure. Minerals, metals, ceramics, and water are examples of inorganic compounds. Most tend to be very stable and persistent because they oxidize slowly or not at all. *See also* Organic compound.

Integrated design team. All individuals involved in a project from very early in the design process, including the design professionals (architects, engineers, landscape architects, and interior designers), the owner's representatives (investors, developers, building users, facility managers, and maintenance personnel), and the general contractor and subcontractors.

Kiln-dried. A method of drying wood in an oven after sawing. Kiln-drying results in 10 percent or less moisture content, which makes the wood more dimensionally stable and better able to resist fungus in storage.

Lacquer. A glossy liquid finish for woods or metals traditionally prepared from plant resins. Nitrocellulose lacquer, made from wood or cotton fiber treated with acid and dissolved in butyl acetate (lacquer thinner), is a more typical formulation today. Lacquer also refers to many types of hard, high-gloss industrial finishes, such as acrylic auto finishes.

Laminate. A thin layer of material (veneer) bonded to another surface. Wood and plastics are both commonly laminated.

Lamp life. The useful operating life of lamps.

Lamps. Devices that use electricity to produce light in any of several ways: by heating a wire for incandescence, by exciting a gas that produces ultraviolet light from a luminescent material, by generating an arc that emits visible light and some ultraviolet light, or by inducing excitation of mercury through radio frequencies.

Latex. A substance that remains flexible at room temperature. Natural latex, derived from rubber trees, a naturally occurring, sticky resin from rubber tree sap used for rubber products, carpet backing, and paints.

It is associated with a rare yet severe allergic response in some people. Synthetic latex is often called simply "latex," but is usually derived from petrochemicals, for example styrene butadiene. *See also* Styrene butadiene rubber.

Lead. A heavy metal that may be hazardous to health if breathed or swallowed. Lead can bioaccumulate in fish and wildlife.

Leadership in Energy and Environmental Design (LEED). USGBC's Green Building Rating System for green building design, a voluntary, consensus-based national standard for developing high-performance, sustainable buildings. LEED standards were created to define green building by establishing common standards of measurement, promote integrated whole-building design practices, recognize environmental leadership within the building industry, stimulate green competition, and raise consumer awareness of green building benefits.

LEED Accredited Professionals (APs). Individuals who have successfully completed the LEED professional accreditation exam.

Life-cycle analysis (LCA). A process or framework to evaluate the environmental burdens associated with a product, process, or activity by identifying, quantifying, and assessing its energy and material usage and environmental releases in order to identify opportunities for environmental improvements. Extraction and processing of raw materials, manufacturing, transportation and distribution, use/reuse/maintenance, recycling, and final disposal are all considered.

Life-cycle cost. Total cost of a product or material, including the initial cost of materials extraction, transportation, manufacturing, maintenance, and operations and end use. This approach can often be used to justify more expensive and energy-efficient systems that save money over the life of the product.

Linseed oil. Nontoxic oil from the seed of the flax plant used in paints, varnishes, linoleum, and synthetic resins.

Low-toxic. A lower degree to which a product is poisonous to people or other living organisms.

Lumen (lm). A unit of measurement of the rate at which a lamp produces light. A lamp's light output rating expresses the total amount of light emitted in all directions per unit time.

Material safety data sheets (MSDS). An MSDS is a legal requirement for all potentially hazardous products. The data sheet indicates the risks from using and disposing of the product and recommends safe practices. It identifies hazardous chemicals and health and physical hazards, including exposure limits and precautions for workers who may come into contact with these chemicals. Review product MSDS when specifying materials and require their submittal during the shop drawing phase.

Medium-density fiberboard (MDF). A manufactured board that is made with very small particles of wood held together with a binder. *See also* Fiberboards.

Melamine. A polymer used for plastics and paints made from formaldehyde, ammonia, and urea. similar to urea formaldehyde resin. Melamine is nontoxic once heated and cured.

Mercury. A neurotoxic heavy metal. It is toxic if breathed or ingested at sufficiently high concentrations. Because of its common use, mercury is released during garbage incineration and through the combustion of fuels such as coal and wood for energy production. Mercury readily bioaccumulates in all aquatic organisms.

Metamorphic. Relating to a change of physical form, structure, or substance especially by supernatural means or a striking alteration in appearance, character, or circumstances.

Methylene diphenyl isocyanate (MDI). The other type of binder used in structural engineered wood products today is polymeric diphenyl methylene diisocyanate (PMDI, sometimes referred to as MDI). This is a polyurethane-type binder that is totally waterproof and contains no formaldehyde. Designers involved with green building like PMDI binders because they emit no formaldehyde. This binder is used in Medite medium-density fiberboard and all of the straw particleboard products, but among structural engineered wood products, only OSB and TimberStrand LSL are available made with PMDI binder.

Mica. A naturally occurring silica mineral used as a filler in paints, gypsum fillers, and as electrical insulation. Low toxicity, but the dust is hazardous.

Mitigation. To make something less severe or painful and cause it to become less harsh or hostile.

Mortar. A cement-based mixture used to lay stone or ceramic tiles, or for use as a grout for these materials.

Multiple chemical sensitivity (MCS). People affected by MCS have severe sensitivity or allergy-like reactions to a number of chemicals at very low concentrations. There are numerous views about the existence, potential causes, and possible remedial actions regarding this phenomenon.

Mutagen. An agent, such as a chemical, ultraviolet light, or a radioactive element, that can induce or increase the frequency of mutation in an organism.

Naphtha. A colorless or reddish brown highly volatile, flammable liquid mixture of hydrocarbons distilled from petroleum, coal tar, and natural gas and used as fuel, as solvents, and in making various chemicals. It is used widely as a solvent for various organic substances such as fats and rubber and in the making of varnish. Used as a cleaning fluid because of its dissolving property, it can also be found in certain laundry soaps. Considered to be an irritant of the skin, eyes, and mucous membranes and a central nervous system depressant.

Nasopharyngeal cancer. Develops in the nasopharynx, an area in the back of the nose toward the base of the skull. Considered an oral cancer, it is not often treated by surgery and has differing risk factors than most oral cancers.

Natural. A substance or material taken from nature as directly as possible, with minimal intervention of processing or chemical synthesis.

Natural capitalism. Natural resources and ecological systems that provide vital life-support services to our planet. *Natural Capitalism*, the book, describes a future in which business and environmental interests increasingly overlap and in which businesses can better satisfy their customers' needs, increase profits, and help solve environmental problems, all at the same time.

Natural resources. Materials or substances such as minerals, forests, water, and fertile land that occur in nature and can be used for economic gain.

Neurotoxin. Toxic substances that target the nervous system and disrupt the signaling that allows nerve tissue to function effectively.

Nonrenewable. A finite resource that does not replenish itself easily, or at all (e.g., stone).

Off-site salvaged materials. Materials recovered from an off-site source and reused.

On-demand heaters. Heaters that heat water only when it is needed and then apply only the amount of heating required to satisfy the user's immediate needs.

On-site salvaged materials. Materials recovered from and reused at the same building site.

Organic compound. Any chemical compound based on the carbon atom. Organic compounds are the basis of all living things; they are also the foundation of modern polymer chemistry. Several million are known and their characteristics vary widely.

Organically grown. Products grown with minimal use of synthetic fertilizers or pesticides. Various state and industry definitions are used to determine which products can be sold as "organically grown."

Oriented strand board (OSB). A manufactured wood product that contains a binder. OSB is usually made with fast-growing farmed trees instead of old-growth trees.

Outdoor air. The ambient air that enters a building either through a ventilation system (with intentional openings) for natural ventilation or by infiltration. (ASHRAE 62.1–2004).

Outgas. The release of gases or vapors from solid materials. It is a form of evaporation, or slow chemical change, that will produce indoor air pollution for prolonged periods after installation of a material. Sometimes referred to as off-gas.

Ozone layer. The protective layer of atmosphere, 15 miles above the Earth, that absorbs some of the sun's ultraviolet rays, thus reducing the amount of potentially harmful radiation from reaching the Earth's surface. Ozone depletion is caused by the breakdown of certain chlorine and/or bromine-containing compounds such as chlorofluorocarbons or halogens.

Particulates. Particles of dust, mold, mildew, and so on small enough to become suspended in air. Very small particulates (less than .005 millimeter) can be inhaled deep into the lungs. Particulates containing plant or animal proteins are allergenic, while those containing mineral fiber (silica, asbestos) cause lung disease or cancer.

Passive solar. Solar energy is a radiant heat source that causes natural processes upon which all life depends. Some of the natural processes can be managed through building design in a manner that helps heat and cool the building. The basic natural processes that are used in passive solar energy are the thermal energy flows associated with radiation, conduction, and natural convection. When sunlight strikes a building, the building materials can reflect, transmit, or absorb the solar radiation. Additionally, the heat produced by the sun causes air movement that can be predictable in designed spaces. These basic responses to solar heat lead to design elements, material choices, and placements that can provide heating and cooling effects in a home.

Pentachlorophenol. Formerly one of the most widely used biocides in the United States, it is now a restricted use pesticide and is no longer available to the general public. It was primarily used as a wood preservative. Pentachlorophenol is extremely toxic to humans from acute (short-term) ingestion and inhalation exposure.

Perchloroethylene (PERC). A chlorinated solvent used mostly in the dry-cleaning process. PERC is implicated in 90 percent of all groundwater contamination.

Perlite. A volcanic glass, which is expanded and used as a plaster additive and fire-resistant insulation.

Petrochemical fertilizers and pesticides. Fertilizers and pesticides made from chemical substances obtained from petroleum or natural gas as gasoline, kerosene, or petrolatum.

Phenol formaldehyde. An adhesive resin used for exterior plywood and other wood products. It is dark brown in color and low in formaldehyde emissions.

Phenols. Hydrocarbons used to make resins and glues. They are usually very toxic and output volatile organic compounds.

Photovoltaic (PV). The capacity of photocells to generate electricity from the sun's energy.

Phthalates. A group of chemicals used to make plastics more flexible and harder to break. They are often called plasticizers. Some phthalates are used as solvents (dissolving agents) for other materials. They are used in hundreds of products, such as vinyl flooring, adhesives, detergents, lubricating oils, automotive plastics, plastic clothes (raincoats), and personal-care products (soaps, shampoos, hair sprays, and nail polishes). Because phthalates do not permanently bind chemically with the polyvinyl chloride, they are able to leach from the plastic into fluids that come in contact with them or to attach to dust particles and loft into air.

Picocurie. A unit for measuring radioactivity, often expressed as picocuries per liter (pCi/L) of air.

Plasticizer. A chemical such as a phthalate added to a plastic or rubber to keep it soft and flexible, particularly common in vinyl upholstery and flexible floor coverings. The plasticizers outgas slowly.

Plumbing fixtures and fittings. Receptacles, devices, or appliances that are either permanently or temporarily connected to the building's water distribution system and receive liquid or liquid-borne wastes and discharge wastewater, liquid-borne waste materials, or sewage either directly or indirectly to the drainage system of the premises. They include water closets, urinals, lavatories, sinks, showers, and drinking fountains.

Pollution prevention. Reducing the amount of energy, materials, packaging, or water in the design, manufacturing, or purchasing of products or materials in an effort to increase efficient use of resources, reduce toxicity, and eliminate waste.

Polybrominated diphenyl ether (PBDE). A flame retardant commonly used in plastics and foam, especially in consumer products such as furnishings and electronics. PBDE is similar in chemical structure to PCB (polychlorinated biphenyl) and PBB (polybrominated biphenyl), both banned in many countries for their toxicity to humans and to the environment. PDBE has been found in concentrations in human breast milk, as well as remote environmental locations, and is also strongly suspected as a hazard. Its use is under review, and some types of PDBE are already banned from use in products such as mattresses.

Polyethylene. A chemically simple, semitransparent plastic used widely as a vapor barrier sheet over insulation, for packaging film, and containers. There are both high-density (HDPE) and low-density (LDPE) varieties. It is a low-toxicity material and produces low-risk vapors when it is burned.

Polyethylene terephthalate (PET). A polyester plastic used widely in soft drink bottles.

Polyurethane. A particular type of plastic known as a "thermoset." Polyurethane is formed by reacting a polyol (an alcohol with more than two reactive hydroxyl groups per molecule) with a diisocyanate or a polymeric isocyanate in the presence of suitable catalysts and additives. Polyurethane can be found in liquid coatings and paints, tough elastomers such as rollerblade wheels, rigid insulation, soft flexible foam, elastic fiber, or as an integral skin.

Polyvinyl butral (PVB). A resin usually used for applications that require strong binding, optical clarity, adhesion to many surfaces, toughness, and flexibility. PVB is prepared from polyvinyl alcohol by reaction with butanal. The major application is laminated safety glass for automobile windshields.

Polyvinyl chloride (PVC). A polymer derived from oil or liquid natural gas and sodium chloride. The liquid natural gas or petroleum is refined and reacted with chlorine from the salt to form vinyl chloride monomer. Vinyl chloride monomer, a known carcinogen, is polymerized to form PVC resin. It is typically very durable and chemically stable, unless plasticized to keep it soft, and is the basis of most flexible flooring, plastic upholstery, and plastic siding. As defined by the EPA, PVC is a tough, environmentally indestructible plastic that releases hydrochloric acid when burned.

Portland cement. A kind of cement made by burning limestone and clay in a kiln. It is the base for most concrete, mortar, and floor tile grouts.

Postconsumer. A material or finished product that served its intended use as a consumer item. It may be recycled and incorporated into building materials, after which it may be identified as containing postconsumer recycled content or recovered material.

Postconsumer content. The percentage of material in a product that is recycled from consumer waste.

Postindustrial waste (also called preconsumer waste). Refers to waste produced during the manufacturing process of virgin material and rerouted from one step in the process to the next. This is not the same as recycled material.

Potable water. Water suitable for drinking that meets or exceeds EPA drinking water standards; it is supplied from wells or municipal water systems.

ppm. Parts per million.

Preconsumer material. Material diverted from the waste stream during the manufacturing process. Excluded is reutilization of materials such as rework, regrind or scrap generated in a process and capable of being reclaimed within the same process that generated it.

Preconsumer recycled content. Containing materials generated in manufacturing, such as damaged or obsolete products, overruns and trimmings. Does not include materials commonly reused in the manufacturing process.

Propylene glycol. An oily alcohol used in paints, waxes, and sealers. Unlike ethylene glycol, it is low toxicity, and approved as a food additive.

Radon. A radioactive, colorless, odorless gas formed in the decay of uranium. The radon decay products (also called "radon daughters" or "progeny") can be breathed into the lungs, where they continue to release radiation as they further decay. Radon passes from some soil types into buildings and is often found in basements or sublevel rooms. Concentrations build up when trapped within, can cause health hazards, and may cause cancer.

Rapidly renewable. Materials that are not depleted when used, but are typically harvested from fast-growing sources and do not require unnecessary chemical support, such as bamboo, flax, wool, and certain types of wood.

Recirculated air. Air removed from a space and reused as supply air, delivered by mechanical or natural ventilation.

Reclaimed. Material that is recovered for reuse or another purpose, such as wood barn siding that becomes flooring. *See also* Salvaged.

Reclaimed water. Wastewater that has been treated and purified for reuse.

Recyclable. The capability of a product or material to be recovered or otherwise diverted from the solid wastestream for the purpose of recycling.

Recycled content. The proportion, by mass, of recycled material in a product or packaging. Only preconsumer and postconsumer materials are considered recycled content.

Recycled/recovered materials. Waste materials and by-products that have been recovered or diverted from solid waste, not including those materials and by-products generated from and commonly reused within an original manufacturing process.

Recycling. The process of converting waste into a reusable product. A series of activities including collection, separation, and processing by which products or materials are recovered from the solid wastestream for use in the form of raw materials in the manufacture of new products other than fuel for producing heat or power by combustion.

Red List. A list composed of chemicals that have been identified to be phased out of production due to health/toxicity concerns. It is updated as new science emerges. The list is written by the Living Building Challenge.

Renewable energy. Energy harvested from sources that are not depleted when used, typically causing very low environmental impact, such as solar energy, hydroelectric power, and wind power.

Resilient. Capable of withstanding shock without permanent deformation or rupture. Rubber, vinyl, and linoleum floor coverings are called resilient because they are elastic.

Resin. A sticky substance that flows from certain plants and trees, especially pine and fir. Resin is used in paints and varnish. Artificial resins, used in the manufacture of plastics and synthetic finishes, are usually petroleum-based polymers.

Resource efficiency. A practice in which the primary consideration of material use begins with the concept of "reduce, reuse, recycle, repair," stated in descending order of priority. This concept may be applied in everyday life to help promote a sustainable society. In design, begin by reducing the amount of material that is specified; find ways to reuse materials, recycle products or product waste; specify products made from recycled materials; and repair or restore products instead of replacing them.

Retrofit. Any change to an existing facility, such as the addition or removal of equipment or a required adjustment, connection, or disconnection of equipment.

Reuse. Method of returning materials to active use in the same or a related capacity and thus extends the lifetime of materials that would otherwise be disposed. Examples of ongoing consumables that can be reused include binders, staplers, and other desk accessories, whether they are reused on- site or donated to other facilities.

Rugmark. A global nonprofit organization working to end illegal child labor and offer educational opportunities for children in India, Nepal, and Pakistan. The Rugmark label is an assurance that no illegal child labor was employed in the manufacture of a carpet or rug.

R-value. A unit of thermal resistance; the opposite of thermal conductance. The higher the R-value, the greater the insulating quality. By knowing the resistance of a material, it is possible to predict how much heat will flow through it and to compare it with other materials. A high R-value indicates a low rate of heat transfer.

Salvaged. Material that is recovered or reclaimed for possible reuse or recycling.

Scientific Certification Systems (SCS). The nation's first third-party certifier for testing pesticide residues in fresh produce, established in 1984. Since 1996, the company has evolved to become a certifier of multiple facets of the food industry and of the environmentally sound management of forests, marine habitats, and a wide variety of manufacturing-related businesses.

Semivolatile organic compound (SVOC). An organic compound that has a boiling point higher than water and that may vaporize when exposed to temperatures above room temperature. Many are manmade and used and produced in the manufacturing industry (e.g., in plastic, pharmaceutical, and pesticide manufacture). SVOCs are typically industrial plasticizers (e.g., phthalates) or by-products of the incomplete combustion of fossil fuels (e.g., benzo(a) pyrene).

Set points. Normal ranges for building systems and indoor environmental quality outside of which action is taken.

Shellac. Purified lac (a resin from a beetle) is used for making varnishes and leather polishes. Shellac is dissolved in methyl alcohol and can be thinned with safer ethyl alcohol. Low toxicity.

Sick building syndrome (SBS). The occurrence of health complaints such as nasal congestion, headache, irritated eyes, lethargy, and tiredness that are difficult to medically diagnose but are present in individuals when they are within a building and disappear or diminish once they leave the building. The cause of SBS is suspected to be poor air quality and conditions within the building and related to the construction and mechanical systems of the building.

Silicone. Organic compounds of silicon used for caulking and flexible plastics, lubricating oils, and sealers. A very low-toxicity material.

Sink. In buildings, surfaces that tend to capture volatile organic compounds from the air and release them later. Carpets, gypsum board, ceiling tile, draperies, and upholstery are all sinks. Also, a place in the environment where a compound or material collects, as defined by the EPA.

Sizing. A temporary, formaldehyde-based liquid treatment that seals a surface against absorption of adhesive. Sizing adds stiffness or shine, particularly to fabrics and wallpaper, providing "tooth" for the wallcovering. Fabric sizing is very irritating to some people.

Slake. To combine lime chemically with water or moist air.

SmartWood. An independent agency, accredited by the Forest Stewardship Council, that certifies for chain-of-custody and rediscovered wood products. Through independent auditing, certification and the promotion of certified forest products, SmartWood's purpose is to improve forest management by providing economic incentives to businesses that practice responsible forestry. SmartWood is a program of the Rainforest Alliance, a global nonprofit conservation organization.

Solvents. Petroleum-based liquids that can dissolve solids and keep them in solution. Solvents may contribute to pollution through evaporation.

Styrene-butadiene rubber (SBR). A synthetic latex formed from petroleum and used for carpet backings and elastic fabrics. SBR has a characteristic pungent odor and releases several irritating gases. The earliest synthetic rubbers were styrene-butadiene copolymers, Buna S, and SBR, whose properties are closest to those of natural rubber. SBR is the most commonly used elastomer because of its low cost and good properties; it is used mainly for tires.

Suberin. A waxy, waterproof substance present in the cell walls of cork tissue in plants.

Sunspace. A well-glazed space, generally south-facing, that collects heat and supplies some of it to another space (typically adjoining). Temperatures within sunspaces are not normally controlled; they float daily and seasonally.

Sustainability. Meeting or satisfying the needs of the current generation without diminishing or compromising the ability of future generations to meet their own needs (World Congress of Architects, Chicago, June 1993).

Sustainable. An ecosystem condition in which bio-diversity, renewability, and resource productivity are maintained over time.

Sustainable yield forestry. A type of forestry dictating that the same numbers of trees cut down are also planted. "Clear-cutting with 100 percent replanted" is an example of sustainable yield. It differs from ecologically sustainable forestry, which dictates the management of a productive forest that supports a healthy ecosystem.

Terpenes. Organic, aromatic substances found in the sap of softwoods, and in linoleum. Terpenes can be highly irritating to sensitive people.

Terrazzo. Marble or granite chips embedded in a binder that may be cementitious, noncementitious (epoxy, polyester, or resin), or a combination of both. Terrazzo can be used with divider strips of brass, zinc, or plastic.

Thermal comfort. The appropriate combination of temperatures, warm or cool, combined with airflow and humidity, which allows one to be comfortable within the confines of a building. This comfort is not usually achieved by the fixed setting of thermostats but through careful design and planning.

Thickset method. Installation procedure used for uneven material, such as ungauged stone. The mortar bed is $3/_4$ to $1\text{-}1/_4$ in. thick (2 to 3 cm), often using cement based mortar.

Thinset method. Installation procedure used for evenly gauged material, such as ceramic or granite tile. A mortar as thin as $3/_{32}$ in. (.24 cm) is used, often containing an acrylic adhesive.

Titanium dioxide. A white pigment used in paint, vitreous enamel, linoleum, rubber and plastics, printing ink, and paper. It has low toxicity but high covering power, brilliance, reflectivity, and resistance to light and fumes. Production creates large quantities of toxic waste.

Toluene. An aromatic component of petroleum with a strong solvent odor. Highly flammable and moderately toxic, toluene is used as a solvent for adhesives and inks. May cause lung cancer.

Toxic. Any substance that causes harm to living organisms. There is a wide range of toxicity, from very low to extremely high.

Traditional materials. Materials that have been used for several generations. Their properties and toxicity are known from experience.

Trombe wall. A masonry wall that is usually separated from the outdoors by a glass wall and is designed to absorb solar heat and release it into the interior of a building.

Tung oil. Oil obtained from the seed of the tung tree, widely used as a drying oil in paints and varnishes and as a waterproofing agent.

Ultraviolet (UV). Short-wavelength, high-energy invisible light responsible for sunburn, skin cancer, and bleaching and deterioration of many materials.

Undercushion. A padding material laid prior to laying a carpet. Foamed plastic, rubber, and felts are the most common types. All tend to capture dust and deteriorate with time.

Underlayment. A sheet material, usually wood or wood fiber, laid under resilient flooring, carpet, or tile to minimize irregularities in the subfloor or to add acoustic separation.

Urea formaldehyde. An inexpensive polymer used widely as glue for interior wood products. A source of toxic formaldehyde gas. *See also* Formaldehyde.

U-value (Btu/hr-ft2-F). Measures the energy flowing through a wall, roof, window, door, or floor per hour per each degree of temperature difference between the inside and outside air temperatures. The most technical literature describes the thermal characteristics of wall or roof systems in terms of heat flow coefficient, *U*, rather than the total thermal resistance, or R-value. *See also* R-value.

Vapor barrier. In addition to the moisture carried into building cavities by air movement, a small amount is also transferred by vapor diffusion. Because water vapor tends to move from a moist area to a dryer one, it can be forced through permeable materials such as wood and plaster. A vapor barrier is a material that resists moisture movement in materials.

Veneer. A thin sheet of high-grade wood formed by cutting a thin strip from it. The veneer is applied to thicker wood or paper to make plywood and decorative wood-surfaced panels for furniture and doors. Also, a plastic sheet, typically melamine.

Ventilation. The provision and removal of air to control air contaminant levels, humidity, or temperature within an indoor space. Ventilation is measured in air changes per hour—the quantity of infiltration air in cubic feet per minute (cfm) divided by the volume of the room.

Ventilation rate. The rate at which indoor air enters and leaves a building, expressed in one of two ways: the number of changes of outdoor air per unit of time (air changes per hour, or *ach*) or the rate at which a volume of outdoor air enters per unit of time (cubic feet per minute/cfm).

Volatile organic compounds (VOCs). Substances that are indoor air pollutants or chemical compounds that exist as vapor or gases at normal temperatures. VOCs are carbon-based molecules typically used as solvents in products such as household cleaners, paints, inks, and dyes. Many are irritants; some are toxic. Sources of VOCs include formaldehyde (a suspected carcinogen), xylene, toluene, benzene (a known carcinogen), and acetone. Indoors, VOCs are major air pollutants; outside, VOCs react with other pollutants, producing ground-level ozone.

Waste. All materials that flow from the building to final disposal. Examples include paper, grass trimmings, food scraps, and plastics.

Waste diversion. A management activity that disposes of waste other than though incineration or landfilling. Examples are reuse and recycling.

Waste equals food. A principle of natural systems that eliminates the concept of waste, whereby waste produced is used as the raw materials for another process. In this design strategy, all materials are viewed as continuously valuable, circulating in closed loops of production, use, and recycling.

Waste reduction. A process to reduce or eliminate the amount of waste generated at its source or to reduce the amount of toxicity from waste or the reuse of materials. The best way to reduce waste is not to create it in the first place.

Wastestream. The total flow of solid waste from homes, businesses, institutions, and manufacturing that is recycled, burned, or disposed of in landfills.

Wastewater. Water that has been used and contaminated. Wastewater must be purified before being used again or before being returned to the environment.

Well-managed forest. A forest that has been cared for with particular concern for conserving biological diversity and functioning ecosystems, maintaining high conservation-value forests, advancing the economic and social well-being of workers, local communities, and indigenous groups, and establishing sound and long-term management practices.

Xylene. An aromatic component of petroleum; it has a sharp solvent odor. Xylene is moderately toxic and is used as a solvent for dyes, inks, paints, and adhesives.

Zero-VOC. Having volatile organic compounds (VOCs) outgassing levels that are so low as to not be measurable by standard EPA methods.

Zinc oxide. A white pigment used in paints, ointments, plastics, and rubber that resists ultraviolet light and mold growth. Low toxicity, but the dust is hazardous.

INDEX

Page numbers in *italic* type refer to illustrations.